WISCONSIN LAW OF TRUSTS AND ESTATES: CASES AND MATERIALS

WISCONSIN LAW OF TRUSTS AND ESTATES: CASES AND MATERIALS

JOSEPH GORDON HYLTON
PROFESSOR OF LAW
MARQUETTE UNIVERSITY

VANDEPLAS PUBLISHING, LLC
UNITED STATES OF AMERICA

Wisconsin Law of Trusts and Estates: Cases and Materials

Hylton, Joseph Gordon

Published by:

Vandeplas Publishing, LLC – August 2013

801 International Parkway, 5th Floor
Lake Mary, FL. 32746
USA

www.vandeplaspublishing.com

ISBN 978-1-60042-201-0

TABLE OF CONTENTS

INTRODUCTION xiii

CHAPTER 1. PROPERTY AND DEATH 1

I. THE CONSTITUTIONAL RIGHT TO MAKE A WILL 1

Estate of Ogg 2

II. THE PROBATE PROCESS 8

A. PROBATE 8

B. NOTICE TO CREDITORS 10

C. CONSTITUTIONAL LIMITATIONS 12

Tanner v. Fessler 12

Note on Tulsa Collections v. Pope 20

D. VALID AND INVALID CLAIMS AGAINST AN ESTATE 21

Estate of Steffes 21

III. THE LAWYER'S ROLE 22

A. SOLICTING BUSINESS AND SAFEGUARDING WILLS 25

State v. Gulbankian 26

Note on Safeguarding Wills 31

B. ATTORNEY LIABILITY TO INTENDED DEVISEES 32

Auric v. Continental Casualty Co 32

C. CONFLICTS OF INTEREST 38

Office of Lawyer Regulation v. Felli 38

Apyan v. Easton 59

D. LAWYER-CLIENT CONFIDENTIALITY 61

Estate of Boerner 62

CHAPTER 2. INTESTACY: DISTRIBUTION BY DEFAULT 65

I. DEFINING HEIRS 65

A. THE INTESTACY STATUTE 65

Estate of Szaczywka 67

Estate of Rhodes 69

B. THE VOCABULARY OF INHERITANCE 74

C. CALCULATING HEIRS 76

Table of Consanguinity 76

D. IDENTIFYING HEIRS 77

Kleiber v. Ecker 81

II. PROBLEMS RELATED TO INTESTACY 83

A. SIMULTANEOUS DEATH 83

Estate of Villwock 86
B. INHERITANCE RIGHTS OF ADOPTED CHILDREN 89
Winiarski v. Miicke 91
C. ADVANCEMENTS 92
Arthur v. Arthur 96
D. DISCLAIMER 99
Goldhammer v. Goldhammer 104
E. THE SLAYER DILEMMA 107
Whaley v. Avery 110
Jackson v. Gray 117
F. ESCHEAT 122
In re Estate of Kavanaugh 122
G. NEGATIVE DISINHERITANCE 125
In re Will of Rosnow 125

CHAPTER 3. WILLS: DISTRIBUTION BY CHOICE 129
I. INTENTION AND CAPACITY 129
A. TESTAMENTARY INTENT 129
Estate of Beale 129
B. TESTAMENTARY CAPACITY 139
In re Estate of Dobrecevich 139
C. INSANE DELUION 142
In re Estate of Evans 142
D. UNDUE INFLUENCE 151
Estate of Malnar 151
II. WILL FORMALITIES 158
A. REQUIREMENTS FOR A VALID WILL 158
In re Wilcox's Estate 161
Estate of Wilm 162
B. HOLOGRAPHIC AND ORAL WILLS AND WILLS FROM OTHER JURISDICTIONS 164
In re Estate of Warner 167
C. WITNESSES 172
Will of Johnson 172
D. AMENDMENT AND REPUBLICATION BY CODICIL 185
Fairweather v. Love 185
Lonsdorf v. Citizens State Bank & Trust Co 189
III. REVOCATION OF WILLS 196

A. SIMPLE REVOCATION 196
In re Estate of Haugk 197
In re Byrne's Will 206
B. REVOCATION BY MARRIAGE OR DIVORCE 209
Allstate Life Ins. Co. v. Hanson 211
C. DEPENDENT RELATIVE REVOCATION AND REVIVAL 213
Estate of Alburn 213
IV. RULES AFFECTING ADMISSIBILITY TO PROBATE 217
A. LOST WILLS 217
Hanusa v. Intestate Heirs of Ewer 217
B. WILL CONTESTS 231
In re Keenan's Will 231
C. WILL CONTRACTS AND JOINT WILLS 235
Estate of Shultz 236

CHAPTER 4. INTERPRETING WILLS 239
I. UNDERSTANDING WILLS 239
A. INCORPORATION BY REFERENCE 239
Skinner v. American Bible Society 241
B. THE OPERATIVE DATE OF WILLS AND ACTS OF INDEPENDENT SIGNIFICANCE 244
Estate of Zink 245
C. AMBIGUOUS LANGUAGE 248
In re Estate of Ganser 249
D. CORRECTING MISTAKES 254
In re Southard's Will 254
Krause v. Krause 256
E. EXONERATION OF LIENS 260
F. MISCELLANEOUS STATUTORY PROVISIONS AFFECTING THE INTERPRETATION OF WILLS 261
II. ACCOUNTING FOR CHANGED CIRCUMSTANCES 266
A. LAPSE 266
Firehammer v. Marchant 268
B. ADEMPTION 270
Estate of Boerner 273
C. PRETERMITTED SPOUSES 277
In re Estate of Jones 278
D. PRETERMITTED CHILDREN 281
Sandon v. Sandon 283

In re Read's Will 285
E. ABATEMENT 290
Drews v. Marwede 291

CHAPTER 5. LIMITS ON TESTAMENTARY FREEDOM 297
I. FAMILY OBLIGATIONS 297
A. OBLIGATIONS TO CHILDREN 297
In re Will of Mattes 298
B. FAMILY MAINTENANCE 303
Estate of Sullivan 307
II. SPOUSAL CLAIMS 309
A. THE TRADITIONAL ELECTIVE SHARE 309
Uihlein v. Uihlein 311
B. PROBLEMS WITH THE ELECTIVE SHARE 320
C. WISCONSIN MARITAL PROPERTY 321
In re the Matter of the Estate of Lloyd 326
D. SURVIVORSHIP MARITAL PROPERTY 339
Wonka v. Estate of Bierbrauer 341
E. DEFERRED MARITAL PROPERTY 345
In re estate of Hemmrich 357
F. ADDITIONAL PROTECTIONS FOR MARITAL PROPERTY 359
III. LIMITATIONS ON SPOUSAL CLAIMS 360
A. INVALID MARRIAGES 360
B. MARITAL AND PRENUPTIAL AGREEMENTS 361
Estate of Stocking v. Stocking 372
IV. PUBLIC POLICY LIMITATIONS ON TESTAMENTARY FREEDOM 379
A. CONDITIONAL BEQUESTS 379
Webster v. Morris 381
In re Paulson's Will 386
B. RESTRICTIONS ON THE RIGHT TO MARRY 392
In re Estate of Heller 392

CHAPTER 6. WILL SUBSTITUTES 397
I. DONATIVE TRANSFERS IN ANTICIPATION OF DEATH 397
A. INTER VIVOS GIFTS 397
Aprahamian v. Brown 397
B. GIFTS CAUSA MORTIS 400

In re Estate of Hansen 400
C. DISCLAIMERS OF *INTER VIVOS* GIFTS 405
D. ANATOMICAL GIFTS 410
II. FUTURE INTERESTS 412
A. REMAINDERS IN LIEU OF WILLS 417
In re Estate of Carpenter 417
B. TESTAMENTARY DEEDS 422
III. CONCURRENT ESTATES 424
A. JOINT TENANCIES AND TENANCIES IN COMMON 424
Aaby v. Citizens National Bank of Stoughton 429
B. SURVIVORSHIP MARITAL PROPERTY 430
Moen v. Moen 432
IV. PAYABLE ON DEATH ACCOUNTS 434
A. FINANCIAL ACCOUNTS 435
Tucker v. Simrow 441
Bruckner v. Prairie Federal Sav. & Loan Asso 443
B. ANNUITIES AND INSURANCE CONTRACTS 447
Reichel v. Jung 447
V. REVOCABLE TRUSTS 458
A. THE TRUST CONCEPT 458
McMahon v. Standard Bank and Trust Co. 461
B. LIVING TRUSTS AS WILL SUBSTITUTES 474
In re Estate of Steck 475
C. POUR OVER WILLS 480
VI. THE INTERPLAY BETWEEN WILLS AND WILL SUBSTITUTES 483
A. LIVING TRUSTS AND THE LAW OF WILLS 484
In re Estate of Cayo 484
Taylor v. Marshall & Isley Trust Co. 487
B. WILL SUBSTITUTES AND TAXES 493
Estate of Sheppard v. Schleis 493

CHAPTER 7. AN OVERVIEW OF THE LAW OF TRUSTS 507
I. ELEMENTS OF TRUSTS 508
A. INTENTION TO CREATE A TRUST 509
Wyse v. Puchner 509
B. THE TRUST RES 513
Warsco v. Oshkosh Sav. & Trust Co 513
C. THE BENERFICIARY 515
Tharp v. Seventh Day Adventist Church 515

D. THE TRUSTEE 520
In re Sensenbrenner 524
II. LIMITATIONS ON THE BENEFICIARY'S INTEREST 536
A. SPENDTHRIFT TRUSTS 536
Resop v. McCoy 540
In re Trust of Talmage 547
B. DISCRETIONARY AND SUPPORT TRUSTS 553
In re Walker's Will 554
C. THE ENFORCEMENT OF TRUSTS 564
In re Estate of Becker 566
III. REVOCATION AND MODIFICATION OF TRUSTS 574
A. THE CLAFLIN DOCTRINE 574
In re Hamburger's Will 577
B. INSUFFICIENT TRUST RES 585
Schmidt v. Higgins 586
C. THE WISCONSIN RULE AGAINST PERPETUITIES 587
In re Will of Walker 589
IV. RESULTING AND CONSTRUCTIVE TRUSTS 593
A. PURCHASE MONEY RESULTING TRUSTS 594
Masino v. Sechrest 594
B. CONSTRUCTIVE TRUSTS 600
Hendricks v. McCormick Memorial Home 600
C. ORAL TRUSTS AND OTHER SECRET TRUSTS 606
In re Estate of Liginger 606

CHAPTER 8. POWERS AND DUTIES OF TRUSTEES 609
I. TRUSTEE POWERS 609
A. TRADITIONAL POWERS 609
In re Boyle's Estate 609
B. STATUTORY POWERS 613
II. TRUSTEE DUTIES 616
A. FIDUCIARY DUTIES OF TRUSTEES AND EXECUTORS 616
United States Bank v. Sullivan 620
B. DUTY OF LOYALTY 626
Berg v. Berg 626
C. TRUST MANAGEMENT AND THE DUTY TO DIVERSIFY 631
In re Mueller's Trust 637
D. DUTY TO DIVIDE PRINCIPAL AND INTEREST 648
In re Will of Clarenbach 672

E. THE DUTY TO ACCOUNT 676
In re Trust Estate of Martin 676
III. REMOVAL OF TRUSTEES 680
A. REMOVAL OF TRUSTEE WITH CONSENT OF THE SETTLOR 681
In re Trust of Charitable v. Bowen 681
B. REMOVAL OF TRUSTEE WITHOUT SETTLOR CONSENT 685
Bramen v. Angelopulos 685

CHAPTER 9. CHARITABLE TRUSTS 695
I. CREATING CHARITABLE TRUSTS 695
A. WHAT MAKES A TRUST CHARITABLE? 695
Webster v. Morris 696
B. CHARITABLE INTENT 699
In re Estate of Raulf 700
C. MIXED PURPOSE TRUSTS 702
In re Estate of Frautschy 703
D. DISCRIMINATORY TRUSTS 708
II. THE MODIFICATION OF CHARITABLE TRUSTS 709
A. ADMINSTRATIVE DEVIATION 710
Estate of Robinson v. Webster 710
B. *CY PRES* 716
Estate of Bletsch 716
In re Oshkosh Foundation 720
C. ENFORCEMENT OF CHARITABLE TRUSTS 722
Estate of Sharp 723
D. HONORARY TRUSTS 728
Krawcyzk v. Bank of Sun Prairie 729
E. CHARITABLE FOUNDATIONS 731

CHAPTER 10. POWERS OF APPOINTMENT 733
I. OPERATION OF POWERS OF APPOINTMENT 733
A. DEFINITION 733
B. SPECIFIC VERSUS GENERAL POWERS OF APPOINTMENT 735
In re Estate of Trainer 736
C. EXERCISING THE POWER OF APPOINTMENT 742

In re Estate of Sheppard v. Sheppard 743
II. FAILURE TO EXERCISE A POWER 751
A. TAKERS IN DEFAULT 751
Derse v. Derse 752
B. DONEE RELEASE OF A POWER OF APPOINTMENT 754
In re Cudahy's Trust 755
C. RIGHTS OF CREDITORS 757

INTRODUCTION

This is a casebook about death and property and greed. The dance inevitably comes to an end, and the furnishings have to be distributed to others. The line forms quickly.

Those who are fortunate to accumulate more property than they use up during their lifetimes have to decide how to dispose of what they own. If they do nothing, it passes according to their home state's law of intestacy. Otherwise, they can give it away during their lifetime, or they can dictate the ways in which it will be distributed after their death through the use of a will or a will substitute. There are restrictions on how the property can be distributed, but not very many.

These materials illustrate the way that one American state (Wisconsin) has chosen to regulate the process by which property is distributed from one generation to the next. The first half of the book focuses upon the formal transfer of property at death through the probate process. The second concentrates on alternatives to the probate system with a special focus on trusts.

This is an old-fashioned casebook in a number of respects. First of all, its focus is on the law of trusts and estates, and it is not primarily designed to expose students to the mechanics of modern estate planning practice. Second, it is a traditional casebook, in the pre-1970's sense. Its contents are almost exclusively published judicial opinions and statutes, and there are no excerpts from treatises, law review articles, or other scholarly sources. Notes are kept to a minimum and usually are historical in their focus.

Its third distinctive feature is that it focuses on the law of a single jurisdiction. Casebooks on the law of an individual state were not uncommon in the first half of the twentieth century, but they largely disappeared after 1950 as legal publishing became increasingly centralized and thus national in its focus. Students who use this book and end up practicing law in Wisconsin will benefit from learning a great deal of the actual law of the jurisdiction, but that is not the primary purpose of its Wisconsin-centric focus. Students who end up in Wisconsin or elsewhere will benefit from exposure to the interaction of actual cases and actual statutes drawn from a single jurisdiction rather than being asked to assimilate a model statute and a variety of cases drawn from many different jurisdictions. The single state focus of the materials also makes it easier to document how the law of wills and trusts responded to changing social and economic conditions over the past century and a half.

I have taught courses entitled Trusts and Estates, Decedent's Estates, Decedents Estates and Trusts, and Wills and Trusts on a regular basis since 1991, and my views on this subject matter have been shaped by exchanges with more than 1000 students and by conversations with my colleagues at various law schools, especially Alan Madry, Patricia Bradford, Julian Kossow, Vada Lindsey, David Papke, and Judi McMullen at Marquette; Phil Hablutzel and Jeffrey Sherman at Chicago-Kent; David Becker and Frances Foster at Washington University; Bob Danforth, Ned Henneman, and Robin Wilson at Washington and Lee; and Barry Cushman, Alex Johnson, and John Morley at the University of Virginia. Although never formal colleagues, I have similarly benefitted from such conversations with Al Brophy, Danaya Wright, and Michael Wolf. I also continue to owe a great debt to my own law school T&E professor, the late Charlie Whitebread. To the extent that this is also a book about the social and economic history of Wisconsin, I have greatly benefitted from what is now at 15-year running conversation on Wisconsin legal history with lawyer-historian Jay Ranney.

I owe an enormous debt to library staff at the Marquette University Law School, to my research assistants Ellison Hitt and Andrea Austin, and to my students at Marquette who worked their way through the manuscript version of these materials in the summer of 2013,

Greatest appreciation, however, goes to my wife Monica Walker who has supported me throughout this project as she has through many others.

Gordon Hylton
Milwaukee, Wisconsin and Charlottesville, Virginia
July 2013

CHAPTER 1.
PROPERTY AND DEATH

I. THE CONSTITUITONAL RIGHT TO MAKE A WILL

Do property owners have a constitutional right to control the distribution and use of their property after their deaths? The traditional answer to this question by American constitutional theorists was that they did not. Whatever constitutionally protected property rights one might have while alive, it was widely accepted that any control that an owner had over its property could be terminated at death if the sovereign so desired. Even the United States Supreme Court embraced this position. In *Irving Trust Co. v. Day,* 314 U.S. 556 (1942), Justice Owen Roberts, writing for a unanimous court, stated, "Rights of succession to the property of a deceased, whether by will or by intestacy, are of statutory creation, and the dead hand rules succession only by sufferance. Nothing in the Federal Constitution forbids the legislature of a state to limit, condition, or even abolish the power of testamentary disposition over property within its jurisdiction." *Id.* at 562.

This was, in the American context, an entirely theoretical question, since no state ever sought to eliminate the rights of inheritance and testation. However, in 1987, in the case of *Hodel v. Irving,* 481 U.S. 704, the United States Supreme Court implicitly overruled the *Irving Trust* decision (or at least the above quoted language) when it recognized that the protections of the Fifth and Fourteenth Amendments extended to the "transfer of property after death" situation, at least in limited form. In *Hodel,* the Court invalidated Section 207 of the Indian Consolidation Act of 1983, by which Congress had dictated that very small real property interests (having an annual income of less than $100) would "escheat" to the Native American tribe to which the deceased owner had belonged, rather than to the owner's descendants. In her opinion for the Court, Justice Sandra Day O'Connor acknowledged that "complete abrogation of both the descent and devise of a particular class of property may be a taking." *Id.* at 717.

In contrast to the relatively late recognition by the United States Supreme Court, the right of testation and the right to inherit have long been recognized as constitutionally protected rights in Wisconsin. The Wisconsin Supreme Court proclaimed this fact as early as the 1879 case of *Dodge v. Williams,* 46 Wis. 70, 50 N.W. 1103, and resolutely confirmed the position in *Numenmacher v. State,* 129 Wis. 190, 108 N.W. 627 (1906). In the following opinion, the mid-twentieth century Wisconsin Supreme Court reiterates the special role of testamentary freedom in the state's constitutional framework.

Estate of Ogg

Supreme Court of Wisconsin
262 Wis. 181, 54 N.W.2d 175 (1952)

CURRIE, J. Counsel for the respondents contend that sec. 310.25, Stats., gives Grace L. Ogg, as next of kin of the testator, the unqualified right to name the attorneys for the bank, as administrator with the will annexed, even though testator in his will directed that Mr. Biart be employed as legal counsel by the administrator with the will annexed and trustee. Sec. 310.25, provides as follows:

"Whenever a firm or corporation of any kind is named as administrator or executor of an estate, he or she who is nearest of kin and who receives any interest in the estate, and if there be no bequest of any kind, then the party receiving the largest amount or interest from the estate, shall name the attorney who shall represent the estate in all proceedings of any kind or nature, unless good cause be shown before the court why this should not be done. . . ."

The point in issue in this case is one of first impression in this court. We believe that the advisable approach in passing upon such question is to first determine whether the direction of the testator, that Mr. Biart be employed by the executor (administrator with the will annexed) as counsel in the administration of the estate, would be enforceable in the absence of sec. 310.25, Stats.; and, if the conclusion is that it would be enforceable under the facts in this case in the absence of the statute, then to consider whether such result would be affected by reason of the existence of the statute.

Wisconsin has taken a more advanced position in carrying out the intent of the testator as expressed in his will than probably any other state. The following statement from 1 Page, Wills (2d ed.), p. 37, sec. 22, recognizes this:

"According to the great weight of authority in the United States, the right to make a will is in no sense a property right or a so-called natural right. It did not exist for realty at common law, nor at one time for more than a fraction of a testator's personalty. It is therefore not a right protected by any of the constitutional provisions whereby property is protected, which is sometimes expressed by saying that it is not a natural right; but it is purely a statutory right, subject to the complete control of the legislature.

"On the other hand, the courts of Wisconsin have dissented sharply from this theory and have held that the power to make a will is an inherent power and not a statutory power. They hold that the right to make a will is secured by the constitution, and that the legislature can regulate succession by will or descent in intestacy within reasonable limits, but that it cannot impair such rights substantially or take them away entirely.

"Under this theory, every person of mature age and sound mind has a right, conformably to statutory regulations designed to safeguard such right, to make his own will, and have it carried out according to his intent; and the constitutional right to make a will includes the right to have a valid will so given effect as to enforce the intention of the testator." (Emphasis supplied.)

This court, in Will of Rice (1912), 150 Wis. 401, 444, 447, 136 N. W. 956; modified, 150 Wis. 484, 137 N. W. 778, stated:

"The right to make a will is more sacred than the right to make a contract. . . .

". . . the right to make a will and have it allowed and carried out is a constitutional right, affirmed by statute law, and which courts and parties are powerless to take away."

As recently as 1948, this court in its decision in Will of Szperka (1948), 254 Wis. 153, 157, 35 N. W. (2d) 209, reiterated the principle, that the right to make a will is one that is guaranteed by the constitution, as follows:

"It has often been held by this court that one of the most important rights that a normal adult person has is his power to dispose of his property by will as he chooses. In fact, it has been referred to by this court as a 'sacred right' and one that is guaranteed by the constitution. Will of Rice (1912), 150 Wis. 401, 136 N. W. 956; modified, 150 Wis. 484, 137 N.W. 778; Upham v. Plankinton (1913), 152 Wis. 275, 140 N. W. 5; Will of Ball (1913), 153 Wis. 27, 141 N. W. 8; Duncan v. Metcalf (1913), 154 Wis. 39, 141 N. W. 1002; Will of Schaefer (1932), 207 Wis. 404, 241 N. W. 382."

Not only is the right to make a will a sacred right guaranteed by the constitution, but, as stated in Will of Rice, supra (pp. 447, 450), such right:

". . . subsists after the death of the testator, he being recognized as having, in effect, given the court irrevocable power of attorney to carry out his wishes, but not to violate them. . . .

"So we must conclude, not only that there is a constitutional right to make a will but that such right includes a right of equal dignity to have it carried out. There seems to be no escape from the conclusion."

Likewise in Will of Dardis (1908), 135 Wis. 457, 463, 115 N. W. 332, this court stated:

"His [the testator's] right is recognized to direct at least the method of management and disposal of his property after his decease, which courts cannot be compelled to disregard to accommodate the wishes of some or even all parties having pecuniary interest in the property."

In the instant case the respondent bank, as administrator with the will annexed, has voiced no objection against employing Attorney Biart as its counsel in administrating testator's estate, and stated in its petition to the trial court that it is willing to so employ him as its counsel if the court should so instruct it. In the absence of any statute to the contrary, we would have no hesitation in reaching the conclusion that the expressed request of testator contained in his will, that Mr. Biart be retained as counsel, would take precedence over the request of his sister as next of kin and a legatee under the will, that the firm of Ela, Christianson & Ela be employed as such counsel.

This court, in Will of Ball (1913), 153 Wis. 27, 31, 141 N. W. 8. stated:

". . . in a very high degree, the testamentary right, as compared with that of the mere subjects of testamentary charity or bounty, is the superior."

Testator expressly states in his will the reasons he requested that Mr. Biart be employed as counsel, such reasons being that Mr. Biart had an intimate knowledge of testator's affairs, views, and wishes respecting many matters that might arise in the probating of the instrument, the administration of the estate, and the execution of the trusts. On the other hand, the record is silent as to what reason respondent Grace L. Ogg had for opposing Mr. Biart's appointment as counsel and requesting the employment of other attorneys, but such reason would be immaterial unless good cause could be shown by her why it would be inimical to the interests of the estate that Mr. Biart be employed as counsel by the bank.

However, the fact that Miss Ogg, in her letter to the bank requesting the naming of other counsel, mentioned that she had been considering contesting the will indicates disappointment on her part as to the extent of the testator's bounty provided for her under the will, thus permitting the inference to be drawn that her antipathy to Mr. Biart may possibly have been due to a belief on her part that he had assisted testator in drafting a will of which she disapproved. Public policy would clearly seem to require that the expressed views of testator, based on the sound reasons he advanced in his will for naming Mr. Biart as counsel who was to assist the administrator with the will annexed in the administration of the estate, should take precedence over the contrary wishes of his sister as next of kin, in the absence of any showing of good cause for disregarding testator's request.

In the instant case it is also of some significance that testator did not name an executor, thereby leaving it to the court to appoint the administrator with the will annexed, so that the only person he did name who was to take part in the administration of the estate was Attorney Biart. Counsel for the respondent urge that to give recognition to the expressed request of testator, that Mr. Biart act as counsel for the bank in the administration of the estate, is directly contrary to the great weight of authority, and cites us to an annotation in 166 A. L. R. 491, on the subject. All of the decisions, including one English case, with the single exception of those of Louisiana, are cited therein as supporting the following principle:

"Provisions of a will naming an attorney to represent the executor in the probate of the will and the administration of the estate, or requesting the employment of a named attorney by the executor, are merely suggestive, precatory in nature, and not binding upon the executor, who is at liberty to disregard such provisions and to select an attorney of his own choice."

We have examined all of the cases cited in such annotation in support of the above-quoted principle, and find that in none of them was there a fact situation similar to the instant case in which the executor was willing to employ the attorney named by testator in his will. In a few cases the issue was raised collaterally, such as determining whether the attorney named had sufficient interest to bar him from acting as a witness to the will. In practically all the other cases, the executor, or executors, had either objected to carrying out the request of testator, or had engaged counsel other than named in the will. None of such cases is in point as to the instant case in which the administrator with the will annexed is willing to employ as counsel the attorney named by testator in his will.

Examination of the cases so cited in such annotation (166 A. L. R. 491) discloses that the courts in those cases have based their decisions, that the executor can disregard the request of testator that a certain attorney be employed by the executor, on one, or both, of the following two grounds: (1) That the request is merely suggestive or precatory in nature, or (2) that the executor is responsible for the dereliction or negligence of counsel employed, and therefore the executor should not be forced against his will to employ as counsel someone in whom the executor has no confidence.

In the instant case we have no difficulty in reaching the conclusion that the words used by testator in requesting the appointment of Mr. Biart as counsel are more than precatory, and are in the nature of a direct request, the words being, "I hereby declare it to be my express desire." In Will of Platt (1931), 205 Wis. 290, 296, 237 N. W. 109, it was stated:

"Here it is manifest from the whole will and the circumstances that the words 'it is my desire' indicate an intent as distinguished from a mere wish. The words are therefore mandatory."

In other words, the bank being willing to carry out this expressed desire of testator, the intent of the testator is mandatory as to all other persons.

We now come to the question of what effect the provisions of sec. 310.25, Stats., have upon the result in this case. The author of a note appearing in 31 Marquette Law Review, 231, 236, states that the purpose underlying the enactment of this statute was "for the protection of the interests of the heirs, and to prevent a monopoly of the probate business by counsel appointed by such [corporate] executors." In other words, the statute was aimed to prevent the real, or fancied, evil of corporations acting as executors playing favorites in selecting counsel, thus tending to create a monopoly in probate business by such favorite counsel. It assuredly was not aimed at preventing a corporate executor from selecting as its counsel to probate an estate the attorney whom testator had requested in his will be so selected.

It is a principle of statutory construction that the rules of common law are not to be changed by doubtful implication. Leach v. Leach (1952), 261 Wis. 350, 52 N. W. (2d) 896, and authorities cited therein. The common law that this principle has reference to is, of course, the common law of Wisconsin, and not that of other states, in a field in which Wisconsin, by court decisions, has taken a different stand than the courts of other jurisdictions. Should this principle of statutory construction be applied in construing sec. 310.25, Stats., so as to hold that that statute has no application to a situation in which testator has named the attorney for the corporate executor and such corporate executor is willing to abide thereby? We conclude that it should be so construed, in view of the serious doubts we entertain as to the validity of the statute if it were not thus construed.

In view of the fact that Wisconsin is unique in holding that the right to make a will and have it carried out is a sacred right guaranteed by the constitution, it necessarily follows that any regulation or limitation of such right by the legislature must be of a reasonable nature. Nunnemacher v. State (1906), 129 Wis. 190, 202, 108 N. W. 627.

Inasmuch as this court has held that the right of testator to dispose of his property as he sees fit is paramount to the right of the object of his bounty, such as his next of kin or legatee, it would appear to be an unreasonable limitation of this right of testator for the legislature to legislate that the right of a next of kin, named as legatee in a will, to select counsel for the executor, supersedes any testamentary direction of testator in such respect.

In Will of Risher (1938), 227 Wis. 104, 111, 277 N. W. 160, this court stated: "Anything designed to defeat the intent of the testator is against public policy."

For these reasons, we conclude that sec. 310.25, Stats., must be construed as having no application to a situation, such as in the instant case, in which the testator, by his will, has designated the counsel for the executor, and the executor is willing to employ as counsel the attorney so designated by testator. It is our duty to so construe this statute as to uphold its validity, if the resulting construction is one that is reasonable and does not lead to an absurd result. …

[The Court next rejected the respondents' claim that the appellant was not a "person aggrieved" within the meaning of the controling statute and thus had no standing to bring an action of this sort to the court. Having disposed of respondent's various objections, the court then returned to the question of whether the testator's wishes should be followed. It concluded:]

We hold that the orders of the trial court appealed from should have instructed the administrator with the will annexed to employ Mr. Biart as its counsel. Orders reversed and cause remanded with directions to enter a new order in conformity with this opinion.

II. THE PROBATE PROCESS

A. PROBATE

Although the concept of probate is often not very well understood by Americans; the term *probate* invariably carries decidedly negative connotations. Not only does the word usually imply the death of a loved one, but it is synonymous with unnecessary delay, unnecessary expense, and disappointment. At least since the publication of non-lawyer Norman Dacey's *How to Avoid Probate* in 1965—a work that sold millions of copies—many Americans have been convinced that the avoidance of probate should be a top priority.

In reality, probate is just a state-mandated process to guarantee that property is transferred from one generation to the next in an orderly fashion. As the Wisconsin Court System's webpage states, "Probate is the court-supervised process for the orderly transfer of a decedent's assets to those who are entitled to receive them."* In order insure that the deceased property is directed to the proper party and that it is protected during the interim period, Wisconsin and every other American state has adopted a detailed set of rules governing the probate process. In the *Wisconsin Statutes,* these rules occupy sixteen chapters, beginning with Chapter 856 and continuing through Chapter 882. (For some reason there are no Chapters numbered 864, 866, 869-876, and 880.)

The principal purposes of probate are to pay the creditors of the deceased, to satisfy any tax liability to the United States or Wisconsin governments, and to distribute the remainder of the deceased property is to the next lawful owners. The probate process is normally initiated by the relatives of the deceased, and it is managed by a court-appointed administrator, known as the executor or administrator in most states, but in Wisconsin, called the *personal representative*. (In an earlier era, the terms *executor* and *administrator* were also used in Wisconsin). The personal representative is ordinarily a close relative of the deceased who possesses the requisite managerial ability to shepherd the property through the process. When there is a valid will, courts will normally appoint the individual named as personal representative in the document itself. In addition, where there is a will, there is an initial procedure, usually fairly *pro forma*, to determine preliminarily that the will is valid.

* http://www.wicourts.gov/services/public/selfhelp/probate.htm

The probate process typically begins after the funeral of the deceased, although if issues arise, it can start even earlier. Probate may be formal or informal depending on the complexity of the estate. Either way, a personal representative is appointed, and once named the personal representative collects the property owned by the deceased, posts the required notice of the death of the individual, begins paying off the creditors, makes certain that surviving family members have sufficient assets to live on, and manages the deceased's property while the probate process is ongoing. The personal representative, who is treated as a fiduciary, has the power to hire lawyers, accountants, or other service providers necessary to complete the probate process. In addition, the personal representative is normally paid a percentage of the estate for his or her or its services.

Probate proceedings are normally initiated in the Wisconsin county in which the deceased was domiciled at the time of death. If the deceased was not a Wisconsin resident, then probate takes place in any county in which he or she owned real, and sometimes personal, property. Other aspects of the probate process will be explored in subsequent chapters. Because of the costs and delays associated with probate, modern estate planning often focuses on alternatives to probate and property arrangements that allow the assets controlled by the deceased to pass outside of the probate system. These alternatives are examined in Chapter 6 of these materials.

In contemporary Wisconsin, the probate process is overseen by the circuit court judges. Probate issues are tried before the circuit court, ordinarily without a jury. Probate can be formal or informal, with the latter reserved for estates where the assets are relatively limited and where there are unlikely to be disputes regarding the distribution of property. When probate is formal, the personal representative is almost always represented by an attorney who is authorized to act on his or her account. In an earlier area, probate was the special province of the county courts, a branch of the Wisconsin judiciary that was essentially eliminated with the 1959 and 1977 court reorganizations.

There is nothing inevitable about the Anglo-American system of probate. Most of the world, including Louisiana, gets along quite well without it. As an alternative, most civil law countries use a process known as *universal succession* in which title to property passes to the new owners immediately at death, and the new owners handle all issues related to creditors and taxes. Something like universal succession exists in a few states, including California and Wisconsin. In California, no probate is required if the estate passes in its entirety to the surviving spouse. In that situation, the spouse takes full responsibility for any debts owed by the deceased. Cal. Prob. Code §§13500-13650 (2013). The situation in Wisconsin is slightly more complicated, but under Wis. Stat. §766.58(3)(f), married couple are permitted to enter into a "marital property agreement" under which the parties agree that "upon the death of either spouse any of either or both spouse's property, including after-acquired property, passes without probate to a designated person, trust or other entity by nontestamentary disposition." (Marital property agreements are discussed in Chapter 5.)

B. NOTICE TO CREDITORS

One of the primary functions of the probate process is to make sure that the debts of the decedent are paid in a timely fashion. The following statutes deal with the need to expedite this process.

Wis. Stat. 859.01. Time for Filing Claims

When an application for administration is filed, the court, or the probate registrar under informal administration proceedings, shall by order set a date as the deadline for filing a claim against the decedent's estate. The date shall be not less than 3 nor more than 4 months from the date of the order. If a claim is not filed by the deadline, the consequences provided in s. 859.02 apply.

Wis. Stat. 859.02. Limitation on claims.

(1) Except as provided in sub. (2) and s. 859.03, all claims against a decedent's estate including claims of the state and any subdivision thereof, whether due or to become due, absolute or contingent, liquidated or unliquidated, are barred against the estate, the personal representative and the heirs and beneficiaries of the decedent unless filed on or before the date set under s. 859.01.

A claim against a decedent's estate that is not filed on or before the date set under s. 859.01 is not barred if:

(a) It is a claim based on tort, on a marital property agreement that is subject to the time limitations under s. 766.58 (13) (b) or (c), on Wisconsin income, franchise, sales, withholding, gift or death taxes, or on unemployment insurance contributions due or benefits overpaid; a claim for funeral or administrative expenses; a claim of this state under s. 46.27 (7g), 49.496 or 49.682 or rules promulgated under s. 46.286 (7); or a claim of the United States; or

(b) All of the following circumstances exist:

1. On or before the date set under s. 859.01, the personal representative knew, or in the exercise of reasonable diligence should have known, of the existence of the potential claim and of the identity and mailing address of the potential claimant.

2. At least 30 days prior to the date set under s. 859.01, the personal representative had not given notice to the potential claimant of the final day for filing his or her claim and the court in which the estate proceeding was pending.

3. At least 30 days prior to the date set under s. 859.01, the claimant did not have actual knowledge that the estate proceeding was pending and of the court in which that proceeding was pending.

(2m)

(a) A claim based on a tort is subject to s. 859.45.

(b) A claim of a creditor without notice is subject to s. 859.48.

(3) Failure of a claimant timely to file a claim against a decedent's estate does not bar the claimant from satisfying the claim from property other than the decedent's estate.

Wis. Stat. 859.07. Notice; publication.

(1) Notice of the deadline for filing a claim under s. 859.01 shall be given by publication, under s. 879.05(4), and may be given with the notice for granting letters. The first insertion shall be made within 15 days of the date of the order under s. 859.01.

(2)

(a) The personal representative shall provide notice of the date set under s. 859.01 to the department of health services, the department of children and families, or the department of corrections, as applicable, and to the county clerk of the decedent's county of residence, as defined in s. 49.001 (6) if, at any time prior to or at the time of the decedent's death, any of the following applied:

1. The decedent was a patient or inmate of any state or county hospital or institution.

2. The decedent was responsible for any obligation owing to the state or a county under s. 46.03 (18), 46.10, 48.36, 49.32 (1), 49.345, 301.03 (18), 301.12, or 938.36.

3. The decedent or the decedent's spouse received the family care benefit under s. 46.286, medical assistance under subch. IV of ch. 49, long-term community support services funded under s. 46.27 (7), or aid under s. 49.68, 49.683, or 49.685.

(b) The notice under par. (a) shall comply with all of the following:

1. The notice shall be in writing on forms provided by the applicable department or county clerk.

2. The notice shall be sent by registered or certified mail not less than 30 days before the date set under s. 859.01.

(3) The personal representative may at any time give notice to any potential claimant of the deadline for filing a claim against the estate under s. 859.01 or 859.48 and of the court in which the estate proceeding is pending.

C. CONSTITUTIONAL LIMITATIONS

William B. Tanner Co. v. Estate of Fessler

Supreme Court of Wisconsin
100 Wis. 2d 437, 302 N.W.2d 414 (1981)

Beilfuss, C.J. This is a review of a decision of the court of appeals which affirmed the judgment of the Circuit Court for Dane County, Robert R. Pekowsky, Circuit Judge.

This matter concerns the denial of a claim filed in probate court against the Estate of Earl W. Fessler, deceased. The claim was filed by the William B. Tanner Company, Inc. The claimant is a Tennessee corporation which engages in the business of providing promotional advertising and other services to various radio and television stations throughout the United States.

The record reflects that the decedent was the owner and operator of radio station WMFM, Madison, Wisconsin. In this capacity he contracted with the William B. Tanner Company, Inc. (Tanner) for a service program known as a "Creative Sales Service." In consideration for this service program, the decedent agreed to pay a monthly sum and agreed to provide a series of "one-minute spots" to be used by Tanner for advertising purposes during the radio station's broadcasting programs. There was no time limitation on the use of these spots and under the contract they remained valid until used. The parties initially contracted for a one-year term in 1968. A second contract was entered into in 1969. This was a two-year contract.

Tanner alleges that $11,287.20 is owed to it under the terms of the contracts. This sum represents both the monthly payments remaining due under the agreements and the value of the unused "one-minute spots" that were to be provided by the decedent to Tanner.

The decedent died on November 27, 1977. A petition for the probate of his will was filed on December 14, 1977. On that same date, pursuant to secs. 859.01 and 859.05,

Stats., the probate court entered an order limiting the time for the filing of claims by creditors. According to the order, claims were to be filed by March 28, 1978. Notice of this limitation was ordered to be published in the Wisconsin State Journal once a week for three consecutive weeks. A notice was in fact published in accord with sec. 859.07.

On December 26, 1978, almost nine months after the final date for filing claims as ordered by the court, Tanner filed a claim against the estate in the amount of $11,287.20. The personal representative, Mrs. Earl W. Fessler, objected to the allowance of Tanner's demand as an untimely claim barred by the operation of sec. 859.01, Stats.

A hearing was held on the claim on February 28, 1979. Tanner argued that before a creditor's rights may be extinguished by operation of sec. 859.01, Stats., notice which is reasonably calculated to advise the creditor of the pending probate proceeding is required by the due process clause of the fourteenth amendment. It was contended that notice by publication alone under the terms of sec. 859.07 was not constitutionally valid. The personal representative argued that the notice scheme was not unconstitutional and that Tanner's claim was barred by the time limitation under the probate code.

Although Tanner's argument challenged the constitutionality of the notice provisions of sec. 859.07, Stats., no notice was served upon the attorney general to afford the state an opportunity to be heard at the probate proceedings.

The probate court disallowed the claim, and Tanner appealed. While this matter was pending before the court of appeals, the attorney general was notified and was given an opportunity to participate in the appellate proceedings. In response to this invitation the attorney general maintained that the court of appeals had no jurisdiction to hear the appeal in light of Tanner's failure to give the state notice of the lower court proceeding wherein the statutes were originally challenged as unconstitutional.

Addressing the merits of Tanner's claim, the attorney general adopted the argument of the personal representative as an ample presentation of the case law and policy considerations in support of the constitutionality of the notice provisions under ch. 859, Stats. The court of appeals dismissed the appeal in light of the lack of the attorney general's participation at the trial court level. The opinion was unpublished. We subsequently granted Tanner's petition for review.

This case presents three issues:

1. Whether the failure to notify the attorney general of the proceedings prior to the time the cause reached the court of appeals requires the dismissal of Tanner's appeal.

2. Whether a creditor is entitled as a matter of due process of law to be notified of an order under sec. 859.05, Stats., limiting the time for the filing of claims.

3. Whether the notice provisions of ch. 859, Stats., unduly "fetter" the flow of interstate commerce so as to be violative of the commerce clause of the federal constitution.

The personal representative asked that we dismiss this review due to Tanner's failure to provide the attorney general with an opportunity to participate in the initial challenge to the constitutionality of the notice provisions of ch. 859, Stats., in the probate court. It is claimed that this result is required by the rule of Kurtz v. City of Waukesha, 91 Wis.2d 103, 280 N.W.2d 757 (1979). However, the Kurtz Case was decided several months after judgment was entered against Tanner, and Tanner argues that the retroactive application of the holding in that case to this proceeding would violate the due process clause of the fourteenth amendment.

Although the arguments of counsel have focused upon the retroactivity of the Kurtz decision, we conclude that even if it is assumed that that decision has retroactive effect, the Kurtz rule does not bar our consideration of the merits of Tanner's claims.

Prior to our decision in Kurtz v. City of Waukesha, supra, this court recognized the importance of allowing the attorney general to participate in proceedings wherein a statute was challenged as invalid. In Kenosha v. Dosemagen, 54 Wis.2d 269, 195 N.W.2d 462 (1972), the court considered the constitutional validity of several statutes. It was noted that participation by the attorney general in such cases was desirable. "It is the attorney general who should be afforded the opportunity to act in a representative capacity in behalf of the legislature and the people of the state to uphold the constitutionality of a statute of statewide application." Id. at 271. The court concluded that it may in the future direct the state to file a brief amicus curiae when the attorney general has not been made a party to the action. Id.

The notice requirement in a nondeclaratory action was reviewed and changed several years after the decision in Kenosha v. Dosemagen, supra. In Kurtz v. City of Waukesha, 91 Wis.2d 103, 280 N.W.2d 757 (1979), this court ruled that it would not consider the constitutionality of the Fair Employment Act, sec. 111.31 et seq. Stats., due to the failure of the parties to notify the attorney general of the constitutional challenge to the statute and to allow him to be heard on the issue. The court wrote:

"We conclude that cogent reasons exist for the application of the service requirement in all cases involving constitutional challenges . . . Because we hold that the service requirement is applicable to this case and the record is devoid of evidence of service on the attorney general, it follows that the trial court could not properly consider the constitutional issue raised by the demurrer. We therefore cannot review that issue." 91 Wis.2d at 117.Under the Kurtz rule a party will be foreclosed from challenging the validity of a statute unless the attorney general is given an opportunity to appear before the court and defend the law as constitutionally proper.

There is no dispute in this case that notice to the attorney general was not given and that the Kurtz rule was not complied with. The question which must be resolved is whether notice which was first given in this case while the cause was pending before the court of appeals cured the defect created by the failure to give notice to the attorney general at the probate court level.

Although the Kurtz rule is closely akin to the notice of requirement under sec. 806.04(11), Stats., and although the failure of notice in a sec. 806.04 declaratory action would require dismissal for lack of jurisdiction, we conclude the same result is not required in this case. In a declaratory action the failure to give the notice required by sec. 806.04(11) is fatal to the jurisdiction of the court. O'Connell v. Board of Education, Joint Dist. No. 10, 82 Wis.2d 728, 735, 264 N.W.2d 561 (1978); Town of Center v. City of Appleton, 70 Wis.2d 666, 669, 235 N.W.2d 504 (1975); Bollhoffer v. Wolke, 66 Wis.2d 141, 144, 223 N.W.2d 902 (1974).

This conclusion is mandated by the language in sec. 806.04(11). See Bollhoffer v. Wolke, supra at 143. Because the declaratory action itself is a creature of statute, the maintenance of a declaratory action requires strict compliance with sec. 806.04. O'Connell v. Board of Education, Joint Dist. No. 10, supra at 735. Unlike the notice requirement under the statutes, the Kurtz rule is a judicially mandated rule of procedure. Lack of compliance with this rule will not preclude review of a constitutional issue because of a failure of jurisdiction.

The purpose of the Kurtz rule is to allow the state to defend the validity of its statutes. Kenosha v. Dosemagen, supra, 54 Wis.2d at 271. It is intended to afford the court an opportunity to analyze questions of constitutional dimension from a perspective that is not limited to the narrow interests and views of the private parties to the action. In this case we conclude that the failure to notify the attorney general of the probate court proceedings was a defect which was cured by virtue of the subsequent invitation to the attorney general to participate in the court of appeals' proceedings. In light of the opportunity which was given to the attorney general, and in the absence of any claim or evidence that the interests of the state have been prejudiced by its lack of participation in the probate proceedings, the purpose of the Kurtz rule has been fulfilled. There is no reason for refusing to consider Tanner's claims on their merits.

Tanner's principal argument on this review is that the Due Process Clause of the Fourteenth Amendment to the United States Constitution requires more than notice by publication under sec. 859.07, Stats., to apprise creditors of the opportunity to present proof of their claims and to inform them of the fact that claims will be barred if not timely submitted. In support of this argument, principal reliance is placed upon the United States Supreme Court decision in Mullane v. Central Hanover Trust Co., 339 U.S. 306 (1950). Tanner also notes that the Mullane rule has been applied by this court in the context of proceedings to admit a will to probate. See In re Estate of Phillips, 92 Wis.2d 354, 284 N.W.2d 908 (1979). It is therefore argued that the Mullane rule applies in similar fashion to the notice which is given to creditors under sec. 859.07.

We do not agree with Tanner's view of the notice requirements due to a creditor under ch. 859, Stats. As set forth below, we conclude that the Mullane rule does not control the disposition of this case. As a matter of due process of law, notice of the operation of sec. 859.01 is not required.

In the case of Mullane v. Central Hanover Trust Co., 339 U.S. 306 (1950), the court considered the validity of a New York state court judgment which finalized the accounts of the trustees of a common trust fund established under the laws of New York. This judgment foreclosed every right which the beneficiaries would have had against the trustee of the common fund. The beneficiaries were numerous, and many were not residents of New York. Notice of the proceeding to finalize the fiduciary accounts was given by publication as required by state law. Although the names and addresses of many of the beneficiaries were known, no attempt was made to notify these individuals by personal service or by mail. The United States Supreme Court held that the state court judgment was not binding on the beneficiaries whose addresses were known to the trustee of the common trust fund. As to these individuals, the judgment was obtained in violation of the due process law. The court wrote:

An elementary and fundamental requirement of due process in any proceeding which is to be accorded finality is notice reasonably calculated, under all the circumstances, to apprise interested parties of the pendency of the action and afford them an opportunity to present their objections. Milliken v. Meyer, 311 U.S. 457; Grannis v. Ordean, 234 U.S. 385; Priest v. Las Vegas, 232 U.S. 604; Roller v. Holly, 176 U.S. 398. The notice must be of such nature as reasonably to convey the required information, Grannis v. Ordean, supra, and it must afford a reasonable time for those interested to make their appearance, Roller v. Holly, supra, and cf. Goodrich v. Ferris, 214 U.S. 71." Id. at 314.

The court viewed the publication notice as a hollow formality and concluded that "when notice is a person's due, process which is a mere gesture is not due process." Id. at 315.

In the thirty years since it was decided, Mullane v. Central Hanover Trust Co., 339 U.S. 306 (1950), has been the controlling precedent in a number of United States Supreme Court cases. In Schroeder v. City of New York, 371 U.S. 208 (1962), the court held that a condemnation proceeding which was predicated upon notice by publication was violative of due process. A similar conclusion was reached in Covey v. Town of Somers, 351 U.S. 141 (1956). In that case the court concluded that a proceeding to enforce a tax lien which resulted in a judgment of foreclosure was not binding upon a legally incompetent person who was without a guardian and who had been notified of the action by mail.

The United States Supreme Court has also held that a court decree terminating the parental rights of a natural parent and establishing those rights in an adoptive parent was violative of due process in that the termination/adoption proceeding was not preceded by actual or constructive notice to the natural parent. See Armstrong v. Manzo, 380 U.S. 545 (1965). Most recently, in Memphis Light, Gas & Water Div. v. Craft, 436 U.S. 1 (1978), the court ruled that a termination notice sent out by a municipal utility does not comport with constitutional requirements when it does not advise the customer of the availability of a procedure for protesting a proposed termination of utility service as unjustified. In that case the Mullane rule was held to require notice of that which the court viewed as an informal due process hearing. See Id. at n. 17.

These cases make it clear that when the rights or interests of a person are sought to be affected by judicial or quasi-judicial decree, due process requires that the individual be given notice reasonably calculated to inform the person of the pending proceeding and to afford him or her an opportunity to object and defend his or her rights. This is the essence of the rule of Mullane v. Central Hanover Trust Co., 339 U.S. 306 (1950), and its progeny. It is evident upon a reading of these cases that the scope of the Mullane rule is limited to those rights or interests jeopardized by judicial or quasi-judicial actions or proceedings. It is therefore crucial to this review to determine whether or not Tanner's claim has been extinguished by adjudication or by some other means.

Tanner's claim was extinguished by operation of sec. 859.01, Stats. This section requires that claims in probate be filed within a specified period of time, and if a claim is not filed it is barred forever. It is settled law in Wisconsin that this statute is essentially a statute of limitations. Estate of Palmer, 68 Wis.2d 101, 107, 227 N.W.2d 680 (1975); Estate of Lathers, 215 Wis. 151, 251 N.W. 466 (1934).

The bar created by operation of a statute of limitations is established independently of any adjudicatory process. It is legislative expression of policy that prohibits litigants from raising claims -- whether or not they are meritorious -- after the expiration of a given period of time. See Gamma Tau Educational Foundation v. Ohio Cas. Ins. Co., 41 Wis.2d 675, 683, 165 N.W.2d 135 (1969). See also Denzer v. Rouse, 48 Wis.2d 528, 534, 180 N.W.2d 521 (1970). Under Wisconsin law the expiration of the limitations period extinguishes the cause of action of the potential plaintiff and it also creates a right enjoyed by the would-be defendant to insist on that statutory bar. See Pulchinski v. Strnad, 88 Wis.2d 423, 276 N.W.2d 781 (1979). The passage of time itself destroys the right and remedy of the injured party.

We conclude that Tanner's probate claim was cut off by operation of a statute of limitation and not by action of a judicial body. Therefore, the Mullane rule has no application. Of course this is not true of all aspects of the probate process. As we recognized in In re Estate of Phillips, 92 Wis.2d 354, 284 N.W.2d 908 (1979), the Mullane rule operates where the powers of the court are invoked to pass judgment on the validity of a will. However, Mullane does not require that a person be notified of the running of a statute of limitations.

This is not to say that the due process clause has no application to a discussion of the operation of a limitations statute. Once a cause of action accrues it may not be divested except by operation of the due process of law. Hunter v. School District of Gale-Ettrick-Trempealeau, 97 Wis.2d 435, 443, 293 N.W.2d 515 (1980). However, the focus of our attention must now shift to a consideration of whether the legislature may, consistent with notions of due process, divest a person of his cause of action even though he may not precisely know the time within which he must assert his claim to preserve it.

In the case of Rod v. Farrell, 96 Wis.2d 349, 291 N.W.2d 568 (1980), this court rejected the "discovery rule" as it related to the accrual of a cause of action in a medical malpractice case. The court adhered to its previous rulings which held that the statute of limitations for a medical malpractice claim begins to run at the time the negligent act occurs with accompanying injury. Id. at 352. In Rod v. Farrell, it was alleged that the defendant negligently performed surgery on the plaintiff in 1951 thereby causing the plaintiff to become sterile. This sterility was not discovered until 1975. Suit was filed in 1976. Despite the fact that the statutory limit to the plaintiff's action had expired years before his injury was even discovered, we concluded that the operation of the limitation statute did not offend the due process clause of the federal constitution. Id. at 356.

In this case Tanner knew of the existence of its claim and failed to assert it within the limits imposed by sec. 859.01, Stats., only because of a failure to keep in close enough contact with the decedent to know that he had died. Having concluded that the operation of the statute of limitations in the Rod v. Farrell Case was not violative of due process, it would be inconsistent to find such a constitutional violation under the facts and circumstances of this case.

The conclusion which we have reached in this case is in accord with the determinations of courts from other jurisdictions. In the case of Gano Farms, Inc. v. Estate of Kleweno, 2 Kan. App. 506, 582 P.2d 742 (1978), the Kansas Court of Appeals considered the validity of the operation of a probate code statute requiring only notice by publication as a means of notifying creditors of their time to file claims. The court ruled that the creditor's claim was barred by the nonclaim statute and not by virtue of being made a party to a judicial proceeding requiring Mullane-type notice. Id. at 508. Other courts have reached similar conclusions in similar cases. One such case was Baker National Bank v. Henderson, 151 Mont. 526, 445 P.2d 574 (1968). Since the Montana Supreme Court ruled against the creditor on due process grounds in that controversy, an appeal was taken to the United States Supreme Court. The appeal was dismissed for want of a substantial federal question. Baker National Bank v. Henderson, 393 U.S. 530 (1969). As compared to the denial of a writ of certiorari, the dismissal of an appeal is an adjudication on the merits of the controversy. Hicks v. Miranda, 422 U.S. 332 (1975). Although entitled to less precedential weight than would be accorded a decision accompanied by a full opinion, the dismissal of the appeal by the United States Supreme Court is authority which supports our conclusion that no due process violation has occurred in this case.

Tanner's final argument is that it is a violation of the commerce clause to allow an out-of-state creditor's claim to be extinguished by virtue of the operation of sec. 859.01, Stats., without notice to the creditor which is reasonably calculated to inform the potential claimant of the operation of a nonclaim statute. The thrust of this argument is that notice by publication alone is no notice at all to out-of-state creditors and this unduly fetters interstate trade or commerce. Tanner argues that the United States Supreme Court decisions in Allenberg Cotton Co. v. Pittman, 419 U.S. 20 (1974), and Shafer v. Farmers Grain Co., 268 U.S. 189 (1925), require us to rule in its favor.

This claim is without merit. The cases cited to us involve the question of a state's authority to regulate intrastate activities which are part and parcel of the flow of interstate commerce. Based on the record in this case, we know only that a nonresident creditor entered into two contracts with a resident radio station owner, and claims for a breach of these agreements were extinguished by operation of a probate statute. We are at a loss to understand how this record establishes a violation of the commerce clause. A state does not lose its authority to regulate matters of contract and probate law simply because the disputed transaction involves a nonresident. To the extent that it is argued that lack of sufficient notice "fetters" interstate commerce, we view this claim as a due process argument clothed in the guise of an alternative constitutional provision.

The denial of Tanner's claim violated no provision of the federal constitution. The rule of the Mullane decision does not limit the authority of the legislature to extinguish a claim by virtue of the operation of a limitations statute. Tanner was divested of his claim in a manner not offensive to notions of due process. Finally, the state is not deprived of authority to regulate the administration of the estate merely because the decedent's creditors were not Wisconsin residents. No violation of the commerce clause was involved in this case. The decision of the Court of Appeals is modified and, as modified, affirmed.

NOTE ON TULSA PROFESSIONAL COLLECTIONS SERVICES v. POPE

The Wisconsin Supreme Court's *Tanner v. Fessler* decision was handed down prior to the United States Supreme Court's decision in *Tulsa Professional Collection Services, Inc. v. Pope*, 485 U.S. 478 (1988), in which the court held that a known creditor's Fourteenth Amendment due process rights were violated by a statutory bar on claims, if the only notice to creditors was publication. In *Pope,* the complaining creditor was, ironically, the Tulsa, Oklahoma hospital in which the deceased, H. Everett Pope, had died on April 2, 1979. Nevertheless, the hospital, which had not been directly notified of the death by the executor, had failed to file a claim against Pope's estate within the prescribed period. As a result, the estate, administered by Pope's widow, refused to pay the claim.

Under the controlling Oklahoma "nonclaim" statute in effect at the time, most claims against the estate, to be valid, had to be filed within two months of publication of a notice of death in a local Oklahoma newspaper. The Oklahoma Supreme Court upheld the constitutionality of the statute, and in so doing, ruled that *Mullane v. Central Hanover Bank and Trust Co.,* 339 U.S. 306 (1950), was not applicable. In its analysis, the court relied specifically upon *Tanner v. Fessler*, along with similar cases from Washington and Kansas. *Tulsa Professional Collection Services, Inc. v. Pope,* 733 P.2d 396 (Okla. 1986).

Although language in the United States Supreme Court's *Pope* decision appeared to distinguish the existing Wisconsin statute from its Oklahoma counterpart, the Wisconsin legislature enacted current Wis. Stat. 859.02(2)(b) (set out below) in 1989 in response to the *Pope* decision. That this was the Wisconsin response to *Pope* was acknowledged by the Wisconsin Supreme Court in *Sears, Roebuck & Co. v. Plath*, 161 Wis.2d 587, 592, 598, 468 N.W.2d 689, 691, 693 (1991). The current Wisconsin statute differs from many of its counterparts in other states in that it gives the supervising judicial official some discretion in determining the proper length of the claim period.

D. VALID AND INVALID CLAIMS AGAINST AN ESTATE

The personal representative that handles probate is obligated to pay the lawful debts of the decedent, but it is not always clear what is a lawful debt and what is not, as the following case illustrates.

In re Estate of Steffes

Supreme Court of Wisconsin
95 Wis. 2d 490, 290 N.W.2d 697 (1980)

Abrahamson, J. The question on appeal is whether the plaintiff, who engaged in an adulterous relationship with the deceased, may recover from the estate for unpaid salary, wages or other compensation for personal services rendered to the deceased within the two-year period preceding his death.

Virgil Steffes died without a will on July 17, 1976. His gross estate was valued at $733,644.65. Steffes was survived by a son, who is an heir and the personal representative of the estate, and children of a deceased son, who are heirs. The plaintiff, Mary Lou Brooks, filed a claim against the estate in the amount of $29,200.00 for personal services rendered to the deceased during the last two years of his life (July 17, 1974-July 17, 1976). The estate refused to pay the claim and this litigation ensued. The trial court rendered judgment allowing the claim against the estate in the amount of $14,600.00.

There is no dispute that plaintiff rendered services for Steffes on the farm and in his home and that she gave him excellent nursing care during his lengthy last illness. Steffes' son had been a guest in his father's home before his father's death, and he testified that he had eaten meals cooked by the plaintiff, that his father's home was kept in good condition, and that the plaintiff took good care of his ill father.

The son, as personal representative, appeals the judgment on three grounds: (1) that the facts do not sustain the trial court's findings that the plaintiff rendered services at the request of and with the knowledge of the deceased and with the expectation of compensation; (2) that any services rendered are presumed to be gratuitous because plaintiff lived for more than six years as a member of Steffes' household and that the requirement that there be an express promise to pay for such services was not met; and (3) that the plaintiff cannot recover compensation for the work she performed in the house and on the farm, because Steffes and the plaintiff had engaged in sexual intercourse.

We affirm the judgment of the trial court. The facts are not in dispute. Mary Lou Brooks, the plaintiff, met Virgil Steffes, the deceased, in 1969, while the plaintiff was working in a tavern, and soon thereafter she moved to Steffes' farm home where she resided until his death. Plaintiff and Steffes were each married to other persons. Plaintiff knew Steffes was a married man, and he continued to be married until his wife died in 1974. The plaintiff had been married in 1963 and had two children. She continued to be married while she lived in the deceased's house, initiating divorce proceedings after Steffes' death. Plaintiff admitted having sexual relations with Virgil Steffes until about a year before Steffes' death. Plaintiff and numerous witnesses testified that neither plaintiff nor Steffes had represented her as Mrs. Virgil Steffes.

According to the plaintiff's undisputed testimony she performed the following chores in the house and on the farm: she cleaned the house, did the cooking, washing, and ironing; she helped fix farm fences; she picked the corn crop; she ran the combine and loaded the corn into a "semi" during late 1974; she chased animals which escaped from the pasture; from the end of October until May (1974-1975) she loaded silage; she aided the deceased in pouring concrete walls around the feedlot; she aided the deceased in remodeling his home by "tearing out partitions" and by setting forms, pouring concrete, and pulling the forms; she wrote all the deceased's checks (with one or two exceptions) under the deceased's direction over the two-year period in question, signing his name along with her initials; and she cleaned and prepared machinery for the April 1975 farm sale.

The amount of work performed by the plaintiff may be gauged by the size of the farming operation. In July, 1974, there were 80 head of Charolais cattle and approximately 20 registered Morgan horses on the farm. There were also 325 acres of corn on the farm in the spring of 1975.

The plaintiff also described the nursing care she gave Steffes. In the fall of 1974, his health began to deteriorate. He suffered from headaches and dizzy spells. In March, 1975 he was hospitalized and tests revealed a brain tumor; surgery was performed. Plaintiff stayed in a chair beside Steffes' bed for four days and nights while he was in the hospital. For twenty-eight consecutive days after Steffes' surgery, plaintiff drove him to the hospital for cobalt treatments. Steffes' condition continued to worsen during 1976 and plaintiff's care continued. …

[The opinion's description of the care provided by the plaintiff during Steffes' last months is omitted.]

Plaintiff testified that she received the following items from the deceased during this two-year period: food and lodging; approximately $7,200.00 from the sale of horses and cows which deceased had given to plaintiff to take care of; $3,200.00 towards a $4,544.00 Pontiac which was purchased June 22, 1976 and titled in the plaintiff's name.

The trial court summarized the plaintiff's efforts as follows: "Now this lady although she was not a mason [she] did cement work, and although she was not a carpenter she did carpentry work, and although she wasn't an accountant she did bookkeeping work, although she was not a nurse she rendered nursing services."

Plaintiff testified that she expected to receive something for the services she performed for Virgil Steffes during the last two years of his life. The deceased's brother-in-law and friends of both the plaintiff and the deceased testified that Steffes had indicated that he wanted to provide for the plaintiff and that he wanted her to have the house and farm on his death. However, Steffes did not execute a will and sold part of the farm on land contract and gave the purchasers an option to purchase farm property.

The trial court found that the plaintiff went into the deceased's home as a housekeeper, that the housekeeping, farming and nursing services "rendered by her were performed at the instance and with his knowledge of the decedent;" and that the plaintiff expected compensation for these services over and above room and board and the gratuities she received from Mr. Steffes. These findings are significant because this court, in a long line of cases, has held that where services are performed at the special instance of the deceased and with his knowledge and are performed by the claimant with expectation of reasonable compensation, recovery may be allowed on the basis of a contract to pay, implied in fact or law.

The trial court concluded that a contract for services can be implied from the facts and can also be implied in law (quasi-contract) on the ground of unjust enrichment and that plaintiff can recover the reasonable value of services rendered to the deceased.

The personal representative asserts that the evidence does not support the trial court's findings of fact that the services were rendered at the instance of and the knowledge of the decedent and with the expectation of compensation. …

[After an analysis of the evidence pertaining to the personal and business relationship between the plaintiff and the deceased and of the Court's prior decisions regarding implied contracts and the claims of service providers, the majority rejected the personal representative's argument that the plaintiff had no reason to have expected that she would be compensated for her assistance of the deceased during their "relationship," after which the Court continued:]

In the case at bar the plaintiff had been employed in a tavern when she met the deceased. The trial court concluded that she left a paying job to take care of deceased's home; that she went to the deceased's farm and performed labor usually performed by a housekeeper, farm-hand, mason, carpenter, bookkeeper and nurse; and that she worked long and hard doing heavy work and performing unpleasant tasks. She testified she expected compensation.

Witnesses testified that the decedent said he wanted to leave real estate to her and wanted to provide for her. Several of the services plaintiff performed were of a commercial variety, and the deceased hired employees to perform services similar to those rendered by the plaintiff. … We hold that there is sufficient evidence in the case at bar to support the trial court's finding that there was an implied promise to pay for the services plaintiff rendered.

The personal representative's final argument is that because the plaintiff voluntarily and knowingly lived in an adulterous relationship with the decedent she cannot recover on implied contract for her household, farm or nursing services.

In support of its contention, the estate quotes the following language from Estate of Fox, 178 Wis. 369, 371, 190 N.W. 90 (1922):

"Courts are practically unanimous in holding that when a woman voluntarily and knowingly lives in illicit relations with a man, she cannot recover on implied contract during the period of such relationship."

This language was obiter dicta. In the Fox case, this court permitted a woman who in good faith believed she was married to a man, though she was not, to recover for services rendered during the illicit relationship. Our court refused to adopt the harsh Massachusetts rule that the woman could not recover because the law can imply no agreement when no compensation was contemplated by the parties. Instead, our court held that the determination of whether a woman who lived in an illegal relationship with a man could recover from the man on the theory of implied contract turns on the equities of the situation. In the Fox case we held that the woman could recover under a theory of implied contract because denying recovery would unjustly enrich his estate at her expense. We said "equity demands that she shall be made whole . . . . It is inferred from the nature of the transaction, and the supposed husband is held to have assumed to pay because in point of law and equity it is just that he should pay."

The trial court in the case at bar looked at the equities and decided that unless plaintiff was compensated for her services the Steffes' estate would be unjustly enriched. The trial court concluded that fairness and justice required that her claim be paid. The trial court stated:

". . . I don't think that there is a person that could sit here in the courtroom today and listen to what I heard too today and listen to all the work that Mary Lou Brooks did for Virgil Steffes during his lifetime and conclude that anything other than that estate has been enriched by reason of her services. Had he hired somebody to do this he would have had to pay them for that and to the extent that he has not paid for those services that estate has been enriched. He was just as much a party to the illicit relationship as this lady was. The question I have in mind is why should the estate be enriched when that man was just as much a part of the illicit relationship as she was and not let her have her fair dues. I don't understand that law that would interpret unjust enrichment that way and deprive one and let the other benefit and do it on the basis that there was an illicit relationship but not equally held against the both. . . ." **[The remainder of the Court's discussion of this issue is omitted.]**

In the case at bar the trial court found that the illicit relationship was incidental to the plaintiff's performance of lawful services and was not a condition of, nor a consideration for, the deceased's implied promise to compensate. In view of the trial court's findings and the facts of this case, we conclude that it is not contrary to public policy to permit the plaintiff to recover the reasonable value of the lawful services performed for the deceased. For the foregoing reasons, we affirm the judgment of the trial court.

[Justice Coffey dissented, in a lengthy opinion that took issue with most of the majority's analysis and which included the following observation:]

"I believe the majority has resorted to an unfortunate form of judicial surgery that can only serve to accelerate the growth of the self-destructive cancer of the '70's "immorality" and the decline of the family. If there is to be a direct, frontal assault on the traditional values, principles, ideals and pattern of family life, the very lifeline and backbone of our American society, it should be accomplished within the confines of the legislative halls -- not in the courts." …

III. THE LAWYER'S ROLE

A. SOLICTING BUSINESS AND SAFEGUARDING WILLS

The following case was decided several years before the landmark decision of *Bates v. State Bar of Arizona,* 433 U.S. 350 (1977), in which the United States Supreme Court ruled that lawyers had a First Amendment right to advertise that could not be impaired by the state bars. Before *Bates,* most states prohibited virtually all forms of advertising and solicitation by lawyers on the grounds that such activities were "unprofessional" and a disservice to the public. However, the two appellants in the Bates case were young lawyers who had been disciplined by the Arizona bar for running a small informational advertisement listing fees for legal services in a Phoenix newspaper.

The full impact of the *Bates* decision was initially unclear. Whether the First Amendment also proscribed restrictions on the solicitation of business had not been directly addressed by the Court. However, the following year, the Supreme Court drew a line between advertising and face-to-face solicitation of clients in *Ohralik v. Ohio State Bar Assn.*, 436 U.S. 447 (1978). While lawyers had a constitutional right to advertise the availability of their services in a non-misleading way, the potentially coercive nature of *in personam* solicitation justified a state ban on such activities.

In addition to the prohibitions on advertising and solicitation, lawyers in the era of *Tanner* and *Bates* were required to avoid conduct that might appear inappropriate (even if it was not). Canon 9 of the American Bar Association's *Model Code of Professional Responsibility,* which had been adopted in Wisconsin, provided that "A Lawyer Should Avoid Even the Appearance of Professional Impropriety." While retaining the original of a client's will was a widely used practice by American lawyers, few considered it "inappropriate" before this case. (Interestingly, the phrase "appearance of impropriety" does not appear in the current Wisconsin Rules of Professional Conduct for Attorneys or in the American Bar Association's Model Rules of Professional Conduct on which they are based. However, the phrase still appears in the ABA's Model Code of Judicial Conduct.)

State v. Gulbankian

Supreme Court of Wisconsin
54 Wis. 2d 605, 196 N.W.2d 733 (1972)

PER CURIAM. Gulbank K. (George) Gulbankian was admitted to practice law in Wisconsin in 1926 and practiced alone in Racine until his sister Miss Vartak Gulbankian was admitted to practice law in 1935. They shared offices until 1955 when they commenced to practice law as partners and have so practiced until the present time. The complaint alleges the Gulbankians have solicited the probate of estates by inserting in the wills which they draft a provision that they should be the attorney for the executor and in some wills the executor or executrix. The answer denies any solicitation and alleges their designation as attorneys or executor in the wills was at the request of the respective clients.

From January 1, 1955, through January 23, 1971, the Gulbankians filed for probate in the county court of Racine county 147 wills, of which 135 were drafted by them. Of these 135 wills, 71 directed the employment of one or the other of the Gulbankians for the purpose of probating the estate. Twenty-six of the wills directed the employment of Gulbank K. Gulbankian and four directed the appointment of Vartak Gulbankian; in 41 wills Akabe Gulbankian, a sister of the attorneys, was appointed either executrix or coexecutrix; and in three wills Vartak Gulbankian was named executrix. Prior to 1957 about 50 percent of the wills drawn contained a provision for the employment of either Gulbank or Vartak Gulbankian, but since that time in about 94 percent of the wills the executor was instructed to retain either G. K. Gulbankian or Vartak Gulbankian as attorney. Only one will drafted after 1957 failed to name a member of the Gulbankian family to some fiduciary capacity. On the basis of this record it is argued that because such a large percentage of wills drawn by the Gulbankians contain a direction to the executor to retain them as attorneys, an inference must of necessity be drawn that the

Gulbankians at the time the wills were drafted suggested to or solicited the testators to provide for their employment to probate the estates. Such conduct it is argued amounts to unprofessional conduct.

It is, of course, unprofessional to solicit professional employment, not only by advertisement, touters or runners, but also by personal communication or interviews. Canon 27, Canons of Ethics of the American Bar Association. The new Code of Professional Responsibility, Disciplinary Rules DR 2-103, provides in paragraph. (A) that a lawyer shall not recommend employment of himself or his partner or associate to a nonlawyer who has not sought his advice regarding the employment of a lawyer. The object of these canons is to prevent lawyers from engaging in competitive advertising and from attempting to explain to the public why they could serve better or accomplish more than other lawyers could. Such advertising is the lifeline of business, but it has traditionally been prohibited in the professions. While solicitation of cases may not involve the high degree of moral turpitude which fraud does, nevertheless solicitation is considered inimical to the good reputation of the legal profession and likely to bring the profession into disrepute.

The narrow question in this case is whether this court should draw an inference of solicitation on the record. This matter was referred to and heard by the Honorable John K. Callahan, a reserve judge, as referee. We have great respect for his judgment. He does not find actual solicitation but he does think that lay people might infer solicitation if they were not cognizant of the facts.

The Gulbankians claim they did not suggest the inclusion of such a clause but rather their clients spontaneously directed that they put in the will the requirement that they be retained to take care of the probate or that they act as executor. They point out many of their clients are of Armenian descent and have difficulty conversing in English; and because of the common ethnic background, there is a closer relationship between the Gulbankians and their clients than ordinarily exists between other attorneys and clients.

The Gulbankian family were Armenian immigrants to America, coming here to escape the massacre by the Turks in the early part of the 20th Century. Their family presently consists of two attorneys (the defendants), a sister Akabe who is engaged as a real estate saleswoman and does income tax work, and a sister Rose who for the most part is the housekeeper for the family. There was also a brother Harry who was the first of the family to come to this country but who is now deceased. The Gulbankians arrived in this country as penniless immigrants and settled in Racine county, where there is now a large population of Armenians, Slovaks, Greeks, and southern Europeans.

Apparently the Gulbankians have helped the Armenian community, gained the confidence of a large segment of the foreign-speaking people in the area, and for many years were the only Armenian attorneys in Racine. The defense produced several clients who have had their wills prepared by the Gulbankians and who testified they wanted the Gulbankians to probate their estates as well.

We are asked to consider that the clients of the Gulbankians' firm are different than the average law client in that they place unusually great trust in their attorneys and look to them for counsel and advice in many areas, some of which do not involve legal matters. This confidence is based not only on the fact the Gulbankians are professional people but also on language and ethnic affinity. The record shows the Gulbankians have a substantial probate practice in the county of Racine and are well respected and regarded by the community. The referee was impressed with these features of the case.

As a part of their defense, the Gulbankians claim there is a custom in Racine county for attorneys to name themselves attorneys for the estate in some form of language. The defendants' exhibits show that 23 to 71 percent of the wills drafted by other law firms in the Racine area contain a provision for employment to probate the estate. There is oral testimony tending to prove a practice in Racine county of attorneys putting in a clause directing he be retained to probate the estate in five to 50 percent of the wills. There was other testimony that one attorney seldom put the clause in a will and never without a voluntary direction by the client. Of course, the extensiveness of a practice does not mean the practice is legitimate if in fact the practice amounts to solicitation of business. It is most difficult to determine from statistics whether the recurrence of such clauses is the result of voluntary and unsuggested directions from the testator or whether such recurrence reflects the effectiveness of subtle suggestions.

It is clear an attorney cannot solicit either directly or by any indirect means a request or direction of a testator that he or a member of his firm be named executor or be employed as an attorney to probate the estate. In those fairly rare cases where a client, because of the unusual familiarity of the attorney with the testator's business or family problems or because of a relationship which transcends the ordinary client-attorney relationship, asks his attorney to act as executor or to provide for his employment to probate the estate, there is no solicitation. A gray area, however, exists when an attorney explains the duties of an executor and the question is reached concerning probate. In preparing a will the attorney must know the identity of the executor. In many cases the testator is unfamiliar with the duties of an executor. It is the lawyer's right and duty to advise the testator what the duties of the executor are, to explain that the executor may hire an attorney to help him probate the estate, and that in the case of a corporate executor that sec. 856.31 Stats. (effective April 1, 1971), may apply. When the section is applicable, the person receiving the largest interest may name the attorney unless good cause is shown otherwise. Whether the naming of the attorney by the testator constitutes such good cause has raised problems but so have directions to a noncorporate executor to hire a designated attorney.

This problem must be discussed by the attorney and his client objectively and uninfluenced by any desire of the attorney to eventually probate the estate. An attorney should not use a will form which provides for a designation of an attorney for the probate of the estate or executor for submission to the testator on the theory it is properly a part of a standard form of a will; no such form of suggestion may be used. An attorney, merely because he drafts a will, has no preferential claim to probate it. *Estate of Ainsworth* (1971), 52 Wis. 2d 152, 187 N. W. 2d 828. Nor do we approve of attorneys' "safekeeping" wills. In the old days this may have been explained on the ground many people did not have a safe place to keep their valuable papers, but there is little justification today because most people do have safekeeping boxes, and if not, sec. 853.09, Stats., provides for the deposit of a will with the register in probate for safekeeping during the lifetime of the testator. The correct practice is that the original will should be delivered to the testator, and should only be kept by the attorney upon specific unsolicited request of the client.

We emphasize that while an attorney is discussing the identity and the duties of an executor, he must especially be careful that his conversation does not intimate or suggest or solicit, directly or indirectly, his employment as the possible attorney to assist the executor in the probate of the estate or his appointment as executor. We realize this is an area in which it is difficult to police professional standards, but circumstantial evidence as well as direct testimony may be relied upon to prove that solicitation has occurred.

Upon this record this court is constrained not to draw an inference the Gulbankians solicited the probate of estates by drafting wills designating themselves as executors or to be retained as attorneys by the executor. We are concerned, however, that the high percentage of such provisions in the wills drafted by the Gulbankians and by other attorneys in Racine county might well lead lay people and the public generally to conclude there has been solicitation. A lawyer must not only avoid solicitation but also the appearance of solicitation so as not to damage the confidence the public has in the legal profession. We do not hold that a lawyer may not draft a will in which he is designated as executor or contains a direction to the executor to employ him in suggestive or even the mandatory language required by the *Estate of Sieben, supra*, if in fact that is the unprompted intent of his client; but the number of times this will occur will be few and the percentage in total of such wills drawn low.

Because this is the first disciplinary case which raises this important issue, we have spent some time giving guidelines for the future. This may not be the total answer to the problem and improvements may be worked out on a case-to-case basis in the future.

Therefore, It Is Ordered And Adjudged that the complaint herein be, and it is hereby, dismissed.

NOTE ON SAFEGUARDING WILLS.

If it is not proper to leave the original copy of the will with the lawyer who drafted it, where should the will be stored? Wis. Stat. 853.09 provides one answer, although the evidence suggests that few Wisconsin testators take advantage of the opportunity.

Wis. Stat. § 853.09. Deposit of will in circuit court during testator's lifetime.

(1) DEPOSIT OF WILL.

Unless provided otherwise by county ordinance, any testator may deposit his or her will with the register in probate of the court of the county where he or she resides. The will shall be sealed in an envelope with the name and address of the testator, and the date of deposit noted thereon. If the will is deposited by a person other than the testator, that fact also shall be noted on the envelope. The size of the envelope may be regulated by the register in probate to provide uniformity and ease of filing. A county board may, by ordinance, provide that wills may not be deposited with the register in probate for the county. Wills deposited with the register in probate prior to the effective date of that ordinance shall be retained by the register in probate as provided under sub. (2)

(2) DUTY OF REGISTER IN PROBATE.

The register in probate shall issue a receipt for the deposit of the will and shall maintain a registry of all wills deposited. The original will, unless withdrawn under sub. (3) or opened in accordance with s. 856.03 after death of the testator, shall be kept on file for the period provided in SCR chapter 72; thereafter the register may either retain the original will or open the envelope, copy or reproduce the will for confidential record storage purposes by microfilm, optical disk, electronic format or other method of comparable retrievability and destroy the original. If satisfactorily identified, the reproduction is admissible in court for probate or any other purpose the same as the original document. Wills deposited with the county judge under s. 238.15, 1967 stats., shall be transferred to the register in probate and become subject to this section.

(3) WITHDRAWAL.

A testator may withdraw the testators will during the testators lifetime, but the register in probate shall deliver the will only to the testator personally or to a person duly authorized to withdraw it for the testator, by a writing signed by the testator and 2 witnesses other than the person authorized.

B. ATTORNEY LIABILITY TO INTENDED DEVISEES

It has long been accepted that lawyers owe a duty of reasonable care to their clients, including individuals for whom they draft wills. If they fail to exercise reasonable care in the provision of legal services, they can be sued in tort for malpractice. However, it was historically less clear whether or not this legal duty extended to non-client, third parties, like the intended devises in a will who were left out of the document because of the lawyer's carelessness. The following case represented a turning point in the way in which Wisconsin courts viewed this issue.

Auric v. Continental Casualty Co.

Supreme Court of Wisconsin
111 Wis. 2d 507, 331 N.W.2d 325 (1983)

Day, J. This is an appeal from a judgment of the circuit court for Racine County, James W. Wilbershide, Judge, which dismissed Robert Auric's (Auric) complaint. Auric appealed and filed a petition to bypass the court of appeals pursuant to sec. 808.05, Stats. 1979-80. This court granted the petition on November 8, 1982.

There are three issues to be considered on appeal. The first issue is: May an attorney who drafted a will be held liable to a beneficiary of the will not in privity with the attorney for the attorney's negligence in failing to properly supervise the execution of the will? The second issue is: Should the respondent be allowed to challenge a trial court order denying his motion for summary judgment when he has failed to file a notice of cross-appeal pursuant to sec. 809.10(2) (b), Stats. 1979-80. The final issue is: When does the statute of limitations in sec. 893.52, Stats. 1979-80, commence to run in an action by a will beneficiary against an attorney for negligently supervising the execution of a will?

We conclude that the beneficiary of a will may maintain an action against an attorney who negligently drafted or supervised the execution of the will even though the beneficiary is not in privity with that attorney. We deny plaintiff-appellant's motion to dismiss the defendant-respondent's cross-appeal because the defendant failed to file a cross-appeal under sec. 809.10(2) (b), Stats., but raised the issue for the first time in his brief on appeal. We also conclude that the plaintiff, Auric's, action was commenced within the period of the statute of limitations. Accordingly, we reverse the decision of the trial court and direct the trial court to enter judgment in favor of the plaintiff in the amount of $25,000, the amount bequeathed to him in the invalid will. We remand the case to the trial court to determine whether an award of prejudgment interest should be made.

This action was tried on stipulated facts as follows. The testator, Frank P. Goldstein, died on April 13, 1975. Prior to his death, the decedent had attorney Timothy P. Crawford draft a new Will and Revocable Living Trust to replace a previous will dated April 30, 1970. On July 24, 1973, Mr. Crawford had the decedent come to his office to execute the new will and trust. Crawford explained the provisions of the trust to the decedent, had him sign the document, and then both Crawford and his secretary signed the trust document as witnesses. Crawford then explained the provisions of the will to the decedent and had him sign that document. Crawford then signed as a witness. However, because of what was characterized as either "confusion" or a "mistake of the moment," Crawford's secretary failed to sign the will.

The 1973 will contained a specific bequest of $25,000 to Robert Auric, who was Mr. Goldstein's brother. The 1970 will contained no such bequest. On July 1, 1975, the Racine County Probate Court ordered the 1970 will admitted to probate and denied admission to the 1973 will because it was not executed as required by sec. 853.03(2), Stats. 1971, which required two subscribing witnesses. Crawford specifically stipulated that his action in failing to obtain the signature of a second witness to the July 24, 1973 will was negligent but "clearly not fraudulent."

On March 12, 1981, Auric filed an action against Crawford. His action contained two claims -- one based on a theory of breach of an implied contract and the other based on negligence. On June 1, 1981, Crawford moved for summary judgment on the grounds that both claims were barred by the statute of limitations. On October 29, 1981, Judge Wilbershide issued a written decision granting Crawford's motion on the contract action but denying the motion on the negligence action. Judge Wilbershide reasoned that the breach of contract occurred on the date of the negligent act, July 24, 1973, and thus an action for breach of contract which was commenced on March 12, 1981, was brought well after the six-year statute of limitations for actions on contracts. Judge Wilbershide, however, also concluded that the statute of limitations for the negligence action did not commence to run until the date Goldstein died, April 13, 1975, and thus the negligence action was commenced within the six-year period.

The case was then submitted to the trial court on the stipulated facts. The trial court issued a written decision on April 30, 1982, in which it ruled that Crawford was not liable to Auric for his negligent act because no privity existed between the two. The court therefore dismissed Auric's complaint in an order dated May 17, 1982. Auric appealed and this court granted his petition to bypass the court of appeals.

The first issue is whether an attorney may be held liable to a beneficiary of a will not in privity with the attorney for the attorney's negligence in drafting or supervising the execution of the will. While it has long been the general rule that an attorney is not liable to third parties for acts committed in the exercise of his duties as an attorney, this rule is not without exceptions. Where fraud has been involved, attorneys have been held liable to third parties. Scandrett v. Greenhouse, 244 Wis. 108, 11 N.W.2d 510 (1943). This exception was reaffirmed in Goerke v. Vojvodich, 67 Wis. 2d 102, 108, 226 N.W.2d 211 (1975), a case in which the court affirmed a trial court's dismissal of a third-party complaint against an attorney because the complaint failed to state a cause of action in fraud or wrongful conduct.

The question is should an exception be recognized to the general rule of attorney nonliability to third parties to allow a beneficiary of a will to sue an attorney for his negligence in drafting or supervising the execution of a will. This court has frequently stated that it is a question of public policy -- and, thus, one appropriate for a determination by this court -- as to whether liability should not be imposed even though damage is caused by the negligent act of another. Kornitz v. Earling & Hiller, Inc., 49 Wis. 2d 97, 102-103, 181 N.W.2d 403 (1970); Coffey v. City of Milwaukee, 74 Wis. 2d 526, 541, 247 N.W.2d 132 (1976); Ollerman v. O'Rourke Co. Inc., 94 Wis. 2d 17, 51, 288 N.W.2d 95 (1980). The question of whether to impose liability upon the attorney here is one that involves a consideration of public policy.

Jurisdictions which have considered this question are divided on the issue. See Annot., Attorneys-Liability to Third Parties, 45 A.L.R.3d 1181. Where courts have shied away from allowing the imposition of liability, concern has been expressed that such liability may conflict with the duty an attorney owes to his client. Clagett v. Dacy, 47 Md. App. 23, 420 A.2d 1285, 1289-1290 (1980). Courts that have allowed the imposition of liability seem to recognize that it will make attorneys more careful in the execution of their responsibilities to their clients. Lucas v. Hamm, 56 Cal. 2d 583, 15 Cal. Rptr. 821, 364 P.2d 685, 688 (1961), cert. denied 368 U.S. 987 (1962); Licata v. Spector, 26 Conn. Sup. 378, 381, 225 A.2d 28 (1966). This is especially true where the beneficiaries of wills have been the injured third parties because, as the court in Licata wrote, "public policy would seem to favor the court's extending its equitable arm to assist innocent parties seeking just damages resulting from an error committed by another and affecting their rights, which error those innocent parties were never themselves able to correct." 26 Conn. Sup. at 382.

In this state, there is a constitutional right to make a will and to have it carried out according to the testator's intentions. Cowie v. Strohmeyer, 150 Wis. 401, 136 N.W. 956 (1912); Estate of Ogg, 262 Wis. 181, 186, 187, 54 N.W.2d 175 (1952); Will of Wright, 12 Wis. 2d 375, 380, 107 N.W.2d 146 (1961). This right reflects a strong concern that people should be as free as possible to dispose of their property upon their death. Allowing a will beneficiary to maintain a suit against an attorney who negligently drafts or supervises the execution of a will is one way to make an attorney accountable for his negligence.

Accountability should result in increasing the care with which attorneys draft wills and see to their execution. It is consistent with and promotes this state's long-standing public policy supporting the right of a testator to make a will and have its provisions carried out. Public policy supports the imposition of liability on an attorney who acts negligently in drafting or supervising the execution of a will resulting in a loss to a beneficiary named therein. Therefore the lack of privity should not be a bar to this action.

Such a determination is consistent with decisions of other jurisdictions which have abandoned a strict privity test in will beneficiary suits against attorneys. Many of those courts have relied upon a balancing of the factors set out in Lucas. Those factors are: "the extent to which the transaction was intended to affect the plaintiff, the foreseeability of harm to him, the degree of certainty that the plaintiff suffered injury, the closeness of the connection between the defendant's conduct and the injury, and the policy of preventing future harm." 364 P.2d at 687.

Examining these factors in light of the stipulated facts in this case, it is clear that this will was intended to bring direct benefit to the plaintiff. It was foreseeable that if the will was not admissible in probate it would cause harm to him. It is also clear that the plaintiff suffered a loss of his $25,000 bequest and that loss resulted directly from the defendant's negligence. Finally, in order to prevent future harm to others similarly situated, the imposition of liability is proper.

Although the lack of privity does not bar this action, there remains the question of whether liability should be imposed in this specific case. Normally, such a factual determination would be one for the trial court to make. However, because this case is before the court on stipulated facts, the only task that remains is to apply the law to undisputed facts. Here Crawford admits that he negligently supervised the execution of the will. That negligence resulted in the loss to Auric of a $25,000 bequest. Since neither Crawford's liability nor the amount of damage is in dispute, we reverse the decision of the trial court and direct it to enter judgment in the plaintiff's favor in the amount of $25,000. However, because of a factual dispute between the parties on the question of whether prejudgment interest should also be awarded, we remand the case to the trial court for a decision on that issue.

The second issue on appeal is whether the respondent's challenge to a trial court order denying his motion for summary judgment based on the defense of the running of the statute of limitations should be allowed where he has failed to raise the issue on cross-appeal under sec. 809.10(2) (b), Stats. Crawford raised the defense in his brief on appeal. The appellant raised this issue in this court by a motion to dismiss the respondent's "attempted cross-appeal" and strike those portions of his brief relating to this question. We ordered the motion be held in abeyance until the case could be considered on the merits.

Section 809.10(2) (b), Stats., governs cross appeals and requires that a respondent who seeks modification of an order entered in a proceeding from which the appellant appealed must file a notice of cross-appeal within thirty days after filing of a notice of appeal. The defendant failed to do this but now seeks in his brief to raise the issue of the trial court's denial of his motion for summary judgment. In State v. Alles, 106 Wis. 2d 368, 316 N.W.2d 378 (1982), this court discussed the cross-appeal requirement contained in sec. 809.10(2) (b).

It is clear that orders challenged on cross-appeal need not be final orders. It is also true that a respondent may raise an issue in his briefs without filing a cross-appeal "when all that is sought is the raising of an error which, if corrected, would sustain the judgment. . .". This Court wrote in Alles,

"The reason for this is the accepted appellate court rationale that a respondent's judgment or verdict will not be overturned where the record reveals the trial court's decision was right, although for the wrong reason. An appellate court, consistent with that percept [sic], has the power, once an appealable order is within its jurisdiction, to examine all rulings to determine whether they are erroneous and, if corrected, whether they would sustain the judgment or order which was in fact entered." Alles, 106 Wis. 2d at 391.

Here, were we to conclude that the trial judge erred in denying Crawford's motion for summary judgment on the grounds that the negligence action was barred by the statute of limitations, such a decision would sustain the decision of the trial court. The issue is one that under Alles can be raised for the first time in briefs on appeal without having filed a cross-appeal. We therefore deny the appellant's motion.

The final issue is when did the statute of limitations under sec. 893.52, Stats., commence to run in a negligence action by a will beneficiary against an attorney who drafted and supervised the execution of the will. Under sec. 893.52, an action must be commenced within six years after the cause of action accrues. In Boehm v. Wheeler, 65 Wis. 2d 668, 223 N.W.2d 536 (1974), an action for damages for legal malpractice, this court held that for purposes of sec. 893.52 (then sec. 893.19(5)), it was the date of injury rather than the date of the negligent act which commenced the running of the period of limitations. Wheeler, 65 Wis. 2d at 676-677. In the present case the negligent act occurred on July 24, 1973, the date attorney Crawford negligently supervised the execution of the will. The question is whether the injury to Auric occurred on the same date as the negligent act.

We conclude that Auric was not injured on the date of Crawford's negligent act but rather was injured on the date of Frank Goldstein's death for it was only after that date that Auric would have had an enforceable right under the July 24, 1973, will. As the court of appeals properly determined in Estate of Eisenberg, 90 Wis. 2d 620, 630, 280 N.W.2d 359 (1979), "a will does not create an enforceable right in a beneficiary until the testator has died." Therefore, Auric could suffer no injury before Goldstein died for at any point up until Goldstein's death, the will could have been changed and the bequest removed. Since Goldstein died on April 13, 1975, and the action was filed on March 12, 1981, the action was commenced within the six year period set out in sec. 893.52 (then sec. 893.19(5)).

Judgment of the trial court is reversed with directions to enter judgment in favor of the plaintiff in the amount of $25,000 and cause remanded for further proceedings not inconsistent with this opinion.

C. CONFLICTS OF INTEREST

Rules 20.1-7, 20.1-8, and 20.19 of the *Wisconsin Rules of Professional Conduct for Attorneys* prohibit lawyers from representing clients in situations where the lawyer's judgment and neutrality may be influenced by the existence of conflicts of interest between the lawyer and the client. Such conflicts may be the result of the lawyer's personal business interests, family relationships, or duties to other clients, past and present. Representing clients in matters related to estate planning, especially when the lawyer may be representing multiple members of the same family can pose special challenges.

Lawyers can be disciplined in a number of ways. They can be sanctioned by judges in matters in which they represent clients in the judge's court. They can be sued by their clients for malpractice, and they can disciplined by the state bar itself. The following decision is the result of an appeal to the Wisconsin Supreme Court of a severe punishment handed down by the Wisconsin Office of Lawyer Regulation, the regulatory arm of the Wisconsin State Bar.

Office of Lawyer Regulation v. Felli

Supreme Court of Wisconsin
291 Wis. 2d 529, 718 N.W.2d 70 (2006)

ATTORNEY disciplinary proceeding.

PER CURIAM. Attorney Jay Andrew Felli has appealed from a referee's report concluding that he engaged in professional misconduct and recommending that his license to practice law in Wisconsin be suspended for a period of 18 months. The Office of Lawyer Regulation (OLR) has cross-appealed, arguing that the referee's findings that there was insufficient evidence to prove three of the counts alleged in the OLR's complaint are clearly erroneous. In addition, the OLR asserts that the recommended 18-month suspension inadequately addresses the severity of the misconduct and that the gravity of the offenses supports revocation of Attorney Felli's license to practice law.

We conclude that all of the referee's findings of fact, including those challenged by the OLR, are supported by satisfactory and convincing evidence. We also agree with the referee's conclusions of law that Attorney Felli engaged in professional misconduct. We conclude, however, that the appropriate discipline for the misconduct is a three-year suspension of Attorney Felli's license to practice law rather than the 18-month suspension recommended by the referee. We further agree with the referee that the costs of the proceeding, which total $33,400.72 as of January 19, 2006, should be assessed against Attorney Felli.

Attorney Felli was admitted to practice law in Wisconsin in 1994 and practices in Brookfield. In 1998 he received a private reprimand for failure to timely pay his Wisconsin State Bar dues. In 2005 he received a public reprimand for failing to act with reasonable diligence and promptness in representing a client and making misrepresentations to the OLR. See In re Disciplinary Proceedings Against Felli, 2005 WI 58, 281 Wis. 2d 25, 697 N.W.2d 42.

On December 30, 2004, while the prior disciplinary proceeding was still pending, the OLR filed a second complaint against Attorney Felli and also filed a motion seeking a temporary suspension of Attorney Felli's license on the ground that his continued practice of law posed a threat to the interests of the public and the administration of justice. This court denied the OLR's motion for a temporary suspension, but concluded that the motion raised significant concerns such that the court deemed it appropriate to expedite the disposition of the underlying proceeding.

The OLR's complaint alleged 15 counts of misconduct involving three client matters. All of the cases involved estate planning. Two financial planners, Stanley Zurawski and Ramzi Raad, were partners in a company called Lincoln Financial Planning. Zurawski and Raad presented financial planning seminars to target audiences 55 years of age and older. Sometime between 1995 and 1997 they decided to include an attorney in their seminars so they could refer clients back and forth. They asked Attorney Felli, who was married to Zurawski's cousin, to join them in the financial planning seminars.

The first client matter detailed in the OLR's complaint involved Attorney Felli's representation of R.W. In 1996 R.W. had executed a will, filed with the Milwaukee County Probate Court, leaving her estate, which was valued at more than one million dollars at the time of her death two years later, to the Wisconsin Conservatory of Music and the Milwaukee Ballet Company. R.W. appointed her neighbor and his wife as her personal representatives.

R.W. attended an estate planning seminar at which Attorney Felli and Zurawski made presentations. Attorney Felli and Zurawski recommended that R.W. use trusts to carry out the charitable bequests. Attorney Felli prepared a revocable living trust and a charitable remainder unitrust that R.W. executed on June 18, 1997. The Wisconsin Conservatory of Music was named as the sole beneficiary under both trusts. R.W.

herself was named as the original trustee of the living trust, with her neighbor and his wife as successor trustees. The neighbors were also appointed as the trustees of the charitable unitrust. R.W. executed a pour-over will that left any remaining assets at the time of her death to the living trust. A year later Attorney Felli prepared amendments to the trusts that deleted the Wisconsin Conservatory of Music as the sole beneficiary and substituted Civic Music as the beneficiary.

In June 1998 Zurawski's sister founded and incorporated a new piano school. Zurawski was initially on the school's board of directors. On July 13, 1998, less than one month after the last amendments to R.W.'s estate planning documents had been prepared and executed, Attorney Felli prepared new amendments removing Civic Music as the beneficiary of the trusts and naming Zurawski's sister's piano school as the sole beneficiary. The piano school did not apply for tax-exempt status until September 1998 and did not receive tax-exempt status until March 1999. The amendments dated July 13, 1998, also changed the trustees of both trusts and removed the neighbor's wife as a co-trustee and appointed Attorney Felli as co-trustee of R.W.'s charitable remainder unitrust and as successor co-trustee of her living trust upon R.W.'s disability or death.

Attorney Felli did not discuss with R.W. any alternative trustees, such as financial institutions, nor did he question her about her reasons for appointing him as co-trustee with her neighbor, nor did he suggest that the neighbor might serve as sole trustee.

R.W. died on September 19, 1998, without having executed further changes to her estate plan and leaving the piano school as the sole beneficiary. Upon R.W.'s death, Attorney Felli served as co-trustee for both trusts, did legal work for the estate and trusts, and managed the estate and trust bank accounts. Zurawski handled trust investment accounts.

An attorney sent a copy of R.W.'s obituary notice to the Milwaukee County Probate Court and wrote to the Wisconsin Conservatory of Music and the Milwaukee Ballet Company to inform them that R.W. had a will on file with the court naming their organizations as beneficiaries of her estate. In January 1999 those organizations filed a petition for administration of R.W.'s 1996 will. On February 23, 1999, Attorney Felli filed the 1997 pour-over will, an objection to the probate of the 1996 will, and a petition for probate of the 1997 will. Various challenges to the 1997 will and trusts ensued, all of which were eventually settled with payments to the challengers by the estate and/or trusts. Attorney Felli retained outside counsel to represent the estate and trusts in those contests.

A section of the living trust document required the trustees to submit at least a semiannual report to beneficiaries regarding trust receipts, disbursements, and distributions. The trust's books and records were also to be made available for inspection by the trust beneficiaries. The piano school received some distributions from the R.W. living trust between 1998 and 2001. Apparently no distribution was larger than $25,000.

In late 2001 Attorney Felli gave instructions to Zurawski to liquidate about $130,000 in trust assets. On December 19, 2001, the piano school's attorney wrote to Attorney Felli requesting that the school's accountant be allowed to review trust accounting records. The following day Attorney Felli informed the piano school it was being terminated as a trust beneficiary. The piano school was never provided with any accountings or records, and it received no further distributions from the trusts other than a lump sum payment in settlement of a civil action subsequently brought by the school. Upon termination of the piano school as a beneficiary, for a period of time there were no beneficiaries to whom the trustees were required to make distributions or accountings.

In January 2004 a grievance was filed with the OLR by Zurawski's sister. In the course of the OLR's investigation, Attorney Felli was requested to provide, among other things, trust documents, an accounting of the $130,000 that had been liquidated, an inventory of trust and estate assets, and an accounting of all legal fees, trustee fees, and other amounts Attorney Felli had paid himself or his law firm out of R.W.'s trust and estate assets.

Attorney Felli responded to the OLR on March 30, 2004, but failed to provide any documents. After a follow-up request on April 16, 2004, Attorney Felli provided documents related to the living trust but not to the charitable remainder unitrust. In response to a third request from the OLR, on June 2, 2004, Attorney Felli provided a copy of the charitable remainder unitrust document and one amendment that was dated after R.W.'s death. Attorney Felli explained his initial failure to provide unitrust documents by representing to the OLR that the charitable remainder unitrust had been combined with the living trust at the time of R.W.'s death, but this statement was false since Attorney Felli had executed an amendment to the unitrust six months after R.W.'s death and assets were still being held in a separate unitrust investment account as late as 2002, four years after R.W. died.

With regard to the OLR's request for an accounting of the $130,000 in funds that Zurawski said he had liquidated in the latter part of 2001, Attorney Felli originally represented that he had used the $130,000 to pay approximately $35,000 for legal fees to outside counsel, $2500 for legal fees to himself, and $50,000 to $55,000 for distributions to the piano school. Attorney Felli represented that the balance was held in the trust's operating account. When the OLR requested more information, Attorney Felli provided a second accounting. Rather than showing that he had received $2500 for legal fees as he had represented in the first accounting, the second accounting itemized five checks payable to Attorney Felli's law firm totaling over $26,000.

Bank account records established that neither of Attorney Felli's accountings was correct. After subpoenaing bank records, the OLR learned that during the same time period covered by Attorney Felli's accounting, he wrote checks to himself or his law firm in excess of $86,000. Attorney Felli's accounting to the OLR misrepresented the payee on two checks he had written to himself. Attorney Felli's accounting showed that check 1087 for $7961 was payable to the Gonyo Law Offices, when in fact the check was payable to the Felli Law Offices. Attorney Felli's accounting also showed that check 1090 for $5000 was paid to Attorney David DeToffel, when in fact that check was also payable to the Felli Law Offices.

Attorney Felli's accounting referenced two liquidations from trust investment accounts: $60,000 that was liquidated in April of 2001 and $65,000 that was liquidated in May of 2001. The bank records showed that in addition to these two liquidations, another $100,750 was liquidated between July and December 2001. Attorney Felli's accounting made no reference to receiving the latter funds and offered no accounting of how the funds were disbursed.

The OLR also requested Attorney Felli to produce a schedule of assets transferred to the R.W. living and charitable remainder unitrust during R.W.'s lifetime, an inventory of trust assets at the time of R.W.'s death, and an inventory of R.W.'s estate assets. Attorney Felli never provided the OLR with any of this information.

With respect to the OLR's request for an accounting of all legal fees Attorney Felli had paid himself from R.W.'s estate and trusts, Attorney Felli provided the OLR with a billing printout showing that during a 14 1/2 month period starting just before R.W. died, from mid-September 1998 through November 30, 1999, Attorney Felli had earned and billed legal fees of $105,961.56. He also provided the OLR with sporadic bills between May 1, 2000, and July 31, 2001. He provided no billing records after August 1, 2001, although he apparently continues to represent the trusts, and the R.W. probate proceeding is still pending.

The OLR's complaint alleged the following counts of misconduct with respect to Attorney Felli's representation of R.W.:

> COUNT ONE-By preparing trust documents and subsequent trust amendments that named himself as a co-trustee of the [R.W.] Living Trust and the [R.W.] Charitable Remainder Unitrust, Felli prepared legal documents which required that the lawyer's services be used in relation to that document, in violation of SCR 20:7.3(f).
>
> COUNT TWO-By charging over $105,000.00 for legal fees to the [R.W.] estate and trusts for a 14 1/2-month period, Felli charged fees that were unreasonable and clearly excessive, in violation of SCR 20:1.5.
>
> COUNT THREE-By representing [R.W.], her trusts and estate when Felli's independent professional judgment on behalf of his client was influenced by his own pecuniary interests in acquiring control and possession of [R.W.]'s assets for himself and for the family of a financial advisor with whom he had a close working relationship, Felli's representation of [R.W.], her trusts and estate was materially limited by the interests of a third party and his own financial interests, in violation of SCR 20:1.7(b).
>
> COUNT FOUR-By administering [R.W.]'s trusts in such a way that he terminated all trust beneficiaries and then paid himself at least $374,000 of [R.W.]'s assets, Felli engaged in conduct which involved dishonesty, fraud, deceit, or misrepresentation, in violation of SCR 20:8.4(c).
>
> COUNT FIVE-By willfully failing to provide relevant information, answer questions fully, and furnish requested documents in his responses to OLR, and by making misrepresentations in his disclosures to OLR, Felli violated SCR 22.03(6).
>
> The second client matter detailed in the OLR's complaint involved Attorney Felli's representation of L.D. L.D. was introduced to Attorney Felli in early 1998. L.D. had been blind since she was ten years old and was living at the Badger Home for the Blind. In a will dated May 14, 1987, L.D. had appointed her brother, A.D., to be her personal representative. On March 12, 1998, L.D. executed a will prepared by Attorney Felli. The will included bequests to family members and several charities and named A.D. as personal representative. On the same date, L.D. executed documents making her brother her financial and health care power of attorney.

In early 1999 Attorney Felli and Zurawski met with L.D. to discuss the creation of a charitable remainder unitrust to carry out L.D.'s charitable bequests. At that time, according to a memo prepared by Zurawski, L.D.'s primary assets consisted of some annuities and a brokerage account totaling $136,000. On February 17, 1999, L.D. executed a will and charitable remainder unitrust prepared by Attorney Felli. The will appointed L.D.'s brother as her personal representative, and the trust document appointed Attorney Felli as trustee. Attorney Felli acknowledged to the OLR that he did not discuss with L.D. any alternatives to his appointment as trustee, such as the use of a corporate trustee, friend, or relative.

Attorney Felli does not have billing records for the L.D. matter but said he received legal fees of between $1500 and $2000 for his work. After the charitable remainder unitrust was executed, Attorney Felli never spoke with L.D. again. Pursuant to the unitrust, Attorney Felli, as trustee, was required to make annual distributions to L.D. in the amount of 5 percent of the market value of the trust assets, as valued on the first day of each taxable year. Attorney Felli and Zurawski arranged to have an annual disbursement equal to 5 percent of the trust's initial total value taken from one fund that charged no penalty for withdrawal. Attorney Felli should have performed an annual accounting allowing him to make annual adjustments and ensure that L.D. was receiving 5 percent, but he failed to perform such accountings. He also never filed fiduciary income tax returns for the trust.

The L.D. trust granted "reasonable compensation" to the trustee. Zurawski arranged for disbursements totaling 2 percent of the initial trust value to Attorney Felli, from which Attorney Felli was to draw his fees. In the beginning of calendar year 2000, Attorney Felli received an annuity check payable to the trust in the amount of $2395.72. Attorney Felli opened a checking account as trustee and deposited the annuity payment to that account. He then wrote two checks to himself for trustee fees, one in the amount of $720 and another in the amount of $1125. In 2001 Attorney Felli deposited another check in the amount of $2395.72 into the checking account and again wrote two checks to himself for trustee fees, one for $500 and the other for $2000. In 2002 Attorney Felli deposited another $2395.72 check and wrote himself checks for $800 and $2000.

On November 7, 2002, L.D. removed Attorney Felli as trustee of her trust and replaced him with her brother. Attorney Felli was notified of his removal via a letter from the brother's attorney dated November 18, 2002.

The OLR's complaint alleged the following counts of misconduct with respect to Attorney Felli's representation of L.D.:

> COUNT SIX-By preparing a charitable remainder unitrust that named himself as trustee, Felli drafted a legal document which required that the lawyer's services be used in relation to that document, in violation of SCR 20:7.3(f).

COUNT SEVEN-By failing to investigate and inform [L.D.] of the suitability of a charitable remainder trust, by failing to advise [L.D.] about the risks of creating a charitable remainder trust with respect to her potential eligibility for Title XIX benefits, by failing to advise [L.D.] that she could consider corporate trustees or individuals other than Felli as a trustee, by failing to see that assets named in Schedule A of the trust were timely transferred to the trust, by transferring an asset to the trust that was not included in Schedule A without the knowledge or consent of the donor, by failing to file tax returns for the trust, and by failing to prepare annual trust accountings and make quarterly distributions to [L.D.] as required under the terms of the trust, Felli failed to provide competent representation to a client, in violation of SCR 20:1.1.

COUNT EIGHT-By failing to investigate and inform [L.D.] of the suitability of a charitable remainder [19] trust, by failing to advise [L.D.] about the risks of creating a charitable remainder trust with respect to her eligibility for Title XIX benefits, and by failing to advise [L.D.] that she could consider corporate trustees or individuals other than Felli as trustee, Felli failed to explain a matter to the extent reasonably necessary to permit the client to make informed decisions regarding the representation, in violation of SCR 20:1.4(b).

COUNT NINE-By failing to arrange timely transfer of trust assets to [L.D.]'s trust and by failing to obtain a timely employer identification number for the trust, Felli failed to act with reasonable diligence and promptness in representing a client, in violation of SCR 20:1.3.

COUNT TEN-By having a personal pecuniary interest in receiving annual trustee fees from a trust he created for [L.D.] without determining whether the trust was in his client's best interests, Felli represented a client when the representation of that client might be materially limited by his own interests, in violation of SCR 20:1.7(b).

COUNT ELEVEN-By creating a Charitable Remainder Unitrust for [L.D.], that provided no financial or tax benefits to his client but personally benefited Felli; by paying himself over $7,000.00 from a trust annuity when he rendered little or no trustee services to warrant such payment; by failing to provide his client or successor counsel with any accounting information including checks written to himself; and by failing to turn over to the successor trustee an annuity check that was sent to Felli after he had been discharged as trustee, Felli engaged in conduct involving dishonesty, fraud, deceit, or misrepresentation, in violation of SCR 20:8.4(c).

The final client matter detailed in the OLR's complaint involved Attorney Felli's representation of W.G. W.G. used Raad's services to handle investments for her. Sometime in 2001 W.G. and Raad discussed the possibility of her giving him a gift or bequest in addition to the commissions he earned on her transactions. Raad had researched how W.G. might properly give him such a benefit and determined it should be done through a trust. In April 2002, when W.G. was in her 80s, Raad purchased an annuity worth about $30,000 for her. Raad suggested to W.G. that she change her estate plan to include a trust, and W.G. agreed. Raad told her she could appoint as trustee of the trust the lawyer who would draft the trust, and he recommended Attorney Felli. Raad's purpose in referring W.G. to Attorney Felli was to have him set up a trust that would facilitate W.G. giving Raad money.

Attorney Felli prepared estate planning documents for W.G., which she signed in May 2002. The documents included a new will, a living trust, a financial power of attorney, and a health care power of attorney. A provision in the trust was a bequest to Raad giving him the proceeds of the annuity he had purchased for W.G. about a month earlier. Although Attorney Felli had met W.G. less than a month before preparing the documents, the documents he prepared appointed himself not only as successor trustee to W.G. for her living trust, but also as personal representative of her estate, as her financial power of attorney with immediate authority to act on her behalf, as nominated guardian in the event she became incompetent, and as her alternative health care power of attorney.

Attorney Felli said he did not solicit appointment to the various fiduciary positions in W.G.'s estate plan, but that Raad had done so. Attorney Felli said he did discuss alternatives with her, but that discussion failed to elicit the name of I.B., a personal friend of W.G. for 50 years and the person named as her personal representative in her 1998 will, as well as her power of attorney and health care power of attorney. Attorney Felli said I.B.'s name never came up in his discussions with W.G.

The W.G. living trust was 66 pages in length. W.G. did not sign or initial any of the first 65 pages, and her signature appeared only on the last page. Attorney Felli was the only witness to the document. The will Attorney Felli prepared for W.G. left all of her estate assets to the living trust "dated May 15, 2002," although the living trust W.G. signed was dated May 16, 2002. Raad and Attorney Felli served as witnesses to W.G.'s signature on the will.

The trust was funded with all of W.G.'s property that was permitted by law to be held in trust. The will poured over any of W.G.'s assets at the time of her death to the living trust. The living trust gave all trust property not previously distributed, such as the specific bequest to Raad, to W.G.'s minor grandnieces and nephews on her death. It gave her trustee significant discretion as to what distributions would be made to those heirs before each reached age 25.

W.G.'s health care power of attorney named a friend of W.G. as her primary health care agent and named Attorney Felli as her alternate health care agent. The primary health care agent was not provided with a copy of the document or asked to sign it. The only agent who signed the document and agreed to act as W.G.'s health care agent was Attorney Felli. Raad and Attorney Felli served as witnesses to W.G.'s signature on the health care power of attorney and stated they were not entitled to, and did not have a claim on, the principal's estate. Both Attorney Felli and Raad were aware that Raad had been left a substantial bequest under W.G.'s trust. I.B. was never informed she had been replaced as the personal representative in W.G.'s will and as her power of attorney and health care power of attorney.

On May 24, 2002, an insurance company issued a $1750 check to W.G. for a policy she had acquired through Raad. The check was endorsed by W.G. and signed over to the Felli Law Offices, evidently as payment for Attorney Felli's legal services. Using his power of attorney, Attorney Felli sent a change of beneficiary form to the insurance company changing the primary beneficiary to the W.G. Living Trust dated May 16, 2002, J.A. Felli, Trustee. In fact, W.G., not Attorney Felli, was the trustee of the trust at that time. Attorney Felli did not provide the insurance company with a copy of the trust agreement as they required.

After preparing the May 2002 documents, Attorney Felli had no further contact with W.G. beyond a possible phone call or two related to the insurance check or the transfer of assets to the trust. Around April 2003 I.B. spoke to W.G. about her taxes and W.G. showed I.B. the documents that had been prepared by Attorney Felli. I.B. then worked with another attorney to prepare new estate planning documents for W.G., effectively voiding all documents prepared by Attorney Felli.

The OLR's complaint alleged the following counts of misconduct with respect to Attorney Felli's representation of W.G.:

> COUNT TWELVE-By preparing a will that appointed Felli as personal representative of [W.G.]'s estate, by preparing a living trust that appointed Felli as successor trustee upon [W.G.]'s death or disability, by preparing a power of attorney that gave Felli immediate authority to handle [W.G.]'s financial affairs and authority to immediately act as trustee of [W.G.]'s living trust, and that nominated him to serve as guardian in the event of [W.G.]'s incapacity, and by preparing a medical power of attorney that appointed Felli as a health care

> agent, Felli drafted legal documents which require or imply that the lawyer's services are to be used in relation to that document, in violation of SCR 20:7.3(f).
>
> COUNT THIRTEEN-By preparing a will for [W.G.] that gave her assets to a nonexistent May 15, 2002, living trust; by failing to have the primary health care agent execute [W.G.]'s health care power of attorney; by appointing himself, a stranger to [W.G.], as proposed guardian, power of attorney, and alternative health care agent; by using a witness to [W.G.]'s health care power of attorney who falsely stated that he did not have a claim on [W.G.]'s estate; and by preparing a trust that Felli himself acknowledged he expected [W.G.] to change at any time, Felli failed to provide competent representation to a client, in violation of SCR 20:1.1.
>
> COUNT FOURTEEN-By preparing estate planning documents under which Felli and the financial advisor, who was a business associate of Felli's, stood to financially benefit from execution of the documents, Felli represented a client in such a way that his representation of the client was materially limited by the interests of a third party and the lawyer's own interest, in violation of SCR 20:1.7(b).
>
> COUNT FIFTEEN-By preparing legal documents for [W.G.], an 87-year-old woman whom Felli had just met, that gave Felli immediate financial control over all of [W.G.]'s assets and appointed Felli as personal representative of [W.G.]'s estate, trustee of her trust, health care power of attorney, and nominated guardian upon [W.G.]'s incapacity and by bequeathing to the financial advisor and business associate of Felli, an annuity that the financial advisor had just sold to [W.G.], Felli engaged in conduct involving dishonesty, fraud, deceit, or misrepresentation, in violation of SCR 20:8.4(c).

Attorney John Nicholas Schweitzer was appointed referee in the matter and a hearing was held in April 2005. The referee issued his report on May 31, 2005. The referee noted that the central activity that led to all of the charges in the OLR's complaint was Attorney Felli's preparation of estate plans that required or implied his services, a prima facie violation of SCR 20:7.3(f). The referee said the dispute between the OLR and Attorney Felli centered on the exception to SCR 20:7.3(f) created by this court in State v. Gulbankian, 54 Wis. 2d 605, 196 N.W.2d 733 (1972). The referee noted that Gulbankian explained:

> It is clear an attorney cannot solicit either directly or by any indirect means a request or direction of a testator that he or a member of his firm be named

> executor or be employed as an attorney to probate the estate. In those fairly rare cases where a client, because of the unusual familiarity of the attorney with the testator's business or family problems or because of a relationship that transcends the ordinary client-attorney relationship, asks his attorney to act as executor or to provide for his employment to probate the estate, there is no solicitation.
>
> . . . .
>
> . . . We do not hold that a lawyer may not draft a will in which he is designated as executor or contains a direction to the executor to employ him . . . if in fact that is the unprompted intent of his client; but the number of times this will occur will be few and the percentage in total of such wills drawn low.

Id. at 610-12.

The referee said Gulbankian stands for the proposition that there must be a legitimate reason for the attorney to be chosen over all other potential executors or trustees. He said that in the absence of evidence that Attorney Felli had a significant relationship or an unusual familiarity with the testator's affairs, he must be found to have violated the prohibition on drafting documents, especially wills or trusts, that require or imply the use of his own services.

The referee noted that the OLR presented expert testimony on the topic from Attorney Lewis Perlson, who specializes in estate planning and wrote part of a handbook on estate planning in Wisconsin. Attorney Perlson expressed the opinion that many of Attorney Felli's actions violated supreme court rules, although Attorney Perlson himself testified that he serves as trustee on a small number of trusts set up by his clients.

The referee noted that at the time of the hearing in this case all three of Attorney Felli's clients were unavailable as witnesses. R.W. had died, L.D. was in a nursing home with a poor memory, and W.G. was in a care facility with the beginning of dementia at age 90. Other witnesses were called to testify about Attorney Felli's representation of those three clients, and evidence was presented from three other clients on the question of whether Attorney Felli routinely suggested himself as trustee or personal representative or power of attorney without exhaustively exploring other alternatives.

The referee said the question of whether Attorney Felli or Raad suggested appointing Attorney Felli in the various fiduciary capacities was irrelevant since Gulbankian prohibits both direct and indirect solicitation; Attorney Felli made as many as 400 joint presentations with Raad and Zurawski; and the business relationship that existed between Attorney Felli and Raad and Zurawski meant that the suggestion by Raad or Zurawski that Attorney Felli be appointed would qualify as an indirect solicitation.

The referee noted that the testimony of three of Attorney Felli's other clients showed a pattern in which Attorney Felli failed to investigate alternative trustees and either offered his own services or allowed Raad and Zurawski to make the suggestions. The referee reasoned that the testimony from these other clients reinforced the likelihood that on the three occasions charged in the OLR's complaint, Attorney Felli either offered his services or made only a halfhearted effort to investigate other alternatives.

The referee said the fact Attorney Felli was unaware of the existence of W.G.'s friend, I.B., showed that Attorney Felli "failed miserably to meet his obligation" to investigate other alternatives to appointing himself in various fiduciary capacities. The referee said Raad's testimony regarding his involvement in the W.G. case was at points to be self-serving, and the referee said Raad's testimony that he did not really know he was being left something by W.G. was patently false and established Raad as a person whose truthfulness was not to be relied upon. In the referee's opinion, Attorney Felli's representation of W.G. represented the "clearest and worst violation of the three presented in the complaint." The referee found that all four counts in the OLR's complaint relating to Attorney Felli's representation of W.G. were proven by clear, satisfactory, and convincing evidence.

With respect to Attorney Felli's representation of L.D., the referee found that Counts Six, Seven, and Eight of the OLR's complaint were proven by clear, satisfactory, and convincing evidence. The referee said there was no evidence that Attorney Felli discussed any alternatives to naming himself as trustee, and the referee found that Attorney Felli failed to explain matters to the extent reasonably necessary to permit L.D. to make informed decisions.

The referee found there was insufficient evidence to support the allegations contained in Counts Nine, Ten, and Eleven of the OLR's complaint regarding Attorney Felli's handling of the L.D. matter. The referee said the arrangement whereby 2 percent of the trust value was withdrawn annually to cover Attorney Felli's fees was not shown to be fraudulent, and he found there was insufficient proof that the $7145 Attorney Felli received during the three years he served as trustee of L.D.'s trust was unreasonable.

With respect to Attorney Felli's representation of R.W., the referee found there was sufficient proof to support the allegations in Counts One, Three, and Five of the OLR's complaint. The referee said there was no evidence that Attorney Felli discussed any alternative to himself serving as trustee and that Attorney Felli violated SCR 20:7.3(f) in preparing R.W.'s estate plan. The referee also found that by representing R.W., her trust and estate, when Attorney Felli's independent professional judgment on behalf of R.W. was influenced by the pecuniary interests of the family of a financial advisor with whom Attorney Felli had a close working relationship, Attorney Felli's representation was materially limited by the interests of a third party and by his own financial interests, in violation of SCR 20:1.7(b). The referee further found that by willfully failing to provide relevant information, failing to answer questions fully, failing to furnish requested documents in his responses to the OLR, and by making misrepresentations to the OLR, Attorney Felli violated SCR 22.03(6).

The referee concluded that the OLR failed to meet its burden of proof with respect to Counts Two and Four of the complaint. The referee said the OLR's allegations that Attorney Felli charged the R.W. estate fees that were unreasonable was too speculative to satisfy the burden of proof. The referee said Attorney Felli's testimony regarding the allegedly chaotic state of affairs in R.W.'s house and in her finances after her death was unrefuted, and Attorney Felli testified that he invested hundreds of hours defending the trust against the various lawsuits that were filed. The referee agreed, however, that Attorney Felli's accounting was incomplete and confusing and that some of the testimony strongly suggested a misappropriation of funds, as alleged in Count Four of the complaint, and an attempt by Attorney Felli to escape detection by preventing the examination of trust records by the piano school or others.

In discussing the appropriate discipline to be imposed for Attorney Felli's misconduct, the referee noted that the OLR requested the revocation of Attorney Felli's license. Attorney Felli asked for a public reprimand or, at most, a 60-day suspension. The referee noted that the purpose of discipline is to prevent further misconduct by the attorney, deter other attorneys from engaging in similar misconduct, and to foster the rehabilitation of the offender. The referee said anything less than a lengthy suspension would fail to impress on Attorney Felli the need to practice law with more attention paid to the rules of procedure and professional conduct. The referee said:

> This referee's visceral reaction to the evidence of an attorney feathering his own nest, and the nests of his close associates, at the expense of his clients and their best interests, was that revocation would be too lenient. This is partly because Mr. Felli showed no hint of acknowledging that he might have overstepped the bounds, nor any remorse over having tried to take advantage of a vulnerable population and a very small loophole in the law, which he stretched to the breaking point and far beyond, for his own benefit and the benefit of his business associates. Revocation would also be lenient, however,

> in that it would leave him in various positions of trust granted to him by a still-unknown number of clients, for which he could not be held accountable as a member of the legal profession.
>
> Although Mr. Felli's reprehensible actions amply justify revocation, it is possible that he can learn to conform his behavior to accepted standards. This suggests leaving open the possibility of reinstating his license in less than five years for the purpose of rehabilitation. In addition, the prospect of reinstating his license might encourage him to discharge his various duties under some of his clients' estate plans conscientiously and punctiliously, and to prepare an accounting of his management of the assets placed in his care . . . I recommend a suspension of eighteen months.

The referee also recommended that Attorney Felli pay the full costs of the proceeding.

Attorney Felli has appealed all of the referee's conclusions of law finding that he violated any supreme court rules. Attorney Felli's principal argument is that the referee misinterpreted and misapplied SCR 20:7.3(f) and this court's decisions in Gulbankian and Schmeling v. Devroy, 109 Wis. 2d 154, 325 N.W.2d 345 (1982). Attorney Felli notes that in Gulbankian, the attorneys filed 135 wills, 71 of which directed their employment. The Gulbankians contended their clients had spontaneously directed that they appoint themselves, and they noted since they spoke the same language as their clients and shared a common ethnic background they shared a closer relationship than ordinarily exists between other attorneys and clients. This court declined to infer that the Gulbankians solicited the probate of the various estates.

Attorney Felli argues that Gulbankian did not hold that an attorney is presumed to have acted unethically and bears the burden of proving he had a significant relationship or an unusual familiarity with the testator's affairs. He argues one reason R.W., L.D., and W.G. all selected him to serve in a fiduciary capacity was because there was no other logical choice since none of the women had husbands, none had children, R.W. and W.G. had no family members living in Wisconsin, and L.D. had only a distant relationship with a brother in the state.

Attorney Felli points out that the referee found that the practice of the OLR's expert witness also appeared to be improper as indirect solicitation. Attorney Felli asserts that any error on his part should be seen as a product of the uncertainty as to the interpretation and scope of the rules rather than a disregard for or intentional violation of the rules. He contends there is no direct evidence that he persuaded any of the clients to name him in any fiduciary capacity. He says even assuming his testimony in this regard is not accepted, there is no evidence as to how and why the various appointments were made (since none of the three clients were available to testify at the hearing) and he argues the OLR cannot prove allegations by clear, convincing, and satisfactory evidence by an inference of questionable value without any substantiating testimony. Attorney Felli asserts he did have a substantial relationship with all three clients and that he worked with R.W. for at least 13 months and had been L.D.'s lawyer for over one year at the time he prepared the charitable trust for her.

Attorney Felli also argues that the OLR failed to meet its burden of proof of showing he violated SCR 20:1.7(b) in his handling of the R.W. and W.G. matters by having his professional judgment influenced by his relationship with the Zurawski family. He again notes that since R.W. did not testify, it can never be known for sure why she chose the piano school run by Zurawski's sister as the beneficiary. Attorney Felli also asserts he did not have a conflict of interest in the W.G. matter simply because Raad, with whom Attorney Felli had a longstanding business relationship, stood to financially benefit from the W.G. trust.

Attorney Felli further argues that the referee's finding that he willfully failed to cooperate with the OLR during its investigation is clearly erroneous. He contends there was ample evidence that he tried to satisfy the OLR's numerous, detailed requests for information. He also asserts that there is insufficient proof that he violated SCR 20:1.1 by not providing L.D. with competent representation. He says he was not a tax expert, but Zurawski's wife, an accountant, who did L.D.'s personal taxes, failed to remind him that the split interest tax form had to be filed.

Attorney Felli says if L.D. was harmed in any way it was only that she was assessed a modest annual fee and any shortcomings in his performance with regard to the tax forms do not rise to the level of a disciplinary rule violation. With respect to the OLR's claim that Attorney Felli failed to provide competent representation because he did not prepare an annual trust accounting for L.D., Attorney Felli says it was not improper for him to rely on Zurawski to do the mathematical calculations and paperwork.

Attorney Felli also asserts there was insufficient proof that he violated SCR 20:8.4(c) by allowing Raad to witness W.G.'s power of attorney and by failing to identify W.G. as a client during the OLR's investigation. Attorney Felli says the evidence shows that Raad's attestation, when he witnessed W.G.'s power of attorney, that to the best of his knowledge he was not entitled to and had no claim on the principal's estate, was "technically true" since no one ever told Raad he was a beneficiary under W.G.'s estate plan. Attorney Felli says even assuming Raad knew he was going to benefit from the W.G. trust, there was still nothing improper about Raad signing the W.G. health care power of attorney as a witness.

Attorney Felli argues that even if all counts of misconduct found by the referee should be affirmed by this court, the recommended 18-month suspension is much too harsh. He notes that nearly all of the counts of misconduct found by the referee concerned the solicitation claim and he argues that the limits as to when and in what context a lawyer can mention to a client that the lawyer could serve as a trustee are unclear, so the discipline imposed in this case should be mitigated by the fact that it occurred in a "gray area" in legal ethics.

In response to the arguments raised in Attorney Felli's appeal, the OLR argues the referee appropriately interpreted and applied existing law in determining that Attorney Felli violated SCR 20:7.3(f) as to each of the three clients. The OLR says Gulbankian was one of those "rare cases" where the attorney and clients had a common ethnic background and a close personal relationship leading to this court's conclusion that solicitation had not occurred. The OLR says the facts of this case are dramatically different. It says in each instance, Attorney Felli met the elderly clients at financial planning seminars at which he worked "hand in glove" with Raad and Zurawski.

The OLR says in each instance Attorney Felli had no pre-existing personal or professional relationship with the elderly clients. The OLR says Attorney Felli and the financial planners made income off the efforts of the other. The OLR says there was no legitimate reason for Attorney Felli, a virtual stranger, to be chosen by these clients over other potential executors or trustees; Attorney Felli directly, or indirectly through the financial planners, solicited his service in such capacities, and contrary to Attorney Felli's statements, there were other logical choices, individuals or institutions, to serve in the fiduciary capacities filled by Attorney Felli.

The OLR also argues that Attorney Felli's representation of R.W. and W.G. was materially limited by the interests of third parties and by Attorney Felli's own financial interests, in violation of SCR 20:1.7(b). The OLR argues at no time did Attorney Felli make sufficient written disclosures to his clients concerning these conflicts. The OLR also argues that by failing to provide the OLR with relevant information and by making misrepresentations to the OLR, Attorney Felli violated SCR 22.03(6).

The OLR cross-appealed the referee's legal conclusions that there was a failure of proof as to Counts Two, Four, and Ten of the OLR's complaint. The OLR also appealed from the referee's recommended 18-month license suspension and asserts that revocation of Attorney Felli's license is appropriate.

The OLR argues that the evidence submitted in the R.W. matter supports a finding that Attorney Felli's fees were unreasonable. The OLR notes that the referee acknowledged the investigator's challenge in making sense of records that bore almost no relationship to information she had received from Attorney Felli, and the OLR says in effect Attorney Felli has received the benefit on the fee question out of the confusion he created. The OLR says the only thing that is speculative is how much more money Attorney Felli may have received from the R.W. estate and trusts beyond what he admits charging. The OLR says the figures the investigator used to determine that Attorney Felli had taken at least $374,000 from the R.W. estate and trust are fully documented.

The OLR notes the only independent expert testimony on the subject of the reasonableness of Attorney Felli's fees was offered by the OLR's expert, Attorney Perlson, who said it seemed to be impossible that someone would take so long a time to carry out the duties that were described in the billings. The OLR says although Attorney Felli spoke in general terms about the chaotic state of affairs in R.W.'s house and finances following her death, he produced nothing at the hearing that would substantiate or justify the amounts he charged. The OLR says while the referee found its investigator's conclusions about the billings were too speculative based on the information provided, it was Attorney Felli himself who provided the information.

The OLR says the referee's findings of fact essentially lead to but one conclusion: Attorney Felli acted dishonestly or deceitfully in handling R.W.'s affairs and paying himself fees. The OLR contends there was a premeditated scheme on Attorney Felli's part to systematically acquire control over R.W.'s assets over a period of time. It says the piano school was named a beneficiary under circumstances suggesting a cozy relationship between Zurawski's family and Attorney Felli. Once the piano school was in place as a beneficiary, the OLR says even Zurawski and his sister became suspicious of Attorney Felli's activities and one day after the piano school requested an opportunity to review trust accountings, as it was entitled to do under the trust, Attorney Felli sent a letter summarily suspending the school as a beneficiary.

The OLR says Attorney Felli clearly did not want anyone to obtain an accounting of the R.W. trust since such an accounting would have shown significant withdrawals of funds by Attorney Felli. The OLR says in the course of its investigation it repeatedly asked Attorney Felli to provide an accounting of the assets he was administering and the amounts he had paid himself and he offered various excuses why he could or would not do so: his co-trustee objected, he did not keep the information in the ordinary course of business, and he was still in the process of assembling information. The OLR says it presented Attorney Felli with its calculations, which showed he had taken at least $374,000 from the R.W. estate and trust, and while he offered general criticism he provided no specific information concerning any inaccuracies nor any independent summaries or conclusions of his own. The OLR says the documents in the record lead to but one conclusion: Attorney Felli used his control over R.W.'s assets to pay himself a sizable percentage of her estate.

The OLR also argues it is undisputed that Attorney Felli had a personal pecuniary interest that conflicted with L.D.'s interests, in violation of SCR 20:1.7(b). The OLR says given L.D.'s modest income there were no significant tax savings resulting from a possible charitable deduction and the result is that Attorney Felli prepared trust documents which were of no benefit to L.D. but which served as a vehicle for Attorney Felli to receive ongoing annual trustee fees of over $2000 per year at L.D.'s expense.

The OLR argues that the referee's recommended 18-month suspension inadequately addresses the severity of Attorney Felli's misconduct. The OLR says contrary to Attorney Felli's argument that any misconduct he might have committed occurred in a "gray area" in ethics, Attorney Felli positioned himself in a fiduciary capacity in his clients' estates contrary to the unambiguous guidelines set forth in Gulbankian. It says there is a pattern of misconduct with respect to the three clients since all of them were unmarried, elderly, and without any close family. The OLR says after being introduced to the three women by financial planners with whom he had a long and close professional relationship, over time Attorney Felli positioned himself in various fiduciary capacities permitting him to make important personal decisions for his clients and to avail himself of their assets. The OLR notes that Attorney Felli is an experienced attorney who does not have available the defense of being a novice who was in over his head. It argues that under the circumstances revocation of Attorney Felli's license is appropriate.

This court will adopt a referee's findings of fact unless they are clearly erroneous. Conclusions of law are reviewed de novo. See In re Disciplinary Proceedings Against Eisenberg, 2004 WI 14, P5, 269 Wis. 2d 43, 675 N.W.2d 747. The court may impose whatever sanction it sees fit regardless of the referee's recommendation. See In re Disciplinary Proceedings Against Widule, 2003 WI 34, P44, 261 Wis. 2d 45, 660 N.W.2d 686. The referee's findings of fact are not clearly erroneous, and we adopt them. We also agree with the conclusions of law that flow from the referee's findings of fact.

Attorney Felli's conduct in appointing himself as a trustee and/or personal representative in the three client matters violated SCR 20:7.3(f) and did not fall under the limited exceptions carved out in Gulbankian. Unlike the attorneys in Gulbankian, who shared a common ethnic background with their clients and had served as longtime attorneys for the clients, Attorney Felli's contact with the three clients was very limited. He met all three women at financial planning seminars conducted jointly with Raad and/or Zurawski, and he drafted the wills and trusts naming himself in various fiduciary capacities soon after meeting the women. The unusual familiarity with the testators' affairs that excused the attorney's conduct in Gulbankian simply does not exist here.

We also agree with the referee's conclusion that Attorney Felli violated SCR 20:1.7(b) by representing R.W. under circumstances where Attorney Felli's independent professional judgment was influenced by his own pecuniary interests in acquiring control of R.W.'s assets for himself and/or for Zurawski's sister's piano school. Similarly, we agree that by preparing estate planning documents for W.G. under the terms of which both Attorney Felli and his associate, Raad, stood to benefit financially, Attorney Felli also violated SCR 20:1.7(b).

The referee's other findings of fact, which led to his conclusion that Attorney Felli violated SCR 22.03(6) by making misrepresentations to the OLR in the R.W. matter; that he violated SCR 20:1.1, by failing to provide competent representation to L.D. and W.G.; and that he violated SCR 20:8.4(c), by engaging in conduct involving dishonesty, fraud, deceit or misrepresentation in his representation of W.G. are also supported by the record and we adopt them.

After careful review of the record, we reject the arguments made in the OLR's cross-appeal, and we affirm the referee's findings of fact which led to his conclusions of law that the OLR failed to meet its burden of proof with respect to Counts Two, Four, and Ten of the complaint. We uphold the referee's conclusions with respect to Counts Two and Four of the complaint with some reluctance.

The evidence regarding the amounts Attorney Felli charged the R.W. estate and trusts is very disturbing. The OLR's expert witness, Attorney Perlson, opined that the fees charged by Attorney Felli were unreasonable and clearly excessive. The referee said Attorney Felli's testimony about the chaotic state of affairs in the R.W. case was unrefuted. While the referee agreed that the accounting provided by Attorney Felli in the R.W. matter was incomplete and confusing, and that some of the evidence strongly suggested Attorney Felli misappropriated funds, he ultimately concluded that the OLR failed to prove by clear, satisfactory, and convincing evidence that Attorney Felli engaged in conduct involving dishonesty, fraud, deceit or misrepresentation.

As previously noted, the referee found that Attorney Felli engaged in misconduct by failing to fully cooperate with the OLR in its investigation of the R.W. case, and the referee speculated that Attorney Felli might have made a conscious tradeoff and decided not to provide complete information to the OLR to prevent the referee from finding that Attorney Felli mishandled R.W.'s funds. We concur with the referee's comment that it is possible such a conscious tradeoff was made, and we are deeply troubled by that possibility. However, we are required to adopt a referee's findings of fact unless they are clearly erroneous and based on the record before us we are unable to say that the referee's findings of fact with respect to Counts Two and Four of the complaint were clearly erroneous. Consequently, we are required to adopt the findings of fact as well as the resulting conclusions of law.

Even though we adopt all of the referee's findings of fact and conclusions of law, we disagree with the referee as to the appropriate sanction. The misconduct found by the referee is extremely serious. Along with the two financial planners, Attorney Felli targeted vulnerable elderly women and either directly or indirectly through the financial planners solicited his service in various fiduciary capacities. Unlike the situation in Gulbankian, Attorney Felli did not have a close personal relationship with any of these clients. At the time Attorney Felli drafted the will and trust for R.W., she already had two trustees. After the co-trustees divorced, the husband could have continued as the sole trustee and there was no particular reason to appoint Attorney Felli. L.D. had a brother who had been named a fiduciary in her prior wills. W.G. had previously named her friend, I.B., as her fiduciary. There is no reason those persons could not have continued to act in a fiduciary capacity, nor is there any evidence that Attorney Felli discussed the possibility of naming those persons or naming an institution to serve in the fiduciary capacities ultimately filled by Attorney Felli himself.

In light of the seriousness of Attorney Felli's misconduct, we believe that the 18-month suspension recommended by the referee is too lenient. Instead, given the egregiousness of Attorney Felli's behavior, we conclude that a three-year suspension of his license to practice law in this state is called for. We hope that that period of suspension will help him understand and accept the responsibilities of the legal profession and the ethical constraints placed upon its practice. In addition, we agree with the referee that Attorney Felli should pay the full costs of the proceeding.

IT IS ORDERED that the license of Attorney Jay Andrew Felli to practice law in Wisconsin is suspended for three years commencing July 27, 2006, as discipline for his professional misconduct.

IT FURTHER ORDERED that within 60 days of the date of this order, Attorney Jay Andrew Felli pay to the Office of Lawyer Regulation the costs of this proceeding. If the costs are not paid within the time specified and absent a showing to this court of his inability to pay the costs within that time, the license of Jay Andrew Felli to practice law in Wisconsin shall remain suspended until further order of the court.

IT IS FURTHER ORDERED that Jay Andrew Felli comply with the provisions of SCR 22.26 concerning the duties of a person whose license to practice law in Wisconsin has been suspended.

Apyan v. Easton

Wisconsin Court of Appeals
296 Wis. 2d 419, 722 N.W.2d 400 (2006)

PER CURIAM. Carol J. Apyan appeals from an order awarding $72,000 in attorney's fees to Attorney George H. Easton for his work on the probate estate of her late father. We affirm.

Sarkis Apyan had three children, Paul, Carol and Roseanne. Sarkis established a revocable trust and designated Paul as the trustee, and Sarkis' will named Paul as the special administrator of his estate. In February 2003, shortly after Sarkis' death, Paul contacted Attorney Easton regarding estate work. In November 2003, Paul, as special administrator of Sarkis' estate, entered into an agreement with Attorney Easton to pay him $72,000, a fee which the agreement deemed fair and reasonable to resolve issues involving Sarkis' estate based upon the time and labor required to resolve issues, Attorney Easton's relevant experience, and the complexity and novelty of the issues.

Over more than two years, Attorney Easton provided legal services. When he sought payment pursuant to the fee agreement, Carol objected on the grounds that the trust's beneficiaries had not agreed to pay attorney's fees in the amount of $72,000. Paul countered that Carol and Roseanne had joined him at a meeting with Attorney Easton in February 2003 and discussed Attorney Easton's request for a $72,000 fee. Paul stated that everyone present agreed that this was a reasonable fee and agreed to pay the fees out of the trust's assets. Attorney Easton responded that he had spent countless hours on the case and that the estate work was highly contentious, particularly where Carol was concerned.

In its memorandum decision, the circuit court resolved numerous issues in dispute, including the attorney's fees to be paid to Attorney Easton. The court acknowledged Carol's objection to Attorney Easton's $72,000 fee as unreasonable and excessive, and the contention of Paul and Roseanne that the fee was agreed upon by all, including

Carol. The court found that Attorney Easton is honest, ethical and competent, and that he undertook the representation "in good faith and with the understanding that the fee charged would approximate the value of the legal services performed." The court noted that in light of Carol's objection, it had to review the services provided pursuant to Wis. Stat. § 851.40(1) (2003-04).

The court required Attorney Easton to reconstruct his time records so that the court could evaluate the scope of work required by the estate. The court stated that it would not use the time records to attempt a mathematical calculation as to time spent and the applicable hourly rate. Rather, the court intended to use the reconstructed time records to develop a better, general understanding of the complexity of the issues and the labor expended by Attorney Easton. The court found that such a review was required because of the suggestion that the $72,000 fee was a percentage of the estate, a disfavored practice under Lontkowski Law Office v. Estate of Konopka, 175 Wis. 2d 100, 103, 498 N.W.2d 853 (Ct. App. 1993).

On February 9, 2005, in response to the circuit court's decision, Attorney Easton filed an estimate of the time he spent on the estate. Attorney Easton stated that this was the most involved and contentious estate he had ever worked on because nearly every issue was contested. Attorney Easton estimated that he spent 401 hours on the estate. On February 22, Carol filed an objection to Attorney Easton's submission, arguing that the fees were excessive and asking the court to review the appropriateness of the fees "based upon the existing trial record and Attorney Easton's memorandum." On April 19, Attorney Easton submitted a proposed order approving the fees. On April 25, the court entered an order approving the $72,000 fee to Attorney Easton based upon the proceedings held, the estimated time spent on the matter, the fee agreement, and the letters of counsel. Carol appeals.

We begin our review by noting that Carol does not challenge the validity of the fee agreement between Paul and Attorney Easton. Therefore, we focus on the circuit court's approval of the $72,000 fee after Attorney Easton submitted time records.

The reasonableness of fees for an attorney providing services to an estate under Wis. Stat. §851.40 is within the circuit court's discretion. See Anderson v. Anderson, 147 Wis. 2d 83, 93-94, 432 N.W.2d 923 (Ct. App. 1988).

On appeal, Carol complains that the circuit court's order approving the $72,000 fee does not state any findings or reasons. The court's order approving Attorney Easton's fees cited the proceedings held, the estimated time spent on the matter, and the fee agreement and the letters of counsel. We do not agree with Carol that the fee order is devoid of findings or reasons.

Additionally, we search for reasons to sustain a discretionary decision. See J.A.L. v. State, 162 Wis. 2d 940, 960-61, 471 N.W.2d 493 (1991). The circuit court presided over this case for more than two years. The court was aware of the issues and their complexity and the extent of Attorney Easton's efforts. In addition, the court previously found that Attorney Easton is honest, ethical and competent and that he undertook the representation "in good faith and with the understanding that the fee charged would approximate the value of the legal services performed." The court observed the quantity and quality of the services rendered and had "the expertise to evaluate the reasonableness of the fees with regard to the services rendered." Standard Theatres, Inc. v. DOT, 118 Wis. 2d 730, 747, 349 N.W.2d 661 (1984).

Carol argues that Attorney Easton's time records do not describe the amount and character of the legal services or the complexity of the issues, and he did not meet his burden to establish the reasonableness of the fees. Carol did not raise these complaints in the objection she filed in the circuit court. We conclude that they are raised for the first time on appeal and are therefore waived. See Segall v. Hurwitz, 114 Wis. 2d 471, 489, 339 N.W.2d 333 (Ct. App. 1983).

Carol also argues that she did not have the opportunity to challenge and contest Attorney Easton's submission in support of his fee request. However, Carol never asked to be heard further, and the objection she filed on February 22 invited the circuit court to decide the attorney's fee issue "based upon the existing trial record and Attorney Easton's memorandum." This issue is also waived. See id.

Essentially, the court confirmed that the fee agreement bore a relation to the work performed in the case. The circuit court did not misuse its discretion in awarding Attorney Easton $72,000 in attorney's fees.

D. LAWYER-CLIENT CONFIDENTIALITY

While lawyers who counsel clients in estate planning matters are expected to retain their client's confidences in general, the duty of confidentiality does not prevent a lawyer from testifying as to statements made by the client during the drafting of a will as a way of establishing testamentary intent. This issue is examined in *Estate of Boerner* below. A more extensive excerpt from the *Boerner* case can be found in Chapter 4.

Estate of Boerner

Supreme Court of Wisconsin
46 Wis. 2d 183, 174 N.W.2d 457 (1970)

This is an appeal of a trial court order on a petition for construction of a will, particularly paragraph two, which provides:

"Second, I give and bequeath the securities issued in my name and held for safekeeping by Walter J. Brand & Co., Sheboygan, Wisconsin, to my nephew, John A. Boerner, of Lakewood, California, if living; if not, then to his children in equal shares."

On March 30, 1964, the testator, John B. Boerner, owned 963 shares of Boston Fund, Inc., a mutual fund. The six stock certificates, evidencing such ownership, were in his possession. On March 31, 1964, he executed an agreement which placed him in a so-called Cumulative Investment Program of Boston Fund, Inc. Under such agreement, future dividends on Boston Fund shares would be automatically reinvested in additional shares of the fund. The agreement, executed with Walter J. Brand & Co., provided for the New England Merchants National Bank in Boston, Massachusetts, as agent of the dealer, to reinvest the dividends in Boston Fund shares. Under the cumulative investment program, the testator was sent regular notices by the bank of dividends accruing and certificates of ownership of shares purchased for him by the bank, the certificates being retained by the bank. As of May 31, 1968, the testator had 260.764 shares of Boston Fund on deposit with the bank in Boston. On May 31, 1968, the testator also had the certificates for the 963 shares of Boston Fund, these being in his possession. Thus his total holding of Boston Fund shares on May 31, 1968 amounted to 1223.764 shares.

On June 29, 1968, the testator purchased an automobile, on which a balance of $ 2,581 was due. On July 1, 1968, the testator withdrew this amount from his savings account. On the same day he notified Walter J. Brand that he wished to "cash in" the 260.764 shares in the Boston Fund held by the Boston bank. On July 11, 1968, the testator received the proceeds of the sale of such shares, amounting to $ 2,375.56, which amount he deposited in his savings account. On July 12, 1968, he died.

On August 13, 1968, his will was admitted to probate. On November 6, 1968, the final account in the probate proceedings was filed, and the hearing set for December 3, 1968. The final account excluded the nephew, John A. Boerner, as a legatee under the will, and he filed a petition for construction of the will. The trial court held him to be excluded under the will. Petitioner appeals.

Hansen, J.

[The bulk of the court's opinion has to do with the interpretation of paragraph two of Boerner's will (quoted above) and the admissibility of extrinsic evidence to establish its meaning. However, during the trial, the attorney who drafted the will was permitted to testify to the intentions of the testator over the objections of the executor of the estate. In the following portion of the opinion, Justice Hansen addressed the issue of the confidentiality of lawyer-client conversations in the context of the will drafting process.]

Confidential communication.

The executor argues that the attorney who drafted the will was improperly allowed to testify as to statements made by the testator during the drafting of the will. It is contended that such testimony violates the attorney-client privileged communication rule. If this objection is a valid one, the construction given the will as expressing the established intent of the testator would be fatally weakened for it rests in no inconsiderable measure upon the testimony of the lawyer who drafted the will as to statements made by the testator when the will was prepared. However, this court has several times held that communications between an attorney and a client concerning a last will and testament, the transactions which led to the execution of the will, and the circumstances surrounding the execution of the will, do not enjoy the status of privileged communications after the client's death in a suit between the testator's heirs, devisees, legatees or other parties who claim through him. …

CHAPTER 2.
INTESTACY: DISTRIBUTION BY DEFAULT

In every state, property belonging to individuals .who die without valid wills is distributed in accordance with the rules of intestacy. Although there are variations, intestacy statutes commonly define the right to inherit as a consequence of family relationships with spouses and descendants given priority over parents, grandparents and siblings who in turn are given priority over most distant relatives: aunts, uncles, and cousins of various degrees.

The drafters or revisers of intestacy statutes have to answer a number of questions. What should be the order of inheritance? What if some individuals who would have inherited had they not predeceased the decent are themselves survived by descendants? Is there a limit to how far removed an heir can be and still have the right to inherit? What should be the effect of an adoption on inheritance rights relative to both the birth and adoptive parents? Intestacy statutes normally favor the spouse and the decedent's descendants. If there is no souse and no descendants, then ancestors and the deceased's collateral relatives will inherit the property, albeit in accordance with a somewhat complicated formula which may vary from state to state. In 2009, Wisconsin's intestacy statute was amended to recognize the inheritance rights of registered same sex partners (itself a newly created legal status).

I. DEFINING HEIRS

A. THE INTESTACY STATUTE

Wis. Stat. 852.01. Basic rules for intestate succession.

(1) WHO ARE HEIRS.

Except as modified by the decedent's will under s. 852.10 (1), any part of the net estate of a decedent that is not disposed of by will passes to the decedent's surviving heirs as follows:

(a) To the spouse or domestic partner:

1. If there are no surviving issue of the decedent, or if the surviving issue are all issue of the surviving spouse or surviving domestic partner and the decedent, the entire estate.

2. If there are surviving issue one or more of whom are not issue of the surviving spouse or surviving domestic partner, one-half of decedent's property other than the following property:

a. The decedent's interest in marital property.

b. The decedent's interest in property held equally and exclusively with the surviving spouse or surviving domestic partner as tenants in common.

(b) To the issue, per stirpes, the share of the estate not passing to the spouse or surviving domestic partner, under par. (a), or the entire estate if there is no surviving spouse or surviving domestic partner.

(c) If there is no surviving spouse, surviving domestic partner, or issue, to the parents.

(d) If there is no surviving spouse, surviving domestic partner, issue, or parent, to the brothers and sisters and the issue of any deceased brother or sister per stirpes.

(f) If there is no surviving spouse, surviving domestic partner, issue, parent, or issue of a parent, to the grandparents and their issue as follows:

1. One-half to the maternal grandparents equally if both survive, or to the surviving maternal grandparent; if both maternal grandparents are deceased, to the issue of the maternal grandparents or either of them, per stirpes.

2. One-half to the paternal relations in the same manner as to the maternal relations under subd. 1.

3. If either the maternal side or the paternal side has no surviving grandparent or issue of a grandparent, the entire estate to the decedent's relatives on the other side.

(2) SURVIVORSHIP REQUIREMENT.

Survivorship under sub. (1) is determined as provided in s. 854.03

(2m) HEIR WHO KILLS DECEDENT.

If a person under sub. (1) killed the decedent, the inheritance rights of that person are governed by s. 854.14

(3) ESCHEAT.

If there are no heirs of the decedent under subs. (1) and (2), the net estate escheats to the state to be added to the capital of the school fund.

Wis. Stat. 852.03. Related rules.

(1) PER STIRPES.

If per stirpes distribution is called for under s. 852.01 (1) (b), (d) or (f), the rules under s. 854.04 apply.

(3) RELATIVES OF THE HALF BLOOD.

Inheritance rights of relatives of the half-blood are governed by s. 854.21 (4)

(4) POSTHUMOUS HEIRS.

Inheritance rights of a person specified in s. 852.01 (1) who was born after the death of the decedent are governed by s. 854.21 (5)

(5) RELATED THROUGH 2 LINES.

Inheritance rights of a person who is related to the decedent through 2 lines of relationship are governed by s. 854.21 (6)

(6) TAKING THROUGH OR BY ALIEN.

No person is disqualified from taking as an heir because the person or a person through whom he or she claims is not or at some time was not a U.S. citizen. The rights of an alien to acquire or hold land in the state are governed by ss. 710.01 to 710.03

Estate of Szaczywka

Supreme Court of Wisconsin
270 Wis. 238, 70 N.W.2d 600 (1955)

Steinle, J. The sole question involved on this appeal is: When a decedent is survived only by a first cousin and by second cousins who are children of a first cousin who predeceased the decedent, does the first cousin inherit all of the decedent's estate to the exclusion of the second cousins' right to inherit the share their parent would have taken had he survived?*

Sec. 237.01, Stats., provides in part:

When any person shall die seized of any lands, tenements, or hereditaments or any right thereto or entitled to any interest therein, in fee simple, not having lawfully devised the same, they shall descend, . . . in the manner following:

"(1) In equal shares to his children and to the lawful issue of any deceased child by right of representation; and if there be no child of the intestate living at his death his estate shall descend to all his other lineal descendants; and if all the said descendants

---

* **Ed. Note:**: The children of one's first cousins are first cousins once removed, not second cousins, as the court incorrectly states above. However, this mistaken characterization has no effect on the resolution of the case, which would be the same where the potential heirs in question were first cousins once removed or second cousins.

are in the same degree of kindred to the intestate they shall share the estate equally, otherwise they shall take according to the right of representation.

"(3) If the intestate leave no lawful issue nor widow nor widower nor father nor mother the estate shall descend in equal shares to the intestate's brothers and sisters and to the lineal descendants of any deceased brother or sister by right of representation.

"(4) If the intestate leave no lawful issue, widow, widower, father, mother, brother, nor sister the estate shall descend to the intestate's next of kin in equal degree, except that when there are two or more collateral kindred in equal degree, but claiming through different ancestors, those who claim through the nearest ancestor shall be preferred to those claiming through an ancestor more remote; provided, however, . . ."

Sec. 237.07, Stats., provides that:

"Inheritance, or succession by right of representation, takes place when the descendants of any deceased heir take the same share or right in the estate of another person that their parent would have taken if living; posthumous children are considered as living at the death of their parents."

The provisions of sec. 237.01 (4), Stats., apply to the situation in the case at bar.

Under the clear and express language of sec. 237.01 (4), Stats., the estate descends to the intestate's next of kin in equal degree. The item of "succession by right of representation" as defined in sec. 237.07 and as applicable in sec. 237.01 (1) and (3) is absent in sec. 237.01 (4). By virtue of such omission it is clear that the legislature intended that only the deceased's next of kin in equal degree are to share in the estate. As was held in *Estate of Reil* (1949), 70 Idaho 64, 211 P.2d 407, 19 A. L. R. (2d) 186, a statute defining the term "by right of representation" has no application to a statute which does not provide for descent by right of representation, but restricts descent to "next of kin in equal degree."

Sec. 237.03, Stats., provides:

"Degrees of kindred, how computed. The degrees of kindred shall be computed according to the rules of the civil law; and kindred of the half-blood shall inherit equally with those of the whole blood in the same degree unless the inheritance came to the intestate by descent, devise, or gift of some one of his ancestors; in which case all those who are not of the blood of such ancestors shall be excluded from such inheritance."

In 2 Gary, Wisconsin Probate Law (5th. ed.), p. 117, sec. 628, the author points out that the rule of the civil law, used in computing degrees of kinship in this state, is to count up the degrees, from one of the persons related, to the common ancestor, and down to the other from the common ancestor, adding the number of degrees in both lines. Under this method (illustrated by diagram in the author's text), a cousin is one degree nearer of kin than is a cousin's child.

Had Kajeton Makarewicz, father of the appellants and brother of Josephine Maejeck, survived the intestate, Ignatz Szaczywka, it is plain that he would have shared the estate per capita with Josephine Maejeck for the reason that he was of equal degree with her in kinship to the deceased. Had neither Josephine Maejeck nor Kajeton Makarewicz survived the intestate, then appellants would have been the next of kin of equal degree and would have shared per capita. However, since the legislature has limited the descent to the next of kin of equal degree, and because appellants are not of equal degree with Josephine Maejeck, who has survived the decedent, but are in fact a degree removed, the trial court properly determined that she was entitled to the entire distribution of the estate. Order affirmed.

Estate of Rhodes

Supreme Court of Wisconsin
271 Wis. 342, 73 N.W.2d 602 (1955)

BROWN, J. The will was signed by the testatrix September 18, 1935. The part for which construction was demanded reads as follows:

"*Second:* -- I hereby give, devise and bequeath all the rest, residue and remainder of my said estate, both real, personal and mixed, to my beloved sister, Mrs. Louise Welch, residing at number 2031 Loomis street, in the city of La Crosse, county of La Crosse and state of Wisconsin, and to my beloved brother, Herman Kletcka, residing at number 1433 Badger street in the city of La Crosse, county of La Crosse and state of Wisconsin, to each an undivided one half thereof, share and share alike, and in case either of my said heirs shall be deceased at the time of my said death, the share of such deceased brother or sister to go to his or her natural heirs, as defined in the Wisconsin laws of descent and distribution."

Edith Rhodes, who died October 7, 1954, never had children of her own. She had sisters, Louise Welch and Bertha Borger, and a brother, Herman Kletcka. Louise Welch never had natural children and when the will was executed she was fifty-eight years old. She had adopted Meta Howard on March 3, 1914, more than twenty years before the date of the will. This fact was well known to Mrs. Rhodes then and thereafter.

Mrs. Welch died during Mrs. Rhodes' lifetime leaving the adopted daughter who has also survived Mrs. Rhodes. She is the respondent. Testatrix's sister, Bertha Borger, died during Mrs. Rhodes' lifetime leaving three daughters who still survive. They are appellants Jessie Wege, Sophia Uehling, and Lulu Zeichert. Neither Mrs. Borger nor her daughters are named or referred to in the will.

Herman Kletcka died during the lifetime of the testatrix leaving two daughters who still survive. They are appellants Helen Frisch and Thelma Moen.

The trial court found as a fact and also as a conclusion of law that it was the intent of Mrs. Rhodes to include as a beneficiary of her will Meta Howard and to exclude the children of the deceased Bertha Borger. The controversial part of the judgment is as follows:

". . . that paragraph second of the last will and testament of Edith Rhodes should be and hereby is construed to mean that in the event that either or both her brother, Herman Kletcka, and her sister, Louise Welch, should die prior to the death of the testatrix, such share or shares should go to the person or persons entitled to take in accordance with the laws of descent and distribution in the state of Wisconsin, as such law existed at the time of the death of the testatrix; that the testatrix, Edith Rhodes, intended that a determination of the heirs of her brother, Herman Kletcka, and her sister, Louise Welch, as defined by the laws of descent and distribution in Wisconsin, should be made as of the date of her death, and did not intend to exclude Meta Howard, the adopted daughter of Louise Welch; that the testatrix, Edith Rhodes, intended thereby that the daughters of her deceased sister, Bertha Borger, be excluded from sharing in her estate; that testatrix intended that in determining the person or persons entitled to take under the laws of descent and distribution of Wisconsin, section 322.07 of the Wisconsin statutes should apply and be read in conjunction therewith; and that testatrix, Edith Rhodes, thereby intended that the residue of her estate should go one half (1/2) to Meta Howard, adopted daughter of Louise Welch, one fourth (1/4) to Helen Frisch, daughter of Herman Kletcka, and one fourth (1/4) to Thelma Moen, daughter of Herman Kletcka."

The question here is who gets the share of the residue primarily designed for Louise Welch. The will directed that, if Mrs. Welch did not survive, the share should go to Mrs. Welch's natural heirs as defined in the Wisconsin laws of descent and distribution. The appellants contend they are the natural heirs because they are related by blood to their aunt, Mrs. Welch.

It is presumed that every word of a will is used advisedly and with its ordinary meaning. It is the duty of the court first to read the will giving ordinary meaning to its words and, if this produces a plain result, that result must prevail and be taken to express the testator's intent. This principle, under varying circumstances, has been repeatedly declared by this court. *Estate of Treat* (1948), 253 Wis. 527, 530, 34 N.W.2d 685; *O'Hearn v. O'Hearn* (1902), 114 Wis. 428, 432, 90 N.W. 450; *Estate of Gray* (1953), 265 Wis. 217, 221, 222, 61 N.W.2d 467; *Will of Petit* (1945), 246 Wis. 620, 622, 18 N.W.2d 339; *Holmes v. Walter* (1903), 118 Wis. 409, 413, 95 N.W. 380.

Counsel on both sides praise the rule and each contends that the provisions of the will are so clearly in favor of his client that there is no room for a construction. We find the question more difficult. Reading the words of the controversial disposition we turn, as the will directs, to the Wisconsin laws of descent and distribution, chs. 237 and 318, Stats.

Sec. 237.04, Stats., refers us to sec. 322.07 for the right of descent from and to an adopted person, which section declares in sub. (1):

"Except as otherwise provided in this section, the effect of the order of adoption is to completely change the legal status of the adopted person from that of a child of the natural parents to that of a child of the adoptive parents; and to free the adopted person from all legal obligations to or on account of the natural parents, and *vice versa*."

Statutory directions follow covering various contingencies, but nowhere do we find the promised definition of the term "natural heirs." Contrary to the contentions of both counsel, by reason of its reference to a nonexisting definition or standard, a reading of the will does not provide a plain meaning. We turn then to the dictionaries and from Webster's New International Dictionary find that "natural" in its reference to persons is defined as "of, from or by, birth; . . . existing or characteristic from birth;" also as "actually begotten by one [opposite to adopted]." "Natural heirs" does not appear in Webster but it does in 2 Bouvier, Law Dict. (3d ed.), p. 2297, where we find "Natural heirs. As used in a will and by way of executory devise, they are considered as of the same legal import as 'heirs of the body.'" To like effect are most of the citations found in 28 Words and Phrases (perm. ed.), p. 56, under the term "Natural Heir" though there are examples where, for lack of an heir got by or on the body of the ancestor, some other person, not so engendered, was held to have been intended by the testator in his use of the term. So, in *Ludlum v. Otis* (1878), 15 Hun 410, the testator's mother and sister were allowed to take as "natural heirs" in preference to cousins. We regard the will as ambiguous for lack of "natural heirs as defined by Wisconsin laws of descent," etc., or by dictionary definition. We must construe in an effort to ascertain the testatrix's intent.

Since neither appellants nor respondent fulfill the ordinary meaning of "natural heirs" as construed and applied by the courts, it might be held that an intestacy has occurred and Mrs. Welch's share should be distributed generally to the heirs of the testatrix as prescribed by the statutes governing the distribution of intestate estates. To do this is to confess that we cannot find within the four corners of the will, read in the light of the circumstances surrounding the testatrix when she executed it, the person or persons to whom she intended to give this share, notwithstanding her evident purpose to make provision for its devolution if Louise Welch did not survive her. The court "'. . . must look to the language of the whole will and read it in the light of the circumstances surrounding the testator, in order to discover what was apparently in his mind at the time he made it, and thus ascertain his intention.'" *Estate of Britt* (1947), 249 Wis. 602, 607, 26 N.W.2d 34. Under such conditions the trial court properly turned to the surrounding circumstances and on competent evidence found that Mrs. Welch never had any children of her own but that some twenty years before the will was signed, and forty years before Mrs. Rhodes' death, to Mrs. Rhodes' knowledge, Mrs. Welch had adopted a daughter, Meta Howard. It found, too, that when the will was executed Louise Welch was fifty-eight years old [and presumably past childbearing]. It noted that the will did not provide for Mrs. Rhodes' sister, Mrs. Borger, nor for Mrs. Borger's natural heirs, as it had done for testatrix's other sister and her brother and their natural heirs.

While the various parties seek to take under the will and not under the statutes regulating inheritance through intestacy, the will's reference to the Wisconsin statutes of descent and distribution cannot be ignored. Even though they do not *define* "natural heirs," as the will supposed, the key to the intent of the testatrix must be in such statutes. By this reference we consider she meant to call attention to the fact that between Mrs. Welch and Meta Howard the relationship was that of mother and daughter and that the latter had the *status* of a natural daughter and heir. The trial court held that she was "the equivalent" of a natural daughter, which is a phrase to which appellants object though we consider it appropriate to their relationship. There is no thought here of making Meta Howard a "natural niece," or its equivalent, of the testatrix. By the adoption laws the legislature did not make, or purport to make, blood relatives of those who are strangers nor prevent testators from preferring relatives by birth to those by adoption. *Estate of Uihlein* (1955), 269 Wis. 170, 68 N.W.2d 816. But by its reference to the statutes the will calls attention to the fact that Mrs. Welch has a daughter, an heir, exactly as though the daughter was born to her.

We cannot read into this will, -- from the language "natural heirs of Louise Welch," or otherwise, -- any intent to benefit the children of Bertha Borger, nor does such benefit follow by operation of law. They are not Louise's natural heirs nor do the circumstances reveal an intent to treat them as such, as they do in the case of Meta Howard. We are confined to a choice between a partial intestacy and a designation of Louise Welch's adopted daughter as Louise's "natural heir" within the meaning Mrs. Rhodes ascribed to the words. The testatrix was providing against intestacy and, under the conditions surrounding her when she made her will, we conclude that it was her intent, in making a contingent bequest to the "natural heirs" of Louise Welch, to leave the deceased Mrs. Welch's share of the residue to the daughter who, *as between such mother and daughter* had the status of natural relationship.

The judgment determining heirship included beneficiaries under the will in addition to heirs at law, who take intestate realty, and next of kin, who take intestate personalty. *Will of Bray* (1951), 260 Wis. 9, 49 N.W.2d 716. It also stated that Louise Welch and her deceased husband adopted Meta Howard who "is the sole issue and lineal descendant of Louise Welch." Appellants have appealed from this determination as so expressed.

As to the inclusion of beneficiaries, that is, those who take by will, in a judgment determining heirship, we regard this as improper, but harmless in this instance where all those named in the judgment actually are heirs at law and next of kin. It might be otherwise if persons who could take only by virtue of the will were included.

As to the designation of Meta Howard as Mrs. Welch's issue and lineal descendant, for the purpose of intestacy, which is what proof of heirship deals with, she has that *status* by virtue of sec. 322.07, Stats. *Estate of Holcombe* (1951), 259 Wis. 642, 49 N.W.2d 914, and *Estate of Nelson* (1954), 266 Wis. 617, 64 N.W.2d 406. If the judgment had recited that this status was by virtue of the adoption we would not criticize it. But the bald statement that Meta Howard was issue and lineal descendant of Mrs. Welch is contrary to fact and no statute could alter her actual birth. Sec. 322.07 does not purport to do so. *Estate of Uihlein, supra*, page 173. However, this, too, becomes inconsequential where, as here, distribution is determined by a will. Judgment affirmed.

B. THE VOCABULARY OF INHERITANCE

Wis. Stat. 854.01. Definitions.

In this chapter **[Transfers at Death – General Rules]**:

(1) "Extrinsic evidence" means evidence that would be inadmissible under the common law parole evidence rule or a similar doctrine because the evidence is not contained in the governing instrument to which it relates.

(2) "Governing instrument" means a will; a deed; a trust instrument; an insurance or annuity policy; a contract; a pension, profit-sharing, retirement, or similar benefit plan; a marital property agreement under s. 766.58 (3) (f); a beneficiary designation under s. 40.02 (8) (a); an instrument under ch. 705; an instrument that creates or exercises a power of appointment; or any other dispositive, appointive, or nominative instrument that transfers property at death.

(3) "Revocable," with respect to a disposition, provision, or nomination, means one under which the decedent, at the time referred to, was alone empowered, by law or under the governing instrument, to change or revoke, regardless of whether the decedent was then empowered to designate himself or herself in place of a former designee, and regardless of whether the decedent then had the capacity to exercise the power.

Wis. Stat. 854.02. Scope.

This chapter applies to all statutes and governing instruments that transfer property at death.

Wis. Stat. 854.04. Representation; per stirpes; modified per stirpes; per capita at each generation; per capita.

(1) BY REPRESENTATION OR PER STIRPES.

(a) Except as provided in subs. (5) and (6), if a statute or a governing instrument calls for property to be distributed to the issue or descendants of a designated person "by representation," "by right of representation," or "per stirpes," the property is divided into equal shares for the designated persons surviving children and for the designated persons deceased children who left surviving issue. Each surviving child and each deceased child who left surviving issue are allocated one share.

(b) The share of each deceased child allocated a share under par. (a) is divided among that persons issue in the same manner as under par. (a), repeating until the property is fully allocated among surviving issue.

(2) MODIFIED PER STIRPES.

(a) Except as provided in subs. (5) and (6), if a statute or a governing instrument calls for property to be distributed to the issue or descendants of a designated person by "modified per stirpes", the property is divided into equal shares at the generation nearest to the designated person that contains one or more surviving issue. Each survivor and each deceased person in that same generation who left surviving issue are allocated one share.

(b) The share of each deceased person allocated a share in par. (a) is divided among that person's issue in the same manner as under par. (a), repeating until the property is fully allocated.

(3) PER CAPITA AT EACH GENERATION.

(a) Except as provided in subs. (5) and (6), if a statute or a governing instrument calls for property to be distributed to the issue or descendants of a designated person "per capita at each generation," the property is divided into equal shares at the generation nearest to the designated person that contains one or more surviving issue. Each survivor in that generation and each deceased person in that generation who left surviving issue are allocated one share. The shares of the deceased persons in that same generation who left surviving issue are combined for allocation under par. (b)

(b) The combined share created under par. (a) is divided among the surviving issue of the persons whose shares were combined in the same manner as under par. (a), as though all of those issue were the issue of one person. The process is repeated until the property is fully allocated.

(4) PER CAPITA.

Except as provided in sub. (6), if a statute or governing instrument calls for property to be distributed to a group or class "per capita", the property is divided into as many shares as there are surviving members of the group or class, and each member is allocated one share.

(5) CERTAIN INDIVIDUALS DISREGARDED.

For the purposes of subs. (1) to (3), all of the following apply:

(a) An individual who is deceased and who left no surviving issue is disregarded.

(b) An individual who has a surviving ancestor who is an issue of the designated person is not allocated a share.

(6) CONTRARY INTENT.

If the transfer is made under a governing instrument and the person who executed the governing instrument had an intent contrary to any provision in this section, then that provision is not applicable to the transfer. Extrinsic evidence may be used to construe the intent.

C. CALCULATING HEIRS: THE TABLE OF CONSANGUINITY

The Table of Consanguinity pictured below, is used to calculate the identity of collateral heirs under both the *parentelic* and *degree-of-relationship* systems. This calculation is necessary when the intestate deceased has no surviving spouse or issue (descendants). Under the *parentelic* system, intestate property passes to the potential heir who shares the closest common ancestor with the deceased. Consequently, siblings, nieces and nephews, and their children take first because they are all descended from the deceased's parents. The next group of eligible relations would be those who were descended from the deceased's grandparents (i.e., uncles and aunts, first cousins, and their children). If no one is a first (descendant of

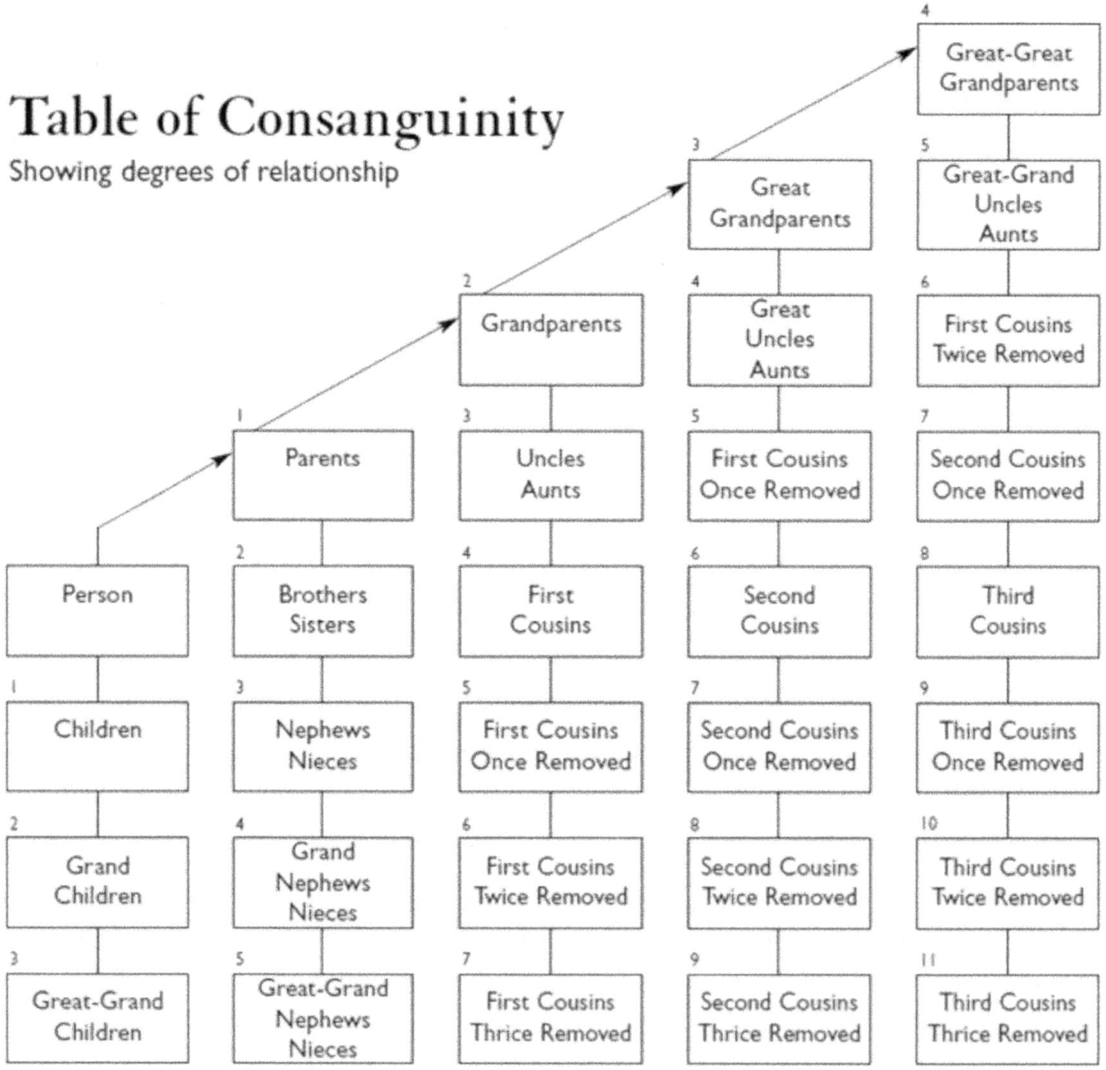

parents) or second line collateral (descendant of grandparents), then the property would pass to the third line collaterals: descendants of the deceased great-grandparents (great uncles and aunts, certain first cousins once removed, second cousins, and their descendants). Unless the state cuts off inheritance rights (as Wisconsin does at the level of second line collaterals) this process would continue until an heir is located.

In a *degree-of-relationship* system, the heir is the closest relative as measured by the number of steps away from the deceased as measured through common ancestors. Consequently, a sibling is two steps removed from the deceased—one step from the sibling to the common parent and then another from the parent to the deceased. A first cousin, in contrast, is four steps removed: (1) from the cousin to the aunt or uncle; (2) from the aunt or uncle to the grandparent; (3) from the grandparent to the parent; and (4) from the parent to the deceased. The small number above the upper left hand corners of the "rectangular boxes" on the Table of Consanguinity indicate the number of degrees of relationship between that particular category and the deceased.

The two systems can produce different results in the identification of the heir. Suppose the deceased is survived only by a first cousin (a not uncommon scenario) and one of his great grand parents (a possibility, though unlikely). Under a parentelic system, the heir would be the first cousin because she is a second line collateral while the great grandparent is a third line collateral. However, in a degree-of-relationship system, the great grandparent would be the heir as he or she is only three degrees of relationships removed while the first cousin is four degrees removed.

In addition to the parentelic and degree of relationship systems, some states use a hybrid system. Massachusetts, for example, is a degree-of-relationship jurisdiction, but if there are two potential heirs of equal kinship, the one who is a closer line collateral will be the heir. For example, an uncle and a nephew are both three degrees removed from the deceased, but because the nephew is a first line collateral and the uncle a second, the nephew will be the heir, not the uncle. This was the system in force in Wisconsin at the time of the *Estate of Rhodes* case, *supra*.

D. IDENTIFYING HEIRS

It is one thing to say that the heir is a spouse or a child, but it is not always a simple matter to know who qualifies as a spouse or a child, as the case of *Kleiber v. Ecker,* below, illustrates. It is normally not enough to be thought of as a spouse or a child; rather the person claiming on the basis of family relationship must demonstrate that they meet the legal definition of the status claimed. The following constitutional and statutory provisions define husband-wife and parent-child relationships in Wisconsin.

Wis. Const. Art. XIII, §13

Only a marriage between one man and one woman shall be valid or recognized as a marriage in this state. A legal status identical or substantially similar to that of marriage for unmarried individual shall not be valid or recognized in this state.

Wis. Stat. 765.01. [Marriage] A civil contract.

Marriage, so far as its validity at law is concerned, is a civil contract, to which the consent of the parties capable in law of contracting is essential, and which creates the legal status of husband and wife.

Wis. Stat. 765.02. Marriageable age; who may contract.

(1) Every person who has attained the age of 18 years may marry if otherwise competent.

(2) If a person is between the age of 16 and 18 years, a marriage license may be issued with the written consent of the person's parents, guardian, custodian under s. 767.225 (1) or 767.41, or parent having the actual care, custody and control of the person. The written consent must be given before the county clerk under oath, or certified in writing and verified by affidavit or affirmation before a notary public or other official authorized to take affidavits. The written consent shall be filed with the county clerk at the time of application for a marriage license. If there is no guardian, parent or custodian or if the custodian is an agency or department, the written consent may be given, after notice to any agency or department appointed as custodian and hearing proper cause shown, by the court having probate jurisdiction.

Wis. Stat. 765.03. Who shall not marry; divorced persons.

(1) No marriage shall be contracted while either of the parties has a husband or wife living, nor between persons who are nearer of kin than 2nd cousins except that marriage may be contracted between first cousins where the female has attained the age of 55 years or where either party, at the time of application for a marriage license, submits an affidavit signed by a

physician stating that either party is permanently sterile. Relationship under this section shall be computed by the rule of the civil law, whether the parties to the marriage are of the half or of the whole blood. A marriage may not be contracted if either party has such want of understanding as renders him or her incapable of assenting to marriage.

(2) It is unlawful for any person, who is or has been a party to an action for divorce in any court in this state, or elsewhere, to marry again until 6 months after judgment of divorce is granted, and the marriage of any such person solemnized before the expiration of 6 months from the date of the granting of judgment of divorce shall be void.

Wis. Stat. 852.05. Status of child born to unmarried parents for purposes of intestate succession.

(1) A child born to unmarried parents, or the child's issue, is treated in the same manner as a child, or the issue of a child, born to married parents with respect to intestate succession from and through the child's mother, and from and through the child's father if any of the following applies:

(a) The father has been adjudicated to be the father in a paternity proceeding under ch. 767 or by final order or judgment of a court of competent jurisdiction in another state.

(b) The father has admitted in open court that he is the father.

(c) The father has acknowledged himself to be the father in writing signed by him.

(2) Property of a child born to unmarried parents passes in accordance with s. 852.01 except that the father or the fathers kindred can inherit only if the father has been adjudicated to be the father in a paternity proceeding under ch. 767 or by final order or judgment of a court of competent jurisdiction in another state or has been determined to be the father under s. 767.805 or a substantially similar law of another state.

(3) (a) This section does not apply to a child who becomes a marital child by the subsequent marriage of the child's parents under s. 767.803 (b) The status of a child born to unmarried parents who is legally adopted is governed by s. 854.20

Wis. Stat. 854.21. Persons included in family groups or classes.

(1) ADOPTED PERSONS.

(a) Except as provided in sub. (7), a gift of property by a governing instrument to a class of persons described as "issue," "lawful issue," "children," "grandchildren," "descendants," "heirs," "heirs of the body," "next of kin," "distributees," or the like includes a person adopted by a person whose birth child would be a member of the class, and issue of the adopted person, if the conditions for membership in the class are otherwise satisfied and at least one of the criteria under s. 854.20 (1) (b) 1., 2., and 3. is satisfied.

(b) Except as provided in sub. (7), a gift of property by a governing instrument to a class of persons described as "issue," "lawful issue," "children," "grandchildren," "descendants," "heirs," "heirs of the body," "next of kin," "distributees," or the like excludes a birth child and his or her issue otherwise within the class if the birth child has been adopted and would cease to be treated as a child of the birth parent under s. 854.20 (2)

(2) INDIVIDUALS BORN TO UNMARRIED PARENTS.

(a) Subject to par. (b) and sub. (7), individuals born to unmarried parents are included in class gifts and other terms of relationship in accordance with s. 852.05 (b) In addition to the requirements of par. (a) and subject to the provisions of sub. (7), in construing a disposition by a transferor who is not the birth parent, an individual born to unmarried parents is not considered to be the child of a birth parent unless that individual lived while a minor as a regular member of the household of that birth parent or of that birth parents parent, brother, sister, spouse or surviving spouse.

(3) RELATIVES BY MARRIAGE.

Subject to sub. (7), terms of family relationship in statutes or governing instruments that do not differentiate between relationships by blood and relationships by marriage are construed to exclude relatives by marriage.

(4) RELATIVES OF THE HALF-BLOOD.

Subject to sub. (7), terms of family relationship in statutes or governing instruments that do not differentiate between relationships by the half-blood and relationships by the full-blood are construed to include both types of relationships.

(5) POSTHUMOUS ISSUE.

Subject to sub. (7), if a statute or governing instrument transfers an interest to a group of persons described as a class, such as "issue", "children", "nephews and nieces" or any other class, a person conceived at the time the membership in the class is determined and subsequently born alive is entitled to take as a member of the class if that person otherwise satisfies the conditions for class membership and survives at least 120 hours past birth.

(6) PERSON RELATED THROUGH 2 LINES.

Subject to sub. (7), a person who is eligible to be a transferee under a statute or governing instrument through 2 lines of relationship is limited to one share, based on the relationship that entitles the person to the larger share.

(7) CONTRARY INTENT.

If the transfer is made under a governing instrument and the person who executed the governing instrument had an intent contrary to any provision in this section, then that provision is inapplicable to the transfer. Extrinsic evidence may be used to construe the intent.

KLEIBER v. ECKER

Supreme Court of Wisconsin
174 Wis. 432; 182 N.W. 977 (1921)

APPEAL from a judgment of the circuit court for Manitowoc county. Affirmed.

Joseph Ecker died intestate April 30, 1918, his wife having died some years before. He left surviving his sister, the appellant, and several children of a deceased brother. There were no children as a result of his marriage.

It appears that in 1866 one Mary Halda made a complaint before a justice of the peace in which she charged that the deceased, Joseph Ecker, was the father of her unborn child. A warrant was issued. Subsequently Mary Halda gave birth to a male child and named him Adolph Ecker, by which name he has ever since gone. Soon after the birth of Adolph, Mary Halda married one Frank Steinfest, leaving the child Adolph with her parents, where he remained until he was four years of age.

The maternal grandparents then took Adolph to the residence of Joseph Ecker, who in the meantime had married, and Adolph thereafter remained as a member of the family of Joseph Ecker and was in all respects treated by Joseph Ecker as his son. Adolph subsequently married a daughter of a neighboring farmer and ever since his marriage has resided in the neighborhood where Joseph Ecker lived. Joseph Ecker was never adjudged the father of Adolph, and Joseph never adopted Adolph in the manner prescribed by statute.

Upon the death of Joseph Ecker, Adolph Ecker made a petition to the county court of Manitowoc county for the administration of the estate of Joseph Ecker, alleging that he was the only heir at law of the deceased, and shortly thereafter Elizabeth Kleiber, the appellant, petitioned the county court for administration of the estate of Joseph Ecker and alleged that she was one of the heirs at law and the only surviving sister of Joseph Ecker. The case was tried in the county court and judgment was entered in favor of Adolph. An appeal was then taken to the circuit court, where the case was tried before the court without a jury, and the circuit court also found in favor of Adolph, and from the judgment entered Elizabeth Kleiber, the sister, appeals.

ROSENBERRY, J. While the finding of the court that *Adolph Ecker* is the son of Joseph Ecker is assigned as error by the appellant, that fact is so conclusively established that it may be treated as a verity in this case. In every possible way over a long period of time, with the single exception of formally adopting him or acknowledging him as his son by some formal document, Joseph Ecker treated *Adolph* as his son. *Adolph* was born January 2, 1866, so that the witnesses to the transactions which occurred at the time *Adolph* became a member of the family of Joseph have passed away with the exception of Mary Halda, the mother, who appeared at the trial and testified in behalf of *Adolph. Adolph* was received as a son, lived as a member of the family of Joseph Ecker until his marriage, and thereafter the relationship which would naturally exist between a father and an adult son continued down to the time of the death of Joseph. The decisive question in this case is, Did Joseph Ecker acknowledge himself to be the father of *Adolph Ecker* so as to entitle *Adolph* to the benefit of the provisions of sec. 2274, Stats.?

"Every illegitimate child shall be considered as heir of the person who shall, in writing signed in the presence of a competent witness, have acknowledged himself to be the father of such child."

The evidence to sustain the finding upon this branch of the case was practically without dispute, and the question is, "Did the writings amount to a compliance with the statute?" The court found:

"8. That about twenty years before the time of this trial said Joseph Ecker and his son *Adolph Ecker* entered into a written contract with one F. F. Stelling for the purchase from said Stelling of a threshing machine; that in the body of that contract it was stated that Joseph Ecker and son were the purchasers of the machine. That the contract was signed by said Joseph Ecker and *Adolph Ecker* and said F. F. Stelling; that the said contract in writing was signed by the said Joseph Ecker and *Adolph Ecker* in the presence of said F. F. Stelling and that he, F. F. Stelling, was a competent witness thereto. That said written contract has since been lost, and after due search could not be found to be produced at the trial.

"9. That while the said *Adolph Ecker* was a boy and was living with said Joseph Ecker, said Joseph Ecker on frequent occasions wrote out a slip of paper, an order addressed to a saloonkeeper at Brillion, to deliver a keg of beer to said *Adolph* for said Joseph Ecker. These orders *Adolph* took to the saloonkeeper and procured the beer. On some of these occasions said *Adolph Ecker* was accompanied by Fred Wolfe and at other times by John Schreiber. One of these orders for beer was written by the said Joseph Ecker in the presence of said Fred Wolfe; others of these orders were written by said Joseph Ecker in the presence of said John Schreiber. Said Fred Wolfe and said John Schreiber were competent witnesses. Said orders were written by said Joseph Ecker in the German language; one of them was read by said Schreiber and its meaning in the English language is, 'Give my son *Adolph* a keg of beer on my name. Joseph Ecker.'

That order was signed by Joseph Ecker in the presence of said John Schreiber, and he was a competent witness thereto."

The trial court held that these writings constituted a sufficient acknowledgment on the part of Joseph Ecker that he was the father of *Adolph* and that *Adolph* thereby became entitled to inherit in accordance with the provisions of sec. 2274.

The provisions of sec. 2274 were quite fully discussed in *Richmond v. Taylor,* 151 Wis. 633, 139 N.W. 435. It is there stated:

"It is not essential that the written acknowledgment shall be made for the express purpose of establishing heirship or of a compliance with the statute. It may be made in entire ignorance of the statutory requirements and for purposes other than that of creating heirship. . . . It does not require that the witness should attest or subscribe the writing or acknowledgment--only that the person making it shall sign in the presence of the witness. . . . Neither does it require that the acknowledgment of paternity shall be in precise formal language. It is sufficient if it appear with reasonable clearness and certainty from the written words that the paternity of the child is acknowledged."

It is considered that the trial court correctly held that the writings referred to in the findings were a sufficient acknowledgment. Our attention has been called to many cases in other jurisdictions where conclusions have been reached which are at variance with those reached in the case of *Richmond v. Taylor.* We see no reason, however, for disturbing the ruling made in that case. Judgment affirmed.

II. PROBLEMS RELATED TO INTESTACY

A. SIMULTANEOUS DEATH

Determining the sequence of death when two people die close together in time can be almost impossible. Even so, knowledge of the order of death was long a necessary prerequisite for the application of the intestacy statute when the deceased were heirs to each other, but otherwise had no common heirs. For example, if H and W are a married couple without children or grandchildren, they are each other's heirs. Were H to die first and intestate, then his property would pass to W and then, following her death, to her heirs. Were W the first to die, her property would end up with H's heirs through a similar sequence. But how is the estate to be distributed if the order of death is not known, as when they both die in a common disaster like a plane crash or a ship sinking at sea?

Courts were traditionally forced to make the best guess that they could from the available evidence. However, the problem was ultimately resolved by the promulgation of the Uniform Simultaneous Death Act in 1940, which took the seemingly contradictory position that each spouse could be treated as though they had predeceased the other. Although the statute was originally designed to apply only in situations where the two deaths were nearly simultaneous and the order was not known, the advantages of a survival requirement became increasingly apparent. Individuals who died testate, i.e., with a will, could always incorporate such a provision into the will, as in "to Rodney, if he survives me by five days or more."

What was originally a statutory answer to a factual question that could not otherwise be answered has evolved in most states into a general 120 hour (or five-day) survivorship requirement that applies whether or not the sequence of death is at issue or whether the two deceased parties died in a common accident or incident.

The *Villwock* case, set out below, deals with the complications surrounding an attempt to determine the sequence of death in a simultaneous death situation prior to the adoption of the current version of Wis. Stat. § 854.03. Under the earlier version of the statute, the "presumption" that each party predeceased the other applied only if the order of death could not be conclusively determined.

Wis. Stat. 854.03. Requirement of survival by 120 hours.

(1) REQUIREMENT OF SURVIVAL.

Except as provided in sub. (5), if property is transferred to an individual under a statute or under a provision in a governing instrument that requires the individual to survive an event and it is not established that the individual survived the event by at least 120 hours, the individual is considered to have predeceased the event.

(2) CO-OWNERS WITH RIGHT OF SURVIVORSHIP.

(a) In this subsection, "co-owners with right of survivorship" includes joint tenants, owners of survivorship marital property and other co-owners of property or accounts that are held under circumstances that entitle one or more persons to all of the property or account upon the death of one or more of the others.

(b) Except as provided in sub. (5), if property is transferred under a governing instrument that establishes 2 or more co-owners with right of survivorship, and if at least one of the co-owners did not survive the others by at least 120 hours, the property is transferred to the co-owners in proportion to their ownership interests.

(3) MARITAL PROPERTY.

Except as provided in subs. (4) and (5), if a husband and wife die leaving marital property and it is not established that one survived the other by at least 120 hours, 50% of the marital property shall be distributed as if it were the husbands individual property and the husband had survived, and 50% of the marital property shall be distributed as if it were the wife's individual property and the wife had survived.

(4) LIFE INSURANCE.

Except as provided in sub. (5), if the insured and the beneficiary under a policy of life or accident insurance have both died and it is not established that one survived the other by at least 120 hours, the proceeds of the policy shall be distributed as if the insured had survived the beneficiary. If the policy is the marital property of the insured and of the insured's spouse and there is no alternative beneficiary except the estate or the personal representative of the estate, the proceeds shall be distributed as marital property in the manner provided in sub. (3)

(5) EXCEPTIONS.

(am) This section does not apply if any of the following conditions applies:

1. The statute or governing instrument requires the individual to survive an event by a specified period.

2. The statute or governing instrument indicates that the individual is not required to survive an event by any specified period.

3. The statute or governing instrument deals with simultaneous deaths or deaths in a common disaster and the provision is relevant to the facts.

4. The imposition of a 120-hour survival requirement would cause a nonvested property interest or a power of appointment to fail to be valid, or to be invalidated, under s. 700.16 or under the rule against perpetuities of the applicable jurisdiction.

5. The application of this section to more than one statute or governing instrument would result in an unintended failure or unintended duplication of a transfer.

6. The application of this section would result in the escheat of an intestate estate under s. 852.01 (3)

7. The statute or governing instrument specifies that this statute, or one similar to it, does not apply.

8. The imposition of a 120-hour survival requirement would be administratively cumbersome and would not change the identity of the ultimate beneficiaries of the property or the property that each beneficiary would receive.

(bm) If the transfer is made under a governing instrument and the person who executed the governing instrument had an intent contrary to any provision in this section, then that provision is not applicable to the transfer. Extrinsic evidence may be used to construe the intent.

(6) EVIDENTIARY STANDARD.

Unless the statute or governing instrument provides otherwise, proof that an individual survived the period required under subs. (1) to (4) must be by clear and convincing evidence.

ESTATE OF VILLWOCK

Court of Appeals of Wisconsin
142 Wis. 2d 144, 418 N.W.2d 1 (1987)

LaRocque, J. Mary Hintz, Roy Villwock's daughter by a previous marriage, appeals an order that her father's estate be probated in accord with the trial court's finding that Roy preceded his wife, June, in death. The effect of the order is to pass Roy's entire estate to June's estate and in turn to June's heirs as directed by her will. The trial court's determination of the time of Roy's death is a finding of fact and is not clearly erroneous. Section 805.17(2), Stats. Because the trial court found that Roy died before his wife, the provisions of the Uniform Simultaneous Death Act, sec. 851.55(1), Stats., are inapplicable. We affirm.

Roy and June Villwock, critically injured but alive and conscious after a head-on car crash on July 25, 1985, were transported together to a Rhinelander hospital. All five emergency medical technicians on board agreed that Roy suffered cardiopulmonary failure minutes before June similarly failed. Upon arrival at the hospital, each was taken to a separate treatment room where CPR, begun in the ambulance, was continued. A physician eventually pronounced June dead at 8:23 p.m. Another physician, Dr. Bruce Kotila, after giving advanced CPR to Roy, pronounced him dead at 8:34 p.m.

A probate hearing was held to determine the time of Roy's death. Dr. Kotila testified that Roy's heart and lung failure in the ambulance was irreversible despite the efforts to revive him. The trial court accepted Dr. Kotila's testimony and found that Roy died in the ambulance, while his wife was undisputedly still alive and conscious. Roy's will left everything to June and contained no contingency that she need survive him any period of time in order to take under the will. There were no other dispositive provisions in the will. There were no children born to the marriage of Roy and June. June's will left everything to specific members of her family.

Section 146.71, Stats., provides:

Determination of Death. An individual who has sustained either irreversible cessation of circulatory and respiratory functions or irreversible cessation of all functions of the entire brain, including the brain stem, is dead. A determination of death shall be made in accordance with accepted medical standards.

Prior to the adoption of this statute in 1981, the Wisconsin courts declined to define death. *Cranmore v. State*, 85 Wis. 2d 722, 774, 271 N.W.2d 402, 428 (Ct. App. 1978). The Wisconsin statutory definition of death adopts the uniform Act approved by the National Conference of Commissioners on Uniform State Laws. Modern advances in life-saving technology have prompted adoption of this uniform law. *See* Prefatory Note to Uniform Determination of Death Act, 12 U.L.A. 286 (Supp. 1986). The statute allows for two alternative definitions of death. We are only concerned here with the first alternative, which essentially codifies the common law: death is the irreversible failure of the cardiorespiratory system.

Hintz contends that Dr. Kotila's testimony determining Roy's time of death must be disregarded as a matter of law because it is contradictory and speculative. She then concludes that, under the terms of the Uniform Simultaneous Death Act, sec. 851.55, "there is no sufficient evidence that [Roy and June] have died otherwise than simultaneously." We reject her argument.

Dr. Kotila's original death pronouncement of 8:34 p.m. conflicts with his ultimate opinion that death occurred earlier in the ambulance. There also is arguably an inconsistency between his ultimate opinion and his administration of advanced CPR for an hour at the hospital. Dr. Kotila, however, offered explanations for these conflicts. Dr. Kotila explained that his original death pronouncement was not intended to preclude a reevaluation to establish death at an earlier time. Given the demands upon an emergency room physician in a time of crisis, it is not difficult to accept his explanation. Dr. Kotila also explained that CPR was continued for an hour or more to preclude any possibility of an erroneous judgment of death made in haste. This explanation is not incredible as a matter of law. The determination of credibility is the sole province of the trial court. *Estate of Sensenbrenner v. Sensenbrenner*, 89 Wis. 2d 677, 700, 278 N.W.2d 887, 898 (1979).

Hintz further insists that it is beyond the ability of any medical scientist to fix at a precise moment in time when cardiopulmonary failure was "irreversible." Dr. Kotila testified, however, that the extent of a person's injuries is "a very big factor" in deciding irreversibility. Roy's injuries were undisputedly extensive. The drafters of the Uniform Determination of Death Act contemplated disputes over irreversibility. The determination of death must be made in accordance with accepted medical standards. "This Act is silent on acceptable diagnostic tests and medical procedures. It sets the general legal standard for determining death, but not the medical criteria for doing so. The medical profession remains free to formulate acceptable medical practices and to utilize new biomedical knowledge, diagnostic tests, and equipment." Prefatory Note to Uniform Determination of Death Act, 12 U.L.A. at 287.

Dr. Kotila is a licensed physician, board certified in internal medicine with nine years' experience in emergency room practices. Although the trial court did not explicitly find that the medical evidence was in accord with accepted standards, it did so implicitly. This court may assume that a missing finding was determined in favor of the order or judgment. *Sohns v. Jensen*, 11 Wis. 2d 449, 453, 105 N.W.2d 818, 820 (1960). Based upon the qualifications of the expert witness and the fact that his opinion was unchallenged by any other witness or evidence, we will assume that the trial court found that the determination of death was in accord with accepted medical standards.

Given the few minutes between Roy's cardiopulmonary failure and that suffered by June, the margin for error, when measured by time, is admittedly narrow. The narrow margin for error is no reason to reject the trial court's fact finding. The problem is that the facts are forever gone and no scientific method of inquiry can ever be devised to produce facsimiles that bring the past to life. The judicial process deals with probabilities, not facts, and we must therefore be on guard against making fact skepticism our main preoccupation. However skillfully, however sensitively we arrange a reproduction of the past, the arrangement is still that of the theater. We acknowledge as much when we speak of re-enacting the crime or the accident or perhaps some everyday event; we know better than to speak of reliving it. The most we can hope for is that witnesses will be honest and reasonably accurate in their perception and recollection, [and] that triers of fact will be honest and intelligent in their reasoning, ...

R. Traynor, *Fact Skepticism and the Judicial Process*, 106 U. Pa. L. Rev. 635-36 (1958). The "fact" of the time of Roy's death has been adequately established in this case.

The Simultaneous Death Act is inapplicable. The Villwocks did not die simultaneously. The statute's nontechnical words, if not specifically defined, will be given their ordinary and accepted meaning, which may be ascertained from a recognized dictionary. *State v. Wittrock*, 119 Wis. 2d 664, 670, 350 N.W.2d 647, 651 (1984). Webster's Third New International Dictionary 2122 (1975) defines "simultaneous" as "occurring at the same time . . . ." Based on the trial court's finding, the deaths here did not occur at the same time.

B. INHERITANCE RIGHTS OF ADOPTED CHILDREN

The traditional view of adoption is that it cuts off all inheritance rights between the adopted individual and his biological parents. The adopted child becomes the legal child of the adoptive parents, and a new web of kinship relations is substituted for the one that existed prior to the adoption. Ordinarily, this works for the benefit of the adoptive child, but on occasions, adoption has the consequence of preventing the adopted child from taking an inheritance for which he or she would have been eligible. The situation becomes more complicated when a step-parent is the adopting parent and one of the biological parents remains in place as the legal parent. If the original parents divorced, then the former parent presumably consented to the adoption, but if the original parent is deceased, no such consent is attainable. Many states, including Wisconsin, have addressed this issue by adopting special rules in cases of step-parent adoption. Additional complications can arise when the adopted individual is already an adult.

854.20. Status of adopted persons.

(1) INHERITANCE RIGHTS BETWEEN ADOPTIVE PERSON AND ADOPTIVE RELATIVES.

(a) Subject to par. (b) and sub. (5), a legally adopted person is treated as a birth child of the persons adoptive parents and the adoptive parents are treated as the birth parents of the adopted person for purposes of transfers at death to, through, and from the adopted person and for purposes of any statute or other rule conferring rights upon children, issue, or relatives in connection with the law of intestate succession or governing instruments.

(b) Subject to sub. (5), par. (a) applies only if at least one of the following applies:

1. The decedent or transferor is the adoptive parent or adopted child.

2. The adopted person was a minor at the time of adoption.

3. The adoptive parent raised the adopted person in a parent-like relationship beginning on or before the child's 15th birthday and lasting for a substantial period or until adulthood.

(2) INHERITANCE RIGHTS BETWEEN ADOPTED PERSON AND BIRTH RELATIVES.

(am) Subject to sub. (5), a legally adopted person ceases to be treated as a child of the person's birth parents and the birth parents cease to be treated as the parents of the child for the purposes specified in sub. (1) (a), except:

1. If the parent-child relationship between the child and one birth parent is replaced by adoption, but the relationship to the other birth parent is not replaced, then for all purposes the child continues to be treated as the child of the birth parent whose relationship was not replaced.

2.

a. Subject to subd. 2. b. and c., if a birth parent of a child born to married parents dies and the other birth parent subsequently remarries and the child is adopted by the stepparent, the child continues to be treated as the child of the deceased birth parent for purposes of transfers at death through that parent and for purposes of any statute or other rule conferring rights upon children, issue or relatives of that parent under the law of intestate succession or governing instruments.

b. Subd. 2. a. applies only if the adopted person was a minor at the time of adoption or if the adoptive parent raised the adopted person in a parent-like relationship beginning on or before the child's 15th birthday and lasting for a substantial period or until adulthood.

c. Subdivision 2. a. does not apply if the parental rights of the deceased birth parent had been terminated.

(bm) Subject to sub. (5), if an adopted child is subsequently adopted by another person, the former adoptive parent is considered to be a birth parent for purposes of this subsection.

(5) CONTRARY INTENT.

If the transfer is made under a governing instrument and the person who executed the governing instrument had an intent contrary to any provision in this section, then that provision is not applicable to the transfer. Extrinsic evidence may be used to construe the intent.

Wis. Stat. 882.01. Adoption of adults.

An adult may be adopted by any other adult, who is a resident of this state.

Wis. Stat. 882.02. Consent.

The consent of the adult to be adopted and the consent of the spouse of the petitioner, if that spouse has not joined in the petition under s. 882.01, shall be filed in writing with the court.

Wis. Stat. 882.03. Jurisdiction and venue.

The circuit court shall have jurisdiction to order an adoption. The petition shall be filed in the county where the petitioner resides.

Wis. Stat. 882.04. Hearing and order.

After a hearing on the petition, which may be held in chambers and which shall be attended by the petitioner and the adult to be adopted, unless the court orders otherwise, and after such investigation as the court considers advisable, if the court finds that it is to the best interests of the persons involved, an order of adoption may be granted which shall have the same legal consequences as an order of adoption of a minor under ch. 48.

WINIARSKI v. MIICKE

Court of Appeals of Wisconsin
186 Wis. 2d 409, 521 N.W.2d 162 (1994)

FINE, J. James J. Winiarski, as successor personal representative of the Estate of Lorenz E. Jank, appeals from a trial-court order declaring Gerald J. Miicke to be an "interested party" in the Jank estate. Underlying this determination was the trial court's finding that Miicke was Mr. Jank's heir. We reverse.

The facts material to this appeal are few and undisputed. Miicke was born in 1931 to the decedent, Lorenz E. Jank, and his wife Helen Jank, who died in childbirth. In 1933, Miicke was adopted by his maternal grandparents. Mr. Jank died intestate in 1991. Winiarski contends that Miicke's right to inherit from Mr. Jank by intestate succession was terminated by §851.51(2), STATS., which provides, with exceptions not relevant here, that a lawfully adopted child may not take by intestate succession from his or her birth parents. Section 851.51(2) became effective on February 8, 1970. The trial court's ruling was premised on its belief that §851.51(2) was prospective only, and therefore did not apply to Miicke's situation.

Whether §851.51(2), STATS., cuts off the intestate-succession rights of those persons lawfully adopted prior to its effective date is a matter of first impression. We decide this legal issue *de novo. See Schulz v. Ystad*, 155 Wis.2d 574, 596, 456

N.W.2d 312, 320 (1990)(whether statute applies retroactively is a question of law decided by appellate courts *de novo*).

Statutes affecting substantive rights are not applied retroactively, unless the legislature clearly so intended. *Schulz*, 155 Wis.2d at 597, 456 N.W.2d at 320 ("no law should be enforced before people can learn of its existence and conduct themselves accordingly"); *Bair v. Staats*, 10 Wis.2d 70, 78, 102 N.W.2d 267, 272 (1960). When Miicke was adopted by his maternal grandparents, the law in Wisconsin permitted an adopted child to inherit from his or her birth parents. *Sauer v. Goetsch*, 216 Wis. 289, 257 N.W. 28 (1934). Nevertheless, the right to take by intestate succession does not exist until the decedent dies intestate. *Stein v. Meyer*, 206 Wis. 227, 234-235, 239 N.W. 448, 450-451 (1931). Thus, intestate succession is governed by statutes "in force at the time of the death of the intestate." *Hull v. Collins*, 259 Wis. 453, 455, 49 N.W.2d 483, 484 (1951).

Accordingly, a statute enacted after an adoption that alters the effect of the adoption on the right to inherit from a intestate decedent is *prospective, not retroactive*, as long as the statute was effective before the intestate's death. *Stein*, 206 Wis. at 234-236, 239 N.W. at 450-451. Although Miicke was adopted in 1933, and, therefore, may have had an expectancy of being able to take from Mr. Jank by intestate succession, that expectancy disappeared upon the enactment of §851.51(2), STATS. At that point, Mr. Jank could have accomplished what Miicke now seeks by the simple expedient of making a will and naming Miicke as a beneficiary.

Although there might be problems with applying a law limiting intestate succession so as to adversely affect circumstances that became fixed prior to its enactment, *cf. Schulz*, 155 Wis.2d at 597, 456 N.W.2d at 320 ("as a matter of justice, no law should be enforced before people can learn of its existence and conduct themselves accordingly"), this is not the case here.

C. ADVANCEMENTS

Sometimes an individual will desire to transfer property to one or more of her heirs with the understanding that the transfer is an advancement on the heir's inheritance and that when the property owner dies, the intestate share of the heir is reduced accordingly. (The same principle also applies to devisees of money or the equivalent in a will.) Often, however, the transfer will be made without clear evidence as to whether or not it was intended to be an advancement on one's inheritance or bequest in a will or simply an inter vivos gift. The traditional rule was that all gifts to heirs were presumed to be advancements unless it could be shown otherwise by a preponderance of the evidence. This presumption in favor of advancement still exists in some states, but it has been abandoned in a majority of jurisdictions, including Wisconsin. Today, in most states in-life transfers are assumed to be gifts unless there is written documentation to the contrary, and the writings are often required to be roughly contemporaneous with the transfer.

Hotchpot.[*] When an advancement can be established, the total sum of all advancements is added to the total of the assets in the decedent's probate estate. (The advancements are not literally returned, but the personal representative or administrator of the estate simply does the calculations.) In a process traditionally known as *hotchpot*, the estate with the advancements added is divided among the heirs with each heir who received an advancement having his share proportionately reduced. For example if A, B, and C are the heirs of D, and A received an advancement of $10,000, and B, $20,000, and D died with a probate estate worth $270,000. The sum of the probate estate plus the advancements is $300,000, so A, B, and C would each have a combined share of $100,000. Subtracting the advancements, A would receive $90,000; B would receive $80,000, and C would receive the full $100,000 from the probate assets.

What happens if an heir receives an advancement greater than his or her intestate share? Suppose that A receives an advancement of $300,000, and that B and C receive no advancements and that D dies with probate assets of $300,000. Adding the probate estate to the advancement gives a combined total of $600,000, which would ordinarily mean that each of the three heirs would be entitled to a total of $200,000. However, the estate has only $300,000 to distribute, and A will never be required to return any part of his advancement. Since B and C are entitled to equal shares, they will split the $300,000, which works out to $150,000 each, and A receives nothing from the probate estate.

The doctrine of advancements is limited to the law of intestacy and does not apply to estates where there are valid wills. As the Wisconsin Supreme Court noted in *Estate of Pardee,* 240 Wis. 19, 1 N.W.2d 803 (1942), the doctrine of advancements, whether rooted in the common law or in statute, is applied only in cases of intestacy. There is, however, a corresponding doctrine in the law of wills known as *ademption by satisfaction* which applies when a still living testator "advances" (rather than gives)

---

[*] **Ed. Note:** Although *hotchpot* is the traditional term for the distribution of an estate from which there have been advancements, there appears to be no reported Wisconsin appellate court opinion where the specific term is used.

money or its equivalent to someone who is entitled to a similar devise under the testator's will.

Wis. Stat. 852.11. Advancement.

The effect of a lifetime gift by the decedent on the intestate share of an heir is governed by s. 854.09

Wis. Stat. 854.09. Advancement; satisfaction.

(1) A gift that the decedent made during his or her lifetime, including an incomplete gift that became complete on the decedent's death, is treated as a full or partial satisfaction of a transfer at death to an heir under s. 852.01 (1) or a transferee under a governing instrument executed by the decedent only if at least one of the following applies:

(a) The governing instrument, if any, either expressly or as construed from extrinsic evidence, provides that the gift be taken into account.

(b) The decedent declared in a document, either expressly or as construed from extrinsic evidence, that the gift is in satisfaction of, or an advance against, what the transferee would receive at the decedent's death, whether or not the document was contemporaneous with the gift.

(c) The transferee acknowledged in writing before or after the decedent's death, either expressly or as construed from extrinsic evidence, that the gift is in satisfaction of, or an advance against, what the transferee would receive at the decedent's death.

(2) For partial satisfaction, property given during life is valued as of the time that the transferee came into possession or enjoyment of the property or at the death of the person who executed the governing instrument, whichever occurs first.

(3) If the transferee fails to survive the person who executed the governing instrument and his or her issue take a substitute transfer under intestacy or under a governing instrument, the issue receive the same transfer that the named transferee would have received had the transferee survived, unless the transferor declared otherwise in a document, either expressly or as construed from extrinsic evidence.

Wis. Stat. 852.12. Debts to decedent.

If an heir owes a debt to the decedent, s. 854.12 governs the treatment of that debt.

Wis. Stat. 854.12. Debt to transferor.

(1) HEIR UNDER INTESTACY.

(a) If an heir owes a debt to the decedent, the amount of the indebtedness shall be offset against the intestate share of the debtor heir.

(b) In contesting an offset under par. (a), the debtor heir shall have the benefit of any defense that would be available to the debtor heir in a direct proceeding by the personal representative for the recovery of the debt, except that the debtor heir may not defend on the basis that the debt was discharged in bankruptcy or on the basis that the relevant statute of limitations has expired. If the debtor fails to survive the decedent, the court may not include the debt in computing any intestate shares of the debtor's issue.

(2) TRANSFEREE UNDER REVOCABLE GOVERNING INSTRUMENT.

(a) Subject to par. (c), if a transferee under a revocable governing instrument survives the transferor and is indebted to the transferor, the amount of the indebtedness shall be treated as an offset against the property to which the debtor transferee is entitled. If multiple revocable governing instruments transfer property to the debtor, the debt shall be equitably allocated against the various instruments.

(b) Subject to par. (c), in contesting an offset under par. (a), the debtor shall have the benefit of any defense that would be available to the transferee in a direct proceeding for the recovery of the debt, except that the transferee may not defend on the basis that the debt was discharged in bankruptcy, unless that discharge occurred before the execution of the governing instrument, or on the basis that the relevant statute of limitations has expired. If the transferee fails to survive the decedent, the debt may not be included in computing the entitlement of alternate beneficiaries.

(c) If the person who executed the governing instrument had an intent contrary to any provision in this subsection, then that provision is not applicable to the transfer. Extrinsic evidence may be used to construe the intent.

(3) PROPERTY NOT DISTRIBUTED BECAUSE OF OFFSET.

The property not distributed to the debtor becomes part of the residue of the entity that holds the debt. If the debt is not held by an entity, then the property not distributed to the debtor becomes part of the residue of the decedent's probate estate.

Arthur v. Arthur

Supreme Court of Wisconsin
143 Wis. 126, 126 N.W. 550 (1910)

KERWIN, J. The question in this case is whether the transfer of $5,000 worth of property to each of the three sons of John Arthur--Samuel, Charles, and Harry--amounted to an advancement to each of them which should be charged against him in the settlement of the estate of his father. The court below in a lengthy and able opinion held that the sums given were advancements and not gifts; therefore that each should be charged with the amount so advanced in the settlement of John Arthur's estate.

The grounds of decision of the court below are, in effect, that the evidence tends to show that John Arthur desired to distribute his property equally, and the court recites the certificate set out in the findings, made at least four months after the transfers, to the effect that John Arthur had made advancements to each of his four sons of $5,000; that, independent of the statute regarding proof of advancements (sec. 3959, Stats. 1898), a presumption is raised upon the facts that the gifts were advancements, and that such presumption is controlling unless rebutted by evidence; and that but for sec. 3959, Stats. (1898), he would hold that the gifts to Charles, Samuel, and Harry were advancements under the evidence.

The court below then proceeds to discuss sec. 3959, Stats. (1898), and the effect of the certificate referred to and put in evidence, and argues that the statute does not require the charge to be made at the time of making the gifts; that, since the facts and circumstances show that the gifts were intended as advancements, there is nothing in the language of the statute or in reason why the parent afterwards may not in writing declare the gifts to have been advancements, and thereby comply with the statute. Pomeroy v. Pomeroy, 93 Wis. 262, 67 N.W. 430, and Ludington v. Patton, 121 Wis. 649, 99 N.W. 614, are referred to and held not controlling.

It may be that, in the absence of a statute prescribing the manner of proving advancements, the proof would have been sufficient to support the findings and judgment below. But in the face of our statute (sec. 3959) we cannot find that it is. The assignments of the $5,000 interest to each of the three sons bear upon their face no evidence that they were advancements. True, the age of John Arthur when the assignments were made, the fact that the property assigned amounted to more than half of his estate, and that he was averse to making a will, and perhaps some other facts and circumstances appearing in evidence, might be sufficient to raise a presumption that the gifts were advancements without the certificate of October 28, 1905, were it not for the statute referred to. But in face of the statute we fail to find sufficient proof, unless the certificate was admissible in evidence. The statute (sec. 3959) provides:

"All gifts and grants shall be deemed to have been made in advancement if they are expressed in the gift or grant to be so made or if charged in writing by the intestate as an advancement or acknowledged in writing as such by the child or other descendant. . . . "

This statute at least by implication excludes other proof of advancement and provides for proving an advancement. Bulkeley v. Noble, 2 Pick. 337; Barton v. Rice, 22 Pick. 508. In Massachusetts the statute is the same as our own, and in Barton v. Rice, supra, the court said:

"The statute does not expressly declare that an advancement shall not be proved in any other manner, but that undoubtedly is the meaning of the statute."

And in Bigelow v. Poole, 10 Gray 104, 105, it is said: "It is the settled law of this commonwealth that an advancement, whether of real or personal property, made by an intestate to his child or other descendant, must be proved by the evidence prescribed by our statutes, and by no other."

The construction placed upon the statute by the Massachusetts court has been adopted by this court. In Pomeroy v. Pomeroy, 93 Wis. 262, at page 266 (67 N.W. 430, at page 431), this court said:

"It follows that the construction given to this statute by the Massachusetts court became, on its adoption here, a part of the law of this state. We therefore hold that parol evidence is inadmissible to prove an advancement; that, though the statute does not expressly declare that an advancement shall not be proved in any other manner than that indicated therein, such is undoubtedly its meaning; that, by prescribing a particular manner for proving an advancement, by implication all other evidence is excluded."

To the same effect is Ludington v. Patton, 121 Wis. 649, 662, 99 N.W. 614.

Since the evidence independent of the certificate was not sufficient to establish that the transfers were advancements, the question arises whether the certificate was competent. This certificate was made some four months after all the transfers were completed and delivered, and it is insisted by respondent that it was competent as tending to show the intention of John Arthur and in harmony with the statute, because the statute does not provide when the charge shall be made. The statute, however, has been construed by this court in two cases (Pomeroy v. Pomeroy, 93 Wis. 262, 67 N.W. 430, and Ludington v. Patton, 121 Wis. 649, 662, 99 N.W. 614) contrary to the contention of the respondent. In the Pomeroy Case, after reviewing the Massachusetts cases under a similar statute, it is held that parol evidence is inadmissible to prove an advancement, and that all other evidence than that prescribed by the statute is excluded by implication. And in the Ludington Case it was held that t§§he charge in writing must be made at the time of delivery of the property. The court said (121 Wis. 649, 99 N.W. 614):

“The statute is mandatory and must be enforced as written. Pomeroy v. Pomeroy, 93 Wis. 262, 67 N.W. 430. It clearly contemplates that a delivery of property by one to another, the latter having claims upon the former's bounty, is not to be deemed an advancement unless it is given that character at the time of such delivery, either by a declaration in the writing making the bestowal, or by an acknowledgment in writing at that time by the recipient of the bounty, or by an expression of the donor in respect to the matter in charging the property to the person receiving the same."

But it is said in the opinion of the learned trial judge, and so argued by counsel here, that the question as to when the charge of advancement must be made was not involved in the Ludington Case. The question of the construction of the statute (sec. 3959) was involved and under consideration, and it is clear from the briefs of counsel in the case that whether the writing or charge referred to in the statute should be contemporaneous with the advance was also regarded in the case by counsel as necessarily considered in construing the statute as applied to the facts of the case then under consideration.

It is also clear from the opinion that this court regarded the point as necessarily in the case and one of the propositions upon which the decision of the court rested. But even if we should consider what was said in the Ludington Case on the point as obiter, we see no reason to depart from the conclusion reached and declared by the court, and we adhere to the construction put upon the statute in that case.

The manifest purpose of the statute in making the charge in writing evidence of an advancement is that the charge must be made contemporaneously with the advancement. This is in harmony with the rule respecting book accounts. In Marshall v. Coleman, 187 Ill. 556, at page 580 (58 N.E. 628, at page 636), the court said:

"Book accounts are only admissible in favor of the party who keeps them when the entries are made contemporaneously with the transactions recorded, and the same rule applies to books and entries of deceased persons. 1 Greenl. Ev. (13th ed.) §118; 1

Whart. Ev. §§246, 688; 2 Woerner, Adm'n (2d ed.) §558; Nelson v. Nelson, 90 Mo. 460, 2, 2 S.W. 413 S. W. 413. 'Declarations or book entries of the donor subsequent to the transaction are inadmissible unless they are of the res gestoe or against interest.' 2 Woerner, Adm'n (2d ed.) §558." See, also, Young v. Young, 204 Ill. 430, 68 N.E. 532; Nelson v. Nelson, 90 Mo. 460, 2 S.W. 413.

Nor were declarations of John Arthur made after the transfers admissible to prove advancements. Kimball v. Leland, 110 Mass. 325; Harness v. Harness, 49 Ind. 384; Thornton, Gifts & Advancements, p. 198, §224; Howard v. Howard, 101 Ga. 224, 28 S.E. 648. It will be seen that the cases from other jurisdictions are in harmony with the decisions of this court heretofore cited. Indeed, it is unnecessary to go outside of the decisions of this court. The Pomeroy and Ludington Cases are decisive of the propositions involved.

It follows that there is not sufficient evidence to support the findings or conclusions of the court below to the effect that the transfers to the sons of John Arthur, deceased, were advancements, or to warrant the court below in reversing the judgment of the county court in part. The judgment below must therefore be reversed.

The judgment of the court below is reversed, and the cause remanded with directions to affirm the judgment of the county court and for further proceedings according to law

D. DISCLAIMER

No one can be required to accept property that they do not want, even if they inherit it. If the heir or prospective owner wishes to renounce any claim to ownership, this can be done by *disclaiming* the property. While disclaimers are sometimes used to avoid taking undesirable property, like kittens or land with badly polluted soil, there are often strategic reasons, frequently tax or creditor related, for choosing to disclaim an interest in property.

Wis. Stat. 852.13. Right to disclaim intestate share.

Any person to whom property would otherwise pass under s. 852.01 may disclaim all or part of the property as provided under s. 854.13

Wis. Stat. 854.13. Disclaimer of transfers at death.

(1) DEFINITIONS.

In this section:

(a) "Beneficiary under a governing instrument" includes any person who receives or might receive property under the terms or legal effect of a governing instrument.

(b) [Left blank.]

(c) "Power" has the meaning given in s. 702.01 (4)

(2) RIGHT TO DISCLAIM.

(a) In general.

1. In this paragraph, "person" includes a person who is unborn or whose identity is unascertained.

2. A person who is an heir, recipient of property or beneficiary under a governing instrument, donee of a power created by a governing instrument, appointee under a power exercised by a governing instrument, taker in default under a power created by a governing instrument or person succeeding to disclaimed property may disclaim any property, including contingent or future interests or the right to receive discretionary distributions, by delivering a written instrument of disclaimer under this section.

(b) Joint tenants. Upon the death of a joint tenant, a surviving joint tenant may disclaim any property that would otherwise accrue to him or her by right of survivorship and that is the subject of the joint tenancy by delivering a written instrument of disclaimer under this section.

(c) Survivorship marital property. Upon the death of a spouse, the surviving spouse may disclaim the decedent spouse's interest in survivorship marital property.

(d) Partial disclaimer. Property may be disclaimed in whole or in part, except that a partial disclaimer of property passing by a governing instrument or by the exercise of a power may not be made if partial disclaimer is expressly prohibited by the governing instrument or by the instrument exercising the power.

(e) Spendthrift provision. The right to disclaim exists notwithstanding any limitation on the interest of the disclaimant in the nature of a spendthrift provision or similar restriction.

(f) Disclaimer by guardian or conservator. A guardian of the estate or a conservator appointed under ch. 54 or ch. 880, 2003 stats., may disclaim on behalf of his or her ward, with court approval, if the ward is entitled to disclaim under this section.

(g) Disclaimer by agent under power of attorney. An agent under a power of attorney may disclaim on behalf of the person who granted the power of attorney if all of the following apply:

1. The person who granted the power of attorney is entitled to disclaim under this section.

2. The power of attorney specifically grants the power to disclaim.

(gm) Disclaimer by trustee. The trustee of a trust named as a recipient of property under a governing instrument may disclaim that property on behalf of the trust if the trust authorizes disclaimer by the trustee. If the trust does not authorize disclaimer by the trustee, the trustees power to disclaim is subject to the approval of the court.

(h) After death. A person's right to disclaim survives the person's death and may be exercised by the person's personal representative or special administrator upon receiving approval from the court having jurisdiction of the person's estate after hearing upon notice to all persons interested in the disclaimed property, if the personal representative or special administrator has not taken any action that would bar the right to disclaim under sub. (11g) (i) Disclaimer of inter vivos transfers. A person who is a recipient of property under an inter vivos governing instrument, as defined in s. 700.27 (1) (c), may disclaim the property as provided in s. 700.27

(3) INSTRUMENT OF DISCLAIMER.

The instrument of disclaimer shall do all of the following:

(a) Describe the property disclaimed.

(b) Declare the disclaimer and the extent of the disclaimer.

(c) Be signed by the disclaimant.

(d) Be delivered within the time and in the manner provided under subs. (4) and (5)

(4) TIME FOR EFFECTIVE DISCLAIMER.

(a) Present interest. An instrument disclaiming a present interest shall be executed and delivered not later than 9 months after the effective date of the transfer under the governing instrument. For cause shown, the period may be extended by a court of competent jurisdiction, either within or after the 9-month period, for such additional time as the court considers just.

(b) Future interest. An instrument disclaiming a future interest shall be executed and delivered not later than 9 months after the event that determines that the taker of the property is finally ascertained and his or her interest indefeasibly fixed. For cause shown, the period may be extended by a court of competent jurisdiction, either within or after the 9-month period, for such additional time as the court considers just.

(c) Future right to income or principal. Notwithstanding pars. (a) and (b), an instrument disclaiming the future right to receive discretionary or mandatory distributions of income or principal from any source may be executed and delivered at any time.

(d) Persons under 21. Notwithstanding pars. (a) and (b), a person under 21 years of age may disclaim at any time not later than 9 months after the date on which the person attains 21 years of age.

(e) Interests arising by disclaimer. Notwithstanding pars. (a) and (b), a person whose interest in property arises by disclaimer or by default of exercise of a power created by a governing instrument may disclaim at any time not later than 9 months after the day on which the prior instrument of disclaimer is delivered, or the date of death of the donee of the power.

(5) DELIVERY AND FILING OF DISCLAIMER.

(a) Delivery. In addition to any requirements imposed by the governing instrument, the instrument of disclaimer is effective only if, within the time specified under sub. (4), it is delivered to and received by any of the following:

1. The transferor of the property disclaimed, if living.

2. The personal representative or special administrator of the deceased transferor of the property.

3. The holder of legal title to the property.

(b) Delivery to trustee. If the trustee of any trust to which the interest or power relates does not receive the instrument of disclaimer under par. (a), a copy shall also be delivered to the trustee.

(c) Filing. When delivery is made to the personal representative or special administrator of a deceased transferor, a copy of the instrument of disclaimer shall be filed in the probate court having jurisdiction.

(d) Failure to deliver or file. Failure to deliver a copy of the instrument of disclaimer to the trustee under par. (b) or to file a copy in the probate court under par. (c), within the time specified under sub. (4), does not affect the validity of any disclaimer.

(e) Recording. If real property or an interest in real property is disclaimed, a copy of the instrument of disclaimer may be recorded in the office of the register of deeds of the county in which the real estate is situated.

(6) PROPERTY NOT VESTED.

The property disclaimed under this section shall be considered not to have been vested in, created in or transferred to the disclaimant.

(7) DEVOLUTION.

(a) In general. Subject to pars. (bm) and (c) and subs. (8), (9), and (10), unless the governing instrument provides otherwise, either expressly or as construed from extrinsic evidence, the disclaimed property devolves as if the disclaimant had died before the decedent. If the disclaimed interest is a remainder contingent on surviving to the time of distribution, the disclaimed interest passes as if the disclaimant had died immediately before the time for distribution. If the disclaimant is an appointee under a power exercised by a governing instrument, the disclaimed property devolves as if the disclaimant had died before the effective date of the exercise of the power. If the disclaimant is a taker in default under a power created by a governing instrument, the disclaimed property devolves as if the disclaimant had predeceased the donee of the power.

(bm) Devolution to issue of the disclaimants. Unless the governing instrument provides otherwise, either expressly or as construed from extrinsic evidence, if, by law or under the governing instrument, the issue of the disclaimant would share in the disclaimed interest by any method of representation had the disclaimant died before the time the disclaimed interest would have taken effect in possession or enjoyment, the disclaimed interest passes only to the issue of the disclaimant who survive when the disclaimed interest takes effect in possession or enjoyment.

(c) Disclaimer of a devisable future interest.

1. In this paragraph, "devisable future interest" is a future interest that can be passed under the will of the person who holds the future interest.

2. If the disclaimed interest is a devisable future interest under the law governing the transfer, then the disclaimed interest devolves as if it were a nondevisable future interest.

(8) DEVOLUTION OF DISCLAIMED INTEREST IN JOINT TENANCY.

Unless the decedent provided otherwise in a governing instrument, either expressly or as construed from extrinsic evidence, a disclaimed interest in a joint tenancy passes to the decedent's probate estate.

(9) DEVOLUTION OF DISCLAIMED INTEREST IN SURVIVORSHIP MARITAL PROPERTY.

Unless the decedent provided otherwise in a governing instrument, either expressly or as construed from extrinsic evidence, a disclaimed interest in survivorship marital property passes to the decedent's probate estate.

(10) ACCELERATION OF SUBSEQUENT INTERESTS WHEN PRECEDING INTEREST IS DISCLAIMED.

(a) Subsequent interest not held by disclaimant. Unless the governing instrument provides otherwise, either expressly or as construed from extrinsic evidence, upon the disclaimer of a preceding interest, a subsequent interest not held by the disclaimant and limited to take effect in possession or enjoyment after the termination of the interest that is disclaimed accelerates to take effect as if the disclaimant had died immediately before the time when the disclaimed interest would have taken effect in possession or enjoyment or, if the disclaimant is an appointee under a power exercised by a power of appointment, as if the disclaimant had died before the effective date of the exercise of the power.

(b) Subsequent interest held by the disclaimant. Unless the governing instrument provides otherwise, either expressly or as construed from extrinsic evidence, upon the disclaimer of a preceding interest, a subsequent interest held by the disclaimant does not accelerate.

(11g) BAR.

Bars to a person's right to disclaim property include, but are not limited to, any of the following:

(a) The person's assignment, conveyance, encumbrance, pledge, or transfer of the property or a contract for the assignment, conveyance, encumbrance, pledge, or transfer of the property.

(b) The person's written waiver of the right to disclaim.

(c) The person's acceptance of the property or benefit of the property.

(11p) EFFECT OF DISCLAIMER OR WAIVER.

The disclaimer or the written waiver of the right to disclaim is binding upon the disclaimant or person waiving and all persons claiming through or under him or her.

(12) NONEXCLUSIVENESS OF REMEDY.

(a) This section does not affect the right of a person to waive, release, disclaim or renounce property under any other statute, the common law, or as provided in the creating instrument.

(b) Any disclaimer that meets the requirements of section 2518 of the Internal Revenue Code, or the requirements of any other federal law relating to disclaimers, constitutes an effective disclaimer under this section or s. 700.27

(13) CONSTRUCTION OF EFFECTIVE DATE.

In this section, the effective date of a transfer under a revocable governing instrument is the date on which the person with the power to revoke the transfer no longer has that power or the power to transfer the legal or equitable ownership of the property that is the subject of the transfer.

GOLDHAMMER v. GOLDHAMMER

Court of Appeals of Wisconsin
138 Wis. 2d 77, 405 N.W.2d 693 (1987)

This case tests whether a debtor can disclaim a bequest received in a will in order to defeat an action begun by a judgment creditor under sec. 813.026, Stats. We hold that unless barred by statute, the disclaimer can defeat the creditor's action. We affirm here because no allegation was made that the disclaimer was barred under a specific statutory provision.

The Deere Credit Company obtained a judgment against Robert J. Goldammer in the sum of $11,978.00. Subsequently, Goldammer's mother died, leaving a will giving him an interest amounting to in excess of $20,000. John Deere filed an action under sec. 813.026, Stats., which allows the heir's creditors to reach the interest to the extent of the debt. Goldammer then filed a disclaimer under sec. 853.40, Stats., renouncing his interest. The issue is whether the disclaimer overrides the sec. 813.026 action.

Section 813.026, Stats., provides:

In an action, in a court of record, for damages founded upon contract or upon a judgment, when it appears that the defendant is interested, as heir, legatee or devisee, in the estate of a decedent and that the defendant's property liable to execution is probably insufficient to satisfy the plaintiff's claim for damages, *the defendant may be enjoined by the court, pending the action, from assigning or otherwise disposing of his interest in such estate; and a receiver therefor may be appointed. The judgment may compel the defendant to transfer sufficient of his interest to satisfy the judgment or may adjudge such transfer*. The remedy given by this section is in addition to that given by proceedings supplementary to execution under ch. 816. If a receiver is appointed, he shall give prompt notice thereof to the administrator or executor. [Emphasis added.]

The disclaimer statute, sec. 853.40, Stats., in pertinent part, provides:

(2) RIGHT TO DISCLAIM. (a) *In general.* A person who is an heir, person succeeding to a disclaimed intestate interest, beneficiary under a will, person succeeding to a disclaimed interest created by will, donee of a power created by will, appointee under a power exercised by will or taker in default under a power created by will, may disclaim any property or interest in property, including contingent or future interests or the right to receive discretionary distributions, by delivering a written instrument of disclaimer under this section.

. . . .

(6) EFFECT OF DISCLAIMER. (a) *Property not vested.* The property or interest disclaimed under this section shall be deemed not to have been vested in, created in or transferred to the disclaimant.

(b) *Devolution.* Unless the deceased transferor of the property or deceased donee of the power has otherwise provided, the property or interest disclaimed devolves as if the disclaimant had predeceased the deceased transferor of the property . . . . *A disclaimer relates back for all purposes* to the date of death of the deceased transferor of the property or the deceased donee of the power . . . . [Emphasis added.]

John Deere argues that even if neither of these statutes expressly mentions that a creditor's lien overrides disclaimers, there is a "common law lien," equitable in nature, that must be read into the statute. This lien operates against the interests of the beneficiary, is codified by sec. 813.026, Stats., and makes the disclaimer under sec. 853.40, Stats., ineffectual.

As conceded by John Deere, however, no previous Wisconsin common law involves the creditor's pursuit of the debtor's interest in an estate when a disclaimer has been made. Further, neither statute's history discusses placing the creditor's actions in a superior position to disclaimers.

Rather, sec. 853.40(6), Stats., expressly provides that the property or interest disclaimed shall be deemed not to have been vested in, created in or transferred to the disclaimant. Instead, the disclaimer relates back "for all purposes." If a disclaimer is filed, therefore, the beneficiary has no property interest to which an "equitable lien" can attach. The only way that a creditor can defeat a disclaimer is if there is a specific bar under the statute that is alleged and proven by the creditor. Section 853.40(7)(a) and (b) provides:

(a) *Method.* A person's right to disclaim property or an interest in property is barred by the person's:

1. Assignment, conveyance, encumbrance, pledge or transfer of the property or interest or a contract therefor;

2. Written waiver of the right to disclaim; or

3. Acceptance of the property or interest or benefit of the property.

(b) *Payment of debt. A person's right to disclaim property or an interest in property is barred if there is a pending proceeding under s. 863.46 for the payment of a debt.* [Emphasis added.]

Section 863.46, Stats., provides in part:

(1) If any legacy or distributive share of any estate belongs to any debtor who has absconded from or is a nonresident of this state, any of his or her creditors may petition to intervene in the probate proceedings to compel the application of the legacy or distributive share to the payment of his or her debt.

Since Goldammer apparently resides out of state, John Deere may have been able to allege a bar to disclaimer under sec. 853.40(7)(b), Stats. Belatedly, on appeal and after briefing has been completed, John Deere makes that exact claim before us. It now asks us to consider this statutory bar as an alternative argument to its equitable lien theory.

As pointed out by Goldammer, however, it is clear from the record that there was not a "pending proceeding" under sec. 863.46, Stats. Use of that section was never pled or argued at the trial court level; it is raised for the first time on appeal. We will not now review whether John Deere is protected under sec. 853.40(7)(b), Stats., because the issue presented to the trial court and to us was whether it was protected by sec. 813.026, Stats., under the equitable lien theory.

Order affirmed.

E. THE SLAYER DILEMMA

Whether or not an heir who murders an ancestor (or a devisee under a will who murders the testator) should still inherit or receive the property was a complicated question in 19th Century America. The problem was made difficult because few American jurisdictions had statutes disqualifying the killer in this situation, and courts were often reluctant to simply impose an additional penalty on the killer in the absence of legislative authorization. (The long standing American rejection of the common law principle of "corruption of the blood," under which the commission of a felony resulted in the perpetrator's forfeiture of all of his property, was also a factor.) Some of these cases, especially *Riggs v. Palmer,* 115 N.Y. 506, 22 N.E. 188 (1889), have become important landmarks in the history of American jurisprudence.

The issue was particularly compelling in Wisconsin because of the view that such cases involved constitutional rights on the part of both the slayer and victim. *Whaley v. Avery,* reproduced below, is the "not quite so well known" Wisconsin version of *Riggs v. Palmer.* Today, every American state has a slayer statute. Frequently at issue, however, in what types of homicides trigger the forfeiture. Because "slayer rule" cases are not themselves criminal cases, they are typically tried in civil courts by civil standards, including the *preponderance of the evidence* standard for proof of guilt, rather than the *beyond a reasonable doubt* standard of criminal cases.

Wis. Stat. 854.14. Beneficiary who kills decedent.

(2) REVOCATION OF BENEFITS.

Except as provided in sub. (6), the unlawful and intentional killing of the decedent does all of the following:

(a) Revokes a provision in a governing instrument that, by reason of the decedent's death, does any of the following:

1. Transfers or appoints property to the killer.

2. Confers a power of appointment on the killer.

3. Nominates or appoints the killer to serve in any fiduciary or representative capacity, including personal representative, trustee, or agent.

(b) Severs the interests of the decedent and killer in property held by them as joint tenants with the right of survivorship or as survivorship marital property and transforms the interests of the decedent and the killer into tenancies in common or marital property, whichever is appropriate.

(c) Revokes every statutory right or benefit to which the killer may have been entitled by reason of the decedent's death.

(3) EFFECT OF REVOCATION.

Except as provided in sub. (6), provisions of a governing instrument that are revoked by this section are given effect as if the killer disclaimed all revoked provisions or, in the case of a revoked nomination in a fiduciary or representative capacity, as if the killer predeceased the decedent. Except as provided in sub. (6), the killers share of the decedent's intestate estate, if any, passes as if the killer had disclaimed his or her intestate share under s. 854.13

(3m) ADDITIONAL EFFECTS IF DEATH CAUSED BY SPOUSE.

(a) Definitions. In this subsection:

1. "Owner" means a person appearing on the records of the policy issuer as the person having the ownership interest, or means the insured if no person other than the insured appears on those records as a person having that interest. In the case of group insurance, the "owner" means the holder of each individual certificate of coverage under the group plan and does not include the person who contracted with the policy issuer on behalf of the group, regardless of whether that person is listed as the owner on the contract.

2. "Ownership interest" means the rights of an owner under a policy.

3. "Policy" means an insurance policy insuring the life of a spouse and providing for payment of death benefits at the spouse's death.

4. "Proceeds" means the death benefit from a policy and all other economic benefits from it, whether they accrue or become payable as a result of the death of an insured person or upon the occurrence or nonoccurrence of another event.

(b) Life insurance.

1. Except as provided in sub. (6), if a noninsured spouse unlawfully and intentionally kills an insured spouse, the surviving spouse's ownership interest in a policy that designates the decedent spouse as the owner and insured, or in the proceeds of such a policy, is limited to a dollar amount equal to one-half of the marital property interest in the interpolated terminal reserve and in the unused portion of the term premium of the policy on the date of death of the decedent spouse. All other rights of the surviving spouse in the ownership interest or proceeds of the policy, other than the marital property interest described in this subsection, terminate at the decedent spouse's death.

2. Notwithstanding s. 766.61 (7) and except as provided in sub. (6), if an insured spouse unlawfully and intentionally kills a noninsured spouse, the ownership interest at death of the decedent spouse in any policy with a marital property component that designates the surviving spouse as the owner and insured is a fractional interest equal to one-half of the portion of the policy that was marital property immediately before the death of the decedent spouse.

(c) Deferred employment benefits. Notwithstanding s. 766.62 (5) and except as provided in sub. (6), if the employee spouse unlawfully and intentionally kills the nonemployee spouse, the ownership interest at death of the decedent spouse in any deferred employment benefit, or in assets in an individual retirement account that are traceable to the rollover of a deferred employment benefit plan, that has a marital property component and that is attributable to the employment of the surviving spouse is equal to one-half of the portion of the benefit or assets that was marital property immediately before the death of the decedent spouse.

(d) Deferred marital property. Except as provided in sub. (6), if the surviving spouse unlawfully and intentionally kills the decedent spouse, the estate of the decedent shall have the right to elect no more than 50 percent of the augmented deferred marital property estate, as determined under s. 861.02 (2), as though the decedent spouse were the survivor and the surviving spouse were the decedent. The court shall construe the provisions of ss. 861.03 to 861.11 as necessary to achieve the intent of this paragraph.

(4) WRONGFUL ACQUISITION OF PROPERTY.

Except as provided in sub. (6), a wrongful acquisition of property by a killer not covered by this section shall be treated in accordance with the principle that a killer cannot profit from his or her wrongdoing.

(5) UNLAWFUL AND INTENTIONAL KILLING; HOW DETERMINED.

(a) A final judgment establishing criminal accountability for the unlawful and intentional killing of the decedent conclusively establishes the convicted individual as the decedent's killer for purposes of this section.

(b) A final adjudication of delinquency on the basis of an unlawful and intentional killing of the decedent conclusively establishes the adjudicated individual as the decedent's killer for purposes of this section.

(c) In the absence of a judgment establishing criminal accountability under par. (a) or an adjudication of delinquency under par. (b), the court, upon the petition of an interested person, shall determine whether, based on the preponderance of the evidence, the killing of the decedent was unlawful and intentional for purposes of this section.

6) EXCEPTIONS.

This section does not apply if any of the following applies:

(a) The court finds that, under the factual situation created by the killing, the decedent's wishes would best be carried out by means of another disposition of the property.

(b) The decedent provided in his or her will, by specific reference to this section, that this section does not apply.

Whaley v. Avery

Supreme Court of Wisconsin
192 Wis. 111, 211 N.W. 652

This appeal is by the administrator with the will annexed of the estate of Athanacios Kurasethas, deceased, from part of a decree of the county court construing the will of one Edith Wilkins, deceased.

The will of Edith Wilkins, deceased, among other things, provided for a legacy of $ 5,000 to Kurasethas, hereinafter referred to as "K.," and he was also named as beneficiary, with others, under the residuary clause of the instrument. It is conceded that K. murdered Edith Wilkins, and immediately thereafter committed suicide. The county court, upon an application made to construe the will, decreed that K. could not and did not take thereunder.

DOERFLER, J. The sole question presented on this appeal involves the effect to be given to those provisions of the will which provide certain bequests for K., under the peculiar facts and circumstances heretofore related. Our Reports contain no precedent, and the question to be determined is one of first impression in this state. The exhaustive briefs presented by counsel have been of great aid to the court and have lightened its burdens.

The record does not disclose that K. when he committed the murder had knowledge of the will, so that in that respect the case differs from a number of others in foreign jurisdictions where the murderer, with knowledge of the contents of a will, commits the act for the express purpose of preventing the testator from changing his will to his detriment.

In the case of Nunnemacher v. State, 129 Wis. 190, 108 N.W. 627, it is said:

"The right to take property by inheritance or by will is a natural right protected by the constitution which cannot be wholly taken away or substantially impaired by the legislature. . . .

"So clear does it seem to us from the historical point of view that the right to take property by inheritance or will has existed in some form among civilized nations from the time when the memory of man runneth not to the contrary, and so conclusive seems the argument that these rights are a part of the inherent rights which governments, under our conception, are established to conserve, that we feel entirely justified in rejecting the dictum so frequently asserted by such a vast array of courts that these rights are purely statutory and may be wholly taken away by the legislature."

In Will of Rice, 150 Wis. 401, 136 N.W. 956, 137 N.W. 778, this court held:

"The right to make a will is more sacred than the right to make a contract. The right to make a will is incidental to the right to acquire property and so is one of the inherent rights guaranteed by the constitution. It antedates common and civil law. It is sacred in all nations and under all conditions. It is guaranteed by sec. 1, art. I, of the constitution and also by sec. 13, art. XIV."

The language thus quoted is clear and explicit. It contains no ambiguities, and it is expressive of a constitutional guaranty relating both to personal rights and rights of property. So firmly are the foregoing doctrines, expressed in the Nunnemacher and Rice Cases and in numerous other cases decided by this court, entrenched in the jurisprudence of this state, that any attempt at this date to modify or upset them must be deemed futile.

This sacred right to make a will rests entirely with the testator, who under our law can dispose of his property in accordance with his volition, excepting only as to certain rights which are extended by statute to a specified class of persons, designed for their protection as a matter of public policy. Under this exception comes the right of a widow to renounce the provisions of the will by accepting her statutory rights of dower. A testator may ignore wholly, if he desires, those in close relation to him by ties of blood, and he may bestow his devises and bequests upon persons who are ordinarily not deemed the objects of his bounty. Nor is any one permitted to make a will for him; neither can the courts change or modify a will, or substitute in its place one which they deem more equitable and just, for to permit this would destroy the sacredness of a will and would substitute in its place the will of another.

In approaching, therefore, the consideration of the important issue confronting us, we must not lose sight of these and other fundamentals, and we will endeavor to harmonize our holding with them instead of modifying or upsetting them. It is said that "law" is the perfection of human reason. In a democratic form of government like our own, it is designed to promote human welfare. It recognizes the rights of persons and of property, and to vindicate such rights and to secure remedies for the infringement thereof courts are created and established. Each branch of the government is supreme in its field, and if one branch invades the territory of another, contrary to the fundamental law, it results in an attack upon the very foundation of the government itself, and the result must necessarily be disastrous and revolutionary in its nature.

Under the provisions of sec. 238.14 of the Statutes "The power to make a will implies the power to revoke the same." Edith Wilkins, therefore, not only had the sacred right to make the will in question, but she also possessed the right and power at any time during her life to revoke the same, and the power of revocation is equally as sacred as the power of making. It not infrequently happens that a testator arrives at a determination to revoke or modify his will, but before he is enabled to effectuate a change or revocation he meets with sudden death by accident or disease. Such occurrences, however, cannot affect the enforcement of the will so made, regardless of the high degree of proof that may be offered with respect to the testator's determination. In instances like these, sec. 238.14 comes into operation, for it determines how a will or any part thereof may be revoked or modified. A beneficiary under a will may be guilty of the commission of an atrocious crime upon the testator which may result in suffering and eventual death. Still, if the testator lives a reasonable time after the commission of the offense, and during such time retains his competency to make a new will or to revoke or modify the one already made, but fails or refuses to make a change, the will nevertheless becomes effective and must be enforced in accordance with its terms, and the offender will take thereunder, provided he is a beneficiary, notwithstanding his offense.

The commission of crime does not disqualify one from taking under a will, unless it be under facts and circumstances as appear in the instant or similar cases. Under the facts in the instant case, the shooting of Edith Wilkins resulted in instantaneous death. K. survived her but a few seconds at most, and his act of suicide by shooting also resulted in instantaneous death. Had the death of both parties resulted from disease or from accident, there can be no question but that the survivor would take, even though he survived for the short period of a second. Edith Wilkins lost her life as the result of the premeditated act of K., and such fact distinguishes this case from the other incidents above alluded to. By the commission of murder she was, by the very act of the murderer, deprived of the sacred right to change her will in accordance with her volition. Such a right, as has already been stated, was inherent in her, was sacred, and of this right she was deprived.

Under the civil law as it obtained for centuries in European countries where it was adopted, a murderer could not take property devised or bequeathed to him in a will under circumstances existing in the instant case. Such was and is also the rule under the Code Napoleon. This is likewise true under the common law in England. In fact, this seems to be the rule quite generally recognized in the law of all civilized nations. See the following cases and authorities cited in respondent's brief, viz.: Riggs v. Palmer, 115 N.Y. 506, 22 N.E. 188; Wall v. Pfanschmidt, 265 Ill. 180, 106 N.E. 785; 28 Ruling Case Law 75; 40 Cyc. 1063; Wharton, Homicide (3d ed.) § 665. In 40 Cyc. 1063, it is said:

"Under the civil law one cannot take property by inheritance . . . from one whom he has murdered. And the few common-law decisions on the subject hold that a beneficiary under a will who murders the testator to make the will operative, or who is guilty of a lower grade of crime, such as manslaughter, in killing the testator, cannot take under the will. The principle upon which the beneficiary is held incapable of taking under the will of the person he kills is that no one can take advantage of his own wrong."

In Riggs v. Palmer, decided in 1889 and reported in 115 N.Y. 506, 22 N.E. 188, and in 5 L.R.A. 340, the defendant, Elmer E. Palmer, was a beneficiary under the will of Francis B. Palmer. The defendant murdered the testator, knowing that he was a beneficiary under the will, with the intention of preventing the testator from revoking or modifying the same. We have, therefore, under the facts presented in the Riggs Case, one similar in all respects to the instant case, with one exception: that in the latter the murderer had no knowledge of the provisions of the will and that he did not commit the crime for the purpose of preventing the testatrix from revoking or modifying her will. The action was brought by the plaintiff in the Riggs Case in a court of equity in order to restrain the defendant from taking anything under the will. In the opinion in that case the court says:

"Here there was no certainty that this murderer would survive the testator, or that the testator would not change his will, and there was no certainty that he would get this property if nature was allowed to take its course. He therefore murdered the testator expressly to vest himself with an estate. Under such circumstances, what law, human or divine, will allow him to take the estate and enjoy the fruits of his crime? The will spoke and became operative at the death of the testator. He caused that death, and thus by his crime made it speak and have operation. Shall it speak and operate in his favor? If he had met the testator, and taken his property by force, he would have had no title to it. Shall he acquire title by murdering him? If he had gone to the testator's house, and by force compelled him, or by fraud or undue influence had induced him, to will him his property, the law would not allow him to hold it. But can he give effect and operation to a will by murder, and yet take the property? To answer these questions in the affirmative, it seems to me, would be a reproach to the jurisprudence of our state, and an offense against public policy."

The opinion in the Riggs Case has been criticised by a number of courts, yet in the main we consider the logic of that case substantially sound and irrefutable. Note the language above quoted in the opinion in the Riggs Case: "The will spoke and became operative at the death of the testator. He caused that death, and thus by his crime made it speak and have operation. Shall it speak and operate in his favor? " The Riggs Case is based upon the theory that, notwithstanding the murder, the will spoke and became operative instantaneously upon the death of the testator, but that the murderer by his act, under the equitable doctrine that a man shall not profit by his own wrong, shall not be permitted to enjoy the fruits resulting from his wrong. That such is the holding of the Riggs Case is further made clear in the opinion in Ellerson v. Westcott, 148 N.Y. 149, 42 N.E. 540, where the facts involved were similar to those in the Riggs Case. Briefly stated, these New York cases hold that equity comes into operation upon the very threshold of the murderer's taking and "stays his hand." That this constitutes good, equitable doctrine cannot be denied. It is our view, however, that the act of vesting and that of taking are simultaneous; that there can be no vesting without a taking, even if that taking be only for the short period of a second; that if there [118] be a vesting, even for the shortest unit of time, there is visited upon the criminal a punishment in addition to that provided for by law. In other words, it amounts to an attainder or a corruption of blood, prohibited by the constitution. While it must be conceded in the instant case that the will remained in force up to the time of the death of the testatrix, it became wholly inoperative, in so far as the rights of K. were concerned, at the very moment of her death, and if this be so, there was neither a vesting nor a taking in contemplation of law.

And here it must be borne in mind that the crime committed by K. did not directly affect any of the provisions of the will other than those in which he was interested, but that such other provisions became fully operative and must be given effect, to the same extent as though Edith Wilkins had died a natural death or as the result of an accident. If, notwithstanding the murder, it be held that K. can take under the will and that the will becomes operative as to him, then it follows as a logical consequence that a murderer, under the facts herein, can deprive a testator of the sacred right to revoke a will or to modify it, and no logical distinction can be drawn between a case where the murder is committed expressly for the purpose of coming into an untimely possession of a bequest or devise, and one where the offense is committed where the murderer has not this specific intent. In either event the effect is the same, and in both instances the testator is deprived of the same right.

In this state the county court has jurisdiction to construe a will, and where this court can afford as complete a remedy as is granted to the circuit court its jurisdiction is exclusive. Such appears not to be the case in New York, where a separate action is begun in equity in a court of general jurisdiction, as will appear in the Riggs and Ellerson Cases, supra. But when the county court, in proceedings therein brought to construe a will, acts, it does so pursuant to the equitable powers possessed by it. All of the doctrines and maxims of equity applicable to courts of equity generally, are applicable in a county court when it proceeds in matters of will construction. When the proceedings in the matter of the construction of the will of Edith Wilkins came before the county court of Rock county for hearing, the judge thereof became the chancellor, and by his decree he in effect held that the will became inoperative at the time of the death of the testatrix, in so far as the rights of K. were concerned, and with this holding we fully agree.

The equitable doctrine that a man shall not profit by his own wrong dates back centuries in the history of the common law, and is as old as equity itself. It is recognized, as far as we are able to determine, in the laws of all civilized communities. It lies at the foundation of every religious faith, and may be said to be one of the corner-stones of the Christian religion.

It is vitally essential to the administration of justice, and a careful search of our statutes fails to reveal that it was ever modified or abrogated. It therefore exists at the present day in Wisconsin, with all the force which it possessed throughout the ages, and this court in holding as it does in this opinion does not entrench upon the legislative field, but, on the contrary, its holding is in harmony with the spirit and intent of the legislature. No system of laws permits a criminal to profit by his own crime, for if this were so, the very object of all law would be subverted.

It is argued by respondent that under the provisions of sec. 238.14 of the Statutes it may be held that this will was revoked as to the provisions contained therein for the benefit of K. The section referred to deals with the manner in which wills may be revoked, and the statute contains an exception which reads as follows: "excepting only that nothing contained in this section shall prevent the revocation implied by law from subsequent changes in the condition or circumstances [120] of the testator." The language used in the exception is broad and general. It was construed in Will of Battis, 143 Wis. 234, 126 N.W. 9, where it is said:

"The rule rests on the idea that the changed condition and circumstances of the testator respecting his property, his family or beneficiaries, imposing different moral and legal duties, affords strong evidence that the testator intended that his will should become revoked as to the provisions affected by such subsequent change."

In the Battis Case the court had before it the effect of a divorce granted by the court after the execution of the will, and it was there held that such divorce constituted such a change in the condition or circumstances of the testator as would operate to revoke the will with respect to the provisions therein contained affecting the other spouse. The rule as above stated in the Battis Case is substantially like the one contained in 28 Ruling Case Law on page 186. It becomes apparent, however, from a reading of the authorities which deal with this exception that neither the text-writers nor the courts had in view a situation such as is presented by the instant case. We therefore deem it advisable to rest our decision in chief on the views heretofore expressed; however, we are not prepared to say that the exception could not logically be construed to operate as an implied revocation of the provisions of the will in the instant case in so far as they affect K.

The language of the statute appears to be broader than the rule as above quoted from the Battis Case, for it says, "excepting only that nothing contained in this section shall prevent the revocation implied by law from subsequent changes in the condition or circumstances of the testator." (Italics ours.) The sudden and unexpected killing of the testatrix by K. clearly effected a change in the condition of the testatrix. It deprived her of a valuable and sacred right, viz. the right to modify or change her will. The last sentence of the statute referred to reads: "The power to make a will implies the power to revoke the same." Here it must be reiterated [121] that it was K. who deprived the testatrix of this sacred right to revoke her will, thus producing a changed situation not contemplated by the testatrix.

In view, however, of the construction placed upon this exception by the authorities, we have concluded primarily to rest our decision upon the theory chiefly treated in this opinion.

Numerous cases have been referred to in the briefs of counsel involving insurance contracts, where the beneficiary under an insurance policy murdered the insured in order to obtain the insurance. The decisions of the courts are uniform to the effect that the murderer cannot take under such circumstances, because he cannot obtain the benefits of a contract by the commission of crime. Numerous other cases involving the right of a murderer to take under the statutes of descent are referred to.

Whether or not the doctrine herein invoked would affect the murderer's right to take under the statute of descent involves a question with which we are not concerned in this case, and our decision upon this question will be reserved until that issue is presented.

The portion of the decree from which this appeal has been taken is affirmed.

JACKSON V. GRAY

Wisconsin Court of Appeals
212 Wis. 2d 436, 569 N.W.2d 467 (1997)

WEDEMEYER, P.J. James Earl Jackson appeals from a judgment disqualifying him from inheriting a portion of his wife Diane's intestate estate. James Earl claims that the trial court erred as a matter of law when it concluded that the killing of Diane was unlawful and intentional for the purposes of §852.01(2m)(br), STATS. Because the content of the final written order of the motion court, which declares that James Earl unlawfully and intentionally killed his wife, prevails over an earlier finding of the court regarding James Earl's "mental purpose to kill," we affirm.

I. BACKGROUND

James Earl was convicted of first-degree reckless homicide of his wife, Diane. Her death occurred shortly after a high-speed chase when James Earl, while pursuing Diane's vehicle, struck her vehicle causing it to go out of control. Diane's car then hit a traffic median and rolled over several times before coming to rest. Diane died intestate. James Earl, as her spouse, would normally be entitled to inherit a portion of her estate, with the balance going to her children from a previous marriage. See §852.01(1)(a)2 & (b), STATS.

This is the second appeal in this matter. As noted in this court's first decision, *Jackson v. Jackson*, 186 Wis. 2d 439, 440, 521 N.W.2d 173 (1994), Diane's children sought an order disqualifying James Earl as an heir. The trial court granted the motion without an evidentiary hearing. We reversed and remanded holding that James Earl's conviction for reckless homicide was not conclusive for the purposes of §852.01(2m), STATS., and that he was entitled to an evidentiary hearing pursuant to §852.01(2m)(br). *Id.; see also, Safran v. Safran*, 102 Wis. 2d 79, 98, 306 N.W.2d 27, 36 (1981). On remand after the hearing, the court concluded as a matter of law that "the estate at this Evidentiary Hearing, by clear and convincing evidence has proved that the killing of the decedent was unlawful and intentional for purposes of Sec. 852.01 (2m) (br), Stats." James Earl once again appeals.

II. ANALYSIS

James Earl asserts that §852.01(2m), STATS., prohibits a beneficiary from inheriting only when he or she "has unlawfully and intentionally killed" the decedent. He reasons that the plain meaning of the statute requires disqualification only when the beneficiary has caused the death of the decedent with the intent to kill the decedent and where such intentional killing was unlawful. He claims that the trial court found that he never intended to kill his wife and therefore should not be disqualified from inheritance. To support his analysis, he points to the following colloquy that took place between his counsel and the court during the motion hearing on remand:

[James Earl's Counsel]: ... The court is not making a finding that Mr. Jackson formed the mental purpose to kill his wife, correct?

The Court: Correct. I am stating that he did an intentional act which caused the death. I presume that would be the appealable issue. That's why I asked if you wanted to make a settlement.

(Capitalization modified). From this exchange, James Earl argues that the trial court found that he did not intend to kill and, therefore, that under the statute he is not disqualified from inheriting a portion of Diane's estate. James Earl's contention, however, is based on a single question and answer at the hearing. A review of the entire motion hearing record, plus the contents of the final written findings of facts, conclusions of law and order, together with the current statutory scheme affecting "intent to kill" reveals a different view of the court's intention. We shall address the claim of error from three perspectives.

First we examine James Earl's claim from the standpoint of what effect the oral finding had on the final order. Near the end of the hearing, James Earl's counsel asked the court whether it was making a finding that James Earl formed the mental purpose to kill his wife. In doing so, he sought to avoid application of the element of "intent to kill," found in §940.01, STATS., and as defined in §939.23, STATS. This attempt was to prevent James Earl's disqualification as an intestate heir. The court's response to counsel's query consisted of the direct response "correct," in juxtaposition to the sentence, "I am stating he did an intentional act which caused the death."

When we examine a trial court's decision-making process for review purposes, we are obliged to comply with certain rubrics of accepted appellate procedure. Initially, we observe that the written and signed findings of fact and conclusions of law of a court take precedence over a court's previously issued memorandum decision. *See Gordon v. Gordon*, 270 Wis. 332, 348, 71 N.W.2d 386, 394 (1955).

Here the basis for James Earl's claim is an oral finding of the court in response to a late query from counsel. After the court responded to James Earl's counsel, it ordered counsel for Diane's estate to prepare written findings and conclusions of law and submit them to opposing counsel for review. There were no objections to the proposed findings and conclusions, and, thus, they were approved as filed.

Pertinent to this appeal, the hearing court found or concluded that: (1) James Earl's auto came into contact with Diane's while she was parked in a filling station; (2) from the station James Earl chased Diane in his car at a high rate of speed; (3) on more than one occasion his car made contact with hers; (4) one of the contacts caused Diane's vehicle to go out of control, which caused her death; (5) Diane died when the car she was driving was struck by James Earl, her husband; (6) the high rate of speed and contact was intentional and, as a matter of law, the estate of Diane had proven that the killing was unlawful and intentional for the purposes of the statute; and (7) James Earl was disqualified for inheritance purposes.

Although *Gordon* established that a court's final written findings of fact and conclusions of law take precedence over an earlier written memorandum, the principle established in *Gordon* has all the more effect when applied to a single oral finding not repeated in the final order. Under this form of analysis, we conclude that the contents of the final order prevail. The final order clearly states that the estate proved by clear and convincing evidence that the killing of Diane was unlawful and intentional for purposes of §852.01(2m)(br), STATS. Accordingly, James Earl is disqualified as an heir.

Next, because the parties did not address the clarity of the trial court's oral remarks which precipitated this appeal, we are not obligated to do so. *See Wirth v. Ehly*, 93 Wis. 2d 433, 443-44, 287 N.W.2d 140, 145 (1980). Nevertheless, in the interests of completeness, we choose to engage in such analysis. When there is a conflict between an ambiguous oral pronouncement and the written judgment, the intent of the judge controls the determination. *See State v. Lipke*, 186 Wis. 2d 358, 364, 521 N.W.2d 444, 446 (Ct. App. 1994). "Where the oral pronouncement is ambiguous, it is proper to look at the written judgment to ascertain the court's intention." *Id.*

Putting aside for a moment the language contained in the final order, we revisit the oral comments of the trial court. The court stated the incident was "intentionally caused," "the intentional high-speed chase ... was an intentional act so far as the civil court is concerned," and "that ... by clear and convincing evidence ... the killing was unlawful and intentional for the purpose of this subsection." Later, however, in response to appellant's attorney's question as to whether the court was finding that

James Earl did not "form the mental purpose to kill his wife," the trial court stated "correct." The court then expanded its answer to explain, "I am stating that he did an intentional act which caused the death." A reasonable reading leads us to conclude that the oral pronouncement of the court is ambiguous in nature and content.

In contrast, the final order of the court expressly declared that the high-speed chase and collision were intentional acts, and that the "estate ... by clear and convincing evidence has proved that the killing was unlawful and intentional for purposes of Sec. 852.01(2m) (br), Stats." Although *Lipke* concerned a criminal sentencing discrepancy, whereas this is a civil matter, we conclude that the same principles apply. Here, the written order for judgment is unambiguous. It clearly expresses the court's intent in concluding that the killing was unlawful and intentional. Therefore, in discerning the true intention of the court pursuant to *Lipke*, the final order must prevail. Under this analysis, James Earl is likewise disqualified as an heir.

Last, we examine this claim of error in the context of its statutory setting. James Earl's counsel asked the trial court for a specific finding that he did not "form the mental purpose to kill his wife." In doing so, he was attempting to avoid application of the element of "intent to kill," found in §940.01, STATS., and as defined in §939.23, STATS., to prevent James Earl's disqualification as an intestate heir. James Earl's application, however, is too narrowly formulated. In 1987 the legislature amended §939.23(4), STATS., to read as follows: "'With intent to' or 'with intent that' means that the actor either has a purpose to do the thing or cause the result specified, or *is aware that his or her conduct is practically certain to cause that result.*" (Emphasis added).

The introductory comments to the new homicide law in the Wisconsin Criminal Jury Instructions are instructive: The new phrase-"aware that his conduct is practically certain"-is based on the Model Penal Code, sec. 2.02(2)(b)ii, where almost identical language is used to define "knowingly." Acting either with "mental purpose" or "knowingly" is sufficient for liability for most offenses defined by the Model Code. The basis for this approach is the conclusion that acting with awareness that one's conduct is "practically certain" to cause a result is as blameworthy as acting with the purpose to cause that harm. WIS J I--CRIMINAL 1000 (II)(C).

Thus, we must recognize that "with intent to" has a broader connotation than that argued by James Earl. To illustrate the implications of the new definition of "intent to kill," the Criminal Jury Instruction committee has provided the example of the arsonist who is being paid to burn down a building. *Id.* He knows there are people in the building, but he starts the fire anyway. *Id.* He does not have the purpose to cause their death, and he hopes they are able to escape. *Id.* If "intent to kill" was limited to "purpose to cause the death of another," there would be no "intent to kill." Yet, he is "aware that his conduct is practically certain" to cause death and, therefore, his act is with the intent to kill under the current Model Penal Code formulation.

Another example is the person who, from medium to short range, fires numerous times at a person and then exclaims, "yes, I fired the gun at him, but I didn't intend to kill him." The principle behind the expanded definition of "with intent to" allows the finder of fact to determine whether, under the circumstances, the accused is aware that his or her conduct is practically certain to cause death.

In conducting the remand hearing, the trial court succinctly and correctly stated its task, i.e., to determine whether the killing was intentional for the purposes of §852.01(2m)(br), STATS. It then reviewed the record relating to the incident. The record contains police reports of batteries to Diane, and a threat to take her in a car and kill her. Prior to the last high-speed chase, James Earl observed Diane's car in a filling station and bumped into it. In the high-speed chase that ensued, James Earl intentionally caused his car to physically crash into Diane's car more than once-the last contact between the two vehicles caused Diane's car to go off the road, over a traffic median, and to roll over several times. Based on this record and the court's findings, the trial court concluded not only that the high-speed chase and collision was intentional, but also that the killing of Diane was intentional and unlawful thereby satisfying the disqualification criteria.

Although the trial court did not make a specific finding that James Earl was aware that his conduct was practically certain to cause Diane's death, the evidence would support such a finding. "This court may affirm the judgment if '[a] perusal of the evidence shows that the court reached a result which the evidence would sustain if specifically found.'" *Grimh v. Western Fire Ins. Co.*, 5 Wis. 2d 84, 89, 92 N.W.2d 259, 262 (1958) (citations omitted); *see also Sohns v. Jensen*, 11 Wis. 2d 449, 453, 105 N.W.2d 818, 820 (1960) (This court may assume when "a finding [of fact] is not made on an issue which appears from the record to exist, that it was determined in favor of or in support of the judgment.").

Moreover, when faced with ambiguous findings, "that one of two or more reasonable probable meanings of the language used should be adopted which will make the same material and will support the judgment rather than one which will defeat it, and in solving the matter resort should be had to the evidence dealt with by the finding." *Bautz v. Adams*, 131 Wis. 152, 159, 111 N.W. 69, 72 (1907).

Therefore, even though the specific query that James Earl relies on in support of his argument may raise some ambiguity with regard to the trial court's findings pertaining to "intent," we conclude that the trial court resolved that ambiguity when it rendered the final judgment. The evidence is sufficient to support a finding that the trial court found the "intent" element of the probate statute was satisfied because James Earl was aware that his conduct was practically certain to cause the death. He repeatedly and intentionally crashed into Diane's car during a high-speed chase. In the past, he expressed intent to harm her, even kill her. When an automobile traveling at a high rate of speed is operated with animus to intentionally collide with another vehicle, it is practically certain that the driver may lose control and crash, and that the occupants will be killed.

This inference is abundantly supported in the record. Therefore, under this analysis, we conclude that the killing of Diane "was unlawful and intentional for purposes" of §852.01(2m)(br), STATS., and James Earl was properly disqualified as an heir.

F. ESCHEAT

If someone dies intestate, and there are no heirs eligible to inherit, or the eligible heirs cannot be located, the property passes to the state under the principle of escheat. (In Wisconsin, it specifically goes to the state school fund.) The current Wisconsin escheat statute can be found at Wis. Stat. 852.01(3) (reproduced above). Escheat is rarely a desired result, even from the point of view of the state's own courts, as the following case illustrates.

In Re Estate of Kavanaugh

Supreme Court of Wisconsin
11 Wis. 2d 629, 106 N.W.2d 405 (1960)

Martin, C. J Katherine Kavanaugh died in January, 1953. A claim was filed in her estate by one Frances Brennan and on October 13, 1955, the court disallowed said claim and found that the deceased died intestate and without any known heirs-at-law. A final decree was entered in 1959 directing the entire estate to be distributed to the state of Wisconsin under sec. 237.01 (7), Stats., which provides that the estate of an intestate leaving no heirs shall escheat to the state and be added to the capital of the school fund. The official receipts of the state treasurer for said funds are dated June 8 and November 12, 1959, respectively, and total $86,127.43. Respondents' petition was filed October 29, 1959.

Sec. 318.03 (4), Stats., provides:

"The moneys received by the state treasurer pursuant to secs. 237.01, 238.136, and 318.03 (1) shall be paid to the owner on proof of his right thereto. The claimant may, within seven years after the date of publication by the treasurer of notice of receipt thereof as provided by sec. 14.42 (15), file in the county court in which the estate was settled, a petition alleging the basis of his claim to the residue or to the legacy or share. The court shall order a hearing upon the petition; and twenty days' notice thereof shall be given by the claimant to the attorney general, who shall appear for the state at the hearing. If the claim is established it shall be allowed without interest; and the court shall so certify to the director of budget and accounts, who shall audit and the state treasurer shall pay the same. . . ."

The proceedings provided for therein were followed in this matter. It is admitted by the state that Chauncey B. Corcoran and his sister, Theresa Marie Gombeau, now deceased, were heirs of Katherine Kavanaugh. It contends, however, that the petitioners are not entitled to the residue of her estate because they have not established, in a proper proceeding, that there are no living heirs with prior claims to the money.

There was evidence that Katherine Kavanaugh had two nieces, Ethel Haggerty and Helen Kavanaugh. An heirtracer, who made a search of several months' duration for heirs of Miss Kavanaugh, was unable to locate any relatives other than the petitioner and his sister. It was shown that Ethel Haggerty, born in 1894, left the home in Chicago where she lived with her parents after her parents' death in 1930, and was not heard from thereafter. The other niece, Helen Kavanaugh, disappeared from her home around 1908 and has not been heard from since that time. The trial court found both of the nieces are dead and the only known living heirs of Katherine Kavanaugh at the time of her death were Chauncey B. Corcoran and Theresa Marie Gombeau.

That finding is challenged by the state both on the ground that the county court had no jurisdiction to make a finding of death based on absence in proceedings under sec. 318.03 (4), Stats., and on the ground that the evidence on which the court based that finding was insufficient to support it. In our opinion the state has no appealable interest in this matter. It not only concedes that there is evidence to sustain the finding that respondents were heirs of the deceased, but it admits that legal heirs exist. That being so, it is no longer a party in interest. The state takes and holds escheated property as a trustee. *Estate of Payne* (1932), 208 Wis. 142, 242 N.W. 553. If there is an heir, there can be no legal escheat. 19 Am. Jur., Escheat, p. 413, sec. 52. In *Estate of Rade* (1951), 259 Wis. 169, 173, 47 N.W.2d 891, this court held:

"The state contends that, even though there are known heirs of a decedent and even though there has been a determination of heirship, the residue of the estate does not automatically become the property of such heirs and that it becomes the property of an heir only when it is claimed 'by the heir' as provided by said statute. We cannot agree with this strict construction. *When it is established that a decedent leaves known heirs the state has no interest in the residue of said estate* except in remote instances where no claim is made for the share of a known heir. [Emphasis supplied.]"

Here the state maintains that its duty to protect the school fund entails the preservation of the interests of other potential claimants. We do not agree. If other heirs appear -- and we are advised that one has appeared and is petitioning the county court of Milwaukee county for vacation of the judgment here appealed from -- they have a right to claim against Chauncey B. Corcoran and the estate of Theresa Marie Gombeau. As stated in 19 Am. Jur., Escheat, p. 414, sec. 53:

"Claimants who were not parties to, and had no notice of, escheat proceedings in which other heirs were found to be entitled to the property may sue such persons for a share in the property within the period allowed heirs to recover escheated property."

The attorney general's appearance at a hearing under sec. 318.03 (4), Stats., is to protect the state against spurious claims. Once it is established that there are heirs to escheated property, the state no longer has any right or interest in the property. The attorney general has no duty and no authority to contest the distribution of the estate on the ground that other heirs may exist who have a better claim.

If there are any heirs at all, the state has no right to the property and it is for the court, not the attorney general, to determine which of the heirs is entitled to it. Under the statute, the state is protected from future claims by the certification of the court to the director of budget and accounts and the state treasurer, ordering audit and payment of the property to those it has adjudged entitled thereto.

As mentioned above, this court is advised that one Kathleen Whitehead English is petitioning the lower court to vacate its judgment, alleging she is the great-niece of Katherine Kavanaugh. This opinion is without prejudice to the petition of Mrs. English, and we assume the county court of Milwaukee County will afford said petitioner the opportunity to establish her claim. Appeal dismissed.

G. NEGATIVE DISINHERITANCE

Under the traditional law of inheritance, an heir could not be disinherited by a will or will-like document whose only purpose was to disinherit a particular individual or group of heirs. To be effective, the disinheriting document had to also devise the property to someone else. Otherwise, the attempt to disinherit an heir simply failed, and the heir took the property anyway through partial intestacy. Wisconsin, like most states, has reversed this rule by statute, although as the case below indicates, the traditional rule was once in force within the state.

Wis. Stat. 852.10. Disinheritance from intestate share.

(1) A decedent's will may exclude or limit the right of an individual or class to succeed to property passing by intestate succession.

(2) The share of the intestate estate that would have passed to the individual or class described in sub. (1) passes as if the individual or each member of the class had disclaimed his or her intestate share under s. 854.13

(3) This section does not apply if the individual or all members of the class described in sub. (1) predecease the testator.

In re Will of Rosnow

Supreme Court of Wisconsin

273 Wis. 438, 78 N.W.2d 750 (1956)

Proceeding for construction of a will. William Rosnow executed his will on January 18, 1949. He died in November, 1954. His wife had died sometime previously. The heirs-at-law and next of kin who survived him were his sons, Arthur and Leonard, and his grandchildren, Norman and Noami, who were children of William, Jr., a deceased son of the testator. The paragraphs of the will material to this appeal are:

First: A legacy of $ 500 to Norman.

"Second: I hereby mention the name of my granddaughter, Noami Rosnow, of Clintonville, Wisconsin, in loving remembrance, it being my will that she shall share in no part of this my estate.

"Fourth: I hereby mention the name of my son, Leonard Rosnow, of Milwaukee, Wisconsin, in loving remembrance, it being my will that he shall share in no part of this my estate.

"Tenth: All the rest, residue and remainder of my property of whatsoever kind, nature or description and wherever the same may be situated, I give, devise and bequeath, in equal and undivided shares, share and share alike, to my following named children, i. e., to my beloved daughter, Meta Larson of Clintonville, Wisconsin, an undivided one-half (1/2) share; to my beloved son, Arthur Rosnow, of Cecil, Wisconsin, an undivided one-half (1/2) share.

"In the event, however, that my son, Arthur Rosnow should predecease me, then, and in that event, I will and direct that the share which my son Arthur Rosnow receives under the third and tenth paragraphs of this my last will and testament, be assigned and belong to my beloved grandson, Gerald Rosnow."

Meta having died without issue before the death of the testator, this proceeding was brought to construe paragraph Tenth. The trial court determined that the share of Meta in the residue lapsed and adjudged that it be distributed as intestate property, that is, the son Arthur would take one third of Meta's half, the son Leonard would take one third, and the grandchildren Norman and Noami would divide equally the one third which their father, testator's son, William, would have been entitled to if he had survived the testator. Arthur has appealed in his capacity of executor. He points out that this construction gives a portion of the estate to Leonard and Noami notwithstanding the provisions of paragraphs Second and Fourth.

The appellant submits that persons expressly disinherited are disqualified from receiving any part of the estate under any theory and, preferably, the entire residue should be assigned to the only surviving individual mentioned in the residuary clause; that is, Arthur. Or, less desirable but still acceptable, Meta's share of the residue should be distributed among the next of kin who have not been disinherited by the will. He relies mainly on Will of Nielsen (1950), 256 Wis. 521, 41 N. W. (2d) 369, in which we gave great consideration to extrinsic facts and circumstances and reached a conclusion that the death of one of the residuary heirs did not result in a lapsed legacy but brought into effect a presumed wish of the testator's that some, but not all, of his heirs-at-law should divide the residue though there were no express terms of the will excluding any of them. The extrinsic considerations in Will of Nielsen, supra, seem now to be much less persuasive to the result then reached than they did when the case was determined. On the other hand, Will of Ziehlke (1939), 230 Wis. 574, 284 N. W. 497, which is not referred to in the Nielsen opinion presents the same problems as the case at bar and disposes of them according to what we consider must be the rule when, by lapse of a legacy a partial intestacy has occurred. In Ziehlke, paragraph Fourth described a residuary legatee but no person fulfilled the description when the testator died. There was a residue for division and there were nieces and nephews who were heirs-at-law but it was contended that they could not share in the division because of a paragraph in Mr. Ziehlke's will reading (p. 575):

"'Fifth: For reasons known to all, it is my will and I hereby direct that no part of my estate shall go to any of my nieces or nephews.'"

Mr. Justice Wickhem spoke for the court, saying (p. 579):

"The trial court appears to have been impressed by the fifth clause in which the testator disclosed a positive intention that his nieces and nephews take nothing under his will. The answers to this are, (1) that they do not take under the will, and (2) that this paragraph throws no light upon the meaning of the fourth paragraph as applied to the present situation. If one of the nieces had actually nursed him during his last illness, the fifth clause might be effective to exclude her as a beneficiary under the fourth clause. Here, however, the nieces and nephews do not take under the will but by law. The fourth paragraph being the residuary clause and the gift failing, the residue goes by operation of the law of descent. No doubt this is not what testator intended, but the only way in which he could vary the rules of descent would be by making an effective gift at variance with these. This he did not do." (Our emphasis.)

We find no escape from the logic of that opinion if we are to refrain, as we ought, from writing a new will for the testator. Therefore, we conclude that in the instant will the rules of descent take over when the testator made no provision for distribution of Meta's share of the residue in the event he outlived her. That law directs the distribution of her share in the manner directed by the learned trial court.

We are asked by respondents to inform the trial court upon remand that the executor's (appellant's) costs and disbursements must be paid by him personally, and not allowed as a charge against the estate, because of his strong personal interest in the success of his appeal. We do not attempt to control the trial court's discretion in its allowance of the executor's account until it becomes manifest that discretion has been abused.

Order affirmed.

CHAPTER 3. WILLS: DISTRIBUTION BY CONSCIOUS CHOICE

As Chapter 1 illustrated, the right to make a will disposing of one's belonging has long been viewed as a fundamental right in Wisconsin. However, to be valid, a will has to comply with the requirements of the Wisconsin statutes. This chapter explores the various rules governing the use of wills.

I. INTENTION AND CAPACITY

A. TESTAMENTARY INTENT.

For a will to be valid, it must be executed with the intention that it be a will. A will that is signed by an actor in a play is not a valid will, even if the actor signs the will with his own name. A trial draft of a will is not a valid will even if signed, unless the testator signed with the intention that he was executing a valid will. (Situations like the one just described can create almost insurmountable problems of proof, since a will that appears to be validly executed starts with a presumption of legitimacy.). The following is one of the most famous wills cases in Wisconsin history. The testator was the noted University of Wisconsin professor, Howard K. Beale (1899-1959), who was one of the most highly regarded American historians of the middle third of the twentieth century. His 1958 work, *The Critical Year: A Study of Andrew Johnson and Reconstruction* remains one of the most influential works written about the Civil War and Reconstruction era.

ESTATE OF BEALE

Supreme Court of Wisconsin
15 Wis. 2d 546, 113 N.W.2d 380 (1962)

BROWN, Justice. IS THIS AN UNNATURAL WILL?

Appellant begins with the assertion that the 1959 will is an unnatural one in that it disinherited Beale's ten year old son. Then he states his proposition that 'proponents of an unnatural will have burden to give a reasonable explanation for its unnatural provisions.' The learned trial court filed a written decision which demonstrated the meticulous study which the court gave to the will itself and to the evidence adduced in the several hearings, and the court concluded that the will was not 'unnatural.' Thomas' inheritance was reduced by the 1959 will to a contingent remainder but whether this rendered the will an unnatural one seems to us to be immaterial in the absence of any contention by appellant that, because of testamentary incapacity, undue influence or other factors appearing in the evidence, the will does not express the testator's true desires and intent. There are present no such factors to impugn the conclusion that the 1959 will exactly stated Professor Beale's own wish and purpose in respect to provision for his son Thomas. As the provisions or the lack of them are within the permission of the law neither Beale nor anyone else has to justify them or please any other person.

Appellant's brief further informs us that 'the right to make a will is not a constitutional or natural right, but a 'creature of statutory law', citing a Pennsylvania case. We have frequently held to the contrary, even so recently as in Estate of Ogg (1952), 262 Wis. 181, 54 N.W.2d 175, and Will of Wright (1961), 12 Wis.2d 375, 107 N.W.2d 146. See also Will of Rice (1912), 150 Wis. 401, 450, 136 N.W. 956, 137 N.W. 778. In each of those cases we have emphasized that the right to make a will is a sacred and constitutional right, which right includes a right of equal dignity to have the will carried out. And see Will of Hopkins (1956), 273 Wis. 632, 639, 79 N.W.2d 131, where we said:

Appellant claims that the will was an unnatural will, because after the administration of the specific bequests, the bulk of which was to the Masons, no residue remained to distribute to the surviving relatives. When a valid last will and testament has disposed of the owner's estate, the interest of surviving relatives is controlled by its provisions and not by the statute of descent. As said by the trial court, 'the law gives the testator the right to dispose of his property in any manner he may desire as long as it is his own act and free will, and the court is fully satisfied in this instance that the testator knew what he was doing at the time he signed his will and disposed of his property in the manner indicated therein * * * it is the responsibility of this court to respect his wishes.'

In the Rice case, supra, at page 446, 136 N.W. at page 974, we cited with approval Will of Dardis (1908), 135 Wis. 457, 115 N.W. 332, 23 L.R.A.,N.S., 783, to the effect that '* * * regardless of holdings elsewhere, in this state a will, once validly made and subsisting to the death of the testator, must be taken and judicially enforced according to his intent, if that can be ascertained; * * *.'

The long line of Wisconsin decisions does not permit the probate court to entertain the argument that a will can be denied probate only because it appears to be unjust to a natural object of a testator's bounty. Here appellant has made no attack on the testamentary capacity of Beale nor has he claimed he was unduly influenced. Will of Dobson (1951), 258 Wis. 587, 46 N.W.2d 758, states the following, relying upon Will of Schaefer (1932), 207 Wis. 404, 241 N.W. 382:

'* * * We might, without great difficulty, conclude that in equity the instrument provides an unjust distribution of the estate. However, we may not consider it in the light of what we may deem just or unjust. If it was made by Joseph Dobson with full testamentary capacity, expresses his desires and is not the result of undue influence, it is our duty to give it effect. That it does not divide the estate equally between the natural objects of testator's bounty is not controlling.'

Thus this court, as well as the county court, is precluded from considering whether Professor Beale's 1959 will is an 'unnatural will', with a view to denying probate to it.

EXECUTION OF WILL

While appellant concedes, or at least does not dispute, that when Professor Beale signed the purported 1959 will he had testamentary capacity and was not subject to undue influence appellant vigorously denies that the 14 pages of the 1959 instrument were legally published and declared to be his will and legally signed and witnessed as such and, in the alternative, that these pages did not constitute his will at the moment of execution.

In this record there are a few indisputable facts. From then there are a number of conflicting inferences reasonably to be drawn.

It cannot be questioned that on June 16 or 17, 1959, Professor Beale dictated a 14 page Document in the form of a last will, revoking all prior wills; that his secretary typed the original will, with three carbon copies, and delivered all of them to him in looseleaf form the afternoon of June 20th; that Beale was in New York City at the home of a friend, a professor of Columbia University, on the evening of June 21st and on that evening he exhibited 'a pile' of sheets of paper and declared to his three friends that this was his will and desired them to witness his will; that they saw him sign the sheet which was on top of the pile and that immediately thereafter, at his request, they signed as witnesses in his presence and in the presence of each other; that the place where they put their signatures was immediately below the usual testamentary clause declaring this to be Professor Beale's will; that none of the witnesses paid any detailed attention to the number of pages in the pile nor could they identify later any of the pages except the one where they had written their names; that when all four participants had signed, Beale put all papers in his briefcase and the meeting ended.

It is uncontradicted that on the next day, or shortly thereafter, Beale and his two sons left by plane for Moscow; that a few days after June 21st Mrs. Burleigh, Beale's secretary, received a letter from him on Columbia University note paper, bearing date June 21, 1959, mailed in New York or in London on a day not given; that the letter asked Mrs. Burleigh to make several changes in pages 12 and 13 of the will which she had previously typed, to carry out marginal penciled notes in Beale's handwriting on those pages; that enclosed with the letter were the original pages 12 and 13; that Mrs. Burleigh made the alterations as directed and mailed them back to him in Moscow; that these pages were later found in a sealed envelope addressed to Beale in Beale's handwriting and mailed from London, England to him at his Madison address.

There is nothing legally invalid in the execution of a will because the separate pages of the will have not been fastened together. It is a requirement, though, that all the pages be present at the time of execution.

Thompson on Wills (3rd Ed.), sec. 124, page 197, states:

* * * It is not necessary that they [the witnesses] see or examine all the pages of the will to see that all the sheets of paper were in place when the will was executed. * * *' Citing In Re Sleeper's Appeal, 129 Maine 194, 151 Atl. 150, 71 A.L.R. 518.

In Sleeper's Appeal, supra, the court stated:

* * * nor is it essential that the witnesses should see and examine all the pages of a will at the time of execution, if the court is satisfied, from other evidence or the circumstances surrounding the execution, that all the sheets of paper offered for probate were present at the time of execution. * * *'

2 Page on Wills (Bowe-Parker Revision), sec. 19.147, page 277, is to the same effect, citing Sleeper's Appeal, supra, and 11 B.U.L.Rev. 148; 5 Temp.L.Q. 152; 17 La.L.Rev. 69; and 40 Yale L.J. 144.

In the case at bar the witnesses are unable to say whether or not the 14 pages were on the table before them when, on June 21st, they signed the last page. The determination then, comes down to the reasonable inferences to be drawn from the established facts. Appellant relies on the undisputed fact that two pages of the will were received in Madison within a few days following June 21st, enclosed in a letter dated June 21st. And appellant infers that those two pages had already been sent off to Madison when, late in the evening of June 21st, the testator and witnesses signed the last page.

On the other hand the trial court put weight on the fact that all 14 original pages are clearly identified and legible as they were dictated by Beale before the corrections or amendments. This intact original was handed to Beale by his secretary and was taken by him to New York. The very next day Beale presented 'a pile' of papers to his witnesses and declared that such papers were his will. It is not impossible or improbable that Beale was speaking the truth and the pile of pages were the complete 14 page will, as the trial court found. The fact that Beale sent off two pages to Mrs. Burleigh with a letter dated June 21st may raise an inference that Beale did this before he went to the party and he had there only the remaining pages, which he falsely declared to be his will. Certainly that is not the only permissible inference. When Beale and his friends had signed the will and he had gathered up the pages and departed June 21st was not over; Beale could still have written the letter, less than 100 words, on that date after the party and enclosed with it pages 12 and 13. There is no evidence at all of when the letter and the pages were mailed and there is some evidence that they were mailed in London.

The question is one of inference and when the inferences can reasonably go either way the appellate court must adopt the view taken by the trial court.

1. It is the function of the trial court, in cases tried to the court, to draw such inferences from the established facts as deemed proper, and the supreme court cannot disturb the same unless they are against the great weight and clear preponderance of the evidence.' Hull v. Pfister & Vogel Leather Co. (1940), 235 Wis. 653, 294 N.W. 18, (Headnote).

As the trial court's function is to determine the facts and to weigh them, In re Will of Russell, 1950, 257 Wis. 510, 44 N.W.2d 231, so, too, the inferences to be drawn from established facts are for the trier of the fact, in this case the trial court. Its findings in these respects should not be interfered with unless contrary to the great weight and clear preponderance of the evidence, * * *.' Estate of Miller (1953), 265 Wis. 420, 424-425, 61 N.W.2d 813.

'It is well established that findings of a trial court are not to be disturbed on appeal unless they are contrary to the great weight and clear preponderance of the evidence. Swazee v. Lee, 1951, 259 Wis. 136, 137, 47 N.W.2d 733.' Drott Tractor Co. v. Kehrein (1957), 275 Wis. 320, 323, 81 N.W.2d 500.

* * * The most that can be said is that on some of the contested issues of fact, the proof might have sustained a finding contrary to that made by the court. Upon such a state of the record this court may not disturb the findings of the trial court.' Drott Tractor Co. v. Kehrein, supra, p. 328, 81 N.W.2d p. 504.

While the present facts permit the inference urged by appellant they do not compel that inference in opposition to the one drawn by the trial court, and the evidence and reasonable inferences sustain the trial court's conclusion that the entire original will, as dictated by Professor Beale to his secretary, was before the witnesses and the execution of that will complied with the requirements of law.

ANIMUS TESTANDI

Appellant, however, has other shots in his locker, the first of which is that even if the entire 14 pages of the will, as originally typed, were before the testator and witnesses at the time of execution the fact that Beale so quickly chose to make changes in it must persuade the court that at the moment of execution Beale did not intend this to be his will, no matter what he may have declared. The burden is on appellant to show that although Beale had himself dictated this will in the very recent past and had declared it to his three friends to be his will, he had already changed his mind concerning it.

As before, the court might have drawn that inference but it was not compelled to do so. The trial court considered Beale's express declaration that this was his will as of that moment was entitled to the greater weight. That court said, in its written decision:

'The objectors contend that the proper *Animus Testandi* is lacking in this case. Such an objection cannot be sustained. It certainly cannot be said that a man who dictates a document consisting of fourteen pages which purports to be his last will and testament, takes the finished typewritten document from Madison, Wisconsin to New York City, secures three personal friends to witness the document, telling them it is his will, all of which takes place shortly before he is to take a long trip to a foreign land, lacks the necessary testamentary intent to make that document his last will. The necessary testamentary intent existed at the time the will was executed, and that is all that is required.

The inference drawn by the trial court is reasonable and we must adopt its conclusion.

REVOCATION

Next, appellant submits that Beale had revoked the 1959 will. Sec. 238.14, Stats. of 1959, states:

'*Will, how revoked.* No will nor any part thereof shall be revoked unless by burning, tearing, canceling or obliterating the same, with the intention of revoking it, by the testator or by some person in his presence and by his direction, or by some other will or codicil in writing, executed as prescribed in this chapter, or by some other writing, signed, attested and subscribed in the manner provided in this chapter for the execution of a will; excepting only that nothing contained in this section shall prevent the revocation implied by law from subsequent changes in the condition or circumstances of the testator. The power to make a will implies the power to revoke the same.'

These are the only ways by which a will can be revoked in this state. Deck v. Deck (1900), 106 Wis. 470, 82 N.W. 293. The burden is upon the objectors to establish by competent evidence that there was a valid and effective revocation. Estate of Sweeney (1946), 248 Wis. 607, 22 N.W.2d 657, 24 N.W.2d 406.

In contending that Beale intended to revoke the 1959 will, appellant first points to the several alterations requested by Beale and the fact that the date was changed from June 21st to June 22nd. Beale, himself, never said or wrote that he intended to revoke the will. He wrote a direction to modify one sentence. Such attempted alterations, according to appellant, were themselves sufficient to revoke the 1959 will. None of these alterations pertained to the distribution of Beale's property. As already mentioned, the change in executors was the only significant substitution. Such a change does not operate as a revocation of the will in its entirety. 57 Am.Jur., Wills, sec. 510, page 355, states:

'Clearly, a will is not revoked in its entirety by the act of the testator in striking out the name of the person designated executor and writing in the name of another person as executor, notwithstanding this occurs after the will has been executed and attested and without a reattestation or republication. * * *'

Respondents contend that the substitution of executors, as it did not comply with statutory will standards (sec. 238.06, Stats.), is invalid. Thus, the attempted changes cannot have the effect of invalidating the will. Even if the changes were valid they would have no effect on the property distribution directed by the will. Will of Home (1939), 231 Wis. 227, 233, 284 N.W. 766, 285 N.W. 754, held: 'Aside from this the alterations have no effect to invalidate the will as a whole. They would only invalidate the change.' In the same case we said, page 234, 284 N.W. page 768: '* * * The recent case of Byrne's Will, 223 Wis. 503, 271 N.W. 48, clearly implies that alterations in a will do not render it void and have no effect except as they operate as partial revocations. * * *'

2 Page on Wills, sec. 537, pages 3-4, says:

'If the will which is altered by testator after execution is one which is required, by statute, to be attested and subscribed by witnesses, interlineations which testator makes after execution, are of no effect unless the will is subsequently re-executed or republished; and such a will must be admitted to probate as though the interlineations had never been made. * * *

'If the name of an executor is added after execution, such addition is of no effect. * * *

Will of Marvin (1920), 172 Wis. 457, 179 N.W. 508, (headnotes 1 and 2) states:

'If a testator cancels or destroys a will with the present intention of making a new disposition of his property, and the proposed new disposition fails to be carried into effect, the presumption in favor of a revocation by the canceling is repelled, and the will stands as originally made.

'Where testatrix left all her property to one of four grandchildren, and after her death the will was found to have pencil marks through the words bequeathing the property to such grandchild, and below the attestation clause there was written with a pen a clause in the handwriting of the testatrix giving all her property, after payment of all her debts, to an orphans' home, but such clause was not signed by testatrix nor witnessed, the attempted changes did not become effective and the will remained as originally drawn.'

We determine that the 1959 will was not revoked by the alterations nor were the attempted modifications effective.

We then come to a fact whose effect, if any, until now we have found no occasion to consider, viz.:

Promptly after Professor Beale's death his family searched his office in the University Library for a will. What they found there was the 1959 will, without the *first* page, and a complete copy of the will, including the first page. Several months later the missing original first page was discovered in a folder containing Beale's notes for a history lecture. These papers were found in Beale's second office in another university building. This page was delivered to the court and the complete will as originally transcribed and legible in spite of the alterations was then before the county court.

Page 1 contained the introductory clause revoking all prior wills. Appellant submits that the abstraction of this page from the remainder of the will manifested Beale's intent to destroy the will of which page 1 was a part. The trial court concluded that page 1 had merely been misplaced and no contrary intent has been proved. Once the execution and validity of a will has been established, valid and effective revocation is a burden which falls upon the objectors. Estate of Sweeney, supra. The county court's conclusion that appellant has not met this burden is consistent with the proof. A contrary view, that revocation by this means was intended, depends not even upon inference but on mere speculation.

EPILOGUE

At least one more mystery appears worth mentioning, although in our view it presents no fact to affect the outcome:

A few days before Christmas, 1959, Beale, who had returned to Madison, directed Mrs. Burleigh to re-type the altered pages 12 and 13 on the same typewriter she had used when she first typed the will. We may guess that Beale wanted pages which did not show they had been tampered with, as was apparent on the two original sheets now showing erasures and re-typed corrections. We may guess, further, that Beale intended to insert in the will without discovery the new pages without republication and re-execution of the will. This is no more than guesswork and is of no consequence. Before Mrs. Burleigh typed the two new sheets Beale's death intervened on December 27, 1959. Whatever his purpose, nefarious or not, he did not accomplish it. Mrs. Burleigh had not begun this final typing when she was told that Professor Beale had died. She then typed the two pages as Professor Beale directed and gave them to Beale's son, Henry. There were then no marginal initials on them. These pages are in evidence and, although Professor Beale never in his life had them or saw them, his initials are now on the margin of each of these pages and, as Mrs. Burleigh testified, are in his handwriting.

We began with a consideration of the unnatural. At the end we are confronted by the supernatural. We consider ourselves fortunate that this weird addition to the facts turns out to be immaterial.

We conclude that the trial court's findings and conclusions are not against the great weight and the clear preponderance of the evidence and the judgment admitting the will to probate as the will existed when it was executed and as Mrs. Burleigh first typed it must be affirmed.

CURRIE, Justice (dissenting). On the record here presented, the paramount issue is whether, at time of execution of the 1959 will, testator intended the then existing fourteen typewritten pages to be his will. As the majority opinion intimates, if it was testator's intent to keep the instrument ambulatory in character, so that from time to time he could substitute pages for any except the last, which bore the signature of himself and witnesses, then this instrument would not qualify as his last will and testament because the requisite testamentary intent would be lacking. The crucial piece of evidence on this issue is testator's letter of June 21, 1959, to Mrs. Burleigh forwarding for retyping the two pages on which he had made alterations. If this letter was written before testator and the witnesses affixed their signatures, it would carry great weight in establishing that testator had intended an ambulatory instrument.

The June 21st letter was written on Columbia University stationery. A reasonable inference is that he procured this stationery at the apartment of his friend, Professor Forcey, a member of the Columbia University faculty, and the host of the June 21st party given in honor of testator. However, Professor Forcey, who testified as a subscribing witness to the 1959 will, was asked no questions about furnishing stationery to testator or about whether he possessed any knowledge concerning the writing of the June 21st letter.

Forcey did testify that both Howard Kennedy Beale, Jr., and Henry Barton Beale were present with their father in the Forcey apartment at the June 21st party. Neither of these two sons of testator were called as witnesses at the trial. The general rule is that failure of a party to call a material witness within his control, or whom it would be more natural for such party to call than the opposing party, raises an inference against such party. Feldstein v. Harrington (1958), 4 Wis.2d 380, 388, 90 N.W.2d 566; 2 Wigmore, Evidence (3rd ed.), p. 162, et seq., secs. 285, 286. This rule is applicable in situations of family relationship, such as parent and child. Anno., 5 A.L.R.(2d) 893, 934. Thus, the failure to call either of these two sons as a witness raised an inference against the proponents of the 1959 will. However, the trial court's memorandum opinion does not comment upon the fact that these two older sons were not called to testify as to their knowledge with respect to the writing of the June 21st letter.

It may very well be that the *guardians ad litem* for all three sons interviewed the two older sons about the June 21st letter and found they possessed no knowledge or recollection with respect to their father writing it. However, this is a situation where the trial court might very well have drawn the opposite inference from that which it did. Additional testimony with respect to the June 21st letter might have tipped the scales the other way. This is very important considering the fact that a ten year old boy, who is a ward of the court, has been virtually disinherited by his father's will.

Under these circumstances I would exercise our discretionary power under sec. 251.09, Stats. to reverse and remand for the purpose of taking the testimony of the two older boys with respect to the June 21st letter. I am authorized to state that DIETERICH, J., joins in this dissenting opinion.

B. TESTAMENTARY CAPACITY

For a will to be valid, it not only has to be executed in compliance with the formalities of the Wisconsin Wills Act (discussed below), it also has to have been intended as a will and must be the product of the testator's conscious intent. If it can be shown that the testator lacked testamentary capacity (a legal standard), suffered from an insane delusion (in the legal sense) or was improperly coerced or influenced in the drafting of a will by a third party, the will is not valid. Wisconsin also requires a minimum age of 18 for testamentary capacity and does not recognize an exception for individuals who are under 18 but legally married (as some states do.) The following cases illustrate how these principles have been applied by Wisconsin courts.

Wis. Stat. 853.01. Capacity to make or revoke a will.

Any person of sound mind 18 years of age or older may make and revoke a will.

IN RE ESTATE OF DOBRECEVICH

Supreme Court of Wisconsin

14 Wis. 2d 82, 109 N.W.2d 477; 1961

BROWN, J.

Execution of the Will.

The document was signed by Rade Dobrecevich at the Farmers & Merchants Bank in Menomonee Falls, Waukesha County, on March 31, 1954, in the presence of Robert Goode and Bernard Bellin, who were officers of the bank for many years. These officers testified that Dobrecevich and the two witnesses all signed in the presence of each other. Mr. Bellin testified directly that he remembered Rade's statement to the witnesses that this paper was his will.

The objector's contention is that the witnesses had no present recollection of the execution of the will, that the attesting witnesses did not read the will and could not now say that they knew this to be a will at the time they witnessed it, and they did not read the attestation clause and therefore there was no presumption of fact in the declarations of the standard attestation clause. Whether they read the attestation clause or not, both bank officers testified that they were accustomed to act as witnesses to wills and that they knew this was a will presented to them to be witnessed. It is extremely improbable that bank officers would put their names to documents about whose nature and purpose they did not know and understand, in addition to which the testimony, particularly of Mr. Bellin, shows that Rade published and declared this paper to be his will and asked them to be witnesses to his signing it. There is no contrary testimony and the appellant's objection to this feature of the case rests only on an inference that the witnesses could not have remembered the transaction. The court did not draw that inference but did believe the witnesses. The court's finding that the execution conformed to the statute, sec. 238.06, was sufficiently proved.

Testamentary Capacity.

The decisions dealing with testamentary capacity are so numerous and the law so well established that it hardly seems necessary to review them again at length. The question of competency to make a will is to be determined as of the time of the execution of the will; the credibility of witnesses and the weight to be given to their testimony are matters for the trial court, as are the inferences to be drawn from the evidence. The findings of the trial court must be affirmed unless contrary to the great weight and clear preponderance of the evidence. *Estate of Fuller* (1957), 275 Wis. 1, 81 N. W. (2d) 64. The party contesting the will because of alleged lack of testamentary capacity has the burden of proving the incapacity by clear and satisfactory evidence and the question of mental competency is to be determined as of the time of the execution of the will. *Estate of Kaiman* (1961), 13 Wis. (2d) 201, 108 N. W. (2d) 379.

As witnesses to establish Rade Dobrecevich's incompetency, the objector called his brother and his two sisters, as well as numerous other witnesses, all of whom testified that Rade drank heavily and when drunk behaved in a most disorderly manner. In this respect the effect of such testimony is very similar to that on the issue of testamentary capacity in the *Kaiman Case, supra*. It may be conceded that a fastidious hostess would not want Rade to be her house guest but this testimony bears little relationship to the testator's competency to make a valid will distributing his property after death. Neither is there much probative force in the fact that in the years after the will was executed Rade's drinking habits got worse and a year and half after the date of the will his children determined that he was wasting his money and they thought it advisable that he should be put under guardianship as a spendthrift. On the petition of his daughter, Anna, the Waukesha county court, November 1, 1955, found Rade to be incompetent to have the care and management of his property because of his being an habitual drunkard and spendthrift and letters of guardianship were issued to Anna Brandt. Long ago we determined that the mere fact that a person is under guardianship as to his person and property does not incapacitate him to make a valid will. *Will of*

Slinger (1888), 72 Wis. 22, 37 N. W. 236. The distinction between incapacity to handle his finances and incapacity to comprehend the conditions of his property, his relationship to the natural objects of his bounty, and the disposition actually made of his property by a will still holds good.

The objector also charged that Rade suffered from insane delusions and that such delusions produced the distribution which the will made in the estate. No delusions whatever are in evidence. The objector has attempted to work the problem backwards by a course of reasoning which starts by a will unsatisfactory to the objector, from which he argues that the testator must have been motivated by an insane delusion that the children, other than Anna, persecuted him and he resented it. There is no testimony that Rade had any such thoughts or beliefs.

Under the evidence adduced in the trial of this case we find no merit in objector's contention that Rade lacked testamentary capacity.

Testator's Ability to Understand the Will.

The objector also submits that even if Rade's competency was such as to enable him to make a valid will there is insufficient proof that he did intentionally and understandingly make this will. This rests on a theory that Rade, who was of Serbian birth, could not communicate satisfactorily in the English language and, therefore, Rade was not able to express his wishes to the scrivener who drafted the will and who understood and spoke only English, nor could Rade understand the will when the scrivener read it back in English to him nor could he read the will for himself. It must be conceded Rade could not have read the will but it is not one difficult to understand. The scrivener, Attorney Higgins, testified that he was able to understand what Rade wanted and that Rade understood the will which Higgins prepared and read to him. Numerous other witnesses called by Anna, the proponent, testified that Rade could understand and be understood in the English language when conversing on simple subjects. He could make purchases in stores and argue about his tax bills. Such witnesses testified that Rade was able to express himself in English and to understand what was said to him in English in the everyday pursuits of his life.

Rade came alone to the office of Attorney Higgins to have a will prepared and it was Rade and no one else who told Higgins how the property should be distributed. Inspection of the will shows that Rade was able to tell Higgins who his children were and their addresses. The will omitted none of them. (Helen Lucas is one of Rade's married daughters.) In fact, except for the size of the respective bequests, the objector does not contend that Rade did not communicate accurate information to the attorney whom he asked to prepare the will.

A few days after the first interview, Rade came to the attorney's office to sign the will, when Higgins told him the will would be ready. Evidently Rade had understood the necessity of this second visit. This occurred in the evening and there were no available witnesses, so Mr. Higgins gave Rade the will, told him to get two good men to be witnesses and when he and the witnesses had signed the will he should mail it back to Mr. Higgins in an envelope which Higgins gave Rade for the purpose. The next day Rade asked his daughter, Anna, if she could take him to two good men to be witnesses to a paper which he was going to sign. Anna said that she was going to the bank and would take him there. The trip to the bank and the execution followed as already described. When the signing had been attended to, Rade asked Anna where he could mail the paper back to Mr. Higgins and Anna took him to the Menomonee Falls post office and pointed out the place where the envelope could be deposited. The will reached Mr. Higgins in the mail in due course. It appears, therefore, that Rade was able to understand the instructions which Mr. Higgins had given him and that he followed the instructions exactly. There can be no question but what Rade could understand Mr. Higgins in that matter and there is not the slightest reason to suppose that Rade did not understand the very simple bequests which Mr. Higgins testified that he read to Rade and that the written will expressed Rade's wishes.

We conclude that the testator had testamentary capacity in general and, particularly, at the time of the preparation and the execution of the will, and was able to communicate his wishes to the scrivener and to understand and approve what the scrivener had written for him in respect to the testator's directions. ...

[The Court also concluded that the charges that Dobrecevich was susceptible to undue influence and had been improperly influenced by his daughter Anna were not supported by the evidence.]

C. INSANE DELUSION

In re Estate of Evans

Supreme of Wisconsin
83 Wis. 2d 259, 265 N.W.2d 529 (1978)

Hansen, J. The appellants are adult daughters of the testator, John C. Evans, deceased. They filed objections to the admission of his last will and testament to probate on the grounds that he was suffering under an insane delusion, lacked testamentary capacity, and was unduly influenced by the beneficiaries.

The will, dated April 25, 1972, left his estate, of an approximate value of $32,000, to certain of his nieces and nephews. It made no provisions for his two daughters, Blanche, born in 1914, and Patricia, born in 1936.

Evans was born June 23, 1889; was educated through the sixth grade; and was married on October 29, 1913, to Dorathea Evans (hereinafter Dorathea). For the next forty-seven years, he and Dorathea worked a farm near Briggsville, Wisconsin. Their two daughters, who remained unmarried, resided with them and helped work the farm for many years without compensation. In 1960, a land contract was executed for the sale of the farm, and the farm equipment was sold at auction. Evans, then seventy years old, told the buyers that he was getting too old to handle farm work. Following the sale of the farm, the daughters obtained fulltime employment off the farm for the first time. Until 1963, the Evans family continued to reside in the farm house, renting it from the buyers under the land contract. In 1963, they purchased and moved to a residence in nearby Briggsville.

Numerous witnesses testified that the Evans family appeared to be a close and loving family, and that they participated in many activities together. Beginning in approximately 1966, however, the family relationship became increasingly strained. The source of this strain is at issue.

The appellants contend that Evans' behavior underwent a sudden and irrational change, and that he became obsessed with an insane delusion that his wife and daughters were stealing his assets. The evidence shows that he became mistrustful of the financial records kept by his wife, and that he was convinced that money was being withheld from him. There is also evidence, however, that he was concerned about a lack of sexual relations with his wife, and that he attributed the family's troubles to the presence in the household of his daughters, particularly the older daughter, Blanche, whom he considered domineering.

Whatever the source of the trouble, it became serious. Evans repeatedly accused Dorathea of failing to account for family funds. At Dorathea's request, the family lawyer and a minister met twice with Evans and Dorathea to review the books kept by Dorathea. Although they found no errors, and attempted to persuade him that he was not being cheated, he remained unconvinced. Evans began demanding that his wife and daughters leave the family home. On one occasion, he excluded his wife and daughter from the family home by barring the door with a shotgun. At another time

Blanche returned home to find that her father had trapped her mother behind a bedroom door, and Blanche called the sheriff to release her.

Evans suffered from a number of medical problems and was hospitalized several times early in 1967. His hospital records show, among other things, that he was suffering from arteriosclerosis, and after his release from the hospital he mentioned to a friend that he had hardening of the arteries. His hospital records also show that he was very despondent about family problems.

In March, 1967, Evans was hospitalized for psychiatric evaluation. His medical records state that this hospitalization was the result of "a somewhat chaotic family situation," and that one of his daughters had called the hospital "and, in effect, demanded that the patient be hospitalized." These medical records also show that Dorathea informed the hospital staff that he had accused her of squandering funds, and that he verified the fact that he believed his wife and daughters had "'plotted against him.'"

Upon his discharge, on March 18, 1967, Evans did not resume residence in the family home, but instead went to live with his brother, Louis, about four miles from Briggsville. He was later to state that he had been driven from his home. Twelve days later, on March 30, 1967, Dorathea commenced an action for legal separation. By judgment entered February 15, 1968, Dorathea was granted an absolute divorce, and the family property was divided equally between Evans and his wife.

Evans was soon convinced, and remained convinced to his death, that he had not received his full share in the division of the property. There followed an extensive and confusing exchange of correspondence in which his lawyer identified what Evans insisted were family assets in a total amount of $74,500, and in which Dorathea's lawyer offered detailed explanations of the various items. It is sufficient to observe here that some of these claims were clearly erroneous, and that Evans denied receiving some payments even though cancelled checks and the testimony of disinterested witnesses show that the payments were in fact made. Nevertheless, he persisted in the belief that he had not received his half of the property.

Following the divorce, the daughters remained in the Briggsville house with their mother, who suffered from diabetes, which left her unable to work around the house. In June of 1968, part of her leg was amputated, and she was confined to a wheelchair. She died on June 25, 1970, and her entire estate was devised and bequeathed to the two daughters.

After the divorce, Evans lived with his brother, Louis Evans, for about two months. He then lived with his sister, Alice Ramsey, and her husband for approximately one year. Except for a short period before his last illness, when he lived with his nephew, Orville Evans, he lived the remainder of his life, slightly more than six years, by himself in a rented apartment in Briggsville. Although he saw his daughters often in Briggsville, he had little contact with them. He occasionally spoke with them on the street. They visited him a number of times in the hospital and were seen visiting with him while playing cards at parties and public gatherings. However, neither of them ever visited him in his apartment, allegedly for fear that he would accuse them of stealing.

Evans' health failed somewhat each year. Various witnesses testified that he showed a general loss of interest in life, that he became forgetful, and that he frequently became confused. He showed a lack of concern for his personal cleanliness. He lost weight, his eyesight became poor, he had difficulty breathing, and he sometimes fell. During February of 1972, while vacationing in Florida, he fell and broke several ribs and punctured a lung. He was hospitalized for three weeks. In April, 1972, after returning to Wisconsin, he was hospitalized for one week and was diagnosed as having Hodgkin's Disease.

On April 25, 1972, five days after his release from the hospital, Evans visited Howard Latton, then a practicing lawyer, to have a will drawn. He had not met Latton before and did not see him again after that day. Latton testified that Evans told him he had been married and divorced, that the divorce had caused bitterness and that his two daughters had had nothing to do with him since the divorce. Evans told Latton that he had a previous will which made no provision for his daughters and which benefited certain of his nieces and nephews, but that he wanted to revise his will to provide greater benefit to certain other nieces and nephews who were close to him.

The earlier will, executed July 17, 1967, after Evans left the family home in Briggsville but prior to the judgment of divorce, made no provision for the wife or daughters, and left his entire estate in equal shares to his nephews, Harley Evans and Orville [Orvel] Evans, and to his nieces Eva Ramsey and Helen Treadwell. The will drawn by Latton on April 25, 1972, made no provision for his two daughters "for reasons which I consider sufficient." Instead, it left his estate to seven nieces and nephews.

Latton testified that he met with Evans for approximately seventy minutes in total; that Evans identified the intended beneficiaries, discussed the fact of his divorce, and also discussed burial plans. After the will was typed, Latton reviewed it with the testator, paragraph by paragraph, and asked him a series of questions to confirm that Evans had read the will and understood it; that it was as he wanted it; and that no one had influenced him in making it.

Latton also testified that it was his opinion, based on his observation of Evans, that he had a sufficiently active memory to comprehend, without prompting, the condition of his property, his relation to his children and other possible beneficiaries, and the scope and bearing of his will; to perceive the relation of these things to each other; and to form a rational decision in reference to them. In forming this opinion, however, Latton apparently did not know that Evans had been discharged from a hospital only five days earlier.

Although Latton formed an impression that Evans' assets were in the range of $20,000 to $30,000, he did not make a record of the assets of Evans and their value, and Evans apparently did not identify his property in detail. In addition, a memorandum prepared by Latton for his files recites that Evans said his wife had obtained a divorce "and that she and the two daughters got most of the property and since then the daughters have paid no attention to him." In fact, as previously stated, the divorce judgment had provided for an equal division of the property.

Following the execution of the will, Evans' health continued to fail. In May, 1972, he was hospitalized for a radical mastectomy which revealed a malignant lymphoma. His x-ray reports also showed "sclerotic changes," or hardening, of the aorta.

Evans died on September 22, 1974, at the age of eighty-five, and his last will and testament was subsequently admitted to probate.

Additional facts are set forth in discussion of the issues, which are:

1. Was the testator suffering from an insane delusion which materially affected his will?

2. Did the testator lack testamentary capacity?

3. Was the testator's will the product of undue influence by the beneficiaries?

After an extended trial and in a detailed memorandum decision, the trial judge found as facts that the will was not obtained as the result of undue influence, that Evans was mentally competent when he executed the will, and that he was not affected by an insane delusion.

The findings of the trial court were based on conflicting evidence. The test on this appeal, therefore, is whether a judicial mind could, on due consideration of the evidence as a whole, reasonably have reached the same conclusions. This court will defer to the fact findings of the trial court, and they will not be upset on appeal unless they are clearly erroneous and against the great weight and clear preponderance of the evidence. In re Estate of Taylor, 81 Wis.2d 687, 696, 697, 260 N.W.2d 803 (1978).

The question on appeal is not whether this court would reach the same findings, but whether the findings should be affirmed as not being contrary to the great weight and clear preponderance of the evidence. In Matter of Estate of Becker, 76 Wis.2d 336, 346, 251 N.W.2d 431 (1977). On appeal this court examines the record, not for evidence to support findings which the trial court did not make, but for facts to support the findings which the trial court did make. In Matter of Estate of Becker, supra, at 347. Applying these standards to the record on this appeal dictates that the judgment admitting the will to probate be affirmed.

INSANE DELUSION.

It has been stated that an insane delusion is a false belief which would be incredible to the victim if he were of sound mind, and from which he cannot be dissuaded by any evidence or argument. Will of Riemer, 2 Wis.2d 16, 19, 85 N.W.2d 804 (1957). The test of whether an erroneous belief is an insane delusion is whether a sane person could have formed such a belief from the evidence. Will of Wicker, 15 Wis.2d 86, 112 N.W.2d 137 (1961); Will of Quam, 10 Wis.2d 21, 102 N.W.2d 217 (1960); Will of Riemer, supra.

In the present case, there does not appear to be any substantial question but what Evans entertained a mistaken belief regarding the family finances. The trial court stated in its opinion:

". . . The record is clear that beginning in, at least, 1966 Mr. Evans and his wife and daughters had continual disagreements as to money. Mr. Evans believed that he was not and did not receive all the property he had coming. The record is also clear that he did receive all of such money."

This finding of the trial court is amply supported by the evidence.

The trial court concluded that this erroneous belief did not constitute an insane delusion and thus invalidate the will. However, in arriving at this conclusion, the trial court emphasized that Evans' disposition of his property could be explained by the fact that his wife had brought a divorce suit against him, and that his daughters had sided with his wife, leaving him to live alone and never coming to visit him in his nearby apartment. Suspicion and bitter accusations often attend divorces, the trial court observed, and it was natural under such circumstances for a testator to remember those who were kind to him in his last years.

It would be difficult to sustain the decision of the trial court if it were based solely on the conclusion that the divorce and the resultant attitude toward the daughters overrode or negated the testator's delusions regarding their role in the handling of the family finances prior to the divorce.

In Estate of Joslin, 4 Wis.2d 29, 89 N.W.2d 822 (1958), this court considered a will in which an elderly testatrix had made no provision for her husband of fifty-five years. The testatrix had been afflicted with delusions that her eighty-year-old husband was carrying on adulterous relations with other women in their home after she had retired for the night. As a result of these delusions, the testatrix and her husband had made an equal division of their property some six years prior to the execution of the will.

The division of property did not alter the effect of the insane delusion or explain the exclusion of the husband from the will, this court held. The court said:

"The trial court, as a reason for holding that the insane delusion of Mrs. Joslin did not materially affect the testamentary disposition of her property whereby she bequeathed nothing to her husband, stressed the property division of 1947 which took place between the parties. However, the motivating cause for such property division was Mrs. Joslin's harboring of the delusion that her husband was squandering money on other women. This was what prompted her in denying him funds to carry on his business which in turn precipitated the property division. We thus consider it to be logically impossible to separate the delusions from the property division and to hold that one was a motivating force in the making of the will and not the other." Estate of Joslin, supra, at 34. See also, Will of McGovern, 241 Wis. 99, 3 N.W.2d 717 (1942).

By the same reasoning, where a divorce is logically inseparable from an insane delusion, or where the delusion is the motivating cause of the divorce, the divorce cannot be said to negate the effect of the delusions on a subsequent will.

In the present case there was persuasive evidence to support the contention that Evans suffered from an obsession that the family was secreting assets from him. However, an objector cannot succeed by merely showing that the testator had an insane delusion. His testamentary document will not be disallowed unless is also shown that the insane delusion materially affected the disposition embodied in the will. Will of Quam, supra, at 28, 29.

The daughters cannot prevail, therefore, unless it is reasonably certain that, but for the insane delusion, they would have received a materially larger portion of the estate. See: Will of Wicker, supra, at 90; Will of Riemer, supra, at 32. When the evidence shows that for other reasons the testator would have made the same disposition of his property in his will, the will should be admitted to probate, as was the will here.

The daughters rely on the Will of Elbert, 244 Wis. 175, 11 N.W.2d 626 (1943), in which this court affirmed a judgment denying probate of a will where the testatrix was influenced by the insane delusion that her children were stealing from her. There, however, this court emphasized that the delusion was ". . . the only possible cause for cutting off her children in the will. . . ." This court concluded that ". . . except for these insane delusions, there existed no ground of estrangement between her and her children and no other way to account for the disposition made of her property. . . ." Will of Elbert, supra, at 177.

In contrast, the record in the present case contains substantial evidence of other grounds for estrangement between Evans and his daughters. Therefore, it cannot be said that the great weight and clear preponderance of the evidence is contrary to the conclusion of the trial court that any insane delusion regarding the family finances did not materially affect the will.

The record contains considerable evidence that Evans attributed the breakdown of his marriage to the presence of his unmarried daughters, and particularly the older daughter, in the home. The bill of particulars, filed by his lawyer in the divorce proceedings, attributes the collapse of the marriage to the allegedly domineering influence of the older daughter. The medical records of his hospitalization in 1967, for psychiatric evaluation, the testimony of his bookkeeper, the family lawyer and numerous other witnesses, attribute the source of the family breakdown to the presence of the two daughters in the home.

There is considerable credible evidence that he was treated unkindly by both daughters. The evidence does not compel the conclusion that Evans' feelings toward his daughters were groundless or that, in the same circumstances, a sane person would not have become estranged from his daughters.

On this record, the finding of the trial court that Evans' beliefs on money matters did not materially affect his will is not contrary to the great weight and clear preponderance of the evidence.

The daughters further argue that Evans' will was affected by a second insane delusion, and that he believed that Blanche was not his daughter. This argument is founded entirely on the purported testimony of Donald Hollman, the former family lawyer, in response to the question whether, in the trial of the divorce action, Evans ever testified to the effect that he was not the father of Blanche. The transcript prepared by the court reporter showed no answer to this question.

The daughters have moved to insert the answer "yes" to conform to what they contend was the answer of the witness. Five affidavits, including an affidavit of the witness, have been filed in support of this contention. In addition, the contention is supported by the fact that after the question was asked, the daughters' lawyer offered Blanche's birth certificate and other statements of Evans showing that he was in fact her father. The trial court entered an order denying the motion to amend the transcript, and the daughters ask that this order be reversed.

It is unnecessary to determine whether the order of the trial court was erroneous because, even if Hollman did testify that Evans once gave testimony "to the effect that" Blanche was not his daughter, this would not constitute sufficient evidence to establish an insane delusion.

An insane delusion is a belief from which the victim cannot be dissuaded by any evidence or argument. Will of Riemer, supra, at 20. A belief must have a rigid or persistent quality, and must be unreasonably adhered to, over time, if it is to assume the status of an insane delusion.

Even if it is assumed that Evans once denied that Blanche was his daughter, the record is devoid of any indication that he persisted in any such belief or that he ever repeated it. On the contrary, the record is replete with accounts of his statements about his "daughters," Blanche and Patricia. There is therefore no basis for the argument that he was subject to an insane delusion that Blanche was not his daughter.

[For similar reasons, the Court in *Estate of Evans* also concluded that the record justified the trial court's findings that Evans possessed testamentary capacity and was not the subject of undue influence.]

D. UNDUE INFLUENCE

Estate of Malnar

Supreme Court of Wisconsin
72 Wis. 2d 192, 243 N.W.2d 435 (1976)

Heffernan, J. This is an appeal from an order denying the petition of appellant-proponent and sole beneficiary, Genevieve Malnar, to admit a document dated July 30, 1973, to probate as the will of the deceased, Frances Malnar.

The trial court denied admission of the will to probate because (1) there was insufficient evidence that the deceased, Frances Malnar, understood the contents of the will when she executed it; and (2) the proponent, Genevieve Malnar, had failed to overcome the inference of undue influence arising from a confidential relationship between proponent and deceased and from suspicious circumstances surrounding the drafting and execution of the will. We affirm.

The deceased, Frances Malnar, was a seventy-four-year-old widow, suffering from advanced liver disease. At the time the will was executed, she was staying at the Marshfield Convalescent Center. Her deceased husband was the uncle of Emil Malnar, the proponent's husband. The proponent, Genevieve Malnar, is the daughter of Mary Miksha, a friend of Frances Malnar for over thirty years. Mary Miksha was not related to the testatrix, Frances Malnar.

Frances Malnar had no children. She did have one sister, who was living in Yugoslavia. This sister had several children, all living in Yugoslavia. Frances also had two brothers who predeceased her, both of whom were survived by children. The majority of the nieces and nephews lived in Illinois. There was testimony that Frances and the nieces and nephews were on good terms and that they corresponded with one another several times yearly. Several of the nieces and nephews would occasionally visit Frances, and Frances would occasionally visit them. Frances would send gifts to her nieces and nephews on birthdays and Christmas.

There was testimony that Frances Malnar was a strong-willed woman, who wanted to control her own affairs. At the time that the will was executed, however, she was a very sick and very weak individual. She was able to speak little English, but could write her name. Her native language was Croatian.

Frances owned a home in Greenwood, Wisconsin. In 1970, she was hospitalized at St. Joseph's Hospital in Marshfield for about two weeks as a result of a liver condition.

When she returned to her home in Greenwood, she was weak and had problems maintaining her house-hold.

In July 1971, Frances Malnar executed a will in which she left most of her estate to her living nieces and nephews. One of the nephews, Ralph Stimac, was appointed as the executor of the will. A sum of $100 was devised and bequeathed to St. Mary's Catholic Church of Greenwood, to be used for masses for the repose of her soul and that of her previously deceased husband, Jack Malnar. The document was drafted by her attorney, Clarence Gorsegner.

In March of 1972, Frances Malnar was again hospitalized for two weeks as a result of gastrointestinal bleeding caused by her liver disease. The bleeding was controlled, and she was released from the hospital. Her doctor felt that she should not return home but should enter a nursing home. Genevieve Malnar, the proponent of the 1973 will -- the will in question -- arranged for her to enter the Havenet Nursing Home in Owen, Wisconsin. Frances stayed one week, but returned home because she did not like the surroundings at the nursing home.

After Frances Malnar returned home, Genevieve, who also lived in Greenwood, helped her buy groceries, drove her to the bank in Marshfield and to her doctor appointments, assisted her in taking certain medications, and visited her two or three times a month. In addition, Genevieve talked to her on the telephone almost daily.

In July 1972, Frances Malnar gave Genevieve Malnar a power of attorney. The document was drafted by Attorney Clarence Gorsegner, who had drafted the will executed by Frances in July 1971. Genevieve Malnar used the power of attorney to open a checking account, from which she wrote checks and paid bills for Frances.

On June 18, 1973, Frances was again hospitalized for increasing liver failure. During her stay in the hospital, Frances was visited regularly by her long-time friend, Mary Miksha, the mother of the proponent, Genevieve Malnar. Mary Miksha had been a neighbor of Frances in Willard, Wisconsin, before Mary moved to Marshfield in the early 1950's. After she moved to Marshfield, Mary visited Frances approximately every other week. This had continued for some twenty years. These visits continued while Frances was hospitalized. During a visit to the hospital in June 1973, Frances told Mary she wanted to move in with Mary. Frances did not believe that she could remain in her home in Greenwood any longer, because she was too sick. Mary told Frances that she was welcome to come any time. The two women talked about arrangements for some kind of payment for allowing Frances to move in with Mary, but they did not agree on any specific amount. Frances told Mary that this could be settled when Frances moved in with Mary. Frances was released from the hospital on

July 3, 1973. Instead of moving in with Mary, however, she went to the Marshfield Convalescent Center on the advice of her doctor, Dr. Wyman. She stayed there from July 3, 1973, until her death on September 3, 1973.

Mary Miksha continued to visit Frances Malnar regularly after Frances went to the convalescent center. They had a conversation in Croatian on July 29, 1973. According to Mary, they talked just like two sisters about Frances moving from the convalescent center to Mary's home. Frances told Mary she would sell her house in Greenwood or give it to Mary's daughter, Genevieve. Mary advised her not to do so, because Frances might not like it in Mary's home and if she disposed of her property she would have no place to go. Frances agreed with Mary and decided that she would keep the house.

On July 30, 1973, Genevieve Malnar contacted William J. Dehn, a Marshfield attorney who had previously done some work for Genevieve's mother, Mary Miksha. Dehn did not know Genevieve or Frances Malnar. Genevieve asked Dehn to come to the convalescent center to draft a will for Frances. Dehn went to the center and met Genevieve and her husband, Emil Malnar, a nephew of Frances Malnar by marriage. They went to Frances' room, where Frances was lying in bed. Dehn started to talk to Frances, realized that Frances was not understanding him, and asked Genevieve to translate. Dehn did not speak Croatian nor did he understand it. Through Genevieve, Dehn ascertained that Frances was a widow who had no living children and no brothers and sisters but a large number of nieces and nephews. He also learned through translation that Frances wanted all her property to go to Genevieve and wanted to name Genevieve the personal representative of her estate. Dehn had no knowledge of any prior will. Genevieve and Frances then had a conversation in Croatian. Genevieve informed Dehn that Frances did not want to make a will. Dehn turned to leave. Before leaving the room, however, he turned back to Frances' bed and asked her in English if she wanted to leave all of her estate to Genevieve. Frances nodded yes. He also asked her if she wanted Genevieve to administer the estate. Frances again nodded yes. These questions were put to Frances directly without any translation. Dehn then told Frances in English that this would not be possible unless she made a will, and that if she did not make a will, her property would go to her nieces and nephews. This latter statement was translated by Genevieve. Frances looked at Dehn for a long period of time, then lowered her eyes and spoke something in Croatian. Dehn understood from her expression and demeanor that he was to go ahead and draft the will. Genevieve also translated Frances' direction to draft the will.

Dehn returned to his office, drafted the will and took it back to the convalescent center the same day. Accompanying him was Elmer Martens, the office manager of Dehn's law firm. The two went to Frances' room, where they met Genevieve and Emil

Malnar. Dehn handed Genevieve a copy of the will and addressed Frances in English, while in possession of the original. He summarized the will, but did not attempt to read it line for line. Dehn then asked Genevieve to translate what he had said. After Genevieve completed the translation, Dehn addressed Frances in English, without the aid of translation. Dehn asked Frances if she realized this was her will, and she nodded. He asked her if she realized that, if she signed the will, her nieces and nephews would not receive any of her estate. Frances gave some indication that she did. Dehn then explained that the will would give everything to Genevieve and that Genevieve would be the administrator. He then asked Frances if she was ready to execute the will. She nodded yes. Because Frances was weak and the bed could not be raised, Genevieve and Emil propped her up with pillows and held her. She then tried to sign the will with a ballpoint pen given her by Dehn, but she could not exert enough pressure to make the pen write. Dehn asked her to make an X, which she did, and he marked the will above and below the mark. Martens and Dehn then signed as witnesses.

On the foregoing record, the trial court denied probate of the will. This appeal raises two issues. First, is there sufficient evidence that Frances Malnar understood the contents of her will. Second, did the objector prove undue influence by clear and convincing evidence?

Proof that a will has been duly executed creates a presumption that the will is valid, but this court has held that the presumption is overcome by evidence showing that the testatrix did not know the contents of the instrument at the time of its execution. *Estate of Barnes* (1961), 14 Wis. 2d 643, 112 N. W. 2d 142.

If a will has been duly executed, it is presumed that the testatrix understood the contents of the document she has signed. *Will of Walter* (1885), 64 Wis. 487, 25 N. W. 538. Once the proponent establishes that the will was duly executed, the burden of persuasion shifts to the opponent to bring forth evidence indicating that the nonexistence of the presumed fact (knowledge of contents) is more probable than its existence. Sec 903.01, Stats.

An opponent to the will satisfies this burden by showing that the testatrix did not understand the language in which the will was written. Where this is the case, it is presumed that the testatrix did not understand the contents of the will. *Walter, supra.* Once an opponent to the will shows that the testatrix did not understand the language in which the will was written, the proponent of the will carries the burden of showing that the testatrix was correctly informed of the contents of the will and understood it. Sec. 903.01, Stats.; *Barnes, supra; Will of Arneson: Quale v. White* (1906), 128 Wis.

112, 107 N. W. 21; *Will of Zych* (1947), 251 Wis. 108, 28 N. W. 2d 316. Proponent may satisfy this burden in any number of ways, normally by showing that the contents of the will were communicated to the testatrix in her own language or by showing that the will was drafted according to her directions. *Walter, supra; Quale, supra; Zych, supra.*

In the instant case, the trial court held that there was no proof that the testatrix understood the contents of the will, so that the proponent, Genevieve Malnar, had failed to carry her burden of making satisfactory proof on this issue. The court noted that the contents of the will had only been summarized by Dehn, the draftsman, and that the information had been relayed by Genevieve Malnar, the sole beneficiary, who was foreclosed from testifying as to what she told the deceased under the Dead Man's Statute, sec. 885.16. The court also noted that paragraph 1 of the will refers to nieces and nephews and states that the testatrix had no knowledge of their names and addresses. The court noted that this was not accurate, because in the past she had sent money orders to some and letters to others.

It is clear that the proponent is unable to show that testatrix knew the contents of the will by virtue of Genevieve's translation, as proponent was the translator and was foreclosed, under the Dead Man's Statute, sec. 885.16, from testifying what was translated. Proponent, however, attempts to show that Frances Malnar had knowledge of the contents of the will by arguing that the will was drawn in accordance with her instructions. Proponent contends that testatrix thus had knowledge of the dispositive scheme of the will and thus was aware of the contents of the will. While we agree that a knowledge of the dispositive scheme may suffice to show a knowledge of the contents of the will, we cannot say that testatrix had such knowledge in the present case.

Absent the testimony of the translator in this case, the only evidence indicating that the will was drawn in accordance with the testatrix's instructions or showing testatrix's knowledge of the dispositive scheme comes from Attorney Dehn. Dehn testified that, prior to preparing the will, he asked Frances in English, and without the aid of translation, whether she wanted to leave all of her estate to Genevieve and whether she wanted Genevieve to administer the estate. Dehn testified that Frances nodded yes to both of these inquiries. Dehn also testified that, just prior to the execution of the will, he explained that the will gave everything to Genevieve and nothing to her nieces and nephews. Dehn then asked Frances in English whether she realized this was her will and whether she was ready to execute the will, to which Frances nodded yes.

While the above testimony is certainly probative of testatrix's knowledge of the contents of the will, the trial court felt that it was insufficient to show clearly that the testatrix was accurately informed of the contents and meaning of the will. This is what is required. *Walter, supra; Quale, supra.* A finding of fact by the trial court will not be upset on appeal unless it is against the great weight and clear preponderance of the evidence. *Estate of Velk* (1972), 53 Wis. 2d 500, 192 N. W. 2d 844.

On appeal we examine the record, not for facts to support a finding the trial court did not make or could have made, but for facts that support the finding the trial court did make. *Estate of Hamm* (1975), 67 Wis. 2d 279, 282, 227 N. W. 2d 34. Given the fact that the testatrix spoke very little English and given the error appearing on the face of the will in regard to testatrix's knowledge of the addresses of her nieces and nephews, as well as the other circumstances present here, we cannot say that testatrix's nods to the several inquiries put to her in English by Attorney Dehn concerning the dispositive scheme of the will were sufficient to show clearly testatrix's knowledge of the contents and meaning of the will. In any event, we cannot say that the trial court's finding to the contrary was against the great weight and clear preponderance of the evidence.

Apart from the question of testatrix's knowledge of the contents and meaning of the will, the will was properly denied admission to probate because of undue influence in the execution of the will. Ordinarily, the test of undue influence on a testatrix is fourfold: (1) was there opportunity to influence, (2) was there a disposition to influence, (3) was there susceptibility to influence, and (4) was a coveted result obtained. An opponent to the will must prove each of these elements by clear, satisfactory, and convincing evidence. *Estate of Von Ruden* (1972), 55 Wis. 2d 365, 373, 198 N. W. 2d 583.

Undue influence may also be proved under a second approach. Where the relationship between the testatrix and the principal beneficiary is "confidential or fiduciary" in nature, that fact, "coupled with the existence of 'suspicious circumstances,'" is enough to create the presumption or inference of undue influence. *Von Ruden, supra*, p. 373.

An examination of the record in the instant case clearly shows that the opponent of the will was entitled to invoke the presumption of undue influence. Genevieve Malnar was given a power of attorney for Frances Malnar in July 1972. Thus, there was a fiduciary relationship between the proponent -- sole beneficiary -- and the testatrix. *Estate of Von Ruden, supra*, p. 377.

Furthermore, there existed a confidential relationship between testatrix and the person who engaged in procuring the drafting of the will and who took a benefit thereunder -- Genevieve Malnar. Frances Malnar relied heavily on Genevieve Malnar for transportation, maintaining her household, assisting her in taking medication, making translations for her, and assisting her in financial matters. These factors indicate the presence of a confidential relationship. *Will of Cooper* (1965), 28 Wis. 2d 391, 137 N. W. 2d 93; *Estate of Steffke* (1970), 48 Wis. 2d 45, 179 N. W. 2d 846.

The record is also replete with suspicious circumstances surrounding the execution of the will. Proponent procured the drafting of the will and participated in the drafting and execution of the will in which she was the sole beneficiary. The attorney who drafted the will was not the personal attorney of the deceased. Rather, he was the attorney of the proponent's mother and had never met the testatrix. Proponent did all of the translation required in the execution of the will. Attorney Dehn was informed by Genevieve, translating for Frances, that Frances had no sisters when she did have a sister living in Yugoslavia. There was no explanation given for the sudden change in the attitude of the testatrix from that expressed in the 1971 will, which bequeathed her estate to nieces and nephews as well as leaving money to the church of which she was a member. The 1973 will eliminated the nieces and nephews as well as the church and substituted proponent as the sole beneficiary.

The will was made in haste -- the discussion of the terms of the will and its execution were completed on the same day. Testatrix showed some reluctance in making the will and, in fact, at first refused to do so, but suddenly and without explanation changed her mind. The testatrix was in such a weak and debilitated condition that she had to be held up in bed, and even then did not have the strength to sign her name. At the funeral, Genevieve told one of the nephews that she knew that Frances left a will naming her as personal representative, but did not know the contents of the will. None of the nieces and nephews had been informed of the seriousness of testatrix's condition in the summer of 1973 or that testatrix was considering making another will, despite the fact that proponent knew that testatrix was near death. Rather, proponent waited until after testatrix's death to inform the nieces and nephews of what had transpired. Many of these factors have previously been recognized by this court as evidence of suspicious circumstances. *Komarr, supra; Von Ruden, supra; Hamm, supra; Will of Faulks* (1945), 246 Wis. 319, 17 N. W. 2d 423; *Estate of Perssion* (1963), 20 Wis. 2d 537, 123 N. W. 2d 465.

The basis for the undue influence presumption lies in the ease in which a confidant can dictate the contents, and control or influence the drafting, of a will either as the draftsman or as one who procures the drafting. *Hamm, supra*, p. 294. We agree with the trial court that the opponent to the will introduced sufficient evidence to entitle him to the benefit of the presumption.

Once the presumption was established, the burden of persuasion shifted to the proponent, Genevieve Malnar, to introduce sufficient evidence to rebut the presumption. Genevieve had the burden of proving that the nonexistence of the presumed fact (undue influence) was more probable than its existence. Sec. 903.01, Stats.

In attempting to satisfy her burden of persuasion, Genevieve Malnar introduced evidence indicating that testatrix was a strong-willed woman who was not susceptible to influence. Proponent also introduced evidence indicating that the result obtained under the will in question was not unnatural under the circumstances for the proponent expended a significant amount of time caring for Frances and that Frances viewed the proponent as a daughter. Such evidence, though highly probative on the question of undue influence (*Perssion, supra; Hamm, supra*), does not necessarily overcome the presumption of undue influence. *Komarr, supra.*

The dispositive issue is whether the trial court's finding of undue influence on the part of Genevieve Malnar was contrary to the great weight and clear preponderance of the evidence. *Hamm, supra.* The trial court could not find that the evidence adduced by proponent was sufficient to overcome the presumption of undue influence by Genevieve Malnar.

While the evidence presented by the proponent could support a finding of a lack of undue influence, we cannot conclude that the trial court's finding of undue influence is against the great weight and clear preponderance of the evidence.

II. WILL FORMALITIES

A. REQUIREMENTS FOR A VALID WILL

For a will to be valid, it must comply with the terms of the Wills Act of the jurisdiction in which the will is executed. American wills acts were originally based on the 1677 English Statute of Frauds, which significantly limited the use of oral wills and which required wills devising real property to be in writing, signed by the testator or by someone on his behalf and at his direction, and attested by at least three witnesses who signed in the presence of the testator who "published" (i.e., declared the will to be valid) in the presence of the witnesses. The requirements were extended to personal property by the British Wills Act of 1837, which also added the requirement that the will be signed at the bottom but reduced the number of subscribing witnesses from three to two and relaxed the requirement that the will be "published."

Until relatively recently, the requirements of the Wisconsin Wills Act reflected the concerns of these earlier English statutes, especially the view that formal requirements could be used to protect against fraud and to convince testators that the drawing of a will was a serious matter. However, in recent years, the emphasis on will formalities has been reduced in Wisconsin, as it has in many United States jurisdictions. Overall, this "revolt against formalism" has argued for a *reduction in the number of formalities*, for the doctrine of *substantial compliance,* which holds that strict formal compliance is not necessary, so long as the general purpose of the will formalities are accomplished, and, at least in some quarters, the adoption of the *dispensing power,* which was developed in Australia and which gives courts the authority to admit to probate documents that clearly do not meet the requirements of the wills act, so long as the proponents of the document can establish by *clear and convincing evidence* that the deceased intended the document to be his or her will.

Wisconsin has clearly followed the movement to reduce the number of will formalities. It long ago renounced the requirement that the will be formally published by the testator or signed in the presence of the witnesses. Before 1997, wills in Wisconsin had to be signed by two witness, each of whom signed in the presence of the other and the testator (the traditional English requirement), but this requirement has also been abolished. Essentially, the only formalities in Wisconsin are that the will be in writing, that it be signed, and that it be witnessed by two disinterested witnesses.

The Wisconsin Supreme Court was also an early advocate of the principle of substantial compliance, stating in *In re Noon's Will*, 115 Wis. 299, 91 N.W. 670 (1902), that a will was valid so long as it was "executed *in substantial conformity* to the statutory requirements," 114 Wis. At 303 (emphasis added). However, as the contrasting results in the two following cases indicate, the standards for "substantial conformity" are, to say the least, somewhat vague in Wisconsin. To date, Wisconsin has not embraced the dispensing power, or what the Uniform Probate Code refers to as the "Harmless Error" rule. Nor has it modified its Wills Act to accommodate notarized, electronic, or filmed or videotaped wills. While at one time the state accepted the legitimacy of holographic wills—wills that are unwitnessed but in the handwriting of the testator—this exception to the wills act formalities was abolished long ago, as was any recognition of oral wills.

Wis. Stat. 853.03. Execution of wills.

Every will in order to be validly executed must be in writing and executed with all of the following formalities:

(1) It must be signed by the testator, by the testator with the assistance of another person with the testator's consent or in the testator's name by another person at the testator's direction and in the testator's conscious presence.

(2) (am) It must be signed by at least 2 witnesses who signed within a reasonable time after any of the following:

1. The signing of the will as provided under sub. (1), in the conscious presence of the witness.

2. The testator's implicit or explicit acknowledgement of the testator's signature on the will, in the conscious presence of the witness.

3. The testator's implicit or explicit acknowledgement of the will, in the conscious presence of the witness.

(bm) The 2 witnesses required under par. (am) may observe the signing or acknowledgement under par. (am) 1. to 3. at different times.

Uniform Probate Code 2-503. Harmless Error. [Not adopted in Wisconsin.]

Although a document or writing added upon a document was not executed in compliance with Section 2-502, the document or writing is treated as if it had been executed in compliance with that section if the proponent of the document or writing establishes by clear and convincing evidence that the decedent intended the document or writing to constitute: (1) the decedent's will, (2) a partial or complete revocation of the will, (3) an addition to or an alteration of the will, or (4) a partial or complete revival of his [or her] formerly revoked will or of a formerly revoked portion of the will.

Wis. Stat. 853.04. Self-proved will.

(1) ONE-STEP PROCEDURE.

A will may be simultaneously executed, attested and made self-proved by the affidavit of the testator and witnesses. The affidavit must be made before an officer authorized to administer oaths under the laws of the state in which execution occurs and must be evidenced by the officer's certificate, under official seal, in substantially the following form: **[omitted].**

(2) TWO-STEP PROCEDURE.

An attested will may be made self-proved at any time after its execution by the affidavit of the testator and witnesses. The affidavit must be made before an officer authorized to administer oaths under the laws of the state in which the affidavit occurs and must be evidenced by the officer's certificate, under official seal, attached or annexed to the will in substantially the following form: **[omitted].**

Wis. Stat. 853.50-853.62. Sample Will with Trust

These provisions of the Wisconsin statutes contain the text of, and instructions for, a sample will designed to meet the needs of the typical Wisconsin citizen. Although endorsed by the Wisconsin legislature, its usage garners no special benefits for the testator when the will is submitted to probate.

In re Wilcox's Estate

Supreme Court of Wisconsin
215 Wis. 341, 254 N.W. 529 (1934)

WICKHEM, J.

Testatrix executed a will in January, 1930; a second will February 26, 1930, and a third will November 21, 1930. Objections to the will of November 21st were made upon the grounds that testatrix was mentally incompetent, and that the execution of the instrument was secured by undue influence. The trial court found against the contestants upon all these issues after a lengthy trial, during the course of which the mental state of the testatrix during the entire period covered by the three wills was disclosed, as well as the circumstances under which each will was executed.

So far as the questions of mental competency and undue influence are concerned, the issues are solely of fact and no useful judicial service will be performed by a review of the evidence, which occupies six hundred pages of the record. Suffice to say that we do not consider the findings of the trial court to be contrary to the great weight and clear preponderance of the evidence. Were this the only issue here presented, there would be no occasion for an opinion.

However, appellants' contention that the will of November 21st was not properly executed, presents an issue of law to which an opinion may usefully be addressed. At the time of the execution of this will testatrix was aged and infirm, and had suffered a stroke of paralysis. She was physically unable to write her signature or, unaided, even to make her mark. There is no evidence of an express request that the scrivener make this mark for her. Sec. 238.06, Stats., provides:

"No will made . . . shall be effectual to pass any estate . . . unless it be . . . signed by the testator or by some person in his presence and by his express direction. . . ."

It is clear that the statute is not satisfied by anything short of an express direction. It is in evidence, however, that while the scrivener made the mark for her, testatrix touched the pen while this mark was being made. It is earnestly and ably contended that the touching of the pen does not constitute the making of the mark by the testatrix, and that since there was no express direction to the scrivener or to any one else to make the mark for testatrix, the execution does not satisfy the statutory requirements.

Since there was no express direction to the scrivener to make the mark, the question is whether the touching of the pen by testatrix, as the scrivener made the mark, was a sufficient participation in the act to warrant a holding that the mark was that of the testatrix and not the scrivener. In *Will of Grant,* 149 Wis. 330, 135 N.W. 833, it was said:

"It is the common and usual practice for the scrivener to make the mark, the party merely touching the pen while it is being made."

The implication is that this is a sufficient satisfaction of the statutory requirements. It is our conclusion that such an execution satisfies the statute; that such a participation in the making of the mark, makes the act that of the testatrix. It furnished objective evidence of assent, and doubtless represented as much participation in the act as testatrix was physically capable of.

Estate of Wilm

Supreme Court of Wisconsin
182 Wis. 242, 196 N.W. 255 (1923)

APPEAL from a judgment of the county court of Milwaukee County: M. S. SHERIDAN, Judge. Affirmed.

Proceedings for the probate of the will of Charles Wilm, deceased. The testator made his will about 8:30 o'clock a. m. March 14, 1922, and died about 11 o'clock p. m. on the same day. When the will was executed by him and signed by the witnesses he was sitting up in a bed located in the northwest corner of a bedroom about ten feet square. In the center of the south wall was a door leading out into the living room, which was about the size of the bedroom. Near the northwest corner of the living room a door led out to the kitchen. A little west and north of this door and in the center of the kitchen stood a table. After the testator had signed the will sitting up in the bed, the scrivener, Max Gruenwald, took the will and requested a witness, Edward Johnson, who had been standing near the door leading from the bedroom to the living room, to follow him to the kitchen, which he did. Here upon the kitchen table the two signed the will as witnesses. A third witness, Anton Ernst, came in later and signed it.

The court found:

"That Max Gruenwald and Edward Johnson signed said instrument in the presence of each other, but not in the presence of said Charles Wilm, and that Anton Ernst thereafter signed said instrument, not in the presence of Charles Wilm, and that he did not see either Max Gruenwald or Edward Johnson sign said instrument, the same having been signed by them before his entry into the kitchen, and that none of the witnesses to said instrument signed said instrument in the presence of the testator, and that neither one of said witnesses was personally or directly requested to sign said instrument as a witness by said Charles Wilm, and that said Charles Wilm did not declare, in the presence of either Edward Johnson or Anton Ernst, that said instrument was his last will and testament."

The court denied the probate of the will because it was not executed in the manner provided by law, and the proponent appealed.

VINJE, C. J. The question raised by the appeal is whether the witnesses, or any of them, signed in the presence of the testator as required by sec. 2282, Stats. Were this a case of first construction of the statute it might well be that the facts bring the attestation within the statute, giving to the word "presence" the broad liberal meaning that some courts have given it. But our court in an early day in the case of *Will of Downie,* 42 Wis. 66, decided in 1877, held that the witnesses must subscribe in a place where the testator, if not blind, may, if he so desires, see them sign, and that the statute is not satisfied by the will being brought to the testator after it is subscribed by witnesses in an adjoining room where he cannot see them, though he assents to and approves of the attestation. This rule seems a harsh one, but it is prescribed by the legislature and it must be given the construction that the language naturally requires. An act cannot be said to be done in the presence of another when it is outside of his range of vision and beyond his sense of hearing. Even if the word "presence" is construed to mean within a sphere where the senses of the testator can inform him of the performance of the act, the present case would not come within the statute, for he could neither hear ordinary conversation in the kitchen nor see what was being done on the kitchen table from any point in the bedroom he occupied. It is true the distance from the kitchen table through the wall of the bedroom to the bed was perhaps less than ten feet, but the solid wall prevented both the senses of hearing and seeing from ascertaining what was being done. Of course a man both deaf and blind may make a valid will, because the statutory test of presence is based upon a normal human being. If it is within his presence then it is equally within the presence of a blind or deaf man or one who is both.

When a will for the purpose of attestation is taken to a place where a testator of normal senses, though he desires so to do, cannot by his own act or by the aid of others in moving him either hear what is said or see the execution of the attestation, it must be deemed to be not within his presence. To hold otherwise would be to permit a will to be taken entirely away from the testator for purposes of attestation. It was the purpose of the statute to require the attestation of the witnesses to be in the presence of the testator as the word "presence" is ordinarily used, that is, in a place where the testator can by the use of his senses ascertain what is being done. When the place is beyond the reach of any of his senses it is no longer within his presence. That it need not necessarily be in the same room is established by the case of *Will of Meurer,* 44 Wis. 392. The case of *Will of Downie,* 42 Wis. 66, contains a detailed discussion of the reasons for the rule there announced and no restatement of such reasons will here be made. For a good discussion of the subject by other courts see *Riggs v. Riggs,* 135 Mass. 238; *Cook v. Winchester,* 81 Mich. 581, 46 N.W. 106, 8 L. R. A. 822, and note.

It is urged that since the attestation clause imports verity and that in the case of the death of the witnesses before probate the presumption that they signed in the presence of the testator would be sufficient to admit the will to probate, it should be admitted under the evidence as it stands. The answer to that is that we must decide the case upon the evidence in the record, and not upon evidence as it might have been had it been impossible to secure the evidence of the witnesses to the will. Judgment affirmed.

B. HOLOGRAPHIC AND ORAL WILLS AND WILLS FROM OTHER JURISDICTIONS

At one time Wisconsin also accepted unwitnessed wills written in the testator's handwriting (holographic wills) as alternatives to wills executed in compliance with the Wills Act, but that option was eliminated for Wisconsin residents in 1896. Similarly, oral wills were once eligible for probate in Wisconsin, albeit only under extremely limited circumstances, primarily when they were formulated by soldiers and sailors during combat and then only to transfer tangible personal property. However, since 1969, all forms of oral wills have been prohibited in Wisconsin.

On the other hand, under certain circumstances, Wisconsin will accept a holographic will for probate, if it were executed by an individual who was domiciled in Wisconsin at the time of his or her death, but who had been domiciled in a state where holographic wills were permitted when the will at issue was executed. (Almost half of the states currently permit holographic wills.). Furthermore, a holographic will that it valid in the state in which the testator was domiciled at death can be admitted to probate in Wisconsin for purpose of transferring Wisconsin real property. If A, a Virginia resident, dies owning land in Wisconsin, his valid Virginia holographic will can be used in Wisconsin as a basis for transferring the Wisconsin real estate to the next owner.

As a general rule, wills of Wisconsin residents can be submitted to probate in Wisconsin so long as they were validly executed in the state in which the testator resided when the will was executed.

Wis. Stat. 853.05. Execution of wills outside the state or by nonresidents within this state.

(1) A will is validly executed if it is in writing and any of the following applies:

(a) The will is executed according to s. 853.03 (b) The will is executed in accordance with the law, at the time of execution or at the time of death, of any of the following:

1. The place where the will was executed.

2. The place where the testator resided, was domiciled or was a national at the time of execution.

3. The place where the testator resided, was domiciled or was a national at the time of death.

(2) Any will under sub. (1) (b) has the same effect as if executed in this state in compliance with s. 853.03

Wis. Stat. 868.01. Uniform probate of foreign wills act

(1) PROBATE ON PROOF OF DOMICILIARY PROBATE; EFFECT. The written will of a testator who died domiciled outside this state, which upon probate may operate upon any property in this state, shall be admitted to probate upon proof that it stands probated or established in the jurisdiction where the testator died domiciled and is not being contested there. A will probated under this subsection is sufficient to operate on any property within the terms of the will, subject to any limitations upon its operation imposed by the law of the jurisdiction where the testator died domiciled. Rights to take against the will are not affected by this subsection.

(2) LOCAL CONTEST LIMITED; SETTING ASIDE LOCAL PROBATE. A will offered for probate under sub. (1) may be contested only upon the ground that the conditions of that subsection are not met or that it has been finally rejected from probate in this state; but probate under sub. (1) shall be set aside upon proof that probate or establishment of the will has been set aside in the jurisdiction where the testator died domiciled, if, within one year after such probate in this state under sub. (1), application is made in this state to set aside such probate upon such ground, or verified notice that proceedings have been taken to contest the will in the jurisdiction where the testator died domiciled, is filed, and in the case of real property, also recorded as provided in sub. (3)

(3) PROTECTION OF PROBATE UNDER SUB. (1)

If within one year after probate under sub. (1), verified notice that proceedings have been taken to contest the will in the jurisdiction where the testator died domiciled is filed in the court of this state where probate was granted, and, in the case of real property, also recorded in the office of the register of deeds in the county where the real property is located, the protection of probate ceases until proof that the domiciliary proceedings have been terminated in favor of the will or were never actually taken is filed and, in the case of real property, also recorded as provided herein.

(4) EFFECT OF REJECTION OF WILL AT DOMICILE. Final rejection of the will from probate or establishment in the jurisdiction where the testator died domiciled is conclusive in this state except where the will has been rejected solely for a cause which is not ground for rejection of a will of a testator who died domiciled in this state, in which case the will nevertheless may be admitted to probate under sub. (5)

(5) ORIGINAL PROBATE; WHEN ALLOWED. Original probate of the will of a testator who died domiciled outside this state, which upon probate may operate upon any property in this state and is valid under the laws of this state, may be granted if the will does not stand rejected from probate or establishment in the jurisdiction where the testator died domiciled, or stands rejected from probate or establishment in the jurisdiction where the testator died domiciled solely for a cause which is not ground for rejection of a will of a testator who died domiciled in this state. The court may delay passing on the application for probate under this

subsection pending the result of probate or establishment or contest at the domicile or on the application for probate under sub. (1)

(6) PROOF OF WILL BY PROBATE IN NONDOMICILIARY JURISDICTION. If a testator dies domiciled outside this state, an authenticated copy of the testator's will and of the probate or establishment thereof in a jurisdiction other than the one in which testator died domiciled shall be sufficient proof of the contents and legal sufficiency of the will to authorize the admission of the will to probate under sub. (5) if no objection is made thereto. This subsection does not authorize the probate of any will which would not be admissible to probate under sub. (5), nor, in case objection is made to the will, to relieve proponent from offering proof of the contents and legal sufficiency of the will except that the original will need not be produced unless the court so orders.

(7) AUTHENTICATION AND TRANSLATION. Proof contemplated by this section may be made by authenticated copies of the will and the records of judicial proceedings with reference thereto. If the will has not been probated but is otherwise established under the laws of the jurisdiction where the testator died domiciled, its contents and establishment may be proved by the authenticated certificate of the notary or other official having custody of the will or having authority in connection with its establishment. If the respective documents or any part thereof are not in the English language, verified translations may be attached thereto and shall be regarded as sufficient proof of the contents of the documents unless objection is made thereto. If any person in good faith relies upon probate under this section the person shall not thereafter be prejudiced because of inaccuracy of such translations, or because of proceedings to set aside or modify the probate on that ground.

(8) GENERAL LAW TO APPLY. Except where otherwise provided, the law of this state relating to wills and to the probate, contest and effect thereof shall apply in case of a testator who died domiciled outside this state.

(9) UNIFORMITY OF INTERPRETATION. This section shall be so interpreted and construed as to effectuate its general purpose to make uniform the law of those states which enact it.

In re Estate of Warner

Wisconsin Court of Appeals

161 Wis. 2d 644, 468 N.W.2d 736 (1991).

Cane, J. Clarence Dennis, who sought to be named personal representative of Rachel Warner's estate, appeals an order rejecting his petition for original probate of Warner's will pursuant to sec. 868.01(5), Stats. We concur with the court's characterization of the issue on appeal as whether it abused its discretion by rejecting the petition for administration. Because the court failed to examine the relevant facts necessary in determining whether to grant or refuse original probate, we reverse and remand the matter for further proceedings.

Warner died in Arizona. The parties do not dispute that at the time of her death she was domiciled in Arizona and owned a house there. One month before the trial court ruled on the Warner estate's petition for administration, it had admitted to probate the will of Warner's sister, Louise Wight, a domiciliary of Wisconsin. Wight predeceased Warner, leaving all her property to Warner.

Prior to her death, Warner sent a two-page handwritten letter to her Wisconsin attorney who was arranging for probate of the Wight estate. The letter indicated, in pertinent part:

> Clarence is happy to be co-executor and will be at Cable for the summer about the middle of this month. …
>
> Since Louise and I were the last of the Dennis family, we had agreed to leave whatever assets remained of our combined estates to the U of Minn School of Mines in honor of our brother, Richard C. Dennis. There will be no bequests of any kind to my brother Harry's 3 children. As soon as it is feasible to draw up a will to that effect, I hope you will do so. This scholarship is to be granted upon my death.

The letter was written on the front and back of one page of stationery. Warner signed her full name on the front and initialed the reverse side.

Holographic wills are not generally recognized as valid in Wisconsin. See sec. 853.03, Stats. However, a will is valid if executed in accordance with the law of the place where the testator is domiciled at the time of the will's execution. Section 853.05, Stats. Arizona recognizes the validity of holographic wills. Prior to the hearing on his petition, Dennis submitted to the court information on Article 5, Title 14, of the Arizona Revised Statutes, which governs the validity of a holographic will in that state. He also indicated the willingness of August G. Eckhardt, former University of Wisconsin Law School professor and author in the 1960's of the Workbook for Wisconsin Estate Planners, presently practicing in Tucson, Arizona, to provide an affidavit or other certification with respect to the Arizona statutes and interpretive case law involved.

Dennis further provided the court with copies of three prior wills executed by Warner, along with a handwritten letter from one legatee of a previous will indicating that "I do not plan to make a claim on her estate." The record discloses that notice of the hearing, along with a copy of Warner's handwritten letter, was properly given all interested parties.

At the hearing, counsel for the University of Minnesota was briefly heard and requested that the court admit Warner's will to probate. Dennis, a cousin of Warner's and executor of Wight's estate, appeared, along with his wife. Three other witnesses who were represented to the court as capable of giving evidence of Warner's testamentary intent were also present. No party appeared to oppose the petition, and no objection to probate had been made prior to the hearing.

Dennis' counsel argued that a number of concerns favored a conclusion that Wisconsin should exercise original probate jurisdiction in this case: the convenience of the court in administering the Wight and Warner estates concurrently; the convenience of Dennis, who would arguably be named administrator of both estates and who was a resident of Minnesota with a summer home in Wisconsin; and the convenience of the University of Minnesota, the principal legatee under Warner's proffered holographic will. The trial court responded:

> I think there are serious legal issues that have to be decided as to whether or not this will qualify as holographic Will. I have already indicated she was an Arizona resident, she was domiciled in Arizona at the time of death. Arizona law will have to be applied and it is going to be my decision that [the] Arizona Court[ ] will be the one that's going to interpret it. (Emphasis added.)

In its written decision, the court rejected the petition "because decedent's domicile in Arizona makes Arizona the proper state and Wisconsin an improper state for administration." The court noted that it reserved any ruling on the validity of the proffered holographic will.

Section 868.01(5), Stats., provides:

> Original probate; when allowed. Original probate of the will of a testator who died domiciled outside this state, which upon probate may operate upon any property in this state and is valid under the laws of this state, may be granted if the will does not stand rejected from probate or establishment in the jurisdiction where the testator died domiciled, or stands rejected from probate or establishment in the jurisdiction where the testator died domiciled solely for a cause which is not ground for rejection of a will of a testator who died domiciled in this state. The court may delay passing on the application for probate under this subsection pending the result of probate or establishment or contest at the domicile or on the application for probate under sub. (1).

Counsel for the University of Minnesota informed the court at the petition hearing that there was no evidence of any attempt to have Warner's will admitted in probate in Arizona, and no evidence that it had been rejected there.

Dennis contends that sec. 868.01(5), Stats., and interpretative case law grant the estates of nonresident decedents who own Wisconsin property the right to original probate with certain exceptions. In Dennis' view, original probate could be refused where the will stands rejected from probate or establishment in the jurisdiction of the testator's domicile and could be delayed where proceedings for probate, establishment or contest have been initiated in the state of domicile or an application for probate under another statutory subsection has been made. Absent these conditions, he contends the estate has a statutory right to original probate.

Statutory construction is a question of law that we decide de novo. Cornellier Fireworks Co. v. St. Croix County, 119 Wis. 2d 44, 46, 349 N.W.2d 721, 722 (Ct. App. 1984). In construing a statute, we ascertain the intent of the legislature by looking first to the language of the statute itself. Doe v. Roe, 151 Wis. 2d 366, 373-74, 444 N.W.2d 437, 441 (Ct. App. 1989). We assign the statutory language its ordinary and accepted meaning and will resort to outside sources to aid statutory construction only if the language is ambiguous. Id.

We conclude that the language of sec. 868.01(5), Stats., is not ambiguous. The statute instructs that a Wisconsin court "may" grant original probate under certain conditions. Another subsection of the same statute, sec. 868.01(1), directs that a Wisconsin court "shall" admit a will to probate upon proof that it stands probated or established in the jurisdiction where the testator died domiciled and is not being contested there. The word "shall" is generally construed as mandatory and "may" is generally construed as permissive. State v. Camara, 28 Wis. 2d 365, 371, 137 N.W.2d 1, 4 (1965). Such a construction of the word "may" is especially indicated where the word "shall" appears in close juxtaposition in other parts of the same statute. Scanlon v. City of Menasha, 16 Wis. 2d 437, 443, 114 N.W.2d 791, 795 (1962). We conclude that the use of the term "may" in sec. 868.01(5) is permissive and describes action that a Wisconsin court is empowered to take in the exercise of its discretion.

Interpretive case law supports our conclusion that the trial court's decision to grant or refuse original probate is an exercise of discretion. See In re Tressing, 86 Wis. 2d 502, 511, 273 N.W.2d 271, 276 (1979); see also Annotation: Probate, In State Where Assets are Found, Of Will of Nonresident Which Has Not Been Admitted to Probate In State of Domicile, 20 A.L.R.3d 1033, 1058 (1968) ("The courts . . . have . . . taken the position that such jurisdiction may be assumed or declined by the probate court in the exercise of a sound discretion, such discretion being influenced by comity and the distinctive circumstances surrounding each case."). Because the exercise of discretion is not the equivalent of unfettered decision-making, the record must reflect the trial court's reasoned application of the appropriate legal standard to the relevant facts in the case. Hedtcke v. Sentry Ins. Co., 109 Wis. 2d 461, 471, 326 N.W.2d 727, 732 (1982). Factors that may influence a court in determining whether to exercise its discretionary power to admit the will of a nonresident to probate include the relative rights of the parties in interest and the presence or absence in the state of legatees named in the testamentary instrument. In re Lamborn, 168 Misc. 504, 6 N.Y.S.2d 192 (1938), reprinted in 20 A.L.R.3d at 1059.

The trial court here based its ruling entirely on two facts: first, that Warner owned property in Arizona, which meant that a proceeding in Arizona would be required at some point; and second, that there was a question as to the validity of Warner's proffered holographic will under Arizona law. Neither reason determines whether Wisconsin courts should assume original probate jurisdiction.

We note first that Wisconsin courts may act on property within the state, even though the will has not yet been admitted to probate in the state of domicile, provided other conditions of the statutes are met. Tressing, 86 Wis. 2d at 513, 273 N.W.2d at 277. If proceedings are later commenced in the state of domicile, Wisconsin proceedings will become ancillary. In re Joyce, 238 Wis. 370, 376-77, 298 N.W. 579, 582 (1941). The mere fact that proceedings here will not be considered primary when other proceedings are commenced in the state of domicile is not dispositive.

Second, Wisconsin statutes provide that every court of this state shall take judicial notice of the common-law and statutes of every other state. Section 902.02, Stats. Even before the enactment of the Uniform Judicial Notice of Foreign Law Act, common-law provided that the mere fact that a court will be called upon to administer the laws of another state, without more, is not grounds for a discretionary refusal to entertain an action to enforce a right. Eingartner v. Illinois Steel Co., 94 Wis. 70, 80-81, 68 N.W. 664, 667-68 (1896). Here, Dennis attempted to prove the provisions of Arizona law under which Warner's holographic will might be held valid. A Wisconsin court must take judicial notice of applicable Arizona law and can decide questions of the validity of a proffered holographic will. The need to take judicial notice of foreign law is not, without more, grounds for refusal to exercise discretionary jurisdiction.

Our review of the record indicates that those considerations urged by Dennis' counsel at the hearing, the convenience of the court, of Dennis, and of the University of Minnesota as principal legatee, are factors the court should have considered, but did not, when determining whether to assume original probate jurisdiction. We note that no interested party presented a countervailing interest to the court. For these reasons, we conclude that the trial court failed to exercise its discretion. The order of the trial court is therefore reversed, and the matter is remanded for further proceedings consistent with this opinion.

C. WITNESSES

The traditional rule was that to be a valid witness to a will, the witness had to be "disinterested," which was to say that he or she was not to receive any property through the operation of the will that was signed. If the witness' signature was necessary to prove the will—which would be the case unless there were extra witnesses—then the will failed if the witness or witnesses were interested. To prevent this unfortunate result all states, including Wisconsin, adopted *purging statutes* that converted the *interested* witness into a *disinterested* one by negating the devise to the witness completely. However, if there were additional witnesses so that the signature of the interested witness was not necessary, the statute left the devise to that particular interested witness in place. Although a number of states have followed the lead of the Uniform Probate Code and abolished the prohibition against interested witnesses, many states, including Wisconsin, retain the requirement of disinterested witnesses.

Will of Johnson

Supreme Court of Wisconsin
175 Wis. 1; 183 N.W. 888 (1921)

OWEN, J. This is an appeal from an order or decree of the county court of Racine county construing the will of Theodore W. Johnson, deceased. The case was here on a former appeal from an order admitting the will to probate, and is reported in 170 Wis. 436, 175 N.W. 917, to which reference may be had for facts supplemental to those which will appear in this opinion.

The will of Theodore Johnson constituted *Mrs. L. C. Hahn* the principal beneficiary. She was a witness to the will. The question involved on the former appeal was whether she could testify to the execution of the will. It was there held that she could. The question presented on this appeal is whether *Mrs. Hahn* is entitled to the bequest made to her by the terms of the will. The county court held that the devise and legacy to the said *L. C. Hahn* was and is void because she is a subscribing witness to the will and said will is not attested or subscribed by two other competent witnesses.

There is no serious contention but the law as it existed at the time of the death of the testator is the law that governs as to the question whether *Mrs. Hahn* can take under the will.

"A will is ambulatory during the life of its maker. It is, in effect, reiterated as his testament at each moment of his life after its execution, including the last moment, and is governed by the law existing at the time when it takes effect, upon the testator's death." *Will of Kopmeier,* 113 Wis. 233 (89 N.W. 134) at p. 239.

This fact is mentioned at the outset because it is claimed that the statute which, concededly, controls in this case was amended during the interim between the execution of the will and the death of the testator. That statute is sec. 2284. Prior to the enactment of ch. 128, Laws 1905, that section provided as follows:

"All beneficial devises, legacies and gifts whatsoever, made or given in any will to a subscribing witness thereto, shall be wholly void unless there be two other competent subscribing witnesses to the same; but a mere charge on the lands of the devisor for the payment of debts shall not prevent his creditors from being competent witnesses to his will."

By ch. 128, Laws 1905, that section was amended by voiding gifts made to the husband or wife of a subscribing witness, as well as to the subscribing witness himself, and by dropping out the word "subscribing," so that it now provides that such devises, legacies, and gifts "shall be wholly void unless there be two other competent witnesses to the same." As so amended the section now reads as follows:

"All beneficial devises, legacies and gifts whatsoever, made or given in any will to a subscribing witness thereto, or to the husband or wife of a subscribing witness thereto, shall be wholly void unless there be two other competent witnesses to the same; but a mere charge on the lands of the devisor for the payment of debts shall not prevent his creditors from being competent witnesses to his will."

It will be seen that the purpose of the statute is to void gifts made to a witness to a will, so that a subscribing witness may be a competent witness and the will be established by the testimony of the subscribing witness, unless the will cannot be established without his testimony. That, at least, was clearly the purpose of the statute as it existed prior to the amendment of 1905. It is not seriously disputed that such is the present purpose of the statute, but it is contended that the bequest is saved to the attesting witness if there is another person who can testify to facts showing an execution of the will in conformity with the requirements of the statute. This contention is based on the theory that the amendment dropped out the word "subscribing" and hence the bequest is now saved to a subscribing witness if there is any other competent witness to the same.

It is said that it is not necessary that a competent witness be a subscribing witness. Our first suggestion in response to this contention is that the phrase "witness to a will," or any other written instrument, has a well settled meaning not only in common parlance but in the law. A witness to a deed means a witness who has attached his signature to the deed. A witness to a will means one who has attested the will by subscribing his name thereto. Furthermore, the statute as it now exists requires two other competent witnesses to the will. We take it that the term "competent" as used in this connection means something more than a witness who is free from the many disqualifications visited upon persons by the common law; that is to say, it means not only a person who is under no disability to testify generally in a court of justice, but it means a person who is under no disability to give testimony which will establish the instrument as the will and testament of the testator.

It has been the ruling of courts ever since the statute of frauds required certain instruments to be in writing and signed in the presence of witnesses, that the testimony of the subscribing witnesses constituted primary evidence of the execution thereof by the parties bound thereby, and that no other evidence of such fact could be given until the person seeking to establish the instrument demonstrated his inability to produce the subscribing witnesses because of their death, their absence from the jurisdiction of the court, or that they were *non compos mentis.* It has been universally held that until such showing has been made on the part of him who seeks to establish the instrument, secondary evidence could not be introduced to show the fact of execution. 2 Wigmore, Evidence, §1287 *et seq.,* and note to *Garrett v. Hanshue* (53 Ohio St. 482, 42 N.E. 256) 35 L.R.A. 321, where the general rule upon this subject is summed up as follows:

"The general rule is that the attesting witness to a written instrument is regarded as the person who must be called to prove its execution when he can be had, as it is said that the parties selected him to enable them to refer the execution of the document to him in case any question should arise over its execution. His evidence is regarded as the best evidence, and must be used when the execution is in dispute."

This is a general rule applicable to all written documents which by law are required to be attested by subscribing witnesses. From the time when wills were required to be in writing and attested by subscribing witnesses it has been commonly understood that the will must be proved by the testimony of a subscribing witness if he could be produced, and that other or secondary evidence could be resorted to for that purpose only after a showing that the subscribing witness was dead, or beyond the jurisdiction of the court, or was then *non compos mentis.*

Questions have arisen in some jurisdictions as to whether it was necessary to call all of the subscribing witnesses. *Thornton's Ex'rs v. Thornton's Heirs,* 39 Vt. 122; *Denny v. Pinney,* 60 Vt. 524, 12 A. 108; *Chase v. Lincoln,* 3 Mass. 236. But it has never been doubted that the production of some of the subscribing witnesses was necessary if their presence in court could be secured. In the chancery courts of England it was held that all subscribing witnesses must be produced. As that was the only court which could by its decree establish a will, that doctrine has been held to be the common law of this country; and, except where modified by statute, the law is that all of the subscribing witnesses to a will must be produced unless the impossibility of producing them is made to appear. *Thornton's Ex'rs v. Thornton's Heirs, supra;* 1 Redfield, Wills, pp. 34-39.

The only statute of this state bearing upon this question is sec. 3788, which provides that, if no person shall appear to contest the probate of a will, the court may in its discretion grant probate thereof on the testimony of one of the subscribing witnesses only, and that if none of the subscribing witnesses shall reside in this state at the time fixed for proving the will, or if one or more of them shall have gone to parts unknown, and the court shall be satisfied that such witness, after due diligence used, cannot be found, it may, in its discretion, admit the testimony of other witnesses to prove the sanity of the testator and the execution of the will and may admit proof of his handwriting and of the handwriting of the subscribing witness. This is the only modification of the common-law rule requiring all of the attesting witnesses to be called, to be found in the statutes of this state, and it is a clear recognition that the testimony of the attesting witnesses is indispensable to the establishment of a will if they can be produced at the hearing or trial.

This brings us to the question whether a mere bystander is a competent witness to a will. In this case the subscribing witnesses, including *Mrs. Hahn,* testified at the trial upon the question whether the writing propounded was in fact testator's will. Two or three bystanders also testified that they were present at the time the will was signed, and testified to a number, if not all, of the facts required by statute for the legal execution of a will. Now it is said that these bystanders constituted competent witnesses to the will, by reason of which fact there were two other competent witnesses to the will besides *Mrs. Hahn,* satisfying the calls of sec. 2284, so that the bequest to her does not fail. When the will was propounded for probate a contest was interposed. It could not be admitted upon the testimony of one of the subscribing witnesses. If one only were produced the will must be denied probate.

The question immediately confronting the proponents of the will was the production of the subscribing witnesses or a showing that they could not be produced. As a matter of fact they were both produced and both testified. But supposing they had not testified? Could the testimony of these bystanders have been introduced? Universal authority answers the question in the negative. Their testimony would constitute what the courts call secondary evidence of the fact of execution, and could be introduced only upon a showing that the primary evidence could not be produced.

Under the circumstances, therefore, their testimony was incompetent and inadmissible, and they were not competent witnesses to show the fact of a valid execution of the will. The conclusion seems irresistible that these bystanders were not witnesses to the will, much less were they competent witnesses. They witnessed a mere transaction. To become what in common parlance as well as law is known and understood as a witness to the will required their identification therewith by the subscribing of their names thereto. While they may have been able to testify to the fact that the testator signed this document under certain circumstances and in a certain manner, that in nowise identified them with the will so that they may be said to be witnesses to the same.

But it is asked, What was the purpose of the legislature in dropping out the word "subscribing" in its amendment of sec. 2284, Stats., by ch. 128, Laws 1905? One very good answer to this inquiry is that the legislature undoubtedly considered it mere surplusage, which in fact it was, because under the law existing at that time a competent witness to a will must have been a subscribing witness. It is by no means unusual for the statute to use the mere term "witness" to a will when it is plain it means a "subscribing witness" to the will. That is evident from the last part of sec. 2284, which was unaffected by the amendment of 1905, providing: "but a mere charge on the lands of the devisor for the payment of debts shall not prevent his creditors from being competent witnesses to his will." Who will doubt that the words "competent witness" as there used, both before and after the amendment, meant a subscribing witness?

When the word "subscribing" was dropped out of the preceding similar expression in the first part of the section it harmonized with the expression used in the last part of the section. Another instance of where the legislature refers to the subscribing witness to a will by the use of the mere term "witness" is sec. 3292. As a matter of fact, not only statutes but textwriters and judges commonly refer to the subscribing witnesses to a will as "witnesses."

But whether we are correct in our assumption that the legislature dropped out the word "subscribing" because it was mere surplusage, we cannot ascribe to the legislature a purpose of working such a radical change in the law as would result from the construction contended for by appellant. In the first place, the inquiry suggests itself, how, and by whom, and when is it to be determined whether a mere bystander is in fact a witness to a will? Is he a witness to a will because, perchance, he sees a testator sign his will and no more? Is he a witness to a will because he hears the testator declare the document to be his will and request the witnesses to sign the same, but does not see them sign? Is he a witness to a will if he sees one of the attesting witnesses sign, but sees no more?

In order to constitute him a witness to a will, must he be able to testify to all the facts showing a legal execution of the will? And if so, when, and where, and how is his status in such respect to be established? It will ofttimes happen that there will be no occasion for his giving his testimony in court, as where there is no contest, unless, forsooth, this amendment be held to operate to do away with the necessity of producing attesting witnesses to the will upon the probate thereof. Unless his testimony be given sometime during the course of the proceeding upon issues raised or some legitimate subject of inquiry, how is the court to tell whether he was a witness to the will or not? Is the witness at some time to submit to a moot interrogation and cross-examination to enable the court to say whether he was in fact a witness to the will?

Of course if he is to be held competent to take the place of a subscribing witness upon the hearing for the probate thereof, then it may be adjudged from his testimony so given; but is it to be held that the legislature contemplated such a radical change in the law by such inconspicuous action? Did the legislature intend, by the mere dropping out of the word "subscribing" in sec. 2284, to obviate the necessity of calling subscribing witnesses to establish the will, and thus do away with a principle firmly intrenched in the common law and tacitly recognized by the statutes of this state above quoted? The presumption in construing statutes is against any radical change of legislative policy. It is presumed that there is no intention to depart from any established policy of the law; to innovate upon fundamental principles. 2 Lewis's Sutherland, Stat. Constr. (2d ed.) p. 931, §499.

The amendment by which the word "subscribing" was dropped out of sec. 2284 made two changes in that section. It disqualified the wife or the husband of a subscribing witness, in addition to the witness himself, from taking under the will. It also omitted the term "subscribing." If the omission of that word is to have the effect for which appellant contends, it was by far the more important of the two changes and worked a more radical change in the existing law. Nevertheless, the title to the bill resulting in ch. 128, Laws 1905, made no mention of this feature of the bill. It was entitled: "An act amending sections 2284 and 2285 of the statutes of 1898 and making valid wills containing beneficial provisions in favor of husband or wife of a subscribing witness by making such provisions void." Not a word as to qualifying bystanders; not a word as to constituting mere bystanders witnesses to a will; and not a word as to obviating the necessity of producing subscribing witnesses to establish the will. We cannot think the legislature had in mind any such sweeping change or innovation. Had such been its purpose it certainly would have dignified it by some mention of it in the title to the act.

Upon these considerations we cannot impute to the legislature the purpose suggested by the appellant. We do not think it was the intention to change the law with reference to the probate of wills or the competency of witnesses in the least. We do not think it was the intention to designate as witnesses to a will a class of persons who had never before been so regarded since wills were required to be subscribed by attesting witnesses. Judgment affirmed.

ROSENBERRY and ESCHWEILER, JJ., dissented.

ESCHWEILER, J. (dissenting). "All men are liars" sang King David; he said it in haste but permitted it to stand. Nevertheless even under the old Hebrew law that one was financially interested in the result of a lawsuit did not, apparently, prevent his being sworn and giving testimony. Michaelis, Laws of Moses, vol. IV, p. 345, quoting the apostrophe to the man to be honored from Psalm 15, "He that sweareth to his own hurt, and changeth not."

Centuries afterwards and as early as the seventeenth century (1 Wigmore, Evidence, § 575), and at the time when juries first began to consider information as to the issues other than that which they themselves possessed as dwellers in the same neighborhood, this expression of the Hebrew poet was apparently crystallized into the common-law rule of evidence to the effect that a person financially interested in the issue of a lawsuit was unworthy of belief and therefore an incompetent witness.

This common-law rule excluding as incompetent any interested person, whether a party or a mere witness, was to a great extent adopted as part of the law of this state. This rule, however, has been slowly relaxed by legislative enactments. Estate of Johnson, 170 Wis. 436 (175 N.W. 917), at p. 450. The only basis suggested for such statutes as are here involved, under which a person situated as is the appellant Mrs.

Hahn can have objection raised as to her legal capacity to testify concerning the execution of or her right to take under a will, is this old common-law rule excluding as incompetent and unworthy of belief a person having a financial interest in the matter involved. Will of Lyon, 96 Wis. 339, 340, 71 N.W. 362; Will of Hoppe, 102 Wis. 54, 55, 78 N.W. 183.

It may safely be asserted that all the changes, either by statute or judicial decision, from territorial days to the time of the present decision, on the subject of the admissibility of the evidence of one interested in the result, have been in the direction of relaxing and modifying this old common-law rule and permitting such matters to go to the credibility rather than to the admissibility of such evidence. Whether because mankind is slowly growing less prone to lie or more skillful in sifting the wheat from the chaff, it is, fortunately, not necessary to here express an opinion. The fact remains of the steady march, by statute and judicial decisions, in the one direction.

It is held in substance by the majority opinion that the omission by ch. 128, Laws 1905, of the word "subscribing" in the phrase "shall be wholly void unless there be two other competent subscribing witnesses" as it appeared in sec. 2284, Stats., prior to that amendment, was either done inadvertently or because deemed surplusage, or in any event that such omission was not a sufficient declaration of legislative intent to make a substantial change in the law on this point. I cannot concur in any such backhanded compliment to the mental processes of the legislature in this particular instance and for the following among other reasons:

There is a substantial difference between one who is a competent witness to the transaction involved in the making of a last will and one who is a competent subscribing witness to the same. By the very language of the statute as it stood and now stands and from the very nature of things, no one can properly be a subscribing witness to such a document who is not also a competent witness. But by no means does it follow that one who is a competent witness is necessarily only the one who also meets the definition of competent subscribing witness. The term "competent witness" describes the genus, the term "competent subscribing witness" defines the species; the former is the large circle, the latter the smaller and enclosed circle. That these two circles may often, from the very nature of the transaction involved, coincide, so far as contained numbers is concerned, can be readily seen, but that fortuitous coincidence is of no real weight in determining the question here presented.

If a testator desire to have his will admitted to probate and his wishes therein expressed carried out, he must at the time of signing it, from the field of competent witnesses then present, call two at least of such competent witnesses to subscribe their names to such document in his presence and in the presence of each other. Such selection of such particular competent witnesses in nowise creates their competency or lessens the competency of other witnesses equally well qualified in law to testify as to the transaction. They must be competent witnesses or they cannot be competent subscribing witnesses; therefore their competency must exist before and at the time they subscribe; it is neither the gift nor the creation of the testator; it is an attribute of the witness alone.

I think the distinction was clearly recognized by one who surely had a familiarity with the subject and especially in this state, in the expression by the late Mr. Chief Justice CASSODAY in his work on Wills, sec. 210:

"Although other persons besides those who subscribe to the will as witnesses may be competent to testify as to its execution, yet it should be remembered that subscribing witnesses have a special importance in all controversies over the execution of wills."

In the state of Pennsylvania, for instance, from an early date and apparently up to the present moment, it has been held under a statute on this subject containing the following language: "shall be proved by the oaths or affirmations of two or more competent witnesses," that such competent witnesses need not be subscribing witnesses. Frew v. Clarke, 80 Pa. 170, 179, decided as early as 1833. It was also therein declared that although one such competent witness was the sole beneficiary and to a legacy of $ 75,000, his testimony was properly received.

In McClure v. Redman, 263 Pa. 405, 107 A. 25, decided in 1919, the existence of the doctrine was clearly recognized, and it was further held that, even with the provision requiring two or more witnesses, the requirement may be met by circumstantial proof, one witness alone being present at the time of the execution of the will.

Manifestly, in the state of Pennsylvania at least, the use of the term "a witness to a will" would not imply that such witness was a subscribing witness, although much stress is laid in the majority opinion upon what is assumed to be the meaning of the term. It might be noted in passing, as to conveyances, that signing of witnesses is not essential to qualify one to testify as to facts showing the passing of title; such formality of subscription is only necessary in order that the instrument may be recorded. Leinenkugel v. Kehl, 73 Wis. 238, 40 N.W. 683; Eadie v. Chambers, 172 F. 73, 24 L. R. A. N. S. 879, and note.

The making of a last will and testament, which is defined by Blackstone as "the legal declaration of a man's intention, which he wills to be performed after his death," is his act and one thing; the statutory formalities which are necessary in order to permit the court having proper jurisdiction to administer the property under such declaration is another and separate thing and subject entirely to legislative control.

This court has gone as far as any court in the land in declaring the substantial nature of the right existing in the living to make disposition of his property after death and that it is of such a nature that it cannot be taken away by the legislature. Nunnemacher v. State, 129 Wis. 190, 202, 108 N.W. 627.

The solemn duty resting upon the courts in this state to effectuate the testator's lawfully expressed wishes irrespective of the desires of those remembered or unremembered in the document has been repeated so often as to become trite. Will of Dardis, 135 Wis. 457, 115 N.W. 332; Will of Rice, 150 Wis. 401, 405, 136 N.W. 956, 137 N.W. 778; Will of Ball, 153 Wis. 27, 141 N.W. 8; Will of Duncan, 154 Wis. 39, 48, 141 N.W. 1002; Schoenwetter v. Schoenwetter, 164 Wis. 131, 135, 159 N.W. 737; Estate of Staab, 166 Wis. 587, 590, 166 N.W. 326.

It has been declared by the former decisions in this matter that that which was presented as the last will of Theodore W. Johnson was his last will. The intention so declared in that document is now frustrated on the theory that the legislature did not sufficiently express an intention to change the statutory regulation of the formalities surrounding the execution of such a document to now permit the intention of the deceased to be carried out. I can see no substantial reason why a legislative intent to change is not clearly expressed by the change made in the statute by ch. 128, Laws 1905.

For convenience of comparison, that statute before and after the amendment is again here presented:

"All beneficial devises, legacies and gifts whatsoever, made or given in any will to a subscribing witness thereto, shall be wholly void unless there be two other competent subscribing witnesses to the same; but a mere charge on the lands of the devisor for the payment of debts shall not prevent his creditors from being competent witnesses to his will."

"All beneficial devises, legacies and gifts whatsoever, made or given in any will to a subscribing witness thereto, (or to the husband or wife of a subscribing witness thereto), shall be wholly void unless there be two other competent . . . witnesses to the same; but a mere charge on the lands of the devisor for the payment of debts shall not prevent his creditors from being competent witnesses to his will."

It is significant that the word "subscribing" as limiting the term "competent witness" appears twice in the statute before amendment; by the amendment it is stricken out once and again specifically inserted, so that the net result, the descriptive term "subscribing witness," stares one in the face as prominently and as often after the amendment as before. If, as suggested in the majority opinion, the term was considered surplusage in the phrase where it was omitted, the legislative mind evidently did not consider it surplusage in the clause in which it was left in the old statute and in the new clause inserted. From the context it had exactly the same significance--no more, no less--in the phrase in which it was omitted, in the phrase in which it was left, and in the phrase in which it was inserted. To suggest that the legislature had surplusage in their minds in amending this statute and were aiming at brevity of expression only in so omitting it can hardly be considered, to say the least, as flattering to that body. If it was their purpose to merely shorten the statute by such process, that purpose fell stillborn.

No question can be raised but that, if the legislature had in so many words declared that they did intend that a gift should be held valid to one, a competent witness to the transaction involved in the making of a will, and who, at the request of the very testator, also subscribed the same to comply with legislative will, where there were others present just as conversant with what was said and done and whose testimony is available, the court would be bound to so hold. I can see no tremendous upheaval in the law of wills if such a conclusion were now upheld.

As yet neither constitution, statute, nor custom requires that the legislature should give any reasons for their amendments to existing statutes or their passage of new ones. No solemn declaration on their part is required as an explanation of changes made, for such, if given, might but add to the judicial labors.

If we view this question with the not unreasonable assumption that as a foundation of the legislative intent expressed in this amendment there was embodied the thought, as expressed by the late Mr. Chief Justice CASSODAY, supra, and which is recognized as the rule elsewhere, that others than subscribing witnesses could be competent witnesses to testify in a court of justice as to the essential facts concerning what a testator said and did, and further that the legislative mind had become imbued with the lofty and often expressed declarations of this court as to the sanctity to be accorded the wish of a testator, and also wanted to still further encroach upon the old common-law fear of want of credibility in the testimony of interested persons, I can see no more simple and direct way to accomplish such purposes, which are so well and so entirely within the legislative field, than providing, as I think they have done, that when others than a beneficiary who were present at the time of the execution of the will are competent, that is not disqualified by law, and they do testify to sufficient facts to support the will, the wish of the testator and the gift to the beneficiary, although a subscribing witness, should both prevail. That there was no fanfare or flourish of legislative trumpets so declaring is not sufficient, in my view of it, to work what seems to me to be a judicial veto interposed by the majority opinion.

Weight is attached in the majority opinion to the fact that the subscribing witnesses to such a document are required, in case of contest, to be first called and their testimony given or their absence satisfactorily explained. This is entirely a matter of order of proof and has no bearing whatever upon the question of the competency of the witnesses. A person who participates in the making of a contract reduced to writing is no less a competent witness to the transaction because the rules of evidence provide that the document itself is the best evidence and must be first produced or its absence explained before oral testimony is taken as to its contents. The competency of such a witness is not at all dependent upon the production or nonproduction of the document. The same should be held in the instant situation. The mere fact that A. and B. are by certain rules of evidence required to be called as witnesses before C. can be permitted to testify has absolutely no bearing upon the question of the competency of C. under the other and independent rules of evidence. No authority is cited to the effect that a test of competency of a witness is to be determined upon a rule which relates solely to the order of proof or of first or secondary evidence. The competency of a witness does not rest in some twilight zone dependent upon the question as to whether some document or some other witness shall be first produced or sworn.

A mere glance at the statutes and decisions of the different state jurisdictions shows that the requirements of formalities requisite for the probate of a will are as varied as the jurisdictions, and there are none in which such formalities are not constantly changed and without any formidable preambles in the amending statutes either. What is meat in one jurisdiction is poison in another.

In New York two attesting witnesses are required, each of whom shall sign his name as a witness at the end of the will at the request of the testator. They both, however, do not need to be present at the time of signing. Hoysradt v. Kingman, 22 N.Y. 372, 379.

In California, under a substantially similar statute, it was held that they must both be present. Estate of Emart, 175 Cal. 238, 165 P. 707, L. R. A. 1917F, 866.

Under our present statute, sec. 2282, the signing by the witnesses must be done when both are present. Will of Griffith, 165 Wis. 601, 608, 163 N.W. 138. Formerly under the same statute before amendment such subscribing in the presence of both witnesses was not required. Will of Smith, 52 Wis. 543, 547, 8 N.W. 616, 9 N.W. 665.

A substantial difference was recognized at common law and for a long period in many of the states of this country as to wills regarding real property and those regarding personal property, the latter not requiring the same formality as the former. A will that would be void as to real estate for want of proper execution might nevertheless be valid as to personal property. Lake v. Warner, 34 Conn. 483; Ex parte Henry, 24 Ala. 638. The property here involved is substantially all personalty.

Many states expressly provide that a holographic will, that is one written and signed in the proper handwriting of a testator (some requiring that it shall be dated also), shall be valid though not attested or subscribed by a single witness. Rood, Wills, § 268. Such holographic will, valid in France, made by a citizen of Maryland sojourning in France, covering both real and personal property in Maryland, was properly admitted and administered in Maryland. Lindsay v. Wilson, 103 Md. 252, 63 A. 566, 2 L. R. A. N. S. 408, and note.

Undoubtedly the courts in this state would have to hold the same as to such foreign wills under sec. 2283, Stats., providing for recognition of wills executed outside of this state under the there required formalities, conditioned only that it be in writing and subscribed by testator. The provision for subscribing witnesses is here conspicuous by its absence.

In Children's Aid Society v. Loveridge, 70 N.Y. 387, it was held that an executor to a will may nevertheless be a competent subscribing witness under a statute quite similar to the one before us. It would appear furthermore from the language of the decision in that case that other than subscribing witnesses who were present at its execution were sworn upon the hearing just as in the case at bar and their testimony in effect held admissible and sufficient to sustain the will. Page 392.

In Rugg v. Rugg, 83 N.Y. 592, 594, the testimony of the two subscribing witnesses created a doubt as to some of the facts essential to be shown for a proper execution of a will. To supply this defect the executor was held to be a competent witness to testify to the essential features so left in doubt and the will held properly executed. The probate of a will should not be rejected because one of the subscribing witnesses testifies in contradiction to the other and against the document. Will of Grant, 149 Wis. 330, 337, 135 N.W. 833; Matter of Spooner, 13 Mills' Reports (N.Y. Sur.) 482.

These points are dwelt upon merely as indicating the vast variety of legislative and judicial views on the subject of statutory formalities, their flexibility and the constant changes made; that no property rights are considered as invaded or the established order of things overthrown by such changes.

I think the judgment should be reversed and it be held that Mrs. Hahn, as designated beneficiary in the admitted will of Theodore W. Johnson, is entitled to take just as the testator therein declared she should take.

D. AMENDMENT AND REPUBLICATION BY CODICIL

Wills can be amended by codicils, which can add to, subtract from, or even cancel entirely, a prior, validly executed will. While codicils are normally used to modify existing wills, they are testamentary documents that must be independently executed in the same manner as regular wills. A codicil can revoke all or part of the previous will, or it can simply add to it. The codicil also "republishes" the will, so that the effective date of the will becomes the date of the last validly executed codicil. Moreover, if the prior will was defective, either because of improper execution or a lack of testamentary capacity, a valid codicil validates the previously deficient will.

To the extent that the provisions of a codicil contradict those of the original will, the original document is modified by the codicil, even if the codicil fails to explicitly revoke the prior language. In most instances, the revocation of the original will has the effect of revoking the codicil as well. Moreover, there is no limit to the number of codicils that can be attached to an individual will.

Fairweather v. Love (Will of Home)

Supreme Court of Wisconsin
231 Wis. 227, 284 N.W. 766 (1939)

Fowler, J. The case is a will contest grounded on a claim of insufficient execution. Sec. 238.06, Stats., provides:

How wills to be executed. No will made within this state since the first day of January, 1896, except such nuncupative **[i.e., oral]** wills as are mentioned in this chapter, shall be effectual to pass any estate, whether real or personal, or to charge or in any way affect the same unless it be in writing and signed by the testator or by some person in his presence and by his express direction, and attested and subscribed in the presence of the testator by two or more competent witnesses in the presence of each other; if the witnesses are competent at the time of such attesting their subsequent incompetence, from whatever cause it may arise, shall not prevent the probate and allowance of the will if it be otherwise satisfactorily proved."

Two instruments are involved, one purporting to be a will and the other a codicil. Both were admitted to probate. It is claimed that neither was executed according to the statute because not signed by the testatrix in the presence of the witnesses. The purported will is a printed form with blank spaces for the insertion of writing. The material portions are as follows, the italicized portions being in the handwriting of Miss Home:

"I, *Anne E. Home* of *Milwaukee* in the County of *Milwaukee* in the state of *Wisconsin,* being of sound mind and memory, do make, publish and declare this my last will and testament, hereby revoking all former wills, bequests and devises by me made.

"I hereby will and direct the payment of my just debts out of my estate."

Then follows, all in the handwriting of Miss Home, six specific money bequests for educational, religious, and charitable purposes, aggregating $17,500, five specific money bequests to individuals aggregating $7,000, and a residuary clause as follows:

"The residue and remainder of all my estate not disposed of to Red Cross, to Rescue Mission, and Salvation Army."

The only place in the instrument where the signature of Miss Home appears is at the beginning, in the blank space left for the insertion of the name of the testator. The signatures of two persons are affixed to the instrument as witnesses. These witnesses signed in the presence of the testatrix and of each other. Neither witness saw the testatrix sign her name in the blank space at the top. One of them, Miss Van Beckum, a nurse thirty-nine years old, testified that Miss Home said she had signed the will. The other, an elderly woman, Mrs. Krempel, seventy-five years of age, testified that Miss Home said she would sign it. The written portions of the will indicate, except as hereinafter stated, that they were all written by the same pen and with the same ink and at the same time so far as uniform pressure and handwriting characteristics tend to indicate the latter.

When the witnesses signed, the instrument was folded back so that the contents were not observable. According to Mrs. Krempel it was folded back in quarters so that the only portion observable was the portion at the end designated as the place where the witnesses were to sign. Mrs. Krempel had been told a couple of days before by Miss Home that she was going to make her will and was then asked to come to be a witness to it. At the immediate time Miss Home told her maid "to go and get the paper." Miss

Van Beckum testified that Miss Home in the presence of herself and Mrs. Krempel declared the instrument signed by the witnesses to be her last will and testament.

The codicil is not on a printed form and not in the handwriting of the testatrix. It is witnessed by the same persons who witnessed the will. It bears date three years later than the will. Miss Van Beckum testified positively that she saw Miss Home sign the codicil at the time the witnesses signed. In this she is positively corroborated by a Mrs. Alexander upon whose testimony the trial judge stated in an opinion filed that he placed great reliance. Mrs. Alexander as an heir would take about $10,000 if probate of the will were denied. By the codicil to the will she was given a ring worth not over $200. She was characterized in the trial judge's opinion as a highly intelligent person more credible than Mrs. Krempel wherever their testimony differed.

In view of the findings of the trial judge and his definitely expressed opinion as to the comparative credibility of Mrs. Alexander and Mrs. Krempel, we cannot say that the finding of the trial judge is against the "great weight and clear preponderance of the evidence" and must therefore affirm the judgment. It so closely coincides with its facts and the law involved in the cases of *Estate of Lagershausen,* 224 Wis. 479, 272 N. W. 469, and *Will of Johnston,* 225 Wis. 140, 273 N. W. 512, recently decided, that we see no reason to discuss further the law involved.

Two propositions were there decided: That the signature of the testator inserted in the blank space left in a printed form of a will for writing of the testator's name at the beginning of a will, if written as and for his signature to the will in executing it as his will is sufficient, and that if the signature of the testator is on the instrument when the witnesses signed it, it is immaterial that the witnesses did not see him affix the signature or see the signature, if the instrument was at the time declared by the testator to be his will and was signed by the witnesses in his presence and the presence of each other for the purpose of attesting it. We let these propositions stand upon the support given them in those opinions.

It is also claimed by the appellants that two alterations of the will appear upon its face, and that these alterations render the will invalid. Alterations made before execution of the will are of course part of the will as originally executed. Alterations are entirely immaterial unless they were in fact made after the will's execution. Their nature and appearance is sometimes such as to raise a presumption that they were made before the will was executed and sometimes such as to raise a presumption that they were made thereafter. When the latter presumption arises the burden is on the proponent to prove that they were made prior to execution. No proof was produced in the instant case by either side.

A note to the case of *Martin v. Martin,* 67 A. L. R. 1127, 1138, covers the subject of the time of alterations. The cited case is to the effect that an alteration which has no effect upon the dispositive portions of the will and that one that is the mere filling in of a blank require no explanation. Under these rules the alterations here involved require no explanation, as one has no dispositive effect in view of the codicil, and the other merely fills in a blank space left at the time of drafting.

The alterations here involved are of specific legacies. One is as follows: "Miss Marie Volz, three thousand dollars." The word "three" and the figure "3" appear to have been substituted for another word and figure after erasing them. This becomes immaterial because the codicil contains the following clause: "I give devise and bequeath to Marie Volz the sum of two thousand ($2,000) dollars, making five thousand ($5,000) dollars in all and direct my executors to pay the inheritance tax on that sum to be paid to her." Miss Volz therefore takes $5,000 free of inheritance tax under the codicil. The other alteration occupies a single line in the will. "Mrs. Mary Boyd, five hundred dollars." The words "five hundred dollars" and the figures "$500" are written in different ink than the words "Miss Mary Boyd" and the rest of the writing in the body of the will. They are plainly in the handwriting of the testatrix, but in somewhat smaller script than the rest of her writing. The words "five hundred dollars" were obviously written in to fill a blank.

Aside from this the alterations have no effect to invalidate the will as a whole. They would only invalidate the change. Having been made by the testatrix herself in her own handwriting, if they were made after the execution of the will, the effect but for the codicil would be to invalidate the changes and leave the will for probate as it stood when executed. It would leave Miss Volz a legacy of $1,000 instead of $3,000 and leave Mrs. Boyd with no legacy at all. Alterations made after execution "form no part of the will and are of no effect whatever, unless they sufficiently support an inference of cancellation." *City Nat. Bank v. Slocum* (6th Cir.), 272 Fed. 11, 16, *certiorari* denied 257 U.S. 637, 42 Sup. Ct. 49, 66 L. Ed. 409. Moreover the codicil was a republication of the will with the alterations incorporated. *Linnard's Appeal,* 93 Pa. 313.

The recent case of *Will of Byrne,* 223 Wis. 503, 271 N. W. 48, clearly implies that alterations in a will do not render it void and have no effect except as they operate as partial revocations. Even if the legacy to Mrs. Boyd was invalid because the amount of it was written in after the will was executed it would not avail the appellants. They would not be at all affected by such invalidity. Only the residuary legatees would be affected by that, and they are not complaining.

The case of *In re Wilson,* 8 Wis. *171, *175, is relied on by appellants as establishing the law of this state that alteration of the will renders it void and not entitled to probate in its original form. It is true that the court denied probate to a will because of changes made therein by a legatee after it came into his possession. If that be the rule when the will is propounded by the person who made the alterations, it does not follow that a will must be denied probate when the alteration is made by the testatrix and the will is propounded by executors named therein or by beneficiaries thereunder not party to the alterations.

We do not perceive that beneficiaries should be deprived of their rights under a will valid when executed by changes made therein for his own advantage by some other beneficiary. But if that be so, that is not in the instant case. Judge Paine who decided the *Wilson Case, supra,* in the county court, and whose decision after reversal by the circuit court on appeal was reinstated by this court, stated in a written opinion filed:

"I shall not examine what would be the effect if it appeared that these alterations were made by the testator after the execution of the will. . . . Probably in neither case would they invalidate it."

This negatives intent on the part of the county judge and of this court to lay down a rule applicable to this case. The judgment of the county court is affirmed.

Lonsdorf v. Citizens State Bank & Trust Co. (Estate of Erbach)

Supreme Court of Wisconsin
41 Wis. 2d 335, 164 N.W.2d 238 (1969)

Hanley, J.

The following issues are presented on this appeal:

(1) What weight is to be given the trial court's decision on this appeal;

(2) Did the codicil of 1966 incorporate the holographic instrument by reference; and

(3) What effect should be given to certain interlineations and changes which were made in the will of 1945?

Weight of Trial Court's Decision.

This court has often stated that the factual findings of the trial court will not be upset unless they are against the great weight and clear preponderance of the evidence. Schroedel Corp. v. State Highway Comm. (1968), 38 Wis. 2d 424, 157 N. W. 2d 562; Eberle v. Joint School Dist. No. 1 (1968), 37 Wis. 2d 651, 155 N. W. 2d 573. However, this court has also stated:

"The rule that findings of the trial court cannot be set aside unless against the great weight and clear preponderance of the evidence does not apply in a case . . . where the interpretation of a will rests upon the application of legal principles or rules of construction to known facts. Under such circumstances the trial court is in no better position to reach a correct conclusion than is the appellate court." Estate of Holcombe (1951), 259 Wis. 642, 646, 49 N. W. 2d 914. See also: Will of Mechler (1944), 246 Wis. 45, 16 N. W. 2d 373.

Although the facts in this case have not been stipulated, basically the case does not present a factual dispute. The primary problem on this appeal is the legal effect of the holographic instrument. This is a question of law which this court must decide based on the same factual conclusions considered by the trial court. We find the trial court's extensive analysis and weighing of the evidence very helpful.

Incorporation by Reference.

The cases and commentators agree that a validly executed will or codicil can incorporate the language of another document by reference.

". . . Stated generally, the doctrine [of incorporation by reference] is that a will, duly executed and witnessed according to statutory requirements, may incorporate into itself by an appropriate reference a written paper or document which is in existence at the time of the execution of the will, irrespective of whether such document is one executed by the testator or a third person, whether it is executed and attested as a will, or whether it is in and of itself a valid instrument, provided the document referred to is identified by clear and satisfactory proof." 57 Am. Jur., Wills, pp. 193, 194, sec. 233.

"In states which recognize the general doctrine of incorporation by reference, the following requisites must be complied with and satisfied in order to incorporate a nontestamentary document into a will by reference. The will itself must refer to such paper to be incorporated as being in existence at the time of the execution of the will, in such a way as reasonably to identify such paper in the will, and in such a way as to show testator's intention to incorporate such instrument in his will and to make it a part thereof. Such document must in fact be in existence at the time of the execution of the will. Such document must correspond to the description thereof in the will and must be shown to be the instrument therein referred to." 2 Page, Wills (Bowe-Parker rev.), pp. 88, 89, sec. 19.18.

Thus, any writing may be incorporated into a will or codicil. The valid execution of the incorporating document gives testamentary validity to the incorporated document.

The trial court determined that the codicil of 1966 incorporated the will of 1945 and the holographic instrument by reference. The valid execution of the 1966 instrument gave the invalidly executed holographic instrument and the altered will of 1945 testamentary validity. We think the rule was improperly applied to this case.

It cannot be disputed that Wisconsin has adopted the doctrine of incorporation by reference.

"The earlier instrument, dated September 21, 1874, was never so executed as to become a will. But it cannot well be doubted that the later instrument, of October 8, 1883, being sufficiently executed to become a will, has so adopted and incorporated into itself the former writing as that it has become a part of the latter instrument." Skinner v. American Bible Society (1896), 92 Wis. 209, 213, 65 N. W. 1037.

". . . The first will having become legally dead by revocation, we can see no way in which it could be revitalized except by some act which the law recognizes as being equivalent to execution under the statute. A codicil or subsequent writing adopting the former will, duly executed . . . would undoubtedly revive it." Will of Noon (1902), 115 Wis. 299, 303, 91 N. W. 670.

In Estate of Wells (1924), 184 Wis. 242, 199 N. W. 52, the testatrix willed her property to her sons. She provided, however, that their respective shares of her estate should be reduced by the advances they had received.

"'. . . A record of the total amount of these respective advances has been made, and is kept in my lock box at the First National Bank, Monroe, Wisconsin.'" Estate of Wells, supra, at page 243.The court determined that this reference was sufficient to incorporate the record of the advances into the will.

Finally, in Estate of Brandenburg (1961), 13 Wis. 2d 217, 226, 108 N. W. 2d 374, the court stated:

". . . The great majority of states, including Wisconsin, have accepted the doctrine of incorporation by reference."

Although this court has frequently applied the doctrine, it has never discussed the elements which lead to its application. We think the minimum necessary elements should be:

(1) There must be an intention to incorporate;

(2) The incorporated paper or document must be in existence when the incorporated testamentary document is executed;

(3) The incorporated paper or document must be sufficiently identified; and

(4) The incorporating testamentary document must be executed in accordance with statutory requirements.

Clearly, the third requirement of sufficient identification has not been met in this case. By execution of the codicil of 1966, the testatrix could have meant the will of 1945, the holographic instrument of 1965, or, as the trial court held, both of them taken together.

". . . A reference to the will in the codicil constitutes a sufficient identification of the will, even though the instruments are deposited in different places, provided it identifies the will with reasonable certainty." 57 Am. Jur., Wills, p. 415, sec. 605.

“A duly executed codicil operates as a republication of the original will and makes it speak from the new date, in so far as it is not altered or revoked by the codicil, although the codicil is not physically annexed to the will, and although the will is not in the presence of the testator at the time of executing the codicil, where it refers to the will in such a way as to identify that instrument beyond doubt." 57 Am. Jur., Wills, p. 428, sec. 626.

"In order to operate as an incorporation, the will must refer to the instrument to be incorporated and must describe it with sufficient certainty that it may be identified and distinguished from other similar documents." 2 Page, Wills (Bowe-Parker rev.), p. 96, sec. 19.23.In all of the Wisconsin cases approving incorporation, there has been some connection between the incorporating and incorporated documents. In Skinner v. American Bible Society, supra, a second validly executed codicil incorporated an invalid prior codicil because both codicils were on the same piece of paper. Moreover, the second codicil specifically referred to the first. In Estate of Wells, supra, the testatrix referred to a

"'. . . record of the total amount of these respective advances has been made, and is kept in my lock box at the First National Bank, Monroe, Wisconsin.’" In Estate of

Brandenburg, supra, at page 222, the testatrix's will provided that a certain trust corpus should be paid over:

"'. . . to my son's trust estate, which is willed to charities, including those of my choosing . . . .'"

In each of these cases, the incorporated writing was described with sufficient particularity. In this case, however, the codicil of 1966 merely refers to "my Last Will and Testament." The question as to which one is referred to still remains. The trial court was influenced by the fact that both the will of 1945 and the holographic instrument were found folded together. "A paper placed with a will is not a part thereof where the will shows no intention to incorporate it." 2 Page, Wills (Bowe-Parker rev.), p. 115, sec. 19.30.

The codicil itself must clearly identify the incorporated written material. The codicil of 1966 did not incorporate anything by reference because it did not clearly identify what was meant by "my Last Will and Testament." The trial court actually came to this same conclusion:

". . . In the Erbach case it is difficult to ascertain the precise thinking of the testator at the time that she executed the Codicil of June 23, 1966, which Codicil is absent of any reference to any specific instrument and makes only a general statement to 'my Last Will and Testament.' . . ." (Emphasis supplied.) The holographic instrument is not itself properly executed nor is it incorporated by any validly executed testamentary document. Hence its provisions may not form any part of the final decree of the probate court.

Effect of Changes in Will of 1945.

The failure of the codicil of 1966 to refer to a specific will raises an interesting problem. The will of 1945 was executed in accordance with the statutes. It could only be revoked by complying with sec. 238.14, Stats. Since there never was a physical destruction of the will of 1945, nor a validly executed later will, nor a validly executed written statement of revocation, the will of 1945 remained in full force and effect at the testatrix's death.

The will of 1945 is, however, subject to the validly executed codicil of 1966. When a person has two validly executed testaments, the first one is not revoked by the second unless there is a clear statement to that effect or unless the provisions of the second testament are so clearly repugnant to the provisions of the first that they cannot stand together. See 57 Am. Jur., Wills, pp. 331, 332, sec. 474. This is especially true when the second validly executed testamentary instrument is labeled a codicil. In such instances, there is clearly no intention to revoke a prior will. When minor inconsistencies do arise between two or more valid testaments, however, the provisions of the testament executed the latest in time control. Obviously, the appointment of the executor by the codicil of 1966 controls over the executor appointed by the will of 1945.

If the codicil of 1966 had specifically referred to the will of 1945 or the holographic instrument, the entire testamentary document would have been republished as of the date of the codicil. The republishing of the will would validate any changes made between the execution of the will and the execution of the codicil. However, the codicil here did not republish the will of 1945 because there was no specific reference. Therefore, the court must determine the effect to be given certain changes which the testatrix made to the will of 1945 after it had been executed.

The changes which the testatrix made can be divided into two types: crossouts and interlineations. This court has previously determined that interlineations subsequent to execution of a will have no effect. The will is construed as it was originally written. Estate of Beale (1962), 15 Wis. 2d 546, 113 N. W. 2d 380. The interlineations made by the testatrix occurred in Paragraphs 2 and 4 of her will. In Paragraph 2 she wrote in the name of a co-executor. This can be completely disregarded because a validly executed codicil subsequently controlled the appointment of an executor. In Paragraph 4 of the will, the testatrix originally divided the residue of her estate as follows:

". . . in equal shares, unto my grandchildren, Lewis Plisch, Nan Plisch, Susan Plisch, John Erbach, Tom Erbach, and Mariana Erbach, and my nephews, Frank J. Hollfelder and Walter Hauboldt, to wit, each an equal 1/8 share . . . ."

Sometime after the will was executed in 1945 the testatrix wrote in "Veseley" above the name of Nan Plisch, "Langhoff" above the name Susan Plisch, and "Lonsdorf" after the name Mariana Erbach. These changes merely stated the married names of the beneficiaries originally named. Completely disregarding the changes makes no difference in the distribution of the estate. The testatrix made further changes by crossing out names from Paragraph 4 as it is set out above. She completely crossed out the names of Susan Plisch (and the added word "Langhoff" which had previously been written in), and Walter Hauboldt. Both of those persons predeceased the testatrix. The names were heavily crossed out in ink so that the original typewritten names were practically obliterated. The testatrix made one further change. Where Paragraph 4 originally stated "each an equal 1/8 share," the figure "1/8" had been changed to "1/7."

Subsequently the figure "1/7" was heavily crossed out in ink and the figure "1/6" was written in.

The court is again faced with the problem of partial revocation. In Will of Byrne (1937), 223 Wis. 503, 271 N. W. 48, the testatrix crossed out the names of her two brothers in her residue clause. The court held that this was a sufficient partial revocation. The court commented on the Byrne Case, supra, in Will of Home (1939), 231 Wis. 227, 234, 284 N. W. 766, 285 N. W. 754:

". . . The recent case of Will of Byrne . . . clearly implies that alterations in a will do not render it void and have no effect except as they operate as partial revocations." However, in Estate of Holcombe, supra, at page 650, the court stated that crossing out a beneficiary with a lightly drawn pencil mark did not "indicate a finality of decision." The court then concluded, at page 651, that:

". . . all pencil alterations and interlineations on the will are ineffective." (Emphasis supplied.)

We hold that the heavily crossed-out names in Laura Erbach's will certainly indicated a finality of decision. We further hold that the crossing out of the names operated as a partial revocation. The only change in the will which has not been considered is the addition of "1/6" after the figures "1/8" and "1/7" were crossed out. The crossing out of "1/8" and "1/7" operates as a revocation of that part of the will. If the figure "1/6" is deleted, the will would still read "each an equal share" and the will lists six persons who are to share in the residue. Thus the division of the residue remains the same whether the figure "1/6" remains or not.

The court has been requested to consider the problem of fees in this case. One of the respondents was a minor and a guardian ad litem was appointed. The minor would have received $500 under the holographic instrument. Under the 1945 will he receives nothing. Under sec. 251.23 (1), Stats., costs are discretionary with this court. Under sec. 324.13 (2), Stats., the court may allow compensation and expenses to a guardian ad litem out of the estate. We are of the opinion that the guardian ad litem fees and costs should be allowed out of the estate.

It is our opinion that the estate of Laura Erbach should be probated under the will of 1945 with the effective alterations and interlineations, together with the codicil of 1966.

III. THE REVOCATION OF WILLS

A. SIMPLE REVOCATION

Traditionally, wills could be revoked either by a subsequent revocatory writing, executed in compliance with the Wills Act, or by physical act, done for the purpose of revoking a will. Under no circumstances could a will be revoked by an oral statement. Similarly, it was impossible for a will to be "accidentally" revoked.

Wis. Stat. 853.11. Revocation.

(1) REVOCATION BY WRITING.

(a) A will is revoked in whole or in part by a subsequent will that is executed in compliance with s. 853.03 or 853.05 and that revokes the prior will or a part thereof expressly or by inconsistency.

(bm)

1. A subsequent will wholly revokes the prior will if the testator intended the subsequent will to replace rather than supplement the prior will, regardless of whether the subsequent will expressly revokes the prior will.

2. The testator is presumed to have intended a subsequent will to replace, rather than supplement, the prior will if the subsequent will completely disposes of the testator's estate. If this presumption arises and is not rebutted by clear and convincing evidence, the prior will is revoked.

3. The testator is presumed to have intended a subsequent will to supplement, rather than replace, the prior will if the subsequent will does not completely dispose of the testator's estate. If this presumption arises and is not rebutted by clear and convincing evidence, the subsequent will revokes the prior will only to the extent of any inconsistency

(1m) REVOCATION BY PHYSICAL ACT.

A will is revoked in whole or in part by burning, tearing, canceling, obliterating or destroying the will, or part, with the intent to revoke, by the testator or by some person in the testator's conscious presence and by the testator's direction.

(2m) PREMARITAL OR PREDOMESTIC PARTNERSHIP WILL

Entitlements of a surviving spouse or surviving domestic partner under a decedent's will that was executed before marriage to the surviving spouse or before recording of the domestic partnership under ch. 770 are governed by s. 853.12

(3) TRANSFER TO FORMER SPOUSE OR FORMER DOMESTIC PARTNER.

A transfer under a will to a former spouse or former domestic partner is governed by s. 854.15

(3m) INTENTIONAL KILLING OF DECEDENT BY BENEFICIARY.

If a beneficiary under a will killed the decedent, the rights of that beneficiary are governed by s. 854.14

(4) OTHER METHODS OF REVOCATION.

A will is revoked only as provided in this section.

(5) DEPENDENT RELATIVE REVOCATION.

Except as modified by sub. (6) this section is not intended to change in any manner the doctrine of dependent relative revocation.

(6) REVIVAL OF REVOKED WILL.

(a) If a subsequent will that partly revoked a previous will is itself revoked by a revocatory act under sub. (1m), the revoked part of the previous will is revived. This paragraph does not apply if it is evident from the circumstances of the revocation of the subsequent will or from the testator's contemporary or subsequent declarations that the testator did not intend the revoked part of the previous will to take effect as executed.

(b) If a subsequent will that wholly revoked a previous will is itself revoked by a revocatory act under sub. (1m), the previous will remains revoked unless it is revived. The previous will is revived if it is evident from the circumstances of the revocation of the subsequent will or from the testator's contemporary or subsequent declarations that the testator intended the previous will to take effect as executed.

(c) If a subsequent will that wholly or partly revoked a previous will is itself revoked by another, later will, the previous will or its revoked part remains revoked, unless it or its revoked part is revived. The previous will or its revoked part is revived to the extent that it appears from the terms of the later will, or from the testator's contemporary or subsequent declarations, that the testator intended the previous will or its revoked part to take effect.

(d) In the absence of an original valid will, the execution and validity of the revived will or part may be established as provided in s. 856.17

In re Estate of Haugk

Supreme Court of Wisconsin

91 Wis. 2d 196, 280 N.W.2d 684 (1979)

Coffey, J. The appellants, Lutheran Children's Friend Society and the Easter Seal Society of Milwaukee County, appeal from an order denying a petition for probate of the allegedly revoked will of Marie Haugk and further ordering the intestate administration of the decedent's estate. The subject will was duly executed on January 6, 1965 naming the appellants, Lutheran Children's Friend Society and Easter Seal Society of Milwaukee County, Inc., as residual beneficiaries. It is undisputed that the decedent's husband, Horst Haugk, burned the will of 1965 on or about September 2, 1976

The decedent (hereinafter Marie), and Haugk were married in 1959, her second marriage and his third. At the time of their marriage, Marie was sixty-two years of age and childless, and Haugk was fifty-five years of age, and the record contains no indication that he fathered any children in his previous marriages.

The 1965 will provided that Haugk would receive a nominal disposition from his wife's estate, consisting of her household goods and furnishings, as well as her clothing, jewelry and other personal property. Marie's will also provided that Haugk occupy their apartment located in her building, rent free for a period of one year after her death. It was expressly stated in the will that the bequests to her husband did not include any money, securities, evidences of debt, titles or accounts owned by Marie at the time of her death.

The will also provided:

"FOURTH: All the rest, residue and remainder of my estate, of whatsoever kind and wheresoever situated, I direct shall be divided into fifteen (15) equal parts, and I give as follows:

"(a) To JOHN FUCHS, brother, 1 part.

"(b) To RAY SPORS, nephew, 3 parts

"(c) To PAUL SPORS, nephew, 4 parts

"(d) To JOHN FUCHS, Jr., nephew, 2 parts

"(e) To DAVID KJELL, friend, 2 parts

"(f) To SALVATION ARMY, 1 part

"(g) To LUTHERAN CHILDREN'S FRIEND SOCIETY, 1 part

"(h) To EASTER SEAL SOCITY OF MILWAUKEE, 1 part

"In the event HORST HAUGK or DAVID KJELL shall predecease me, his legacy shall lapse and become a part of the residue of my estate. In the event JOHN FUCHS,

RAY SPORS, PAUL SPORS, or JOHN FUCHS, JR. shall predecease me, leaving issue of his own surviving me, then such issue shall take, and if more than one, equally between them as tenants in common, the share which the parent would have taken had he been then living, but if any of said legatees dies before my decease without issue surviving him, the intended bequest shall lapse and become a part of my residuary estate."

The 1965 will was drafted by Atty. Albert Franz who retained a copy of the testamentary document. The original of this will was deposited for safekeeping in the offices of the Milwaukee County Register in Probate on January 7, 1965.

In March, 1976, Marie and Haugk consulted another attorney, Terese Tillman, regarding the drafting of new individual wills. Thereafter, Attorney Tillman met with the Haugks on August 11 and 26 and discussed their intentions in establishing new wills. At the August 26 conference, Marie and Haugk authorized Atty. Tillman to prepare new wills and post-nuptial agreements disclaiming each party's interest in the other's estate.

The next day, after the conference with the new attorney, Haugk attempted to withdraw the 1965 will from the office of the register in probate, but the request was denied as he had not complied with the requirement that he obtain Marie's signature on a power of attorney form provided by the probate office for the withdrawal of a will. A few days later on the 31st of August, 1976, Haugk returned to the probate office and secured the will after producing his wife's signature on the witnessed and notarized probate office power of attorney form.

At the will contest hearing, Haugk testified that at his wife's request he burned the will in the basement incinerator of Marie's apartment building. He also explained that, at the time of the burning of the will in the first week of September, 1976, his wife was not present in the basement as she was suffering from a severe heart condition and thus was unable to climb the thirteen stairs separating the kitchen from the apartment's basement.

A week to ten days after the burning of the will on September 10 and 17, Marie conferred by telephone with Atty. Tillman requesting the delivery and execution of the new will and post-nuptial agreements. In the conversation on the 17th, the attorney told Marie the new will was prepared and scheduled an appointment for its execution on September 20, 1976. The new will, similar in many respects to the provisions contained in the 1965 will, provided for a nominal bequest to Haugk. He was to receive Marie's personal effects and the rent-free use of the apartment for eight months rather than one year. Another change in the new will provided the estate residue was to be divided equally among her nephews, Ray and Paul Spors and John Fuchs, Jr.

Further, in contrast to the earlier 1965 will, the new will withdrew any bequest to the appellant charities, the Easter Seal Society of Milwaukee County, Inc., and Lutheran Children's Friend Society. Haugk explained at the will contest hearing the reason for the withdrawal of the bequest to the appellant charities was because his wife, Marie, had become disenchanted with the charities because of their frequent advertising and solicitation for contributions.

The new will was never executed as Marie died of a heart attack sometime during the day of September 17, 1976, after the phone conversation with Atty. Tillman. Some six days thereafter, on September 23, 1976, Haugk petitioned the court for the probate of his wife's estate. The petition reflects that his wife died intestate leaving property valued at approximately $130,000. Haugk was listed as the estate's sole beneficiary and at his request the court appointed him personal representative.

The Easter Seal Society petitioned the court on January 26, 1977, for admission to probate of a conformed copy of the destroyed will. The charity received this copy of the 1965 will from the drafter of the earlier will, Atty. Albert Franz. Haugk has objected to the charities' petition for probate of the destroyed will.

The Easter Seal Society, in petitioning the court for admission of the 1965 will, stated that: (1) the revocation was ineffective for failure to comply with sec. 853.11(1) (b), Stats., requiring a third party's destruction of a will be at the testator's request and in his or her presence; and (2) that even if the revocation was in accordance with the statute, it was ineffective under the dependent relative revocation theory, sec. 853.11(5), as Marie did not intend the revocation to be effective until the new will had been executed.

After the hearing on the admission to probate of the destroyed 1965 will, the trial court made the following findings: (1) that the removal of the will from safekeeping was proper, (2) that the destruction of the will complied with sec. 853.11(1) (b), Stats., as it was performed at Marie's instruction and in her "constructive presence"; (3) that the destruction of the new will was not dependent upon an effective execution of the 1976 will.

Issues:

1. Was the withdrawal of the will from the probate office invalid pursuant to sec. 853.09(3), Stats., thus making the destruction of the decedent's will ineffective?

2. Did the destruction of the decedent's will comply with sec. 853.11(1) (b), Stats., requiring a third party's destruction of a will to be at the testator's direction and in her presence?

3. Was it the decedent's intention that the destruction of her will be effective only upon the valid execution of a new will?

I. *Was the Testator's Will Properly Withdrawn from Safekeeping?*

The appellants contend that the revocation of the 1965 will should be declared invalid as the power of attorney form used by Haugk for withdrawal of his wife's will from the custody of the register in probate was improper as it did not comply with the requirements of sec. 853.09(3), Stats. The statute provides:

"853.09. Deposit of will in county court during testator's lifetime.

. . .

"(3) Withdrawal. A testator may withdraw his will during his lifetime, but *the register in probate shall deliver the will* only to the testator personally or *to a person duly authorized to withdraw it for the testator, by a writing signed by the testator and 2 witnesses other than the person authorized.*" (Emphasis supplied.)

The appellants maintain that contrary to the two witness requirements in sec. 853.09(3), Stats., the power of attorney form produced by Haugk in securing his wife's will from the probate office was witnessed by only one person. Haugk contends he had the right to rely that the register in probate's delivery of the 1965 will was done in compliance with sec. 853.09(3). Alternatively, he argues that the invalidity of the power of attorney form used in withdrawing the will from the probate office is being raised for the first time on appeal and thus the issue is not properly before this court.

The respondent's allegation that the question of non-compliance with sec. 853.09(3), Stats., was not raised in the lower court cannot be supported, as the record reflects that the validity of the power of attorney form was considered by the trial court. A thorough reading of the record indicates that the trial judge discussed the question of compliance with sec. 853.09, and issued a finding in the following language: "The testimony of the notary public was uncontroverted that the power of attorney authorizing Horst O. Haugk to withdraw the 1965 will from the office of the register in probate was signed by Marie Haugk in the presence only of the notary public, and that there was no influence exerted upon the said Marie Haugk to execute said instrument." Therefore, we conclude that the existence of this finding establishes that the question of the validity of the power of attorney form was addressed by the trial court.

In analyzing this issue, it is undisputed that the power of attorney form produced by Haugk to obtain the 1965 will was signed by the decedent and notarized by Eleanor Nauertz. Further, it is undisputed that she was the only witness as to the proof of Marie's execution of the form. Thus, the signed document bearing the signature of only one witness to the execution to the power of attorney form was in violation of sec. 853.09(3), Stats., that permits the release of the testator's will to a third person only upon compliance with the following condition: that the third person is authorized by a writing signed by the testator and two witnesses, other than the person authorized to receive the will.

Despite this violation of the sec. 853.09(3), Stats., witnessing requirements, we will not declare the revocation of this will invalid on that ground alone. The legislative intent underlying the sec. 853.09(3) witnessing requirements was to prevent the fraudulent procurement and destruction of a testator's will. In this case there is no evidence that the will was obtained from the probate office through fraud. The trial court, in fact, found there was no influence exerted upon Marie to execute the power of attorney form. Further, Eleanor Nauertz, the sole witness to Marie's execution of the form, testified unequivocally that Marie's signing of the document was an act of her own free will.

In the absence of proof establishing that this will was fraudulently obtained from the probate office, we will not declare the revocation of this testamentary document invalid solely on the grounds of non-compliance with the witnessing requirements of sec. 853.09(3), Stats. However, we note that in this case the non-compliance with sec. 853.09(3) could have been avoided by the exercise of greater care by the register in probate's office. In this case an agent of the register in probate's office participated in the non-compliance with sec. 853.09(3) in giving Haugk a power of attorney form with only a single witness signature blank rather than two witness signature blanks as provided in the statute. To compound this problem, the probate office accepted the defective form bearing only one witness's signature rather than two signatures and gave Haugk Marie's 1965 will. Carelessness of this nature will in some instances contribute to a party's fraudulent designs; thus public offices charged with a statutory duty similar to the dictates of sec. 853.09 must exercise greater care in the inspection of legal papers, thereby preventing the improper distribution and receipt of invalid documents. It is indeed fortuitous that Atty. Franz came forward with a copy of the destroyed will, thus preventing the frustration of the decedent's testamentary intentions.

II. *Was the Revocation in Compliance with Sec. 853.11(1) (b), Stats.?*

The common law requirements for revocation of a will by a physical act have been codified in sec. 853.11(1) (b), Stats., which recites:

"853.11 Revocation (1) Subsequent writing or physical act. A will is revoked in whole or in part by:

". .

"(b) Burning, tearing, canceling or obliterating the will or part, with the intent to revoke, by the testator or by some person in the testator's presence and by his direction."

Thus the revocation statute clearly delineates that, in order for the revocation of Marie's will to be effective, Haugk had to burn the will: (1) in Marie's presence, and (2) at her direction. In the *Estate of Beale*, 15 Wis.2d 546, 559, 113 N.W.2d 380 (1962), it was held that the revocation statute recites the "only ways by which a will can be revoked. . . ." Therefore, the statutory requirements in sec. 853.11(1) (b), Stats., mandating that a will's revocation be in the testator's presence and at his direction will be strictly construed by this court as the intent of the statute is to prevent fraud.

Was the will destroyed in Marie's presence?

The record discloses that Marie was in the kitchen of her apartment while Haugk was in the basement burning the will in the incinerator. He explained that Marie's heart condition prevented her from going to the basement because of the strain of climbing the stairs. Contrary to the strict wording of sec. 853.11(1) (b), Stats., the trial court found that Marie, being in near proximity in the same house, 13 steps away, was in Haugk's "constructive presence" at the time the will was destroyed.

In *Estate of Murphy*, 217 Wis. 472, 259 N.W. 430 (1935), this court discussed the necessity of the testator's presence during the destruction of a will. In that case the testator's will was destroyed by his sister not in his presence. The testator learned of the will's destruction sometime afterwards and, although he had ample opportunity to execute a new will, the testator apparently acquiesced to the will's destruction. In *Murphy* the trial court had found that the testator ratified the will's destruction and therefore strict adherence to the statutory requirement of the testator's presence was not essential. This court, recognizing the testator's non-presence during the will's destruction, reversed the lower court and mandated the following requirements for a valid revocation of a will:

"'Inasmuch as revocation involves intention, the inference arises that the physical act must be performed by the testator himself or under his sanction and direction. . . . Both presence and direction of the testator being usually essential where the act is performed by another, a will is not legally revoked, though destroyed by the testator's own order, if burned or torn where he did not or could not see or take cognizance of the deed done, as statutes commonly require the revocation by physical act to be by testator himself or in his presence and in such states cancellation by a third party out of the presence of testator is of no effect, but in other states destruction by direction of the testator outside of his presence may be effective. The local statute must determine whether both presence and direction are here indispensable.'" *Id.* at 480. *See:* Schouler, *Wills*, sec. 587 at 667 (6th ed.).

However, the court in *Murphy* did not define the "testator's presence" as used within the contemplation of the revocation statute. The requirement of "presence" has been defined in will execution cases. These cases require that a valid will must be executed and witnessed in the immediate presence of the testator and two witnesses. In the earlier will execution cases, it was found that the testator and the witnesses must be in a position where they could see the execution and attestations. *Will of Meurer*, 44 Wis. 392, 28 A.R. 591 (1878); *Will of Downie*, 42 Wis. 66 (1877). In later cases this court has construed the requirement as combining physical proximity with the witnesses' awareness that the other witness is signing the testamentary document. *In re Hulett's Estate*, 6 Wis.2d 20, 26, 94 N.W.2d 127 (1959). Again, it is the clear intent of the will execution statute and the construing case law to prevent the fraudulent manipulation of a testator's estate.

In *Estate of Hulett* the court ruled that a valid execution had not taken place as the attesting witnesses, while in the same room, were totally unaware of the testator's and the other witness signing because of the large number of people in the room, preventing the other parties' view. The *Hulett* case, in part, relies on *Estate of Wilm*, 182 Wis. 242, 196 N.W. 255 (1923), which bears some factual similarity to the case at bar. In *Estate of Wilm* the drafting attorney took the will from the presence of the bedridden testator into the kitchen where it was witnessed in the presence of two other people, but out of the hearing and sight of the testator. The testator's bedroom was approximately ten feet from the kitchen, separated by a wall. After considering these facts, the court stated:

"Even if the word 'presence' is construed to mean within a sphere where the senses of the testator can inform him of the performance of the act, the present case would not come within the statute, for he could neither hear ordinary conversation in the kitchen nor see what was being done on the kitchen table from any point in the bedroom he occupied. It is true the distance from the kitchen table through the wall of the bedroom to the bed was perhaps less than ten feet, but the solid wall prevented both the senses of hearing and seeing from ascertaining what was being done." *Id.* at 244.

Thus, in recognition of the case law reviewed above strictly construing the statutory element of "presence" as it relates to testamentary issues, we cannot sustain the trial court's finding that Marie's "constructive presence" satisfies the requirement stated in sec. 853.11(1) (b), Stats. The "testator's presence" as used in sec. 853.11 requires that when another person destroys a will on the behalf of the testator, the testator must be in that party's immediate physical presence and, furthermore, possessing an awareness that the will is being destroyed. To hold otherwise would open the door to enumerable cases of fraud.

In this case, Marie was not in Haugk's physical presence and could not see the burning of the will. Thus, it is evident that she had no knowledge that the will was presently being destroyed. Further, as can be concluded from the *Estate of Wilm, supra*, the testator's limitations of movement due to physical infirmities appear to lack any controlling significance in the consideration of this issue.

In the present case, a valid revocation in compliance with sec. 853.11(1) (b), Stats., could have been achieved if Haugk had torn up and destroyed the will in Marie's presence; thus she would not have had to endanger her health by climbing the basement stairs. It makes even more sense and eliminates all suggestion of fraud if the testator personally revokes the will, defacing each page of the document and placing her initials thereon.

The requirement that a will must be destroyed in the "testator's presence" must be strictly construed. This strict construction is necessary so as to prevent the inadvertent or more importantly the fraudulent destruction of a will contrary to the testator's intentions. Each element recited in the revocation statute must be established by adequate evidence as this court will not adopt a position that will promote either intestacy or the fraudulent destruction of an individual's last will and testament.

We hold the attempted revocation of Marie Haugk's 1965 will was ineffective as the burning of the will was not in her immediate physical presence and thus she had no present knowledge of the will's destruction. Thus, the facts in this case establish a failure to conform with the revocation requirements of sec. 853.11(1) (b), Stats. The trial court's finding that the will was destroyed in the testator's "constructive presence" is contrary to the great weight and clear preponderance of the evidence.

Thus, we do not consider the second statutory element required for a valid will revocation -- whether the will was destroyed at Marie's direction. We also do not reach the appellants' final contention that the doctrine of dependent relative revocation would preclude the valid revocation of the will as Marie did not intend the destruction of the 1965 will to be effective until she had executed her new will. Order reversed and cause remanded for further proceedings not inconsistent with this opinion.

In re Byrne's Will

Supreme Court of Wisconsin
223 Wis. 503, 271 N.W. 48 (1937)

Rosenberry, C. J. The testatrix left an estate of approximately $19,000. She was never married and left as her next of kin her brothers and sisters and their descendants. Upon her death there was taken from her safety-deposit box, the document in question. Mr. Vivian F. Brown, the custodian, delivered it into court. Two other persons had access to this box, C. S. Slichter, husband of the sister of deceased, and Donald C. Slichter, the executor. A photostatic copy of the will appears herewith:

WILL.

I, Isabel T. Byrne, of Madison, Wisconsin, declare this to be my last will and testament.

FIRST. After the payment of all my just debts and funeral expenses, I direct that a Marker be placed at my grave similar to the one placed at the grave of my sister Agnes.

SECOND. I direct that my executor repay to my brothers, George and Patrick, each an amount equal to the amount which either of them has advanced or paid to me from time to time until my death for my support and maintenance.

THIRD. I bequeath to my sisters, Maria E. Odell, Louise Slichter and Ellen Byrne Merrill, all of my household furniture, fixtures, wearing apparel and other personal property connected with my maintaining a home, subject, however, to the conditions of any note or memorandum that I may leave in regard to such articles.

FOURTH. I give, devise and bequeath all the rest and residue of my estate, real and personal, of whatsoever kind and description, to my brothers George and Patrick, and my sisters Maria E. Odell, Louise Slichter and Ellen Byrne Merrill, their heirs, executors, administrators and assigns, absolutely, each share and share alike.

FIFTH. I appoint George g, Merrill executor of this my last will and testament, and request that my said executor be not required to give any bond, and do hereby revoke any and all wills heretofore made by me.

In witness whereof I, Isabel T. Byrne, after this my last will and testament, subscribed my name this 28 day of October, A.D. 1922.

Isabel J. Byrne (Seal)

The only question presented upon the hearing was the form in which the will should be admitted to probate. It was the contention of the executor that the lines in the second paragraph of the will should be omitted and that the words "to my brothers George and Patrick" where they appear in the fourth paragraph should likewise be omitted. The court struck out the second paragraph and struck out the words "my brothers George and Patrick" in the fourth paragraph, and in that form admitted the will to probate.

The appellants contend, (1) that there are no definite cancellations appearing upon the face of the will, and (2) that there is no competent evidence of any intention on the part of the testatrix to revoke portions of the will. In the view which we take of the matter it will be necessary for us to consider only the first contention.

Sec. 238.14, Stats., provides:

"No will nor any part thereof shall be revoked unless by burning, tearing, canceling or obliterating the same, with the intention of revoking it, by the testator or by some person in his presence, and by his direction, or by some other will or codicil in writing, executed as prescribed in this chapter, or by some other writing, signed, attested and subscribed in the manner provided in this chapter for the execution of a will. . . ."

This statute has been in force in Wisconsin since 1849.

The question presented here is whether or not the marks made upon the will are a sufficient compliance with the statute which provides that the will or any part thereof may be revoked by cancellation. In this connection attention should be given to the fact that there was pinned to the codicil a letter addressed to Donald C. Slichter, as follows:

"Dear Donald Slichter:

"After my death when you have paid all the expenses, divide the remainder of the estate in four equal parts. You are to have one fourth, the three sisters each a fourth Ellen Merrill, Maria Odell, Mary L. Slichter each one fourth.

"Jan. 1931.

Isabel Byrne."

The will itself was executed October 28, 1922. At the time the will was executed the decedent had two brothers, George Byrne and Patrick Byrne and three sisters, Louise Slichter, Maria E. Odell and Ellen Byrne Merrill. In January, 1931, Patrick Byrne was dead, but the brother, George Byrne and the sisters, were living. The second paragraph at the time of the execution of the will was inserted for the purpose of repaying any amount to George and Patrick which might be advanced by them to her for her support. The codicil which merely names another executor was executed January 24, 1927.

The testatrix was eighty years of age at the time of the execution of the will. When the codicil was executed she was eighty-five years of age. When the letter was written she was eighty-nine years of age. There is no evidence in the record as to when the marks of cancellation were made. There is no claim that they were made by anyone other than the testatrix. All the evidence with respect to her intent must be derived from the cancellation marks themselves, aided possibly by the contents of the letter.

It may be supposed, but there is no proof of the fact, that the marks of cancellation and the letter were contemporaneous acts. Some argument is made to the effect that the marks of cancellation should not be made effective because the will and the letter indicate that one was dependent upon the other. We find no evidence to sustain that contention. It is apparent that she intended to strike out the provision for her brothers in any event. The fact that she failed to make an efficient provision for her nephew, Donald Slichter, in no way indicates that one act was dependent upon the other.

It is considered that the trial court correctly held that the marks, although they were not drawn as they would have been drawn by a competent scrivener, clearly indicate that the testatrix intended to strike out those provisions of her will which made provision for her brothers. A good deal of speculative comment might be indulged in with respect to the position of the marks upon the will which are fully disclosed by the photostatic copy. The trial court was of the view that the intention of the testatrix was apparent from an inspection of the instrument, and in that view we concur.

B. REVOCATION BY MARRIAGE OR DIVORCE.

In some jurisdictions (Oregon, Rhode Island, England, Australia) the rule is that a subsequent marriage automatically revokes an existing will, unless the existing will was made in contemplation of the marriage. While Wisconsin and most states no longer follow this rule, a subsequent divorce everywhere automatically revokes previously executed will provisions to the benefit of the now ex-spouse (or, in Wisconsin, ex-domestic partner).

Wis. Stat. 854.15 Revocation of provisions in favor of former spouse or former domestic partner.

DEFINITIONS. In this section:

"Disposition of property" means a transfer, including by appointment, of property or any other benefit to a beneficiary designated in a governing instrument.

"Divorce, annulment or similar event" means any of the following:

A divorce, annulment, or other event or proceeding that would exclude a spouse as a surviving spouse under s. 851.30.

A termination of a domestic partnership or other event or proceeding that would exclude a person as a surviving domestic partner under s. 851.295.

"Former spouse" means a person whose marriage to the decedent or domestic partnership with the decedent has been the subject of a divorce, annulment or similar event.

"Relative of the former spouse" means an individual who is related to the former spouse by blood, adoption or marriage and who, after the divorce, annulment or similar event, is not related to the decedent by blood, adoption or marriage.

SCOPE. This section applies only to governing instruments that were executed by the decedent before the occurrence of a divorce, annulment or similar event with respect to his or her marriage to the former spouse.

REVOCATION UPON DIVORCE. Except as provided in subs. (5) and (6), a divorce, annulment or similar event does all of the following:

Revokes any revocable disposition of property made by the decedent to the former spouse or a relative of the former spouse in a governing instrument.

Revokes any disposition created by law to the former spouse or a relative of the former spouse.

Revokes any revocable provision made by the decedent in a governing instrument conferring a power of appointment on the former spouse or a relative of the former spouse.

Revokes the decedent's revocable nomination of the former spouse or a relative of the former spouse to serve in any fiduciary or representative capacity.

Severs the interests of the decedent and former spouse in property held by them as joint tenants with the right of survivorship or as survivorship marital property and transforms the interests of the decedent and former spouse into tenancies in common.

EFFECT OF REVOCATION. Except as provided in subs. (5) and (6), provisions of a governing instrument that are revoked by this section are given effect as if the former spouse and relatives of the former spouse disclaimed the revoked provisions or, in the case of a revoked nomination in a fiduciary or representative capacity, as if the former spouse and relatives of the former spouse died immediately before the divorce, annulment or similar event.

EXCEPTIONS.

This section does not apply if any of the following applies:

The express terms of a governing instrument provide otherwise.

The express terms of a court order provide otherwise.

The express terms of a contract relating to the division of the decedent's and former spouse's property made between the decedent and the former spouse before or after the marriage or the divorce, annulment or similar event provide otherwise.

The divorce, annulment or similar event is nullified.

The decedent and the former spouse have remarried or entered into a new domestic partnership before the death of the decedent.

If the transfer is made under a governing instrument and the person who executed the governing instrument had an intent contrary to any provision in this section, then that provision is inapplicable to the transfer. Extrinsic evidence may be used to construe the intent.

REVOCATION OF NONTESTAMENTARY PROVISION IN MARITAL PROPERTY AGREEMENT. The effect of a judgment of annulment, divorce or legal separation on marital property agreements under s. 766.58 is governed by s. 767.375 (1).

Allstate Life Ins. Co. v. Hanson

United States District Court for the Eastern District of Wisconsin
200 F. Supp. 2d 1012 (2002)

ABELMAN, J.

I. PROCEDURAL BACKGROUND

This case involves a dispute between Misti Hanson, the former wife of Richard Hanson, now deceased, and Elizabeth Hanson, Richard's mother and only heir. The dispute concerns who is entitled to the benefits of Richard's life insurance policy. Misti is the named beneficiary of the policy, but a recently-enacted Wisconsin statute changed the status of former spouses named as beneficiaries of life insurance policies. The new law creates a presumption that divorce revokes the beneficiary status of former spouses; and it applies retroactively.

The case began when plaintiff Allstate Life Insurance Co. filed an interpleader action in Wisconsin state court naming Misti and Elizabeth as defendants. Misti is a citizen of Wisconsin, and Elizabeth is a citizen of Illinois. Elizabeth timely removed the case to federal court. Neither Allstate nor Misti objected to removal or moved to remand the case to state court. The case was assigned to the Hon. John W. Reynolds and, when Judge Reynolds died, was randomly reassigned to me. Allstate deposited the benefits under the policy, $509,189.80, with the Clerk of Court and was dismissed as a party.

Misti now moves for summary judgment, asserting that she is entitled to the proceeds of the policy. She argues that the new law presumptively revoking her beneficiary status violates federal and state constitutional provisions prohibiting the enactment of laws that impair the obligation of contract.

II. SUBJECT MATTER JURISDICTION

[The court first ruled that even though the case was improperly removed from state court to federal court, the problem was not jurisdictional and that both parties has waived their right to object.]

III. FACTUAL BACKGROUND

Misti and Richard married in 1989 and each purchased a $500,000 Allstate life insurance policy naming each other as beneficiary but reserving the power to change the beneficiary designation. In 1997, Misti and Richard divorced. The marital settlement agreement stated that "neither party shall be obligated to maintain life insurance for the benefit of the other party," and awarded each party the life insurance policy in his or her own name. In addition, the agreement stated "each party shall be divested of and each party waives, renounces, and gives up . . . all right, title, and interest in and to property awarded to the other. All property and money received and retained by the parties shall be the separate property of the respective parties, free and clear of any right, title, interest or claim of the other party." Nothing in the agreement or decree expressly changed the beneficiaries in Misti's and Richard's life insurance policies, and Misti and Richard did not expressly change the beneficiaries later.

When Misti and Richard purchased the policies and when they divorced, Wisconsin law presumptively treated each divorced spouse as having pre-deceased the other for purposes of awarding probate assets at death. Wis. Stat. §853.11(3) (1991), amended by Wis. Stat. §854.15 (1998). However, nonprobate assets, such as life insurance policies, were treated differently. See Bersch v. VanKleeck, 112 Wis. 2d 594, 599, 334 N.W.2d 114 (1983). When spouses who had named each other as beneficiaries in life insurance policies divorced, the former spouse remained the presumed beneficiary unless the divorce decree "unequivocally and explicitly" divested the spouse of that interest, and the parties notified the insurance company of the change.

In 1998, the Wisconsin Legislature revised the state probate code bringing it into closer alignment with the Uniform Probate Code. The new provision states that divorce "revokes any revocable disposition of property made by the decedent to the former spouse or a relative of the former spouse in a governing instrument." Wis. Stat. §854.15(3)(a). The effect of this change was to apply the presumption previously applicable to the probate assets of divorcing spouses to nonprobate assets and presumptively treat each divorced spouse as having pre-deceased the other. Thus, under the present law, divorce presumptively revokes the beneficiary spouse's interest in a life insurance policy. The beneficiary spouse can rebut the presumption by showing that the parties expressly agreed otherwise or by offering extrinsic evidence of the decedent's intent. Id. §854.15(5). The legislature also applied the 1998 revisions retroactively. Id. §861.21.

IV. SUMMARY JUDGMENT STANDARD

[The court then summarized the standard for summary judgment in Wisconsin.]

V. DISCUSSION

"The laws which subsist at the time and place of the making of a contract . . . enter into and form a part of it." Gen. Motors Corp. v. Romein, 503 U.S. 181, 188, 117 L.

Ed. 2d 328, 112 S. Ct. 1105 (1991) (quotation marks and citations omitted). Thus, at the time of the divorce Misti retained her interest as the beneficiary of Richard's policy. See Bersch, 112 Wis. 2d at 599. However, §854.15(3)(a) presumptively revokes her interest. The question presented is whether retroactive application of §854.15(3)(a) violates the Contract Clauses of the federal and Wisconsin constitutions. Misti argues that it does. …

[After a lengthy analysis, the Court concluded that the Wisconsin statute, as applied in this case, did not violate the Contract Clause of either the United States or the Wisconsin Constitutions. Consequently, the motion for summary judgment was denied.]

C. DEPENDENT RELATIVE REVOCATION AND REVIVAL

Estate of Alburn

Supreme Court of Wisconsin
18 Wis. 2d 340, 118 N.W.2d 919 (1963)

CURRIE, Justice. This court is committed to the doctrine of dependent relative revocation. Estate of Eberhardt (1957), 1 Wis.2d 439, 85 N.W.2d 483, and Estate of Callahan (1947), 251 Wis. 247, 29 N.W.2d 352. The usual situation for application of this doctrine arises where a testator executes one will and thereafter attempts to revoke it by making a later testamentary disposition which for some reason proves ineffective. In both the Eberhardt and Callahan Cases, however, the doctrine was applied to the unusual situation in which a testator revokes a later will under the mistaken belief that by so doing he is reinstating a prior will. In this unusual situation, the doctrine of dependent relative revocation is invoked to render the revocation ineffective. The basis of the doctrine is stated in Estate of Callahan, supra, as follows (251 Wis. at p. 255, 29 N.W.2d at p. 355):

"The doctrine of dependent relative revocation is based upon the testator's inferred intention. It is held that as a matter of law the destruction of the later document is intended to be conditional where it is accompanied by the expressed intent of reinstating a former will and where there is no explanatory evidence. Of course if there is evidence that the testator intended the destruction to be absolute, there is no room for the application of the doctrine of dependent revocation.'"

The sole question raised by appellant on this appeal is whether the finding of the trial court that deceased revoked the Kankakee will under the mistaken belief that she was thereby reinstating the prior Milwaukee will is against the great weight and clear preponderance of the evidence. This requires that we review the pertinent evidence.

Testatrix was born in Wisconsin. For about thirty years she had resided in San Francisco, California, and later in Cleveland, Ohio. As a widow without children, she came to Milwaukee in the fall of 1954 and lived there with Viola Henkey, her grandniece. While so residing she executed the Milwaukee will on August 12, 1955. The original of this will was left with Attorney George R. Affeldt of Milwaukee, who had drafted it, where it remained until the death of testatrix. Sometime shortly prior to May 22, 1959, testatrix moved to Kankakee, Illinois, and resided there with her brother, Robert Lehmann. On May 22, 1959, she executed the Kankakee will.

On June 28, 1960, testatrix left Kankakee and came to Fort Atkinson, Wisconsin, and lived there with another brother, Edwin Lehmann, until her death in November of 1960. Testatrix was a patient at a hospital in Fort Atkinson during part of October and November of that year. Edwin testified that he had learned of the execution of the Kankakee will prior to the arrival of testatrix on June 28, 1960. On the evening of her arrival, he asked her what she had done with that will, and she replied, 'What do you suppose, I got rid of it.' The next morning testatrix came downstairs with the torn pieces of the Kankakee will tied up in a handkerchief. Edwin provided her with a paper sack in which she deposited the pieces of the will. Edwin then took the sack with the garbage to the dump. There he opened the sack and let the pieces fly in the wind as testatrix had directed him to do.

Edwin was not questioned about any statement regarding the Milwaukee will which testatrix might have made in his presence at Fort Atkinson. He did testify that after her death he searched through her effects for a will but failed to find one. In view of the following testimony given by Olga Lehmann, his wife, this gives rise to an inference that Edwin was searching for the Milwaukee will.

Olga Lehmann was called as a witness by counsel for proponents of the Kankakee will and proved to be a reluctant if not a hostile witness. She was shown a letter dated January 25, 1961, which she had written to Olga Olson, a resident of San Francisco and an old friend of testatrix, and asked if this letter refreshed her memory regarding a statement made by testatrix, about the time of her arrival in Fort Atkinson, in the witness's presence that testatrix wished her Milwaukee will to stand. The witness stated that her memory was not refreshed by this letter although she admitted that the letter bore her signature. The letter of Olga Lehmann to Olga Olson was offered in evidence by counsel for proponents of the Kankakee will but, objection having been made to its admission, the trial court ruled it inadmissible.

Olga Lehmann then testified that the matter of the Milwaukee will was not discussed by testatrix in a conversation with Viola Henkey after June 29, 1960, when the witness was also present. Olga Lehmann was then asked the following questions and gave the following answers thereto:

'Q. Did the deceased ever discuss in your presence the matter of the Milwaukee will at any other time other than the time we are just now referring to?

'A. Yes.

'Q. Who was present at that time?

'A. Just myself.

'Q. What did she tell you concerning the Milwaukee will?

'A. That was the one she wanted to stand.

'Q. Can you tell me in point of time when this might have been?

'A. No, we talked often.

We deem it significant that counsel for appellant did not cross-examine Olga Lehmann with respect to her testimony that testatrix said she wanted the Milwaukee will to stand. Therefore, Olga Lehmann's testimony was not qualified or limited in any way.

This statement by testatrix clearly occurred after her destruction of the Kankakee will. Appellant now attacks this statement on the ground that it was not made contemporaneously with such destruction. In Estate of Callahan, supra, however, the only evidence regarding the intent of testatrix when she destroyed her 1944 will was her husband's statement in her presence after the destruction and her silence indicating acquiescence. The husband stated that they both had destroyed their 1944 wills because they desired to put their son back in the position he occurred under their 1940 wills. Upon this evidence this court determined the doctrine of dependent relative revocation applied and affirmed the judgment of the county court which had admitted the 1944 will of testatrix to probate.

The plan of testamentary disposition under the two wills was in part as follows: The Milwaukee will contained specific bequests of jewelry and household furnishings to Viola Henkey, the grandniece of testatrix, and directed that any indebtedness owing deceased by Viola Henkey and her husband be deemed satisfied. The residuary clause bequeathed one fourth of the estate to her friend Olga Olson, one fourth to Doris Alburn, one fourth to Lulu Alburn, and one fourth to Viola Henkey. The Kankakee will included a bequest to Olga Olson of 38 shares of stock in the Bank of America National Trust & Savings Association and bequests of jewelry to Lulu and Addie Alburn. The remainder of the estate was bequeathed as follows: four tenths to Lulu Alburn, five tenths to Doris Alburn, and one tenth to Robert Lehmann, brother of testatrix. The Alburns are not related to testatrix but are relatives of her deceased husband. Viola Henkey, although a blood relative of testatrix, is not one of her next-of-kin who would inherit in the event testatrix had died intestate.

The next-of-kin consist of four surviving brothers and one sister plus a large number of nieces and nephews of testatrix, the children of four deceased sisters and one deceased brother. Thus under the Milwaukee will, none of the next-of-kin were named as legatees, whereas under the Kankakee will, the only next-of-kin named a legatee was Robert, her brother. His share under the Kankakee will is somewhat less than the one-tenth share of the entire estate which he would receive if testatrix had died intestate. The bulk of the estate under both wills was bequeathed to the Alburns and Olga Olson. This plan of testamentary disposition extended as late as May, 1959.

There is no evidence of any change of circumstances occurring thereafter that would indicate any reason why testatrix should die intestate and nine tenths of her estate go to next-of-kin not named in either will. The one change in circumstance was her leaving the home of her brother Robert and moving in with her brother Edwin. This more might provide a reason for her desiring to revoke the Kankakee will, but certainly not for her wishing to die intestate. The learned trial judge, in the supplemental memorandum decision of December 26, 1961, stated, 'I have a strong conviction that decedent did not want to die intestate.' The evidence fully supports this conclusion despite the fact that testatrix took no steps between June 29, 1960, and her death nearly five months later to draft a new will.

We deem that a reasonable inference, to be drawn from the competent evidence in this case, for her failure to make a new will is her evident belief that her Milwaukee will was still operative. Testatrix must have known that the original of the Milwaukee will was still in possession of Attorney Affeldt and believed that the only impediment to this will was the revocation clause of the Kankakee will. She also knew that the Kankakee will had been destroyed by tearing it in pieces and scattering the pieces so that they could not be found.

We are constrained to conclude that the statement made to Olga Lehmann that testatrix wished her Milwaukee will to stand, the inference that she did not wish to die intestate, and the fact that she took no steps following the destruction of the Kankakee will to make a new will are sufficient evidence to support the finding that she destroyed the Kankakee will under the mistaken belief that the Milwaukee will would control the disposition of her estate. Furthermore there is no evidence which controverts this finding. Therefore, it is not against the great weight and clear preponderance of the evidence.

Counsel for respondents Alburn request a review by this court of several rulings by the trial court which excluded certain evidence pursuant to objections made by counsel for appellant Ruedisili. This excluded evidence related to further statements made by testatrix, after destruction of the Kankakee will, that she then considered her Milwaukee will to be in effect or desired this result. In view of our conclusion that the trial court's determination may be sustained upon the evidence admitted, we find it unnecessary to review these rulings. Judgment affirmed.

IV. RULES AFFECTING ADMISSIBILITY TO PROBATE

A. LOST WILLS

Hanusa v. Intestate Heirs of Ewer

Supreme Court of Wisconsin
95 Wis. 2d 733, 289 N.W.2d 384 (1980)

DYKMAN, J. Appellant appeals from the order of the circuit court of Waupaca County rendered December 21, 1978, denying admission of the lost will of decedent Sadie Ewer into probate, admitting the decedent's codicil into probate and allowing the estate of Sadie Ewer to pass intestate. The appellant is the executor named in decedent's codicil to her lost will and the respondents are decedent's intestate heirs-at-law.

Sadie Ewer, a long-time resident of Clintonville, Wisconsin, died January 26, 1978, at age 77. The Waupaca County Court found her incompetent five months prior to her death and she was placed in a nursing home. Her heirs-at-law are four nieces, including Virginia Kraegenbrink who was appointed guardian of the decedent when she was found incompetent.

On May 3, 1968, Sadie Ewer executed a last will and testament. The will was duly witnessed by her attorney, C. C. Mullarkey, and his secretary. The will named the pastor of the Christus Lutheran Church of Clintonville as the executor and the residuary clause named five churches as beneficiaries: Christus Lutheran Church of Clintonville (the decedent's church), St. Martin Lutheran Church of Clintonville, St. Rose Catholic Church of Clintonville, United Methodist Church of Clintonville, and St. Anthony Catholic Church of Neopit.

On the same day her husband, John Ewer, executed his will which contained provisions identical to those in the will of Sadie Ewer. Mr. Ewer died September 5, 1970.

An unexecuted copy of Mrs. Ewer's will was kept in her attorney's office. Mrs. Ewer retained the original copy of her will. Mrs. Ewer executed a codicil to this will on November 3, 1970, which was revoked by a subsequent codicil executed December 21, 1972. The 1972 codicil named Reverend Ralph Hanusa as executor of her will. He was the pastor at the Christus Lutheran Church but was being transferred to another church outside of Clintonville. Mrs. Ewer wanted to ensure that Reverend Hanusa would be executor of her will since he had been a friend to her and her husband for several years.

After Mrs. Ewer executed the second codicil in 1972, she placed it in a safe deposit box for safekeeping. Mrs. Ewer visited her safe deposit box frequently over the next few years, and had sole access to it until her niece, Mrs. Kraegenbrink, was given power of attorney in March, 1976. Mrs. Ewer continued to visit her safe deposit box until she was admitted to the nursing home in August, 1977. At that time, Mrs. Kraegenbrink and her attorney inventoried the contents of the safe deposit box and found that there were two envelopes, one containing the 1972 codicil and one containing the revoked 1970 codicil. There was no will in the safe deposit box. Upon the death of Mrs. Ewer, Mrs. Kraegenbrink conducted a search for her aunt's will at her aunt's home and could not find the will.

Additional facts will be stated in this opinion.

Appellant requested admission of the decedent's lost will under sec. 856.17, Stats. which provides:

Lost will, how proved. If any will is lost, destroyed by accident or destroyed without the testator's consent the court has power to take proof of the execution and validity of the will and to establish the same. The petition for the probate of the will shall set forth the provisions thereof.

The trial court noted that there is a presumption that a lost will last known to be in the possession of the deceased has been destroyed by the deceased with the intent to revoke the will. The court found that the proponents of the lost will had not met their burden of proving that Sadie Ewer's will was lost, destroyed by accident or destroyed without the testator's consent.

Specifically the trial court found that although the May 3, 1968 will was valid and duly executed, "[t]he record establishes that Sadie Ewer destroyed the will dated May 3, 1968, sometime after December 21, 1972 and before becoming incompetent and that such destruction was with intent to destroy and revoke the will dated May 3, 1968." This finding of fact and the resulting determination must be sustained on appeal unless such finding of fact is against the great weight and clear preponderance of the evidence. *Estate of Jones,* 74 Wis.2d 607, 247 N.W.2d 168 (1976). Before the trial court's finding can be reversed, the evidence supporting a contrary finding must itself constitute the great weight and clear preponderance of the evidence. *Jones,* 74 Wis.2d at 611.

The issues on appeal are: (1) Whether the presumption regarding lost wills applies to this case; and (2) Whether the trial court's finding that the decedent destroyed her will with the intent to revoke it is against the great weight and clear preponderance of the evidence.

Does the Presumption Apply?

It has long been the law in Wisconsin that when a validly executed will, last known to be in the possession of the testator cannot be found upon the death of the testator a rebuttable presumption arises that the testator intended to revoke the will. *In re Will of Valentine,* 93 Wis. 45, 67 N.W. 12 (1896); *Estate of Fonk,* 51 Wis.2d 339, 187 N.W.2d 147 (1971).

The appellant questions the application of the presumption to this case since Sadie Ewer was not the last person to have access to her important papers located in her safe deposit box or at her home. Two years prior to her death, Mrs. Ewer gave her niece, Virginia Kraegenbrink, power of attorney because a pending incompetency investigation caused Mrs. Ewer to become distraught and concerned over her affairs. Five months prior to Mrs. Ewer's death, her niece was named her guardian and Mrs.

Ewer was admitted to a nursing home. Mrs. Kraegenbrink inventoried and emptied Mrs. Ewer's safe deposit box and conducted the search for the will in Mrs. Ewer's home. The appellant claims that Mrs. Ewer did not have final possession of her will.

The record shows however, that no one saw Mrs. Ewer's 1968 will after it was executed and that Mrs. Ewer kept the original will. It cannot be determined whether a document Mrs. Ewer read to her niece in 1974, which the decedent purported to be her will, was in fact her will. Mrs. Kraegenbrink testified that she never actually saw the 1968 will. Thus, there is no affirmative evidence that anyone but the decedent had final possession of the will.

Although Mrs. Kraegenbrink's access to Mrs. Ewer's papers is probative of whether Mrs. Ewer destroyed her will with the intention to revoke it, *Gavitt v. Moulton,* 119 Wis. 35, 96 N.W. 395 (1903), it is not sufficient to reverse a finding that Mrs. Ewer was the last person to have possession of the 1968 will and prevent the initial application of the presumption in this case.

Was the trial court's finding and determination against the great weight and clear preponderance of the evidence?

Appellant contends that sufficient evidence was presented to rebut the presumption thus allowing the court to review all of the evidence free of the presumption. The cases concerning lost wills support this contention. However, sec. 903.01, Stats., which became effective in 1974, and thus applies to this case, alters the effect of common law presumptions in Wisconsin. Section 903.01 provides:

Presumptions in general. Except as provided by statute, a presumption recognized at common law or created by statute, including statutory provisions that certain basis facts are prima facie evidence of other facts, imposes on the party relying on the presumption the burden of proving the basic facts, but once the basic facts are found to exist the presumption imposes on the party against whom it is directed the burden of proving that the nonexistence of the presumed fact is more probable than its existence.

The Wisconsin Supreme Court explained in *Estate of Malnar,* 73 Wis.2d 192, 203, n. 2, 243 N.W.2d 435, 441, n.2 (1976), that under this evidentiary rule the presumption does not disappear "upon the introduction of any evidence that conflicts with the presumption." Instead the rule requires the proponents of the lost will to show by a preponderance of the evidence that it is more probable than not that Mrs. Ewer did not destroy her will with the intent to revoke.

It is not clear whether this new rule regarding presumptions has any impact on the result of this case. The old rule regarding presumptions was easier for the proponents of lost wills to meet only when there was no evidence aside from the presumption that the decedent destroyed the will with the intent to revoke. If the presumption was the only evidence of destruction with intent to revoke, then credible evidence that the will was lost rebutted the presumption and the proponents had met their burden. *Will of Donigian,* 265 Wis. 147, 150, 60 N.W.2d 732 (1953). However, if there was other evidence supporting a conclusion that the decedent destroyed the will with the intent to revoke, the court would have to make a determination based on a preponderance of the evidence. *Will of Donigian,* 265 Wis. at 150. Under the new rule, the court determines whether it is more probable than not that the decedent destroyed the will with the intent to revoke. This determination is the same as the court's consideration under the prior rule of what constituted the preponderance of the evidence.

In this case there was evidence presented both supporting and countering the presumption. Thus, it was for the trial court to determine, based on all the evidence presented, which conclusion was more probable than not. On review in this court, we must determine whether it was against the great weight and clear preponderance of the evidence for the trial court to conclude that the proponent of the lost will did not meet his burden.

The proponent of the lost will may meet his burden of showing that it is more probable than not that Mrs. Ewer did not destroy her will with the intent to revoke it by presenting evidence of several different factors. Although no one factor is determinative, the cases consider a combination of factors and reflect the numerous theories available to meet the burden of proof. Since intent to revoke is required to support the presumption, the proponent of a lost will could show that the decedent lacked the necessary capacity to form that intent. Sec. 853.01, Stats. Usually evidence is presented showing that the testator affirmed the existence of the will after its execution, *Estate of Fonk,* 51 Wis.2d 339; *Estate of Markofske,* 47 Wis.2d 769, 178 N.W.2d 9 (1970); *Will of Donigian,* 265 Wis. 147; *Gavitt v. Moulton,* 119 Wis. 35; that the testator was careless in his or her care of important papers and therefore could have misplaced the will, *Estate of Markofske; Estate of Lambert,* 252 Wis. 117, 31 N.W.2d 163 (1948); that an adverse party had access to the lost will and an opportunity to destroy or misplace it, *Estate of Markofske;* that the testator had a history of relying on written wills as the method of disposing with his or her property at death, *Estate of Markofske, Will of Donigian, Will of Lauburg,* 170 Wis. 502, 175 N.W. 925 (1920); and that the nature of the testator's relationship to the beneficiaries of the lost will and the heirs-at-law had not changed since the execution of the will, *Will of Lauburg; Wendt v. Ziegenhagen,* 148 Wis. 382, 134 N.W. 905 (1912).

The proponent of Mrs. Ewer's lost will presented evidence regarding several of these factors.

(1) *Capacity to revoke.* Although the court found that Mrs. Ewer destroyed her will before she was found incompetent five months before her death, appellant presented evidence at trial through the testimony of neighbors, the decedent's banker, attorney and others, that Mrs. Ewer became increasingly confused and partially incapable of caring for herself for about two years prior to her death. As Mrs. Ewer's confusion and forgetfulness increased she had increasing difficulty and distress with her finances and papers. She responded by attempting to simplify her business affairs.

At one point, Mrs. Ewer became upset that her savings were located at different banks and had all of her bonds and notes moved to one bank, even though it resulted in reduced earnings. The testimony relating to the careless manner in which she kept her papers, discussed fully later in this opinion, indicates that Mrs. Ewer had a reduced mental capacity to handle her business affairs after 1974. The testimony is supported by the fact that Mrs. Ewer asked her niece, Virginia Kraegenbrink, to assume power of attorney after being notified of a pending incompetency hearing. This evidence raised an issue of her capacity to form the intent to revoke her will during the last two years of her life.

There was also testimony by these same witnesses that Mrs. Ewer could be quite articulate and at times could remember prior events in detail. The trial court inferred from this testimony that until she was found legally incompetent, Mrs. Ewer was capable of forming the intent to revoke. Although it is impossible to determine at what point Mrs. Ewer in fact could no longer from this intent, it was not against the great weight and clear preponderance of the evidence for the trial court to find that until she was found incompetent there were times when Mrs. Ewer could form the intent to revoke her will.

(2) *Affirmation of the existence of the will.* Appellant presented extensive testimony that Mrs. Ewer told others of her will during the last few years of her life. Respondents concede in their brief that she would tell anyone who would listen about her will. There was a great deal of testimony indicating that Mrs. Ewer was extremely concerned that Reverend Hanusa be the executor of her will. She would ask bank employees and others to look at her condicil and assure her that it said that Reverend Hanusa was her executor. At times she would refer to the codicil as her will. The following testimony presented by appellant indicates that during the last few years of her life the decedent frequently referred to the 1968 will as she and her husband had executed it:

(a) The 1972 codicil affirmed the 1968 will by providing in relevant part:

I, SADIE EWER, of the City of Clintonville, County of Waupaca and State of Wisconsin, being of sound mind and memory, do make, publish and declare the following as and for a Codicil to the Last Will and Testament heretofore by me executed, bearing date of May 3, 1968, hereby revoking all former codicils heretofore made.

FIRST: It is my will and wish that any of the religious institutions named in the residuary clause of my will, if memorials are to be in any manner created for me, that the memorial shall also name my late husband, John D. Ewer.

THIRD: I nominate and appoint *Pastor Ralph Hanusa,* Pastor of the Christus Lutheran Church of Clintonville, Wisconsin, as personal representative of this my Last Will and Testament and I will and direct that he shall not be required to furnish bond.

FOURTH: In all other respects and except as hereinabove set forth, I hereby republish, ratify and confirm my said Will dated the 3rd day of May, 1968.

Thus in 1972 Mrs. Ewer affirmed her 1968 will in a most clear manner: republication through a codicil.

(b) Randy Malueg, an employee at the bank which contained Mar. Ewer's safe deposit box, and with whom Mrs. Ewer frequently discussed her business affairs, testified that during the last three years of her life Mrs. Ewer frequently referred to the will that she and her husband had executed.

(c) Pearl Rekitzke another bank employee, testified that Mrs. Ewer had appeared upset over the apparently excessive amount of money available to her and had asked Ms. Rekitzke what she should do with it. When Ms. Rekitzke suggested that she make a contribution to the church, Mrs. Ewer responded that she had already provided well for the church and did not need to make a contribution to it.

(d) Reverend Hanusa, the appellant, testified that during return visits to Mrs. Ewer after he left Mrs. Ewer's church, between 1973 and 1975, she reasserted that the churches were to be the beneficiaries of her will.

(e) Hildegarde Eggleston, a neighbor who attended church with Mrs. Ewer a few times during the last two or three years of Mrs. Ewer's life, testified that Mrs. Ewer discussed her will with her regularly. Mrs. Ewer told her that she had left the will the way that she and her husband had made it, and that the churches were the beneficiaries. Mrs. Eggleston felt Mrs. Ewer's will was of primary importance to her.

(f) Mrs. Hanusa, wife of appellant, testified that in 1974, Mrs. Ewer mentioned that the churches would be beneficiaries of her will.

(g) Mark Joy, a neighbor of Mrs. Ewer who helped care for her during the last two years of her life, testified that Mrs. Ewer told him that the church was well taken care of after she died. She later expressed a concern to him that she wanted to make sure that the will was carried out.

(h) Ruth Joy, Mark Joy's wife, who also helped to care for Mrs. Ewer from 1976 until she went into the nursing home, testified that Mrs. Ewer told her that her will would be carried out the way she and her husband had made it and on occasion mentioned the churches as her beneficiaries.

(i) Eugene Peterson, the pastor who replaced Reverend Hanusa, testified that he had discussed Mrs. Ewer's will with her and that she had told him that she did not get to church as much as she liked, but that the church would be taken care of after she died.

The court inferred from this testimony that because her primary concern was that Reverend Hanusa be executor of her will, Mrs. Ewer considered the 1972 condicil to be her will, and that her references to her will were actually references to this codicil. The court concluded that the ministers understood Mrs. Ewer to be naming their church only as a beneficiary since she did not mention the other churches to the ministers.

The court in *Estate of Lambert,* 252 Wis. at 126, 31 N.W. at 167-68, agreed with the trial court's conclusion that the presumption had been rebutted where the proponent of the will "established that the deceased made a will and persisted in statements of satisfaction with its contents up to the day of his death."

In *Will of Lauburg,* 170 Wis. at 506, 175 N.W. at 926, the court upheld the trial court's finding that the proponents of the lost will had overcome the presumption when they introduced evidence which showed "that the testatrix up to the time of her death had made declarations tending to show the existence of her will and had no intention of revoking her second will, and that she steadfastly adhered to her purpose of providing for her son Fred and her daughter Lillian, as she had done in this will."

We find that the court's conclusion that Mrs. Ewer was only referring to her 1972 condicil in speaking of her "will" is against the great weight and clear preponderance of the evidence. The testimony showed that she consistently referred to the will as she and her husband had made it, discussed the churches as being the beneficiaries, and never expressed a desire to provide for her heirs-at-law in a different manner than provided in the will. The fact that she only mentioned one church to her ministers does not give rise to the inference that she preferred her heirs-at-law to the churches as beneficiaries.

Thus, this court finds the great weight and clear preponderance of the evidence shows that Mrs. Ewer reaffirmed the existence of her will prior to being found incompetent.

(3) *Carelessness in keeping important papers.* Several witnesses testified to acts by Mrs. Ewer which indicated that during the last few years of her life she was careless and forgetful in the manner in which she kept her papers. Roxanne Wunsck, secretary for Mrs. Ewer's attorney, helped Mrs. Ewer prepare her tax returns until 1975. She stated that when she would go to Mrs. Ewer's house to obtain the necessary papers and information, Mrs. Ewer would bring out piles of papers in a basket or box. Although she was always able to complete the returns accurately, Mrs. Wunsch explained that she used the standard deduction in preparing Mrs. Ewer's returns because she never could have found the necessary papers to do an itemized deduction. Mrs. Wunsch further stated that she stopped doing her returns in part because of the disarray in which Mrs. Ewer maintained the necessary material.

Mrs. Ewer's neighbor, Mark Joy, described her preoccupation with money and how she would sometimes withdraw money from her savings only to redeposit it the same day. Mr. Joy also had to help Mrs. Ewer pay some bills because she was not sure what she had to do. He indicated that she could distinguish between junk mail and business mail but that she could not determine what she was supposed to do when she received bills and other business mail. Mr. Joy testified that one day Mrs. Ewer brought over $14,000 in bonds to his house and asked him if she should keep them or throw them out.

Virginia Kraegenbrink, one of the respondents, testified that her aunt had a habit of tearing things up. When she searched her aunt's home for the will she found torn papers in the heating register including John Ewer's military discharge papers.

Reverend Eugene Peterson testified that when he visited Mrs. Ewer at her home her dining table was strewn with papers.

Ethel Wolf, next door neighbor of Mrs. Ewer, testified that Mrs. Ewer would tear up papers and put them in the hedge between their homes. Mrs. Wolf indicated that although she cleaned up some of the papers, she did not examine them to determine their nature. However, Mrs. Wolf did see Mrs. Ewer one day twisting and rolling a social security check. Eventually, Mrs. Wolf called the police to ask Mrs. Ewer to stop tearing up papers in her yard.

The court found that Mrs. Ewer was not careless in the maintenance of her papers because there was no testimony that she had ever complained of losing or had actually lost, misplaced or accidentally destroyed any important papers and that she kept her important papers in a safe deposit box. It is a logical inference that if a person has not in fact lost, misplaced or accidentally destroyed any important papers that they are careful in the maintenance of their important papers. However, the direct, undisputed testimony regarding Mrs. Ewer's confusion about her business papers, her habit of tearing up papers, her twisting and rolling a social security check and her wondering whether she should throw away $14,000 in bonds negates that inference.

In *Estate of Markofske,* 47 Wis.2d 769, the court found that the careless manner in which the decedent kept stocks and bonds supported the conclusion that her will was not destroyed with the intent to revoke it.

We find that the great weight and clear preponderance of the evidence shows that Mrs. Ewer was not careful in keeping some of her important papers. The evidence supports the inference that she did not destroy her will with the intention of revoking it. Her failure to complain about losing papers is consistent with the inference that she did not think that any of her important papers were missing.

(4) *Access by an adverse party to the decedent's important papers.* Although there was no testimony showing any wrongdoing on the part of Virginia Kraegenbrink, appellant showed that she was an adverse party who had exclusive access to Mrs. Ewer's papers while Mrs. Ewer was in the nursing home, that she emptied the bank safe deposit box and took the contents to her home, and that she conducted the search for the will.

As there was no affirmative evidence of any wrongdoing by Mrs. Kraegenbrink the suspicions raised by the appellant are not sufficient to overturn the trial court's finding that Mrs. Kraegenbrink did not destroy Mrs. Ewer's will.

(5) *Testator's reliance on wills as the method of disposing of her property.* The record shows that Mrs. Ewer was obsessed about her will. She frequently showed what she claimed was her will to the bank employees and discussed it with many people. Up until the time she was found incompetent, she referred to the will as the one that she and her husband had made. The trial court concluded that Mrs. Ewer's many references to her will were actually reaffirmations that Reverend Hanusa would be her executor and not indications that she thought her property would be disposed of by a will.

In the case of *In re Steinke's Will,* 95 Wis. 121, 126, 70 N.W. 61, 62 (1897), the court found that the testator's "declarations upon the subject of the existence or nonexistence of the will, and its custody, up to within a short time previous to her death, are competent evidence to rebut such presumption, and to show that she died in the belief that the will was still in existence, as a valid disposition of her estate."

While the trial court may have been correct in concluding that it is not unlawful for someone merely to name an executor in a will and allow the property to pass intestate, there is no indication in the record that this was Mrs. Ewer's intent. To the contrary, Mrs. Ewer's obsession with her will and her references to it as the one that she and her husband had made show that she intended to have a will dispose of her property. The trial court's finding that Mrs. Ewer intended to use a will only to name an executor and to die intestate is against the great weight and clear preponderance of the evidence.

(6) *Relationship between the testator and the beneficiaries of the lost will and the heirs-at-law.* The testimony showed that Mrs. Ewer did not attend church as frequently after 1972 as she had before. Her neighbors, Mr. and Mrs. Joy and Hildegarde Eggleston testified that when they would take her to church or make sure someone sat with her, then she gladly attended church. She was still a member of the Christus Lutheran Church, one of the beneficiaries of the lost will, at the time of her death. She never indicated that she was displeased about the church to her pastor or neighbors.

Her niece, Virginia Kraegenbrink, and her sister-in-law, Virginia Welter, testified that Mrs. Ewer became disenchanted with the church after she executed her codicil. Mrs. Kraegenbrink testified that her aunt complained to her about a minister with a beard whom she did not like. Although she testified that her aunt never mentioned him by name, Mrs. Kraegenbrink said that Mrs. Ewer told her that he was the minister at her church. In addition, she testified that when Mrs. Ewer asked the minister with a beard to give communion to Virginia's mother (Mrs. Ewer's sister) at the nursing home in 1974, he told Mrs. Ewer he would do it when he made his normal visits to the home but that he would not make a special trip. Mrs. Ewer was upset by this according to her niece. Mrs. Kraegenbrink also testified that her aunt complained that she was never compensated for some work that she had done at the church.

Virginia Welter, Mrs. Ewer's sister-in-law corroborated the testimony about Mrs. Ewer's complaints regarding the bearded minister and working at the church for no compensation.

Ethel Wolf, Mrs. Ewer's next door neighbor implied that the decedent had a change of heart about the church, but could offer no statements made or actions done by Mrs. Ewer as a basis for this inference.

On rebuttal Mark Joy and Reverend Peterson testified that the only pastor at Mrs. Ewer's church who ever had a beard did not grow the beard until August, 1977, after Mrs. Ewer was in the nursing home. This testimony was not disputed. Mr. Joy testified that at one time he had a next door neighbor who was an associate pastor at another church (not named in the will) who wore a beard, bluejeans and drove a pickup truck and whom Mrs. Ewer had complained of to him. The testimony of Virginia Kraegenbrink indicates that Mrs. Ewer was primarily disenchanted with beards, rather than with her church: "She said that--only thing she mentioned to me that she was dissatisfied with the minister with the beard, she detested beards, didn't like anybody with a beard."

Thus the testimony that Mrs. Ewer was disenchanted with her own minister because he wore a beard is incredible since no minister at her church had had a beard at that time, and since Mrs. Ewer was attending church and knew who her ministers were. It appears that Mrs. Ewer was misunderstood by her niece and sister-in-law and that this testimony reflects a case of mistaken identity.

Mrs. Ewer's relationship with her heirs-at-law remained unchanged. The record reflects that Mrs. Ewer disapproved of her niece Mrs. Kraegenbrink in some respects and did not want to leave her money to her. However, she did ask her niece to assume power of attorney since she had done so for Mrs. Ewer's sister. None of the other heirs-at-law became any closer to Mrs. Ewer subsequent to the execution of her codicil. In fact only two of the four nieces attended her funeral.

The trial court concluded that Mrs. Ewer became disenchanted with the church after she executed her codicil, and that this disenchantment is reflected by her complaints relating to the church and by her reduced church attendance.

The Wisconsin Supreme Court has considered whether a testator had any reason to change the disposition of his or her property as a factor in determining whether a testator destroyed a will with an intent to revoke it.

In *Will of Donigian,* 265 Wis. at 154, 60 N.W.2d at 735, the court reversed the trial court and found that the presumption was rebutted "when evidence came in that during Donigian's final days he referred to his will with satisfaction, that no change of intent was ever manifested, or cause for such change arose, and that his papers and effects were so situated that others than himself had access to them."

The court upheld a jury finding that the presumption had been rebutted in *Wendt v. Ziegenhagen,* because the record did not reflect any reason for the testator to change the distribution of his property and because:

The evidence clearly shows that the deceased, many times after the execution of the will, recognized its existence, and not only manifested no disposition to change it, but affirmatively asserted that he did not wish to change it,--that it was all right and should so remain. *Wendt v. Zieganhagen,* 148 Wis. at 389, 134 N.W. at 907.

The testimony regarding Mrs. Ewer's other complaints support the trial court's inference that Mrs. Ewer became disenchanted with the church and thus might have been predisposed to change the will. We do not find the inference that she was disenchanted with the church to be against the great weight and clear preponderance of the evidence.

However, in determining whether Mrs. Ewer destroyed her will with the intention of revoking it, we find that this possibility is outweighed by the balance of the evidence. The decedent reaffirmed the will's existence and provisions up until the time that she went into the nursing home, primarily to her neighbors the Joys. This evidence indicates that she thought that she had a will. Her habit of tearing up papers and keeping loose papers and documents in her home makes it probable that she misplaced or lost her will. Although there is no evidence of wrongdoing, and by no means do we suggest an improper act by anyone, the cases previously cited require us to consider the fact that an adverse party had access to Mrs. Ewer's papers after she was in the nursing home and that this adverse party was responsible for the will search. The affirmance of her will by codicil and her obsession with the will indicate that Mrs. Ewer intended that her property be disposed of by will.

The evidence supporting the trial court's findings includes the following:

(1) Virginia Kraegenbrink's testimony regarding the bearded minister, Mrs. Ewer's encounter with the minister requesting the nursing home visit, and the complaints of Mrs. Ewer regarding uncompensated church work, from which the trial court inferred a disenchantment with the church;

(2) Virginia Welter's testimony supporting the inference that Mrs. Ewer became disenchanted with the church;

(3) Testimony that Mrs. Ewer never complained about losing her will or any other important papers; and, her neighbors the Joys. This evidence indicates that she thought that she had a will. Her habit of tearing up papers and keeping loose papers and documents in her home makes it probable that she misplaced or lost her will. Although there is no evidence of wrongdoing, and by no means do we suggest an improper act by anyone, the cases previously cited require us to consider the fact that an adverse party had access to Mrs. Ewer's papers after she was in the nursing home and that this

adverse party was responsible for the will search. The affirmance of her will by condicil and her obsession with the will indicate that Mrs. Ewer intended that her property be disposed of by will.

The evidence supporting the trial court's findings includes the following:

(1) Virginia Kraegenbrink's testimony regarding the bearded minister, Mrs. Ewer's encounter with the minister requesting the nursing home visit, and the complaints of Mrs. Ewer regarding uncompensated church work, from which the trial court inferred a disenchantment with the church;

(2) Virginia Welter's testimony supporting the inference that Mrs. Ewer became disenchanted with the church;

(3) Testimony that Mrs. Ewer never complained about losing her will or any other important papers; and,

(4) Testimony that no one ever saw the will after it was executed in 1968.

The trial court stated in its decision that the court was also considering the fact that the will was "unnatural" in that it left the bulk of the estate to organizations rather than to family members. The court also noted that widows often change their minds about the contents of their joint wills after their spouses die.

It was improper for the trial court to consider the "unnatural" disposition of the will as a factor in determining whether Mrs. Ewer intended to revoke her will. Absent an attack on the testamentary capacity of Mrs. Ewer or a claim that she was unduly influenced, neither this court nor the trial court should consider the nature of the disposition of Mrs. Ewer's estate in her will in resolving the issue of intent to revoke. *Estate of Beale,* 15 Wis.2d 546, 552-53, 113 N.W.2d 380 (1962).

The only evidence supporting the trial court's conclusion that Mrs. Ewer intended to revoke her will is the testimony giving rise to the inference that she became disenchanted with her church, and the fact that no one saw the will after it was executed in 1968. When weighed against the extensive evidence of references to her will as the one that she and her husband had made, of her erratic behavior regarding papers and her safe deposit box, and of her practice of asking for advice or help when she did not understand her mail or financial papers, the trial court's conclusion is against the great weight and clear preponderance of the evidence. While Mrs. Ewer may have been primarily concerned that the Reverend Hanusa was the executor of her estate, the testimony shows that this was not her only concern relating to the will. The testimony by neighbors, bank employees and ministers regarding Mrs. Ewer's references to the churches as her beneficiaries and her wish that Mrs. Kraegenbrink not receive her money, was undisputed.

Since appellant's evidence constitutes the great weight and clear preponderance of the evidence, he has met his burden of proving that Mrs. Ewer's will was either "lost, destroyed by accident or destroyed without the testator's consent." Sec. 856.17, Stats.

B. WILL CONTESTS

In order to contest a will on the grounds that it was not properly executed or that the testator lacked testamentary capacity, suffered from an insane delusion, or was the victim of undue influence, the challenger must be an heir or someone who would take under a prior valid will. As an alternative to will contests for undue influence or fraud, Wisconsin also recognizes the tort remedy of tortious interference with an expectancy. Ordinarily, this remedy is available only after the statutory period for probate challenges has expired.

Wis. Stat. 854.19. Penalty clause for contest.

A provision in a governing instrument that prescribes a penalty against an interested person for contesting the governing instrument or instituting other proceedings relating to the governing instrument may not be enforced if the court determines that the interested person had probable cause for instituting the proceedings.

In Re Keenan's Will

Supreme Court of Wisconsin

188 Wis. 163, 205 N.W. 1001 (1925)

VINJE, C. J. From the statement of facts it is apparent that we are called upon to decide whether or not a condition in a will providing for the forfeiture of a legacy in case the legatee, upon probable cause and in good faith, contests the probate of the will, is a valid condition and works a forfeiture of the legacy. The result of the decision will depend upon whether such a condition shall be held to be void on the grounds of public policy or whether it is within the legitimate field of private regulation and beyond public concern.

The principal authorities both English and American upon the general subject of the validity of conditions in wills providing for forfeitures of legacies or devises in case of a contest of the will by the legatee or devisee are as follows:

… **[At this point the court summarized an extensive list of English and American cases which revealed disagreement as to whether or not a good faith challenge to a will could result in a forfeiture of a right to property under the will that contain a "no contest" clause.]** …

The precise question presented by this appeal has not been passed upon by our court, hence it has been thought advisable to take a general view of the subject as presented by leading English and American cases. Such view discloses the grounds upon which each line of authorities bases its decisions, and these grounds will not be attempted to be restated except in so far as they form an integral part of the reasons that have actuated us in reaching our conclusion.

What is or is not public policy in a given state may vary, and especially so as between a limited monarchy such as England and a democratic form of government such as we have.

If we recur to our own organic state law we find the fundamental provision that "Every person is entitled to a certain remedy in the laws for all injuries or wrongs which he may receive in his person, property or character; he ought to obtain justice freely and without being obliged to purchase it, completely and without denial, promptly and without delay, conformably to the laws." Sec. 9, art. I, Const. This is a basic and valuable guaranty that the courts of the state should be open to all persons who in good faith and upon probable cause believe they have suffered wrongs. Is it not against public policy to permit one person to deprive another from asserting his rights in court? And especially so before it is ascertained that the prohibition against contest is in fact that of the testator and not that of one exercising undue influence over him, or that he was mentally competent to make it? That was the inquiry in this case when the will was presented for probate. It was claimed that the testatrix was not mentally competent to make the will. True, such claim was negatived after the judicial inquiry, but the claim might have been well founded.

We deem that it is contrary to the public policy of our state to require a litigant to forfeit a substantial sum in case he is not successful in the prosecution in court of a *bona fide* claim of right. *Smith v. Sherry,* 54 Wis. 114, 11 N.W. 465; *Fehrman v. Bissell L. Co., ante,* p. 82, 188 Wis. 82, 204 N.W. 582. And this is especially so as to the probate of a will. Our statutes, secs. 310.01 to 310.03, make it the duty, under heavy penalties for the neglect thereof, of county judges, executors, or other persons who may be in possession of wills to present the same for probate within periods therein named. These sections disclose that it is the public policy of our state that wills should be probated; that the state requires that the succession of property should be conformably to law. And upon this subject our court has spoken in no uncertain terms.

In the case of *Will of Dardis'*, 135 Wis. 457, 115 N.W. 332, it was held that a stipulation as to the mental capacity of a testator was not binding upon the court. On the contrary it was held that the probate of a will was "a proceeding *in rem,* involving considerations of public welfare and policy, and while it affects specific individuals it also affects many other interests, including those of decedent, some of which cannot be ascertained in advance, and the instrument should be established regardless of those directly interested." After enumerating the statutory steps required for the probate of a will the court says: "They evince a clear recognition and declaration of the legislature that there is a public policy involved in the establishment of every legally executed will."

Speaking of this decision in the case of *Will of Rice,* 150 Wis. 401, 446, 136 N.W. 956, 137 N.W. 778, the court said:

"Therefrom the conclusion was reached that regardless of holdings elsewhere, in this state a will, once validly made and subsisting to the death of the testator, must be taken and judicially enforced according to his intent, if that can be ascertained; that parties cannot be permitted, even though all interested join, by any agreement between themselves or any subterfuge to displace the dying wish of the testator; that in respect thereto the public at large are, under the policy of our law, so far concerned in the establishment of such a will that the proceedings to that end are in the nature of an action *in rem,* the whole body of the people being parties."

The doctrine laid down in these two cases has been restated and followed in the cases of *Will of Reynolds',* 151 Wis. 375, 138 N.W. 1019, 138 N.W. 1019; *Schoenwetter v. Schoenwetter,* 164 Wis. 131, 159 N.W. 737; *Estate of Staab,* 166 Wis. 587, 166 N.W. 326; *Estate of Sipchen,* 180 Wis. 504, 193 N.W. 385, and must be considered to be the established policy of this state with reference to the probate of wills.

How jealously public policy guards free access to the courts ordained to administer justice in the respective matters involved is exemplified in the ruling of our supreme federal court holding void legislative enactments of states excluding foreign corporations from the federal courts as a condition upon doing business within the state. *Terral v. Burke C. Co.* 257 U.S. 529, 42 S. Ct. 188, 21 A. L. R. 186, 66 L. Ed. 352, and cases cited. In the latter case the rule was extended to deny the right to a state to revoke the license of a foreign corporation doing intrastate business only, on the ground that it violated the state requirement not to bring a suit in the federal courts. And in the case of *Home Ins. Co. v. Morse,* 87 U.S. 445, 20 Wall. 445, 22 L. Ed. 365, it was held that an agreement between a foreign corporation and the state of Wisconsin that cases should not be removed to the federal courts was void, since the agreement could not confer greater validity than the unconstitutional Wisconsin statute providing that a foreign corporation could not do business within the state unless it stipulated that it would not remove into the federal courts cases begun against it by citizens of the state.

From the foregoing we deem that it is the public policy of our state that our probate courts should be open to all litigants who have probable cause to have their claims adjudicated upon without the incurring of severe penalties; that a sound public policy dictates that the truth of a disputable claim shall be ascertained as the law provides; that since courts are instituted to administer justice within the state there should be no penalties attached to the performance of that function.

Of course we agree with that part of the argument of courts who hold all such conditions valid to the effect that a testator has the right to attach whatever lawful conditions he sees fit to a legacy or devise. But that does not answer the question, What constitutes a lawful condition? Nor does it solve the claim that it is not the condition of the testator because the will is the result of undue influence or the product of an incompetent testator. These latter questions usually lie at the threshold of probate proceedings and can be settled only by a judicial inquiry, and that the inquiry should not be prevented by penalties where there is probable cause to raise such questions.

It is urged by the respondent that an interpretation of the will such as we have reached adds to the condition therein the words "without probable cause." Not so. We are not interpolating such words into the will. We simply say that when the conditions in a will applied to the concrete facts of the case are against public policy they are void. If when so applied they are not against public policy they are valid. Nothing is added to or taken from the letter of the will.

We have been asked by respondent to decide the validity of such conditions in cases where there is no probable cause for a contest and to declare them either valid or void. We do not deem it prudent to decide more than what is involved in this appeal. The opinion, therefore, is limited to a case where the contest was prosecuted in good faith and upon probable cause.

C. WILL CONTRACTS AND JOINT WILLS

While the right to make a will cannot be bargained away, testators can enter into agreements to make a will or to refrain from executing a will or from revoking an existing will. If the contract is breached, the offending will is still valid, but the non-breaching party may have a claim against the testator's estate that will be treated like the claim of any legitimate creditor. If the contract involved a promise to devise the breaching party's entire estate to the other party, the fact that the subsequent will is valid may be meaningless, since the non-breaching party may have a claim against the decedent equal to the entire amount of the estate.

Joint wills are designed to operate as a single will for more than one individual (and a typically used in the context of husband and wife). Although it was once the view that the execution of a joint will created an implicit contract not to revoke on the part of the parties to the will, this view is now frowned upon in most jurisdictions.

Wis. Stat. 853.13. [Will] Contracts.

(1) A contract to make a will or devise, not to revoke a will or devise or to die intestate may be established only by any of the following:

(a) Provisions of a will stating the material provisions of the contract.

(b) An express reference in a will to a contract and extrinsic evidence proving the terms of the contract.

(c) A valid written contract, including a marital property agreement under s. 766.58 (3) (e)

(d) Clear and convincing extrinsic evidence.

(2) The execution of a joint will or mutual wills does not create a presumption of a contract not to revoke the will or wills

Estate of Schultz

Supreme Court of Wisconsin
53 Wis. 2d 643, 193 N.W.2d 655 (1972)

Hanley, J. Three issues are raised on this appeal:

(1) Was it error to admit Frances' will to probate;

(2) Should letters testamentary have been granted to appellants rather than to respondent Molepske; and

(3) Does the probate court have jurisdiction to grant the relief sought by appellants?

Admission of will.

Appellants' first contention is that the joint will should have been admitted to probate, rather than the later will of Frances. We do not agree with this contention. The case of *Doyle v. Fischer* (1924), 183 Wis. 599, 198 N. W. 763, settled the proposition that two persons may enter into an agreement to make joint, mutual and reciprocal wills disposing of their separate estates according to some mutually agreeable plan, and that the agreement becomes binding when partially executed. This doctrine was explained in *Estate of Chayka* (1970), 47 Wis. 2d 102, 176 N. W. 2d 561, as follows:

"Where two parties contract to make a joint, mutual and reciprocal will, each pledges to the other that he will execute a mutually agreeable will, and will have that will in full force and effect at the time of death. The parties may express such contract in a separate document, state in the joint will that it is a contract, or the fact of contract may be conclusively presumed from the fact of the joint will being executed. Such contract becomes partially executed upon the death of one of the parties to the agreement and the acceptance by the survivor of properties devised or bequeathed under the will and pursuant to the agreement to make such joint will. At this point the contract becomes irrevocable, the survivor having received the consideration promised." *Estate of Chayka, supra*, at page 106.

However, the existence of an irrevocable contract governing the disposition of an estate does not affect the right to make or change a will, as stated in *Doyle v. Fischer, supra*, at page 606:

". . . It should be borne in mind that it is the contract and not the will that is irrevocable. The authorities generally hold that the will may be revoked, but the contract stands and will be enforced by equity if it be a valid contract and such enforcement is necessary for the prevention of fraud."

We conclude that it was proper to admit Frances' will to probate. Appellants' remedy is to commence an action in equity to enforce the contract rather than to challenge the later will which expressly revoked the joint will.

Granting letters testamentary.

Appellants contend that by virtue of the joint will, which became irrevocably binding upon the death of Leo and the acceptance by Frances of the properties devised and bequeathed under the will, they are entitled to have letters testamentary granted to them. In essence, they are seeking specific performance of that part of the contractual will which appointed them executors of the estate.

On the present record, however, we think that the trial court did not err in granting letters testamentary to respondent rather than to appellants. The joint will was never offered into evidence or filed with the probate court. Copies of what purport to be the joint will are attached to the briefs submitted to the trial court, but there has never been a judicial determination that this was the will of Leo Schultz or that it was in full force and effect at the time of his death. The bare assertion of the existence of a contractual will is insufficient to entitle appellants to have letters testamentary issued to them by the probate court or to have this court review the order granting letters testamentary to the respondent, since neither the trial court nor this court can rely upon facts outside the record. *Ebert v. Kohl's Food Stores* (1969), 42 Wis. 2d 247, 166 N. W. 2d 169. Obviously, appellants are not entitled to specific performance of a contract until they have proven the existence of the contract in the first instance.

Jurisdiction of probate court.

. . . [After considering the argument that this case was not properly a matter for resolution by the probate court, the Court stated:] We conclude that the jurisdiction of the probate court to hear this matter is clearly established. The jurisdiction is concurrent, and appellants may resort to that court for whatever relief may be appropriate.

CHAPTER 4.
INTERPRETTING WILLS

If the meaning of a will is placed in question, the ultimate resolution of the dispute rests with the court that is called upon to interpret the will. This chapter explores a variety of rules pertaining to the construction and interpretation of testamentary documents.

I. UNDERSTANDING WILLS

While courts traditionally insisted that a will must be interpreted based only upon what appeared within the four corners of the text, external factors always came into play during the process of discerning the testator's intent. References to external documents and events, devisees dying between the execution of the will and the death of the testator, devised property being disposed of by the testator in his own lifetime were just a few of the external factors that were always taken into account during the will interpretation process.

A. INCORPORATION BY REFERENCE

Existing documents can, of course, be copied directly into a will, and once the will is executed they become part of the testamentary document. However, as the case of *Lonsdorf v. Citizens State Bank & Trust Co.* in the preceding chapter indicated, it is not necessary to literally reproduce the external document, since pre-existing documents can be "incorporated" into a will, so long as they are clearly identified by the reference to them in the will.

Wis. Stat. 853.32. Effect of reference to another document.

(1) INCORPORATION.

(am) A will may incorporate by reference another writing or document if all of the following apply:

1. The will, either expressly or as construed from extrinsic evidence, manifests an intent to incorporate the other writing or document.

2. The other writing or document was in existence when the will was executed.

3. The other writing or document is sufficiently described in the will to permit identification with reasonable certainty.

4. The will was executed in compliance with s. 853.03 or 853.05 (bm) A writing or document is incorporated into a will under par. (am) even if the writing or document is not executed in compliance with s. 853.03 or 853.05

(2) DISPOSITION OF TANGIBLE PERSONAL PROPERTY.

(a) A reference in a will to another document that lists tangible personal property not otherwise specifically disposed of in the will disposes of that property if the other document describes the property and the distributees with reasonable certainty and is signed and dated by the decedent. The court may enforce a document that is not dated but that fulfills all of the other requirements under this paragraph.

(am) Another document under par. (a) is valid if it was signed in compliance with s. 853.03 (1) or with the law of the place where the document was signed, or where the testator resided, was domiciled, or was a national at the time the document was signed or at the time of death, even if it was not otherwise executed in compliance with s. 853.03 (2) or 853.05 (b) Another document under par. (a) is valid even if any of the following applies:

1. The document does not exist when the will is executed.

2. The document is changed after the will is executed.

3. The document has no significance except for its effect on the disposition of property by the will.

(c) If the document described in par. (a) is not located by the personal representative, or delivered to the personal representative or circuit court with jurisdiction over the matter, within 30 days after the appointment of the personal representative, the personal representative may dispose of tangible personal property according to the provisions of the will as if no such document exists. If a valid document is located after some or all of the tangible personal property has been disposed of, the document controls the distribution of the property described in it, but the personal representative incurs no liability for the prior distribution or sale of the property, as long as the time specified in this paragraph has elapsed.

(d) The duties and liability of a person who has custody of a document described in par. (a), or information about such a document, are governed by s. 856.05 (e) Beneficiaries under a document that is described in par. (a) are not interested parties for purposes of s. 879.03

(3) TRANSFERS TO LIVING TRUSTS.

The validity and implementation of a will provision that purports to transfer or appoint property to a living trust are governed by s. 701.08

Skinner v. American Bible Society

Supreme Court of Wisconsin

92 Wis. 209, 213, 65 N. W. 1037. (1896)

This is an appeal from a judgment of the circuit court for Milwaukee county which affirmed an order of the county court of Milwaukee county whereby it denied probate to two instruments propounded as the codicil to the last will and testament of Mary W. Leonard, deceased.

The first of such instruments, dated September 21, 1874, is as follows: "Whereas, on the first day of January, 1872, I transferred to Rev. A. M. Stowe the sum of one thousand and five hundred dollars (1,500), to be held by him in trust, to pay the interest to me during my lifetime, and to pay the principal, at my decease,--unless, in the providence of God, I should be under the necessity of using more or less of it to supply my own imperative wants,--to some religious society or societies and for religious uses, but without defining the objects of my bounty, I now, therefore, on the first day of September, 1874, for the purpose of defining and specifying more particularly the religious objects to which such money shall be paid after my death, I hereby make this instrument to declare the objects of such trust; and I do hereby transfer said property to said A. M. Stowe in trust, and I do hereby declare the objects of said trust as follows, to wit: First. The interest of said funds shall be paid to me during my life. Second. After my death the said A. M. Stowe shall pay the said money to the following objects, in the sums hereinafter stated: To the American Bible Society, $250.00; to the Board of Foreign Missions of the Pres. Church, $250.00; to the Presbyterian Committee of Home Missions, $250.00; to the American Tract Society, $250.00; to Auburn Theological Seminary, $250.00; to the Home for Little Wanderers and kindred institutions, $250.00. MARY W. LEONARD. Witnessed by M. A. Webster, Sept. 21, 1874."

The second of such instruments, dated October 8, 1883, and written on the same sheet with the instrument above set forth, is as follows: "Oct. 8, 1883. Since the above instrument was drawn up, I feel that the Lord, by withholding success from my dear brother for many years, thus leaving him to come into a state of utter destitution, has, in his providence, thrown him upon me to a large extent for a support, and especially so if his life is spared after he is unable to do anything to furnish himself with the comforts of life. In the meantime the interest on the above sum, not having been called for by me, has accumulated, and there is now to be added to the above sum, viz. $1,500--$1,000. Now, as I have no other way of assisting my brother, I wish the interest of the whole sum, viz. the $1,500 and the $1,000 added, to be used for my brother as long as he lives, if he needs it; also, any part of the principal which is needed to furnish him not only with the necessaries, but also with the comforts of life; and whatever is left of the sum total after his decease and my own decease, I wish to be given to the Lord, as above stated, viz. the $1,500 to be given to the objects heretofore stated, or, if it has been necessary to use a part of it, that the remainder be given to the six objects mentioned in the same ratio, and whatever is left of the additional $1,000 be divided into five equal parts, and that one fifth be given to the American Bible Society, one fifth to the American Tract Society, one fifth to the Presby. Board of Foreign Missions, and two fifths to the Board of Home Missions. M. W. LEONARD. Witnessed by Lucy Brainard Stowe, Robert B. Perine. "

The probate court considered that these instruments did not constitute a will, because (1) they were wanting of testamentary character and purpose, and (2) by reason of defective execution, and denied them probate.

Whether the will was defectively executed is a mixed question of fact and law, arising upon the evidence. Whether it is of testamentary character is to be determined by the interpretation of the instruments themselves. The evidence which tended to show the proper execution of the instruments as a will was substantially as follows: Lucy Brainard Stowe, one of the subscribing witnesses, testified: "I signed my name as a witness to that instrument in Mrs. Leonard's room, . . . in Mrs. Leonard's presence, and at her request, and in the presence of Robert B. Perine. I do not remember anything she said at the time, . . . except to request Mr. Perine and me to sign, and to hand me the pen, and showing me where to sign. I did not see her sign the instrument. Her name was written at the bottom of the instrument, before Mr. Perine and I signed our names. She saw us both sign, and we signed at the same time." Robert B. Perine, the other subscribing witness, testified: "As I came into her room, Mrs. Leonard was just rising from the table where she was signing her name. I do not remember whether anything was said by Mrs. Leonard, except, perhaps, to tell me where to sign my name. The instrument was lying on the table before me. I signed because Mr. Stowe asked me to. Miss Stowe and I signed in one another's presence. I don't remember that Mrs. Leonard made any statement to me, or in my presence, as to what the instrument was that I had just signed. Mrs. Leonard was present and looking on when Miss Stowe and I signed our names." Alfred M. Stowe testified: "She asked me if I would ask my daughter and Mr. Perine to come to her room. . . . I did as she requested. . . . She told me that was her will, and I stated to the witnesses that she requested me to have them come to her room. Mrs. Leonard was sitting at the table with this will or codicil before her, and when we all three went into the room, and she requested them to sign, I said, 'This is Mrs. Leonard's will, and she wishes you to sign as witnesses;' and she said,

'Yes.' I saw the witnesses sign their names." The subscribing witnesses do not remember that Mr. Stowe was present at their signing. Reversed and cause remanded.

ALFRED W. NEWMAN, J. That the two instruments, together, may constitute the last will and testament of Mary W. Leonard, it needs that the last, or codicil, dated October 8, 1883, shall have been executed with so much of formality as the law prescribes for the execution of a will. In order to execute the instrument as a will, it must be (1) in writing; (2) signed by the testatrix; (3) attested and subscribed, in the presence of the testatrix, by two competent witnesses. R. S. sec. 2282. This instrument was in writing. It is not questioned that it bears the genuine autograph signature of the testatrix, subscribed before the attestation. It was not necessary that she should have affixed her signature in the presence of the witnesses. Cassoday, Wills, § 114. It was subscribed by two competent witnesses, in the presence of the testatrix. What lacks it of being perfectly executed? Obviously, nothing, unless it appears that the subscribing witnesses failed to attest as well as to subscribe it.

It would be difficult, no doubt, to satisfactorily define that element in the attestation of a will which is not also present in the mere subscription to a will. No physical act is required in the one which is not also required in the other, and it is not clear what mental act or fact appropriate to the one is absent from the other. And the definitions of the most recent lexicographers do not make it quite perspicuous. The Century Dictionary defines an *attesting witness* to be "a person who signs his name to an instrument to prove it, and for the purpose of identifying the maker or makers." The Standard Dictionary defines *attestation* to be "the subscription by a person of his name to a written instrument to signify that the same was executed in his presence, or that it is correct."

Since it is well settled in this state that it is not necessary to the validity of a will that the witnesses, at the time when they *attest* it, shall know the nature of the instrument they are attesting (*Allen v. Griffin*, 69 Wis. 529, 35 N.W. 21), it is not clear what, if anything, attestation is intended to add to the mere fact of subscription. However that may be, it is well settled that an instrument in writing, signed by the testator, and subscribed in his presence and at his request, which may be implied from circumstances, by two competent witnesses, is *prima facie*, and so far as formality of execution goes, a valid will. Anything further, in mere form, is not contemplated, and would be mere supererogation.

The earlier instrument, dated September 21, 1874, was never so executed as to become a will. But it cannot well be doubted that the later instrument, of October 8, 1883, being sufficiently executed to become a will, has so adopted and incorporated into itself the former writing as that it has become a part of the latter instrument. Both are testamentary in character, and both together form a codicil to the last will and testament of Mrs. Leonard. *Baker's Appeal*, 107 Pa. 381; *Brown v. Clark*, 77 N.Y. 369; *Vogel v. Lehritter*, 139 N.Y. 223, 235, 34 N.E. 914; Cassoday, Wills, §§ 601-605.

The judgment of the circuit court and the order of the county court are reversed, and the cause is remanded to the county court of Milwaukee county, with directions to so modify its former order or judgment as to admit the instrument propounded as a codicil to the last will and testament of Mary W. Leonard to probate and record as a codicil to the last will and testament of the said testatrix.

B. THE OPERATIVE DATE OF WILLS AND ACTS OF INDEPENDENT SIGNIFICANCE.

While there was an earlier era in which the language of wills disposing of property was read in reference to the date the will was executed, the modern rule of construction is that language in a will deposing of property is normally interpreted as referring to the property owned by the testator at the time of death rather than at the time of the will's execution. Like most presumptions, this rule can be rebutted by evidence of contrary intent on the part of the testator. Moreover, if a will devises property where the recipient is described or is identified by actions or events that are yet to occur, the devise will usually be upheld, if the acts or events have a motive and significance apart from their testamentary impact. A classic example is a will provision devising the contents of a bank safe deposit box to a particular devisee. Even though the testator may move items in and out of the lockbox after the execution of the will, the presumption is that the reason for doing so was based on in-life concerns and were not simply efforts to revise the will, without re-executing it.

Wis. Stat. 853.29. After-acquired property.

A will is presumed to pass all property that the testator owns at the testator's death and that the testator has power to transfer by will, including property acquired by the testator after the execution of the will or acquired by the testator's estate.

Wis. Stat. 853.31. Presumption that will passes all of testator' interest in property

Any gift of property by will is presumed to pass all the estate or interest which the testator could lawfully will in the property unless it clearly appears by the will, interpreted in light of the surrounding circumstances, that the testator intended to pass a less estate or interest.

Wis. Stat. 853.325. Effect of reference to acts or events.

A will may dispose of property by reference to acts or events that have significance apart from their effect on the disposition of property under the will and that do not occur solely for the purpose of determining the disposition of property under the will. Reference to the execution or revocation of another individual's will fulfills the requirements under this section. This section applies whether the acts or events occur before or after execution of the will or before or after the testator's death.

ESTATE of ZINK

Supreme Court of Wisconsin
15 Wis. 2d 527, 113 N.W.2d 420 (1962)

GORDON, Justice. The appellant contends that she is entitled to share equally with her three sisters in the real estate acquired by her father after he had executed his will. These three arguments are advanced in support of her contention: (a) By the terms of the will and the circumstances surrounding its execution it is clear that the testator intended to divide his estate equally among his four daughters; (b) only the property owned by the testator on April 7, 1959, should be distributed under the will because that was the date on which he was declared incompetent; and (c) the testator's intent to pass after-acquired real estate does not manifestly appear by the will as required by sec. 238.03, Stats. The first two points are readily disposed of against the petitioner, but the third contention raises an issue which this court has not heretofore resolved.

Equal Shares Under the Will

There is nothing about the circumstances which are reflected in the evidence to warrant a conclusion that George Zink intended to treat his four daughters equally in the disposition of his estate. There is, indeed, proof that he was on good terms with the petitioning daughter, but it does not follow that his testamentary plans necessarily contemplated her receiving an equal share of his assets. The language of the will clearly contradicts the appellant's claim for an equal share. It even provides a reason for not giving her an equal share; in paragraph 2 of the will the testator stated, after making a specific bequest of $6,000 to the petitioner:

'I have intentionally not made any larger provision for her for the reason that I have loaned to her at various times sums of money * * * which she and her husband have failed and neglected to repay to me.'

In our opinion the will is clear and unambiguous and a construction which proposes that this testator intended equal shares for his four daughters would do violence to the language of the will. In Will of Peters (1937), 223 Wis. 411, 413, 270 N.W. 921, 922, this court stated:

While it is true that a will must be construed in accordance with the evident intention of the testator when that intention is clearly expressed in appropriate language, the instrument admits of no construction.' See also Estate of Gray (1953), 265 Wis. 217, 226, 61 N.W.2d 467. Even if the will results in inequality, the court cannot 'distort its construction to accomplish its own idea of what is equitable'. Will of Richter (1934), 215 Wis. 108, 111, 254 N.W. 103, 104.

The Guardianship of the Testator

A petition was submitted to the Waukesha County Court on March 24, 1959, seeking the appointment of a guardian for George Zink on the ground that he was mentally disturbed and unable to manage his property. On April 7, 1959, he was formally adjudged incompetent and a guardian was appointed. He remained under this guardianship until his death. The fact that George Zink was incompetent to manage his property does not mean that he lacked testamentary capacity. The general test for such capacity has been expressed by this court as follows:

* * * whether testator had sufficient active memory to comprehend, without prompting, the condition of his property, his relations to those who might be his beneficiaries, and to hold these things in mind long enough to perceive their relations to each other and to be able to form some rational judgment in relation to them.' Will of Williams (1950), 256 Wis. 338, 346, 41 N.W.2d 191, 195.

The infirmities which may accompany old age do not necessarily incapacitate a person from making a valid will. A person who is under a guardianship may well have many rational intervals during which time he may be capable of executing a valid will. Estate of Dobrecevich (1961), 14 Wis.2d 82, 86, 109 N.W.2d 477; Will of

Ganchoff (1961), 12 Wis.2d 503, 509, 107 N.W.2d 474; Estate of Schalla (1957), 2 Wis.2d 38, 44, 86 N.W.2d 5; Will of Slinger (1888), 72 Wis. 22, 26, 37 N.W. 236.

The Real Property Acquired After the Execution of the Will

At common law real estate which was received by the testator after the date of his will could not pass thereunder. A will only passed that realty of which the testator was seised at the time of the making of his will. Most jurisdictions have modified this common law rule so as to enable a testator to pass after-acquired realty, provided there is the intention so to do. 75 A.L.R. 474, 484-507 (1931); III American Law of Property sec. 14.9 (1952 ed.); 96 C.J.S. Wills § 756(c), p. 156. The statutes accomplishing this modification of the common law have taken various forms, the Wisconsin statute being sec. 238.03, which provides as follows:

'Any estate, right or interest in lands acquired by the testator after the making of his will shall pass thereby in like manner as if possessed at the time of making the will if such shall manifestly appear by the will to have been the intention of the testator.'

It is apparent that by enacting this section in 1849, the Wisconsin Legislature, as a matter of public policy, intended to modify the common law so as to permit a testator to pass an interest in land even though acquired after the making of his will.

Did George Zink in his will demonstrate an intention to pass after-acquired real estate? In our opinion he did. After making some specific bequests the residue of his estate was disposed of by using the following terminology:

'All the rest, residue, and remainder of my estate, both real, personal, and mixed, and wheresoever situate, I do give and bequeath in the following manner * * *'

We believe that this disposition effectively shows an intention on the part of George Zink to include after-acquired real estate. It meets the standard set down in 3 Restatement, Property, sec. 244g:

Any disposition which gives 'all my property' or employs other words of substantially similar meaning, is construed to make a disposition in accordance with, and subject to modification by, any events which increase or decrease his assets and which occur subsequent to the execution of the will and before the death of the testator.'

This court has frequently expressed itself in favor of a presumption against intestacy, particularly where a residuary clause is involved. Will of Nielsen (1950), 256 Wis. 521, 527, 41 N.W.2d 369. To the same effect is Estate of Britt (1946), 249 Wis. 30, 34, 23 N.W.2d 498, 500, where the court said:

The presumption of the law is against an intended intestacy as to any part of an estate because the will indicates a contrary general intention. This presumption is strengthened by the presence of a residuary clause, one obvious purpose of which is to preclude the occurrence of intestates by unforeseen contingencies.'

We do not regard the case of Will of Smith (1922), 176 Wis. 494, 186 N.W. 180, as resolving the question under consideration. The residuary clause in that will incorporated the word 'expectancy', and the court's conclusion that after-acquired realty passed thereunder does not resolve the question in the case at bar. But cf. 1960 Wis.L.Rev. 345, 347. Several other states with statutes comparable to that of Wisconsin have reached the conclusion that a will with a residuary clause expresses the necessary intention to dispose of the testator's entire property whether acquired before or after the making of the will. In re Little Joe (1931), 165 Wash. 628, 5 P.2d 995; Silverman v. Larson (1927), 124 Kan. 267, 259 P. 707; Whitney v. Whitney (1916), 178 Iowa 117, 159 N.W. 657. But cf. Bedell v. Fradenburgh (1896), 65 Minn. 361, 68 N.W. 41; Raines v. Barker (1856), 54 Va. 128, 67 Am.Dec. 762.

In our opinion the better reasoned decisions sustain the position that where the will evidences an intention to dispose of all his property, whether it be contained in a residuary clause or in some other expression of the will, after-acquired realty does pass under such will. Order affirmed.

C. AMBIGUOUS LANGUAGE

Sometimes, wills are validly executed but they are written in such a way that it is difficult to understand what the testator intended. The problem may be the inadvertent omission of intended text; it may be a simple mistake, like typing "Ellen" instead of the intended "Elise;" and sometimes the difficulty stems from the fact that more than one person or object matches the description in the will. The law of wills traditionally frowned upon the introduction of extrinsic evidence to establish the meaning of a will, even though it was simultaneously acknowledged that the ultimate goal was the implementation of the testator's intent. Concern for administrative efficiency and a desire to discourage perjury probably explain the harshness of the old evidentiary rules. Of course, there are certain circumstances in which it is impossible to determine the wills meaning without taking into account the broader context in which it was written. As *Estate of Boerner* (above) and the following case illustrate, Wisconsin courts have generally been flexible on the issue of the admissibility of extrinsic evidence.

In re Estate of Ganser

Supreme Court of Wisconsin
79 Wis. 2d 180, 255 N.W.2d 483 (1977)

Hanley, J. Two issues are presented on appeal:

1. What was the intention of the testatrix, Alma Ganser, in making the bequests in Clause SEVENTEENTH of her will?

2. Does an award to the respondents constitute an improper application of the doctrine of *cy pres?*

Intent of Testatrix

The paramount object of will construction is the ascertainment of the testatrix's intent. *Estate of Farber*, 57 Wis.2d 363, 368, 204 N.W.2d 478 (1973); *Estate of Southey*, 26 Wis.2d 335, 338, 132 N.W.2d 532 (1965). This intent is determined from the language of the will itself, considered in light of the circumstances surrounding the testatrix at the time of the will's execution. *In re Trust of Pauly*, 71 Wis.2d 306, 316, 237 N.W.2d 719 (1976); *In re Trust of Bowler*, 56 Wis.2d 171, 176, 201 N.W.2d 573 (1972).

Since the language of the will is the best evidence of the testatrix's intent, the court will look to it first, and if there is no ambiguity or inconsistency in the will's provisions, there is no basis for interpretation of the language used or a determination as to the testatrix's actual intent. *Estate of Naulin*, 56 Wis.2d 100, 104, 201 N.W.2d 599 (1972). If, however, an ambiguity exists in the language of the will, reference may then be made to the surrounding circumstances at the time of its execution. If, after such reference, the testatrix's meaning is clear, no further inquiry is necessary. *Estate of Gehl*, 39 Wis.2d 206, 213, 159 N.W.2d 72 (1968). When an ambiguity still persists after consideration of the surrounding circumstances, resort may finally be had to the rules of will construction and extrinsic evidence. *Estate of Mangel*, 51 Wis.2d 55, 65, 186 N.W.2d 276 (1971).

Language is said to be ambiguous when it is subject to two or more reasonable interpretations. "A latent ambiguity exists where the language of the will, though clear on its face, is susceptible of more than one meaning when applied to the extrinsic facts to which it refers." *Estate of Gibbs*, 14 Wis.2d 490, 496, 111 N.W.2d 413 (1961).

In the instant case, a change in circumstances, the severance of formal ties between the University and the Medical College, has occurred since the execution of the will. While there is certainly no question, under the language of the will, as to what the testatrix intended under the circumstances which existed at the time it was executed, the will gives no clear indication as to her intent in the event this particular change in circumstances would take place. The parties' opposing interpretations of Clause SEVENTEENTH, relating to whether the Medical College is "its [the University's] Medical School" and whether the University is "unable" to accept the bequest, considered in light of the 1967 separation of the University and the Medical College, are both reasonable, and it may not be doubted that a latent ambiguity exists.

This case, therefore, turns on the determination of Mrs. Ganser's intent in making the bequest in Clause SEVENTEENTH. The trial court accepted the respondents' contention that the testatrix's intent was "to benefit medical education at the post-graduate level under the aegis of Marquette University in the context of Marquette's educational and philosophical principles." The appellant, on the other hand, argues that the testatrix's intent was to benefit a medical school which was a part of the University, her and her deceased husband's *alma mater*, a private, sectarian institution, the fundamental religious principles of which were of great importance to her.

Consideration of the circumstances surrounding this bequest convinces this court that the Medical College, despite the formal separation from the University, constitutes "its [the University's] Medical School" within the intent of the testatrix, Alma Ganser. The predecessor of the Medical College originated in 1907 when Marquette University and the Milwaukee Medical College joined to create the Medical Department of Marquette University. In 1911, Mrs. Ganser graduated from the Marquette University School of Nursing. When the University acquired the assets of the Wisconsin College of Physicians and Surgeons in 1913, the medical department became the Marquette University School of Medicine. Mrs. Ganser's husband, William J. Ganser, M.D., who predeceased his wife, was a 1913 graduate of the Marquette University School of Medicine. Throughout their lifetimes, Dr. and Mrs. Ganser were active members of the Roman Catholic Faith and made the University and the Marquette University School of Medicine the object of their beneficence, making gifts of not less than $100 on at least eleven occasions from 1939 to 1964.

In 1918 the Marquette University School of Medicine was incorporated and since that time has always been a legal entity separate from, although affiliated with, the University. The Medical College and the University have also since that time maintained separate assets and accounting systems. Prior to 1967, the Medical College operated under Articles of Association which stated the Medical College formed a department of the University. The Articles further provided "that there shall be no deviation from the fundamental, ethical and educational principles established by said Marquette University." Under the Articles, the president of the University was president of the Medical College and an ex officio member of the board of directors of the Medical College; officers of the University and one person nominated by the trustees of the University served as members and directors of the Medical College; the president of the University had the power to appoint Medical College faculty; and the directors of the University had the power to discharge faculty members for breaches of the fundamental, ethical and educational principles established by the University. In addition, it was provided that if the Medical College failed to perform the function for which it was organized, all of its assets would be transferred to the University.

By the adoption of Restated Articles of Incorporation in 1967, the Medical College served all of the above-mentioned ties with the University, eliminating all control which the University had over the Medical College. The Medical College, while always legally separate from the University, became academically independent as well. The Medical College and the University have, however, continued to maintain cooperative joint medical and medically related programs in the basic sciences, benefiting both graduate and undergraduate students. These cooperative efforts include the medical library and programs in physical therapy, medical technology, immunology, biomedical engineering and bionuclear medicine. The Medical College continues to be physically located where it always has been, upon the University campus in the Cramer Building, which is owned by the University and leased to the Medical College.

In light of all of the above circumstances, we hold that the 1967 separation between the University and the College did not alter those aspects of the relationship which motivated Mrs. Ganser to refer to the Medical College as "its" [the University's] Medical School. The appellant contends that the word "its" was used by the testatrix to identify an association between the University and the Medical College by which the University controlled the Medical College or by which the Medical College was a department of the University. It is further contended that it was Mrs. Ganser's intent that if such an association did not exist, the corpus should pass to the appellant by the gift over provision.

The meaning of the words of a will, however, are to be ascertained subjectively. The court does not seek to determine what the usual or dictionary usage of a word may be, but rather the testatrix's individual meaning. *Estate of Gehl, supra* at 211. The separation between the University and the Medical College only eliminated one component of their relationship, that of control of the Medical College by the

University. Other important components remain. The separation involved here could not destroy the parental aspect of the University's relationship with the Medical College, which was originated by the University over sixty years before the separation. The Medical College has always been physically situated on the campus of the University, and the two institutions continue to cooperate in joint medical and medically related programs. These unchanged aspects of the relationship are very significant in light of the fact both Mrs. Ganser and her husband graduated from the University during the period in which the University created the Medical College. Dr. Ganser graduated from the Medical College's predecessor in the first year, 1913, that it was formally a school of medicine. It is perfectly reasonable that an old alumnus such as the testatrix, who was certainly aware of the historical association between the University and the Medical College, would, even after the 1967 separation, still refer to the Medical College as the University's medical school.

This case is very similar to *Estate of Southey, supra*, wherein the will of the testatrix, Miss Southey, contained the following bequest and the following gift over clause:

"'a. one-half (1/2) thereof to Mrs. Louise Baker, in the event that the relationship of employee and employer exists between her and me at the time of my death and that she is actually and actively engaged in the performance and discharge of her duties as housekeeper to me under such employment at the time of my death;

"'In the event that the said Mrs. Louise Baker, at the time of my death, does not sustain the relationship of employee to me and is not then actively and actually engaged in the performance and discharge of duties as my housekeeper, the share of my residuum so bequeathed to her shall be distributed pro-rata to and among the other residuary legatees of my estate.'" *Id.* at 336.

Miss Southey died in 1962. For the period from 1952 to 1960, Mrs. Baker had served as Miss Southey's housekeeper and companion, receiving a weekly salary. In 1960, Miss Southey suffered a serious stroke and was subsequently placed under a guardianship and moved to a nursing home. She was incompetent until her death. During the two years from 1960 to 1962, Mrs. Baker continued to serve as a personal attendant and was paid by the guardians for this service. The residuary legatees, however, contended that Mrs. Baker could not be considered Miss Southey's housekeeper because there was no house to keep and also that Mrs. Baker was not employed by Miss Southey, but rather by the guardians. In *Southey* this court held that while if the terms of the will were interpreted literally, Mrs. Baker could not receive the bequest, it was Miss Southey's intent that Mrs. Baker receive the bequest if she served in the same fashion as she did at the time the will was executed. Having done so, she was entitled to the bequest.

The instant case includes a similar change of circumstances in relation to the status of the legatee, and as in *Southey* that change is not of such a nature that it appears the testatrix did not intend the legatee to receive the bequest under the circumstances. Furthermore, while in *Southey* the condition imposed by the testatrix was clear and definite, in this case the condition imposed, if any is imposed, is very indefinite, based solely on the word "its." Actually, there is nothing to indicate Mrs. Ganser intended the word "its" to be as restrictively interpreted as the appellant contends.

The appellant's reliance upon this court's opinion in *State ex rel. Warren v. Reuter*, 44 Wis.2d 201, 170 N.W.2d 790 (1969) is misplaced. In that case the court evaluated the relationship between the University and the Medical College for the purpose of determining whether a state appropriation to the Medical College was constitutional in light of the establishment of religion clauses in art. I, sec. 18 of the Wisconsin Constitution and the First Amendment of the United States Constitution. The court held in *State ex rel. Warren* that the 1967 separation was complete for the purposes of this constitutional issue. In the instant case, however, the court only seeks to determine Mrs. Ganser's intent. A finding in favor of the University here does not result in the University having it both ways, as the appellant contends, for in this case, it is the intent of the testatrix, not the University, which is effectuated.

Therefore, it is concluded that despite the 1967 separation, the Medical College constitutes "its [the University's] Medical School" within the meaning intended by Mrs. Ganser. The University is, accordingly, able to accept the bequest. An agreement of administration of bequest between Marquette University and the Medical College of Wisconsin was executed on January 15, 1974. No issue has been raised as to the validity of that agreement. Therefore, the court does not pass upon the question of the validity of the agreement of administration in relationship to the testatrix's intent as between those two respondents.

*Cy Pres Doctrine**

[Although all parties agree that the *cy pres* doctrine is inapplicable in this case, the appellant argues that the trial court improperly applied it. It is the appellant's contention that if the respondents receive the bequest, the doctrine of *cy pres* would

* The doctrine of Cy Pres, which normally pertains only to charitable trusts, is examined in greater detail in Chapter 9.

thereby be improperly applied. This contention is not correct. The doctrine of *cy pres* is accurately stated in the Restatement (Second) of Trusts, sec. 399 (1959).

"If property is given in trust to be applied to a particular charitable purpose, and it is or becomes impossible or impracticable or illegal to carry out the particular purpose, and if the settlor manifested a more general intention to devote the property to charitable purposes, the trust will not fail but the court will direct the application of the property to some charitable purpose which falls within the general charitable intention of the settlor."

Under *cy pres* a court's award is made after a determination that it is impossible or impracticable to carry out the particular charitable purpose of the bequest. In the instant case, however, the trial court's conclusion and the conclusion reached above do not involve a determination that the testatrix's particular charitable purpose cannot be carried out, but rather involve the direct effectuation of her particular intent as determined from the language of the will interpreted in light of the surrounding circumstances. The doctrine of *cy pres* has not been applied.

D. CORRECTING MISTAKES

American courts have traditionally resisted correcting mistakes in wills, unless the mistake could be corrected on the basis of information contained in the will itself. This was true even if the mistake was accidentally made by the drafter of the will (a so-called *scrivener's error*). Wisconsin courts appear to have been more willing than most to admit extrinsic evidence for purposes of correcting errors. The modern trend in American law has been to adopt the Wisconsin position. The following two cases involve wills that contained mistakes of varying degrees that affected the identification of the will's intended devisee.

In re Southard's Will

Supreme Court of Wisconsin
208 Wis. 148, 242 N.W. 583 (1932)

FRITZ, J. The provision in question bequeaths a legacy "unto the Congregational Sunday School of the State of Wisconsin . . . for its use generally." The trial court, from all of the evidence and surrounding circumstances, concluded that the testatrix intended the bequest under clause three of her will to be paid to the Wisconsin Congregational Conference, the only organization in Wisconsin which is carrying on a state-wide work for the Congregational Sunday schools in this state; and further concluded that the misnomer of the beneficiary did not defeat the gift.

As was repeated in Will of Scott, 181 Wis. 607, 195 N.W. 843:

"Where a case is presented for judicial construction, a meaning is to be preferred which will sustain testacy and the provisions of the will rather than to defeat them (p. 610).

"The comprehensive and all-dominating rule in construing wills is that the intention of the testator must be ascertained from the words thereof, in the light of all surrounding circumstances, and that intention be given effect" (p. 608).

In the case at bar the evidence established that no association or organization ever existed under the name of "Congregational Sunday School of the State of Wisconsin." On the other hand, testatrix for twenty-five years had been interested in and an annual contributor to the Congregational Church of Lone Rock, where she resided, and had been superintendent and a teacher of its Sunday school, which she had helped organize in 1900 under the direction of Reverend Whitelaw, who was sent there for that purpose by the state-wide Congregational Church organization, which was the predecessor in activities and name of the Wisconsin Congregational Conference. She had participated in the affairs of that organization and knew of its activities, pursuant to its articles of organization, in the carrying on of such religious, benevolent, educational, and philanthropic work as the Congregational churches of Wisconsin might desire to undertake in common, including the work formerly done by a Congregational Sunday School & Publishing Society, which was reorganized as the Sunday School Department of the Wisconsin Congregational Conference; and but recently she had been informed as to certain work which had been done under the guidance and with the financial support of the Wisconsin Congregational Conference in organizing and maintaining Congregational Sunday schools elsewhere in this state.

In the light of all of those circumstances, and with no other organization in existence to which the designation used by the testatrix was at all applicable, the court was warranted in concluding that it was the intention of the testatrix that the bequest was to be paid to the Wisconsin Congregational Conference; and that there was no such misnomer of the beneficiary as to defeat the legacy. Those conclusions were well within the decisions in Will of Scott, 181 Wis. 607, 195 N.W. 843; Giblin v. Giblin, 173 Wis. 632, 182 N.W. 357; Paulson's Will, 127 Wis. 612, 107 N.W. 484; Webster v. Morris, 66 Wis. 366, 28 N.W. 353.

Those cases, as well as the case at bar, are distinguishable from the situation in Tharp v. Seventh Day Adventist Church, 182 Wis. 107, 195 N.W. 331. In that case the misnomer was equally applicable to either of two church organizations, which were not identical in their creeds, and as the testator had not been associated with either and there were no other circumstances to aid in ascertaining his intent, there resulted a fatal ambiguity because no means existed of ascertaining the testator's intention.

Order affirmed.

Krause v. Krause (Estate of Gibbs)

Supreme Court of Wisconsin
14 Wis. 2d 490, 111 N.W.2d 413 (1961)

FAIRCHILD, J.

1. *The intention of the testators as determined from all the evidence*. The evidence leads irresistibly to the conclusion that Mr. and Mrs. Gibbs intended legacies to respondent, and that the use of the middle initial "J." and the address on North Forty-Sixth street resulted from some sort of mistake.

Respondent testified that he met Mr. Gibbs about 1928. From 1930 to 1949 he was employed as superintendent of a steel warehouse where Mr. Gibbs was his superior. They worked in close contact. Until 1945 the business belonged to the Gibbs Steel Company. In that year the business was sold, but Mr. Gibbs stayed on for four years in a supervisory capacity. Respondent remained with the new company until 1960. After 1949 Mr. Gibbs occasionally visited the plant and saw the respondent when there. From 1935 to 1955 respondent took men occasionally to the Gibbs home to do necessary work about the place. He also visited there socially several times a year and saw both Mr. and Mrs. Gibbs. Mrs. Gibbs had made a few visits at the plant before 1949 and respondent had seen her there. Mr. Gibbs did not visit respondent's home, although on a few occasions had telephoned him at home. Mr. Gibbs always called respondent "Bob."

Miss Krueger, who had been the Gibbs housekeeper for twenty-four years up to 1958 and was a legatee under both wills, corroborated much of respondent's testimony. She also testified that Mr. Gibbs had told her he made a will remembering various people including "the boys at the shop," referring to them as "Mike, Ed, and Bob." Miss Pacius, a legatee under both wills, who had been Mr. Gibbs' private secretary for many years while he was in business, testified to Mr. Gibbs' expressions of high regard for respondent. Another former employee also testified to a similar effect.

Of the individuals named in the wills as legatees, all except two were shown to be relatives of Mr. or Mrs. Gibbs, former employees, neighbors, friends, or children of friends. The two exceptions were named near the end of the will and proof as to them may have been inadvertently omitted. "Mike," named in the will, was a warehouse employee under the supervision of respondent.

The attorney who drew several wills for Mr. and Mrs. Gibbs produced copies of most of them. They were similar in outline to the wills admitted to probate except that Mr. Gibbs' wills executed before Mrs. Gibbs' death bequeathed his property to her if she survived. The first ones were drawn in 1953 and each contained a bequest to "Robert Krause, of Milwaukee, Wisconsin, if he survives me, one per cent (1%)." There was testimony that Mrs. Gibbs' will, executed in August, 1955, contained the same language. In the 1957 wills the same bequest was made to "Robert Krause, now of 4708 North 46th Street, Milwaukee, Wisconsin." In several other instances street addresses of legatees were given for the first time in 1957. In the 1958 wills the same bequest was made to "Robert J. Krause, now of 4708 North 46th Street, Milwaukee, Wisconsin." The scrivener also produced a handwritten memorandum given to him by Mr. Gibbs for the purpose of preparing Mr. Gibbs' 1958 will, and the reference on that memorandum corresponding to the Krause bequest is "Bob, 1%." Four bequests (to Gruener, Krause, Preuschl, and Owen) appear in the same order in each of the wills and are reflected in the memorandum referred to as "Fred Gruener, Bob, Mike, and Ed." Gruener, Preuschl, and Owen were former employees of Gibbs Steel Company, as was respondent. Owen's residence is given as Jefferson, Wisconsin, in all the wills. In the 1953 wills, the residence of Gruener, Krause, and Preuschl was given only as Milwaukee, Wisconsin. A street address was inserted for the first time in each case in the 1957 wills, and repeated in the later ones.

Prior to 1950 respondent had lived at several different locations. From 1950 until April, 1960, he lived at 2325 North Sherman Boulevard. We take judicial notice that this address and 4708 North Forty-Sixth Street are in the same general section of the city of Milwaukee, and that both are a number of miles distant from the Gibbs home. We also take judicial notice that the telephone directory for Milwaukee and vicinity listed 14 subscribers by the name of Robert Krause with varying initials in October, 1958, and 15 in October of 1959. The listing for appellant gives his middle initial *J.* as well as his street address.

The only evidence which suggests even a possibility that Mr. or Mrs. Gibbs may have known of appellant may be summarized as follows:

For a time, appellant had a second job as a part-time taxi driver, and he recalled an elderly lady who was his passenger on a lengthy taxi trip in June, 1955. He did not recall where he picked her up. He had driven her across the city, waiting for her while she visited in a hospital, and then driven her back across the city. The place where he let her out, however, was not her home. He did not recall that she had given him her name, but she had inquired as to his. They had conversed about the illness of appellant's wife and his working at an extra job in order to make ends meet. She had expressed sympathy and approval of his efforts. Presumably when he was notified that his name appeared in the Gibbs wills as legatee, he endeavored to find an explanation of his good fortune and concluded that the lady in question must have been Mrs. Gibbs. The 1955 taxi ride, however, could not explain the gift to Robert Krause in the 1953 wills, and it is clear that the same legatee was intended in the Krause bequests in all the wills. Moreover, appellant's description of his taxi passenger differed in several particulars from the description of Mrs. Gibbs given by other witnesses.

2. *Propriety of considering extrinsic evidence*. As stated above, the county court could reach no other conclusion upon consideration of the extrinsic evidence than that Mr. and Mrs. Gibbs intended to designate respondent as their legatee. The difficult question is whether the court could properly consider such evidence in determining testamentary intent.

Under rules as to construction of a will, unless there is ambiguity in the text of the will read in the light of surrounding circumstances, extrinsic evidence is inadmissible for the purpose of determining intent. A latent ambiguity exists where the language of the will, though clear on its face, is susceptible of more than one meaning, when applied to the extrinsic facts to which it refers.

There are two classes of latent ambiguity. One, where there are two or more persons or things exactly measuring up to the description in the will; [3] the other where no person or thing exactly answers the declarations and descriptions of the will, but two or more persons or things answer the description imperfectly. Extrinsic evidence must be resorted to under these circumstances to identify which of the parties, unspecified with particularity in the will, was intended by the testator.

Had the probated wills used the language of the 1953 wills "To Robert Krause of Milwaukee," such terms would have described both appellant and respondent, as well as a number of other people. Upon such ambiguity of the first type above mentioned becoming apparent, extrinsic evidence would be admissible in order to determine which Robert Krause Mr. and Mrs. Gibbs had in mind as their legatee. Had the will said "To my former employee, Robert J. Krause of 4708 North 46th Street," neither appellant nor respondent would have exactly fulfilled the terms. Latent ambiguity of the second type would thus have appeared, and again extrinsic evidence would be admissible to determine what individual testators had in mind.

The wills containing, as they do, similar bequests to a long list of individuals, each bearing some relationship of blood, friendship, or former employment to Mr. or Mrs. Gibbs, come close to implying that every legatee named has some such relationship. Nevertheless the wills do not refer to Krause as standing in any particular relationship. The terms of the bequest exactly fit appellant and no one else. There is no ambiguity.

"An ambiguity is not that which may be made doubtful by extrinsic proof tending to show an intention different from that manifested in the will, but it must grow out of the difficulty of identifying the person whose name and description correspond with the terms of the will."

Under the circumstances before us, can a court properly consider evidence showing that some of the words were used by mistake and should be stricken or disregarded? It is traditional doctrine that wills must not be reformed even in the case of demonstrable mistake. This doctrine doubtless rests upon policy reasons. The courts deem it wise to avoid entertaining claims of disappointed persons who may be able to make very plausible claims of mistake after the testator is no longer able to refute them.

Although the courts subscribe to an inflexible rule against reformation of a will, it seems that they have often strained a point in matters of identification of property or beneficiaries in order to reach a desired result by way of construction. In *Will of Stack* where the will devised "Block 64," the court included part of block 175 in the provision to conform to the unexpressed intent of the testator. In *Will of Boeck* where the will devised the "northeast quarter of the northwest quarter" of a section, which was not owned by the testator, the court held such provision passed the southeast quarter of the northwest quarter, to conform to the misexpressed intent of the testator. In *Moseley v. Goodman* where testator bequeathed property to "Mrs. Moseley," the court denied the claim of Mrs. Lenoir Moseley to the gift and held that Mrs. Trimble had been intended by the testator. Mrs. Trimble was known to the testator by the nickname "Mrs. Moseley."

In *Estate of Miller* testator left property to "William Wilson's children." Relying on evidence that testator frequently confused William Wilson with his brother Seth, the court held the gift should go to the children of Seth Wilson, who had been intended by the testator. In *Groves v. Culph* testator devised a remainder interest in part of lot 15 to his daughter. The court, to conform to testator's true intent, included part of lot 16 in this devise. In *Castell v. Tagg* and *Geer v. Wind,* the testator omitted a child from his will by mistake. The court inserted in the will the gift which had been intended for the child by the parent. In *Beaumont v. Fell* a bequest to "Catharine Earnley" was proven to have been intended for Gertrude Yardley, and was given to the latter, and in *Masters v. Masters* a gift to "Mrs. Sawyer" was given to Mrs. Swopper, because testator knew no one by the former name. In the two cases last mentioned, no one with the name given in the will claimed the gift.

We are also aware of the rule which allows a court in probating a will to deny probate to a provision in the document which was included by mistake. British courts will deny probate to a single word, or part of a sentence, thereby completely altering the provided dispositions.

We conclude that details of identification, particularly such matters as middle initials, street addresses, and the like, which are highly susceptible to mistake, particularly in metropolitan areas, should not be accorded such sanctity as to frustrate an otherwise clearly demonstrable intent. Where such details of identification are involved, courts should receive evidence tending to show that a mistake has been made and should disregard the details when the proof establishes to the highest degree of certainty that a mistake was, in fact, made.

We therefore consider that the county court properly disregarded the middle initial and street address, and determined that respondent was the Robert Krause whom testators had in mind.

E. EXONERATION OF LIENS

Whether or not the executor or personal administrator of the estate was obligated to pay off mortgages or other forms of liens against devised property as part of his duty to pay the debts of the estate was once a thorny question. The resolution of this issue had a profound effect on the interests of residuary devisees and sometimes on the recipients of general and specific devises. Wisconsin, like most states, now allows the indebtedness to pass with the asset when it is devised.

Wis. Stat. 854.05. No exoneration of encumbered property.

(1) DEFINITIONS.

In this section:

(a) "Debt" includes accrued interest on the debt.

(b) "Encumbrance" includes mortgages, liens, pledges and other security agreements that are encumbrances on property.

(2) GENERALLY.

(a) Except as provided in sub. (5), all property that is specifically transferred by a governing instrument shall be assigned to the transferee without exoneration of a debt that is secured by an encumbrance on the property.

(b) If the debt that is secured by the encumbrance on the property is paid in whole or in part out of other assets, the specifically transferred property shall be assigned to the transferee only if any of the following applies:

1. The transferee contributes to the person or entity that held the assets that were used to pay the debt an amount equal to the amount that was paid.

2. The person or entity secures the amount described in subd. 1. through a new encumbrance on the property.

F. MISCELLANEOUS STATUTORY PROVISIONS AFFECTING THE INTERPRETATION OF WILLS

The following provisions from the *Wisconsin Statutes* provide additional rules that are used to interpret testamentary documents. In most cases, a clear expression of a contrary intention in the will itself prevails over the statutory default rule.

Wis. Stat. 854.10. Choice of law.

The meaning and legal effect of a governing instrument are determined by the local law of the state selected by the transferor in the governing instrument, unless the application of that law is contrary to s. 861.02 or 861.31 or any other public policy of this state otherwise applicable to the disposition.

Wis. Stat. 853.40. Disclaimer.

A person to whom property would otherwise pass under a will may disclaim all or part of the property as provided in s. 854.13 **[See Chapter 2.]**

Wis. Stat. 853.15. Equitable election if will attempts to dispose of property belonging to beneficiary.

(1) NECESSITY FOR ELECTION.

(a) Unless the will provides otherwise, this subsection applies if a will gives a devise to one beneficiary and also clearly purports to give to another beneficiary property that does not pass under the will but belongs to the first beneficiary by right of ownership, survivorship, beneficiary designation or otherwise.

(b) If the conditions in par. (a) are fulfilled, the first beneficiary must elect either to take under the will and transfer his or her property in accordance with the will or to retain his or her property and not take under the will. If the first beneficiary elects not to take under the will, unless the will provides otherwise his or her devise under the will shall be assigned to the other beneficiary.

(c) This section does not require an election if the property belongs to the first beneficiary because of transfer or beneficiary designation made by the decedent after the execution of the will.

(2) PROCEDURE FOR ELECTION.

If an election is required under sub. (1), the following provisions apply:

(a) The court may by order set a time within which the beneficiary is required to file with the court a written election either to take under the will and forego, waive or transfer the beneficiary's property interest in favor of the other person to whom it is given by the will, or to retain such property interest and not take under the will. The time set shall be not earlier than one month after the necessity for such an election and the nature of the interest given to the beneficiary under the will have been determined.

(b) If a written election by the beneficiary to take under the will and transfer the beneficiary's property interest in accordance with the will has not been filed with the court within the time set by order, or if no order setting a time has been entered, then prior to the final judgment, the beneficiary is deemed to have elected not to take under the will.

(c) Except as provided above, participation in the administration by the beneficiary does not constitute an election to take under the will.

Wis. Stat. 853.17. Effect of will provision changing beneficiary of life insurance or annuity.

(1) Any provision in a will which purports to name a different beneficiary of a life insurance or annuity contract than the beneficiary properly designated in accordance with the contract with the issuing company, or its bylaws, is ineffective to change the contract beneficiary unless the contract or the company's bylaws authorizes such a change by will.

(2) This section does not prevent the court from requiring the contract beneficiary to elect under s. 853.15 in order to take property under the will; nor does it apply to naming a testamentary trustee as designated by a life insurance policy under s. 701.09

Wis. Stat. 853.18. Designation of beneficiary, payee or owner.

(1) Except as otherwise provided in s. 853.15 or 853.17 (1) or ch. 766, none of the following is subject to or defeated or impaired by any statute or rule of law governing the transfer of property by will, gift, or intestacy, even though the designation or assignment is revocable or the rights of the beneficiary, payee, owner, or assignee are otherwise subject to defeasance:

(a) A written designation in accordance with the terms of any insurance, annuity, or endowment contract.

(b) Any agreement issued or entered into by an insurance company supplemental to or in settlement of any insurance, annuity, or endowment contract.

(c) Any written designation made under a contract, plan, system, or trust providing for pension, retirement, deferred compensation, stock bonus, profit-sharing, or death benefits, or an employment or commission contract, of any person to be a beneficiary, payee, or owner of any right, title, or interest thereunder upon the death of another, or any assignment of rights under any of the foregoing.

(2) This section applies to such designations or assignments made either before or after June 25, 1969, by persons who die on or after that date. This section creates no implication of invalidity as to any designation or assignment, of the nature described in sub. (1), made by any person who dies before that date or as to any declaration, agreement or contract for the payment of money or other transfer of property at death not specified under sub. (1).

Wis. Stat. 853.41. Applicability of general transfers at death provisions.

Chapter 854 applies to transfers under wills, including transfers under a Wisconsin basic will or basic will with trust.

Wis. Stat. 853.33 Gift of securities

Section 854.11 governs gifts of securities under a will.

Wis. Stat. 854.11. Gift of securities.

(1) DEFINITION.

In this section, "securities" includes all of the following:

(a) Any note, stock, treasury stock, bond, debenture, evidence of indebtedness, collateral trust certificate, transferable share or voting trust certificate.

(b) Any certificate of interest or participation in an oil, gas or mining title or lease or in payments out of production under such a title or lease.

(c) Any interest or instrument commonly known as a security.

(d) Any certificate of interest or participation in, any temporary or interim certificate, receipt or certificate of deposit for, or any warrant or right to subscribe to or purchase, any of the instruments or interests specified in pars. (a) to (c)

(2) INCREASE IN SECURITIES; ACCESSIONS.

Except as provided in sub. (4), if a person executes a governing instrument that transfers securities and at the time of the execution or immediately after execution the described securities are in fact governed by the instrument, the transfer includes additional securities that are governed by the instrument at the person's death if all of the following apply:

(a) The additional securities were acquired after the governing instrument was executed.

(b) The additional securities were acquired as a result of ownership of the described securities.

(c) The additional securities are any of the following types:

1. Securities of the same organization acquired as a result of a plan of reinvestment.

2. Securities of the same organization acquired by action initiated by the organization or any successor, related or acquiring organization, excluding any acquired by exercise of purchase options.

3. Securities of another organization acquired as a result of a merger, consolidation, reorganization or other distribution by the organization or any successor, related or acquiring organization.

(3) GIFT OF SECURITIES CONSTRUED AS SPECIFIC.

Except as provided in sub. (4), a transfer of a stated number of shares or amount of securities is construed to be a specific gift if the same or a greater number of shares or amount of the securities was governed by the instrument at the time of, or immediately after, execution of the instrument, even if the instrument does not describe the securities more specifically or qualify the description by a possessive pronoun such as "my".

(4) CONTRARY INTENT.

If the person who executed the governing instrument had an intent contrary to any provision in this section, then that provision is inapplicable to the transfer. Extrinsic evidence may be used to construe the intent.

Wis. Stat. 854.22. Form of distribution for transfers to family groups or classes.

(1) INTERESTS IN HEIRS, NEXT OF KIN AND THE LIKE.

Subject to sub. (4), if a statute or governing instrument specifies that a present or future interest is to be created in a designated individuals "heirs", "heirs at law", "next of kin", "relatives", "family" or a term that has a similar meaning, the property passes to the persons, including the state, to whom it would pass and in the shares in which it would pass under the laws of intestacy of the designated individuals domicile, as if the designated individual had died immediately before the transfer was to take effect in possession or enjoyment. If the designated individuals surviving spouse is living and remarried when the transfer is to take effect in possession or enjoyment, the surviving spouse is not an heir of the designated individual.

(2) TRANSFERS TO DESCENDANTS, ISSUE AND THE LIKE.

Subject to sub. (4), if a statute or governing instrument creates a class gift in favor of a designated individuals "descendants", "issue" or "heirs of the body" the property is distributed among the class members who are living when the interest is to take effect in possession or enjoyment in the shares that they would receive under the laws of intestacy of the designated individuals domicile, as if the designated individual had then died owning the subject matter of the class gift.

(3) DOCTRINE OF WORTHIER TITLE ABOLISHED.

The doctrine of worthier title is abolished as a rule of law and as a rule of construction. Language in a governing instrument describing the beneficiaries of a disposition as the transferors "heirs", "heirs at law", "next of kin", "distributees", "relatives" or "family", or a term that has a similar meaning, does not create or presumptively create a reversionary interest in the transferor.

(4) CONTRARY INTENT.

If the transfer is made under a governing instrument and the person who executed the governing instrument had an intent contrary to any provision in this section, then that provision is inapplicable to the transfer. Extrinsic evidence may be used to construe the intent.

II. ACCOUNTING FOR CHANGED CIRCUMSTANCES

A. LAPSE

The lapse principle deals with the situation that occurs when a will submitted to probate includes a devise of property to someone who is no longer living or, in some cases, was not alive at the time the will was executed. The general rule is that such devises fail (or *lapse*), and the property passes into the residue of the estate. If there is no residuary clause, then the property passes by partial intestacy. However, all states have anti-lapse statutes which recognize important exceptions to the general lapse principle. Under the Wisconsin anti-lapse statute (Wis. Stats. § 854.06), gifts to a grandparent of the testator or any descendant of a grandparent of the testator or to a step-child of the testator do not lapse, but pass to the issue of those individuals (if any).

However, the anti-lapse principle is just a default rule, and if the testator wishes a gift to an individual in one of these categories to lapse, the will simply has to say so. Ordinarily, words of survivorship ("if she survives me" or "my surviving brothers") are sufficient to accomplish this purpose, although the criticism is sometimes voiced that wills frequently feature "boilerplate" survivorship phrases that may or may not reflect the wishes of the testator. This criticism notwithstanding, language in a will of the nature of "if she survives me," will almost always be read as per evidence of an intention to negate the anti-lapse statute.

Wis. Stat. 853.27. Lapse

The rights under a will of a beneficiary who predeceases the testator are governed by s. 854.06.

Wis. Stat. 854.06. Predeceased transferee.

(1) DEFINITIONS.

In this section:

(a) "Provision in a governing instrument" includes all of the following:

1. A gift to an individual whether or not the individual is alive at the time of the execution of the instrument.

2. A share in a class gift only if a member of the class dies after the execution of the instrument.

3. An appointment by the decedent under any power of appointment, unless the issue who would take under this section could not have been appointees under the terms of the power.

(c) "Stepchild" means a child of the decedents surviving, deceased or former spouse, and not of the decedent.

(2) SCOPE OF COVERAGE.

This section applies to revocable provisions in a governing instrument executed by the decedent that provide for an outright transfer upon the death of the decedent to any of the following persons:

(a) A grandparent of the decedent, or issue of a grandparent, subject to s. 854.21

(b) A stepchild of the decedent, subject to s. 854.15

(3) SUBSTITUTE GIFT TO ISSUE OF COVERED TRANSFEREE.

Subject to sub. (4), if a transferee under a provision described in sub. (2) does not survive the decedent but has issue who do survive, the issue of the transferee take the transfer per stirpes, as provided in s. 854.04 (1)

(4) CONTRARY INTENT.

(a) Subsection (3) does not apply if any of the following applies:

1. The governing instrument provides that a transfer to a predeceased beneficiary lapses.

2. The governing instrument designates one or more persons, classes, or groups of people as contingent transferees, in which case those transferees take in preference to those under sub. (3) But if none of the contingent transferees survives, sub. (3) applies to the first group in the sequence of contingent transferees that has one or more transferees specified in sub. (2) who left surviving issue.

(bm) If the person who executed the governing instrument had an intent contrary to any provision in this section, then that provision is not applicable to the transfer. Extrinsic evidence may be used to construe the intent.

Firehammer v. Marchant

Court of Appeals of Wisconsin
224 Wis. 2d 673, 591 N.W.2d 898 (1999)

BROWN, J. Jon Firehammer appeals from an order denying his motion for reconsideration of the court's construction of his grandfather's will. The will divides the residual estate into seven shares. It also contains a clause directing that if any beneficiary dies within five months of the testator the beneficiary should be treated as if predeceased. One of the beneficiaries, Firehammer's mother, a daughter of the testator, died six days after the testator. The court ordered that the daughter's share be divided among the six surviving beneficiaries. Firehammer argues that the share should have passed to him under the anti-lapse statute. We see the will as unambiguous and agree with Firehammer that his mother's share should have passed to him. We thus reverse.

Leo Arthur Smith is the testator in this case. He died on August 6, 1996. In his will, he split the residue of his estate into seven shares. One share went to each of his two daughters, one to a sister, and one to a niece. The other three were placed in trust for his three grandchildren, to be distributed to them when the youngest reaches age forty. On August 12, 1996, one of Smith's daughters died. Smith's will has a provision that if any beneficiary dies within five months after his death, "any interest which would have passed to said beneficiary under other provisions of this Will are to be disposed of according to the plan of distribution which would have been effective ... if such beneficiary had predeceased me." The personal representative thus distributed Smith's deceased daughter's share to her son, Firehammer, pursuant to Wisconsin's anti-lapse statute, § 853.27, Stats. (1995-96). Smith's other daughter, Nancy Marchant, filed a motion seeking to prevent this distribution. She argued that the share that would have passed to Firehammer's mother should not pass to him, as the will stated an intent contrary to the anti-lapse statute. The trial court determined that it was Smith's intent to split the share among the surviving residual beneficiaries and gave an order to that effect.

Firehammer's attorney had not received notice of the hearing on Marchant's motion to prevent distribution. Therefore, Firehammer was not present to oppose that motion. When Firehammer received a copy of the proposed order, his attorney contacted the court and requested an opportunity to be heard on the matter. This the court granted. However, the court did not change its position on the intent demonstrated by the will.

The construction of a will is a question of law we review without deference to the trial court. *See Furmanski v. Furmanski*, 196 Wis. 2d 210, 214, 538 N.W.2d 566, 567 (Ct. App. 1995). Our task in construing a will is to determine the testator's intent, and the best evidence of this is the language of the document itself. *See Lohr v. Viney*, 174 Wis. 2d 468, 480, 497 N.W.2d 730, 735 (Ct. App. 1993). When the will is unambiguous, there is no need to look any further to ascertain the testator's intent, as it is clearly stated in the will. *See id.*

Here, Smith's will contains a clause stating that the share of any beneficiary who dies within five months of his death is "to be disposed of according to the plan of distribution which would have been effective under this Will if such beneficiary had predeceased me." There is no ambiguity in this statement. And in Wisconsin, if a relative is a beneficiary under the will, predeceases the testator and has issue who survive the testator, then "the issue ... are substituted for the deceased relative under the will and take the same interest as the deceased relative would have taken had the deceased relative survived the testator," "unless a contrary intent is indicated by the will." Section 853.27, Stats. (1995-96). A testator is presumed to know the law, so Smith knew about the anti-lapse statute. *See Lohr,* 174 Wis. 2d at 485, 497 N.W.2d at 736. Nowhere else in Smith's will is there a provision for a predeceased beneficiary. Thus, the statute clearly controls the disposition of the property in this case. The issue of Smith's daughter, Firehammer, takes her share.

Marchant argues that the will expresses two desires on the part of Smith that are frustrated by the above interpretation. "First, he intended to treat the seven residuary beneficiaries equally. Second, when it came to his grandchildren he made certain that they would not fritter away ... his bequests to them." While it is true that the will expresses an intent to treat each beneficiary equally, the testator did not say that this equality would continue even if one of the beneficiaries predeceased him. Rather, he wrote that any beneficiary who died within five months after his death would be treated as though that beneficiary had predeceased him. And the rule of law in this state is, as we have already stated, that if a beneficiary predeceases a testator, the anti-lapse statute works to give the share to the issue, not to the surviving beneficiaries, unless a contrary intent is clearly established.

If Smith had intended that a deceased beneficiary's share be returned to the residue to be split six ways, he would have said so. He did not. We will not rewrite the will to create language that is not there. *See Furmanski*, 196 Wis. 2d at 216, 538 N.W.2d at 568 (reversing lower court ruling that functionally rewrote will). To us, the result is axiomatic: the anti-lapse statute controls unless a contrary intent is clearly expressed by the testator. No contrary intent having been written, the statute controls. Because the trial court's distribution order contradicted the clear language of the will, we reverse.

We remand for the predeceased beneficiary's share to be distributed in accord with this opinion. Order reversed and cause remanded.

B. ADEMPTION

There are two basic forms of ademption: *ademption by extinction* and *ademption by satisfaction.* The traditional rule of ademption by extinction was that devisees of specifically devised property that had been disposed of by the testator subsequent to the execution of the will or codicil received nothing. The only exception to this was the so-called "change of form rather than substance" exception. For example, if a testator devised his "red wagon" to A, but before his death painted the red wagon green, A would still receive the wagon.

Similarly, and more importantly, stock splits and stock exchanges prompted by corporate mergers or takeovers are normally treated as changes in form, rather than substance. Transfers of general or demonstrative devises made to the devisee by the testator prior to death also nullify the transfer mentioned in the will. This process is essentially the same as an advancement of part of one's intestate share, but in the will context it is called ademption by satisfaction.

Wis. Stat. 853.35. Nonademption of specific gifts in certain instances.

The rights of a beneficiary with respect to a specific gift that is destroyed, damaged, sold or condemned before the testator's death are governed by s. 854.08

Wis. Stat. 854.08. Nonademption of specific gifts in certain cases.

(1) ABROGATION OF COMMON LAW.

The common law doctrine of ademption by extinction, as it might otherwise apply to the situations governed by this section, is abolished.

(2) PROCEEDS OF SALE.

(a) Subject to sub. (6), if property that is the subject of a specific gift is sold by the person who executed the governing instrument within 2 years of the person's death, the specific beneficiary has the right to the following amounts if available under the governing instrument:

1. Any balance of the purchase price unpaid at the time of death, including any security interest in the property and interest accruing before death, together with the incidents of the specific gift.

2. A general pecuniary transfer equivalent to the amount of the purchase price paid to, or for the benefit of, the person within one year of the seller's death.

(b) Acceptance of a promissory note of the purchaser or a 3rd party is not considered payment, but payment on the note is payment on the purchase price; and for purposes of this section property is considered sold as of the date when a valid contract of sale is made. Sale by an agent of the person who executed the governing instrument or by a trustee under a revocable living trust created by the person is a sale by the person for purposes of this section.

(3) PROCEEDS OF INSURANCE ON PROPERTY.

Subject to sub. (6), if insured property that is the subject of a specific gift is destroyed, damaged, lost, stolen or otherwise subject to any casualty compensable by insurance, the specific beneficiary has the right to the following amounts, if available under the governing instrument, reduced by any amount expended or incurred to restore or repair the property:

(a) Any insurance proceeds paid with respect to the property after the decedents death, together with the incidents of the specific gift.

(b) A general pecuniary transfer equivalent to any insurance proceeds paid to, or for the benefit of, the decedent within one year of the decedents death.

(4) CONDEMNATION AWARD.

(a) Subject to sub. (6), if property that is the subject of a specific gift is taken by condemnation prior to the death of the person who executed the governing instrument, the specific beneficiary has the right to the following amounts if available under the governing instrument:

1. Any amount of the condemnation award unpaid at the time of death.

2. A general pecuniary transfer equivalent to the amount of an award paid to, or for the benefit of, the person who executed the governing instrument within one year of that person's death.

(b) In the event of an appeal in a condemnation proceeding, the award is, for purposes of this section, limited to the amount established on the appeal. Acceptance of an agreed price or a jurisdictional offer is a sale under sub. (2)

(5) PROPERTY UNDER GUARDIANSHIP, CONSERVATORSHIP, OR POWER OF ATTORNEY.

(a) In this subsection, "agent" means an agent under a durable power of attorney, as defined in s. 244.02 (3) (b) Subject to pars. (c) and (d) and sub. (6), if property that is the subject of a specific gift is sold or mortgaged by a guardian, conservator, or agent of the person who executed the governing instrument, or if a condemnation award or insurance proceeds are paid to a guardian, conservator, or agent, the specific beneficiary has the right to a general pecuniary transfer equivalent to the proceeds of the sale, mortgage, condemnation award, or insurance proceeds, reduced by any amount expended or incurred to restore or repair the property or to reduce the indebtedness on the mortgage, if the funds are available under the governing instrument.

(c) Paragraph (b) does not apply with respect to a guardian or conservator if, subsequent to the sale, mortgage, award, or receipt of insurance proceeds, the person who executed the governing instrument is adjudicated competent and survives such adjudication for a period of one year; but in such event the rights of the specific beneficiary shall be determined as though the proceeds were paid to the owner under sub. (2), (3), or (4) (d) Paragraph (b) does not apply with respect to an agent if the person who executed the governing instrument is competent at the time of the sale, mortgage, award, or receipt of insurance proceeds but in such event the rights of the specific beneficiary shall be determined as though the proceeds were paid to the owner under sub. (2), (3), or (4)

(6) LIMITATIONS.

(ag) This section is inapplicable if the person who executed the governing instrument gives property during the person's lifetime to the specific beneficiary with the intent of satisfying the specific gift and the requirement under s. 854.09 (1) is satisfied.

(ar) If the person who executed the governing instrument had an intent contrary to any provision in this section, then that provision is inapplicable to the transfer. Extrinsic evidence may be used to construe the intent.

(b) If part of the property that is the subject of the specific gift is destroyed, damaged, sold or condemned, the specific gift of any remaining interest in the property is not affected by this section; but this section applies to the part affected by the destruction, damage, sale or condemnation.

(c) The amount that the specific beneficiary receives under subs. (2) to (5) is reduced by any expenses of the sale, by the expenses of collection of the proceeds of insurance, sale, or condemnation award and by any amount by which the income tax of the decedent or the decedents estate is increased because of items covered by this section. Expenses include legal fees paid or incurred.

Wis. Stat. 853.19. Advancement.

The effect of a lifetime gift by the testator on the rights of a beneficiary under the will is governed by s. 854.09. **[See Chapter 2.]**

Estate of Boerner

Supreme Court of Wisconsin
46 Wis. 2d 183, 174 N.W.2d 457 (1970)

[For a more detailed statement of the facts of this case, see Chapter 1, part III.]

Hansen, J. The executor takes the position that the legacy to the California-based nephew in paragraph two of the will refers only to those shares in the Boston Fund that had been held by the bank in Boston. Since such shares, acquired through dividend reinvestment, had been sold by the bank, the executor argues that the specific legacy to the nephew is adeemed by extinction.

The petitioner contends that paragraph two was intended by the testator and should be construed to refer to all of the shares in Boston Fund owned by the testator at his death. Such contention apparently concedes that the sale by the testator of a portion of his Boston Fund holdings works an ademption by extinction on the part sold, but seeks the award of the remainder of the Boston Fund shares to him. The appeal raises certain definite issues, each made narrow and close by the facts of this case.

Appealability.

Not briefed nor argued by either party is the question of appealability. Since appealability goes to jurisdiction, the duty of this court is to independently examine the record to determine if the appeal is proper. The appeal is from a memorandum decision, and no subsequent order was entered. Probate is a special proceeding, terminated by order rather than by a judgment. Although the better procedure would have been to enter a separate order, the memorandum decision here clearly was intended to be a final ruling, so we treat it as an order, and, therefore, appealable.

Latent ambiguity

The construction of the terms of a will involves ascertaining the intention of the testator, but such intention is to be determined from the words of the document and the surrounding circumstances at the time of its execution. Extrinsic evidence, ordinarily inadmissible to determine intent .may be offered as to actual intent in cases involving a latent ambiguity, defined by this court to be:

". . . where the language of the will, though clear on its face, is susceptible of more than one meaning, when applied to the extrinsic facts to which it refers.

"There are two classes of latent ambiguity. One, where there are two or more persons or things exactly measuring up to the description in the will; the other *where no person or thing exactly answers the declarations and descriptions of the will, but two or more persons or things answer the description imperfectly*. Extrinsic evidence must be resorted to under these circumstances to identify which of the parties, unspecified with particularity in the will, was intended by the testator." (Emphasis supplied.)

In the case before us, such latent ambiguity arises from the fact that no securities held by the testator, either at the time of his death or at the time of executing the will, exactly answer the description given in paragraph two of the will. All of the Boston Fund certificates were, of course, issued in his name, but none were, in the words of the will, "held for safekeeping by Walter J. Brand & Co." 963 such shares were issued in his name, and were in his safe-deposit box at the time of his death. 764 shares, purchased for him by the bank in Boston from the proceeds of dividends, had been held for him by the bank, with periodic statements furnished to inform the testator of the exact amount of such bank-retained shares.

Neither his Boston Fund shares held by the bank nor those found in his safe-deposit box exactly answer the description in the will; either or both do so only imperfectly. Which group of shares did the testator intend to refer to when he bequeathed "securities issued in my name and held for safekeeping by Walter J. Brand & Co.?" Or did he intend to refer to both groups, his entire holdings of Boston Fund shares? Enough of a latent ambiguity exists, in identifying exactly the securities referred to, to warrant the holding of the trial court that extrinsic evidence could be introduced as to the intent of the testator.

Intent of testator

The issue of admissibility of extrinsic evidence resolved, it becomes important to review the evidence made part of this record relating to the actual intent of the testator in paragraph two of the will. The securities dealer, Walter J. Brand, took the witness stand to testify that the only stocks owned by the testator were his shares in the Boston Fund. He testified that his company never kept stocks for safekeeping for any of their clients or customers. He further testified that it was his belief that the bank in Boston acted for the dealer in all of the shares involved in the cumulative investment program, whether held by the bank or the customer.

The principal witness on the issue as to intent was the attorney who drafted the will. He testified that he was a friend of the testator, that the testator often had done personal favors for him, and that he drafted the will in return for the favors done him by the testator. It was his testimony that the only shares of securities to which the testator referred were the ones specified in paragraph two and, on the direct point involved here, that the testator considered the Boston Fund securities to be one block, not to be two separate groups or blocks.

When asked where such Boston Fund securities, referred to in the will, were located, the attorney answered, "I can tell you where he thought they were. Walter J. Brand, as stated in paragraph two." The attorney testified that the testator believed that all of his Boston Fund securities were held by Walter J. Brand. The then recent execution of the agreement with Walter J. Brand & Co., whereby the testator would no longer receive dividends in cash, might well be the basis for the mistaken belief that all Boston Fund shares were with Brand for safekeeping.

However, the issue here is not one of credibility as between contradictory testimony or evidence. The evidence as to the intention and beliefs of the testator is uncontradicted. It stands uncontroverted either by other testimony or by physical facts or circumstances. The testimony of the attorney who drafted the will, corroborated in some measure by the testimony of the securities broker, leads to but one conclusion, that the testator intended to bequeath his shares in the Boston Fund to his nephew, all of them and not part of them.

This court has many times said that in a situation of this kind the court ". . . attempts to place itself in the position of the testator when he made his will . . . " Doing that in this case requires the conclusion that the testator intended paragraph two to cover his Boston Fund shares, those acquired by purchase and those purchased for him from dividends. The only testimony as to intent present in this record supports this interpretation. There is no testimony to support any other interpretation or conclusion.

Confidential communication.

The executor argues that the attorney who drafted the will was improperly allowed to testify as to statements made by the testator during the drafting of the will. It is contended that such testimony violates the attorney-client privileged communication rule. If this objection is a valid one, the construction given the will as expressing the established intent of the testator would be fatally weakened for it rests in no inconsiderable measure upon the testimony of the lawyer who drafted the will as to statements made by the testator when the will was prepared.

However, this court has several times held that communications between an attorney and a client concerning a last will and testament, the transactions which led to the execution of the will, and the circumstances surrounding the execution of the will, do not enjoy the status of privileged communications after the client's death in a suit between the testator's heirs, devisees, legatees or other parties who claim through him.

While the disagreement here is between the executor and a named legatee under the will, the outcome of this suit will be determinative of whether the property in question passes to the specific legatee, who is the petitioner here, or to the residual legatee. So the petition for construction of the will involves the respective rights of the specific and the residual legatee. As such, it clearly comes within the exception above noted and the testimony of the attorney as to statements made to him by the testator are admissible on the question of intent, once such extrinsic evidence became admissible. The trial court must be affirmed in holding that extrinsic evidence, including the testimony of the attorney who drafted the will, was admissible as to the intent of the testator. The trial court must be reversed in not accepting what such extrinsic evidence, uncontradicted and uncontroverted, clearly established as to such intent of the testator.

Doctrine of ademption.

There is and can be no real dispute as to the application to this case of the concept of ademption by extinction. Under the construction of paragraph two urged by the executor, the entire bequest to the nephew would be extinguished, all of the property referred to had been disposed of by the testator during his lifetime. Under the construction of the will urged by the petitioner, and adopted by this court, the Boston Fund shares sold to pay for the auto are no longer available to pass under the specific bequest, but the balance of the Boston Fund shares remaining in the estate at the time of death are bequeathed to the nephew under paragraph two.

So we have only a partial ademption by extinction. In applying the ademption concept, only two determinations are to be made: (1) Whether there has been a specific devise or bequest; and (2) whether the particular asset is in the testator's estate at the time of his death. Here it is clear that we are dealing with a specific bequest, ". . . a gift by will of a particular thing, or specified part, of the testator's estate, . . ."

Difficulty arises in distinguishing it from other parts of the estate, but, once paragraph two has been construed, the difficulty vanishes and clearly we deal here with a specific bequest. Under the second prong of the ademption test, it is likewise clear that, as to those shares of Boston Fund held and later sold by the bank in Boston, they were not in the testator's estate at the time of his death. So there remains, under paragraph two as herein construed, the 963 shares of Boston Fund found in the deposit box of the testator, which are bequeathed to the petitioner-nephew. When a part of a specific legacy is not in existence at the time of death, that part which still is in existence as part of the estate passes to the legatee under the will. It follows that 963 shares of Boston Fund shares pass to John A. Boerner under paragraph two of the will as herein construed.

Order reversed, with directions to enter an order providing that 963 shares of Boston Fund, Inc., pass to John A. Boerner under paragraph two of the will of John B. Boerner.

C. PRETERMITTED SPOUSES

The *pertermitted* problem occurs when someone with a valid will subsequently marries or has a child and fails to revise the will accordingly. Unlike the case when a testator knowingly omits an existing spouse or child from a will, it is not at all clear that the failure to revise a will is an expression of a desire to disinherit. More likely, it represents nothing more than a failure to take the time necessary to revise the will. All states have statutes that in such situations attempt to adjust the will in a way that a typical testator would have wanted. Of course, it is possible that the testator considered, but chose not to revise his or her will. If the will contains evidence of such an intention or if the testator provides for the after-acquired spouse or the after-born child through non-probate means (such as life insurance or the beneficial interest in a trust or a Payable on Death account), the statute may not apply.

In states with elective shares, pretermitted spouses are still entitled to elect against the estate if they choose. Because the elective share is now normally calculated on the basis of the augmented estate while the pretermitted share is of the ordinary probate estate, a detailed calculation may be necessary before the pretermitted spouse can determine which election is in his or her economic best interest.

Wis. Stat. 853.12. Premarital will or pre-domestic partnership will.

(1) ENTITLEMENT OF SURVIVING SPOUSE OR SURVIVING DOMESTIC PARTNER. Subject to sub. (3), if the testator married the surviving spouse or recorded a domestic partnership under ch. 770 with the surviving domestic partner after the testator executed his or her will, the surviving spouse or surviving domestic partner is entitled to a share of the probate estate.

(2) VALUE OF SHARE. The value of the share under sub. (1) is the value of the share that the surviving spouse or surviving domestic partner would have received had the testator died with an intestate estate equal to the value of the testator's net estate, but the value of the net estate shall first be reduced by the value of all of the following:

(a) All devises to or for the benefit of the testator's children who were born before the marriage to the surviving spouse or the domestic partnership with the surviving domestic partner and who are not also the children of the surviving spouse or surviving domestic partner.

(b) All devises to or for the benefit of the issue of a child described in par. (a) (c) All devises that pass under s. 854.06, 854.07, 854.21, or 854.22 to or for the benefit of children described in par. (a) or issue of those children.

(3) EXCEPTIONS.

Subsection (1) does not apply if any of the following applies:

(a) It appears from the will or other evidence that the will was made in contemplation of the testator's marriage to the surviving spouse or domestic partnership with the surviving domestic partner.

(b) It appears from the will or other evidence that the will is intended to be effective notwithstanding any subsequent marriage or domestic partnership, or there is sufficient evidence that the testator considered revising the will after marriage or domestic partnership but decided not to.

[There is no subsection (3)(c).]

(d) The testator and the spouse have entered into an agreement that complies with ch. 766 and that provides for the spouse or specifies that the spouse is to have no rights in the testator's estate.

(4) PRIORITY AND ABATEMENT. In satisfying the share provided by this section:

(a) Amounts received by the surviving spouse under s. 861.02 and devises made by will to the surviving spouse or surviving domestic partner are applied first.

(b) Devises other than those described in sub. (2) (a) to (c) abate as provided under s. 854.18

In re Estate of Jones

Supreme Court of Wisconsin
74 Wis. 2d 607, 247 N.W.2d 168 (1976)

This proceeding seeks to deny admission to probate of the will of Theodore Jones, hereinafter referred to as decedent or testator. Judgment was entered in the probate branch of the Juneau county court in favor of plaintiff-respondent Frances Jones, decedent's surviving wife, denying admission of the will to probate. Defendant-appellant Lee E. Jones, brother of decedent and sole heir named in the contested will, appeals from that judgment.

On February 19, 1958, decedent executed his last will and testament at the office of his attorney, Roland W. Vieth, in Mauston, Wisconsin. It is undisputed that the will was validly executed and witnessed. The will devised the entire estate to a brother, Lee E. Jones, making no mention of wife or wife-to-be. On March 30, 1958, decedent, then age 54, married respondent, Frances Jones, then age 55. This was thirty-nine days after the execution of the will. Frances Jones remained married to decedent until his death on December 30, 1974 -- a period of approximately seventeen years. There was no mention of wife-to-be, Frances Jones in the will of decedent, and the issue, at trial and on appeal, is whether the will of decedent was revoked by statute due to his subsequent marriage to Frances Jones. Additional facts relevant to that issue will be set forth in the court's opinion.

The trial court found the will was not made in contemplation of marriage and held it was revoked by the subsequent marriage of decedent to Frances Jones. The decedent's brother, Lee E. Jones, sole heir under the will denied admission to probate, appeals.

Hansen, J. Appellant challenges the trial court finding that the will of Theodore Jones was not made in contemplation of marriage and was therefore revoked by the subsequent marriage of the testator. Under existing law in 1958, a subsequent marriage of a testator, without issue, did not revoke a will earlier made. However, in 1971, the legislature changed the consequence of a subsequent marriage. The statute then enacted, sec. 853.11, Stats., and made applicable to the will of any testator dying on or after April 1, 1971, instead provides in pertinent part:

"SUBSEQUENT MARRIAGE. A will is revoked by the subsequent marriage of the testator if the testator is survived by his spouse, unless:

"(a) The will indicates an intent that it not be revoked by subsequent marriage or was drafted under circumstances indicating that it was in contemplation of the marriage or makes provision for issue of the decedent."

In the case before us, the will itself neither indicates an intent that it not be revoked by subsequent marriage nor contains provision for issue of the decedent. So the sole question becomes whether or not it was "drafted under circumstances indicating that it was in contemplation of the marriage."

The trial court found the will here involved was not drafted under such circumstances. This trial court finding of fact and a determination based thereon must be sustained on appeal unless such finding of fact is against the great weight and clear preponderance of the evidence. Our court has held that this does ". . . not mean the evidence in support of the finding must 'constitute the great weight or clear preponderance of the evidence.'" Nor is it sufficient for reversal that "'there is evidence to support a contrary finding.'" Rather, to command a reversal, such evidence in support of a contrary finding must itself "'constitute the great weight and clear preponderance of the evidence.'" This standard, our court has stated, is "heavily weighted on the side of sustaining trial court findings of fact in cases tried without a jury." It is thus the standard to be applied here.

On the question of testator's intent, the only testimony as to the circumstances surrounding the drafting of the will was given by its scrivener, Attorney Roland W. Vieth, who drafted the will. That attorney testified as follows: He met with testator in January or February, 1958, to discuss drafting a will. He again met with testator the day the will was drafted. At that time the scrivener "was under the impression that he [the testator] had just become married, not that he was contemplating marriage." He thought he was aware that the testator had been divorced from his first wife, but that he was not sure that he was divorced and not living with the first wife.

He testified that testator instructed him to draw a will which would limit "his wife's" share to the legal minimum. He never asked testator if he had a wife at the time of drafting the will. The scrivener consulted another attorney with respect to limiting the wife's share because it was "the first time that I had ever been asked to draft a will where the question arose of how much a wife, or widow could be limited to receive. . . ." He probably would have made no provision in the will for the wife if at the time he had believed the testator and his first wife were divorced. Mr. Vieth testified that subsequently, in drafting wills to limit a wife to an elective share, he has specifically included a limiting provision in the will to avoid any misunderstanding. He admitted that testator, in seeking to give a minimum share to his wife, may in fact have been referring to his divorced wife. He had no notes or memoranda concerning his meetings with testator, and was testifying solely from recollection of the events occurring seventeen years prior to the court hearing. He could be wrong in his recollections.

This testimony was confusing if not inconsistent in certain particulars. The trial court was faced with evaluating the credibility of the witness, the weight to be given his testimony, and the inferences to be drawn therefrom. As the trial court's function is to determine the facts and to weigh them, so, too, "'the inferences to be drawn from established facts are for the trier of the fact'" -- here the trial court.

In the case before us it was reasonable to infer from the scrivener's testimony, supported by undisputed facts as to subsequent marriage and the will remaining unchanged, that the testator, in seeking to provide only a minimal "wife's share" in his will, was referring to his wife-to-be, not to his divorced first wife. With such inference drawn, the finding of fact would have to be that this will was drafted in contemplation of marriage. However, we also find it reasonable to infer from the scrivener's testimony that the reference by testator to a minimal "wife's share" was a reference to his divorced first wife, not his wife-to-be. Drawing such inference from the testimony, as the trial court apparently did, warrants the finding of fact was that this will was not drafted in contemplation of marriage.

When inferences from testimony reasonably can go either way, this court must adopt the view taken by the trial court. That the testimony may have also sustained a finding contrary to that made by the trial court does not give this court the right to disturb the inferences drawn and findings made by the trial court. Rather, we are constrained to "indulge all reasonable inferences from the evidence which will support the trial court's decision." Applying this standard we find the inference drawn by the trial court to have been reasonable and the finding of fact and conclusion of law made by the trial court to be proper.

D. PRETERMITTED CHILDREN

The normal presumption is that testators who fail to revise their wills after the subsequent birth of a child would not have wanted to disinherit afterborn or after-adopted children unless there were special circumstances evidenced by the will itself or by the fact that the parent had made other provisions for pretermitted children. The Wisconsin statute also recognizes pretermitted rights for children alive at the time of the will's execution but who were accidentally omitted.

Wis. Stat. 853.25. Unintentional failure to provide for issue of testator.

(1) CHILDREN BORN OR ADOPTED AFTER MAKING OF THE WILL.

(a) Applicability. Except as provided in sub. (5), if a will fails to provide for a child of the testator born or adopted after execution of the will, the child is entitled to a share of the estate unless any of the following applies:

1. It appears from the will or from other evidence that the omission was intentional.

2. The testator provided for the omitted child by transfer outside the will and the intent that the transfer be in lieu of a testamentary provision is shown by the testator's statements or is reasonably inferred from the amount of the transfer or other evidence.

(b) Share if testator had no living child at execution. Except as provided in sub. (5), if a will fails to provide for a child of the testator born or adopted after the execution of the will and the testator had no child living when he or she executed the will, the omitted child receives a share in the estate equal in value to that which the child would have received under ch. 852 This paragraph does not apply if the will devised all or substantially all of the estate to or for the benefit of the other parent of the omitted child and that other parent survives the testator and is entitled to take under the will.

(c) Share if testator had living child at execution. Except as provided in sub. (5), if a will fails to provide for a child of the testator born or adopted after the execution of the will and the testator had one or more children living when he or she executed the will and the will devised property to one or more of the then-living children, the omitted child is entitled to share in the testator's estate as follows:

1. The portion that the omitted child is entitled to share is limited to devises made to the testator's then-living children under the will.

2. The omitted child is entitled to receive the share of the testator's estate, as limited in subd. 1., that the child would have received had the testator included all omitted after-born and after-adopted children with the children to whom devises were made under the will and had given an equal share of the estate to each child.

3. To the extent feasible, the interest granted an omitted child under this section shall be of the same character, whether equitable or legal, present or future, as that devised to the testator's then-living children under the will.

4. In satisfying a share provided by this paragraph, devises to the testator's children who were living when the will was executed abate ratably. In abating the devises of the then-living children, the court shall preserve to the maximum extent possible the character of the testamentary plan adopted by the testator.

(d) Rights of issue. Except as provided in sub. (5), if a child entitled to a share under this section dies before the testator, and the child leaves issue who survive the testator, the issue who represent the deceased child are entitled to the deceased child's share.

(2) LIVING ISSUE OMITTED BY MISTAKE.

(a) Except as provided in sub. (5), if clear and convincing evidence proves that the testator failed to provide in the testator's will for a child living at the time of making of the will, or for the issue of any then deceased child, by mistake or accident, including the mistaken belief that the child or issue of a deceased child was dead at the time the will was executed, the child or issue is entitled to receive a share in the estate of the testator as if the child or issue was born or adopted after the execution of the will, as follows:

1. If no children were included in the will but some or all of those children were omitted by mistake, then sub. (1) (b) provides for the share of any child or issue omitted by mistake.

2. If some children were included in the will but other children were omitted by mistake, then sub. (1) (c) provides for the share of any child or issue omitted by mistake.

(b) Failure to mention a child or issue in the will is not in itself evidence of mistake or accident.

(3) TIME FOR PRESENTING DEMAND FOR RELIEF. A demand for relief under this section must be presented to the court in writing not later than (a) entry of the final judgment, or (b) 6 months after allowance of the will, whichever first occurs.

(4) FROM WHAT ESTATE SHARE IS TO BE TAKEN. Except as provided in sub. (5), the court shall in its final judgment assign a share provided under sub. (1) (b) as follows:

(a) First, from intestate property.

(b) Any balance from each devise to a beneficiary under the will in proportion to the value of the estate each beneficiary would have received under the will as written. If the intention of the testator, shown by clear and convincing evidence, in relation to some specific gift or other provision in the will would be defeated by assignment of the share as provided in this paragraph, the court may adopt a different apportionment and may exempt a specific devise or other provision.

(5) DISCRETIONARY POWER OF COURT TO ASSIGN DIFFERENT SHARE. If in any case under sub. (1) or (2) the court determines that the share is in a different amount or form from what the testator would have wanted to provide for the omitted child or issue of a deceased child, the court may in its final judgment make such provision for the omitted child or issue out of the estate as it deems would best accord with the intent of the testator.

Sandon v. Sandon

Supreme Court of Wisconsin
123 Wis. 603, 101 N.W.2d 1089 (1905)

Robert Sandon died April 7, 1902, leaving a will executed May 14, 1894, which was duly probated September 3, 1902. He left surviving his widow and two married daughters; also an adopted daughter named Ellen Victoria, who had been adopted by due legal procedure May 23, 1894. By his will, after making sundry special bequests to his wife and daughters, his grandchildren, and certain religious societies, he left the residue of his property to his wife, whom he appointed his executrix. The will made no mention of the adopted child, Ellen. On application by said adopted child to the county court for her distributive share of the estate, the county court ruled that she was entitled to the same share of the estate as if the testator had died intestate. This judgment was confirmed by the circuit court, and the executrix appeals.

WINSLOW, J. Sec. 2286, Stats. 1898, provides that "when any child shall be born after the making of his parent's will and no provision shall be made therein for him, such child shall have the same share in the estate of the testator as if he had died intestate; and the share of such child shall be assigned to him as provided by law in case of intestate estates unless it shall be apparent from the will that it was the intention of the testator that no provision should be made for such child." This section appeared in the Revised Statutes of 1849 (sec. 26, ch. 66), and has remained unchanged since that time. Secs. 4021-4024, Stats. 1898, provide for the adoption of children by legal proceedings, and sec. 4024 declares that "a child so adopted shall be deemed, for the purposes of inheritance and succession by such child, . . . and all other legal consequences and incidents of the natural relation of parents and children, the same to all intents and purposes as if the child had been born in lawful wedlock of such parents by adoption," with an exception not affecting the present inquiry.

This court held in Glascott v. Bragg, 111 Wis. 605, 87 N.W. 853, that a legal adoption under this statute was equivalent, save for the exception noted, to the birth of a child in wedlock. In the present case there is no question as to the legal adoption of the child, Ellen, after the making of the will. The will is plain and unambiguous, and distributes the entire estate of the testator to certain devisees and legatees, making no mention of the child subsequently adopted. In this situation, we are unable to see how it can be said to be "apparent from the will that it was the intention of the testator that no provision should be made for such child." There is nothing within the four corners of the written will which gives any intimation of the wish of the testator with regard to an after-born child. As said in Bresee v. Stiles, 22 Wis. 120, "we are not permitted to look outside of the will to ascertain the purpose of the testator upon this point." True, if a will contain ambiguous language, which may or may not refer to an unborn child, extrinsic evidence of the circumstances surrounding the testator when the will was made may be resorted to for the purpose of ascertaining the meaning and intention of such language. Verrinder v. Winter, 98 Wis. 287, 73 N.W. 1007. When that meaning is ascertained, it is deemed in legal effect, to be the meaning expressed in the will itself. In re Donges's Estate, 103 Wis. 497, 79 N.W. 786.

The instrument, as written, has simply been construed. Nothing has been added or changed. Lawrence v. Barber, 116 Wis. 294, 93 N.W. 30. In brief, the rule is that such extrinsic evidence may be received to aid in determining whether any doubtful language in the will shows an intention, but cannot be received to add such intention to a will plain and certain upon its face. The evidence relied upon to show such intention was principally evidence of declarations by the testator concerning the making of a will, and as to intention concerning the child's relation to his estate; and it is very clear that such testimony is inadmissible, even if it were a case where surrounding circumstances were admissible to throw light upon the intent.

It is argued that the order of adoption is insufficient, because it does not, in terms, deprive the natural parents of "all legal rights whatsoever respecting" the child. This claim is untenable. It is true that sec. 4024, supra, provides that "the natural parents of such child shall be deprived by such order of adoption of all legal rights whatsoever respecting such child," etc., but it is quite certain that this is simply a statement of the legal effect of the order when made. Sec. 4023 specifically provides the contents of the order, and the directions therein contained were strictly followed in the order made. Judgment affirmed.

In re Read's Will

Supreme Court of Wisconsin
180 Wis. 497, 193 N.W. 382 (1923)

JONES, J. This proceeding arose on a petition by the guardian of the minor son of the testator praying for a construction of the will. The petition names the heirs at law of the deceased, including his widow, and states that the testator made no provision for any of his children but devised his entire estate to his wife; that the ward of the petitioner was born several years after the execution of the will. The court was asked to determine whether the ward was entitled to a share in the estate. The court found and adjudged that it was apparent from the will of the deceased that it was his intention that no provision should be made for the after-born child; that the omission to provide for him was intentional and not by mistake; and that the entire estate vested in the widow to the exclusion of the after-born child.

Under the civil law the birth of a child or children after the execution of a will operated as an implied revocation of the will. This was on the theory that no parent could intend to exclude unborn children and leave them unprovided for without cause.

At common law, subsequent birth of a child or children did not cause a revocation of a will. At common law both marriage and the subsequent marriage of the testator operated as a revocation. This was the rule which has been generally adopted in this country in the absence of statutes. An extended discussion of this question will be found in an opinion by Chancellor KENT in the case of Brush v. Wilkins, 4 Johns. Ch. (N.Y.) 506.

But in most of the states. statutes have been adopted by which, under the conditions stated in the statute, there is a partial revocation in favor of after-born children. In a few states there have been statutes following the civil-law rule declaring the will revoked by the subsequent birth of children. The following is the statute to be considered in this case:

"When any child shall be born after the making of his parent's will and no provision shall be made therein for him such child shall have the same share in the estate of the testator as if he had died intestate; and the share of such child shall be assigned to him as provided by law in case of intestate estates unless it shall be apparent from the will that it was the intention of the testator that no provision should be made for such child" Sec. 2286, Stats.

Under this statute and the facts already stated this is the question to be decided: When a married man having living children makes a will disposing of all his property absolutely to his wife, does an after-born child take the same share as if his parent had died intestate?

In other states there are two classes of decisions diametrically opposed and which cannot be reconciled. Counsel for the guardian especially relies on two cases in which the statutes under consideration were like our own, and where the testator had a wife and child living and bequeathed all of his estate to his wife. Chicago, B. & Q. R. Co. v. Wasserman, 22 F. 872; Carpenter v. Snow, 117 Mich. 489, 76 N.W. 78.

In both of these cases the court held that it could not look beyond the will; that since no mention was made of after-born children and no provision made for them, it could not be held that the omission to provide for them was intentional. The following cases from other states are also cited by appellant's counsel: Waterman v. Hawkins, 63 Me. 156; Burns v. Allen, 93 Tenn. 149, 23 S.W. 111; McLean v. McLean, 207 N.Y. 365, 101 N.E. 178; Tavshanjian v. Abbott, 200 N.Y. 374, 93 N.E. 978; Lewis v. Hare, 8 La. Ann. 378; Chace v. Chace, 6 R.I. 407, 78 Am. Dec. 446; and Sutton v. Hancock, 115 Ga. 857, 42 S.E. 214; but they so differ from the instant case because of differences in the statutes or the facts involved that it does not seem necessary to state their purport.

Counsel for respondent rely on decisions in Illinois where, under substantially the same state of facts and a statute quite similar to our own, it was held that in order to exclude an after-born child it was not necessary that such exclusion should be expressly declared in the will. Froehlich v. Minwegen, 304 Ill. 462, 136 N.E. 669; Peet v. Peet, 229 Ill. 341, 82 N.E. 376; Lurie v. Radnitzer, 166 Ill. 609, 46 N.E. 1116; Hawhe v. C. & W. I. R. Co. 165 Ill. 561, 46, 46 N.E. 240 N.E. 240. Counsel also cite Leonard v. Enochs, 92 Ky. 186, 17 S.W. 437. In that case the statute provided:

"If a will is made when a testator has a child living and a child is born afterwards, such after-born child, or any descendant of his, if not provided for by any settlement, and neither provided for nor expressly excluded by the will, but only pretermitted, shall succeed to such portion of the testator's estate as he would have been entitled to if the testator had died intestate; towards raising of which portion the devisees and legatees shall, out of what is devised and bequeathed to them, contribute ratably, either in kind or in money, as a court of equity, in the particular case, may deem most proper. . . . " Sec. 25, ch. 113, Gen. Stats. Leonard v. Enochs, 92 Ky. 186, 188, 17 S.W. 437.

There was a living child and the testator willed all his property to his wife. It was held that no direct words of exclusion were necessary, and that the intention appeared from the will; that the exclusion was intended to apply to all his children as a class. The following cases from other states are also cited by respondent's counsel: Whittemore v. Russell, 80 Me. 297, 14 A. 197; Reeves v. Hager, 101 Tenn. 712, 50 S.W. 760.

This is the first time that the question here involved has been presented to this court. Counsel for the guardian rely on two Wisconsin decisions: Sandon v. Sandon, 123 Wis. 603, 101 N.W. 1089, and Bresee v. Stiles, 22 Wis. 120. In both of these cases there were living children for whom provision was made in the will. In these cases it was held, in the absence of ambiguity, that the court could not look outside of the will to ascertain the purpose of the testator on this point, and that there was nothing within the will giving any intimation of the wish of the testator with regard to an after-born child. The last named of these cases was cited in the Michigan case above referred to.

Counsel for respondent rely on the case of In re Donges's Estate, 103 Wis. 497, 79 N.W. 786. In that case the testator was childless when the will was made. There was a devise to his wife of his real estate to hold until the youngest child, if any should be born, should attain the age of twenty-one years, and in case no children were living at his death, to his wife until she remarried. There were legacies to other relatives, one of whom survived, and the wife and two children also survived the testator.

Although the statute now under consideration was to be construed, it will be seen that the facts were quite different from those now before us. It is true also that the question of law involved was not the same, since the problem was whether under the statute there was provision for after-born children. Nevertheless, counsel for respondent relies on language used in the decision as applicable to the instant case. Mr. Justice Dodge said in the opinion:

"The comprehensive and all-dominating rule in construing wills is that the intention of the testator must be ascertained from the words thereof, in the light of all surrounding circumstances, and that intention be given effect." In re Donges's Estate, 103 Wis. 497, 500, 79 N.W. 786.

"It must be borne in mind that the legislative purpose was not to restrict the parent, nor to dictate to him what provision he should make. It was not to control his intention, but to provide for after-born children in the not improbable event of forget fullness or oversight of the parent, upon the very presumption, indeed, that if he had thought of them he would have intended that they should have some share in his estate, and that share the law would then fix. The power of the testator to decide whether anything, and if so how much and in what form, should be given to after-born children, is as uncontrolled as if there were no statute on the subject. . . . It is not apparent why it should not be as much in the power of the testator to place a child, born after the making of his will, in a state of dependency on the mother, as it confessedly is to do so with the child in existence when the will was made. The perils to the child in each case are the same, and the reasons justifying or failing to justify interference by the legislature with the parent's wishes on the subject do not vary in one case from the other." Ibid. 511, 512.

The opinion cited, among other cases, Hawhe v. C. & W. I. R. Co. and Leonard v. Enochs, above referred to. The statement of Mr. Justice Dodge above quoted, in construing this statute to the effect that in construing wills the intention should be ascertained from the words of the instrument in the light of all surrounding circumstances, is the rule often declared by this court. Estate of Boyce, 173 Wis. 575, 181 N.W. 735; Will of Elmore, 165 Wis. 266, 162 N.W. 438; Maxcy v. Oshkosh, 144 Wis. 238, 261, 128 N.W. 899, 1138; 1 Schouler, Wills (5th ed.) § 466; 1 Redfield, Wills (4th ed.) p. 433.

The petition for probate of the will showed that the testator left surviving him six children, including the minor for whom the guardian appears; that the personal property was in excess of $1,000,000; and that the value of the real estate was in excess of $150,000. The petition of the guardian for the construction of the will also names the heirs, including the widow, and states that the ward was born several years after the execution of the will.

The facts stated in this petition were certainly before the court, and we consider that they were proper if not indispensable facts in the proceedings to construe the will. It is a familiar rule that in construing wills the court may place itself in the testator's place in order to determine what his intention was in the light of the circumstances as they existed at the time the will was made. 1 Greenleaf, Evidence (15th ed.) p. 388; 28 Ruling Case Law 270, 271, and cases cited.

There is some conflict in the authorities as to what extent extrinsic evidence may be received under statutes of this kind. It is very clear that declarations of the testator as to his intentions are not admissible, but we cannot agree with the view of counsel for the guardian that in construing a will under this statute no consideration can be taken of the fact that the testator has children living for whom the will makes no provision.

Unlike some statutes, sec. 2286, above quoted, does not contain the unqualified provision that there must be a revocation pro tanto or in toto unless some provision is made in the will for the after-born child, or unless he is expressly excluded. The language is: "unless it shall be apparent from the will that it was the intention of the testator that no provision should be made for such child."

The statute does not ignore the intention of the testator. If the intent to exclude the after-born child is apparent from the will, construed under those rules always applied, it is enough. It is evident that in a proceeding under this statute the evidence as to extrinsic facts should be very carefully limited, and we are not prepared to say that we should approve the admission of some of the evidence received in some of the Illinois cases above cited.

In this case we have the conceded fact that the testator had five living children and a wife when the will was made. He evidently had entire confidence in his wife and presumably he loved his children. He made such a will as those who are so fortunate as to have a trusted wife and children very often make. He bequeathed and devised all he had to his wife, evidently believing that she would deal justly with his offspring. Although the statute must not be disregarded, we are construing the testator's will. In doing so it would violate the most important canon governing the construction of wills if we gave no heed to the intention of the testator as expressed in his will. It seems to us that it would do violence to the parental instinct and to his intention to hold that he excluded the children he knew and loved without also intending to exclude an after-born child whom he might never know or see.

In view of the facts that the testator had living children whom he excluded and that he devised his entire estate to his wife, we think it is the more reasonable construction that it was apparent from the will that it was his intention that no provision should be made for any after-born child; and that the wife should take his entire estate to the exclusion, as a class, of all his children, including the living and after-born alike.

It is not to be understood that in affirming the judgment of the county court we are overruling or in any way departing from the rule declared in the cases of Bresee v. Stiles, 22 Wis. 120, and Sandon v. Sandon, 123 Wis. 603, 101 N.W. 1089. In those cases the court was dealing with facts so unlike those here involved that we do not think the language there used is controlling in this case. Judgment affirmed.

E. ABATEMENT

Categories of devises. Gifts of property by will are classified in regard to the character of the property transferred. Efforts to pass particular items of property by will, whether they be tangible or intangible, are characterized as *specific devises,* and when there is a shortfall of property in the estate, they are given priority over other devises. Some states, though not Wisconsin, make a further distinction between the specific devises of real and personal property, with priority given to protecting the real property.

When the testator intends to dispense a general benefit, usually expressed in terms of money or its equivalent, the devise is said to be *general.* Monetary devises are presumed to be general devises unless there is reason to believe that the testator intended to devise a specific coin or piece of paper money. (A devise to Helen of the testator's prized Confederate five-dollar bill would be a specific devise, while a devise of five dollars would be a general devise.) In most jurisdictions, devises of stocks or bonds are presumed to be general devises on the theory that that they are normally just cash equivalents. Only if the evidence suggests that the testator has in mind specific shares of stock or specific bonds is the devise *specific* (as is "To Thomas, the 100 shares of Microsoft that I received from my mother"). However, in Wisconsin, the devise of stock is a *specific* devise, if the testator owned at least the number of shares of the mentioned stock at the time of the will's execution or shortly thereafter.

A *demonstrative devise* is a hybrid of specific and general devises, in that it represents an attempt to transfer a general benefit derived from a specific source, as in "To John, $10,000 from the sale of Blackacre." The remainder of the sale price would be passed as general assets of the estate. A *residuary devise* transfers the remainder of the testator's estate not otherwise devised. If there are such assets, but there is no residuary clause, the property passes to the heir or heirs by a process known as *partial intestacy.* A *class gift* is a devise to a group of devisees who are united by a common characteristic, like "the daughters of John Jee" or the members of the Waupaca High School class of 1964. Ordinarily, a class gift is divided among the surviving members of the class, although in most states the anti-lapse statute applies to class gifts, so the descendants of a class member may be qualified to take the share of their ancestor. A *class gift* may be in the form of a *specific, demonstrative, general, or residuary devise.*

Wis. Stat. 854.18. Order in which assets apportioned; abatement.

(1) (a) Except as provided in sub. (3) or in connection with the deferred marital property elective share amount of a surviving spouse who elects under s. 861.02, the share of a surviving spouse who takes under s. 853.12, or the share of a surviving child who takes under s. 853.25, shares of distributees abate, without any preference or priority as between real and personal property, in the following order:

1. If the governing instrument is a will, property subject to intestacy.

2. Residuary transfers or devises under the governing instrument.

3. General transfers or devises under the governing instrument.

4. Specific transfers or devises under the governing instrument.

(b) For purposes of abatement, a general transfer or devise charged on any specific property or fund is a specific transfer to the extent of the value of the property on which it is charged, and upon the failure or insufficiency of the property on which it is charged, it is a general transfer to the extent of the failure or insufficiency.

(2)

(a) Abatement within each classification is in proportion to the amount of property that each of the beneficiaries would have received if full distribution of the property had been made in accordance with the terms of the governing instrument.

(b) If the subject of a preferred transfer is sold or used incident to administration of an estate, abatement shall be achieved by appropriate adjustments in, or contribution from, other interests in the remaining assets.

(3) If the governing instrument expresses an order of abatement, or if the transferors estate plan or the purpose of the transfer, as expressed, implied, or construed through extrinsic evidence, would be defeated by the order of abatement under sub. (1), the shares of the distributees abate as necessary to give effect to the intention of the transferor.

Drews v. Marwede (In re Estate of Porath)

Wisconsin Court of Appeals
295 Wis. 2d 842, 721 N.W.2d 158 (2006)

PER CURIAM. Beverly Drews appeals an order construing Marie Porath's will, which determined that a bequest of a sum of money to Beverly was a general bequest that abated because of insufficient assets. We affirm the order.

Marie's will was signed on August 22, 1997. At the time of her death on May 16, 2003, her assets included cash in the amount of $136.76, and an undivided one-half interest in her farm property. Marie's will provided, in article III, as follows:

If my husband, Carl A. Porath, predeceases me, I give all of my property as follows:

A. If I own an undivided one-half (1/2) interest in farm land located in the Northwest 1/4 of Section 17, Township 20 North, Range 17 East, in the Town of Menasha, Winnebago County, Wisconsin. I give my undivided one-half (1/2) interest in said farm to my daughter, CAROL MARWEDE, who already owns the other undivided one-half (1/2) interest.

B. I give to my daughter, BEVERLY DREWS, the sum of Fifty Thousand Dollars ($50,000.00) or a sum equal to fifty (50%) percent of the appraised value in my estate of the undivided one-half (1/2) interest which I own in the above-described farm, whichever is greater.

C. I give the sum of Ten Thousand dollars ($10,000.00) to TRINITY LUTHERAN CHURCH, NEENAH, WISCONSIN, or to its successor or successors.

D. I give the sum of Two Thousand Dollars ($2,000.00) to each of my grandchildren, living at the time of my death.

E. I give the sum of Ten Thousand Dollars ($10,000.00) to be divided equally between those of my great-grandchildren living at the time of my death.

F. I give the sum of Five Hundred Dollars ($500.00) to my niece, SHERYL O'ROURKE LOUGHRIN, presently of Greendale, Wisconsin, or to her issue by right of representation. If she leaves no issue then this bequest is to lapse and become part of the residue of my estate.

It is undisputed that Marie's husband, Carl, predeceased her. It is also undisputed that there were insufficient assets at the time of Marie's death to satisfy all the transfers set forth in the will. The circuit court distributed the specific devise of the farm property to Carol Marwede pursuant to paragraph A of the will. The court concluded that the bequests of sums of money that followed in paragraphs B through F were general bequests that abated because there was insufficient money in the estate to satisfy them. Beverly appeals.

The construction of a will involves a question of law that we review without deference to the circuit court. Firehammer v. Marchant (In re Estate of Smith), 224 Wis. 2d 673,

676, 591 N.W.2d 898 (Ct. App. 1999). Despite our de novo review, we value the analysis of the circuit court. Furmanski v. Furmanski, 196 Wis. 2d 210, 214, 538 N.W.2d 566 (Ct. App. 1995). Our task in construing a will is to determine the testator's intent, and the best evidence of this is the language of the document itself. When the will is unambiguous, there is no need to look any further to ascertain the testator's intent. Smith, 224 Wis. 2d at 676-77.

Beverly argues that the order construing the will is contrary to Marie's intent. Beverly asserts that when read in its entirety, the will evidences Marie's clear intent to treat her daughters equally. Beverly does not dispute that Marie intended to leave her one-half interest in the farm to Carol, as Carol already owned the other half of the farm. However, Beverly contends that abatement "would completely defeat Marie's estate plan" because Carol would receive the farm and Beverly would receive nothing. We disagree.

The plain language of Marie's will leaves the farm property to Carol and sums of money to Beverly and certain others. As the circuit court correctly noted, the bequest to Beverly does not provide that Carol takes the farm property subject to a lien in favor of Beverly, or that Beverly is to be paid upon sale of the farm. Marie's will gives no indication of the source of the sum of money for the bequest to Beverly. Paragraph B simply indicates that Beverly was to receive "the sum of" or "a sum equal to" certain amounts. Paragraphs A and B are not contingent upon each other. The only condition placed on the bequest of the farm property to Carol was that Marie own it at the time of her death. There was no condition that the estate be sufficiently funded to satisfy the cash bequests that followed.

As such, the language of the will, if given its ordinary meaning, is consistent with the circuit court's determination that the bequest of the farm property to Carol was a specific bequest. A specific bequest is "a gift by will of a particular thing, or specified part, of the testator's estate, which is so described as to be capable of being distinguished from all others of the same kind." Estate of Haberli, 41 Wis. 2d 64, 69, 163 N.W.2d 168 (1968) (citation omitted). The farm property was identified in the will by legal description and available to be distributed to Carol. It is a specific bequest of Marie's one-half interest in the farm property.

The issue thus becomes whether the circuit court correctly determined that the bequests of sums of money in paragraphs B through F were general bequests. A general bequest is one that confers a general benefit but not a specific asset. It is characterized by the fact that it does not attempt to dispose of any specific article or be made a charge on such item, but it is payable generally from the estate. Will of Weed,

213 Wis. 574, 578, 252 N.W. 294 (1934). As Professor Howard Erlanger discusses in his handbook for practitioners:

A "general" transfer is one that confers a general benefit but not a specific asset; for example, the transfer of $10,000. Howard S. Erlanger, Wisconsin's New Probate Code, a Handbook for Practitioners, 120 n.167, University of Wisconsin Law School (1998).

Marie's will does not specify an asset that would confer the sum of money bequested to Beverly, nor is the sum of money "charged" to a specific asset.* Rather, it is simply the transfer of a sum not less than $50,000. In Korn v. Friz, 128 Wis. 428, 429, 107 N.W. 659 (1906), the court was presented with the following will provision: "I will, devise, and bequeath to my son William Korn my farm [description omitted] upon the express condition, however, that he shall pay to my daughter, Phillipina Steele, the sum of five thousand ($5,000.00) dollars within one year after the death of my said wife …." The Korn court concluded the testator intended that out of his farm should be paid $5,000 to his daughter. Since the son was to take possession immediately upon the death of his mother and was not required to make payment to his sister until afterwards, the court concluded this was a condition subsequent that conferred upon the sister the right to a lien or "charge" for the sum of $5,000. Id. at 436.

We have no similar declaration in the will we are presently considering. By contrast, Marie's will simply indicates an intention that Beverly and various others receive sums of money. The will does not direct Carol to pay the sums of money, nor is the farm property devised "subject to," "expressly conditioned upon," or "contingent upon" Beverly or the others receiving the monetary sums. The will could have been drafted as such, but it was not. The court "can neither make a will for the testator nor distort its construction to accomplish its own idea of what is equitable." Will of Richter, 215 Wis. 108, 111, 254 N.W. 103 (1934).

Abatement involves the reduction of a legacy because of insufficient assets in the estate to pay all debts, charges and legacies in full. Under the common law, when an estate was "inadequate to meet the calls of the bequests in the will, and no provision having been made by the testatrix as to where the burden of the deficiency should lie, the loss must be borne by those who share in the estate under the general legacies." Will of Weed, 213 Wis. at 578. Wisconsin Stat. § 854.18 3 now codifies the order of abatement. Section 854.18(1)(a), provides that general bequests shall abate prior to specific bequests.

* [Ed. Note: Although the court does not use the term, when it refers to "money 'charged' to a specific asset," it is referring to what is usually called a *demonstrative* devise.]

Marie's will in paragraph A makes a specific bequest of the farm property to Carol. The will then makes general bequests of sums of money to Beverly and various others in paragraphs B through F. Marie's will does not set forth an order of abatement should the estate be inadequately funded. Failure to provide for a contingency in a will is an omission rather than an ambiguity. See Trust of Pauly, 71 Wis. 2d 306, 310, 237 N.W.2d 719 (1976).

Since the assets of the estate are insufficient to satisfy all the bequests, and the will lacked an abatement provision, the general bequests were subject to statutory abatement pursuant to WIS. STAT. § 854.18(1)(a). We agree with the circuit court in so holding.

CHAPTER 5: LIMITS ON TESTAMENTARY FREEDOM

While Americans are normally free to dispose of their property in any way they choose, there are certain limitations that come into place when the disposition is by will. All states but Georgia and a handful of community property jurisdictions place some restrictions on the ability of individuals to disinherit their spouses. Moreover, public policy concerns prevent the enforcement of certain types of prerequisites to the ownership of property: unreasonable restraints on the right to marry, improper restraints on alienation, and requirements of illegal or socially undesirable behavior are all unenforceable restrictions.

I. FAMILY OBLIGATIONS

A. OBLIGATIONS TO CHILDREN

In the United States, parents are free to disinherit their children, regardless of their age, in every state except Louisiana. Even there, the obligation, once lasting for the life of the child, now extends only to age 23. While the disinheritance of children is a widely frowned up practice, the right to do so falls within the bounds of testamentary freedom as it is understood in the United States. This is not, however, a world norm. The law of virtually every European and Latin American country guarantees children a part of their parents' estates, as do the laws of countries as diverse as Japan, Korea, India, Mongolia, and Turkey. (It appears that some sort of forced share for children is the world norm, but not in the United States.)

No Wisconsin statute creates any requirement that a deceased parent has to share part of his or her estate with the children. That this is the approach in Wisconsin was illustrated by the opening paragraphs on the Wisconsin Supreme Court's decision in *Estate of Beale* (1952) (see Chapter 2), in which the Court asserted: "The long line of Wisconsin decisions does not permit the probate court to entertain the argument that a will can be denied probate only because it appears to be unjust to a natural object of a testator's bounty.'' (In his will, the noted professor disinherited his 10-year old son, and left the bulk of his estate instead to the Masonic Order.)

Wisconsin law once provided a possible loophole for omitted children in that former Wis. Stat. §238.10 provided that a child omitted "by mistake or accident" was entitled to a share of the estate equal to what he or she would have received had the parent died intestate. While this may have provided an avenue for a sympathetic court to disingenuously restore omitted children to the estate, the loophole could be closed if the testator specifically stated in the will that he was "disinheriting" all or some of his children. (Contemporary Wis. Stat 853.25 preserves the "accidentally or mistakenly omitted from the will" concept, but the statute now provides only that the omitted child is entitled to share in the devises to other children. If the parent devises nothing to his or her children, then there is nothing for the omitted child to share, even if it is found to have been inadvertently omitted.)

In re Will of Mattes

Supreme Court of Wisconsin
268 Wis. 447, 68 N.W.2d 18 (1955)

Arthur A. Mattes executed a will on July 17, 1944, by the terms of which, after making two specific bequests not material here, he devised and bequeathed the entire residue of his estate to his wife, Meta. He had then living a son by a former marriage, Arthur A. Mattes, the contestant in the instant proceeding. Testator died October 2, 1952. The will was presented for probate and the son filed objection to its allowance, one of the grounds therefor being that the testator omitted to provide for him and that such omission was not intentional but was made by mistake or accident. After trial the court made findings of fact as follows:

"2. The will was drafted on a printed form. Herb. J. Smith, the draftsman, was not advised by the testator, and never knew until after testator's death, that he had a son, Artie. There was little preliminary conversation between testator and Herb. J. Smith about the terms of the will. The will was drawn by the testator in a thoughtless and careless manner.

"3. Testator died on October 2, 1952. He left surviving him a son, Arthur A. Mattes (hereinafter sometimes referred to as 'Artie'), born of a first marriage, and a second wife, Meta. The Meta Mattes named in the will is the second wife of the testator. Artie, his son by his first wife, is not mentioned in any way in the will. Meta Mattes had no children and did not adopt Artie.

"4. Testator's estate consisted of real property owned alone appraised at $11,000, personal property owned alone appraised at $173,378.40, jointly owned real estate having a gross value of $5,000, and jointly owned personal property having a gross value of $47,656.67.

"5. There existed between the testator and his son, Artie, from the time Artie was a small boy until the death of the testator, a strong bond of mutual affection and regard. The testator expressed his pride in the affection for his son to others, frequently.

"6. Testator thought that he had provided for his son, Artie, in his will. As he had not, the omission was not intentional but was made by mistake or accident.

"7. Artie, at the time testator signed the will, was employed by Allis-Chalmers Manufacturing Company of Milwaukee, Wisconsin, as an assistant purchasing agent, at a salary of $250-275 a month. He was then married and had one daughter born February 13, 1940. Two other daughters were born subsequent to the signing of the will. In 1943, Artie purchased a home for $8,600, on which, in 1944, he owed almost $8,400, having financed the down payment by borrowing from a friend. He also owed money on his furniture at that time. He had no other property or assets of any kind.

"8. Meta Mattes, Artie's stepmother, never gave Artie any love or affection, and was always unpleasant to him. Artie was courteous to his stepmother even though she always treated him with cold indifference. She gave all the appearances of being a cold, calculating stepmother, who hated her husband's son by his first wife. Testator knew at the time he signed the will, of the hostile attitude of his wife toward his son, Artie.

"9. Testator, after signing his will in 1944, placed the best securities he owned, representing a substantial sum of money, in joint tenancy, with his wife, so that they would pass to her outside of the will. Meta Mattes had no property of her own. The joint property represented earnings of the testator, Arthur W. Mattes, alone. From the manner in which testator put his property in joint tenancy with his second wife, Meta, I find that he intended to provide for his son, Artie, in his will, and the omission was not intentional, but was made by mistake or accident.

"10. Testator, during the last six months of his life, was ill with cancer of the throat. This he was aware of, and knew that it seriously endangered his life. The conversations testator had during that period with Norbert Brick, Peter J. Petrie, Ralph Cavil, and John Miron, did not relate to what he intended to do in the future, but indicated what he thought he had done in the past. From the testimony of those four witnesses and the other circumstances of the case, I find that testator believed he had named his son, Artie, in his will. I find further that inasmuch as the testator believed he had provided for his son, Artie, in his will, when in fact he had not, that the omission was not intentional, but was made by mistake or accident."

On March 29, 1954, the court entered an order allowing the will to probate, "subject to the son of the deceased, Arthur A. Mattes, having the same share in the estate of the deceased as if he had died intestate, to be assigned as provided in section 238.10, Stats." The widow appeals from that part of the judgment appearing immediately above and in quotation marks.

Gehl, J. The applicable statute is sec. 238.11, which provides as follows:

"238.11 Provision for child omitted by mistake, etc. When any testator shall omit to provide in his will for any of his children or for the issue of any deceased child, and it shall appear that such omission was not intentional but was made by mistake or accident, such child or the issue of such child shall have the same share in the estate of the testator as if he had died intestate, to be assigned as provided in section 238.10."

It is contended that to sustain the claim of the contestant would be to ignore the rule that a person has unquestioned power to disinherit his children without cause. We are not dealing with a will; we are concerned with a statute. The statute was not designed to diminish or annul the right of one to dispose of his property by will; it does not attempt to regulate or control the testamentary disposition of property. Its purpose is to protect the interest of a child who by his parent's failure through accident or inadvertence has not been provided for. The will still stands but the pretermitted child takes as if the testator had left no will. The right of a pretermitted child to take under the statute does not affect the will; it operates only to reduce the amount of testator's testate property. Detroit Trust Co. v. Stoepel, 312 Mich. 172, 20 N. W. (2d) 148.

"Children so situated [omitted] do not set up title under the will but under the statute. The will is used to establish that they have no legacy or devise under it. Then the inquiry arises whether the testator intended to omit them." Coulam v. Doull, 133 U.S. 216, 231, 10 Sup. Ct. 253, 33 L. Ed. 596.

"The purpose of the statute before us seems plain. It was passed to guard against the inadvertent and unintentional omission of children and their issue from the will of the parent or grandparent. Under it, a pretermitted child does not seek to defeat or amend the will itself. He does not seek to impeach it in any way. He seeks to have established a right unaffected by it. He does not seek a right under the will at all, but a right under the statute." In re Dugan's Estate, 108 Vt. 430, 433, 188 Atl. 887.

The underlying question in determining the matter here involved is whether the testator's omission to provide for his son was intentional or accidental. The issue presented is one of fact, Moon v. Estate of Evans, 69 Wis. 667, 35 N. W. 20; Will of Kurth, 241 Wis. 426, 6 N. W. (2d) 233, and may be considered upon extrinsic evidence. Newman v. Waterman, 63 Wis. 612, 23 N. W. 696. That the burden of proof to establish an accidental omission is on the contestant in this case is clear from the language of the statute. The trial court determined that he had met that burden. We may not set aside the findings of ultimate fact, those upon which the son's right to recover necessarily depend, unless they are found to be contrary to the great weight and clear preponderance of the evidence. Swazee v. Lee, 259 Wis. 136, 47 N. W. (2d) 733.

We have set forth the so-called findings at length because they are really a statement of the essential evidentiary facts which the court considered as supporting the ultimate finding; it so appears from a memorandum opinion filed by the judge. There is testimony which supports each of these so called findings. We number the succeeding paragraphs to correspond with those of the so-called findings.

2. Although it does not appear that testator drew the will in a thoughtless manner, the scrivener's testimony indicates that there was no lengthy conversation between them before execution of the will. The scrivener testified that he did not learn of the existence of the son until some considerable time after execution of the will.

3. The facts there recited are undisputed.

4. The statement as to the value of testator's estate and of the property held jointly by him and his wife is correct.

5. There is abundant testimony that the relationship between the testator and his son was very close at all times. In fact, no effort was made to contradict the testimony of the son and several other disinterested witnesses to that effect.

6. The testimony permits of the inference that testator thought that he had provided for his son. Norbert Brick who had been employed by decedent since 1936 testified that in 1951 he had indicated to testator that he might be interested in buying the latter's hardware business; that testator told him that he would give him a chance to buy it; that, when the witness spoke of acquiring the money needed, testator said that he would see that the witness would get a good start and that if something should happen to him, the son Arthur would be there and that the witness would be dealing with him. He testified further that shortly before testator went to a hospital and shortly before his

death the same matter was discussed and again the testator said that if the witness owed anything at the time of his death the son would take care of it.

A neighbor for many years, Peter J. Petrie, testified that on one occasion he and the testator had some conversation with respect to wills. The witness told him that he had made his; the deceased answered that Artie, the son, would have nothing to worry about; when he passed on Artie would be well taken care of.

John Miron, an internal-revenue agent who investigated testator's income-tax returns, testified that on July 9, 1952, in a conversation he had with deceased respecting his income tax returns, the latter told him that he wanted to have a clear slate for Artie when the latter took his place; that he did not know whether the son would be interested in the father's business, but whether he would be interested or not it was going to be his to do as he pleased with; that his only concern was for his son and his granddaughters. These declarations of the testator were properly received in evidence, 57 Am. Jur., Wills, p. 412, sec. 600.

7. There was no dispute as to the son's income and his financial condition.

8. Although it is disputed, there is testimony that the stepmother's attitude toward the son was not friendly. He testified that there was ill-feeling between them during all the time that he lived at his father's home, that it was impossible for him "to do anything right;" that on a number of occasions she called him a "G -- d -- Luloff," the latter being his mother's maiden name; that on another occasion she threw a butcher knife at him.

9. It is not disputed that after executing his will in 1944 testator placed securities of the value of approximately $50,000 in the joint names of himself and his wife.

10. In paragraph numbered 6 we have discussed in more detail the statements to which the trial judge refers.

All of these facts and circumstances to which the trial judge refers were properly considered in determining the ultimate issue.

"Evidence of the circumstances under which the will was executed, the intelligence of the testator, the size of the estate, the relations between the testator and the omitted children at the time of the execution of the will, and declarations of the testator have been held to be not only admissible on the issue whether the failure of the testator to provide for a child or the issue of a deceased child was intentional, irrespective of whether offered by a party seeking to show that the omission was unintentional or by a party seeking to establish that it was intentional; but to be sufficient to establish the intent of the testator in this respect." 57 Am. Jur., Wills, p. 411, sec. 599.

We consider it most significant that after execution of the will the testator placed in the joint names of himself and his wife securities worth about $45,000. If he supposed that he had provided by his will that she should have his entire estate, why these transactions? If he made the change to decrease the amount of state inheritance tax to be paid or to reduce the expense of administration of his estate, why did he not place all of his property in the joint names?

Equally significant are the declarations made by him. They indicate most clearly that the deceased was under the impression that he had made provision for his son.

The trial judge's findings must be sustained and the judgment affirmed.

B. FAMILY MAINTENANCE

In most countries, deceased parents also have an obligation to provide support for the surviving members of their immediate family. In some countries (like the United States), this duty is limited to the probate period; in others, many of which share the United States' common law heritage, the family maintenance obligations extends beyond the period immediately after the deceased parent's death. Such countries include England, Northern Ireland, New Zealand, Singapore, and Malaysia, as well as many of the Canadian provinces and Australian states.

Wis. Stat. 861.31. Allowance to family during administration.

(1m) The court may, without notice or on such notice as the court directs, order payment by the personal representative or special administrator of an allowance as the court determines necessary or appropriate for the support of the surviving spouse or surviving domestic partner and any minor children of the decedent during the administration of the estate. The court shall consider the size of the probate estate, other resources available for support, the existing standard of living, and any other factors it considers relevant.

(2) The court may order that an allowance be made to the spouse or surviving domestic partner for support of the spouse or surviving domestic partner and any minor children of the decedent, or that separate allowances be made to the spouse or surviving domestic partner and to the minor children of the decedent or their guardian, if any, if the court finds separate allowances advisable. If there is no surviving spouse or surviving domestic partner, the court

may order that an allowance be made to the minor children of the decedent or to their guardian, if any.

(3) The initial order for support may not exceed one year but may be extended for additional periods of not to exceed one year at a time, and is subject to revision or termination at any time by further order of the court.

(4) The court may order that the allowance be charged against income or principal, either as an advance or otherwise, but the court may not order that an allowance for support of minor children of the decedent be charged against the income or principal interest of the surviving spouse or surviving domestic partner. The court may order that the allowance for support of the surviving spouse or surviving domestic partner, not including any allowance for support of minor children of the decedent, be applied in satisfaction of any of the following:

(a) Any entitlement of the surviving spouse under s. 853.12

(b) Any right of the surviving spouse or surviving domestic partner to elect under s. 861.02

Wis. Stat. 861.33. Selection of personalty by surviving spouse or surviving domestic partner.

(1) (a) Subject to this section, in addition to all allowances and distributions, the surviving spouse or surviving domestic partner may file with the court a written selection of the following personal property, which shall then be transferred to the spouse or domestic partner by the personal representative:

1. Wearing apparel and jewelry held for personal use by the decedent or the surviving spouse or surviving domestic partner;

2. Automobile;

3. Household furniture, furnishings and appliances; and

4. Other tangible personalty not used in trade, agriculture or other business, not to exceed 3,000 in inventory value.

(b) The selection in par. (a) may not include items specifically bequeathed except that the surviving spouse or surviving domestic partner may in every case select the normal household furniture, furnishings, and appliances necessary to maintain the home. For this purpose antiques, family heirlooms, and collections that are specifically bequeathed are not classifiable as normal household furniture or furnishings.

(2) If it appears that claims may not be paid in full, the court may, upon petition of any creditor, limit the transfer of personalty to the spouse under this section to items not exceeding

5,000 in aggregate inventory value until the claims are paid in full or the court otherwise orders, or the court may require the spouse to retransfer property in excess of 5,000 or, at the option of the spouse, pay the excess in value over this amount.

(3) The surviving spouse may select items not specifically bequeathed of the type specified under sub. (1) (a) 4. exceeding in value the 3,000 limit or obtain the transfer of items exceeding the limit set by the court under sub. (2), by paying to the personal representative the excess of inventory value over the respective limit.

(4) The personal representative has power, without court order, to execute appropriate documents to effect transfer of title to any personal property the spouse selects under this section. A person may not question the validity of the documents of transfer or refuse to accomplish the transfer on the grounds that the personal representative is also the surviving spouse of the decedent.

Wis. Stat. 861.35. Special allowance for support of spouse or domestic partner and support and education of minor children.

(1m) If the decedent is survived by a spouse, domestic partner, or by minor children, the court may order an allowance for the support and education of each minor child until he or she reaches a specified age, not to exceed 18, and for the support of the spouse or domestic partner. This allowance may be made whether the estate is testate or intestate. If the decedent is not survived by a spouse or domestic partner, the court also may allot directly to the minor children household furniture, furnishings, and appliances. The court may not order an allowance under this section if any of the following applies:

(a) The decedent has amply provided for each minor child and for the spouse or domestic partner by the transfer of probate or nonprobate assets, or support and education have been provided for by any other means.

(b) In the case of minor children, the surviving spouse or surviving domestic partner is legally responsible for support and education and has ample means to provide them in addition to his or her own support.

(c) In the case of the surviving spouse or surviving domestic partner, he or she has ample means to provide for his or her support.

(2) The court may set aside property to provide an allowance and may appoint a trustee to administer the property, subject to the continuing jurisdiction of the court. If a child dies or reaches the age of 18, or if at any time the property held by the trustee is no longer required for the support of the spouse or domestic partner or the support and education of the minor child, any remaining property is to be distributed by the trustee as the court orders in accordance with the terms of the decedent's will or to the heirs of the decedent in intestacy or to satisfy unpaid claims of the decedent's estate.

(3) In making an allowance under this section, the court shall consider all of the following:

(a) The effect on claims under s. 859.25 The court shall balance the needs of the spouse, domestic partner, or minor children against the nature of the creditors' claims in setting the amount allowed under this section.

(b) The size of the estate.

(c) Other resources available for support.

(d) The existing standard of living.

(e) Whether the provisions of a marital property agreement will create a hardship for the surviving spouse.

(f) Any other factors that the court considers relevant.

(4) The court may order that the allowance to the surviving spouse or surviving domestic partner, not including any allowance for the support and education of minor children, be applied in satisfaction of any of the following:

(a) Any entitlement of the surviving spouse or surviving domestic partner under s. 853.12 (b) Any right of the surviving spouse or surviving domestic partner to elect under s. 861.02 (1)

Wis. Stat. 861.41. Exemption of property to be assigned to surviving spouse or surviving domestic partner.

(1) After the amount of claims against the estate has been ascertained, the surviving spouse or surviving domestic partner may petition the court to set aside as exempt from the claims of creditors under s. 859.25 (1) (h) an amount of property reasonably necessary for the support of the spouse or domestic partner, not to exceed 10,000 in value, if it appears that the assets are insufficient to pay all claims and allowances and still leave the surviving spouse or surviving domestic partner such an amount of property in addition to selection and allowances.

(2) The court shall grant the petition if it determines that an assignment ahead of creditors is reasonably necessary for the support of the spouse or domestic partner. In determining the necessity and the amount of property to be assigned, the court must take into consideration the availability of a home to the surviving spouse or surviving domestic partner and all other assets and resources available for support

Wis. Stat. 861.43. Authority and powers of conservator, guardian or agent.

A conservator, guardian or guardian ad litem of the spouse or of a child of the decedent, or an agent of the spouse or of a child of the decedent acting under a power of attorney, may on behalf of the spouse or child exercise any of the rights, apply for any of the allowances or make any of the selections that apply to the spouse or child under this subchapter.

ESTATE OF SULLIVAN

Supreme Court of Wisconsin
200 Wis. 590, 229 N.W. 65 (1930)

Action begun February 25, 1929; order entered May 14, 1929. Widow's allowance under sec. 318.01 (2), Stats. John McBride Sullivan was twice married. He was divorced from his first wife on December 26, 1917, and she was given the custody of their two minor children. She has since remarried and now lives in Chicago. In November, 1925, Sullivan married the petitioner Elza, who since the death of Sullivan remarried, her present name being Elza Schultz.

Sullivan was killed on February 21, 1928, and left surviving his widow Elza and an infant son, John McBride Sullivan, aged six months. He left no estate, but there was a claim against the Chicago & Northwestern Railway Company for settlement of which the railway company paid $7,100,--$100 was paid to his estate on account of pain and suffering, $2,000 to the children by the first marriage, and the remainder to the widow and child of the second marriage. He was also a veteran of the World War and there was paid to his estate on account of adjusted service certificate the sum of $1,581 on November 16, 1928. The railway company paid its claim on October 6, 1928. Thereupon the widow petitioned the court for an allowance under sec. 318.01 (2), which provides:

"Allowance to family. The widow and minor children, or either, constituting the family of the deceased testator or intestate, shall have such reasonable allowance out of the personal estate or the income of the real estate of the deceased as the county court shall judge necessary for their maintenance during the progress of the settlement of the estate," etc.

The petition of the widow was disallowed, and from an order disallowing it the widow and the administrator appeal.

ROSENBERRY, C. J. The question presented upon this appeal requires an interpretation of sec. 318.01 (2), Stats., already set out. On behalf of the petitioner it is argued that the statute is mandatory; that it was the duty of the court to make a reasonable allowance out of the estate, and that refusal of the court to make the petitioner any allowance was erroneous. On the other hand, it is argued that the statute is purely discretionary; that the widow has received certain insurance moneys and other resources, and that it would be equitable to deny her support under the statute, under all the facts and circumstances of this case.

It is considered that the object and purpose of the statute is to substitute the estate of the husband for the deceased husband during the progress of the settlement of the estate so far as support of the family is concerned. What allowance should be made is to be determined under all the facts and circumstances. Ordinarily in the case of a solvent estate it would be such sum as would maintain the family in approximately the same degree of comfort in which they were maintained by the husband. Under the statute the widow is entitled to an allowance for her support during the progress of the settlement of the estate and it should be paid when and as there are funds available for that purpose, and the fact that the widow has been able to survive by means of aid extended to her or loans made by her friends or relatives does not deprive her of her rights under the statute. All the facts and circumstances of this case were before the court. It is not necessary to have a rehearing of the matter.

There were originally three appeals in this case--(1st) that of Elza Schultz, (2d) that of G. P. Thiedt, administrator, and (3d) that of Ruby A. Gordon, divorced wife of the deceased. The appeal of Ruby A. Gordon has been abandoned by counsel. Her counsel joined in the brief of the guardian ad litem of Max and Maxine Sullivan, children of Mrs. Gordon. The guardian ad litem contends that the appeal of Elza Schultz should be dismissed because not perfected in accordance with the statute, and that the appeal of G. P. Thiedt, administrator, should be dismissed because he has no right to appeal. The same questions would be raised upon each appeal.

Sec. 324.01 (2) provides:

"In counties having a population of over fifteen thousand, in all cases not otherwise provided for, any executor, administrator, guardian, trustee, or any person aggrieved by any order, judgment, decree, determination or denial of the county court shall have the right to have the same reviewed by writ of error or appeal from the county court to the supreme court."

In McKenney v. Minahan, 119 Wis. 651, 97 N.W. 489, it was said:

"Sec. 4031 [now sec. 324.01] expressly recognizes an administrator standing as the representative of persons who would be injuriously affected by a determination of the county court, if it were allowed to stand, as a party aggrieved. That is the plain meaning of the language: 'In all cases not otherwise provided for, any executor, administrator, guardian, trustee or any person aggrieved,' etc. Plainly, any one of the persons specially mentioned is recognized as a party aggrieved, when any one whose interest he represents is aggrieved. It was the duty of the administrator to preserve the property of the estate, so far as he legally could, for transmission to the heirs of the deceased. In the settlement of claims against the estate he stood for them. Any injury to their interests, in legal effect, was a grievance to him within the meaning of the appeal statute. . . . It is elementary that the legal representative of interests involved in litigation, prejudicially affected by the result, is a party aggrieved within the meaning of appeal statutes."

Within the doctrine of this case the administrator was entitled to take the appeal.

We shall not discuss the proposition that the appeal of Elza Schultz was not perfected. It was quite apparent that it was taken in good faith, and if not perfected it would be our duty under sec. 274.32 to stay the proceedings and permit it to be perfected. All questions presented upon her appeal being presented upon the appeal of the administrator, further consideration is not necessary.

By the Court.--That part of the order appealed from is reversed, and cause remanded with directions to the trial court to make an allowance pursuant to the statute as indicated in this opinion. …

[The concurring opinion by Justice Stevens and the dissenting opinion of Justice Owen are omitted. Both dealt with the question of the right of the administrator of an estate to file an appeal, as was done in this case.]

II. SPOUSAL CLAIMS

A. THE TRADITIONAL ELECTIVE SHARE

Every American state except Georgia accepts the principle that husbands and wives are entitled to share in the property acquired by each other by the time of their deaths. In 40 states and the District of Columbia this takes the form of the separate property *elective share,* which entitles a surviving spouse to a portion of the property controlled by the other spouse at the time of death (or in some states, property disposed of in the two years preceding death). Although the formula used to calculate the elective share varies a great deal from jurisdiction to jurisdiction, the basic premise is that the surviving spouse is entitled to an elective share amount, and if she or he fails to receive that amount from the deceased spouse, the "survivor" can "elect" to receive such an amount in lieu of what, if anything, was provided for them in the will.

Before 1984, Wisconsin had such a statute that guaranteed surviving spouses an amount equal to one-third of the deceased spouse's probate estate. (The probate estate includes all assets that pass through a will or by the process of intestacy following the death of the property owner.) However, in 1984, Wisconsin became the ninth community property state in the United States. (The others are Louisiana, Texas, New Mexico, Arizona, California, Nevada, Washington, and Idaho.) Technically, what happened in 1984, was that Wisconsin became the first, and to date only, state to adopt the Uniform Marital Property Act (UMPA) promulgated by the Uniform Law Commission in 1983, a statute designed to facility the transition from a separate property to a community property jurisdiction.

Like the Uniform Act, Wisconsin's statute does not use the term *community property* but instead substitutes the term *marital property.* The provisions of the UMPA are incorporated into the *Wisconsin Statutes* at Wis. Stats. §§ 766.001-766.097 (2013). Property owned by registered domestic partners is not marital property, and the registered domestic partner obtains no legal interest in property acquired by the other partner. As in other community property jurisdictions, almost all property acquired in Wisconsin by husbands and wives during a lawful marriage is owned in equal shares by both parties, regardless of which spouse purchased the property or in whose name it was acquired. Consequently, when one spouse dies, the couple's marital property is automatically divided equally between the surviving spouse and the estate of the deceased spouse, thereby eliminating, at least in theory, the need for an elective share. From the perspective of the surviving spouse, this system works "best" when the marriage was one of long duration where the parties where continuously domiciled in Wisconsin. It works least well in cases where the marriage was short or where the parties lived in *separate property* states during most of the marriage.

Because property acquired before the effective date of the statute or, while a couple lives in a non-community property state ordinarily does not become community property, Wisconsin also has an elective share provision dealing with the distribution of that property (which is discussed below). Such property is referred to in Wisconsin as *deferred marital property,* and sometimes as *quasi-community property.*

The following case, involving one of Milwaukee's wealthiest families, was decided under the pre-1984 system and illustrates many of the complexities that could arise under the previous system. Features of the elective share system in this case are still in effect in most non-community property states, including all of the states that border on Wisconsin.

Uihlein v. Uihlein

Supreme Court of Wisconsin
264 Wis. 362, 59 N.W.2d 641 (1953)

Currie, J. These appeals raise the following issues:

(1) Is the widow who has elected to take her one-third share of the estate, pursuant to sec. 233.14, Stats., entitled to such share without deduction therefrom of any portion of the federal estate tax?

(2) Does the widow's election to take under the law extinguish the special power given to the widow under the will to appoint the residue of the estate upon her death among the nieces and nephews of the deceased, their descendants, and certain charities?

(3) Does the widow's election to take under the law have the same effect as her death and thereby accelerate the distribution of the remaining estate to the persons named as takers, in default of the exercise of the power of appointment, in the proportions provided in the testator's will?

(4) Inasmuch as the testator failed to dispose of one tenth of the residue of the estate (less $10,000), how is such one tenth (less $10,000) to be assigned in making final distribution of the estate?

(5) Is the widow, who has elected to take under the law, in addition to receiving her homestead rights in the homestead and one third of the personal estate, also entitled as sole heir at law and next of kin of the decedent to share in any intestate property of the deceased?

Impact of Federal Estate Tax

While technically the "gross estate" of the deceased is all of the assets before any deduction for administration expenses, debts, allowances for support, and federal estate tax, we will, for purposes of simplicity of nomenclature in this opinion, designate that part of the total estate remaining after deduction of expenses, debts, and allowances as the "gross estate;" while the term "net estate" will be used to refer to that part of the estate which remains after deduction of the federal estate tax, as well as expenses, debts, and allowances.

The impact of the federal estate tax directly affects the amounts distributable to the widow and other beneficiaries. The trial court determined that the widow's share of the personal estate which she is to receive, by reason of her election to take under the law and not under the will, is one third of the gross estate. The result of this is that none of the impact of the federal estate tax falls upon the widow's share of the personal estate. On the other hand, the guardian ad litem and counsel for beneficiaries other than the widow contend that the widow's share of the personal estate should be determined upon the net estate and not the gross estate.

The difference in result of computing the widow's share of the personal estate under each of these two methods is well illustrated by the following table:

	Widow's Share determined on net estate	Widow's Share determined on gross estate
Gross Estate	$7,078,600	$7,078,600
Debts, expenses, family allowance	265,000	265,000
Adjusted gross estate	6,813,600	6,813,600
Homestead real estate	60,000	60,000
Net personal estate before deducting federal estate tax	6,753,600	6,753,600
Federal estate tax	2,361,038	N/A
Next personal estate after federal tax	4,392,562	6,753,600
Widow's 1/3	1,464,187	2,251,200
Other Beneficiaries	2,928,375	4,502,400
Federal Estate Tax	N/A	1,947,315
Net to beneficiaries other than widow	2,928,375	2,555,085

[Note: The widow's interest in the homestead is terminable and does not qualify for marital deduction.]

The learned trial judge in his memorandum opinion advanced two reasons for relieving the widow's share of the personal estate from all impact of the federal estate tax, viz., (1) that the history of the federal legislation which resulted in the allowance of the marital deduction in determining federal estate tax indicated an intention on the part of congress that a widow's share qualifying for such marital deduction should be free from the impact of the federal estate tax; and (2) the recent decision of the Ohio supreme court in Miller v. Hammond (1952), 156 Ohio St. 475, 104 N. E. (2d) .

Sec. 812 (e) (1) (E) of the Internal Revenue Code (26 USCA) provides in part as follows:

"(E) Valuation of interest passing to surviving spouse. In determining for the purposes of subparagraph (A) the value of any interest in property passing to the surviving spouse for which a deduction is allowed by this subsection –

"(i) *there shall be taken into account the effect which a tax imposed by this chapter, or any estate, succession, legacy, or inheritance tax, has upon the net value to the surviving spouse of such interest*; . . ." (Italics supplied.)

Thus the Internal Revenue Code expressly provides that in computing the value of the interest of a surviving spouse for purposes of the marital deduction in determining the federal estate tax there is to be taken into account the impact of any part of the federal estate tax which falls upon such interest of the surviving spouse. This provision of the federal estate-tax statutes thus would seem to expressly negative any intent on the part of congress that the widow's share of the personal estate in the instant case should entirely escape the impact of all of the federal estate tax.

Furthermore, the United States supreme court in Riggs v. Del Drago (1942), 317 U.S. 95, 97, 98, 63 Sup. Ct. 109, 87 L. Ed. 106, 142 A. L. R. 1131, stated:

"We are of opinion that congress intended that the federal estate tax should be paid out of the estate as a whole, and that the applicable state law as to the devolution of property at death should govern the distribution of the remainder and the ultimate impact of the federal tax; . . .

"Its legislative history indicates clearly that congress did not contemplate that the government would be interested in the distribution of the estate after the tax was paid, and that congress intended that state law should determine the ultimate thrust of the tax."

While the marital deduction provisions of the federal estate-tax law did not come into being until 1948, there is nothing contained in the 1948 amendments to the federal estate-tax law which would render inapplicable the rule laid down in Riggs v. Del Drago, supra. Furthermore, U. S. Treasury Regulations 105, sec. 81.47 (c) clearly recognize that local state law is determinative of the question of whether the widow's one-third share of the personal estate in the instant case, is, or is not, subject to the impact of any of the federal estate tax.

Some states, notably New York, have enacted apportionment-of-federal-estate-tax statutes which specifically provide how the federal estate tax is to be apportioned among various beneficiaries of the estate where the deceased has not directed otherwise by his will. However, no apportionment statute has as yet been enacted in Wisconsin. The appellate courts of several states which are in the identical position of Wisconsin (in that they have no apportionment statute such as the New York statute) have passed upon the question confronting us on this appeal. Kentucky and Ohio reached one result, while North Carolina and Illinois arrived at the opposite conclusion. …

[The court's discussion of these cases is omitted.]

… This court in Will of Kootz (1938), 228 Wis. 306, 280 N. W. 672, rejected the theory that our court should invoke its equity powers to achieve an apportionment of federal estate taxes which would prevent inequities. At page 313 of that decision the court considers an example of a man having ten sons and leaving an estate of $1,000,000 whereby $100,000 is conveyed to each of nine sons, and the residue to the tenth. It is conceded under such example that the federal estate tax would wipe out the residuary share of the tenth son, but the court points out that such inequity is created by operation of federal law and not by state law, and that the testator could obviate such inequitable result by making proper provisions in his will. …

In the absence of statutory enactment directing otherwise, the federal tax must be considered as a charge against the whole of the estate and not against the individual shares (Riggs v. Del Drago, 317 U.S. 95) [63 S. Ct. 109, 87 L. Ed. 106], unless otherwise specifically directed by the testator."

The material part of sec. 233.14, Stats., which governs the method of computing the share of the widow in the instant case, who elected to take under the law and not under the will, reads as follows:

". . . provided, that when he shall have died testate the share of personal estate which she may so take shall not exceed *the one-third part of his net personal estate*, . . ." (Italics supplied.)

It seems to us that the words "net estate" of our statute are clear and unambiguous and are subject to no other interpretation than that they mean that part of the estate which remains after payment of all charges against the entire estate. Federal estate taxes stand in no different category than do debts or administration expenses. We deem that it would be unwarranted judicial legislation for this court to attempt to apportion the impact of the federal estate tax as did the Kentucky and Ohio courts. The legislature has the power to enact an apportionment of federal estate-tax statute providing for a different method of bearing the impact of federal estate taxes if it should determine the same desirable. However, three general sessions of the legislature have been held since congress amended the federal estate-tax statute so as to provide for the marital deduction, and to date our legislature has not seen fit to adopt such apportionment statute.

Counsel for the widow, Frances L. Uihlein, contend, that because the testator included in his will a direction that all estate and inheritance taxes should be paid from the residue of his estate, this amounted to a direct provision by the testator that the burden of the federal estate tax should fall upon the remaindermen taking the residue, and not upon the widow, who has elected to take under the law. They urge that the word "residue" in clause Fifth of the will means that part of the estate which remains after the widow's share, which she takes under the law by reason of her election, has been deducted. In support of this last contention they rely on our decision in Will of Reynolds (1912), 151 Wis. 375, 138 N. W. 1019. Headnote 3 of that case states in part as follows:

"Where the widow so renounces, the 'residue' of the estate consists of the part of the general estate that remains after deducting debts, specific legacies, and the widow's share."

On its face such quoted statement would seem to support the contention made in behalf of the widow. The court, however, in the Reynolds Case was not confronted with the problem of the impact of federal estate tax, but only as to determining what part of the estate passed under the residuary clause where the widow, who had renounced the will, was bequeathed 30 per cent of such residue. The gist of our decision in the Reynolds Case was that the election of the widow to take under the law does not defeat the intended disposition of the testator of his other property, and those provisions of the will, which do not operate for the benefit of the widow, are not affected by such election.

However, by following the construction contended for by counsel for the widow, the widow would stand to benefit by the clause of the will which provided for the payment of federal estate taxes out of the residue. If the widow had not renounced the will by her election she would have taken under the residuary clause after deduction of the federal estate tax, and she ought not to be placed in a more advantageous position, in so far as the impact of such tax is concerned, by such election. In electing to take under the law she is not entitled to claim the benefit of the provision directing payment of federal estate taxes out of the residue. Such clause of the will remains effective as between the recipients of specific legacies and the remaindermen who take the residue, but the widow's renunciation of the will prevents such clause from being operative so as to relieve her share from the impact of the federal estate tax.

Therefore, it is our conclusion that that part of the interlocutory judgment (conclusion of law No. 1), which provides that the widow, Frances L. Uihlein, is entitled to her one-third share, pursuant to sec. 233.14, Stats., without deduction therefrom of the federal estate tax, must be reversed, and the cause remanded in order that the interlocutory judgment may be amended by the trial court so that it is consistent with this opinion.

Extinguishment of Power of Appointment and Acceleration of Payment of Remaindermen's Interests

The question of whether the election by the widow to take under the law accelerated payment of the remaindermen's interest is so closely intertwined with the question of whether such election by the widow extinguishes the special power of appointment that these two questions will be considered together.

Counsel for the adult remaindermen named by testator to share the residue of the estate bequeathed in trust upon the death of the widow, in the event she fails to exercise her special power of appointment, in claiming that acceleration of payment to such remaindermen has resulted from the widow's rejection of the will, rely upon the following general principle stated in 4 Page, Wills (lifetime ed.), p. 89, sec. 1390:

"Where the enjoyment of possession by the remainderman is postponed until after the determination of the particular estate and for no other purpose, and such tenant elects to take against the will, the remainderman enters into enjoyment at once. This principle is called acceleration of the remainders. Renunciation by the particular tenant is said to be equivalent to his death with reference to the remainder's taking effect in possession."

However, there is an exception to such general principle as is well pointed out by this court in its opinion in Will of McIlhattan (1927), 194 Wis. 113, 117, 216 N. W. 130, as follows:

"It is a general rule of law that the election of the widow has the same effect as her death, and accelerates the remainders so that the beneficiaries enter directly into enjoyment thereof. [Citing authorities.] This general rule of law does not apply if the terms of the trust expressly otherwise provide; that is, the intent of the testator must prevail if that intent is manifest from the will itself." (Emphasis supplied.)

The crucial questions on this issue of acceleration are therefore: (1) Did the granting of the special power of appointment to the widow evidence an intent of the testator that the trust so far as it affected the remaindermen should continue until the widow's death; and (2) did the election by the widow extinguish such power? …

[The Court concluded that there was "no acceleration in the payment of the remaindermen's interests and that the special power of appointment in trust vested in the widow was not extinguished by her election to take under the law."·]

Assignment of Portion of Residue Not Specifically Bequeathed by Testator

Under testator's will one fifth of the residue was bequeathed to each of the following four named persons: Henry Uihlein, H. Robert Stoepel, Helen Rohnert Stoepel, and L. James Bulkley, and one tenth to John H. Kopmeier, effective upon the widow's death and subject to the condition that the widow did not exercise her power to appoint otherwise. No specific provision was made by the testator for the disposition of the remaining one-tenth share of the residue in the event the widow failed to exercise her special power of appointment, except $10,000 of such remaining one tenth bequeathed to Hugh McMillan, Sr., in trust for his two children.

The trial court in the interlocutory judgment determined that such remaining one-tenth portion of the residue (less $10,000) should "be distributed among the persons specifically named in said will [the remaindermen] proportionately to their respective parts as are therein now designated" in the event the widow failed to otherwise appoint under her special power of appointment. We believe that this determination by the trial court was erroneous and that the provisions of sec. 232.27, Stats., are controlling. This statute provides as follows:

· Powers of Appointment are discussed in greater detail in Chapter 8.

"If the trustee of a power with the right of selection shall die, leaving the power unexecuted, its execution shall be adjudged in the circuit court for the benefit equally of all the persons designated as objects of the trusts."

This court in its decision in Cawker v. Dreutzer (1928), 197 Wis. 98, 221 N. W. 401, held that the provisions of ch. 232, Stats., apply to personal property as well as real estate. Inasmuch as we have construed the power of appointment given to the widow to be a special power in trust, the provisions of sec. 232.27, Stats., require that the circuit court exercise the power for the equal benefit of all persons in the class to whom the widow might appoint the remaining one tenth of the residue (less $10,000) in the event she should fail to exercise the power.

Such class for whom the power might be exercised consists of the remaindermen named in subparagraph (c) of clause Fifth of testator's will, together with the remaining nephews and nieces of the deceased, and their descendants, living at the time of the death of the widow, and St. Mary's Hospital of Milwaukee, Wisconsin, subject to the provision that the hospital shall not receive more than one twentieth of the residue. However, as the trial court well pointed out in his memorandum opinion, the contingency of the widow failing to exercise her power of appointment is one which is unlikely to happen.

That part of the interlocutory judgment (conclusion of law No. 3 thereof) which provides for the disposition of the one-tenth share in the residue (less $10,000) which the testator did not dispose of in the event the widow fails to exercise her power of appointment as to the same, must be reversed.

Widow Sharing in Intestate Property

Counsel for the widow contend that there are certain parts of testator's estate which descend as intestate property, and, inasmuch as the widow constitutes his only heir at law and next of kin, she takes such intestate property. It is maintained that such intestate property consists of the following:

(1) The remainder interest in the homestead remaining after assignment to the widow of her homestead rights therein by reason of her election to take under the law;

(2) The one-tenth interest (less $10,000) in the residue not specifically bequeathed by testator; and

(3) The lapse of the bequest to the widow of an interest in the residue, i. e., payments of $5,000 per month from the trusts, causes the right to the income from said trusts to descend as intestate property, there being no direction to the contrary in testator's will.

The contention of counsel for the widow with respect to the remainder interest of the homestead descending as intestate property is untenable. A specific bequest or devise which lapses thereby passes under the residuary clause of the will and constitutes part of the residue. Harrington v. Pier (1900), 105 Wis. 485, 82 N. W. 345, and Estate of Schefe (1952), 261 Wis. 113, 52 N. W. (2d) 375.

The contention with respect to the widow sharing in the one-tenth portion of the residue (less $10,000) not specifically bequeathed by testator has already been negatived by our holding that sec. 232.27, Stats., controls the disposition of such portion of the residue in the event the widow fails to exercise her special power of appointment in trust.

The contention that the widow is entitled to the income of the trusts as intestate property, pending the distribution of the residue upon her death to the remaindermen, presents a question which has never been directly determined by this court. Such question is whether a widow who elects to take under the law can also share in the distribution of any intestate property as heir at law, or next of kin, of the deceased. In the cases of Hardy v. Scales (1882), 54 Wis. 452, 11 N. W. 590, and Chapman v. Chapman (1906), 128 Wis. 413, 107 N. W. 668, we were confronted with the reverse of this problem, viz., whether a widow could share in intestate property who elected to take under the provisions of the will made for her benefit by her deceased husband. This court therein held that the sharing under the will and the sharing in intestate property were mutually exclusive under our statutes, and denied the right of the widow who took under the will to share in any intestate property. …

Ronald D. Keberle in a note in 1950 Wisconsin Law Review, 182, comes to the conclusion that the reasoning underlying the decisions in the Hardy v. Scales and Chapman v. Chapman Cases, supra, would be followed by this court if it ever were confronted with the problem of whether a widow electing to take under the law, and not under the will, could share also in any part of the estate of the testator left undisposed of by his will as the heir at law or next of kin of the deceased husband.

We agree with Mr. Keberle's conclusion as we deem it to have been the intention of the legislature, that where a widow elects to take under the law and not under the will, she thereby takes her share in the entire estate (not merely the estate disposed of by will) as the result of such election, and is not entitled to participate further in the estate.

Furthermore, in the instant case the testator did by his will make disposition of the income of the trusts during the widow's lifetime, and such disposition was rendered ineffective only by the election of the widow renouncing the will. It would seem to be a highly illogical result that a widow, whose own act of renouncing the provision made for her benefit by the testator in the will, in addition to receiving the portion of the entire estate due her by her election to take under the law, could also share to a still further extent in that portion of the estate which was rendered intestate by such election on her part.

It is therefore our conclusion that the share of the testator's estate to which a widow becomes entitled, as a result of electing to take under the law and not under the will of her deceased husband, is exclusive, and that she does not take any additional share in any remaining portion of the estate which may be left undisposed of by the will, even though she be the sole heir at law and next of kin of the deceased. …

B. PROBLEMS WITH THE TRADITIONAL ELECTIVE SHARE.

There were a number of problems with the traditional elective share approach. First of all, it was calculated as a percentage of the probate estate, so a spouse, intending to disinherit the other spouse and hoping to keep the elective share to a minimum, could transfer assets into forms of ownership that would allow the property to pass to the designated next owner outside of the probate process [i.e., trusts, payable-on-death accounts, life insurance policies, joint tenancies, and other similar devices]. Secondly, the elective share was independent of the length of the marriage, so that a surviving spouse whose husband died on the day after the wedding was entitled to the same share of the estate as someone who had been married to their spouse for 75 years. Finally, the elective share did not take into account the assets of the surviving spouse, either owned outright or which were received through non-probate transfers.

Whether or not these were perceived as problems was also affected by the fact that there were (and are) competing rationales for the elective share. Traditionally, it was viewed as a mechanism for insuring that surviving spouses—who for biological and cultural reasons were likely to be widows—were capable of supporting themselves. More recently, the statutes have also been justified on the theory that they provide a more equitable distribution of assets of what had been an economic partnership (among other things), but one in which many "joint" assets had been acquired in the name of one spouse only.

The Uniform Probate Code has incorporated a number of suggestions for addressing these problems. More than four decades ago, the UPC introduced the concept of the *augmented estate* which included the probate assets plus assets controlled by the deceased at the time of his death and which passed outside the probate process, as well as gifts made within two years of death. The elective share was then calculated by multiplying the *augmented estate* total (rather than the *probate estate* total) by the elective share percentage. If the surviving spouse received property under the will or through non-probate transfers, but in an amount below the elective share amount, the surviving spouse is entitled to the difference, normally paid out of assets of the probate estate. The *augmented* estate concept has been widely adopted by the states, including Wisconsin, which uses it in regard to its *deferred marital property elective share,* discussed below.

More recently, the Uniform Probate Code has adopted a "sliding scale" approach to the elective share percentage, so that the share increases from a minimal amount at the outset of the marriage to 50% for marriages of 15 years or longer. The UPC has also expanded the *augmented share* to include not just the total assets of the deceased spouse but those of the surviving spouse as well. Consequently, in situations where the assets controlled by the surviving spouse exceed those of the deceased spouse, there is no elective share, regardless of the length of the marriage. The elective share provisions of the current Uniform Probate Code can be found at UPC §§2-202 to 2-208.

In regard to its *deferred marital property elective share* Wisconsin has also embraced the concept of an expanded *augmented estate* which for computational purposes includes the assets of both the deceased and surviving spouses. Wisconsin has not, however, adopted the sliding scale approach to the elective share percentage.

C. WISCONSIN MARITAL PROPERTY

Wis. Stat. 766.31 Classification of property of spouses

(1) GENERAL. All property of spouses is marital property except that which is classified otherwise by this chapter and that which is described in sub. (8)

(2) PRESUMPTION. All property of spouses is presumed to be marital property.

(3) SPOUSE'S INTEREST IN MARITAL PROPERTY. Each spouse has a present undivided one-half interest in each item of marital property, subject to all of the following:

(a) Terminable interest in deferred employment benefit plan. As provided in s. 766.62 (5), the marital property interest of the nonemployee spouse in a deferred employment benefit plan or in assets in an individual retirement account that are traceable to the rollover of a deferred employment benefit plan terminates at the death of the nonemployee spouse if he or she predeceases the employee spouse.

(b) Division based on aggregate value at death.

1. Spouses may provide in a marital property agreement that at the death of a spouse some or all of their marital property will be divided based on aggregate value rather than divided item by item. However, at the death of a spouse, a marital property agreement is not necessary for a division of marital property that is not item by item.

2. The surviving spouse and the successor in interest to the decedent's share of marital property may enter into an agreement providing that some or all of the marital property in which each has an interest will be divided based on aggregate value rather than divided item by item.

3. The surviving spouse and a distributee who is a successor in interest to all or part of the decedent's one-half interest in marital property may petition the court to approve an exchange of interests in the marital property authorized under subd. 1. or 2., but court approval of the exchange is not required for the agreement under subd. 1. or 2. to be effective. If the court approves the exchange, the surviving spouse and the distributee shall exchange their respective interests in 2 or more items of marital property and distribute the items in a manner to conform with the exchange. The exchange shall:

a. Occur before the final distribution of the assets under the governing instrument;

b. Be composed of items which are fairly representative of the appreciation and depreciation that has occurred since the date of death;

c. Be composed of items having a fair market value at the time of exchange equal to what would have been distributed had no exchange request been made, including any money used in the exchange; and

d. Be reported with a written description of each item, its basis and its fair market value at the time of exchange in the manner prescribed by the department of revenue.

(4) CLASSIFICATION OF INCOME. Except as provided under subs. (7) (a), (7p) and (10), income earned or accrued by a spouse or attributable to property of a spouse during marriage and after the determination date is marital property.

(5) TRANSFER TO A TRUST. The transfer of property to a trust does not by itself change the classification of the property.

(6) PROPERTY OWNED AT DETERMINATION DATE.

(a) Date of marriage same as determination date. If the date of marriage is the same as the determination date, the property owned at the determination date is individual property of the owning spouse.

(b) Date of marriage prior to determination date. If the date of marriage precedes the determination date, the property owned at the determination date is not classified by this chapter but is subject to all of the following:

1. Subsections (8) and (9) govern property owned at the time of marriage.

2. Subsections (8) and (9) govern property acquired while the spouses were married but before the determination date if the property would have been individual property had it been acquired after the determination date.

3. Subsections (8) and (9) and s. 861.02 govern property acquired while the spouses were married but before the determination date if the property would have been marital property had it been acquired after the determination date.

(7) INDIVIDUAL PROPERTY AFTER DETERMINATION DATE. Property acquired by a spouse during marriage and after the determination date is individual property if acquired by any of the following means:

(a) By gift during lifetime or by a disposition at death by a 3rd person to that spouse and not to both spouses. A distribution of principal or income from a trust created by a 3rd person to one spouse is the individual property of that spouse unless the trust provides otherwise.

(b) In exchange for or with the proceeds of other individual property of the spouse.

(c) From appreciation of the spouses individual property except to the extent that the appreciation is classified as marital property under s. 766.63

(d) By a decree, marital property agreement or reclassification under sub. (10) designating it as the individual property of the spouse.

(e) As a recovery for damage to property under s. 766.70, except as specifically provided otherwise in a decree or marital property agreement.

(f) As a recovery for personal injury except for the amount of that recovery attributable to expenses paid or otherwise satisfied from marital property and except for the amount attributable to loss of income during marriage.

(7m) PERSONAL INJURY DAMAGES; LOST EARNINGS. To the extent that marital property includes damages for loss of future income arising from a personal injury claim of a surviving spouse, the surviving spouse is entitled to receive as individual property that portion of the award that represents an income substitute after the death of the other spouse.

(7p) UNILATERAL STATEMENT. Income attributable to all or specified property other than marital property, with respect to which a spouse has executed under s. 766.59 a statement unilaterally designating that income as his or her individual property, is individual property.

(8) RIGHTS IN PROPERTY ACQUIRED BEFORE DETERMINATION DATE. Except as provided otherwise in this chapter, the enactment of this chapter does not alter the classification and ownership rights of property acquired before the determination date or the classification and ownership rights of property acquired after the determination date in exchange for or with the proceeds of property acquired before the determination date.

(9) TREATMENT OF PROPERTY ACQUIRED BEFORE THE DETERMINATION DATE. Except as provided otherwise in this chapter and except to the extent that it would affect the spouse's ownership rights in the property existing before the determination date, during marriage the interest of a spouse in property owned immediately before the determination date is treated as if it were individual property.

(10) RECLASSIFICATION. Spouses may reclassify their property by gift, conveyance, as defined in s. 706.01 (4), signed by both spouses, marital property agreement, written consent under s. 766.61 (3) (e) or unilateral statement under s. 766.59 and, if the property is a security, as defined in s. 705.21 (11), by an instrument, signed by both spouses, which conveys an interest in the security. If a spouse gives property to the other spouse and intends at the time the gift is made that the property be the individual property of the donee spouse, the income from the property is the individual property of the donee spouse unless a contrary intent of the donor spouse regarding the classification of income is established.

Wis. Stat. 766.63. Mixed property.

(1) Except as provided otherwise in ss. 766.61 and 766.62, mixing marital property with property other than marital property reclassifies the other property to marital property unless the component of the mixed property which is not marital property can be traced.

(2) Application by one spouse of substantial labor, effort, inventiveness, physical or intellectual skill, creativity or managerial activity to either spouse's property other than marital property creates marital property attributable to that application if both of the following apply:

(a) Reasonable compensation is not received for the application.

(b) Substantial appreciation of the property results from the application.

Wis. Stat. 861.01. Ownership of marital property at death.

(1) SURVIVING SPOUSE'S ONE-HALF INTEREST IN MARITAL PROPERTY.

Upon the death of either spouse, the surviving spouse retains his or her undivided one-half interest in each item of marital property. The surviving spouses undivided one-half interest in each item of marital property is not subject to administration. Ownership and management and control rights are set forth under ss. 857.01 and 857.015

(2) INTEREST OF A 3RD PARTY IN MARITAL PROPERTY.

A 3rd party who is a successor in interest to all or part of the decedent's 50% interest in marital property is a tenant in common with the surviving spouse.

(3m) PERSONAL INJURY DAMAGES; LOST EARNINGS.

Section 766.31 (7m) determines the rights of a surviving spouse to that part of a personal injury claim that represents future lost earnings of the surviving spouse.

(4) ENFORCEMENT OF SURVIVING SPOUSE'S MARITAL PROPERTY RIGHTS IN NONPROBATE ASSETS.

Section 766.70 applies to enforcement of a surviving spouse's marital property rights in nonprobate assets.

(5) DIVISION OF MARITAL PROPERTY ON AGGREGATE BASIS.

Section 766.31 (3) (b) determines how marital property may be divided upon the death of a spouse.

Wis. Stat. 861.015. Satisfaction of nonholding spouse's marital property interest in certain business property.

(1) If following the death of a spouse property is subject to a directive under s. 857.015, the marital property interest of the nonholding spouse in the property shall be satisfied within one year after the decedent spouse's death from other property which is of equal clear market value at the time of satisfaction. Except as provided under sub. (3), if the interest of the nonholding spouse under this section is not satisfied within one year after the decedent spouses death, this section does not apply and the nonholding spouses marital property interest in the property subject to the directive continues as if the directive had not been made.

(2) For purposes of this section, property subject to a directive is valued by its clear market value on the date of the decedent's death. Satisfaction of the nonholding spouse's marital property interest in the property subject to the directive shall be based on that value, plus any income from the property subject to the directive after the death of the decedent and before satisfaction. For purposes of determining the income from the property subject to a directive, such property shall be treated as a legacy or devise of property other than money under s. 701.20

(3) If the interest of the nonholding spouse under this section is not satisfied within one year after the decedent spouse's death because the clear market value of the property subject to the directive has not been determined, the court having jurisdiction of the decedent spouse's estate shall do either of the following:

(a) Order that the interest of the nonholding spouse shall be satisfied after the determination of clear market value, at a date specified by the court.

(b) Order that the interest of the nonholding spouse shall be satisfied before the determination of clear market value based on an estimate of the clear market value, subject to any necessary adjustment upon final determination of clear market value.

(4) The following property is not available to satisfy the nonholding spouses marital property interest in the property subject to the directive:

(a) Property included in an order, or extension or revision of an order, for an allowance under s. 861.31 made before satisfaction of the nonholding spouse's interest.

(b) Property selected under s. 861.33 before satisfaction of the nonholding spouse's interest.

(c) Property included in an order for an allowance under s. 861.35 made before satisfaction of the nonholding spouses interest.

(5) Satisfaction of a nonholding spouses marital property interest under this section shall not adversely affect any of the following:

(a) The nonholding spouses marital property interest in property not subject to the directive.

(b) The nonholding spouses election under s. 861.02 of deferred marital property other than deferred marital property subject to the directive.

Wis. Stat. 766.75. Treatment of certain property at dissolution.

After a dissolution each former spouse owns an undivided one-half interest in the former marital property as a tenant in common, except as provided otherwise in a decree or an agreement entered into by the former spouses after dissolution.

IN RE THE MATTER OF THE ESTATE OF LLOYD

Court of Appeals of Wisconsin
170 Wis. 2d 240, 487 N.W. 2d (1992)

SNYDER, J. This case arises under Wisconsin's marital property law. Wesley Lloyd died in 1990. The dispute before us is between Harold Lloyd, Wesley's nephew, and Christine Lloyd, Wesley's widow. Harold seeks to inherit certain real estate and money from certificates of deposit (CDs) and bank accounts (collectively, "bank accounts") left to him in Wesley's will but claimed by Christine to be marital property.

The trial court determined that Wesley had nearly $330,000 in marital property, $256,000 of which Wesley had attempted to pass to Harold by right of survivorship by establishing joint accounts with Harold. The court concluded that Christine was entitled to half of the $330,000. We affirm the trial court's determinations that some of the accounts either were established with marital property or were so commingled as to defy tracing of a nonmarital component. We reverse as to others, however, because we conclude that the nonmarital component was traced adequately. In addition, we agree with Harold that the real estate is not marital property and we reverse that portion of the judgment.

Wesley and Christine were married on May 14, 1979, the second marriage for both. They were domiciled in Wisconsin throughout the marriage. Although Wesley had no children, Christine had two daughters from her former marriage. Wesley and Christine had no children together. Neither Wesley nor Christine executed a unilateral statement. See sec. 766.59, Stats. Likewise, the spouses did not enter into any type of agreement classifying or reclassifying either their solely or jointly owned property. See secs. 766.585, 766.587, 766.588 and 766.589, Stats.

When Wesley and Christine married, each owned separate residences; Christine also owned a cottage on a lake. Throughout most of the marriage, Christine and Wesley lived together in Wesley's house, which remained titled in his sole name. Christine conveyed her residence to her daughters in 1984, just as she had done in 1980 with her cottage. Christine did not http://www.forbes.com/sites/aliciajessop/2013/07/14/suspending-a-rod-and-ryan-braun-could-jeopardize-the-credibility-of-mlbs-joint-drug-prevention-and-treatment-program/consult or notify Wesley about either conveyance.

In May 1984, Wesley executed a will. The will made specific bequests to certain relatives and friends and provided that the residue should go to Christine. If Christine predeceased Wesley, the residue was to go to Harold.

In 1989, Christine filed for divorce. Wesley then executed a codicil to his will which revoked the provision giving the residue of his estate to Christine, leaving it instead to Harold. About the same time, Wesley instructed Harold, as his power of attorney, to transfer certain assets and change the ownership of some CDs despite a court order prohibiting the transfer and disposal of property during the pendency of the divorce.

Wesley died on March 7, 1990, before the divorce was final. Three months later, Christine filed notice to take under the widow's election of deferred and augmented marital property. See secs. 861.02 and 861.03, Stats. Harold objected. The trial court found that Wesley's residence and most of the over forty bank accounts and CDs were marital property. Harold appeals.

I. STANDARD OF REVIEW

The trial court and the parties term the trial court's determinations that the various assets were marital or nonmarital property "factual findings." That is incorrect. We agree that a trial court's tracing or commingling determinations are findings of fact which will not be set aside unless clearly erroneous. Brandt v. Brandt, 145 Wis. 2d 394, 407, 427 N.W.2d 126, 130 (Ct. App. 1988). However, the legal significance of those facts -- i.e., whether the property is marital or nonmarital property -- is a question of law. See Wierman v. Wierman, 130 Wis. 2d 425, 433, 387 N.W.2d 744, 748 (1986); see also Klinefelter v. Dutch, 161 Wis. 2d 28, 33, 467 N.W.2d 192, 194 (Ct. App. 1991). Also, the issues on appeal require application of the marital property law, ch. 766, Stats., to undisputed facts. This presents a question of law which we review de novo. See Hobl v. Lord, 162 Wis. 2d 226, 233, 470 N.W.2d 265, 268, cert. denied, 112 S. Ct. 440 (1991). We are not bound by the trial court's legal conclusions or by legal conclusions the trial court has denominated factual findings. See Janesville Community Day Care Center, Inc. v. Spoden, 126 Wis. 2d 231, 236-37, 376 N.W.2d 78, 81 (Ct. App. 1985).

II. MARITAL PROPERTY PRINCIPLES

A. Generally

The classification of the property at issue is important because it determines how much, if any, of an asset may be disposed of freely at death. At death, a spouse may freely dispose of only the one-half interest he or she has in each item of marital property. See secs. 766.31(3) and 861.01, Stats. By contrast, the spouse may freely dispose of the whole of each item of his or her nonmarital property. See 1 K. Christiansen, F. Wm. Haberman, J. Haydon, D. Kinnamon, M. McGarity & M. Wilcox, Marital Property Law in Wisconsin sec. 2.161a, at 2-218 (2d ed. 1986). Classification also determines the surviving spouse's elective rights under secs. 861.02 and 861.03, Stats. Generally, the marital property law first applies to spouses on their determination date. Section 766.03(1), Stats. The spouses' determination date is the date on which the last of the following three events occurs: (1) marriage; (2) both spouses are domiciled in Wisconsin; or (3) January 1, 1986. Section 766.01(5), Stats. Wesley's and Christine's determination date thus is January 1, 1986.

The enactment of ch. 766, Stats., by itself does not alter the classification and ownership rights of property acquired before the determination date. Section 766.31(8), Stats. Such property is referred to as "unclassified" or "predetermination date" property. Marital Property Law in Wisconsin sec. 2.10a, at 2-20. Predetermination date property is not individual property, or a type of individual property, nor does it imply a classification all its own. Id., sec. 2.70, at 2-112. Rather, each item of predetermination date property has its own particular incidents of ownership which attached under the law that governed before the determination date and that continue except as altered by ch. 766. Id., sec. 2.70, at 2-112. Although predetermination date property is not individual property, during marriage it is treated as if it were, see sec. 766.31(9), and at death is subject to a deferred marital property analysis if the marital property presumption is overcome. See sec. 858.01(2), Stats.

B. Marital Property

Our analysis begins with the basic premise that unless classified otherwise by ch. 766, Stats., all spousal property either is, or is presumed to be, marital property. Section 766.31(1), (2), Stats. The challenger bears the burden of establishing that the property is not marital. See secs. 766.31(2) and 903.01, Stats. The basic presumption favoring a marital property classification may be rebutted by demonstrating that the time (e.g., before marriage or after dissolution), method (e.g., by gift or inheritance), or source (e.g., purchased with nonmarital assets) of the asset's acquisition establishes it as nonmarital property. To determine what property is to be designated "marital property," we look to sec. 766.31 and focus only on property acquired by the spouses on or after January 1, 1986.

Income earned or accrued by a spouse or attributable to property of a spouse during marriage and after the determination date is marital property. Section 766.31(4), Stats. Consequently, mixing income with any other property reclassifies the other property to marital property if the nonmarital component cannot be traced. Section 766.63(1), Stats. Where it can be traced satisfactorily, the presumption of marital property is rebutted for that component. See id.

Marital property also can be created if, without being reasonably compensated, one spouse applies to either spouse's nonmarital property "substantial labor, effort, inventiveness, physical or intellectual skill, creativity or managerial activity" and the property substantially appreciates as a result. Section 766.63(2), Stats.

In a marital property scheme, title is not synonymous with ownership and proof that title to an asset is in one spouse or the other will not rebut the basic presumption. Marital Property Law in Wisconsin sec. 2.23a, at 2-31. Title functions principally to establish management and control rights. Consistent with this principle, the right to manage and control property neither determines classification nor rebuts the presumption favorable to marital property. Section 766.51(5), Stats.

Applying the law to the facts, then, Wesley could have caused his nonmarital bank accounts to be reclassified to marital property by mixing them with marital property to the extent that the nonmarital component cannot be traced. Further, a marital property component could have been created in Wesley's real estate if either Wesley's or Christine's undercompensated efforts caused the property to substantially appreciate.

C. Deferred Marital Property

If any of the property is determined not to be marital property, our next inquiry is whether it is "deferred marital property." See sec. 858.01(2), Stats. Deferred marital property is "property acquired while spouses are married and while ch. 766 does not apply, which would have been marital property under ch. 766 if it were acquired when ch. 766 applied." Section 851.055, Stats.

Whether deferred marital property exists is considered only at death, and then only in the context of the two elective rights granted a surviving spouse. See secs. 861.02 and 861.03, Stats.; see also Marital Property Law in Wisconsin sec. 2.72, at 2-115 to 2-116. Deferred marital property is not a classification of property. Id., sec. 2.109, at 2-170. In this case, then, we presume that any property acquired between May 14, 1979 (the wedding date) and January 1, 1986 (the determination date) is deferred marital property. Property acquired before May 14, 1979 is not deferred marital property, although it could become so through mixing. Here too, the challenger bears the burden of rebutting the presumption by tracing the property to a nonmarital source.

If we determine that any of the property is deferred marital property, we then must examine whether any of that property is part of the augmented marital property estate. See secs. 861.03 and 861.05, Stats. Section 861.05 recites what types of transfers of property are included in the augmented marital property estate. Under sec. 861.05(2)(c), joint tenancies with third parties are among those transfers. See Legislative Council Note, 1985, Wis. Stat. Ann. sec. 861.05. Section 861.05 applies only to transfers on or after April 4, 1984, however, unless the dispositive provisions in the instrument were materially changed after April 3, 1984. See sec. 861.05(4); see also Marital Property Law in Wisconsin sec. 2.114f, at 2-189 to 2-190. Thus, Christine has no elective rights with respect to lifetime transfers of deferred marital property to joint accounts with Harold before that date.

Finally, if any property has been wrongly transferred, the surviving spouse may pursue remedies against either the decedent's estate or the gift recipient. See sec. 766.70(1), (6)(b), (6)(c), Stats.

D. Tracing Rules

Although ch. 766, Stats., does not specify how tracing is to be done, the general principles can be stated as follows. Acquisition of an asset involves either the payment of money, the exchange of another asset, or the incurrence of an obligation. Marital Property Law in Wisconsin sec. 3.21a, at 3-11. The source of the money or asset exchanged or the classification of the obligation incurred determines the classification of the asset acquired. Id.

The first step, therefore, is to determine the particular property's classification at a particular time, such as on the date of marriage, the determination date, or the date the asset was acquired. Id., sec. 3.20, at 3-8. It is necessary to have records of each transaction from the time a particular asset is acquired until the marriage terminates. Id., sec. 3.21a, at 3-12. If the challenger can trace the source of payment for the acquisition of an asset by a spouse during the marriage and after the determination date to nonmarital assets, the acquired asset is nonmarital. See id., sec. 2.51b, at 2-89. Similarly, if an asset is mixed, tracing to a nonmarital property source preserves the traced component's nonmarital property character. See id.

Direct tracing can be accomplished by using an investment account. Id., sec. 3.21a, at 3-12. Direct tracing constitutes actual proof of the classification from the initial receipt of the funds to the point at issue. Id. Unless a unilateral statement is executed, the spouse not only must record each deposit and each expenditure, but also must maintain a record of interest earned on individual property and predetermination date property. That interest is marital property. Section 766.01(10), Stats. If tracing proves impossible at any point in an asset's history, the asset is transformed to marital property. See sec. 766.63(1), Stats.

If during the marriage and after the determination date an asset constituting predetermination date property is sold and the proceeds reinvested, the newly acquired asset also is predetermination date property. Id., sec. 2.74, at 2-122; see also sec. 766.31(8), Stats. If the property or proceeds cannot be traced to predetermination date property, however, the newly acquired property is presumed to be marital property. See secs. 766.31(2) and 766.63(1), Stats.

No Wisconsin case law has yet developed which interprets the principles of mixing and tracing commingled property in a ch. 766, Stats., setting. While we recognize that chs. 766 and 767, Stats., are intentionally distinct, Kuhlman v. Kuhlman, 146 Wis. 2d 588, 593, 432 N.W.2d 295, 297 (Ct. App. 1988), we nonetheless gain insight from cases which deal with property division in the context of divorce to the extent that they deal with characterizing and tracing property, rather than its ultimate disposition. See, e.g., Bonnell v. Bonnell, 117 Wis. 2d 241, 245-48, 344 N.W.2d 123, 126-27 (1984); Brandt, 145 Wis. 2d at 409-13, 427 N.W.2d at 131-33; Trattles v. Trattles, 126 Wis. 2d 219, 222-28, 376 N.W.2d 379, 381-84 (Ct. App. 1985); and Weiss v. Weiss, 122 Wis. 2d 688, 692-94, 365 N.W.2d 608, 610-12 (Ct. App. 1985).

We conclude that for purposes of the discussion at hand, other than marital property" in the context of ch. 766, Stats., is analogous to "nonmarital property" -- property exempt from division -- in the divorce context. In the divorce context, "nonmarital" property must retain both its character and identity if its exempt status is to be preserved. Brandt, 145 Wis. 2d at 410, 427 N.W.2d at 131.

"Character" addresses the manner in which the parties have chosen to title or treat their assets. Id. at 410, 427 N.W.2d at 132. The transfer of solely owned property into joint tenancy changes the character of the ownership interest in the entire property into marital property, which is subject to division. Trattles, 126 Wis. 2d at 225, 376 N.W.2d at 383. Under sec. 700.17(2)(a), Stats., each joint tenant "has an equal interest in the whole property for the duration of the tenancy, irrespective of unequal contributions at its creation." When determining the character of an asset, the donative intent of the owner of the nonmarital property is an issue. Brandt, 145 Wis. 2d at 410-11, 427 N.W.2d at 132.

Tracing pertains to the identity of the property, not its character. Trattles, 126 Wis. 2d at 227, 376 N.W.2d at 383. "Identity" addresses whether the nonmarital asset has been preserved in some present identifiable form so that it can be meaningfully valued and assigned -- in other words, "traced." See Brandt, 145 Wis. 2d at 412, 427 N.W.2d at 132. Whether the person seeking to establish the character and identity of the property at issue has met the burden of proof is a question of law which we examine de novo. Id. at 408-09, 427 N.W.2d at 131.

III. THE RESIDENCE

The first issue involves the residential property titled in Wesley's name where the spouses lived during most of their marriage. The house was acquired by Wesley before the determination date and before the marriage. Harold argues that the trial court wrongly classified the residence as marital property because Wesley solely owned it on the parties' determination date and paid the household expenses, and the spouses intended to keep their residences as solely owned property.

We begin with the presumption that the house is marital property. That basic presumption easily is rebutted, however, because the residence was acquired before the determination date. The secondary presumption -- that the residence is deferred marital property -- also is rebutted because the acquisition date preceded the date of the marriage as well.

The house is Wesley's predetermination date property because it was acquired before the determination date and before the marriage. As we have stated, the enactment of ch. 766, Stats., by itself does not alter the classification and ownership rights of property acquired before the determination date. Section 766.31(8), Stats. Thus, unless the residence was somehow reclassified, it is nonmarital property.

Here, the trial court made no explicit finding regarding donative intent. It is evident, however, that the spouses meant to keep their respective properties separate. Both Christine and Wesley kept their respective residences titled in their own names. Christine conveyed her residence and her summer cottage to her daughters without notice to Wesley, explaining that she thought it unnecessary to consult him. Also, Christine herself testified that their property was kept separate throughout the marriage. We conclude, therefore, that the residence retained its character as nonmarital property.

The trial court implicitly determined that, through mixing, there was a change in the property's identity. Apparently relying on sec. 766.63(2), Stats., the trial court concluded that this real estate is marital property because there was no testimony that the property was solely maintained since the determination date with the decedent's own funds. The testimony is quite the contrary when Christine Lloyd testified that her funds were used to support her and the decedent and therefore maintaining this real estate where they resided for part of the marriage.

Under sec. 766.63(2), a marital property component in Wesley's house would be created if he or Christine applied labor or skill to the house, the labor was not reasonably compensated, and the property substantially appreciated as a result.

Christine did testify that she assumed the couple's food, clothing and shelter expenses. She also testified that there was no mixing of properties throughout the course of the marriage. Wesley's bank records, by contrast, indicate that utility bills and various miscellaneous household expenses were paid from his checking account.

Although the trial court's finding regarding the parties' relative contributions is not clearly erroneous, such a finding does not satisfy the legal standard set out in sec. 766.63(2), Stats., and thus does not support the court's conclusion that the residence has been reclassified as marital property. The finding does not establish that the applied efforts of either spouse were anything more than performance of usual and normal marital responsibilities. See Haldemann v. Haldemann, 145 Wis. 2d 296, 301-02, 426 N.W.2d 107, 109 (Ct. App. 1988). Likewise, there is no evidence of substantial, or even any, appreciation to the property.

We therefore conclude that the residence is not marital property and reverse that portion of the judgment.

IV. BANK ACCOUNTS AND CERTIFICATES OF DEPOSIT

The second issue concerns the classification of thirty-seven of the bank accounts and CDs. Stripped to its essence, Harold's position is that regardless of whether a marital component was later added, whatever amounts were on deposit in Wesley's accounts on January 1, 1986 should be considered Wesley's solely owned property and should not be subject to Christine's elective rights.

Resolving the issue entails the onerous exercise of unraveling an accounting and historical snarl: some of the CDs were established and held in Wesley's name only; some in Wesley's and Harold's joint names; and some in Wesley's and another third party's joint names. To further complicate matters, Wesley at various times moved funds in and out of joint tenancy with Christine. In considering Harold's argument, it is critical to remember that except for property which is classified otherwise by ch. 766, Stats., all property of spouses, not just that acquired after the determination date or titled to both spouses, is marital property. Section 766.31(1), Stats. We commend the trial court on its efforts in this daunting task.

As we have stated, review of the trial court's tracing or commingling determinations presents a question of fact. Brandt, 145 Wis. 2d at 407, 427 N.W.2d at 130. We will not set aside those findings unless they are clearly erroneous. Id. Our task on appeal is not to independently perform a tracing exercise but to determine if the record supports the trial court's findings. Id. at 412, 427 N.W.2d at 133. We review independently, however, the determinations of whether the assets are or are not marital property. See Wierman, 130 Wis. 2d at 433, 387 N.W.2d at 748.

The accounts fall into several broad categories. The first category is composed of accounts established while the divorce was pending and in violation of a court order. The second category includes accounts held jointly with Harold; the third comprises accounts which at some point in their existence were held jointly with Christine; and the fourth is made up of accounts held in Wesley's name alone.

A. Transfers in Violation of Court Order

The first category is composed of three accounts established while the divorce was pending. The trial court termed these accounts "fraudulent" because they were established in violation of a court order. We agree that all are marital property because they were established after the determination date with funds not clearly shown to be nonmarital. Thus, the transfers also constituted a breach of the spousal duty of good faith. See sec. 766.15, Stats.

B. Joint Accounts with Harold

At the time of Wesley's death, twenty-nine accounts were held in the joint names of Wesley and Harold. The trial court concluded that twenty-three of these accounts were marital property. On some of the twenty-three accounts, the trial court made a finding that there was a "substantial increase in principal since the determination date." On most of them, however, the court stated only that the particular account is marital property "because there was insufficient tracing for the Court to find otherwise," and followed this legal conclusion with a cite to various exhibits.

Where we are faced with inadequate findings, we may examine the record anew to see if the trial court's conclusion is supported by a preponderance of the evidence. See In re T.R.M., 100 Wis. 2d 681, 688, 303 N.W.2d 581, 583 (1981). We reverse as to certain of the accounts because we conclude that the legal conclusion was not so supported.

A joint account is an account, other than a marital account, which is payable on request to one or more of two or more parties whether or not mention is made of any right of survivorship. Section 705.01(4), Stats. At the death of a party to the account, the account presumptively belongs to the surviving party or parties. Section 705.04(1), Stats. If marital property is used to fund the account, it is a gift to the third party which is subject to the nontenant spouse's right of reimbursement. See secs. 705.04(4) and 766.70(6), Stats.

We cite as an example First National Bank CD No. XXX5685. The trial court determined that this CD was marital property because "funds [were] added to the principal since the determination date and there was insufficient tracing for the Court to find otherwise (see Exhibit 30)." Exhibit 30 consists of a series of photocopies of the CD beginning when it was established on January 11, 1977 in Wesley's sole name in the amount of $11,342.68. The balance was unchanged on May 14, 1979, the wedding date. The exhibit shows that the CD was transferred into joint tenancy with Harold on January 11, 1982 in the amount of $13,923.71. The exhibit also shows that the balance was $18,440.68 on January 1, 1986 and $20,687.96 at Wesley's death.

This account clearly was created with Wesley's solely owned property. It is not part of the augmented marital property estate because it was transferred into a joint account with Harold before April 4, 1984. See sec. 861.05(4), Stats. In ch. 766, Stats., language, the account is predetermination date property because it was funded with Wesley's solely owned assets before the marriage and before the determination date. Any interest or unexplained additions to the principal between the date of the marriage and the determination date are deferred marital property, however, just as any interest or unexplained additions to the principal between the determination date and Wesley's death are marital property. Sections 766.31(4) and 851.055, Stats.

We conclude that $11,342.68, the amount on deposit on the marriage date, is traceable to Wesley's nonmarital property. Harold did not successfully show that additions to the principal also were funded by Wesley's solely owned property, however. Consequently, $9345.28 (the difference between the balance on the date of death and the balance on the date of the marriage) is either marital or deferred marital property in which Christine has a one-half interest.

A decision of the Texas Supreme Court supports our conclusion. In McKinley v. McKinley, 496 S.W.2d 540 (Tex. 1973), a widow sought a declaratory judgment that two savings certificates in her husband's estate were community property. One certificate was in the amount of $10,400, the other in the amount of $16,000.

The portion of the $10,400 certificate originally on deposit at the time of the marriage was held to be separate property. It was traced to a $9,500 savings account the deceased husband had prior to January 15, 1965, the date of the marriage. The only deposits made during the marriage consisted of interest earned on the account balance, increasing it from $9,500 to $10,453.81 on December 31, 1967. No withdrawals were made between January 5, 1966 and January 2, 1968, when $10,400 was withdrawn and used to purchase a new certificate in the amount of $10,400. The new certificate remained "on account and untouched" until the husband died on October 15, 1970. Id. at 543. The supreme court concluded that direct tracing identified $9,500 of the $10,400 certificate as the decedent's separate property. Id.

The $16,000 certificate, on the other hand, was held to be community property. The account was established through the consolidation of three smaller certificates, two of which the spouses held in joint tenancy, and the third of which had undergone numerous deposits and withdrawals. Only some of the transactions were attributable to interest; the rest were unexplained. The court stated that because there was no evidence to trace the separate funds initially on deposit in the account, any conclusion about the property's status "would require surmise and speculation." Id. at 543-44. The court held the entire $16,000 to be community property. Id. at 544.

C. Joint Accounts with Christine

The accounts in the third category at some point in their existence were held jointly by the spouses. We affirm as to those because we agree that by commingling the funds in that fashion, the entire account became marital property.

At Wesley's death, no accounts remained in his and Christine's joint names. Wesley either had created new accounts using the funds from those joint accounts, or had renewed the CDs in his name alone or in his and Harold's names. These actions, however, did not serve to reclassify the funds as nonmarital property. The law in Wisconsin used to be that withdrawal of more than an equal share of a joint account without the co-tenant's consent severed the tenancy but did not destroy the cotenant's joint and equal interest. See Estate of Schley, 271 Wis. 74, 81, 72 N.W.2d 767, 770 (1955). The other party thus was permitted to trace the withdrawn funds into subsequently acquired savings certificates. Id.

The court of appeals held recently, however, that sec. 705.03(1), Stats., has abrogated the doctrine of severance and tracing for joint savings accounts. In re Frank, 140 Wis. 2d 429, 433, 410 N.W.2d 621, 623 (Ct. App. 1987). In a nonmarital property context, the court held that sec. 705.03(1) bars any inquiry into the application of funds withdrawn from a joint account by either of the joint parties because application of the doctrine defeats the intent of the parties in establishing a joint account in the first instance. Frank, 140 Wis. 2d at 433, 410 N.W.2d at 623. The court explained that inquiry into use of the funds upon the death of a co-tenant is barred in the same manner as is inquiry into their use while both parties are alive. Id.

That said, we nonetheless conclude that having once established joint accounts with Christine, the marital property law endows Christine with rights to those accounts she otherwise might not have. The transfer of separately owned property into joint tenancy changes the character of the ownership interest in the entire property into marital property. Fowler v. Fowler, 158 Wis. 2d 508, 518, 463 N.W.2d 370, 373 (Ct. App. 1990). Accordingly, once a joint account or joint tenancy was created between Wesley and Christine, each had an equal, undifferentiated interest in the whole of the property. Bonnell, 117 Wis. 2d at 247, 344 N.W.2d at 127. The accounts so treated no longer were solely Wesley's; rather, they became a single estate owned by both Wesley and Christine. See id. at 247, 344 N.W.2d at 126-27.

Nonmarital property must retain both its character and identity to preserve its exempt status. Brandt, 145 Wis. 2d at 410, 427 N.W.2d at 131. While placing separate property into joint tenancy with a spouse converts the entire amount to marital property, we do not believe the opposite is true. Thus, Wesley did not change the character of the accounts by taking them out of joint status with Christine. Having determined that a joint account between spouses serves to change the character of the account, we need not address the identity issue.

We hold, therefore, that once the accounts were held jointly with Christine, the accounts became either marital or deferred marital property. Thus, the new or renewed accounts were funded with either marital or deferred marital property. Consequently, regardless of how those new accounts are titled, the funds in them are marital or deferred marital property.

D. Accounts Titled in Wesley's Name

A number of accounts were titled in Wesley's name alone at the time of his death. The trial court concluded that the post-determination date addition of "interest or marital component" and insufficient subsequent tracing converted the entire account to marital property. We disagree that this conclusion necessarily follows. Commingling, in and of itself, is not necessarily fatal to the nonmarital status of an asset. See Brandt, 145 Wis. 2d at 412, 427 N.W.2d at 132. The critical inquiry is whether, despite the commingling, the nonmarital component nonetheless can be identified and valued. Id. We reverse as to four of the accounts.

We use as an example First National Bank CD No. XXX6247. This account was established in February 1977 with Wesley's separate property. The trial court concluded that "because it has had interest or marital component being added to it since the determination date and there was insufficient tracing to find otherwise," the entire amount was marital property. Whether tracing is sufficient is another way of asking whether the challenger has met his or her burden of proof. That is a question of law. Id. at 409, 427 N.W.2d at 131.

We conclude that the account -- principal and interest -- was Wesley's separate property until the marriage date. Then from that time until the determination date, the interest it bore was deferred marital property, as was any increase in the principal not clearly identified as coming from Wesley's separate property. Similarly, from the determination date until Wesley's death, any unexplained increase in principal and all interest are marital property.

The record does not indicate the value of the CD on May 14, 1979, and we remand for that finding. If it can be shown, that much of the account is Wesley's separate property; the rest is either marital property or deferred marital property. If that value cannot be shown, then we agree with the result reached by the trial court because the marital and nonmarital components will have been too commingled to permit sufficient tracing.

No costs to either party. -- Judgment affirmed in part; reversed in part and cause remanded with directions.

D. SURVIVORSHIP MARITAL PROPERTY

Survivorship marital property is a hybrid form of marital property that combines community property principles with the survivorship rights associated with joint tenancy (which is discussed in Chapter 6). This form of ownership prevents one spouse from disposing of his or her 50% interest in such property by will. Instead, it leaves the surviving spouse with the entire ownership interest immediately upon the death of the first spouse. Survivorship marital property is recognized by the Wisconsin statutes.

Wis. Stat. 766.60. Optional forms of holding property; survivorship ownership.

(1) Spouses may hold marital property in a form that designates the holders of it by the words "(name of one spouse) or (name of other spouse) as marital property".

(2) Spouses may hold marital property in a form that designates the holder of it by the words "(name of one spouse) and (name of other spouse) as marital property".

(3) A spouse may hold individual property in a form that designates the holder of it by the words "(name of spouse) as individual property".

(4)

(a) Spouses may hold property in any other form permitted by law, including but not limited to a concurrent form or a form that provides survivorship ownership. Except as provided in par. (b) and except with respect to any remedy a spouse has under this chapter, whether a tenancy in common or joint tenancy was created before or after the determination date, to the extent the incidents of the tenancy in common or joint tenancy conflict with or differ from the incidents of property classification under this chapter, the incidents of the tenancy in common or of the joint tenancy, including the incident of survivorship, control.

(b)

1. Except as provided in subd. 2. or in a marital property agreement under s. 766.58:

a. If a document of title, instrument of transfer or bill of sale expresses an intent to establish a joint tenancy exclusively between spouses after the determination date, the property is survivorship marital property under sub. (5)

b. If a document of title, instrument of transfer or bill of sale expresses an intent to establish a tenancy in common exclusively between spouses after the determination date, the property is marital property.

2. A joint tenancy or tenancy in common exclusively between spouses which is given to the spouses by a 3rd party after the determination date is survivorship marital property or marital property, respectively, unless the donor provides otherwise.

(5)

(a) If the words "survivorship marital property" are used instead of the words "marital property" in the form described in sub. (1) or (2), the marital property so held is survivorship marital property. On the death of a spouse, the ownership rights of that spouse in the property vest solely in the surviving spouse by nontestamentary disposition at death. The first deceased spouse may not dispose at death of any interest in survivorship marital property. Holding marital property in a form described in sub. (1) or (2) does not alone establish survivorship ownership between the spouses with respect to the property held.

(b) A real estate mortgage, a security interest under ch. 409 or a lien under s. 71.91 (5) (b) or ch. 49 or 779 on or against the interest of a spouse in survivorship marital property does not defeat the right of survivorship on the death of the spouse. The surviving spouse takes the interest of the deceased spouse subject to the mortgage, security interest or lien.

(c) A judgment lien on the interest of a spouse in survivorship marital property does not defeat the right of survivorship on the death of the spouse. If execution on the judgment lien was issued before the spouses death the surviving spouse takes the interest of the deceased spouse subject to the lien. If execution on the judgment lien was not issued before the spouses death, the surviving spouse takes the interest of the deceased spouse free of the judgment lien, unless the judgment lien is on the interests of both spouses in the survivorship marital property and all of the property of the spouses was available under s. 766.55 to satisfy the obligation for which the judgment was rendered.

Wis. Stat. 766.605. Classification of homestead.

A homestead acquired after the determination date which, when acquired, is held exclusively between spouses with no 3rd party is survivorship marital property if no intent to the contrary is expressed on the instrument of transfer or in a marital property agreement. A homestead may be reclassified under s. 766.31 (10)

Wis. Stat. 861.21. Assignment of home to surviving spouse or surviving domestic partner.

(1) DEFINITIONS. In this section:

(a) "Governing instrument" has the meaning given in s. 854.01 (2)

(b) "Home" means any dwelling in which the decedent had an interest and that at the time of the decedent's death the surviving spouse or surviving domestic partner occupies or intends to occupy. If there are several such dwellings, any one may be designated by the surviving spouse or surviving domestic partner. "Home" includes a house, a mobile home, a manufactured home, a duplex or multiple apartment building one unit of which is occupied by the surviving spouse or surviving domestic partner and a building used in part for a dwelling and in part for commercial or business purposes. "Home" includes all of the surrounding land, unless the court sets off part of the land as severable from the remaining land under sub. (5)

(2) DECEDENT'S PROPERTY INTEREST IN HOME. Subject to subs. (4) and (5), if a married decedent or decedent in a domestic partnership has a property interest in a home, the decedent's entire interest in the home shall be assigned to the surviving spouse or surviving domestic partner if the surviving spouse or surviving domestic partner petitions the court requesting such a distribution and if a governing instrument does not provide a specific transfer of the decedent's interest in the home to someone other than the surviving spouse or surviving domestic partner. The surviving spouse or surviving domestic partner shall file the petition within 6 months after the decedent's death, unless the court extends the time for filing.

(4) PAYMENT BY SURVIVING SPOUSE OR SURVIVING DOMESTIC PARTNER. The court shall assign the interest in the home under sub. (2) to the surviving spouse or surviving domestic partner upon payment of the value of the decedent's interest in the home that does not pass to the surviving spouse or surviving domestic partner under intestacy or under a governing instrument. Payment shall be made to the fiduciary holding title to the interest. The surviving spouse or surviving domestic partner may use assets due him or her from the fiduciary to satisfy all or part of the payment in kind. Unless the court extends the time, the surviving spouse or surviving domestic partner shall have one year from the decedent's death to pay the value of the assigned interest.

(5) SEVERANCE OF HOME FROM SURROUNDING LAND. On petition of the surviving spouse or surviving domestic partner or of any interested person that part of the land is not necessary for dwelling purposes and that it would be inappropriate to assign all of the surrounding land as the home under sub. (2), the court may set off for the home as much of the land as is necessary for a dwelling. In determining how much land should be set off, the court shall take into account the use and marketability of the parcels set off as the home and the remaining land.

WONKA v. ESTATE OF BIERBRAUER

Court of Appeals of Wisconsin,
249 Wis. 2d 23, 637 N.W.2d 92 (2001)

HOOVER, P.J. Lynn and Jerome Wonka appeal a summary judgment dismissing their claims against the proceeds from the sale of real estate of the Estate of Edward

Bierbrauer. The Wonkas argue that Edward and Donna Bierbrauer held the property as marital property without survivorship rights until Edward's death. They argue further that Edward's portion of the proceeds was available to satisfy a judgment for damages from a tort claim against him that resulted from an auto accident. Donna and the special administrator of Edward's estate contend that at all times the Bierbrauers held the property as survivorship marital property.

We agree. Ownership of the property appropriately passed to Donna upon Edward's death, and she is entitled to all proceeds from its sale. We affirm the trial court's judgment.

Background

In 1976, Edward and Donna acquired an interest in the Boardman Bar by way of a land contract. The land contract conveyed the real property to "Edward E. Bierbrauer and Donna K. Bierbrauer, husband and wife as joint tenants." Edward and Donna satisfied the land contract in 1991, and the seller conveyed the warranty deed to the Bierbrauers as "husband and wife, as marital property with rights of survivorship."

In 1996, Edward Bierbrauer and Lynn Wonka were involved in an automobile accident. The Wonkas filed a personal injury action in April 1998, alleging that Edward negligently caused the accident. Donna Bierbrauer was not involved in the accident and was not named as a defendant.

Early in 1997, the Bierbrauers entered into a land contract with Lloyd and Ann Anderson for the sale of the Boardman Bar. The Andersons defaulted on the land contract. Six months later, in lieu of foreclosure, the Andersons conveyed their interest in the Boardman Bar back to the Bierbrauers as "husband and wife" by way of a quitclaim deed.

Edward passed away in 1999, and the trial court appointed a special administrator of his estate. The Wonkas continued the suit against Edward's one-half interest in the Boardman Bar.

After Edward's death, Donna filed a "Termination of Decedent's Property Interest" to terminate Edward's interest in the Boardman Bar. The Wonkas then amended their complaint to allege that the property was not survivorship marital property. They claimed that any judgment awarded to them could be satisfied from Edward's interest in the property. Donna and the Estate moved for summary judgment to determine whether the Bierbrauers held the property as survivorship or non-survivorship property.

Subsequently, the Boardman Bar was sold and, pursuant to stipulation, the portion of the proceeds attributable to Edward's interest was held in trust. The parties stipulated that all of the Wonkas' claims were dismissed except for issues surrounding the Wonkas' alleged interest in the money in the trust. The parties agreed to the distribution of the trust money upon the trial court's resolution of the legal issue. In the event the trial court determined that the Boardman Bar was survivorship marital property, the parties stipulated that the sum held in trust would be paid to Donna. In the event it determined the Boardman Bar was owned as non-survivorship marital property at the time of Edward's death, the parties stipulated the sum held in trust would be paid to the Wonkas. The trial court signed the order approving the stipulation.

On December 5, 2000, the trial court granted summary judgment in favor of Donna and the Estate. It concluded that the Bierbrauers held the Boardman Bar as survivorship marital property until Edward's death and that the plaintiffs have no interest in the proceeds from the property's sale. The Wonkas now appeal.

Standard of Review

We review summary judgment dispositions de novo and apply the same methodology used in the trial court. *Green Spring Farms v. Kersten*, 136 Wis. 2d 304, 315, 401 N.W.2d 816 (1987). Summary judgment is granted only when pleadings, depositions, interrogatories, admissions and affidavits show that there is no genuine issue as to any material fact. Wis. Stat. § 802.08(2). When examining material presented, we view all inferences to be drawn from the underlying facts in the light most favorable to the party opposing the summary judgment motion. *Kraemer Bros. v. United States Fire Ins. Co.*, 89 Wis. 2d 555, 567, 278 N.W.2d 857 (1979).

Discussion

The Wonkas argue that, at the time of Edward's death, the Boardman Bar was not survivorship marital property, the 1997 land contract having severed the Bierbrauers' joint tenancy. The Wonkas further contend that the quitclaim deed did not convey a survivorship interest from the Andersons back to the Bierbrauers. We disagree because the land contract transferred only equitable title to the Andersons. We conclude that the Bierbrauers at all times retained legal title to the property as survivorship marital property. Therefore, we affirm the trial court's summary judgment.

When a tortfeasor spouse dies, property that would have been available for satisfaction of the incurred obligation generally continues to be available. Wis. Stat. § 859.18(2).

Survivorship marital property, however, is not available to satisfy the obligation of the deceased tortfeasor spouse. Wis. Stat. § 859.18(4)(a). Whether the Wonkas can access Edward's interest in the sale proceeds to satisfy tort judgments against him turns on whether the Bierbrauers held the Boardman Bar as survivorship marital property at the time of Edward's death.

Once survivorship rights are created, they remain with the titleholders until an act or event severs the joint tenancy. *See Nichols v. Nichols*, 43 Wis. 2d 346, 349-50, 168 N.W.2d 876 (1969). The Bierbrauers established survivorship rights when the 1991 warranty deed vested title "with rights of survivorship."

In a land contract, the vendor holds legal title, while the vendee obtains equitable title. *City of Milwaukee v. Greenberg*, 163 Wis. 2d 28, 39, 471 N.W.2d 33 (1991). Here, then, the land contract conveyed to the Andersons equitable title in the Boardman Bar. In *Simon v. Chartier*, 250 Wis. 642, 645, 27 N.W.2d 752 (1947), our supreme court expressly held that executing a land contract does not constitute severance of a joint estate. Therefore, when the Bierbrauers signed the land contract with the Andersons, they did not sever their joint tenancy with rights of survivorship. *See id.* As long as the Bierbrauers held the legal title, the way in which they held that title remained intact.

"The unexercised power to sell or convey a joint tenancy interest does not sever the joint tenancy; a consummated sale or conveyance does." *Nichols*, 43 Wis. 2d at 350. Because the Andersons did not satisfy the 1997 land contract, no sale was ever consummated. Consequently, the Bierbrauers' joint tenancy was never severed.

The Wonkas view the quitclaim deed as creating new rights, ignoring that, under the land contract, the Bierbrauers retained legal title with survivorship interests. The 1997 quitclaim deed in lieu of foreclosure could not destroy the rights of survivorship because it conveyed only the equitable interests the Andersons had under the land contract. Wis. Stat. § 706.10(4). The Andersons could not convey what they did not own. They did not own legal title. Termination of rights under a land contract (via a quitclaim deed in lieu of foreclosure) puts the vendors back in the same position they were in prior to the execution of the land contract. *See* Simon, 250 Wis. at 645.

This case is not about the creation of survivorship rights. It is about the preservation of existing rights. If the Bierbrauers had no legal interest in the Boardman Bar, the quitclaim deed would have been insufficient to create survivorship rights. However, it was unnecessary for the quitclaim deed to create survivorship rights because the Bierbrauers retained legal title in that form when they entered into the land contract with the Andersons and conveyed an equitable interest in the property. The Wonkas argue that other jurisdictions terminate survivorship rights when a land contract is executed. That, however, is inconsequential. Wisconsin is one of the few states to follow the minority rule that survivorship rights are not extinguished. *See id.* at 645.

In summary, the Bierbrauers always retained legal title to the property, which was held as survivorship marital property. When the quitclaim deed in lieu of foreclosure terminated the land contract between the Andersons and the Bierbrauers, it merely returned to the Bierbrauers the equitable title under the land contract. The quitclaim deed merely returned the Bierbrauers to the same position they were in before the land contract transaction with the Andersons. Judgment affirmed.

E. DEFERRED MARITAL PROPERTY

Rules recognizing the right of a surviving spouse to elect a portion of the deceased spouse's non community property is the current Wisconsin equivalent of the traditional elective share. Wisconsin deferred marital property operates in a way that is consistent with the operation of elective share statutes in separate property states, although the 50% share that it awards the surviving spouse is higher than the percentage in many separate property states.

Wis. Stat. 861.018. Definitions.

In this subchapter:

(1) "Augmented deferred marital property estate" means the property under s. 861.02 (2)

(2) "Deferred individual property" means any property that satisfies all of the following:

(a) Is not classified by ch. 766

(b) Was brought to the marriage or acquired while the spouses were married.

(c) Would have been classified as individual property under ch. 766 if the property had been acquired when ch. 766 applied.

(3) "Nonadverse party" means a person who has a power relating to a trust or other property arrangement but who does not have a substantial beneficial interest that would be adversely affected by exercise or nonexercise of that power, except that "nonadverse party" does not include a person who has a general power of appointment over property, with respect to that property.

(4) "Power" includes a power to designate the beneficiary of a beneficiary designation.

(5) "Power of appointment" includes a power to designate the beneficiary of a beneficiary designation.

(6) "Presently exercisable general power of appointment" means a power of appointment under which, at the time in question, the decedent held a power to create a present or future interest in himself or herself, his or her creditors, his or her estate or creditors of his or her estate and a power to revoke or invade the principal of a trust or other property arrangement, whether or not the decedent had the capacity to exercise the power at the time.

(7) "Property" has the meaning given in s. 851.27 and includes values subject to a beneficiary designation.

(8) "Right to income" includes a right to payments under a commercial or private annuity, an annuity trust, a unitrust or a similar arrangement.

(9) "Transfer" includes, but is not limited to, the following:

(a) An exercise or release of a presently exercisable general power of appointment held by the decedent.

(b) A lapse at death of a presently exercisable general power of appointment held by the decedent.

(c) An exercise, release or lapse of either of the following:

861.02. Deferred marital property elective share amount.

(1) AMOUNT.

The surviving spouse has the right to elect an amount equal to no more than 50% of the augmented deferred marital property estate as determined under sub. (2)

(2) AUGMENTED DEFERRED MARITAL PROPERTY ESTATE.

(a) If the presumption of marital property under s. 766.31 (2) is rebutted as to the classification of an asset or a portion thereof, the asset or portion is presumed to be deferred marital property.

(b) The augmented deferred marital property estate is the total value of the deferred marital property of the spouses, irrespective of where the property was acquired, where the property was located at the time of a relevant transfer, or where the property is currently located, including real property located in another jurisdiction. It includes all types of property that fall within any of the following categories:

1. Probate and nonprobate transfers of the decedent's deferred marital property under s. 861.03 (1) to (3)

2. Decedent's gifts of deferred marital property made during the 2 years before the decedent's death under s. 861.03 (4)

3. Deferred marital property of the surviving spouse under s. 861.04

(3) CALCULATION OF PROPERTY INTERESTS.

Exclusions from the augmented deferred marital property estate, valuation of included property and reduction for expenses and claims are governed by s. 861.05

(4) SATISFACTION.

Satisfaction of the augmented deferred marital property elective share amount is governed by ss. 861.06, 861.07, and 861.11, irrespective of where the property was acquired, where the property was located at the time of a relevant transfer, or where the property is currently located, including real property located in another jurisdiction.

(5) PROCEEDINGS.

Proceedings for the election are governed by ss. 861.08 and 861.09

(6) WAIVER.

Waiver of the deferred marital property elective share amount is governed by s. 861.10

(7) APPLICABILITY OF ELECTION.

(a) Unless the right has been waived under s. 861.10 or other limitations of this subchapter apply, the surviving spouse is eligible to make the election if at the time of the decedent's death the decedent is domiciled in this state.

(b) If a decedent who is not domiciled in this state owns real property in this state, the rights of the surviving spouse in that property are governed by s. 861.20

(8) EFFECT IF DEATH CAUSED BY SPOUSE.

Section 854.14 (2) (c) and (3m) (d) applies to election of deferred marital property if the decedent's surviving spouse unlawfully and intentionally killed the decedent.

861.03. Augmented deferred marital property estate: decedent's probate property and nonprobate or other property transfers.

Subject to s. 861.05, the augmented deferred marital property estate includes all of the following:

(1) DEFERRED MARITAL PROPERTY IN DECEDENT'S PROBATE ESTATE.

The value of deferred marital property in the decedent's probate estate.

(2) DEFERRED MARITAL PROPERTY PASSING NONPROBATE AT DECEDENT'S DEATH.

The value of deferred marital property owned or owned in substance by the decedent immediately before death that passed outside probate at the decedent's death, including the following:

(a) The decedent's fractional interest in deferred marital property that was held by the decedent with the right of survivorship.

(b) The decedent's ownership interest in deferred marital property that was held by the decedent in a form payable or transferable on death, including deferred employment benefit plans, individual retirement accounts, annuities and transfers under s. 766.58 (3) (f), or in co-ownership with the right of survivorship.

(c) Deferred marital property in the form of proceeds of insurance on the life of the decedent, including accidental death benefits, that were payable at the decedent's death, if the decedent owned the insurance policy immediately before death or if the decedent alone and immediately before death held a presently exercisable general power of appointment over the policy or its proceeds.

(d) Deferred marital property over which the decedent alone, immediately before death, held a presently exercisable general power of appointment, to the extent that the property passed at the decedent's death by exercise, release, lapse, default or otherwise.

(3) DEFERRED MARITAL PROPERTY TRANSFERRED WITH RETAINED RIGHTS OR BENEFITS.

(a) The augmented deferred marital property estate includes the value of any deferred marital property transferred by the decedent in which the decedent retained rights or benefits, including but not limited to the following:

1. Deferred marital property in which the decedent retained the right to possession, use, enjoyment or income and that was irrevocably transferred, to the extent that the decedent's right terminated at or continued beyond the decedent's death.

2. Deferred marital property in which the decedent retained the right, either alone or in conjunction with any person, to designate the persons who shall possess or enjoy the property or the income therefrom, to control the time at which designated persons shall possess or enjoy the property or income therefrom, or to alter or amend the terms of the transfer of the property, to the extent that the decedent's right terminated at or continued beyond the decedent's death.

3. Any transfer of deferred marital property, including transfer of an income interest, in which the decedent created a power of appointment, including the power to revoke or terminate the transfer or to consume, invade or dispose of the principal or income, if the power was exercisable by the decedent alone, by the decedent in conjunction with another person or by a nonadverse party, and if the power is for the benefit of the decedent, creditors of the decedent, the decedent's estate or creditors of the decedent's estate.

(b) The amount included under par. (a) 3. is the value of the property subject to the power of appointment if the power of appointment is over property, the value of the property that produces or produced the income if the power of appointment is over income or the power valued at the higher amount if the power of appointment is over both income and property. The value is limited by the extent to which the power of appointment was exercisable at the decedent's death or the property passed at the decedent's death by exercise, release, lapse, default or otherwise.

(4) DEFERRED MARITAL PROPERTY TRANSFERRED WITHIN 2 YEARS PRIOR TO DEATH.

(a) In this subsection, termination occurs:

1. With respect to a right or interest in property, when the right or interest terminates by the terms of the governing instrument or when the decedent transfers or relinquishes the right or interest.

2. With respect to a power of appointment over property, when the power terminates by exercise, release, lapse, default or otherwise.

3. With respect to a power of appointment under sub. (2) (d), when the power terminates by exercise or release.

(b) The augmented deferred marital property estate includes the value of any deferred marital property transferred by the decedent within the 2 years immediately preceding the decedent's death, including the following:

1. Deferred marital property that passed as a result of the termination of a right or interest in, or power of appointment over, property that would have been included in the augmented deferred marital property estate under subs. (2) (a), (b) or (d) or (3), if the right, interest or power had not terminated until the decedent's death. The amount included is the value of the property that would have been included if the property were valued at the time the right, interest or power terminated.

2. Transfers by the decedent of or relating to the deferred marital property component of an insurance policy on the life of the decedent, if the proceeds would have been included under sub. (2) (c) had the transfer not occurred. The amount included is the value of the insurance proceeds to the extent that they were payable at the decedent's death.

3. Any transfer of deferred marital property to the extent that it is not otherwise included in the augmented deferred marital property estate. The amount included is the value of the property at the time of the transfer, but only to the extent that the aggregate transfers to any one donee in either of the 2 years exceeded 10,000.

861.04. Augmented deferred marital property estate: surviving spouse's property and transfers to others.

(1) Subject to s. 861.05, the augmented deferred marital property estate includes the value of any deferred marital property that would have been included under s. 861.03 had the surviving spouse been the decedent.

(2m) When the surviving spouse is treated as the decedent under sub. (1), the decedent is not treated as the surviving spouse for the purposes of s. 861.05 (1) (e) or (2m)

861.05. Augmented deferred marital property estate: calculation of property interests.

(1) EXCLUSIONS.

The following are not included in the augmented deferred marital property estate:

(a) Transfers of deferred marital property to the extent that the decedent received full or partial consideration for the transfer in money or money's worth.

(b) Transfers under the U.S. social security system.

(c) Transfers of deferred marital property to persons other than the spouse who did not make the transfer, with the written joinder or written consent of that spouse.

(d) Transfers of deferred marital property to the surviving spouse under s. 861.33 or 861.41

(e) The deferred marital property component of any deferred employment benefit plan, or of assets in an individual retirement account that are traceable to the rollover of a deferred employment benefit plan, held by the surviving spouse that would have terminated under s. 766.62 (5) had it been marital property.

(2) VALUATION OF DECEDENT'S PROPERTY AND TRANSFERS.

(a) Property included in the augmented deferred marital property estate under s. 861.03 (1), (2) (c) and (4) (b) 2. is valued as of the date of the decedent spouses death.

(b) Property included under s. 861.03 (2) (a), (b) and (d) and (3) is valued immediately before the decedent spouses death.

(c) Property included under s. 861.03 (4) (b) 1. is valued as of the date that the right, interest or power terminated.

(d) Property included under s. 861.03 (4) (b) 3. is valued as of the date of the transfer.

(e) If deferred marital property is commingled with other types of property but the deferred marital property component can be identified, only that component is valued.

(f) The value of property included in the augmented deferred marital property estate includes the commuted value of any present or future interest in deferred marital property and the commuted value of deferred marital property payable under any trust, life insurance settlement option, annuity contract, public or private pension, disability compensation, death benefit or retirement plan or any similar arrangement.

(2m) VALUATION OF SURVIVING SPOUSE'S PROPERTY AND TRANSFERS.

The surviving spouses property included in the augmented deferred marital property estate under s. 861.04 (1) is valued in the same manner as the decedent spouses property included in the augmented deferred marital property estate is valued under sub. (2), subject to the following:

a) The surviving spouse shall be treated as having died after the decedent on the date of the decedent's death notwithstanding the 120-hour survival requirement under s. 854.03 (1)

(b) Life insurance on the surviving spouses life shall have the value of the deferred marital property component of the interpolated terminal reserve and the unused portion of the term premium of the policy as of the date of the decedent's death.

(3) REDUCTION FOR EQUITABLE PROPORTION OF EXPENSES AND ENFORCEABLE CLAIMS.

The value of deferred marital property included in the augmented deferred marital property estate under s. 861.03 or 861.04 shall be reduced by an equitable proportion of funeral and burial expenses, administrative expenses, other charges and fees and enforceable claims.

(4) OVERLAPPING APPLICATION; NO DOUBLE INCLUSION.

If the same property could be included in the augmented deferred marital property estate under more than one provision of s. 861.03 or 861.04, the property is included only once, and it is included under the provision that yields the greatest value.

861.06. Satisfaction of deferred marital property elective share amount.

(1) DEFINITION.

In this section, "property transferred to the surviving spouse" includes outright transfers that have been disclaimed by the surviving spouse. The term does not include transfers in trust that have been disclaimed by the surviving spouse, unless the surviving spouse had a general power of appointment over the property in the trust during his or her lifetime or an interest in the trust after the disclaimer.

(2) INITIAL SATISFACTION OF DEFERRED MARITAL PROPERTY ELECTIVE SHARE AMOUNT.

If the surviving spouse makes the election under s. 861.02, the following categories of property are used first to satisfy the elective share amount:

(a) All property included in the augmented deferred marital property estate under s. 861.04

(b) All marital, individual, deferred marital, or deferred individual property, transferred to the surviving spouse, including any beneficial interest in property transferred in trust:

1. From the decedent's probate estate, other than property transferred under s. 861.33 or 861.41, and other than property transferred to the surviving spouse under s. 861.31 or 861.35 except as ordered by the court under s. 861.31 (4) or 861.35 (4)

2. By nonprobate transfer at the decedent's death.

3. By operation of any state or federal law, other than transfers under the U.S. social security system.

4. By the decedent at any time during the decedent's life, except that the following shall be excluded:

a. The first 5,000 of the value of gifts from the decedent to the surviving spouse each year. Each gift shall be valued as of the date of the gift.

b. Gifts received from the decedent that the surviving spouse can show were subsequently and gratuitously transferred in a manner that, had they been the deferred marital property of the surviving spouse, would not have been included in the augmented deferred marital property estate under s. 861.04

(3) UNSATISFIED BALANCE.

After the property under sub. (2) has been applied toward satisfaction of the deferred marital property elective share amount, the remainder of the elective share amount shall be satisfied proportionally from transfers to persons other than the surviving spouse of property included in the augmented deferred marital property estate under s. 861.03 (1), (2), (3) or (4) (b) 2.

(4) REMAINING UNSATISFIED BALANCE.

After the property under subs. (2) and (3) has been applied toward satisfaction of the deferred marital property elective share amount, the remainder of the elective share amount shall be satisfied proportionally from transfers to persons other than the surviving spouse of property included in the augmented deferred marital property estate under s. 861.03 (4) (b) 1. or 3.

(5) EQUITABLE ADJUSTMENT OF SHARES.

If all or part of a prorated share under sub. (2), (3) or (4) is uncollectible, the court may increase the prorated liability of recipients described under the same or another of the 3 subsections if all of the following conditions are satisfied:

(a) The court finds that an equitable adjustment is necessary to avoid hardship for the surviving spouse.

(b) No recipient or donee of a recipient is liable for an amount greater than the value of the deferred marital property subject to the election that was received.

(6) VALUATION.

The value of property used to satisfy the deferred marital property elective share includes the value of any property transferred outright to the surviving spouse, the commuted value of any present or future interest in property transferred to the surviving spouse, and the commuted value of property payable to the surviving spouse under any trust, life insurance settlement option, annuity contract, public or private pension, disability compensation, death benefit or retirement plan, or any similar arrangement.

Wis. Stat. 861.07. Personal liability of recipients.

(1) DEFINITION.

In this section, "proceeds" includes:

(a) The consideration, in money or property, received in exchange for the property that is the subject of the transfer.

(b) Property acquired with the consideration received in exchange for the property that is the subject of the transfer.

(2) PERSONS LIABLE.

The following persons are liable to make a prorated contribution toward satisfaction of the surviving spouses deferred marital property elective share amount:

(a) Original recipients of the decedent's transfers of deferred marital property to others, irrespective of whether the recipient has the property or its proceeds.

(b) Donees of the recipients under par. (a) if the donees have the property or its proceeds. If a donee has neither the property nor its proceeds but knew or should have known of the liability under this section, the donee remains liable for his or her share of the prorated contribution.

(3) MODE OF SATISFACTION.

(a) Subject to par. (b), a person who is liable under sub. (2) may either give up the proportional part of the decedent's transfers to him or her or pay the value of the amount for which he or she is liable.

(b) On petition of the surviving spouse showing that the mode of satisfaction chosen in par. (a) will create a hardship for the surviving spouse, the court may order that a different mode of satisfaction be used.

(4) EFFECT OF FEDERAL PREEMPTION.

If any provision of this subchapter is preempted by federal law with respect to any property interest or benefit that is included under s. 861.03 and that would pass but for that preemption to a person other than the surviving spouse, the recipient, unless he or she is a recipient for value, is subject to subs. (1) to (3)

Wis. Stat. 861.08. Proceeding for election; time limit.

(1) GENERALLY.

Except as the time may be extended under sub. (3), in order to make the election, the surviving spouse shall, within 6 months after the date of the decedent's death, do all of the following:

(a) File a petition for the election with whichever of the following applies:

1. The court that has jurisdiction of the probate proceedings relating to the decedent's estate if a judicial proceeding has been commenced.

2. The court that has jurisdiction of probate proceedings relating to decedent's estates located in the county of the decedent's residence if no judicial proceeding has commenced.

(b) Mail or deliver a copy of the petition to the personal representative, if any, of the decedent's estate.

(2) NOTIFICATION OF INTERESTED PARTIES.

The surviving spouse shall give notice, in the manner provided in ch. 879, of the time and place set for hearing the petition to any persons who may be adversely affected by the election.

(3) EXTENSION OF TIME FOR ELECTION.

a) Subject to par. (b), the court may grant the surviving spouse an extension for making an election if the surviving spouse petitions the court for an extension, gives notice as specified in sub. (2) and shows cause for an extension.

(b) The petition for extension of the time for making an election must be filed within 6 months after the decedent's death, unless the court finds all of the following:

1. That the surviving spouse was prevented from filing the action or naming a particular interested party for reasons beyond his or her control.

2. That failure to extend the time for making an election will result in hardship for the surviving spouse.

(4) WITHDRAWAL OF ELECTION.

The surviving spouse may withdraw the petition for an election at any time before the probate court has entered the final determination of the distribution of the decedent's estate.

(5) COURT DETERMINATION OF LIABILITY.

(a) After notice and hearing, the court shall determine the deferred marital property elective share amount and shall determine the property that satisfies that amount under ss. 861.06 and 861.07

(b) If the personal representative does not hold the money or property included in the augmented deferred marital property estate, the court shall determine the liability of any person or entity that has any interest in the money or property or that holds that money or property.

(c) The surviving spouse may choose to seek relief from fewer than all recipients. However, any such action shall not cause any other recipients liability to exceed the amount that he or she would have had to pay if all recipients had paid a prorated share.

(6) SUITS AUTHORIZED.

An order or judgment of the court may be enforced in a suit for contribution or payment in other courts of this state or other jurisdictions.

Wis. Stat. 861.09. Right of election by or on behalf of surviving spouse.

The surviving spouse must be living in order for an election to be filed. If the surviving spouse does not personally file the election, it may be filed on the surviving spouses behalf by the spouses conservator, guardian or guardian ad litem, or by an agent of the spouse acting under a power of attorney.

Wis. Stat. 861.10. Waiver of right to elect; failure to elect.

(1) RIGHT TO ELECT MAY BE WAIVED.

The right to elect a deferred marital property elective share amount may be waived by the surviving spouse in whole or in part. The waiver may take place before or after marriage. The waiver must be contained in a marital property agreement that is enforceable under s. 766.58 or in a signed document filed with a court described in s. 861.08 (1) (a) after the decedent's death.

(2) WAIVER OF "ALL RIGHTS".

Unless the waiver provides otherwise, a waiver of "all rights," or equivalent language, in the property or estate of a present or prospective spouse, or in a complete property settlement entered into because of separation or divorce, is a waiver of all rights in the deferred marital property elective share amount.

(3) FAILURE TO ELECT.

Failure of a surviving spouse to elect is not a transfer of property and is not a gift from the surviving spouse to the decedent spouses probate estate or to the beneficiaries of other transfers.

Wis. Stat. 861.11. Protection of payers and other 3rd parties.

(1) DEFINITION.

In this section, "governing instrument" includes a filed verified statement under s. 865.201, a certificate under s. 867.046 (1m) or a recorded application under s. 867.046 (5)

(2) PAYER NOT LIABLE UNTIL NOTICE RECEIVED.

(a) Upon a beneficiary's request for payment, a payer or other 3rd party who has received satisfactory proof of the decedent's death and who has not received written notice that the surviving spouse or his or her representative intends to file a petition for the deferred marital property elective share amount or that a petition for the election has been filed is not liable for any of the following:

1. Causing any payment, item of property or other benefit included in the augmented deferred marital property estate under s. 861.03, to transfer directly to the beneficiary designated in a governing instrument.

2. Any other action in good faith reliance on the validity of a governing instrument.

(b) A payer or other 3rd party is liable for payments made or other actions taken after receipt of written notice of the intent to file a petition for the elective share amount or written notice that a petition for the elective share amount has been filed.

(3) METHOD OF NOTICE TO PAYERS.

A written notice of the intent to file a petition for the election or written notice that a petition for the election has been filed shall fulfill one of the following requirements:

(a) Be mailed to the payers' or other 3rd party's main office or home by registered or certified mail, return receipt requested.

(b) Be served upon the payer or other 3rd party in the same manner as a summons in a civil action.

(4) OPTIONAL PAYMENT OF PROCEEDS TO COURT.

(a) Upon receipt of written notice of the intent to file, or the filing of, a petition for the election, a payer or other 3rd party may pay any amount owed or transfer or deposit any item of property to or with whichever of the following applies:

1. The court that has jurisdiction of the probate proceedings relating to the decedent's estate if proceedings have been commenced.

2. The court that has jurisdiction of probate proceedings relating to decedent's estates located in the county of the decedent's residence, if no judicial proceeding has commenced.

(b) Payments, transfers or deposits made to the court discharge the payer or other 3rd party from all claims for amounts paid or the value of property transferred or deposited.

(c) The court shall hold the funds or items of property. After the court makes its determination under s. 861.08 (5), it shall order disbursement in accordance with that determination. The court shall order disbursement to the beneficiary designated in the governing instrument if either of the following conditions applies:

1. No petition is filed in the court within the specified time under s. 861.08 (1)

2. A petition was filed but withdrawn under s. 861.08 (4) with prejudice.

(d) If payments have been made to the court or if property has been deposited with the court under par. (a), the court may order that all or part of the payments or property be paid to the beneficiary who is designated in the governing instrument, upon that beneficiary's petition to the court. Those payments shall be in an amount and subject to conditions consistent with this subchapter.

(5) PROTECTION OF FINANCIAL INSTITUTIONS.

(a) In this subsection:

1. "Account" has the meaning given in s. 705.01 (1) or 710.05 (1) (a)

2. "Financial institution" has the meaning given in s. 705.01 (3)

(b) Notwithstanding sub. (2), in addition to the protections afforded a financial institution under ss. 701.19 (11) and 710.05 and chs. 112 and 705 a financial institution is not liable for having transferred an account included in the augmented deferred marital property estate under s. 861.03 to a beneficiary designated in a governing instrument, or for having taken any other action in reliance on the beneficiary's apparent entitlement under the terms of a governing instrument, regardless of whether the financial institution received written notice of an intent to file, or the filing of, a petition for the deferred marital property elective share amount.

(c) If a financial institution has reason to believe that a dispute exists as to the rights of parties, or their successors, to an account subject to a governing instrument, the financial institution may, but is not required to, do any of the following:

1. Deposit the account with a court as provided in sub. (4)

2. Refuse to transfer the account to any person.

(d) The protection afforded a financial institution under this subsection does not affect the rights of parties or their successors in disputes concerning the beneficial ownership of accounts.

In re Estate of Hemmrich

Wisconsin Court of Appeals
289 Wis. 2d 220, 709 N.W.2d 113 (2005)

PER CURIAM. Dale Hemmrich appeals an order of the circuit court permitting Delores Hemmrich to elect against her husband's will pursuant to WIS. STAT. § 861.08. Dale contends the circuit court erred when it waived the requirement that a surviving spouse must, within six months of the decedent's death, either make an election or petition for an extension of time to make an election. We disagree and affirm.

BACKGROUND

Walter Hemmrich died on June 20, 2003. He was survived by his wife, Delores, and four children, Dale Hemmrich, Wayne Hemmrich, Richard Hemmrich and Karen Keim. Due to her incompetence, Richard was appointed permanent guardian for Delores on May 19, 2003. A probate action was filed on May 18, 2004. Dale, who was also the main recipient of Walter's assets under the will, was appointed personal representative. After Richard failed to appear or file any elections on Delores's behalf, a guardian ad litem was appointed for Delores. The guardian ad litem was not notified by the probate office of the appointment until November 2004. Upon notification, the guardian ad litem quickly elected against Walter's will on Delores's behalf. Dale objected to the election on the ground that it was not timely, but the circuit court granted the election.

DISCUSSION

Dale contends the circuit court erred when it waived the requirement that a surviving spouse must, within six months of the decedent's death, either make an election or petition for an extension of time to make an election pursuant to WIS. STAT. § 861.08(3). Granting an extension to a statutory limit is within the circuit court's discretion, and we will not disturb the decision unless discretion was erroneously exercised. *See Giese v. Giese*, 43 Wis. 2d 456, 460, 168 N.W.2d 832 (1969).

WISCONSIN STAT. § 861.08(1) requires that a surviving spouse make an election within six months of the decedent's death, unless the surviving spouse qualifies for a time extension. The court may grant the surviving spouse an extension if he or she petitions the court and shows cause for the extension. WIS. STAT. § 861.08(3). The petition for the extension must be filed within six months after the decedent's death, unless the court finds the surviving spouse was prevented from filing the action or naming a particular interested party for reasons beyond his or her control and failure to extend the time would result in hardship for the surviving spouse. WIS. STAT. § 861.08(3)(b). The circuit court reasoned Delores met the requirements of WIS. STAT. § 861.08(3)(b). Delores did not have a guardian ad litem until November 2004, which was beyond the deadlines to make an election or to petition for an extension of time to make an election. *See* WIS. STAT. §§ 861.08(1), 861.08(3)(b). Delores was prevented from filing the action herself due to reasons beyond her control. Failing to extend the deadline would result in hardship because she would be unable to pursue her rights as the surviving spouse.

We agree with the circuit court that an extension was appropriate. Dale argues that Richard, Delores's general guardian, should have made the election prior to the deadline; however, the circuit court was faced with the reality of a guardian who was unresponsive and failed to take any action on Delores's behalf. After the guardian ad litem's appointment, she quickly pursued Delores's right to make the election. As the circuit court noted, it was impossible for Delores to have made the election herself, and until the appointment of the guardian ad litem, no one was acting in her interests. Therefore, extending the deadline was not an erroneous exercise of discretion.

F. ADDITIONAL PROTECTIONS FOR MARITAL PROPERTY

Wis. Stat. 861.17. Rights in property transferred in fraud of surviving spouse.

(1) Nothing in this chapter **[Marital Property]** precludes a court in an equitable proceeding from subjecting to the rights of the surviving spouse under ch. 852 and this chapter any property arrangement made by the decedent in fraud of those rights. A property arrangement in fraud of the rights of the surviving spouse means any of the following:

(a) Any transfer or acquisition of property, regardless of the form or type of property rights involved, made by the decedent during marriage or in anticipation of marriage for the primary purpose of defeating the rights of the surviving spouse under ch. 852 and this chapter.

(b) Any breach of the good faith duty imposed by s. 766.15 made for the primary purpose of defeating the rights of the surviving spouse in or to marital property.

(2) An arrangement made before marriage, or within one year after marriage, or prior to April 1, 1971, to provide for issue by a prior marriage is not a fraudulent property arrangement within the meaning of this section.

(3) If the spouse is successful in an action to reach fraudulent property arrangements, recovery is limited to the amount the spouse would receive under ch. 852 and this chapter. Other rules of this chapter apply so far as possible. A spouse who recovers under this subsection forfeits any power of appointment that the surviving spouse possesses over the remaining portion of the fraudulently arranged property, except a special power.

(3m) If the spouse is successful in an action to reach fraudulent property arrangements involving marital property, recovery is limited to the surviving spouses interest in the marital property. Other rules of this chapter apply so far as possible. Recovery forfeits any power of appointment which the surviving spouse possesses over the remaining portion of the fraudulently arranged marital property, except a special power.

(4) The surviving spouse has no rights against any person dealing with the property without actual knowledge, or receipt of written notice, of the claim of the spouse. A person who has

knowledge of facts and circumstances sufficient to put the person on inquiry as to a claim by the spouse does not have actual knowledge and is not required to make further inquiry. This subsection does not protect a gratuitous donee from the original beneficiary of the fraudulent arrangement.

(5) Every such suit must be brought within 3 years of decedent's death, but may be barred by laches at an earlier date.

Wis. Stat. 861.20. Surviving spouse's right in nondomiciliary decedent's real property in this state.

(1) If a married person who does not have a domicile in this state dies and leaves a valid will disposing of real property in this state which is not the community property or marital property of the decedent and the surviving spouse, the surviving spouse has the same right to elect to take a portion of or interest in that property against the will of the decedent as if the property were located in the decedent's domicile at the decedent's death. The procedure of the decedent's domicile for electing against the will applies to such an election.

(2) If a married person who does not have a domicile in this state dies and has an interest in real property in this state that is subject to administration but not disposed of by will, the surviving spouse has the same right to the property under intestate succession as if the property were located in the decedent's domicile at decedent's death.

III. LIMITATIONS ON SPOUSAL CLAIMS

A. INVALID MARRIAGES

Occasionally, parties will live together as man and wife under the impression that they are lawfully married, even though they are not. The following statute gives Wisconsin courts broad discretion in regard to inheritance rights when such an experience occurs. In situations where the parties divorce, no new marital property is acquired, but previous community property remains jointly held until the conclusion of the divorce settlement. If parties to a marriage have filed for divorce, but one party dies before the divorce decree is final, their marriage remains valid.

Wis. Stat. 766.73. Invalid marriages.

If a marriage is invalidated by a decree, a court may apply so much of this chapter to the property of the parties to the invalid marriage as is necessary to avoid an inequitable result. This section does not apply if s. 767.61 applies to the action to invalidate the marriage.

B. MARITAL AND PRENUPTIAL AGREEMENTS

As the statutes below indicate, rules regarding agreements that alter marital property rights in Wisconsin are extensive. While such agreements are permitted, they are valid only if they are entered into willingly and with each party fully disclosing the extent and nature of the affected assets. The case that follows discusses the legitimacy of prenuptial agreements and also explores the application of the Wisconsin "Deadman's Statute," which contains evidentiary rules that have special application to wills-oriented litigation.

Wis. Stat. 766.17. Variation by marital property agreement.

(1) Except as provided in ss. 766.15, 766.55 (4m), 766.57 (3) and 766.58 (2), a marital property agreement may vary the effect of this chapter.

(2) Section 859.18 (6) governs the effect of a marital property agreement upon property available for satisfaction of obligations after the death of a spouse.

(4m) Except as provided under s. 766.56 (2) (c), no provision of a marital property agreement or of a decree under s. 766.70 adversely affects the interest of a creditor unless the creditor had actual knowledge of that provision when the obligation to that creditor was incurred or, in the case of an open-end plan, as defined under s. 766.555 (1) (a), when the plan was entered into. If a creditor obtains actual knowledge of a provision of a marital property agreement or decree after an obligation is incurred or an open-end plan is entered into, the provision does not adversely affect the interest of the creditor with respect to that obligation or plan, including any renewal, extension, modification or use of the obligation or plan. The effect of this subsection may not be varied by a marital property agreement or a decree. This subsection does not affect the application of ch. 706

Wis. Stat. 766.55. Obligations of spouses. Subsection 4m.

(4m) Except as provided under s. 766.56 (2) (c), no provision of a marital property agreement or of a decree under s. 766.70 adversely affects the interest of a creditor unless the creditor had actual knowledge of that provision when the obligation to that creditor was incurred or, in the case of an open-end plan, as defined under s. 766.555 (1) (a), when the plan was entered into. If a creditor obtains actual knowledge of a provision of a marital property agreement or decree after an obligation is incurred or an open-end plan is entered into, the provision does not adversely affect the interest of the creditor with respect to that obligation or plan, including any renewal, extension, modification or use of the obligation or plan. The effect of this subsection may not be varied by a marital property agreement or a decree. This subsection does not affect the application of ch. 706.

Wis. Stat. 766.58. Marital property agreements.

(1) A marital property agreement shall be a document signed by both spouses. Only the spouses may be parties to a marital property agreement. A marital property agreement is enforceable without consideration.

(2) A marital property agreement may not adversely affect the right of a child to support.

(3) Except as provided in ss. 766.15, 766.55 (4m), 766.57 (3) and 859.18 (6), and in sub. (2), in a marital property agreement spouses may agree with respect to any of the following:

(a) Rights in and obligations with respect to any of either or both spouses' property whenever and wherever acquired or located.

(b) Management and control of any of either or both spouses' property.

(c) Disposition of any of either or both spouses' property upon dissolution or death or upon the occurrence or nonoccurrence of any other event.

(d) Modification or elimination of spousal support, except as provided in sub. (9)

(e) Making a will, trust or other arrangement to carry out the marital property agreement.

(f) Providing that upon the death of either spouse any of either or both spouses' property, including after-acquired property, passes without probate to a designated person, trust or other entity by nontestamentary disposition. Any such provision in a marital property agreement is revoked upon dissolution of the marriage as provided in s. 767.375 (1). If a marital property agreement provides for the nontestamentary disposition of property, without probate, at the death of the 2nd spouse, at any time after the death of the first spouse the surviving spouse may amend the marital property agreement with regard to property to be disposed of at his or her death unless the marital property agreement expressly provides otherwise and except to the extent property is held in a trust expressly established under the marital property agreement.

(g) Choice of law governing construction of the marital property agreement.

(h) Any other matter affecting either or both spouse's property not in violation of public policy or a statute imposing a criminal penalty.

(3m) Chapter 854 applies to transfers at death under a marital property agreement.

(4) A marital property agreement may be amended or revoked only by a later marital property agreement.

(5) Persons intending to marry each other may enter into a marital property agreement as if married, but the marital property agreement becomes effective only upon their marriage.

(6) A marital property agreement executed before or during marriage is not enforceable if the spouse against whom enforcement is sought proves any of the following:

(a) The marital property agreement was unconscionable when made.

(b) That spouse did not execute the marital property agreement voluntarily.

(c) Before execution of the marital property agreement, that spouse:

1. Did not receive fair and reasonable disclosure, under the circumstances, of the other spouses property or financial obligations; and

2. Did not have notice of the other spouse's property or financial obligations.

(7)

(a) Unless the marital property agreement expressly provides otherwise, a marital property agreement that classifies a deferred employment benefit plan or an individual retirement account as marital property does not affect the operation of s. 766.62 (5)

(b) Unless the marital property agreement expressly provides otherwise, marital property agreement that classifies as marital property the noninsured spouses interest in a policy that designates the other spouse as the owner and insured does not affect the operation of s. 766.61 (7) In this paragraph, "owner" has the meaning given in s. 766.61 (1) (a) and "policy" has the meaning given in s. 766.61 (1) (c)

(8) The issue of whether a marital property agreement is unconscionable is for the court to decide as a matter of law. In the event that legal counsel is retained in connection with a marital property agreement the fact that both parties are represented by one counsel or that one party is represented by counsel and the other party is not represented by counsel does not by itself make a marital property agreement unconscionable or otherwise affect its enforceability.

(9)

(a) Modification or elimination of spousal support during the marriage may not result in a spouse having less than necessary and adequate support, taking into consideration all sources of support.

(b) If a marital property agreement modifies or eliminates spousal support so as to make one spouse eligible for public assistance at the time of dissolution of the marriage or termination of the marriage by death, the court may require the other spouse or the other spouse's estate to provide support necessary to avoid that eligibility, notwithstanding the marital property agreement.

(10) If the spouses agree in writing to arbitrate any controversies arising under this chapter or a marital property agreement, the arbitration agreement is enforceable under ch. 788

(11) Married persons or persons intending to marry each other may record a marital property agreement in the county register of deeds office under s. 59.43 (1) (r)

(12)

(a) A provision of a document signed before the determination date by spouses or unmarried persons who subsequently married each other, which provision affects the property of either of them and is enforceable by either of them without reference to this chapter, is not affected by this chapter except as provided otherwise in a marital property agreement made after the determination date.

(b) If a provision or an amendment to a provision in a document described under par. (a) is intended to negate, apply or modify any right or obligation which may be acquired under 1983 Wisconsin Act 186, 1985 Wisconsin Act 37, or a community property system, the provision or amendment is enforceable after the determination date if the document was enforceable when executed or, if it is executed after April 4, 1984, either was enforceable when executed or would be enforceable if it were executed after the determination date.

(c) This subsection does not affect a marital property agreement executed under s. 766.585

(13)

(a) With respect to a provision of a marital property agreement that is effective upon or after dissolution of the marriage or termination of the marriage by death, any statute of limitations applicable to enforcement of the provision is tolled until dissolution of the marriage or termination of the marriage by death, respectively.

(b) After the death of a spouse, no action concerning a marital property agreement may be brought later than 6 months after the inventory is filed under s. 858.01 If an amended inventory is filed, the action may be brought within 6 months after the filing of the amended inventory if the action relates to information contained in the amended inventory that was not contained in a previous inventory.

(c) The court may extend the 6-month period under par. (b) for cause if a motion for extension is made within the applicable 6-month period.

(14) Limitations on the effect of marital property agreements for state income tax purposes are set forth in ch. 71

Wis. Stat. 766.585. Marital property agreements before determination date.

(1) After April 4, 1984, and before their determination date, spouses or unmarried persons who subsequently marry each other may execute a marital property agreement under s. 766.58, which is intended to apply only after their determination date, to the same extent that persons may execute a marital property agreement under s. 766.58 after their determination date. The marital property agreement does not apply before the person's determination date. Upon application, the marital property agreement has the same effect as if executed after the person's determination date.

(2) Notwithstanding the execution of the marital property agreement before the persons determination date and notwithstanding the January 1, 1986, effective date of 1983 Wisconsin Act 186 and 1985 Wisconsin Act 37, the law in effect on the date when the marital property agreement applies, not on the date of execution of the marital property agreement, applies to the execution and enforceability or other legal effect of the marital property agreement.

(3) A document executed by spouses or unmarried persons who subsequently marry each other which is intended to apply in whole or in part before their determination date is governed by s. 766.58 (12)

Wis. Stat. 766.587. Statutory individual property classification agreement.

(1) GENERALLY.

(a) Spouses may execute a statutory individual property classification agreement under this section to classify all the property of the spouses, including property presently owned and property acquired in the future but before the agreement terminates, as the individual property of the owner. Ownership of the property of the spouses is determined as if it were December 31, 1985. Except as provided in this section, s. 766.58 applies to an agreement under this section. Persons intending to marry each other may execute an agreement as if married, but the agreement becomes effective only upon their marriage. The form of the agreement is set forth in sub. (7).

(b) If, while an agreement is in effect, spouses acquire property as a joint tenancy exclusively between themselves or as survivorship marital property, the property is classified as the individual property of the owners and is owned as a joint tenancy. If, while an agreement is in effect, spouses acquire property held in a form as provided under s. 766.60 (1) or (2), the property is classified as the individual property of the owners and is owned as a tenancy in common.

(2) EXECUTION. An agreement under this section is executed when signed by both spouses.

(3) EFFECTIVE PERIOD.

(a) An agreement under this section may be executed on or after January 1, 1986. If executed before January 1, 1986, it is effective on January 1, 1986, or upon the marriage of the parties, whichever is later. If executed on or after January 1, 1986, it is effective when executed or upon the marriage of the parties, whichever is later.

(b) An agreement under this section terminates on January 1, 1987. Termination does not affect the classification of property acquired before termination. Property acquired after termination is classified as provided under this chapter.

(4) ENFORCEABILITY. An agreement under this section is enforceable without the disclosure of a spouses property or financial obligations to the other spouse.

(5) EFFECT ON SUPPORT AND AT DIVORCE. An agreement under this section does not affect the duty of support that spouses have to each other or the determination of property division under s. 767.61 or of maintenance payments under s. 767.56

(6) RIGHTS OF SURVIVING SPOUSE. Notwithstanding the fact that an agreement under this section is in effect at, or has terminated before, the death of a spouse who is a party to the agreement, the surviving spouse may elect under s. 861.02 For the purpose of the election, in addition to the property described in s. 851.055, property acquired during marriage and after the determination date which would have been marital property but for the agreement is deferred marital property.

(7) STATUTORY INDIVIDUAL PROPERTY CLASSIFICATION AGREEMENT FORM. **[Omitted.]**

(8) OTHER MEANS OF CLASSIFICATION. This section is not the exclusive means by which spouses may, before January 1, 1987, classify their property as the individual property of the owner.

Wis. Stat. 766.588. Statutory terminable marital property classification agreement.

(1) GENERALLY.

(a) Spouses may execute an agreement under this section to classify the property of the spouses presently owned and property acquired, reclassified or created in the future, as marital property. Except as provided in this section, s. 766.58 applies to an agreement under this section. The form of the agreement is set forth in sub. (9) Persons intending to marry each other may execute an agreement as if married, but the agreement becomes effective only upon their determination date.

(b) Notwithstanding an agreement under this section:

1. The marital property interest of the nonemployee spouse in a deferred employment benefit plan or in assets in an individual retirement account that are traceable to the rollover of a deferred employment benefit plan terminates at the death of the nonemployee spouse if he or she predeceases the employee spouse; and

2. The marital property interest of a decedent spouse in a life insurance policy which designates the surviving spouse as the owner and insured is limited as provided under s. 766.61 (7)

(c)

1. If property is held as survivorship marital property under s. 766.60 (5) (a) or 766.605 at the time an agreement under this section becomes effective, or if property is held as or acquired as survivorship marital property under s. 766.60 (5) (a) or 766.605 while an agreement is in effect, the property remains survivorship marital property as long as it is so held.

2. A joint tenancy which is held exclusively between the spouses when an agreement under this section becomes effective or while an agreement is in effect is survivorship marital property.

3. A tenancy in common which is held exclusively between the spouses when an agreement under this section becomes effective or while an agreement is in effect is marital property.

4. With respect to a tenancy in common or joint tenancy not described under subds. 2. and 3. in which at least one spouse is a tenant when an agreement under this section becomes effective or while an agreement is in effect, to the extent the incidents of the tenancy in common or joint tenancy conflict with or differ from the incidents of marital property, the incidents of the tenancy in common or of the joint tenancy, including the incident of survivorship, control.

(d)

1. In this paragraph:

a. "Joint account" has the meaning given in s. 705.01 (4)

b. "Marital account" has the meaning given in s. 705.01 (4m)

2. An agreement under this section does not defeat the survivorship feature of a joint account under s. 705.04 (1)

3. An agreement under this section does not affect the ownership, under s. 705.04 (2m), of sums remaining on deposit in a marital account at the death of a party to the account, regardless of when the agreement became effective or the marital account was established.

(2) EXECUTION. An agreement under this section shall be signed by both parties to the agreement. An agreement under this section is executed when the signature of each party to the agreement is authenticated or acknowledged. The agreement executed shall conform to the requirements under sub. (9)

(3) EFFECTIVE DATE AND EFFECTIVE PERIOD.

(a) An agreement under this section is effective when executed or upon the determination date, whichever is later.

(b) If the spouses have not completed the financial disclosure form under sub. (9) before or contemporaneously with execution of the agreement, the agreement terminates 3 years after the date that both spouses have signed the agreement, unless terminated earlier by one of the spouses under sub. (4)

(c) If the spouses have completed the financial disclosure form under sub. (9), the agreement terminates when the terms of the agreement no longer apply after dissolution or the death of a spouse, unless terminated earlier by one of the spouses under sub. (4)

(3m) LIMITATION ON EXECUTION OF 3-YEAR AGREEMENT. If spouses execute an agreement under this section which becomes effective for any period and if the spouses did not complete the financial disclosure form under sub. (9) for that agreement, the spouses may not execute a subsequent agreement under this section for the same marriage unless the financial disclosure form under sub. (9) is completed.

(4) TERMINATION BY ONE SPOUSE.

(a) An agreement under this section terminates 30 days after a notice of termination is given under par. (b) by one spouse to the other spouse. An example of a termination form is set forth in sub. (9) (b) Notice of termination is given to the other spouse on the date:

1. That a signed termination is personally delivered to the other spouse; or

2. That a signed termination is sent by certified mail to the address of the other spouse last known to the spouse giving notice of termination.

(c) This subsection does not affect the ability to amend, revoke or supplement an agreement under this section by separate marital property agreement under s. 766.58 (4) (d) With respect to its effect on 3rd parties, a termination under this section shall be treated as a marital property agreement.

(5) ENFORCEABILITY.

(a) If the spouses do not complete the financial disclosure form under sub. (9), the agreement terminates as provided under sub. (3) (b) and the agreement is enforceable without the disclosure of a spouses property or financial obligations.

(b) If the spouses complete the financial disclosure form under sub. (9), the maximum duration of the agreement is 3 years after both spouses have signed the agreement if the spouse against whom enforcement is sought proves that the information on the disclosure form did not provide fair and reasonable disclosure, under the circumstances, of the other spouse's property or financial obligations. This paragraph applies notwithstanding the fact that a spouse had notice of the other spouse's property or financial obligations.

(c) Section 766.58 (6) (c) does not apply to an agreement under this section.

(6) EFFECT ON SUPPORT AND DIVORCE. An agreement under this section does not affect any of the following:

(a) The duty of support that spouses otherwise have to each other.

(b) The determination of property division under s. 767.61 (c) The determination of maintenance payments under s. 767.56

(7) OTHER MEANS OF CLASSIFICATION. This section is not the exclusive means by which spouses may reclassify their property as marital property.

(8) EFFECT OF TERMINATION. Termination of an agreement under sub. (3) or (4) does not affect the classification of property acquired before termination. Property acquired after termination is classified as provided under this chapter.

(9) STATUTORY TERMINABLE MARITAL PROPERTY CLASSIFICATION AGREEMENT FORM.

[Omitted]

Wis. Stat. 766.589. Statutory terminable individual property classification agreement.

(1) GENERALLY.

(a) For purposes of determining ownership of property classified by an agreement under this section, a spouse owns property if the property is held by that spouse. If property classified by an agreement under this section is not held by either or both spouses, ownership of the property is determined as if the spouses were unmarried when the property was acquired.

(b) Spouses may execute an agreement under this section to classify the marital property of the spouses presently owned and property acquired, reclassified or created in the future that would otherwise be marital property, as the individual property of the owner. At the death of the owning spouse, property classified by an agreement under this section is subject to the rights of the surviving spouse under sub. (7) Except as provided in this section, s. 766.58 applies to an agreement under this section. The form of the agreement is set forth in sub. (10) Persons intending to marry each other may execute an agreement as if married, but the agreement becomes effective only upon their determination date.

(c)

1. If at the time an agreement under this section is executed property is held as survivorship marital property, the property is classified as the individual property of the owners and is owned as a joint tenancy. If at the time an agreement under this section is executed property is held in a form as provided under s. 766.60 (1) or (2), the property is classified as the individual property of the owners and is owned as a tenancy in common. If while an

agreement is in effect spouses acquire property as a joint tenancy exclusively between themselves or as survivorship marital property, the property is classified as the individual property of the owners and is owned as a joint tenancy. If while an agreement is in effect spouses acquire property as tenants in common exclusively between themselves, the spouses respective ownership interests in the property are classified as the individual property of the owners. If while an agreement is in effect spouses acquire property held in a form as provided under s. 766.60 (1) or (2), the property is classified as the individual property of the owners and is owned as a tenancy in common. An agreement under this section does not affect the incidents under ch. 705 of a joint account, as defined in s. 705.01 (4)

2. For purposes of an agreement under this section, to the extent the incidents of a joint tenancy or tenancy in common conflict with or differ from the incidents of individual property, the incidents of the tenancy in common or joint tenancy, including the incident of survivorship, control.

(2) EXECUTION. An agreement under this section shall be signed by both parties to the agreement. An agreement under this section is executed when the signature of each party to the agreement is authenticated or acknowledged. The agreement executed shall conform to the requirements under sub. (10)

(3) EFFECTIVE DATE AND EFFECTIVE PERIOD.

(a) An agreement under this section is effective when executed or upon the determination date, whichever is later.

(b) If the spouses have not completed the financial disclosure form under sub. (10) before or contemporaneously with execution of the agreement, the agreement terminates 3 years after the date that both spouses signed the agreement, unless terminated earlier by one of the spouses under sub. (4) (c) If the spouses have completed the financial disclosure form under sub. (10), the agreement terminates when the terms of the agreement no longer apply after dissolution or the death of a spouse, unless terminated earlier by one of the spouses under sub. (4)

(3m) LIMITATION ON EXECUTION OF 3-YEAR AGREEMENT. If spouses execute an agreement under this section which becomes effective for any period and, for that agreement, do not complete the financial disclosure form under sub. (10), the spouses may not execute a subsequent agreement under this section for the same marriage unless the financial disclosure form under sub. (10) is completed.

(4) TERMINATION BY ONE SPOUSE; GOOD FAITH DUTY.

(a) An agreement under this section terminates 30 days after a notice of termination is given under par. (b) by one spouse to the other spouse. An example of a termination form is set forth in sub. (10)

(b) Notice of termination is given to the other spouse on the date:

1. That signed termination is personally delivered to the other spouse; or

2. That signed termination is sent by certified mail to the address of the other spouse last known to the spouse giving notice of termination.

(c) After notice of termination is given under this subsection and until the agreement terminates, each spouse shall act in good faith with respect to the other spouse in matters involving the property of the spouse who is required to act in good faith which is classified as individual property by the agreement. Management and control by a spouse of that property in a manner that limits, diminishes or fails to produce income from that property does not violate this paragraph.

(d) This subsection does not affect the ability to amend, revoke or supplement an agreement under this section by separate marital property agreement under s. 766.58 (4) (e) With respect to its effect on 3rd parties, a termination under this section shall be treated as a marital property agreement.

(5) ENFORCEABILITY.

(a) If the spouses do not complete the financial disclosure form under sub. (10), the agreement terminates as provided under sub. (3) (b) and the agreement is enforceable without the disclosure of a spouses property or financial obligations.

(b) If the spouses complete the financial disclosure form under sub. (10), the maximum duration of the agreement is 3 years after both spouses have signed the agreement if the spouse against whom enforcement is sought proves that the information on the disclosure form did not provide fair and reasonable disclosure, under the circumstances, of the other spouses property or financial obligations. This paragraph applies notwithstanding the fact that a spouse had notice of the other spouses property or financial obligations.

(c) Section 766.58 (6) (c) does not apply to an agreement under this section.

(6) EFFECT ON SUPPORT AND DIVORCE. An agreement under this section does not affect any of the following:

(a) The duty of support that spouses otherwise have to each other.

(b) The determination of property division under s. 767.61 (c) The determination of maintenance payments under s. 767.56

(7) RIGHTS OF SURVIVING SPOUSE. Notwithstanding the fact that an agreement under this section is in effect at, or has terminated before, the time of death of a spouse who is party to the agreement, the surviving spouse may elect under s. 861.02 For the purpose of the election, in addition to the property described in s. 851.055, property acquired during marriage and after the determination date which would have been marital property but for the agreement is deferred marital property.

(8) OTHER MEANS OF CLASSIFICATION. This section is not the exclusive means by which spouses may reclassify their marital property.

(9) EFFECT OF TERMINATION. Termination of an agreement under sub. (3) or (4) does not affect the classification of property acquired before termination. Property acquired after termination is classified as provided under this chapter.

(10) STATUTORY TERMINABLE INDIVIDUAL PROPERTY CLASSIFICATION AGREEMENT FORM.

[Omitted]

Estate of Stocking v. Stocking

Court of Appeals of Wisconsin
238 Wis. 2d 840, 618 N.W.2d 273 (2000)

PER CURIAM. The Estate of Cynthia M. Stocking appeals from an order of the circuit court determining the authenticity of a document and its legal effect in the course of probate proceedings. We accepted interlocutory appeal by order of this court dated April 12, 1999.

The Estate claims the trial court erred when it: (1) allowed testimony by James Stocking in violation of the deadman's statute; (2) concluded that the challenged document was a valid marital property agreement; and (3) found James's testimony and that of his brother, Daniel Stocking, to be credible.

Because the trial court properly applied the deadman's statute consistent with recent case law, because the trial court reasonably concluded, under the circumstances, that the challenged document served as a marital property agreement, and because the trial court's findings of fact are not clearly erroneous, we affirm.

I. BACKGROUND

James and Cynthia Stocking were married on August 30, 1975. It was a second marriage for both. By James's testimony, the marriage was not a close, loving relationship, although it lasted many years until the parties separated in October 1994. At that time, Cynthia moved into an apartment in Milwaukee. James remained in the River Hills home that he owned prior to the marriage. In June 1996, the parties filed a joint petition for divorce. The petition was later dismissed in hopes of reconciliation.

Nonetheless, a second divorce proceeding was commenced in November 1996. On January 19, 1997, James left Milwaukee for a vacation. During the time he was gone, his brother Daniel, or his nephew Thomas Stocking, visited the River Hills home to collect the mail and check phone messages. When James and his girlfriend, Ms. Buerosse, returned to the River Hills home on February 2, 1997, they found Cynthia's car in the driveway. Cynthia was found in the garage of James's home; she was unconscious in Ms. Buerosse's car and the motor was running. The police were called immediately and they determined that Cynthia's death was an apparent suicide. The police discovered a key to James's home on Cynthia's person. The divorce proceeding was still pending at the time of Cynthia's death.

During a search of Cynthia's apartment, the police discovered a will dated January 20, 1996. The will left personal bequests to nieces, nephews and friends. The balance of the estate was bequeathed to Cynthia's two sisters. The will was admitted to probate and the co-personal representative petitioned for an order pursuant to Wis. Stat. § 857.01 (1997-98) to determine the classification of the property of James and Cynthia.

During the course of discovery in the probate action, James produced a document, which he alleged was a copy of an individual income agreement. He testified that he had prepared the document shortly after the death of his father in November 1985, because he was concerned that income generated from gifts or inheritances would be affected if his marriage failed. He was also concerned about individual income interest being affected by the recently enacted Marital Property Act, which would go into effect on January 1, 1986. James indicated that he drafted the document so that any income earned on his or Cynthia's individual assets would not be classified as marital property. He claimed that the original document was signed on December 21, 1985, by both himself and Cynthia, in the presence of Daniel, who notarized the document. James indicated that Cynthia retained a signed original of the document and that he took a signed original of the agreement and placed it in his will file. James also testified that he put a copy of the original in his 1985 income tax file. James stated that he last saw the original document during an annual audit of his files as late as November or December of 1996.

After Cynthia's death, James checked his will file and could not find the original agreement. He testified that he thoroughly searched his files, but the original could not be located. He did find the photocopy of the original in his 1985 income tax file.

Both sides agreed that the agreement's authenticity and legal effect were critical to classification of James's and Cynthia's property. Therefore, the parties entered into a stipulation bifurcating the issues of the authenticity and legal effect of the document from the probate proceedings. During the trial on the authenticity and legal effect of the document, both James and Daniel testified.

The Estate objected to James testifying in any respect to the document, claiming that his testimony was barred by the deadman's statute. The trial court ruled that the deadman's statute prohibited James from testifying with respect to any "communications or transactions which are, 'personal' with the deceased." However, the trial court determined that "James is not incompetent to testify regarding either his preparation, retention or search for the originals or his confirmation of their subsequent absence. All such testimony relates to activities other than direct communications or transactions between James and Cynthia." The trial court determined that the document produced was the best evidence of a valid marital property agreement.

The Estate appeals from the trial court's order.

II. DISCUSSION

A. Deadman's Statute.

The Estate argues that the trial court erred in allowing James's testimony with regard to the agreement. It contends that the deadman's statute prohibits James from offering any testimony relative to the agreement. The deadman's statute is codified at Wis. Stat. § 885.16. It provides:

> Transactions with deceased or insane persons. No party or person in the party's or person's own behalf or interest, and no person from, through or under whom a party derives the party's interest or title, shall be examined as a witness in respect to any transaction or communication by the party or person personally with a deceased or insane person in any civil action or proceeding, in which the opposite party derives his or her title or sustains his or her liability to the cause of action from, through or under such deceased or insane person, or in any action or proceeding in which such insane person is a party prosecuting or defending by guardian, unless such opposite party shall first, in his or her own behalf, introduce testimony of himself or herself or some other person concerning such transaction or communication, and then only in respect to such transaction or communication of which testimony is so given or in respect to matters to which such testimony relates. And no stockholder, officer or trustee of a corporation in its behalf or interest, and no stockholder, officer or trustee of a corporation from, through or under whom a party derives the party's interest or title, shall be so examined, except as aforesaid.

Application of a statute to a set of facts is a question of law that we review independently. See State v. Vennemann, 180 Wis. 2d 81, 93, 508 N.W.2d 404 (1993). In applying the statute to the facts here, we do so with the knowledge that recent case law expresses disdain for the deadman's statute, and requires courts to construe it narrowly and restrict its application whenever possible. See Havlicek/Fleisher Enters., Inc. v. Bridgeman, 788 F. Supp. 389 (E.D. Wis. 1992).

It is undisputed that the statute precludes James from testifying about any actual communications with Cynthia regarding the agreement, and precludes him from testifying about the transaction of executing or entering into the agreement because James certainly stands to benefit from the agreement. However, the parties dispute whether the statute precludes James from making any reference to the agreement at all. The trial court ruled that the statute did not preclude James from testifying as to the preparation of the agreement, his retention of the agreement, or his search for the original of the agreement. The trial court explained that this testimony did not constitute any personal communication or transaction with Cynthia and, therefore, was not barred by the statute.

We agree with the trial court's interpretation. Wisconsin case law clearly provides that the deadman's statute must be strictly construed and, whenever possible, not be applied to bar testimony. See Hunzinger Constr. Co. v. Granite Resources Corp., 196 Wis. 2d 327, 538 N.W.2d 804 (Ct. App. 1995). The trial court's construction and narrowing of James's testimony conforms with the current treatment of the deadman's statute. Limiting James's testimony to his actions with respect to drafting, retaining and searching for the document is consistent with the plain language of the statute and a narrow application. The trial court did employ the deadman's statute to preclude James from testifying "to communication or transactions had between [him] and Cynthia prior to, at the execution of, or subsequent to the execution of the agreement." The distinction drawn by the trial court clearly gives proper effect to the statute itself, and the case law disfavoring its application.

The Estate contends that allowing James to testify in such a manner implied the existence of the agreement which, in effect, allowed James's testimony to operate as authenticating the document. The Estate suggests then that the trial court relied on James's testimony to allow admission of the agreement. The trial court, however, based its admission of the document on the testimony of Daniel, relying exclusively on Daniel's testimony to establish that James and Cynthia signed the originals of the agreement on December 21, 1985.

The Estate contends that because Daniel had a criminal record and because he could not attest that the agreement produced exactly matched the one he had reviewed in December 1985, Daniel's testimony could not serve to authenticate the document. We disagree. The trial court clearly noted its consideration of Daniel's criminal history in assessing the credibility of his testimony:

> With regard to Daniel Stocking's testimony, the court is, of course, aware of his criminal history and considers how it may impact the credibility of his testimony in this case. However, again the court finds the testimony of Daniel Stocking to be credible, as well. Indeed, if this was, again, an effort to support his brother by perjured testimony, the court would expect testimony from Daniel that was much stronger, much more affirmative. There would be no testimony from Daniel to the effect that he did not closely read the document and, therefore, cannot testify that Exhibit 1 is substantively, absolutely the same as the document that he notarized in December of 1985 but, rather, "appears" to be substantially the same. Were Daniel Stocking attempting to perpetuate a fraud by perjured testimony, it would be, in the court's judgment, testimony with a great deal more clarity and less ambiguity.

The trial court's ruling depended in part on this and other credibility determinations. Such determinations are more appropriately left to the trial court. See Chapman v. State, 69 Wis. 2d 581, 583, 230 N.W.2d 824, 825 (1975) (The trial court is the arbiter of the credibility of the witnesses and its findings will not be overturned on appeal unless they are inherently or patently incredible or in conflict with the uniform course of nature or with fully established or conceded facts.). The trial court's findings are reasonable, and supported by the evidence. Therefore, we will not overturn its credibility determinations.

B. Status of Challenged Document.

The trial court determined that the challenged document was a valid marital property agreement. The Estate argues that the trial court erred in reaching this determination, and that the document should not affect the classification of income because it does not comply with certain statutory requirements. First, the Estate claims that the document, which was titled "Individual Income Agreement," cannot be construed to be a Unilateral Statement as set forth under Wis. Stat. § 766.59 because the document purports to be an agreement between the spouses, rather than an individual declaration.

Wis. Stat. § 766.59(1) provides, "A spouse may unilaterally execute a written statement which classifies the income attributable to all or certain of that spouse's property other than marital property as individual property." We agree with the Estate that the document cannot be construed to be a unilateral statement under this statute. It clearly involved an agreement by both spouses rather than individual action. However, the trial court did not construe the agreement to be a unilateral statement. Rather, it found that the Agreement constituted a marital property agreement.

Second, the Estate contends the trial court erred in finding that the Agreement created an enforceable marital property agreement pursuant to Wis. Stat. § 766.58. The trial court's decision on this issue provides in pertinent part:

> Wis. Stat. § 766.58 … clearly states, "A marital property agreement shall be a document signed by both spouses." That's what happened here. Both spouses have signed the document.
>
> In analyzing the document under Section 766.58 …, the court must find … that the document was signed by both spouses. This is supported by the uncontradicted testimony of Daniel Stocking which the court has previously found to be credible. While the court finds that there is consideration by reason of the mutual benefits to each party in retaining their [sic] own income, nevertheless, the court does note that "a marital property agreement is enforceable without consideration".
>
> The court further finds that the agreement does not violate any public policy or a statute imposing a criminal penalty under Section 766.58 (3) (h). Subsection 6 sets forth the burden the proponent (petitioner) must carry in order to invalidate the marital property agreement. The court is satisfied that the evidence fails to support the petitioner in this regard. The court finds no evidence that the agreement was unconscionable, sub 6(a), no indication that it was executed by the deceased involuntarily, sub 6(b), nor has the petitioner established that there was a failure to fairly and reasonably disclose James Stocking's property or financial obligations, nor that Cynthia did not have notice of James' property or financial obligations, sub 6(c) (1) (2).

The Estate argues that the trial court's findings are erroneous because the document did not comply with certain statutory requirements. Specifically, the Estate argues that the document did not make a fair and full disclosure of the spouse's financial obligations as required by Wis. Stat. § 766.68(6)(c). The trial court, as noted above, found otherwise, and that finding is supported by the record. The record demonstrates that Cynthia was fully knowledgeable about the couple's assets and financial status. She assisted in preparation of joint income tax returns, had access to James's checking account, and was fully aware of James's parents' comfortable financial status. The record also provides that Cynthia served as James's secretary and was familiar with his document filing system.

The Estate also protests the trial court's validation of the document, arguing that the document does not contain any words of agreement, but rather uses the word "wish." The Estate continues, therefore, that the document, without any further action, cannot constitute a valid marital property agreement. We are not persuaded. The circumstances in this case are unique. The evidence presented to the trial court demonstrated that the document was created shortly after James's father's death and shortly before the enactment of the marital property law. James's mother was elderly and James wanted to protect future income generated by his gifted and inherited property. Thus, he drafted the document challenged in this case. It is not unreasonable, given the circumstances presented here, that the document failed to comply with all of what would become the requirements of the marital property law under Wis. Stat. § 766.58. Given the mutuality of the document, and the evidence that both James's and Cynthia's individual ownership of inheritances and income derived therefrom was included, the document could reasonably be interpreted to constitute a marital property agreement. Accordingly, we conclude that the trial court's determination was reasonable and we affirm the order.

C. Credibility Determinations.

The Estate also challenges several of the trial court's credibility determinations. This challenge focuses both on the trial court's finding that James's and Daniel's testimony was credible, and on the trial court's finding that Cynthia had access to James's home. We conclude that the trial court's findings of fact are not clearly erroneous. See Wis. Stat. § 805.17(2).

We have already set forth the trial court's reasoning relative to finding Daniel's testimony credible. We have no basis to overturn that credibility assessment. The trial court similarly found James's testimony to be credible. The trial court recognized that James had a substantial interest in the outcome of the ruling, but found that the creation of the Agreement was consistent with the history of the relationship between James and Cynthia, and James's anticipated substantial inheritance. The trial court ruled:

> Were this entire scenario of the preparation of the Agreement, its execution and the subsequent loss of the originals a total effort to fabricate, it indeed would be a bad one. If this was an effort to fabricate, the court would expect to be looking at a clear, unilateral document, literally conforming to the requirements of Sec. 766.59 W.S. There would be no necessity or showing of the mutuality set out in the

Exhibit 1. The trial court's assessment of credibility was reasonable. Why go to the trouble of creating an imperfect mutual document, when one could create a perfectly conforming unilateral statement?

The trial court's findings in this regard were also supported in part by the evidence submitted relative to Cynthia's access to James's home and certain missing items that were discovered at Cynthia's apartment. During the trial, Cynthia's sister, Corrine Hein, testified that certain Wedgewood china plates and a wooden salad bowl had been in Cynthia's Milwaukee apartment since Cynthia had separated from James in October 1994. James had earlier testified that the plates and bowl were in their normal places in his home just before he left on vacation on January 19, 1997, but that he noticed that these items were missing when he returned from vacation on February 2, 1997. James stated that he next saw the missing items when he visited Cynthia's apartment in April 1997, to do a property inventory. After Hein's testimony contradicting his, James introduced a videotape of Christmas dinner in 1996 at James's home, which showed the missing Wedgewood plates on his dining room table. The trial court found that the videotape supported James's testimony. The trial court also found that the videotape supported the inference that Cynthia had recently accessed James's residence and was taking items from the residence, which arguably could have included the original marital property agreement.

This evidence supported James's testimony, thereby lending credibility to James's version. The trial court's findings are not clearly erroneous. Therefore, we affirm the order.

IV. PUBLIC POLICY LIMITATIONS ON TESTAMENTARY FREEDOM

A. CONDITIONAL BEQUESTS

Not only can testators use wills to determine the next owners of their property, they can also use wills to impose preconditions that must be met before the devise becomes effective. In 1889, for example, the Wisconsin Supreme Court ruled that the recently renamed Downer College* in Milwaukee did not qualify for a $5000 devise in

* Downer College merged with Milwaukee College in 1895, under the name, Milwaukee-Downer College. In 1964, the college merged with Lawrence College of Appleton, Wisconsin,

the will of Alcy E. M. Downer, which was conditioned on the trustees of the Wisconsin Female College renaming their school, Downer College, after her late husband, Jason Downer who had been a justice of the Wisconsin Supreme Court from 1864 to 1867. Justice Downer, who died in 1883, had left the bulk of his estate to the college.

Mrs. Downer's will also stipulated that the name change had to occur in her lifetime. Even though the trustees did change the name to Downer College, the change did not take effect until after Mrs. Downer's death. In an opinion by Downer's former colleague, Chief Justice Orasmus Cole, the Court ruled that the college had not met the condition and that the $5,000 would go to her heirs instead. Even though Mrs. Downer had never informed the trustees of the bequest, and even though the trustees acted quickly to change the name after learning about the devise following her death, the court refused to give the matter what it termed "a liberal construction." *Merrill v. Wisconsin Female College,* 74 Wis. 415 (1889).

Unlike the case with Mrs. Downer's will, conditions are also used to control the conduct of the living after the testator's death. Although such efforts at "dead hand" control are frequently criticized, the conditions imposed will usually be enforced, so long as they do not run afoul of any serious public policy concerns. In the past, such restrictions have often involved marital and religious matters. While conditions absolutely prohibiting marriage or requiring divorce are usually considered to be unenforceable, restrictions requiring devisees to participate in a particular religion, marry someone of a particular faith, or marry or remain married to a particular individual are typically upheld.

A related issue is whether or not an individual has the right to order the destruction of his or her property after death. The general rule is that he or she does not have such a right, as the destruction of valuable property, while within the rights of an owner during life, constitutes "waste," once the owner is no longer around to participate in the destruction. See, for example, *Eyerman v. Mercantile Trust Co.*, 524 S.W.2d 210 (Mo. App. 1975), a case in which the court enjoyed the destruction of the testator's mansion in the Central West End of St. Louis. It does not appear that this issue has been addressed in a Wisconsin reported opinion, although, in *Voss v. State*, 204 Wis. 432; 236 N.W. 128 (1931), the state supreme court rejected the defendant's argument that as the owner of a house he could not be convicted of arson merely for setting fire to his own property. (In *Voss,* the torched home was occupied by tenants

---

and its Milwaukee campus was sold to the University of Wisconsin-Milwaukee.

who were behind in their rent payments; Voss was ultimately sentenced to 12-14 years in prison for his acts.)

Litigation involving conditional devises has been relatively rare in Wisconsin. The following three cases illustrate the approach taken by the Wisconsin Supreme Court over the course of its history.

Webster v. Morris

Supreme Court of Wisconsin
66 Wis. 366, 28 N.W. 353 (1886)

[*Webster v. Morris* is a lengthy and complex case involving a variety of legal issues. The excerpt below contains the parts of the opinion that dealt with the issue of "dead hand" control.]

This action was commenced in the circuit court, for the construction of the last will and testament of Hiram W. Webster, deceased, and for the advice and directions of the court upon certain questions submitted, and for such other or further instructions thereon respecting the execution of the trusts thereby imposed as may seem proper. The will was duly executed **[on November 28, 1883]**, and is in the words and figures following, to wit:

"I, Hiram W. Webster, of the village of Omro, Winnebago county, state of Wisconsin, being of sound mind and memory, and mindful of the uncertainties of human life, do make, publish, and declare this my last will and testament, hereby revoking all former wills, bequests, and devises by me made.

"Fifth. I give, devise, and bequeath out of my estate not hereinbefore disposed of, to Hiram W. Morris, my grandson, and son of Delphina and M. D. Morris, the sum of ten thousand dollars; said sum to be invested and put to use, and the interest arising therefrom, or so much as said child's guardian and my executors, hereinafter mentioned, may consider proper and necessary, be used for the support and education of said child, and at his majority the unexpended interest from said principal sum be paid him, and the interest on said sum annually thereafter until he arrives at the age of thirty years, at which time I will and direct that my executors pay to said Hiram Webster one half of said ten thousand dollars, and one thousand dollars each year thereafter, together with all interest earned, until the balance of said ten thousand dollars hereby willed to him has been paid: provided, however, that said Hiram

Webster has in the meantime learned some useful trade, business, or profession, and is of good moral character, my executors to determine whether said child has fully complied with said proviso before any payments from the principal sum are made to him.

"Sixth. **[This provision of the will contained an identical devise to Edward Morris, the brother of Webster Morris.]**

"Seventh. I will and direct that in case of the death of either child without leaving an heir, and before the said legacies are paid to them or either of them, that the surviving one shall be considered the first heir and have the share of the deceased one, under the same restrictions and upon the same conditions provided for said deceased one's share; but, in case of the death of both without leaving an heir, all remaining payments and legacies to revert back to my estate, and to be expended by my executors for charitable purposes, or given to any of my heirs who are in need or not in very comfortable circumstances, as to my executors seems fit and proper.

***

The court found that the testator died May 14, 1884; that Louisa M. Webster was the widow of the testator; that Edward Morris died before the testator; that Hiram W. Morris was an infant grandson of the testator, and his sole next of kin or heir at law; that M. D. Morris was his father.

***

As conclusions of law the court found, in effect, that the real estate did not pass by the will, but descended to the surviving grandson; that the executors were to retain the legacies mentioned in the fifth, sixth, and seventh paragraphs of the will in trust, but that said grandson had a vested interest therein; that their discretionary power over the same, mentioned in the fifth and sixth paragraphs, and the contingent disposition mentioned in the seventh, in case of the death of both grandsons, were so vague and indefinite as to be wholly void, and hence such trust fund would, in case of the death of both of them, go to the executors; that the residuary provisions in the fifteenth paragraph were void for uncertainty; that the other bequests were valid; and that the personal estate which did not pass by the will should be distributed under the statutes.

From the judgment entered thereon the executors appeal, and the grandson, Hiram W. Morris, and his father, M. D. Morris, also appeal.

CASSODAY, J.

***

3. The grandson Edward Morris, mentioned in the sixth paragraph of the will, having died without issue and before the testator, died "without leaving an heir," within the meaning of the seventh paragraph of the will; and the bequest, which would otherwise have gone to him under the sixth paragraph of the will, now goes, under the seventh paragraph of the will, to the surviving grandson Hiram W. Morris, under the same restrictions and upon the same conditions as to him, if valid, as was provided for said Edward had he continued to live; that is to say, said Hiram W. so takes what would otherwise go to said Edward under the same restrictions and upon the same conditions, if valid, as are applicable to the bequest to said Hiram W. under the fifth paragraph of the will.

In other words, it is the same, in effect, as though the amount named in the fifth paragraph had been twenty thousand dollars instead of ten. So construed, the words "first heir," in the seventh paragraph, had the effect of carrying the bequest to Edward, on his death, over to Hiram W. The result is that $20,000 of said estate is to be invested and put to use, and the interest arising therefrom, or so much as said Hiram W.'s guardian and the executors named in the will may consider proper and necessary, be used for his support and education; and at his majority the unexpended interest from said $20,000 be paid to him; and also the interest on said sum annually thereafter, until he arrives at the age of thirty years; at which time one half of the $20,000 is to be paid over to him, and $2,000 each year thereafter, together with all interest earned, until the balance of said $20,000 be paid to him; unless the payment of such principal sum is defeated by his failure to perform the conditions therein provided, which will now be considered.

Such trusts were in contemplation of the statutes, and hence permissible, even as to real estate. Sec. 2081, R. S.; Scott v. West, 63 Wis. 529, 24 N.W. 161. They were certainly permissible as to personal property. The bequests were vested upon the principles stated, and hence not subject to the doctrine of perpetuities or remoteness.

4. The condition annexed to the bequest is that "provided, however, that said Hiram Webster Morris has in the meantime learned some useful trade, business, or profession, and is of good moral character; my executors to determine whether said child has fully complied with said proviso before any payments from the principal sum are made to him." The argument against the validity of this condition is that it is in terrorem, or against public policy. The authorities, however, seem to be strongly the other way. This is on the theory that every person has a legal right to dispose of his own property as he sees fit.

Thus, conditions annexed to a devise or bequest from a husband to a wife, or a wife to a husband, to be held only so long as he or she remains unmarried, are quite common, and have frequently been held valid. **...** So, conditions that the devisee or legatee shall not marry prior to arriving at a particular age, without the consent of a person named, have been held valid. **...** The age named must, of course, be reasonable; as, for instance, twenty-one years of age. But a condition annexed to a devise or bequest from parent to child in absolute restraint of marriage, has been held void, as against public policy. **....** The same has been held where the devise or bequest was to a widow from her husband, and there was no gift over in case of breach of the condition. **... [Citations from outside of Wisconsin omitted.]**

In Cooke v. Turner, 14 Sim. 493, the will contained a gift over in case the legatee should dispute the will or the testator's competency to make it, or should not confirm it when required by the trustees; and the condition was held valid.

In Dickson's Trust, 1 Sim. Ch. 37, the testator, by a codicil, annexed a condition to the bequest to his daughter to the effect that she should not take in case she became a nun, which she did; and it was held by Lord CRANWORTH that the condition was lawful, notwithstanding there was no gift over on its breach.

That case was followed in Hodgson v. Halford, L. R. 11 Ch. Div. 959, S. C. 32 Eng. (Moak) 918, where the condition annexed to the legacy was, in effect, that it should be forfeited in case the legatee married any person who was not a born Jew, professing the Jewish religion; and it was held valid, and not against public policy. It was there said that all the authorities holding the other way were "cases in which the condition was unquestionably against public morality, and it was on that ground that the court declined to give effect to it."

In the very recent case of Delany v. Delany, L. R. (Ireland), 15 Ch. Div. 55, the will provided: "If my said son Andrew shall in all respects conduct himself to the satisfaction of my executors, I bequeath to him a sum of 2,000 pounds, to be paid when my son Henry shall attain (or would have attained) his age of twenty-one years." He also devised and bequeathed the residue of his property to his executors, upon trust for the use and benefit of all his children, including his son Andrew, in equal shares; and declared that "if it should happen that my said son Andrew shall not conduct himself in all respects to the satisfaction of my said executors, or the survivor of them, then I declare that he shall not be entitled to receive any portion of my said residuary estate; and in that case a declaration in writing signed by my said executors, or the survivors of them, of their, her, or his dissatisfaction with him, shall be conclusive evidence that he is not to receive any portion thereof, and the share to which he would otherwise be entitled shall thereupon go to, and be distributed among, my other children in equal shares." The executors who had qualified, certified that Andrew had not conducted himself to their satisfaction, and he made no denial of his misconduct. The condition was held valid.

In Vidal v. Girard's Ex'rs, 2 How. 127, it was held, in effect, that the provision in Mr. Girard's will excluding all ecclesiastics, missionaries, and ministers, of any sort, from holding or exercising any station or duty in the college, or even visiting the same, with the limitation of the instruction to be given to the scholars to pure morality, general benevolence, a love of truth, sobriety, and industry, were not so derogatory and hostile to the Christian religion as to make the devise void, under the constitution and laws of Pennsylvania.

It was recently held, in effect, in Maryland, that a bequest dependent upon the condition that the legatee should withdraw from the priesthood of the Roman Catholic Church, or membership of any order or society connected with such church, or refrain from forming any such connections, was held to be valid, and not against public policy, on the ground that whatever might be thought of the opinions of the testator, or his prejudices, the law recognized his right to make the enjoyment of his bounty dependent upon such conditions. Barnum v. Mayor of Baltimore, 62 Md. 275.

So, it has recently been held that a bequest on condition that the beneficiary shall be educated in the Roman Catholic faith, is not uncertain, impossible, nor against public policy, nor unconstitutional. Magee v. O'Neill, 45 Am. Rep. 765.

Here the principal sum bequeathed is to remain in the possession of the executors until the legatee becomes thirty years of age. His right to it at that time, and thereafter, is made dependent upon his being of good moral character and having in the meantime learned some useful trade, business, or profession, in the judgment of the executors. Without committing ourselves to the doctrine of all the cases cited, especially such as may be regarded as touching matters of conscience, we must hold that the clause in question is capable of performance by any person of ordinary intelligence, and not contrary to public policy. It is designed to put the beneficiary under wholesome restraint. It is not in contravention of good morals, nor any law, nor any matter of conscience, but is promotive of good moral character.

It is in no sense indefinite nor uncertain. It is left to the determination of executors; but that does not give them the right to exercise an arbitrary power of exclusion, but only a reasonable exercise of judgment. Manifestly, the bequest to Hiram W. Morris is not to be held void on the ground of the probability or improbability of the contingency on which it is limited to take effect. Sec. 2050, R. S.; Scott v. West, 63 Wis. 589, 25 N.W. 18. The condition must therefore be held legal and binding. ...

In re Paulson's Will

Supreme Court of Wisconsin
127 Wis. 612, 107 N.W. 484 (1906)

This action was brought for a construction of the will of Mary J. Paulson, of Cashton, Monroe county, Wisconsin, which reads as follows:

"First. After the payment of my just debts, funeral charges, and expenses of administration, I hereby give and bequeath to the Norwegian Home and Foreign Missionary Association the sum of four hundred ($400) dollars, to be paid by the executrix hereof in four equal annual payments.

"Second. I hereby give and bequeath to my beloved son, Peter Paulson, the sum of fifteen hundred ($1,500) dollars, to be paid to him by said executrix in fifteen annual payments. This bequest is made conditional that my son attend the regular meetings of worship of the Emanuel Church near the village of Cashton, Wisconsin, when not sick in bed, or prevented by accident or other unavoidable occurrence.

"Third. In case my said son should die before the expiration of fifteen years, the remainder of said fifteen hundred ($1,500) dollars shall be paid by the said executrix to his children share and share alike.

"Fourth. If my son does not try in good faith to comply with my wishes in carrying out the above condition upon which his legacy is based, in that case I give and bequeath said fifteen hundred ($1,500) dollars to the Norwegian Lutheran Home and Foreign Missionary Association, to be paid by my said executrix in fifteen equal annual payments, commencing one year after the last payment mentioned in the first clause of this will.

"Fifth. I hereby give, devise, and bequeath all the rest, residue, and remainder of my property and estates of whatsoever kind unto my beloved daughter, Matilda Paulson, with whom I have lived and from whom I have received such thoughtful consideration and tender care in my declining years.

"Sixth. I hereby nominate, constitute, and appoint my beloved daughter Matilda sole executrix of this my last will and testament without bond, and authorize and empower her to settle, compound, or compromise any claim in favor of or against my said estate.

"In witness whereof I have hereunto set my hand and seal this 11th day of September, 1903.

"MARY her X mark J. PAULSON. [Seal.]"

Appellant applied to the county court of Monroe county asking that the bequest to him be construed, and the court held that the conditions attached to such bequest were void. Executrix appealed to the circuit court. Appellant moved to dismiss appeal on the ground that the executrix could not appeal, which motion was denied. The circuit court found that the conditions attached to the bequest to appellant were valid, and directed judgment accordingly, which was entered, from which this appeal is taken.

KERWIN, J.

1. The question raised by the first assignment of error is whether the circuit court erred in not granting the motion of appellant to dismiss the appeal of the executrix from the order and judgment entered by the county court. It is plain from a reference to sec. 4031, Stats. 1898, that the executrix, Matilda Paulson, was an aggrieved party within the meaning of the statute, and as such entitled to appeal. This question was directly passed upon by this court in the late case of McKenney v. Minahan, 119 Wis. 651, 97 N.W. 489, and it was there held that an executor or administrator is an aggrieved party within the meaning of the statute, and has a right to appeal. The court below, therefore, was right in denying the motion to dismiss the appeal.

2. The court found, in effect, that the will was duly executed, and that the testatrix during her lifetime was a member of the Emanuel Church, two and one-half miles from Cashton, Wisconsin, and contributed to its support, which church was known as the "Moen Church;" that appellant, Peter Paulson, was also a member of such church, and that the testatrix paid his membership dues in the church during the year prior to her death; that there is no society known as the "Norwegian Home and Foreign Missionary Association," but that there is a society known as "The Home and Foreign Missions of the United Norwegian Lutheran Church of America," and that such society was connected with the Emanuel Church two and one-half miles southwest from Cashton; that the testatrix contributed to this society, and stated during her lifetime that she was going to make a gift to it; and, as conclusions of law, that the testatrix intended to make a bequest of $1,500 to Peter Paulson upon the condition that he attend the regular meetings of Emanuel Church two and one-half miles southwest from Cashton, known as the "Moen Church," when not sick in bed or prevented by

accident or other unavoidable occurrence; that by the fourth clause of said will the testatrix intended to and did give the bequest over to the Home and Foreign Missions of the United Norwegian Lutheran Church of America; and that the conditions annexed to the bequest to Peter Paulson in the second clause of the will were valid.

The errors complained of by appellant under these findings of fact and conclusions of law involve the following propositions: First. Whether the findings of fact are borne out by the will and the evidence. Second. Whether the will vested in Peter Paulson an absolute title to the gift at the death of the testatrix. Third. Whether the testatrix gave, or intended to give, the Peter Paulson bequest over to the Home and Foreign Missions of the United Norwegian Lutheran Church of America. Fourth. Whether the conditions annexed to the bequest to Peter Paulson are valid.

After a careful examination of the record we are convinced that the findings of fact are fully supported by the evidence, and therefore shall spend no time upon this branch of the case. We are unable to agree with counsel for appellant that the will vested absolute title to the $1,500 legacy in Peter Paulson. The first and most important question for determination is, What was the intention of the testatrix? and we think it clear from the terms of the will that it was her intention that the legacy should pass subject to the conditions specified.

The provision that, if Peter Paulson should not in good faith try to comply with the terms imposed upon him, then and in such case the bequest should go over to the society named in the will, to be paid by the executrix in fifteen equal annual payments, commencing five years after the death of the testatrix, makes manifest her intention that the legacy was upon condition attached to such gift, as found by the court below, and that the control and management of the legacy should remain with the executrix until the condition should be performed, or, in case of Peter's death during the fifteen years, the unpaid portion of such bequest should go to his children, share and share alike.

It is true that legacies payable at a future time certain and not subject to condition precedent are vested, while, on the other hand, legacies made payable on conditions which may never happen and placed in the possession and under the control of a trustee and subject to condition precedent are contingent. Scott v. West, 63 Wis. 529, 566, 24 N.W. 161, 25 N.W. 18. And, when a future time for the payment of a legacy is defined by the will, the legacy may be vested or contingent as may appear to have been the intention of the testator upon a proper construction of the will. Stark v. Conde, 100 Wis. 633, 76 N.W. 600, and cases cited. But in all cases the intention of the testator as expressed in the will must govern. And it is quite clear in the case before us that the testatrix intended the conditions should attach to the gift and defeat it upon failure on the part of the legatee to perform.

For the purpose of enabling the executrix to carry out the trust in accordance with the terms of the will, the testatrix manifestly intended that possession and control of the bequest to Peter Paulson should remain in the executrix during the period necessary for the execution of the trust. Scott v. West, supra. The gift over to the Home and Foreign Missions of the United Norwegian Lutheran Church of America, in case of failure of performance of conditions by Peter Paulson, is definite and certain, and the intention of the testatrix clearly was that the gift over to this society was intended, although another name was inadvertently inserted in the will. Extrinsic evidence was admissible to explain the ambiguity. Webster v. Morris, 66 Wis. 366, 28 N.W. 353; Sherwood v. Sherwood, 45 Wis. 357. It is considered that the court below was right in determining that the testatrix intended to make, and did make, the bequest to Peter Paulson upon the condition named in the will.

3. The main contention on the part of the appellant, and the one upon which he seems to rely for reversal, is to the effect that the condition attached to the bequest to Peter Paulson requiring him to "attend the regular meetings of worship of the Emanuel Church near the village of Cashton when not sick in bed or prevented by accident or other unavoidable occurrence," is void for the reasons (1) that it infringes art. I, sec. 18, Const.; (2) that it is void for uncertainty and indefiniteness.

Under the first head it is insisted that the condition referred to is repugnant to the constitutional provision that "the right of every man to worship Almighty God according to the dictates of his own conscience shall never be infringed, nor shall any man be compelled to attend, erect, or support any place of worship or to maintain any ministry against his consent, nor shall any control of or interference with the right of conscience be permitted. . . ."

It is not easy to see how the conditions attached to the will in any manner infringe this constitutional provision. The condition in question is neither against public policy nor contrary to law, nor can it be said that it interferes with the right of the legatee to worship God according to the dictates of his own conscience. The testatrix had the right to dispose of her property in such lawful manner as she saw fit, and make such person as she desired the object of her bounty, and in so doing attach to the bequest any lawful condition. She attached to the bequest in question a condition that the legatee attend the regular meetings of her church and the church to which he also belonged, so far as the evidence shows.

We are unable to see that this condition contained anything against public policy or was unlawful. The testatrix has the right to so dispose of her property, and the legatee might accept or reject the gift voluntarily, without restriction upon his will or coercion of his conscience. In Barry v. Order of C. K. 119 Wis. 362, 96 N.W. 797, where the articles of incorporation and the constitution of a benefit society organized for the sole benefit of the members of the Roman Catholic Church provided that none but practical Catholics could be admitted, and must remain such in order to participate in the benefits, the applicant, having agreed that upon failure to conform strictly to the constitution he should forfeit all right of membership and benefits, afterwards failed to comply with the conditions, and was excommunicated and ceased to be a Catholic, and it was held that all liability on a benefit certificate ceased, and that the provisions mentioned were not contrary to public policy, and did not interfere with any rights of conscience and imposed no religious test within the meaning of the constitution.

The cases appear to be quite uniform on the subject, and hold that such provisions are not unlawful or against public policy, or any infringement of the constitutional provisions referred to. In Magee v. O'Neill, 19 S.C. 170, 45 Am. Rep. 765, where the bequest was on condition that the beneficiary be educated in the Roman Catholic faith, the court said:

"The power of disposition is general. The power to give includes the right to withhold or to fix the terms of gift, no matter how whimsical or capricious they may be, only provided they do not in any way violate the law. Mr. Magee, in his lifetime, could have given money to educate his granddaughter at a particular school, or he could have withheld it at his pleasure.

Suppose he had entered into a covenant with Elizabeth or her mother that, if she was educated at a particular school named and under certain religious influences, he would, upon her attaining twenty-one years, pay to her $5,000. We suppose that, if she were not so educated, she could not go into the court and recover the money. Suppose, further, that before the time for payment arrived John Magee had died; would that strengthen her claim to recover the money against his personal representatives? We are unable to see any material difference in regard to the necessity of complying with the terms imposed between this supposed case and that of a voluntary gift by will."

The provisions in Girard's Will (Vidal v. Girard's Ex'rs, 2 HOW 127), excluding all ecclesiastics, missionaries, and ministers, of any sort, from holding or exercising any station or duty in the college, or visiting it, or the limitation of the instructions to be given to the scholars to pure morality, general benevolence, sobriety, and industry, were not so derogatory and hostile to the Christian religion as to render the devise void; and in Barnum v. Baltimore, 62 Md. 275, the court held that a devise on condition that the devisee withdraw from the priesthood of the church, or from any society connected therewith, was not unlawful.

In In re Knox (1889) 23 L. R. (Ir.) 542, it was held that a gift to a son on condition that he should marry a Protestant wife, the daughter of Protestant parents, who have always been Protestants, was held to be valid. But it is unnecessary to pursue further the authorities upon this subject. We think it is well established that the condition is not contrary to public policy and does not infringe the constitutional provision. Barry v. Order of C. K. 119 Wis. 362, 96 N.W. 797; Vidal v. Girard's Ex'rs, supra; Barnum v. Baltimore, supra; Dickson's Trust, 1 Sim. (n.s.) 37; Spencer v. See, 5 Redf. 442; In re Knox, supra; Mazurkiewicz v. St. Adelbertus Aid Soc. 127 Mich. 145, 86 N.W. 543; Franta v. Bohemian R. C. C. U. 164 Mo. 304, 63 S.W. 1100.

Nor do we think the contention that the condition is void for uncertainty and indefiniteness tenable. It is said there is nothing to indicate when the attendance at church is to commence, nor how long it is to continue, nor who is to judge whether Peter Paulson has attended the "regular meetings" of the church named, and, if he has not attended, who is to be the judge whether or not he was "sick in bed." But we think all of these questions are properly for the determination of the court in case judicial determination should be necessary.

It does not seem that they are incapable of judicial determination, or that the conditions are so uncertain and indefinite that a court could not determine whether they had been performed. The church is designated. The regular meetings required to be attended are specified. And, while the period of time of attendance is not stated, we think it a proper matter of judicial determination under all the terms of the will. It is reasonable to suppose, in view of the fact that the will provides fifteen annual payments, that the conditions upon which these payments are based should be performed during that period of time at least.

It was also suggested at the bar that the proviso for paying the whole amount over to the society in case of default on Peter Paulson's part was indefinite, since the whole amount could not be paid if a portion had been paid to Peter in annual installments before default. We think the will must be construed to mean that such portion as remained unpaid at time of default should be paid over to the society, and that the performance of the conditions should be continued during the fifteen years designated for the payment of the legacy.

In construing this clause, as in all other questions of construction, the intention of the testatrix must be sought for, and it is very obvious that the inducement for the bequest to Peter was that he be and continue to be a practical member of her church and a regular attendant, not for a limited time, but continually, at least for the period covered by the annual payments; and it is not reasonable to suppose that she intended that payments should continue in default of the performance of the conditions, the main object of the gift obviously being that he continue such attendance.

Moreover, the plain meaning of the language that he attend the regular meetings without limitation as to time must be held to mean, under the circumstances of the case, to require such attendance during the period designated for the payment of the bequest.

We think, therefore, that it was the intention of the testatrix that Peter should continue to perform the conditions of the will during the period of fifteen years while the bequest was being paid to him, and that, if during said time he should fail to do so, the remaining portion of the $1,500 should be paid over to the society named in the will in the manner designated, and, if Peter should die before the expiration of fifteen years, the remainder should be paid to his children, share and share alike. We are therefore of the opinion that the judgment below should be affirmed.

B. RESTRICTIONS ON THE RIGHT TO MARRY

In re Estate of Heller

Supreme Court of Wisconsin
39 Wis. 2d 318, 159 N.W.2d 82 (1968)

This is a proceeding for construction of the will of Lena Heller, who died testate on July 21, 1966. Lena Heller had five daughters, including Katie Mau who lived with her family in the first-floor apartment of a duplex building where Lena Heller occupied the second floor.

On April 8, 1965, Katie Mau commenced a divorce action against her husband, Willard Mau. That action was tried before Judge (now Justice) Robert W. Hansen on April 4, 1966. On May 4, 1966, Katie Mau was granted a divorce on the ground of cruel and inhuman treatment.

On September 23, 1965, the testatrix had executed her will in which she provided that the residue of her estate be left in equal parts to four daughters, or to five in the event

Katie Mau was married to and living with her husband, Willard, at the time of the testatrix's death. Specifically, Article V of the will provided in part:

". . . I intentionally omit from any devise or bequest my daughter, Katie Mau, of Milwaukee, Wisconsin, unless, at the time of my death, she is married to and living with her husband, Willard Mau. If, at that time, she is married to and living with the said Willard Mau, then then [sic] the said Katie Mau shall be included with my other daughters according to the terms applicable thereto as described in this article and shall share equally with them."

Article III of the will also provided:

"I specifically bequeath to my son-in-law, Willard Mau, of Milwaukee, Wisconsin, the sum of One Thousand ($1,000.00) Dollars, and to my granddaughter, Linda Mau, of Milwaukee, Wisconsin, also the sum of One Thousand ($1,000.00) Dollars. If either should predecease me, then the said bequest shall lapse and revert to the residue of my estate to be disposed of according to the terms of Article V herein. In any event, however, the said bequests described in this Article III herein shall become effective only if, at the time of my death, my daughter, Katie Mau, wife and mother respectively of said legatees, shall not be married or living with the said Willard Mau."

Following the demise of the testatrix, Katie Mau petitioned the court for a construction of the will claiming that the provisions relating to the maintenance of her marital state were contrary to public policy and invalid. The trial court held the provisions valid and Katie Mau appeals.

Wilkie, J. One issue is raised on this appeal: Is a testamentary gift, conditioned on the legatee being married to and living with the legatee's named husband on the date of the death of the testatrix, void as against public policy?

Both Article III and Article V are clear and definite; they contain no ambiguity that requires interpretation. The testatrix's intent is clear; she is merely making three conditional legacies, one to her daughter Katie Mau if she is married to and living with Willard Mau at the time of the testatrix's death, one to Willard Mau, and another to Katie Mau's minor daughter, Linda, if Willard is in fact divorced from Katie at the testatrix's death.

Appellant contends that either or both of these provisions constitute an unreasonable restraint on marriage and as such are against public policy and void. Appellant's argument is based on the idea that an unreasonable restraint on marriage can be one which not only inhibits marriage but also compels the continuance of an involuntary marital relationship.

The trial court noted this was the first time he had been confronted with a question about a provision in a will "in which a legacy is conditioned on the continuance of a marriage." We find no Wisconsin cases on the validity of such a provision. Two Wisconsin cases have dealt generally with the topic of testamentary restraints on marriage.

McMichael v. Peterman, (1909), 140 Wis. 589, 123 N. W. 262, involved a will provision which gave the residue of an estate to all of the nieces of the testatrix who were unmarried at a certain date in the future. The appellants, married nieces of the testatrix, claimed that the provision was contrary to public policy because it encouraged unmarried nieces to refrain from marriage and married nieces to return to celibacy by divorce or other elimination of their spouses. The court declined to reach the public policy question, holding that the appellants were actually unaffected by the trial court's order from which they appealed.

In Estate of Hauck, (1942), 239 Wis. 421, 1 N. W. 2d 773, a will provision giving a share of the residue to the testator's daughter upon condition that she be no longer living with her present husband was upheld against the claim that it was contrary to public policy. The court reasoned that to render the provision invalid the intent of the testator to induce his daughter to leave her husband (by divorce or separation, etc.) must be clear. Such an illegal condition could not be presumed under the facts of the case.

The Restatement of the Law on Property surveys the law of testamentary provisions affecting marriage. It points out the following general rules:

(1) A condition rendering a gift contingent upon not marrying anyone is void unless clearly motivated by an intention to provide support until a marriage takes place. This invalidation results from the court's unwillingness to penalize a legatee for his failure to respect the socially undesirable attempt of the testator to use his property as a means of coercing abstention from marriage.

(2) Restraints limited as to person, group or time are valid unless the remaining sphere of permissible marriage is so small that a permitted marriage is not likely to occur. These partial restraints are valid upon the theory that guidance by parents or other donors with respect to a particular marriage is not unreasonable.

(3) Restraints on remarriage may be liberally imposed.

(4) Finally, attempts by testators to break up an already existing marriage, by conditioning a gift on divorce or separation, are invalid. If the dominant motive of the testator, however, is merely to provide support in the event of separation or marriage, the condition is valid.

Thus the Restatement does not deal directly with a situation such as that presented by the instant case. Appellant has not directed the court to any authority that has held a provision such as those before us invalid. Appellant's argument that the provision in Article V in effect discourages divorce, which has been declared to be good public policy (viz., public policy demands an end to intolerable marriages) regarding the marriage of Katie Mau, is not persuasive. The Restatement points out that the existence of statutes which permit divorce or separation of married persons is not an indication of public policy favoring provisions that encourage divorce. Likewise, statutes allowing divorce should not be indicative of a public policy that would attempt to prohibit restraints on the seeking of a divorce.

It is a familiar and well-settled principle of law that a will speaks as of the time of the death of the testator. Therefore, it would not be unreasonable to conclude that a will cannot contravene public policy until it begins to speak. Upon the death of the testatrix, there was nothing Katie Mau could do to increase or diminish the amount she was to receive under the will. Her portion (if any) was fixed absolutely as of the date of the death of the testatrix. It was Katie's status then that determined whether she was a beneficiary.

Katie Mau testified that until the death of her mother she was unaware of the questioned provisions in the will. Therefore, irrespective of the true purpose of those provisions, it is difficult to understand how they could have had any restraining effect, one way or another, on Katie's marriage. Public policy regarding restraints on marriage should only be concerned with continuing inducements and not with a provision, as here, which could never truly be a restraint. A will written and executed is merely the expression of an intention to dispose of one's property in a certain way in the future, provided one does not have a change of mind. Only when death ensues, thus making a change of mind impossible, will these expressions of future intention bring rights into existence. When, as here, those rights become absolutely fixed at death, without a continuing inducement to either do or refrain from doing some act, it is difficult to imagine how a restraint in the true sense of the word could ever arise.

As to Article III, the argument runs that since under that article Willard Mau stands to inherit $1,000 only if he is not married to or living with Katie, the article is contrary to public policy because it tends to encourage divorce. But Katie Mau does not even have an interest which is prejudiced by allowing that article to remain viable. Katie could only take under this will as a residuary legatee under Article V. Had Katie fulfilled the condition in Article V she would have an interest in having Willard's gift under Article III struck, the effect of which would be to add $1,000 to the residue. Because Katie is not a residuary legatee she, like a stranger, is without an interest sufficient to have standing to raise the issue.

Appellant contends that the Heller will attempts to penalize her for prosecuting a cause of action which a court found to be valid. Appellant urges that this situation is analogous to the situation that was before the court in Will of Keenan. In that case the court held a condition in a will, providing for the forfeiture of a legacy in case the legatee upon probable cause and in good faith contested the probate of the will, invalid and contrary to public policy. (The condition in Keenan was a continuing inducement.)

The present situation cannot be equated with that of Keenan. The fundamental right sought to be restricted in Keenan went to the very core of the integrity of the will. The court remarked that if the prohibition were allowed to stand, one could not safely ascertain whether the prohibition was that of the testator or of one exercising undue influence over him, or whether the testator himself had the mental competency to make the will. The narrow issue in Keenan should not be extended to a situation such as that present in the instant case. It is not the availability of the courts that is at issue but whether a conditional legacy is contrary to public policy. Keenan was, and the instant case is not.

If appellant is correct then almost all conditional bequests would be void as against public policy because many donees are forced to forego the exercise of legal rights as a valid condition to taking under a will. The widow whose gift is conditioned on not remarrying is giving up a legal right in exchange for that gift. Yet, the widow's condition would not ordinarily be considered violative of public policy. Judgment affirmed.

CHAPTER 6.
WILL SUBSTITUTES

The desire to avoid the probate process has motivated property owners to search for alternative ways to transfer assets to the designated next owner, either at the time of death or shortly before.

I. DONATIVE TRANSFERS IN ANTICIPATION OF DEATH

A. INTER VIVOS GIFTS

There is no more obvious way to insure that individual items of property avoid the probate process than to give them away while one is alive. There are, of course, downsides to the gifting process. First of all, gifts are, by their very nature, irreversible transfers. Property that has been given away cannot be reclaimed, i.e., there is no such thing as a "conditional gift." Secondly, for substantial gifts, there is the possibility of the federal gift tax. So long as donors give $14,000 or less (the 2013 figure) to individual donees, there are no gift taxes assessed. However, for sums in excess of this amount, there is potential for immediate tax liability, although there is also a lifetime gift tax exemption of several million dollars. If a gift is made, the property immediately belongs to the donee. If, however, there was no present donative intent and/or delivery, then the property remains part of the estate of the donor. A delivery without donative intent ordinarily creates a bailment.

APRAHAMIAN v. BROWN

Wisconsin Court of Appeals
168 Wis. 2d 776, 486 N.W.2d 37 (1992)

PER CURIAM. Edward Aprahamian appeals from a judgment dismissing his complaint against Carol Brown for the repayment of $30,700. The jury found that the money was a gift to Brown. Aprahamian argues that the verdict is not supported by the evidence and that judgment should have been entered in his favor as a matter of law on the theory of unjust enrichment. We affirm the judgment.

Aprahamian and Brown dated intermittently from 1978 until sometime in 1981. Late in 1981, Brown asked Aprahamian for a $30,000 loan for a down payment on her house. A couple months after the loan was made, and after a rift in their relationship, Brown signed a document promising to repay the money at Aprahamian's request. Brown repaid the $30,000 by the end of November 1981.

In mid-1982, the parties renewed their romantic relationship. From May 1982 through September 1983, Aprahamian made various transfers of money to Brown totaling $30,700.[*] After their relationship was terminated, Aprahamian asked Brown to sign a document promising to repay the money. That occurred in November 1985. When Brown did not respond, Aprahamian filed this action alleging that there was an oral promise to repay. The special verdict asked the jury if the transfers were gifts or loans and whether Brown benefited from the money "under such circumstances that it would be inequitable for her to retain it without paying it back."

We first address whether the jury's finding that all the transfers were gifts to Brown is supported by the evidence. The test for determining whether to change an answer in a jury's verdict is to view the evidence in the light most favorable to the verdict and sustain the verdict if supported by any credible evidence. *Bennett v. Larsen Co.*, 118 Wis.2d 681, 705, 348 N.W.2d 540, 554 (1984). Where more than one inference can be drawn from the evidence, this court must accept the inference drawn by the jury. *Id.* at 706, 348 N.W.2d at 554. We need only consider the evidence which supports the verdict. *Chart v. General Motors Corp.*, 80 Wis.2d 91, 106, 258 N.W.2d 680, 686 (1977).

The essential elements of a gift are intention to give, delivery, end of dominion by donor, and creation of dominion in the donee. *Peters v. Peters Auto Sales, Inc.*, 37 Wis.2d 346, 350, 155 N.W.2d 85, 87 (1967). The only disputed element at trial was Aprahamian's donative intent.

There was evidence of donative intent. Brown testified that she never asked Aprahamian for the various sums of money but that he offered it to her when they got into discussions of her financial troubles.

---

[*] In a footnote not reproduced here, the court reported that there were a total of eight transfers, ranging in size from $200 to $17,000. Ed.

Brown also testified that she "did not consider any of these checks loans" because "they were monies that he gave to me, offered to me when I needed them." She indicated that until their relationship was terminated, Aprahamian never pressed her to repay the money he gave her. Further, there was evidence that some of the money was transferred to enable Brown to take trips with Aprahamian. This, coupled with Brown's testimony that the two enjoyed a give and take relationship in which she offered things other than money, supports the inference that Aprahamian gave the money to Brown in an effort to win her affection.

Aprahamian points to Brown's refusal to testify that the transfers were gifts and her admission that "morally I had hoped that I would be able to repay him for the things that he did for me." However, as Brown explained, her refusal to characterize the transfers as gifts was based on her perception that it was for the jury to decide if gifts had been made. Her failure to offer testimony on the ultimate issue does not defeat the verdict. Nor does her admission of a moral obligation to repay. That simply exhibited voluntary repayment and did not negate reasonable inferences of Aprahamian's donative intent.

Finally, Aprahamian argues that there is no credible evidence that the transfers were gifts because Brown characterized them as loans in her divorce proceedings. Evidence regarding the characterization of the transfers in Brown's divorce merely impeached her testimony. It was not controlling evidence. Ultimately the case was a credibility battle between Aprahamian and Brown. The verdict reflects that the jury chose to believe Brown. The credibility of witnesses and the weight given to their testimony are matters left to the jury's judgment. *Bennett*, 118 Wis.2d at 706, 348 N.W.2d at 554. When the verdict is supported by evidence the jury could believe, it must be affirmed. *See Lawlis v. Thompson*, 137 Wis.2d 490, 505, 405 N.W.2d 317, 322-23 (1987).

Having concluded that the evidence was sufficient to support a finding that gifts were made, we need not address Aprahamian's claim that he was entitled to a $24,000 judgment as a matter of law on the theory of unjust enrichment. A finding of gift defeats a claim for unjust enrichment. *See Lawlis*, 137 Wis.2d at 496, 405 N.W.2d at 319. Aprahamian's argument that Brown has "unclean hands" and should not, in equity, be allowed to benefit from her conflicting characterization of the transfers simply falls out of play. Likewise, it is inappropriate to consider his contention that the couple exchanged equivalent nonmonetary gratuities such that Brown is unjustly enriched. Equity cannot force the repayment of a gift.

B. GIFTS *CAUSA MORTIS*

Gifts causa mortis, also known as *donatio causa mortis,* are gifts made in contemplation of immediate death. As such, they have long been recognized as an alternative to a will for someone facing imminent death who may not have the time or strength to prepare a traditional will. The concept originated in Roman Law as a way of allowing husbands and wives to avoid the formal requirements of Roman succession. It was incorporated into English law through the ecclesiastical courts and was approved of by Blackstone in his *Commentaries*.

Although the legal device is rarely used today (and is clearly frowned upon as an estate planning technique), it is still widely accepted in the common law world as legitimate means of transferring property. Its use is, however, normally restricted to situations where death appears to be certain and soon, and it is usually limited to the transfer of personal property (and sometimes, only to tangible personal property). In this regard, it is unlike the Roman doctrine which permitted any form of property that could be passed by will to be the subject of *donation causa mortis.* Moreover, while the delivery requirement of a gift *causa mortis* is clearly relaxed, some form of delivery is still required. Finally, the transfer is only valid if the donor actually dies; if he or she survives, the gift is cancelled. In the case that follows, part of the problem lies with the subject matter of the alleged gift in contemplation of death.

IN RE ESTATE OF HANSON

Wisconsin Court of Appeals

118 Wis. 2d 823, 349 N.W.2d 109 (1984)

VERGERONT, J. The issue on this appeal concerns the doctrine of gift causa mortis, also called gift in contemplation of death. Under this doctrine, a gift made during the life of the donor becomes effective upon the donor's death if certain requirements are met. The circuit court concluded that Roger Hansen, the decedent, had made gifts causa mortis to three nieces and a great-nephew and therefore that property was not part of Hansen's estate. We conclude the circuit court erred because, based on the undisputed facts, there was no delivery of the gifts during Hansen's life, a requirement for a gift causa mortis. Accordingly, we reverse the order excluding this property from the inventory of Hansen's estate and remand for further proceedings.

BACKGROUND

Roger Hansen died intestate at the age of eighty-eight. Within the four months preceding his death, he met with an attorney on several occasions for the purpose of making a will, but he died shortly before the appointment at his attorney's office at which he was to sign the last draft his attorney had prepared. Hansen was survived by a brother, Lyle, a sister, their children, and the children of siblings who had predeceased him. During Hansen's lifetime, he made mortgage loans to Lyle's three daughters and was the vendor on a land contract with a grandson of Lyle. At the time of his death, the total outstanding debt on these four notes was approximately $278,000. Lyle, as Hansen's personal representative, included these four notes in Hansen's probate estate.

The debtors and their spouses (collectively, the Netzers) moved to strike the notes from the inventory on the ground that Hansen forgave these debts prior to his death and that the pardons amounted to gifts causa mortis. Therefore, according to the Netzers, these notes are not part of Hansen's estate. The Netzers contended that a notation Hansen made on an early draft of his will, directions in a letter to his attorney, and Hansen's approval of the resulting revisions made by his attorney show that Hansen intended to forgive these debts. Peggy Meegan, the daughter of one of Hansen's deceased siblings, opposed the motion. The circuit court agreed with the Netzers and concluded that the affidavits established gifts causa mortis forgiving these debts. Therefore, the court granted the motion to strike these notes from the inventory. Meegan contends that the evidence does not satisfy any of the elements of a gift causa mortis for any of the four notes. Therefore, according to Meegan, the four notes are properly part of the inventory of Hansen's estate and the court erred in striking them. The Netzers respond that the circuit court correctly decided that the evidence establishes all elements of a gift causa mortis for each of the four notes.

Because resolution of this issue requires the application of a legal standard to undisputed facts, our review is de novo. *See Kersten v. H.C. Prange Co.*, 186 Wis. 2d 49, 56, 520 N.W.2d 99 (Ct. App. 1994). In the following paragraphs we first provide background law on the doctrine of gift causa mortis and then focus on the element requiring delivery of the gift during the donor's lifetime. For the reasons we explain, we conclude that the undisputed facts do not establish the delivery element. Because the absence of proof of this element is dispositive, we do not decide whether the evidence establishes the other elements.

The general rule is that a testamentary disposition (a disposition that takes effect upon the death of the person making the disposition) must comply with the statutory requirements for the execution of wills. *See Waukesha State Bank v. Moore,* 86 Wis. 2d 593, 598, 237 N.W.2d 329 (1979). There are, however, exceptions to this general rule. A gift causa mortis has been characterized as an exception. *Will v. Vander Zanden*, 251 Wis. 90, 97, 28 N.W.2d 360 (1947) (noting that a gift causa mortis takes effect upon death and stating this doctrine "appears to be an exception to the rule against testamentary disposition except by will").

The requirements of a valid gift causa mortis are: (1) the donor has an intention to make a gift effective at death; (2) the donor makes the gift "with a view to the donor's death from present illness or from an external and apprehended peril"; (3) the donor must die of that ailment or peril; and (4) there must be a delivery. *Id.* (citing *Hoks v. Wollenberg*, 209 Wis. 276, 243 N.W. 219 (1932)). Although a gift causa mortis does not take effect until the donor's death, the donee has an interest in the gift during the lifetime of the donor. This interest has been described as "an inchoate title which ripens into absolute title at the donor's death from the illness or peril which [the donor] apprehended in making the gift." *Id.* at 96. Another way of expressing this concept is that a gift causa mortis is "'a gift absolute in form, made by the donor in anticipation of [the donor's] speedy death, and intended to take effect and operate as a transfer of title only upon the happening of the donor's death.'" *Id.* (quoting *Crook v. First Nat'l Bank of Baraboo*, 83 Wis. 31, 36, 52 N.W. 1131 (1892)). The *Crook* court clarifies the meaning of "absolute" when used to describe a gift causa mortis: "The gift must be absolute, with the exception of the conditions inherent in its nature, and a delivery of the article donated is a necessary element; but it may be revoked by the donor, and is completely revoked by [the donor's] recovery from the sickness or escape from the danger in view of which it was made." *Crook*, 83 Wis. at 36.

Turning our attention to the delivery requirement of a gift causa mortis, we begin with the principle that this requirement is the same as it is for a gift inter vivos where the subject matter of the gift is the same. *Hartwig v. East Wisconsin Tr. Co.*, 223 Wis. 218, 228, 270 N.W.2d 71 (1936). Therefore, in analyzing the delivery requirement here, we may look to cases that concern gifts inter vivos as well as to cases that concern gifts causa mortis. The essential requirement for delivery of a gift is that it be "made as the nature of the subject sought to be bestowed reasonably admits." *Baltes v. Klief,* 188 Wis. 626, 629, 206 N.W. 877 (1926) (quoting *Opitz v. Karel*, 118 Wis. 527, 530, 95 N.W. 948 (1903)).

In this case the subject matter claimed to be the gift causa mortis is the forgiveness of a debt. The forgiveness of a debt may be a gift. *Hoks v. Wollenberg*, 209 Wis. 276,

280, 243 N.W. 219 (1932). The Netzers contend, and the circuit court agreed, that delivery of the forgiveness of the debts occurred when Hanson wrote a notation on a draft of his will prepared by his attorney and delivered a letter to his attorney. Specifically, on a draft of Hansen's will prepared by his attorney, Hansen wrote: "Wendy, Shelly and Rhonda [Lyle's daughters] will have their property cleared." Then, after receiving a revised draft with that change incorporated, Hansen wrote a letter to his attorney and dropped it off at his attorney's office.

> 2/16/09
>
> Dear Lan
>
> I think the way this will has been put together looks good to me. We did however forget to include the land contract between Roger T. Hansen and Shirley P. Hansen as tenants in common and Brad Sillman [Lyle's grandson]. In the event of my death I direct that my personal representative cancel and forgive any indebtedness to me at the time of my death by Brad Sillman. This will omit my monthly payment but still have an obligation to Shirley P. Hansen.
>
> Roger T. Hansen

The Netzers' theory of delivery has two components. First, they contend that *Hoks* and *Baltes*, read together, establish that writings extrinsic to the debt instrument—writings like Hansen's notation on the draft will and the letter to his attorney—may be the means of canceling a debt, and that delivery of a gift of forgiveness of a debt may be accomplished without surrendering the debt instrument. Second, they contend that, under *Prosser v. Nickolay*, 249 Wis. 75, 23 N.W.2d 403 (1946), the gifting instruments—Hansen's notation on the draft will and his letter—may be delivered to a third-party trustee instead of directly to the donees; and, they assert, Hansen's attorney is a third-party trustee.

We agree with the Netzers to the extent they argue that delivery of a gift of forgiveness of a debt may be accomplished by means other than delivering the debt instrument with signed writing on it canceling the debt. *See Hoks*, 209 Wis. at 282 (concluding that delivery requirement for a gift causa mortis canceling a debt was satisfied by the following events: the donor had a written statement prepared in which she stated that upon her death an identified mortgage and note and "all indebtedness therein" was canceled; she signed the statement; and the statement, the mortgage, and the note were delivered to the debtor); *see also Baltes*, 188 Wis. at 628-29 (concluding that a gift inter vivos forgiving a land contract debt was complete when the vendor directed the vendee to write on the back of the his monthly check "paid in full on home at [address of the property]," and the vendor then endorsed his name on the back of the check, deposited it, and received payment in the check amount).

Whether Hansen's notation on the draft will and his letter to his attorney are analogous to the writings and documents in *Hoks* or *Baltes* is a more difficult issue. However, we need not decide that issue because the more fundamental problem with the Netzers' theory is that these writings of Hansen were not delivered to the debtors. *Prosser* does not support the Netzers' position that the delivery to Hansen's attorney of Hansen's notation on the draft will regarding Lyle's daughters and the letter regarding Lyle's grandson constitute delivery of the gifts of forgiveness of those persons' debts. In *Prosser*, the question presented was whether an attempted conveyance of real property was valid. *Prosser*, 249 Wis. at 76.

The decedent, shortly before his death, instructed his attorney to prepare a deed conveying certain property to his wife. *Id.* The attorney did so, the decedent and witnesses signed the deed, and it was notarized. *Id.* At the time the deed was executed, the legal description of the property was not available. *Id.* The decedent instructed his attorney to obtain the proper description, insert it, record the deed, and deliver it to his wife. *Id.* The attorney took the deed to his office and inserted the proper description before the decedent's death but did not record the deed or deliver it to the decedent's wife until after the decedent died. *Id.*

The validity of the conveyance was challenged on two grounds: (1) the deed was not duly executed because at the time it was executed it was missing the legal description of the property; and (2) there was no valid delivery of the deed to the decedent's wife prior to the decedent's death. *Id.* at 76-77. The court rejected both challenges, noting that the property description was later added to complete the conveyance and citing case law establishing that "a deed delivered to a third person with instructions to record it and deliver it to the grantee after the grantor's death *becomes effective upon delivery to the third person who thereafter holds as trustee for the grantee.*" *Id.* at 77 (emphasis added) (citations omitted). Consequently, once the missing description was added, the property conveyance was complete because the deed contained all required information and the attorney held the deed as trustee for the decedent's wife. *Id.*

The facts in this case are not analogous to those in *Prosser*. A complete delivery occurred in *Prosser* at the point in time when the attorney held a completed deed *with instructions to deliver it to the donee. Id.* In contrast, in this case Hansen did not instruct his attorney to deliver to the debtors his notation on the draft will and the letter to his attorney. Indeed, that was plainly not the purpose for which Hansen gave his attorney these writings. Hansen's purpose for giving his attorney these writings was so that his attorney could include provisions to this effect in his will.

There is no factual basis for asserting that Hansen's attorney held these writings in trust for the debtors. Thus, the delivery to the attorney, with no instruction for delivery to any debtor, does not constitute delivery to any debtor.

We recognize that on this record it is undisputed that Hansen intended that, upon his death, the debts owed him by Lyle's daughters and grandson would be forgiven. It is unfortunate for the debtors that he died before his will to this effect was validly executed. However, the statutory requirements must be fulfilled in order for a will to be valid, regardless of the evidence of the decedent's intent. Similarly, in the absence of a valid will, testamentary dispositions must meet the particular requirements of the exception invoked—here, gift causa mortis. The delivery requirement for a gift causa mortis is not satisfied by Hansen's written instructions to his attorney to include in his will provisions forgiving the debts of his nieces and great-nephew.

CONCLUSION

We reverse the court's order excluding from the inventory the three mortgage notes from Hansen's nieces and the land contract note from Hansen's great-nephew, and we remand for further proceedings.

C. DISCLAIMERS OF *INTER VIVOS* GIFTS

Just as the recipient of a devise or an inheritance is not required to accept ownership of property, gifts can also be disclaimed. A similar set of rules apply.

Wis. Stat. 700.27. Disclaimer of transfers during life.

(1) DEFINITIONS.

In this section:

(a) "Beneficiary under an inter vivos governing instrument" includes any person who receives or might receive property under the terms or legal effect of an inter vivos governing instrument.

(b) "Extrinsic evidence" has the meaning given in s. 854.01 (1) (c) "Inter vivos governing instrument":

1. Means a gratuitous deed, inter vivos trust instrument, insurance policy, contract, inter vivos instrument that creates or exercises a power of appointment, or any other dispositive, appointive, or nominative instrument that transfers property other than a governing instrument as defined in s. 854.01 (2)

2. Includes an inter vivos gift that is not subject to a written instrument.

(d) "Power" has the meaning given in s. 702.01 (4)

(2) RIGHT TO DISCLAIM.

(a) In general.

1. In this paragraph, "person" includes a person who is unborn or whose identity is unascertained.

2. A person who is a recipient of property or beneficiary under an inter vivos governing instrument, donee of a power created by an inter vivos governing instrument, appointee under a power exercised by an inter vivos governing instrument, taker in default under a power created by an inter vivos governing instrument, or person succeeding to disclaimed property created by an inter vivos governing instrument may disclaim any property, including contingent or future interests or the right to receive discretionary distributions, by delivering a written instrument of disclaimer under this section.

(b) Partial disclaimer. Property transferred under an inter vivos governing instrument may be disclaimed in whole or in part, except that a partial disclaimer of property passing by an inter vivos governing instrument or by the exercise of a power may not be made if partial disclaimer is expressly prohibited by the inter vivos governing instrument or by the instrument exercising the power.

(c) Spendthrift provision. The right to disclaim exists notwithstanding any limitation on the interest of the disclaimant in the nature of a spendthrift provision or similar restriction.

(d) Disclaimer by a guardian or conservator. A guardian of the estate or a conservator appointed under ch. 880, 2003 stats., or ch. 54 may disclaim on behalf of his or her ward, with court approval, if the ward is entitled to disclaim under this section.

(e) Disclaimer by an agent under power of attorney. An agent under a power of attorney may disclaim on behalf of the person who granted the power of attorney if all of the following apply:

1. The person who granted the power of attorney is entitled to disclaim under this section.

2. The power of attorney specifically grants the power to disclaim.

(f) Disclaimer by trustee. The trustee of a trust named as a recipient of property under an inter vivos governing instrument may disclaim that property on behalf of the trust if the trust authorizes disclaimer by the trustee. If the trust does not authorize disclaimer by the trustee, the trustees power to disclaim is subject to the approval of the court.

(g) After death. A person's right to disclaim survives the person's death and may be exercised by the person's personal representative or special administrator upon receiving approval from the court having jurisdiction of the person's estate after hearing upon notice to all persons interested in the disclaimed property, if the personal representative or special administrator has not taken any action that would bar the right to disclaim under sub. (9) (h) Disclaimers of transfers at death. A person who is a recipient of property under a governing instrument, as defined in s. 854.01 (2), may disclaim the property as provided in s. 854.13

(3) INSTRUMENT OF DISCLAIMER.

The instrument of disclaimer must meet the provisions of subs. (4) and (5) and s. 854.13 (3) (a) to (c)

(4) TIME FOR EFFECTIVE DISCLAIMER.

(a) Present interest. An instrument disclaiming a present interest shall be executed and delivered not later than 9 months after the effective date of the transfer under the inter vivos governing instrument. For cause shown, the period may be extended by a court of competent jurisdiction, either within or after the 9-month period, for such additional time as the court considers just.

(b) Future interest. An instrument disclaiming a future interest shall be executed and delivered not later than 9 months after the event that determines that the taker of the property is finally ascertained and his or her interest indefeasibly fixed. For cause shown, the period may be extended by a court of competent jurisdiction, either within or after the 9-month period, for such additional time as the court considers just.

(c) Future right to income or principal. Notwithstanding pars. (a) and (b), an instrument disclaiming the future right to receive discretionary or mandatory distributions of income or principal from any source may be executed and delivered at any time.

(d) Persons under 21. Notwithstanding pars. (a) and (b), a person under 21 years of age may disclaim at any time not later than 9 months after the date on which the person attains 21 years of age.

(e) Interests arising by disclaimer. Notwithstanding pars. (a) and (b), a person whose interest in property arises by disclaimer or by default of exercise of a power created by an inter vivos governing instrument may disclaim at any time not later than 9 months after the day on which the prior instrument of disclaimer is delivered, or the date on which the donee's power lapses.

(5) DELIVERY AND FILING OF DISCLAIMER.

(a) Delivery. In addition to any requirements imposed by the inter vivos governing instrument, the instrument of disclaimer is effective only if, within the time specified under sub. (4), it is delivered to and received by any of the following:

1. The transferor of the property disclaimed.

2. The transferors legal representative.

3. The holder of legal title to the property.

(b) Delivery to trustee. If the trustee of any trust to which the interest or power relates does not receive the instrument of disclaimer under par. (a), a copy shall also be delivered to the trustee. Failure to deliver a copy of the instrument of disclaimer to the trustee within the time specified under sub. (4) does not affect the validity of any disclaimer.

(c) Recording. If real property or an interest in real property is disclaimed, a copy of the instrument of disclaimer may be recorded in the office of the register of deeds of the county in which the real estate is situated.

(6) PROPERTY NOT VESTED.

The property disclaimed under this section shall be considered not to have been vested in, created in, or transferred to the disclaimant.

(7) DEVOLUTION.

(a) In general. Subject to sub. (8), unless the inter vivos governing instrument provides otherwise, either expressly or as construed from extrinsic evidence, the disclaimed property devolves as if the disclaimant had died before the effective date of the transfer under the inter vivos governing instrument. If the disclaimed interest is a remainder contingent on surviving to the time of distribution, the disclaimed interest passes as if the disclaimant had died immediately before the time for distribution. If the disclaimant is an appointee under a power exercised by an inter vivos governing instrument, the disclaimed property devolves as if the disclaimant had died before the effective date of the exercise of the power. If the disclaimant is a taker in default under a power created by an inter vivos governing instrument, the disclaimed property devolves as if the disclaimant had predeceased the donee of the power.

(b) Devolution to issue of the disclaimants. Unless the inter vivos governing instrument provides otherwise, either expressly or as construed from extrinsic evidence, if, by law or under the inter vivos governing instrument, the issue of the disclaimant would share in the disclaimed interest by any method of representation had the disclaimant died before the time the disclaimed interest would have taken effect in possession or enjoyment, the disclaimed interest passes only to the issue of the disclaimant who survive when the disclaimed interest takes effect in possession or enjoyment.

(c) Disclaimer of a devisable future interest.

1. In this paragraph, "devisable future interest" is a future interest that can be passed under the will of the person who holds the future interest.

2. If the disclaimed interest is a devisable future interest under the law governing the transfer, then the disclaimed interest devolves as if it were a nondevisable future interest.

(8) ACCELERATION OF SUBSEQUENT INTERESTS WHEN PRECEDING INTEREST IS DISCLAIMED.

(a) Subsequent interest not held by disclaimant. Unless the inter vivos governing instrument provides otherwise, either expressly or as construed from extrinsic evidence, upon the disclaimer of a preceding interest, a subsequent interest not held by the disclaimant and limited to take effect in possession or enjoyment after the termination of the interest that is disclaimed accelerates to take effect as if the disclaimant had died immediately before the time when the disclaimed interest would have taken effect in possession or enjoyment or, if the disclaimant is an appointee under a power exercised by a power of appointment, as if the disclaimant had died before the effective date of the exercise of the power.

(b) Subsequent interest held by disclaimant. Unless the inter vivos governing instrument provides otherwise, either expressly or as construed from extrinsic evidence, upon the disclaimer of a preceding interest, a subsequent interest held by the disclaimant does not accelerate.

(9) BAR.

Actions that bar disclaimer are as provided in s. 854.13 (11g)

(10) EFFECT OF DISCLAIMER OR WAIVER.

The effect of the disclaimer on the disclaimant and any successors in interest is as provided in s. 854.13 (11p)

(11) NONEXCLUSIVENESS OF REMEDY.

(a) This section does not affect the right of a person to waive, release, disclaim, or renounce property under any other statute or the common law, or as provided in the creating instrument.

(b) Any disclaimer that meets the requirements of section 2518 of the Internal Revenue Code, or the requirements of any other federal law relating to disclaimers, constitutes an effective disclaimer under this section or s. 854.13

(12) CONSTRUCTION OF EFFECTIVE DATE.

In this section, the effective date of a transfer under an inter vivos governing instrument is the date on which the transfer is a completed gift for federal gift tax purposes.

D. ANATOMICAL GIFTS

It was a rule of traditional Anglo-American property law that there was no property interest in a human body after the death of the person who had previously inhabited it. Consequently, no one could will or otherwise give away his or her body after death, because there was no legally recognized interest that could be transferred. To provide some security against pranksters, the law did recognize a quasi-property interest in the corpse on the part of the executor or administrator of the estate who had the right to claim the body for burial.

Obviously, there is an inconsistency between this principle and modern science and technology which has developed a wide variety of uses for human tissue, even after the "owner" is deceased. Almost twenty years ago, E. Richard Gold argued in his book, *Body Parts: Property Rights and Human Biological Material* that there is a deep inconsistency between traditional property law concepts and this new technology. Most Americans today would acknowledge that there is value to the body after death, although there is a general squeamishness about the topic. Few are troubled by the fact that a living human can sell regenerative organs like hair and blood; but the sale of non-regenerative organs, even those that are not essential for life, like the spleen and the second kidney, is troubling to many and is frequently illegal.

Many American states have addressed the issue of post-mortem transplant technology by adopting the Uniform Anatomical Gift Act, which is incorporated into the law of Wisconsin in 1971. Although there have been several versions of the Act promulgated, all but six states have adopted it in one form or another. Most statutes, like the Wisconsin Act, have been amended many times. (In Wisconsin, the most recent amendments came in 2011.) The current form of the statute, which is exceptionally lengthy and detailed, can be found at Wis. Stat. §157.06.

Like so-called "living wills" (that have to do with late in life medical decisions) and durable powers of attorney for health care, anatomical gifts often are prompted by the same mortality-related concerns that prompt individuals to seek out assistance in disposing of their property after their deaths. Clients frequently seek assistance on both subjects from the same lawyer.

Wis. Stat. 157.06. Anatomical gifts (excerpts)

(4) WHO MAY MAKE AN ANATOMICAL GIFT BEFORE DONOR'S DEATH

Except as provided in subs. (7) and (8), any of the following may during the life of a donor make an anatomical gift of the donors body or part in the manner provided in sub. (5):

(a) The donor, if he or she is at least 15 and one-half years of age or is an emancipated minor.

(b) An agent of the donor, unless the donors power of attorney for health care instrument under ch. 155 or some other record prohibits the agent from making an anatomical gift.

(c) A parent of the donor, if the donor is an unemancipated minor and does not object to the making of the anatomical gift.

(d) A guardian of the donor unless a health care agent under ch. 155 has authority to make an anatomical gift of the donor's body or part.

(5) MANNER OF MAKING AN ANATOMICAL GIFT BEFORE DONOR'S DEATH.

(a) A donor under sub. (4) (a) may make an anatomical gift by doing any of the following:

1. Affixing to, or authorizing a person to imprint on, the donors driver's license or identification card a statement or symbol that indicates that the donor has made an anatomical gift.

2. Including an anatomical gift in his or her will.

3. If the donor has a terminal illness or injury, communicating the anatomical gift by any means to at least two adults, at least one of whom is a disinterested witness.

4. Signing a donor card or other record that includes an anatomical gift or, if physically unable to sign a record, by directing another individual to sign the record as provided in sub. (2m)

5. Authorizing a person to include in a donor registry a statement or symbol that indicates that the donor has made an anatomical gift.

(b) A person under sub. (4) (b) to (d) may make an anatomical gift of a donors body or part during the donors life by doing any of the following:

1. Signing a donor card or other record that includes an anatomical gift or, if physically unable to sign a record, by directing another to sign the record as provided in sub. (2m)

2. Authorizing another to include in a donor registry a statement or symbol that indicates that the person has made an anatomical gift of the donors body or part.

(c) The revocation, suspension, expiration, or cancellation of a driver's license or identification card on which an anatomical gift has been made does not invalidate the anatomical gift.

(d) An anatomical gift made by will takes effect upon the donors death whether or not the will is probated. Invalidation of the will after the donors death does not invalidate the anatomical gift.

(6) AMENDING OR REVOKING ANATOMICAL GIFT BEFORE DONOR'S DEATH.

(a) Subject to sub. (8), a donor may amend an anatomical gift of his or her body or part by doing any of the following:

1. Signing a record that amends the anatomical gift or, if physically unable to sign, directing another to sign the record as provided in sub. (2m)

2. Subsequently executing a record of gift that amends a previously executed anatomical gift or a portion of a previously executed anatomical gift either expressly or by inconsistency.

3. If the anatomical gift was not made in a will and the donor has a terminal illness or injury, communicating in any manner an amendment of the anatomical gift to at least two adults, at least one of whom is a disinterested witness.

4. If the anatomical gift was made in a will, amending the will.

II. FUTURE INTERESTS

When the owner of land transfers a remainder interest that follows an estate for years or a life estate, the recipient holds a future interest which will vest in a right of possession at some point. When the owner of the present estate dies, the property passes to the remainderman, not through the probate estate, but by the vesting in possession of the future interest. Should O wish to give Blackacre to A, but wants to retain the use of it for the rest of his life, he can reserve a life estate for himself while transferring a vested remainder to A. This will work to avoid Blackacre having to go through probate, but there are disadvantages. Depending on the value of the remainder (and of Blackacre), there may be gift tax consequences to the transaction, and O would subject himself to the doctrine of waste, which could limit the usages to which Blackacre could be put during the remainder of his life.

Wis. Stat. 700.01. Definitions.

In this chapter, unless the context indicates otherwise:

(1) "Bill of sale" means an instrument evidencing a sale of tangible personal property which names the seller and buyer and describes the property sold.

(2) "Document of title" means a document which is evidence of ownership of certain kinds of personal property, tangible or intangible, the ownership of which may be transferred by transfer of the document; it includes but is not limited to an investment security, a negotiable

instrument and a certificate of title to tangible personal property; it does not include items excepted in s. 700.22

(3) "Instrument of transfer" means an instrument which is effective to transfer an interest in property; it includes but is not limited to a will, a deed, a contract to transfer, a real estate mortgage and an instrument creating a security interest in personal property under ch. 409

(4) "Interest" means an interest in property.

(5) "Property" means real or personal property.

(6) "Successors in interest" means persons who obtain a reversionary interest by transfer or operation of law.

(7) "Transfer" means a transfer effective during the lifetime of the transferor or by reason of the transferor's death.

Wis. Stat. 700.02. Classification of interests in property as to duration.

Interests in property are classified as to duration as:

(1) A *fee simple absolute*;

(2) A *defeasible fee simple* which may be a *fee simple determinable* automatically expiring upon the occurrence of a stated event, a *fee simple subject to a condition subsequent* with a power in the transferor or the transferors successors in interest to reacquire the fee by reason of a breach of the condition, or a *fee simple with a remainder* over to a person other than the transferor or the transferors successors in interest to take effect upon the occurrence of a stated event; for purposes of this subsection, a stated event can be either the happening, or the nonhappening, of a specified occurrence, and can be either certain or not certain to happen;*

(3) An interest for life, which may be created for the duration of a life or lives of one or more human beings;

(4) An interest for years, which is any interest the duration of which is described in units of a year or multiples or divisions thereof;

(5) A periodic interest, which will continue for successive periods of a year, or successive periods of a fraction of a year, unless terminated;

* Emphasis added. With the use of the term *fee simple with a remainder* rather than *fee simple subject to an executory limitation* Wisconsin departs from the more conventional practice.

(6) An interest at will, which is terminable at the will of either the transferor or the transferee and has no designated period of duration.

Wis. Stat. 700.03. Classification of present and future interests.

Interests in property are classified as to time of enjoyment as:

(1) A present interest, which entitles the owner to the present possession or enjoyment of the benefits of property; or

(2) A future interest, which does not entitle the owner to possession or enjoyment of the benefits of property until a future time.

Wis. Stat. 700.04. Classification of future interests.

Future interests are classified as:

(1) A reversionary interest left in the transferor or the transferors successors in interest, either as a reversion, a possibility of reverter upon the simultaneous creation of a fee simple determinable, or a power of reacquisition; or

(2) An interest created in a person other than the transferor or the transferor's successors in interest, called a remainder, to take effect at the termination of a preceding interest created at the same time or without the intervention of such a preceding interest.*

Wis. Stat. 700.05. Classification of remainders.

Remainders are classified as:

(1) Indefeasibly vested, if the interest is created in favor of one or more ascertained persons in being and is certain to become a present interest at some time in the future;

(2) Vested subject to open, if the interest is created in favor of a class of persons, one or more of whom are ascertained and in being, and if the interest is certain to become a present interest at some time in the future, but the share of the ascertained remaindermen is subject to diminution by reason of other persons becoming entitled to share as members of the class;

(3) Vested subject to complete defeasance, if the interest is created in favor of one or more ascertained persons in being and would become a present interest on the expiration of the

---

* Wisconsin uses the term *power of reacquisition* rather than *right of entry* or *power of termination,* and all *executory interests* are classified as *remainders.*

preceding interests but may end or may be completely defeated as provided by the transferor at, before or after the expiration of the preceding interests;

(4) Subject to a condition precedent, if the interest is created in favor of one or more unborn or unascertained persons or in favor of one or more presently ascertainable persons upon the occurrence of an uncertain event.*

Wis. Stat. 700.06. Interest for life of another; succession.

An interest measured by the life of a person other than the owner of the interest passes on the death of the owner, if the owners death is prior to the death of the person who is the measuring life, as an asset of the owners estate and is realty or personalty according to the nature of the property subject to the interest.

Wis. Stat. 700.07. Transferability of future interests.

A future interest is transferable during the lifetime of the owner and passes on the owners death by will or under the law of intestate succession in the same manner as a present interest; but this section does not make an interest transferable if a valid condition or limitation restricts transfer, nor permit an interest to pass at death if the interest ends at death.

Wis. Stat. 700.08. Estate tail becomes fee simple; effect of gift over after attempted estate tail.

The use of language in an instrument appropriate to create a present or future interest in fee tail, such as to a named person "and the heirs of his body" or "and the heirs of her body" or "and his issue" or "and her issue", creates a present or future interest in fee simple. If the same instrument attempts to create a future interest after the interest that is made a fee simple by reason of this section, the future interest is valid.

---

* Note that *contingent remainders* and *executory interests* are referred to in Wisconsin as *remainders subject to a condition precedent.*

Wis. Stat. 700.09. Interest contingent on death without issue.

If an instrument transfers an interest expressly contingent upon the death of a person without "heirs of the body", "descendants", "issue", "children" or relatives described by other terms, the interest takes effect only if that person dies not having such a relative living at the time of death, or conceived then and born alive thereafter.

Wis. Stat. 700.10. Remainder to heirs of owner of life interest; abolition of rule in Shelley's case.

If an instrument purports to transfer an interest for life to one person and a remainder to that persons heirs or the heirs of that person's body, a remainder is created in that person's heirs or heirs of that person's body.

Wis. Stat. 700.11. Interests in "heirs" and the like.

(1) If a statute, inter vivos governing instrument, as defined in s. 700.27 (1) (c), or governing instrument, as defined in s. 854.01 (2), specifies that property is to be distributed to, or a future interest is to be created in, a designated individuals "heirs," "heirs at law," "next of kin," "relatives," "family," or a term that has a similar meaning, or if a class gift in favor of "descendants," "issue," or "heirs of the body" does not specify the manner in which the property is to be distributed among the class members, the property is distributed according to s. 854.22

(2) The common law doctrine of worthier title is abolished under s. 854.22 (3) Situations in which the doctrine may have applied are governed by s. 854.22 (1)

Wis. Stat. 700.13. Remainders presumed not to shorten prior interest; acceleration of remainders.

(1) If an instrument transfers an interest for life or years and a future interest to take effect on a stated contingency not defeating or avoiding the prior interest transferred, and the stated contingency occurs before the normal termination of the prior interest transferred, the future interest takes effect at the normal termination of the prior interest.

(2) The effect of a renunciation or release of an interest for life or years is as provided in ss. 700.27 (8) and 854.13 (10).

Wis. Stat. 700.14. Indestructibility of contingent future interests.

No future interest is destroyed merely by the termination in any manner of any or all preceding interests before the happening of a contingency to which the future interest is subject.

Wis. Stat. 700.15. Nominal conditions not enforced.

A condition imposed by the transferor is not enforceable if it is or becomes merely nominal and of no actual or substantial benefit to the transferor or other person in whose favor it is to be performed.

A. REMAINDERS IN LIEU OF WILLS

IN RE ESTATE OF CARPENTER

Court of Appeals of Wisconsin
1997 Wisc. App. LEXIS 386

ROGGENSACK, J. In this consolidated appeal, James Gratz and his wife, Therese, appeal two judgments: 1) one declaring that Harold, Edwin and Kerry Gratz hold title to the Carpenter farm, and 2) a second judgment denying James' objection to the inventory filed in the estate of his grandmother, Hattie Carpenter, because the Carpenter farm was not listed. James claims title to the Carpenter farm should have passed to Hattie through the laws of intestacy because his mother, Nellie Gratz, predeceased Hattie. However, because we conclude that Nellie's ownership of the farm had vested before her death and that the final judgment in the probate of her estate barred relitigation of the legality of Nellie's ownership and that of her distributees of the Carpenter farm, we affirm the trial court on both judgments.

BACKGROUND

The chain of title to the Carpenter farm worked its way through a tangled web of wills and quit claim deeds. Its tortuous course began when Charles Carpenter died on January 20, 1971. Charles and Hattie Carpenter had one daughter, Nellie. She and her husband, Harold Gratz, worked the Carpenter farm at the time of Charles' death. They had four children: Charles, James, Sharon and Edwin. Charles' will bequeathed the Carpenter farm to Hattie and Nellie under the following terms:

"IV. All the rest, residue and remainder of my estate, I give, devise and bequeath unto my wife, Hattie L. Carpenter, so long as she remains my widow, and if she does not remarry, then for her natural lifetime. And in case she does not remarry, then upon her death unto my daughter, Nellie L. Gratz, her heirs and assigns forever.

"V. But in case my widow should remarry, then upon such remarriage, I give, devise and bequeath said rest, residue and remainder equally unto my said widow and daughter absolutely and forever, in fee simple absolute. And if my daughter should then be dead, then her one-half (1/2) share of the rest, residue and remainder of my said estate, I give, devise and bequeath one-third (1/3) thereof to my son-in-law, Harold Gratz, and the remaining two-thirds (2/3) of said one-half (1/2) to the children of my daughter, in equal shares." The will also provided that Hattie could not sell or mortgage the real estate which comprised the Carpenter farm during her lifetime. However, it was silent about the disposition of Charles' property in the event that Hattie remained unmarried and Nellie predeceased her.

In 1972, as soon as Charles' estate had been settled, Hattie quit claimed all of her interests in the Carpenter farm to Nellie. On November 7, 1984, Nellie quit claimed her interest in the Carpenter farm to herself and Harold, as tenants in common. Nellie died on November 21, 1987, predeceasing her mother, Hattie. Nellie's will devised her interest in the Carpenter farm to Harold for life, with the remainder to their son, Edwin, who was then farming the Carpenter farm. James was also a successor in interest to Nellie's estate and received the remainder interest in the Miller farm, the farm James worked and in which Nellie also held an interest. On February 1, 1990, James waived, consented and approved the final account and entry of the final judgment in Nellie's estate. The judgment described Nellie's interest in the Carpenter farm as an undivided one-half interest as tenant in common, and transferred it to Edwin, with a life estate reserved to Harold.

Hattie died on July 22, 1994, without remarrying. Hattie's will provided in relevant part:

"All of the property which I own at my death is hereby given to my four grandchildren, namely: Charles Gratz, James Gratz, Sharon Ohnstad and Edwin Gratz, in equal shares, share and share alike."

When Hattie's personal representatives filed an inventory of estate in probate court, James objected because the Carpenter farm was not included. On January 6, 1995, Harold quit claimed one-half of his interest in the Carpenter farm to Edwin and Kerry, reserving a life estate for himself. Harold, Edwin and Kerry then filed an action to declare their interests in the Carpenter farm. The trial court granted summary judgment to them, declaring Harold has an undivided one-fourth interest and a life estate in the remaining three-quarters interest in which Edwin and Kerry are remaindermen. In Hattie's probate proceeding, the trial court also dismissed James' objection to the inventory, concluding Hattie held no interest in the Carpenter farm at her death. James and Therese appeal both judgments.

DISCUSSION

Standard of Review.

We review a decision to grant summary judgment *de novo*, applying the same standards employed by the trial court. *Brownelli v. McCaughtry*, 182 Wis. 2d 367, 372, 514 N.W.2d 48, 49 (Ct. App. 1994). These standards have been repeated in many cases, so we need not repeat them here. When we construe a statute, our aim is to ascertain the intent of the legislature; and, in doing so, our first resort is to the language of the statute itself. *State v. Eichman*, 155 Wis. 2d 552, 556, 456 N.W.2d 143, 149 (1990). When the language of the statute is unambiguous, we will not look beyond the statute's plain language to determine legislative intent. *In re Jamie L.*, 172 Wis. 2d 218, 225, 493 N.W.2d 56, 59 (1992).

Summary Judgment.

The material facts are not in dispute. It is the legal consequences which flow from those facts which are contested. Our examination of the complaint and the answer in the declaration of interests action demonstrates that a claim for relief has been stated and issue has been joined. Harold, Edwin and Kerry's submissions in support of their motion for declaratory relief make a *prima facie* case for summary judgment, if they are correct in their interpretation of the law. They argue that it is undisputed that Nellie conveyed her interest in the Carpenter farm when the judgment in the probate of her estate was entered on April 2, 1990. James argues that she had only a contingent interest which lapsed when she predeceased Hattie, so the probate judgment passed no interest in the farm.

Wisconsin law favors early vesting of interests received from a decedent. *See Estate of James'*, 273 Wis. 50, 54, 76 N.W.2d 553, 555 (1956). Unless a contrary intent of the testator is proven, interests that are contingent vest on the death of the testator, subject to being defeated by a condition set by the testator. *See Will of Roth*, 191 Wis. 366, 374, 210 N.W. 826, 828 (1926); *Weymouth v. Weymouth*, 165 Wis. 455, 460, 161 N.W. 373, 375 (1917). Additionally, §700.05, STATS., provides that a remainder interest is vested subject to defeasance if it is created in favor of an ascertainable person and would become a present interest after the expiration of a certain other interest.

Charles' will, which was incorporated into the probate judgment, evinced his clear intent to leave all of his property to his wife and their only child. Under the final judgment, Nellie received a remainder interest that would become a present interest when Hattie's life estate terminated at her death. Therefore, because Nellie was an ascertainable person who had received an interest that would become a present interest at a later date, also through the operation of §700.05, STATS., Nellie's remainder interest vested when Charles died. Additionally, it is undisputed that Hattie never remarried and that in 1972 she quit claimed to Nellie all interest, of any type, which she had in the Carpenter farm. When a remainderman receives the present interest in the real property, merger occurs. *See Bailey v. Wells*, 8 Wis. 141 (1857); *Wagner v. Maskey*, 353 N.W.2d 891, 893 (Iowa App. 1984). Therefore, we conclude that the remainderman's interest in the Carpenter farm, which Nellie received from Charles, merged with the interests of Hattie, creating a fee simple interest in Nellie, due to Hattie's quit claim deed.

We next examine what happened to the Carpenter farm at Nellie's probate. Title to real estate passes by a duly probated will. *Malzahn v. Teagar*, 235 Wis. 631, 638, 294 N.W. 36, 39 (1940). The preclusive effect of a judgment in probate is established by statute in §863.31(1), STATS. It provides:

The final judgment [of the probate court] is a conclusive determination of the persons who are the successors in interest to the estate of the decedent and of the extent and character of their interests therein, subject only to the right of appeal and the right to reopen the judgment. It operates as an assignment or final adjudication of the transfer of the right, title and interest of the decedent to the distributees therein designated.

The probate court determines the testator's intent and construes the will to assign the estate in accordance with that intent. *Estate of Yates*, 259 Wis. 263, 270-71, 48 N.W.2d 601, 604 (1951); §861.31(1). If the testator's words are repeated in the assignment clause of the final judgment, and any ambiguity remains, evidence of the testator's intent may be used to clarify the meaning of the judgment in a subsequent proceeding. *Estate of Yates*, 259 Wis. at 271-72, 48 N.W.2d at 605.

To begin our analysis, we note that the probate court which settled Nellie's estate was one of competent jurisdiction under §856.01, STATS., and no allegations of fraud were made in connection with its final judgment. Furthermore, Therese is the only party in this appeal who was not an interested party in Nellie's probate proceedings. However, because her interest in the Carpenter farm is only derivative of any interest James may have a right to claim, he was her privy in the probate of Nellie's estate. *See Hernke v. Coronet Ins. Co.*, 72 Wis. 2d 170, 175, 240 N.W.2d 382, 385 (1972). Therefore, our conclusions about James' rights and obligations in Nellie's probate apply to Therese as well.

The final judgment of the probate of Nellie's estate was entered April 2, 1990. It specifically described her interest in the Carpenter farm and transferred it to James' brother, Edwin, and his father, Harold. Additionally, the judgment was consented to in writing by James. James does not contend that the judgment is ambiguous. Rather, he now claims the right to look behind the judgment because, as he asserts, Nellie had no interest in the Carpenter farm at her death. He contends she had only the interest of a life tenant measured by the life of Hattie, which reverted to her father's estate when she died. As set forth above, we disagree with James' legal analysis of the interest Nellie held at her death. **[In a footnote not reproduced here, the Court also noted that, "James ignores the remainderman interest Nellie received directly from her father's estate, and the right to receive Hattie's one-half interest in fee, if Hattie remarried. The later interest Hattie quit claimed to Nellie in 1972, together with her life estate."]**

And, even if James' contentions were correct, he had the opportunity to raise them during the course of the probate of his mother's estate. Because he chose not to do so, it does not follow that he may collaterally attack that judgment by objecting to the inventory in the probate of his grandmother's estate or by contesting the issue of his mother's ownership of the Carpenter farm in Harold, Edwin and Kerry's action for declaratory relief. *See Estate of Yates*, 259 Wis. at 270, 48 N.W.2d at 604. Additionally, §863.31, STATS., is a clear expression of legislative intent that probate judgments are final in regard to the interests in property those judgments purport to convey. Subsection (1) states that the probate judgment makes a "conclusive determination" of the property the successors in interest to the estate receive. James, Harold and Edwin were all successors in interest to the estate of Nellie. Subsection (2) establishes that those who purchase from distributees of estate property "may rely on the final judgment as conclusive insofar as it purports to transfer to the distributees any title which the decedent held in the real estate at the time of the decedent's death." Were that not the case, every property interest which had been part of an estate would be rendered uncertain.

Therefore, we conclude that James cannot now claim that his mother's interest in the Carpenter farm was other than as described in the final judgment of her estate. Any right to do so was relinquished when the time for appealing or setting aside the judgment in Nellie's probate expired. In light of our decision, we decline to address Harold, Edwin and Kerry's alternate claim that they acquired title to the Carpenter farm by adverse possession.

CONCLUSION

We conclude that because Nellie had a fully vested interest in the Carpenter farm at the time of her death and because James had notice of and waived any right to object to the inclusion of the Carpenter farm in the final judgment of his mother's estate, he is now barred by §863.31, STATS., from arguing that she conveyed no interest in the farm to Edwin and Harold. Title to the farm is vested in Harold, Edwin and Kerry, as determined by the trial court. Based upon that decision, Hattie had no interest in the Carpenter farm at her death and the trial court properly dismissed James' objection to the inventory.

B. TESTAMENTARY DEEDS

Landowners, looking for a way to transfer land at death while avoiding probate, have in the past come up with the idea of preparing a deed for the land for the intended next owner, signing it, and then placing it in a safe place so that it can be delivered to the new owner once the current owner dies. Unfortunately, this attempted land transfer usually failed because it did not meet the delivery requirement for the deed. To be valid, a deed must be delivered and accepted while the grantor is still alive. The "deed in the drawer" was, alas, simply an unexecuted testamentary document, so the land passed through the probate process after all.

However, since 2006, Wisconsin has permitted a type of testamentary deed, now known as a Transfer on Death deed (or a TOD deed). Under the provisions of Wis. Stat. §705.15, a parcel of land can be transferred without probate to a designated beneficiary if the provisions of the statute are followed. Most importantly, for the

TOD deed to be valid, it must be recorded in the county in which the land is located. No property interest comes into effect until the death of the grantor, and if the grantor changes his mind, he can file a new deed that names a new grantee or simply revokes the TOD designation altogether.

Wis. Stat. 705.15. Nonprobate transfer of real property on death.

(1) An interest in real property that is solely owned, owned by spouses as survivorship marital property, or owned by 2 or more persons as joint tenants may be transferred without probate to a designated TOD beneficiary as provided in this section on the death of the sole owner or the last to die of the multiple owners.

(2) A TOD beneficiary may be designated on a deed that evidences ownership of the property interest in the owner or owners by including the words "transfer on death" or "pay on death," or the abbreviation "TOD" or "POD," after the name of the owner or owners of the property and before the name of the beneficiary or beneficiaries. The designation may be included on the original deed that passes the property interest to the owner or owners or may be made at a later time by the sole owner or all then surviving owners by executing and recording another deed that designates a TOD beneficiary. A TOD beneficiary designation is not effective unless the deed on which the designation is made is recorded.

(3) The designation of a TOD beneficiary on a deed does not affect ownership of the property until the owner's death. The designation may be canceled or changed at any time by the sole owner or all then surviving owners, without the consent of the beneficiary, by executing and recording another deed that designates a different beneficiary or no beneficiary. The recording of a deed that designates a TOD beneficiary or no beneficiary revokes any designation made in a previously recorded deed relating to the same property interest.

(4) On the death of the sole owner or the last to die of multiple owners, ownership of the interest in the real property passes, subject to any lien or other encumbrance, to the designated TOD beneficiary or beneficiaries who survive all owners and to any predeceased beneficiary's issue who would take under s. 854.06 (3) If no beneficiary or predeceased beneficiary's issue who would take under s. 854.06 (3) survives the death of all owners, the interest in the real property passes to the estate of the deceased sole owner or the estate of the last to die of the multiple owners.

(5) A TOD beneficiary's interest in the property on the death of the sole owner or the last to die of multiple owners may be confirmed as provided in s. 863.27, 865.201, or 867.046

(6) Chapter 854 applies to transfers on death under this section.

III. CONCURRENT ESTATES

A. JOINT TENANCIES AND TENANCIES IN COMMON

One of the most common ways to avoid probate is to own property in *joint tenancy,* which in most states carries with it a right of survivorship. If A and B are joint tenants, and A dies, B automatically assumes the entirety of A's interest, so there is nothing for A to pass along via a will or intestacy. Most marital homes are owned in joint tenancy. *Tenancy by the entirety* is a form of joint tenancy limited to married couples that provides a level of protection against the creditors of either spouse that is not a characteristic of a joint tenancy. While its creditor protection features make it a desirable form of ownership for married couples, tenancy by the entirety does not exist in many states, including Wisconsin. *Tenants in common,* in contrast to joint tenants or tenants by the entirety, share a common ownership interest in the same property but do not have a right of survivorship. While the ownership interests of holders of concurrent interests in joint tenancies and tenancies by the entirety are required to be identical—if, for example, there are three joint tenants, each must have a 1/3 undivided interest in the property-- the ownership interests of tenants in common can be of any size. Together, these three estates are known as *concurrent estates.*

Wisconsin's law of property recognizes both joint tenancy and tenancy in common. In both situations, concurrent owners hold undivided interests in the property. Interests in tenancies in common belong to the individual owners and can be alienated either in life or by wife. Joint tenancies, as mentioned above, include a right of survivorship. The estate of tenancy by the entirety (or entireties), a special form of joint tenancy limited to married couples, is no longer recognized in the state, but it was at the time of *Aaby v. Citizens National Bank of Stoughton,* excerpted below. *Aaby* illustrates the operation of concurrent estates in general, and provides a reminder of the extent to which property rights in Wisconsin and elsewhere were defined by gender in the not too distant past.

Wis. Stat. 700.17. Classification and characteristics of certain concurrent interests.

(1) CLASSIFICATION OF CONCURRENT INTERESTS.

Interests in property may be owned concurrently by 2 or more persons as joint tenants or as tenants in common. A joint tenancy or tenancy in common established exclusively between spouses after the determination date is classified as provided under s. 766.60 (4) (b)

(2) CHARACTERISTICS OF JOINT TENANCY.

(a) Each of 2 or more joint tenants has an equal interest in the whole property for the duration of the tenancy, irrespective of unequal contributions at its creation. On the death of one of 2 joint tenants, the survivor becomes the sole owner; on the death of one of 3 or more joint tenants, the survivors are joint tenants of the entire interest. If a survivor disclaims under s. 854.13 (2) (b), the joint tenancy is severed as of the date of death with respect to the disclaimed interest.

(am) Survivorship under par. (a) is governed by s. 854.03 (2) (b) If a joint tenant unlawfully and intentionally kills another joint tenant of the same property, the disposition of the deceased joint tenants interest in the joint tenancy is governed by s. 854.14

(3) CHARACTERISTICS OF TENANCY IN COMMON.

Each of 2 or more tenants in common has an undivided interest in the whole property for the duration of the tenancy. There is no right of survivorship incident to a tenancy in common, but a remainder may be created to vest ownership in the survivor of several persons who own as tenants in common other preceding interests, such as a life interest, in the same property.

Wis. Stat. 700.18. Determination of cotenancy generally

Two or more persons named as owners in a document of title, transferees in an instrument of transfer or buyers in a bill of sale are tenants in common, except as otherwise provided in s. 700.19 or ch. 766

Wis. Stat. 700.19. Creation of joint tenancy.

(1) GENERALLY.

The creation of a joint tenancy is determined by the intent expressed in the document of title, instrument of transfer or bill of sale. Any of the following constitute an expression of intent to create a joint tenancy: "as joint tenants", "as joint owners", "jointly", "or the survivor", "with right of survivorship" or any similar phrase except a phrase similar to "survivorship marital property".

(2) HUSBAND AND WIFE.

If persons named as owners in a document of title, transferees in an instrument of transfer or buyers in a bill of sale are described in the document, instrument or bill of sale as husband and wife, or are in fact husband and wife, they are joint tenants, unless the intent to create a tenancy in common is expressed in the document, instrument or bill of sale. This subsection applies to property acquired before January 1, 1986, and, if ch. 766 does not apply when the property is acquired, to property acquired on or after January 1, 1986.

(2m) DOMESTIC PARTNERS.

If persons named as owners in a document of title, transferees in an instrument of transfer, or buyers in a bill of sale are described in the document, instrument, or bill of sale as domestic partners under ch. 770, or are in fact domestic partners under ch. 770, they are joint tenants, unless the intent to create a tenancy in common is expressed in the document, instrument, or bill of sale.

(3) COMORTGAGEES.

If covendors owned realty as joint tenants and a purchase money mortgage names the covendors as mortgagees, the mortgagees are joint tenants, unless the purchase money mortgage expresses an intent that the mortgagees are tenants in common.

(4) COFIDUCIARIES.

Notwithstanding s. 700.18 and subs. (1) to (3), co-personal representatives and cotrustees hold title to interests in property as joint tenants.

(5) CHANGE IN COMMON LAW REQUIREMENTS.

The common law requirements of unity of title and time for creation of a joint tenancy are abolished.

Wis. Stat. 700.20. Extent of undivided interests in tenancy in common.

The extent of the undivided interests of tenants in common for the duration of the tenancy is determined by the intent expressed in the document of title, instrument of transfer or bill of sale; if no intent is expressed in the document, instrument or bill of sale, tenants in common are presumed to own equal undivided interests for the duration of the tenancy.

Wis. Stat. 700.21. Covendors in contracts to transfer.

(1) If 2 or more persons are named as covendors in a contract to transfer an interest in property which they own as joint tenants, the purchase price is payable to them as joint tenants, unless

the contract expresses a contrary intent. If 2 or more persons are named as covendors in a contract to transfer an interest in property which they own as tenants in common, the purchase price is payable to them according to their interests, unless the contract expresses a contrary intent.

(2) If 2 or more persons are named as covendors in a contract to transfer an interest in property which is owned by less than all of the covendors, the purchase price is payable to the owner or owners of the interest in property to which the contract relates, unless the contract expresses an intent that the purchase price is payable to the covendors as joint tenants or as tenants in common.

Wis. Stat. 700.215. Exception for equitable rights of cotenants and 3rd persons.

Nothing in ss. 700.17 to 700.21 prevents an equitable lien arising in favor of one cotenant against another tenant or tenants because of events occurring after the establishment of the cotenancy relationship nor prevents imposition of a constructive trust in favor of a 3rd person in an appropriate case.

Wis. Stat. 700.22. Exception for bank deposits, checks, government bonds and vehicles.

(1) (a) In this subsection, "deposits" include checking accounts or instruments deposited into or drawn on checking accounts, savings accounts, certificates of deposit, investment shares or any other form of deposit.

(b) Nothing in ss. 700.17 to 700.21 governs the determination of rights to deposits in banks, building and loan associations, savings banks, savings and loan associations, credit unions or other financial institutions.

(2) Nothing in ss. 700.17 to 700.21 applies to United States obligations to the extent they are governed by law of the United States.

(3) Nothing in ss. 700.17 to 700.21 governs the transfer of interest in a vehicle for purposes of s. 342.15 (1) (d)

Wis. Stat. 700.23. Liability among cotenants for rents and profits.

(1) The provisions of this section apply only in the absence of a valid agreement to the contrary between the cotenants. As used in this section, "proportionate share" means a share determined by the number of joint tenants, in the case of a joint tenancy, and the extent of a tenant in commons undivided interest, in the case of a tenancy in common.

(2) If land belonging to 2 or more cotenants is rented to a 3rd person, any cotenant may recover that cotenants proportionate share of the net rents collected by another cotenant after deduction of property taxes, maintenance costs and any other proper charges relating to the property.

(3) If land belonging to such cotenants is occupied by one cotenant and not by another, any cotenant not occupying the premises may recover from the occupying cotenant:

(a) A proportionate share of the reasonable rental value of the land accruing after written demand for rent if the occupying tenant manifests an intent to occupy the premises to the exclusion of the other cotenant or cotenants;

(b) A proportionate share of the net profits if the occupying cotenant engages in mining, cutting of timber, removal of sand or gravel, or any similar operation resulting in diminution of the value of the premises. In such a case, the occupying cotenant must render an accounting to the other cotenant, showing all receipts and expenditures, and is entitled to deduct a reasonable amount for the value of services provided by the occupying cotenant; but any other cotenant may in the alternative elect to recover that cotenants proportionate share of the amount which that cotenant can prove would have been received by licensing a 3rd party to carry on the same operation.

(4) If one cotenant has leased the premises from another cotenant, upon expiration of the lease it is presumed that the cotenant who has leased the premises from the other cotenant continues to hold over as provided in s. 704.25, unless that cotenant gives to the other cotenant prior to the expiration of the lease a written notice to the contrary, by one of the methods under s. 704.21.

Wis. Stat. 700.24. Death of a joint tenant; effect of liens.

A real estate mortgage, a security interest under ch. 409, or a lien under s. 72.86 (2), 1985 stats., or s. 71.91 (5) (b), ch. 49 or 779 or rules promulgated under s. 46.286 (7) on or against the interest of a joint tenant does not defeat the right of survivorship in the event of the death of such joint tenant, but the surviving joint tenant or tenants take the interest such deceased joint tenant could have transferred prior to death subject to such mortgage, security interest or statutory lien.

Aaby v. Citizens National Bank of Stoughton

Supreme Court of Wisconsin
197 Wis. 56, 221 N.W. 417 (1928)

CROWNHART, J. The sole question before us is: Is there an estate by the entirety in personal property, recognizable by our law?

There was such an estate by the common law, and the common law prevails in Wisconsin until changed by statute. The appellant claims that since estates by the entirety in realty were abolished by the Married Women's Act (*Wallace v. St. John,* 119 Wis. 585, 97 N.W. 197), the reason of the common law has ceased to exist as to personal property, and it was therefore the intention of the legislature to abolish such estates in personal property. Prior to the Married Women's Act, estates of joint tenancy in husband and wife were held to be estates by the entirety at common law, and as such estates by the entirety in Wisconsin. *Wallace v. St. John, supra.* But in that case this court, in construing the Married Women's Act in connection with the amended chapter of 1878 on real estate, which changed the real estate chapter from "this chapter" to "these statutes," and in consideration of the revisor's notes thereto, held that estates by the entirety in real estate no longer existed. Personal property was not there involved.

The Married Women's Act, sec, 246.03, Stats., applies to both real estate and personal property, and within the reasoning of *Wallace v. St. John, supra,* there can be no estate by the entirety either in real estate or in personal property. Sec. 246.03, Stats., reads:

"Any married female may receive by inheritance or by gift, grant, devise or bequest from any person, hold to her sole and separate use, convey and devise real and personal property and any interest or estate therein of any description, including all held in joint tenancy with her husband, and the rents, issues and profits thereof in the same manner and with like effect as if she were unmarried, and the same shall not be subject to the disposal of her husband nor be liable for his debts. Any conveyance, transfer or lien executed by either husband or wife to or in favor of the other shall be valid to the same extent as between other persons."

In *Will of Ray,* 188 Wis. 180, 205 N.W. 917, the language of the court is broad enough to include both personal and real property, although only real estate was there involved. The plaintiffs rely upon *Dupont v. Jonet,* 165 Wis. 554, 162 N.W. 664, where this court said:

"As to real estate, our statute has substituted joint tenancy for tenancy by entireties in case of a conveyance to husband and wife, but there has been no such change as to personal property," citing *Wallace v. St. John, supra.*

But it seems that the court there overlooked the reasoning of the *Wallace Case.* The language of the Married Women's Act is plain and unambiguous. It is reinforced by sec. 6.015, Stats., and *First Wis. Nat. Bank v. Jahn,* 179 Wis. 117, 190 N.W. 822, and *Wait v. Pierce,* 191 Wis. 202, 209 N.W. 475, 210 N.W. 822. Estates by the entirety no longer exist in this state either in real or personal property. Anything in *Dupont v. Jonet, supra,* inconsistent with this opinion is overruled.

It is contended by the respondents that the fund is exempt because it arose from a sale of their homestead. It is true that the fund is exempt from seizure "while held, with the intention to procure another homestead therewith, for a period not exceeding two years." Sec. 272.20, Stats. But the law makes no restriction on the voluntary disposition of the fund. The defendant Huber has a lien for attorney's fees on the funds in dispute, in the amount of $100, about which there does not appear to be any contest. He appears here, and he appeared in the court below, to secure the advice of the court as to a proper disposition of the trust funds held by him. He is entitled to retain his fee out of the trust funds, together with his costs to be taxed. The judgment of the circuit court is reversed, with directions to enter judgment in accordance with this opinion.

B. SURVIVORSHIP MARITAL PROPERTY.

In Wisconsin, married persons each own an undivided fifty percent interest in most property acquired during the marriage, regardless of which spouse literally acquired title to it. Consequently, when one spouse dies, the survivor takes half the marital property and the remainder becomes part of the estate of the deceased. However, if the spouses prefer, they can delegate all or part of the marital property as *survivorship marital property.* Such property automatically passes in its entirety to the surviving spouse. The Wisconsin system of marital property and survivorship property is discussed in greater detail in Chapter 5. The case below illustrates the similarities between survivorship marital property and the traditional common law concurrent estates.

Wis. Stat. 766.60. Optional forms of holding property; survivorship ownership.

(1) Spouses may hold marital property in a form that designates the holders of it by the words "(name of one spouse) or (name of other spouse) as marital property".

(2) Spouses may hold marital property in a form that designates the holder of it by the words "(name of one spouse) and (name of other spouse) as marital property".

(3) A spouse may hold individual property in a form that designates the holder of it by the words "(name of spouse) as individual property".

(4)

(a) Spouses may hold property in any other form permitted by law, including but not limited to a concurrent form or a form that provides survivorship ownership. Except as provided in par. (b) and except with respect to any remedy a spouse has under this chapter, whether a tenancy in common or joint tenancy was created before or after the determination date, to the extent the incidents of the tenancy in common or joint tenancy conflict with or differ from the incidents of property classification under this chapter, the incidents of the tenancy in common or of the joint tenancy, including the incident of survivorship, control.

(b)

1. Except as provided in subd. 2. or in a marital property agreement under s. 766.58:

a. If a document of title, instrument of transfer or bill of sale expresses an intent to establish a joint tenancy exclusively between spouses after the determination date, the property is survivorship marital property under sub. (5)

b. If a document of title, instrument of transfer or bill of sale expresses an intent to establish a tenancy in common exclusively between spouses after the determination date, the property is marital property.

2. A joint tenancy or tenancy in common exclusively between spouses which is given to the spouses by a 3rd party after the determination date is survivorship marital property or marital property, respectively, unless the donor provides otherwise.

(5)

(a) If the words "survivorship marital property" are used instead of the words "marital property" in the form described in sub. (1) or (2), the marital property so held is survivorship marital property. On the death of a spouse, the ownership rights of that spouse in the property vest solely in the surviving spouse by nontestamentary disposition at death. The first deceased spouse may not dispose at death of any interest in survivorship marital property. Holding marital property in a form described in sub. (1) or (2) does not alone establish survivorship ownership between the spouses with respect to the property held.

(b) A real estate mortgage, a security interest under ch. 409 or a lien under s. 71.91 (5) (b) or ch. 49 or 779 on or against the interest of a spouse in survivorship marital property does not defeat the right of survivorship on the death of the spouse. The surviving spouse takes the interest of the deceased spouse subject to the mortgage, security interest or lien.

(c) A judgment lien on the interest of a spouse in survivorship marital property does not defeat the right of survivorship on the death of the spouse. If execution on the judgment lien was issued before the spouse's death the surviving spouse takes the interest of the deceased spouse subject to the lien. If execution on the judgment lien was not issued before the spouse's death, the surviving spouse takes the interest of the deceased spouse free of the judgment lien, unless the judgment lien is on the interests of both spouses in the survivorship marital property and all of the property of the spouses was available under s. 766.55 to satisfy the obligation for which the judgment was rendered.

Moen v. Moen

Wisconsin Court of Appeals
308 Wis. 2d 395, 746 N.W.2d 605 (2008)

PER CURIAM. Joyce Moen appeals from an order denying her motion to reopen the probate of the estate of her husband, Lester Moen. The dispositive issue is whether the marital property agreement reclassified certain property as non-survivorship marital property. We conclude it did, and therefore we affirm.

Joyce filed a motion to reopen the estate under WIS. STAT. §879.31 (2005-06), which incorporates the standards provided in WIS. STAT. §806.07. The motion asserted that, as to a property the parties refer to as "Farm No. 3," Joyce succeeded to Lester's interest in the farm upon his death by right of survivorship, and therefore the Estate had no legal interest in the farm, and the personal representative had no legal authority to convey any interest in the farm to heirs under the will. The circuit court denied the motion. On appeal, Joyce frames her argument for reopening in various ways, but all of them ultimately rely on the assertion that she had a survivorship interest in Farm No. 3. We conclude that this assertion is in error.

In March 2000, Joyce and Lester received a warranty deed on Farm No. 3, which titled the property in their names, with the further notation "Husband and Wife as Survivorship Marital Property." In May 2000, they executed a marital property agreement. The respondents argue that this agreement reclassified Farm No. 3 in a manner that extinguished Joyce's survivorship right that was provided in the title. We agree.

Construction of a marital property agreement is a question of law. Gardner v. Gardner, 190 Wis. 2d 216, 240, 527 N.W.2d 701 (Ct. App. 1994). This case hinges on the distinction between "marital property" and "survivorship marital property." For both forms of marital property, each spouse normally has a present undivided one-half interest in each item. WIS. STAT. §766.31(3). The difference is at the death of one spouse. If property is held in the names of the spouses "as marital property," that phrase does not alone establish survivorship ownership. WIS. STAT. §766.60(5)(a). However, if the property is instead described as "survivorship marital property," the ownership rights of the decedent spouse vest solely in the surviving spouse by nontestamentary disposition. Id.

The marital property agreement in this case provides in paragraph 3.II.A. that the parties "designate the following property as marital property: All real estate owned by them or either of them." Farm No. 3 fits within the description of "real estate owned by them." We conclude that by describing this property as "marital property," rather than "survivorship marital property," the marital property agreement had the effect of altering the form in which the property was held. In other words, for purposes of determining survivorship rights, the agreement had the effect of modifying the form of ownership that was earlier established in the title.

Joyce argues that this interpretation of the agreement is erroneous because, in her view, the agreement actually confirms the existing forms of ownership and survivorship as to all real estate, by expressly confirming the primacy of any designation set forth in the title. In support of this contention she quotes a sentence from paragraph 3.III: "All other property shall be classified as marital property unless otherwise titled." Because Farm No. 3 was "otherwise titled," Joyce argues that the title controls. However, we conclude that Joyce is reading this sentence too broadly. In the context of paragraph 3.III., it is clear that this sentence is part of the provisions regarding "property acquired by them together or individually after the date of this agreement." (Emphasis added.) Therefore, this provision is irrelevant to Farm No. 3, which was acquired before the agreement.

Joyce also argues that the court erred by deciding her motion to reopen without permitting her to take discovery on her allegation that the personal representative may have committed fraud in the classification of Lester's interest in Farm No. 3 as an asset of the Estate. We conclude that this issue is resolved by our conclusion that the personal representative's treatment of Lester's interest was legally correct. Even if we assume for purposes of argument that the personal representative reached that result by fraud, that would not be a ground to reopen the estate, since the result as to Joyce would still be the same in the absence of any fraud. Order affirmed.

IV. PAYABLE ON DEATH ACCOUNTS

Payable on death (P.O.D.) and transfer on death (T.O.D.) accounts are created by contractual arrangements. Under such agreements, a party holding assets of value belonging to another agrees to deliver the assets to a named beneficiary upon the death of the property owner. (The classic example is a bank account with a P.O.D. designation.) Accounts of this nature exist in a variety of forms including what are commonly (but not correctly) called "joint bank accounts;" stock certificates, mutual fund shares, and pension plans. For all practical purposes, any type of financial account controlled by its owner can be designated to transfer automatically, and outside the probate process, to a third party immediately upon the death of the owner.

At one time, P.O.D. accounts were viewed as invalidly executed wills, in that they were revocable designations for the transfer of property to take effect on the death of the owner, but were not likely to executed and witnessed in compliance with the Wills Act. Nevertheless, the devices were popular, and Wisconsin adopted legislation in 1951 declaring some forms of P.O.D. accounts to be non-testamentary. Today, Wisconsin and most other states exempt such accounts and instruments from the requirements of the Wills Act.

It is somewhat ironic that the P.O.D. account apparently flourished even when it was legally unenforceable in most states. Since the beneficiaries on such accounts were commonly the heirs or likely devisees of the owner, they had no incentive to challenge the validity of the transfer from which they benefitted by having the assets pass outside of probate. For similar reasons, the banks and insurance companies and other entities that offered such arrangements had no reason to emphasize their presumed "illegality." The following case reflects the traditional approach to these types of arrangements. However, five years after the decision, its holding was superseded by a P.O.D. account-friendly statute. The second case represents the contemporary approach.

A. FINANCIAL ACCOUNTS

Wis. Stat. 705.01. [Multi-Party and Agency Accounts] Definitions.

As used in this subchapter, unless the context otherwise requires:

(1) "Account" means a contract of deposit of funds between a depositor and a financial institution, and includes a checking or savings account, certificate of deposit, share account and other like arrangement. All such contracts in which there are 2 or more parties or one or more agents shall be evidenced by a writing signed by each party making a deposit to the account, prior to or within a reasonable time after such deposit, containing language in substantially the form set forth in s. 705.02 For purposes of this subchapter, the term "account" does not include contracts established for the deposit of funds of a partnership, joint venture, or other association for business purposes, accounts controlled by one or more persons as the duly authorized agents or trustees for a corporation, limited liability company, unincorporated association, or charitable or civic organization, or regular fiduciary or trust accounts where the relationship is established other than by deposit agreement.

(2) "Agent" means a person who, by the terms of an account, has a present right, subject to request, to payment therefrom as agent for all of the parties to the account.

(3) "Financial institution" means any organization authorized to do business under state or federal laws relating to financial institutions, including, without limitation, banks and trust companies, savings banks, building and loan associations, savings and loan associations and credit unions.

(4) "Joint account" means an account, other than a marital account, payable on request to one or more of 2 or more parties whether or not mention is made of any right of survivorship. "Joint account" also means any account established with the right of survivorship on or after January 1, 1986, by 2 parties who claim to be husband and wife, which is payable on request to either or both of the parties.

(4m) "Marital account" means an account established without the right of survivorship on or after January 1, 1986, by 2 parties who claim to be husband and wife, which is payable on request to either or both of the parties and which is designated as a marital account. An account established by those parties with the right of survivorship under s. 766.58 (3) (f) or 766.60 is a joint account.

(5) "Net contribution" of a party to a joint account as of any given time is the sum of all deposits made by or for the party, less all withdrawals made by or for the party which have not been paid to or applied for the use of any other party, plus a proportional share of any interest or dividends included in the current balance as adjusted to reflect time of deposit. It includes

any proceeds of deposit life insurance added to the account by reason of the death of the party whose net contribution is in question.

(6) "Party" means a person who, by the terms of an account, has a present right, subject to request, to payment therefrom other than as agent. A beneficiary of a P.O.D. account is a party only after the account becomes payable to the beneficiary by reason of the beneficiary's surviving the original payee. A minor may be a party to an account, subject to the withdrawal restrictions of s. 705.04 (2) Unless the context indicates otherwise, "party" includes a guardian, conservator, personal representative or assignee, including an attaching creditor, of a party.

(7) "Payment" of sums on deposit includes withdrawal, payment on check or other order of a party, any pledge of sums on deposit by a party and any setoff, or reduction or other disposition of all or part of an account pursuant to a pledge.

(8) "P.O.D. account" means an account payable on request to one person during lifetime and on the person's death to one or more P.O.D. beneficiaries, or to one or more persons during their lifetimes and on the death of all of them to one or more P.O.D. beneficiaries. It includes an account in the name of one or more parties as trustee for one or more beneficiaries where the relationship is established by the form of the account and the deposit agreement with the financial institution and there is no subject of the trust other than the sums on deposit in the account. It includes a marital account for which a party named one or more P.O.D. beneficiaries for that party's interest.

(9) "P.O.D. Beneficiary" means a person designated on a P.O.D. account as one to whom all For part of the account is payable on request after the death of one or more parties.

(10) "Request" means a proper request for withdrawal, or a check or other order for payment, which complies with all conditions of the account, including special requirements concerning necessary signatures and regulations of the financial institution. Unless the signature card, passbook, contract or instrument evidencing the account clearly provides to the contrary, a request by all parties to a joint or marital account is required for payment if the account is designated with their names conjunctively joined by the word "and". If the financial institution conditions withdrawal or payment on advance notice, for purposes of this subchapter the request for withdrawal or payment is treated as immediately effective and a notice of intent to withdraw is treated as a request for withdrawal.

(11) "Sums on deposit" means the balance payable on a multiple-party account including interest, dividends, and any deposit life insurance proceeds added to the account by reason of the death of a party.

Wis. Stat. 705.04. Right of survivorship.

(1) Sums remaining on deposit at the death of a party to a joint account belong to the surviving party or parties as against the estate of the decedent unless there is clear and convincing

evidence of a different intention at the time the account is created. If there are 2 or more surviving parties, their ownership interests during lifetime shall remain subject to s. 705.03 (1); and the right of survivorship continues between the surviving parties.

(2) If the account is a P.O.D. account, on the death of the original payee or the survivor of 2 or more original payees, all of the following apply:

(a) If there is one P.O.D. beneficiary and he or she survives, he or she is entitled to payment of all sums remaining on deposit.

(b) If there are 2 or more P.O.D. beneficiaries and they all survive, they are entitled to payment of the sums on deposit in accordance with any written instructions that the owner filed with the financial institution or, if the owner left no written instructions, to payment in equal shares.

(c) If 2 or more persons succeed to ownership of the account, there is no further right of survivorship unless the terms of the account expressly provide for survivorship or for the accounts continuance as a joint account.

(d) Subject to the rights of financial institutions under s. 705.06 (1) (c), if any P.O.D. beneficiary predeceases the original payee or the survivor of 2 or more original payees, the amount to which the predeceased P.O.D. beneficiary would have been entitled passes to any of his or her issue who would take under s. 854.06 (3) (e) If no P.O.D. beneficiary or predeceased P.O.D. beneficiary's issue who would take under s. 854.06 (3) survives the death of all owners, the account belongs to the estate of the deceased sole owner or the estate of the last to die of multiple owners.

(f) Payment may be made to a minor P.O.D. beneficiary only in accordance with a procedure approved under ch. 54 (g) If the P.O.D. account is a marital account, this section applies only to the 50 percent of the account not owned by the surviving spouse named as a party on the account.

(2g) Notwithstanding subs. (1) and (2), the department of health services may collect, from funds of a decedent that are held by the decedent immediately before death in a joint account or a P.O.D. account, an amount equal to the medical assistance that is recoverable under s. 49.496 (3) (a), an amount equal to aid under s. 49.68, 49.683 or 49.685 that is recoverable under s. 49.682 (2) (a), an amount equal to long-term community support services under s. 46.27 that is recoverable under s. 46.27 (7g) (c) 1. and that was paid on behalf of the decedent or the decedent's spouse or an amount equal to the family care benefit under s. 46.286 that is recoverable under rules promulgated under s. 46.286 (7) and that was paid on behalf of the decedent or the decedent's spouse.

(2m) Unless a marital property agreement under s. 766.58 provides otherwise, after deducting all payments and certifications made under s. 404.405 50% of the sums remaining on deposit at the death of a party to a marital account belongs to and may, upon the maturity of the account, be withdrawn by the surviving spouse and 50% belongs to and may, upon the maturity of the account, be withdrawn by the decedent's estate. No financial institution is liable for any amount withdrawn under this subsection by a party who falsely claims to be the decedent's spouse.

(3) Subject to s. 853.15, a right of survivorship arising from the express terms of the account or under this section, or a P.O.D. beneficiary designation, cannot be changed by will. Any transfers resulting from the application of this section are not to be considered testamentary dispositions.

(4) As to any deposit made on or after January 1, 1986, a surviving spouse who is not a party to the account may recover under s. 766.70 (6)

Wis. Stat. 705.05. Designation and powers of agent.

(1) A party to an account, notwithstanding such party's minority, or if the account has multiple parties, all of them acting in concert, may appoint one or more agents for purposes of making withdrawals from the account. The authority of an agent to make withdrawals from an account may be terminated by any party to the account upon written notice to the financial institution, and this shall not preclude a party's liability for wrongful termination of such agency.

(2) The uses and purposes for which withdrawals may be made by an agent to an account shall be governed by agency principles of general application. The application of any sum withdrawn from an account shall only be subject to inquiry by a party to the account, and such party shall have the burden of proving breach of the agency relationship. A minor party may not disaffirm the appointment of an agent, but the period within which the minor party may inquire into the propriety of any withdrawal shall be governed by s. 893.16 or 893.18 Unless there is clear and convincing evidence of a different intent, if the agent is a spouse of a party, the sums so withdrawn may be used, but not by way of limitation, for the support and maintenance of either spouse or any common minor children.

(3) The parties to an account may provide, by the terms of the account or by independent written power of attorney which, if later, shall have precedence over the terms of the account, that the authority conferred upon an agent shall be exercisable notwithstanding any party's legal disability. In such case the authority of the agent is also exercisable notwithstanding later uncertainty as to whether a party is dead or alive. Absent a written direction to the contrary, the foregoing power of withdrawal shall exist without the necessity of written provision if the agent is the spouse of a party, but in such a case funds so withdrawn, the application of which may be inquired into only as provided in sub. (2), may only be used for the support and maintenance of either spouse and any common minor children. This subsection shall apply to all accounts created prior to and after July 1, 1975.

Wis. Stat. 705.06. Protection of financial institutions.

(1) In accordance with the terms of an account, and subject to this subchapter, ch. 112 and the duties prescribed for personal representatives in ch. 72 and unless otherwise ordered by a court of competent jurisdiction:

(a) A financial institution may on request pay any sums on deposit in the account to any party or agent; and the financial institution shall not be required to look into the source of funds received for deposit or the proposed application of any funds withdrawn or requested to be withdrawn.

(b) Any sums in a joint account may be paid, on request, to any party without regard to whether any other party is under legal disability or is deceased at the time the payment is requested.

(c) Any sums in a P.O.D. account may be paid, on request, to the P.O.D. beneficiary upon presentation to the financial institution of proof of death showing that the P.O.D. beneficiary survived all persons named as original payees of the account. If more than one P.O.D. beneficiary is named and at least one of them is predeceased, sums in the account may be paid to the surviving P.O.D. beneficiary or beneficiaries upon presentation of proof of death of the other beneficiary, without regard to claims by the issue of a predeceased beneficiary under s. 705.04 (2) (d) If none of the named beneficiaries survive, the sums in the account may be paid to the estate of the deceased sole owner or the estate of the owner who was the last to die of multiple owners, without regard to claims by the issue of a predeceased beneficiary under s. 705.04 (2) (d) If the P.O.D. account is a marital account, this paragraph applies only to the 50 percent of the account not owned by the surviving spouse named as a party on the account.

(d) Any sums in a marital account may be paid, on request, to either party without regard to whether the other party is under legal disability or is deceased, unless the financial institution receives actual notice that the other party is deceased. After receipt of actual notice of the death of one party to a marital account, the financial institution may pay on request not more than 50% of the sums on deposit to the surviving party, and 50% of that amount to the personal representative of the deceased party or if applicable to any P.O.D. beneficiary of the deceased party's interest, unless before payment is made the financial institution receives a verified statement under s. 865.201 or a certified copy of a certificate or recorded application concerning survivorship rights under s. 867.046, in which case the financial institution shall make payment as provided in that document.

(2) Payment made under this subchapter discharges the financial institution from all claims for amounts so withdrawn. If the institution has reason to believe that a dispute exists as to the rights of the parties to an account or their successors it may, but shall not be required to, refuse to pay funds in the account to any persons pending instructions from a court, or it may pay the proceeds to a court. An institution may but need not recognize the authority of an agent, other than one with continuing authority under s. 705.05 (3), until it knows of the fact of death or

adjudication of incompetence of all parties appointing such agent and has reasonable opportunity to act.

(3) The protection provided by this section shall have no bearing on the rights of parties or their successors in disputes concerning the beneficial ownership of funds in or withdrawn from an account.

Wis. Stat. 705.07. Rights of creditors.

(1) Only the creditors of any living party to an account may subject the entire sums on deposit to their claims, as if such sums resulted solely from contributions made by the debtor party. If a joint or P.O.D. account requires the signatures of all of the parties for purposes of withdrawal, such account shall not be subject to the claims of creditors of a debtor party to the extent of the net contributions of the other parties to the account. Such other parties shall have the burden of proving their net contributions by clear and convincing evidence.

(2) For purposes of ch. 242, a debtor party shall be deemed to have made a transfer only at the time some other party withdraws all or part of the sums on deposit, or at the time of the debtor party's death as to sums not previously withdrawn. In the case of a withdrawal while the debtor party is living, the sole grounds for determining any such transfer to be fraudulent shall be whether the debtor party is or will be thereby rendered insolvent under s. 242.05 (1) or whether the debtor party is engaged or is about to engage in a business or transaction for which the assets remaining in the debtor party's hands after the transfer are unreasonably small under s. 242.04 (1) (b) 1. In the case of a transfer by reason of the death of the debtor party, the sole ground for determining any such transfer to be fraudulent shall be whether the debtor party's estate subject to administration is insolvent under s. 242.02 For purposes of this subsection, the amount transferred shall be deemed to consist of those assets which the creditors of the debtor party could have made subject to their claims immediately prior to the transfer, less any sums which such creditors could have made so subject to their claims immediately after the transfer.

Wis. Stat. 705.08. Construction

This subchapter shall be construed in such a manner as to ensure reasonable certainty of legal result for those who establish a multiple-party or agency account.

Wis. Stat. 705.09. Applicability of general transfers at death provisions.

Chapter 854 **[Transfers at Death – General Rules]** applies to transfers at death under this subchapter.

Wis. Stat. 705.10. Non probate transfers on death

(1) A provision for a nonprobate transfer on death in an insurance policy, contract of employment, bond, mortgage, promissory note, certificated or uncertificated security, account agreement, custodial agreement, deposit agreement, compensation plan, pension plan, individual retirement plan, employee benefit plan, trust, conveyance, deed of gift, marital property agreement, or other written instrument of a similar nature is nontestamentary. This subsection governs a written provision that:

(a) Money or other benefits due, controlled by or owned by a decedent before death must be paid after the decedents death to a person whom the decedent designates either in the instrument or in a separate writing, including a will executed either before or at the same time as the instrument, or later;(b) Money due or to become due under the instrument ceases to be payable in the event of death of the promisee or the promisor before payment or demand; or(c) Any property controlled by or owned by the decedent before death which is the subject of the instrument passes to a person whom the decedent designates either in the instrument or in a separate writing, including a will executed either before or at the same time as the instrument, or later.

(2) This section does not limit rights of creditors under other laws of this state.

(3) Chapter 854 applies to transfers at death under this section.

(4) A transfer under this section does not require confirmation in any procedure under s. 867.01, 867.02, or 867.03 or ch. 856 or 865 A transfer under this section may be confirmed under s. 867.046 (1m) or (2)

Tucker v. Simrow

Supreme Court of Wisconsin

248 Wis. 143, 21 N.W.2d 252 (1946)

Wickhem, J. The facts are undisputed and are not complicated. Augusta Sands had savings and checking accounts in the State Bank of Elcho. She married Frank Simrow and had the accounts changed to "Mrs. Frank Simrow." On December 1, 1936, after consultation with the bank cashier she signed a paper containing the following directions applicable to the accounts:

"Effective as of this date you are hereby directed to add the following to my savings account No. 659:

"In case of death one half (1/2) of this account to be payable to Frank Simrow, husband; one fourth (1/4) to Florence Tucker Wirth, daughter; one fourth (1/4) to Clarence Tucker, son.

"You are also directed to add the following to my checking account:

"In case of death same to be payable to Frank Simrow, husband.

"(Signed) Mrs. Frank Simrow,

Mrs. Frank Simrow."

Appellant argues that under the facts above there was a contract between the bank and depositor for the benefit of third parties (namely the persons named in Exhibit C), and that under the logic of the decisions in Estate of Staver, 218 Wis. 114, 260 N. W. 655, and Estate of Skilling, 218 Wis. 574, 260 N. W. 660, the balance in these accounts remaining at the death of depositor should be paid according to the terms of the contract. Tweeddale v. Tweeddale, 116 Wis. 517, 93 N. W. 440.

The trial court held that the directions in Exhibit C were ineffective testamentary dispositions by testator. We consider that this ruling was correct. In the Staver Case, supra, this court dealt with the question whether a joint deposit was effectively created without delivery of certificates of deposit evidencing the account. This court held that no delivery was necessary, since the contract between the bank and depositor created the chose in action which was the subject of the gift, as well as an immediate present interest in the persons named as joint tenants; that since no transfer of a chose in action was involved, the terms of the contract itself determined its scope, effect, and validity and there was nothing to deliver and requirements as to gifts of specific personal property are inapplicable.

The doctrine of Koppelkam v. First Wisconsin Trust Co. 240 Wis. 254, 3 N. W. (2d) 350, and Warsco v. Oshkosh Savings & Trust Co. 183 Wis. 156, 196 N. W. 829, is to the effect that, where substantially entire control of the property disposed of is retained by the person making the deposit until his death, a testamentary disposition has been attempted and any document making such disposition must satisfy the statute governing execution of wills. The distinction is between cases like the Staver and Skilling Cases, supra, where a present interest is created in the person alleged to be a joint tenant and those where complete control over the property or chose is retained until death by the donor. Judgment affirmed.

Bruckner v. Prairie Federal Sav. & Loan Asso.

Supreme Court of Wisconsin

81 Wis. 2d 215, 260 N.W.2d 256, (1977)

HEFFERNAN, J. The questions presented are whether a "payable on death" savings account is permissible in a federal savings and loan association and, if it is, whether there is sufficient evidence to show that the decedent, John L. Bruckner, created a savings account with the Prairie du Chien Federal Savings and Loan Association payable on his death to Lee J. Bruckner, a nephew.

We conclude that, as a matter of state law, an account "payable on death" to designated beneficiaries is permissible in a federal savings and loan association, but we also conclude that there is insufficient evidence to show that John L. Bruckner created such an account payable upon his death to Lee J. Bruckner or that he intended to create such account. Accordingly, we affirm the trial court judgment, which directed that the proceeds of the account be paid to Richard A. Bruckner as personal representative of the estate of John L. Bruckner.

The admitted facts show that John L. Bruckner, who died on July 8, 1974, opened a savings account, in his own name only, on November 9, 1959, at the savings and loan association. On that latter date, he executed a signature card, and he received a passbook. On the same date, the association opened a ledger card, which thereafter purported to reflect deposits and withdrawals in respect to John L. Bruckner's account. It is undisputed that, at the time the account was opened, only John L. Bruckner was referred to on the association's records.

Upon the death of John L. Bruckner in 1974, Richard A. Bruckner, as personal representative, presented the passbook to the association and asked that the amount on deposit (in excess of $18,000) be delivered to him for inclusion in the estate assets.

The association refused to turn over the assets, because of an entry on the signature card which recited "POD to Lee J. Bruckner." The same entry appears on the second of three pages of the association's ledger card in respect to the Bruckner account.

When the association refused to turn over the money to the personal representative, he commenced this action against the savings and loan association, asserting that POD accounts were not permissible in federal savings and loan associations and, in addition, that the evidence was insufficient to show that John L. Bruckner had set up an account payable on his death to Lee J. Bruckner. Lee J. Bruckner was joined as a third-party defendant.

The evidence at trial showed that initially the signature card and the ledger card did not include a POD entry. No association employee had any recollection when the POD entries were made on the signature and ledger cards. It was shown, however, that the typed addition to the cards was made by a typewriter which was not acquired by the savings and loan association until 1966.

Each year the savings and loan association, for tax purposes, sent its members federal interest report forms 1099. Copies of these forms were placed in evidence at trial. Only for the two years, 1969 and 1973, did the forms refer to the account as a POD account.

Because the typewriter used to make the signature and ledger card entries was acquired in 1966 and the earliest date that there was reference to the POD nature of the account in the 1099 forms was 1969, it is reasonable to assume that the entry was made on the cards sometime between 1966 and 1969.

There was no evidence to show that John L. Bruckner had ever requested or applied for a POD account, and no employee of the association had any recollection of making the POD entries on the cards.

Because the origin of the POD card entries could not be demonstrated, the trial judge ruled that the cards were not admissible to show the POD entries. Such entries, he held, were not authenticated, but the cards, exclusive of the POD reference, were admissible for the limited purpose of showing the creation of the account and the ensuing ledger entries only. Objection had been made by the plaintiff to the POD portion of the entry under sec. 909.01, Stats., which requires that evidence be identified or authenticated as a precondition to admissibility.

Because there was, therefore, no evidence admitted which showed that an account payable on death to Lee J. Bruckner was ever created, the trial judge held that the proceeds of the account were properly payable to the personal representative of John L. Bruckner and ordered the claim of Lee J. Bruckner dismissed.

This appeal could be disposed of on an evidentiary basis only, i.e., assuming the propriety of establishing a POD account in a federal savings and loan association, there was no evidence to show that John L. Bruckner had created or attempted to create a POD account.

Both parties, however, have extensively briefed the question of whether POD accounts are permitted in federal savings and loan associations doing business in Wisconsin. The appellant, Lee J. Bruckner, contends they are permitted; and the respondent, personal representative, contends they are not. Were we to conclude as a matter of law that POD accounts are impermissible, the question whether from an evidentiary viewpoint John L. Bruckner intended to create a POD account or followed the procedure necessary to create one, if permissible, would be irrelevant.

We, accordingly, address ourselves to the permissibility of creating POD accounts in federal savings and loan associations in Wisconsin.

While, at one time, accounts payable on death were held void in Wisconsin because, under the rationale of Tucker v. Simrow, 248 Wis. 143, 21 N.W.2d 252 (1946), they sought to make a testamentary disposition without complying with the statute of wills, POD accounts were specifically permitted after the passage of sec. 215.14 (2), Stats., in 1951. That renumbered statute applicable to this case provides:

"215.14(13) Accounts Payable to Another Person Upon Death. Savings accounts may be issued to a member payable upon death to another person. Upon the death of the member such other named person shall become the owner thereof, and the payment of the withdrawal value of the savings accounts to such person shall be made under s. 72.29, but no new owner shall have right superior or prior to the rights of the deceased member. Such savings accounts shall be considered a part of the deceased member's estate and subject to the payment of his just debts." (Stats. 1973)

From the effective date of that statute POD accounts were permissible for state savings institutions (Estate of Fucela, 26 Wis.2d 476, 132 N.W.2d 553 (1965)), but were they also thereafter permissible in federal savings and loan associations doing business in Wisconsin? We conclude that they were.

The parties agree that no federal statutes or regulations prohibit or authorize POD accounts. Our independent investigation corroborates the research of the parties. The federal law is silent on the subject of POD accounts.

In Kaski v. First Federal Savings & Loan Association of Madison, 72 Wis.2d 132, 240 N.W.2d 367 (1976), we indicated that, in respect to the regulation of lending practices of federal savings and loan associations, the federal law was pervasive and preempted any state regulation in the field. We clearly implied, however, that federal savings and loan associations were subject to state laws in some respects. Kaski, supra, at 141. We said therein, quoting Pearson v. First Federal Savings & Loan Asso. (Fla. App. 1963), 149 So.2d 891, 894-95:

"'It is a well-established rule that federal savings and loan associations are subject only to state law which does not interfere with the purposes for which it was created, does not destroy its efficiency, and does not conflict with paramount federal law.'"

In the context of this case we are not concerned with any state regulatory power that conflicts with federal legislation. Our question here is solely one of state laws -- by what means, other than by will, can property be passed to another upon the death of the owner.

The federal law, while demonstrating an interest in the taxability of such transfers, has never sought to limit the methods of testamentary transfers in respect to federally franchised institutions or otherwise.

While the federal law is silent in respect to POD accounts, the State of Wisconsin by sec. 215.14(13), Stats., in effect at the time it is alleged the POD account was created, has announced that POD accounts are not contrary to Wisconsin public policy and are permitted by Wisconsin law.

Although the state law does not purport to regulate the lending practices of federal savings and loan associations, it does recognize property interests that may be created or transferred by federal savings and loan associations. The creation and transfer of these interests are regulated by state law. The federal government has no concern with these matters.

We accordingly conclude that federal savings and loan associations doing business in Wisconsin may issue accounts to a member with the provision that, upon the death of the association member, the proceeds of the account will be payable to a named beneficiary.

Did John L. Bruckner provide for such an account? There is no admissible evidence which shows that he did. …

[In the remainder of its opinion, the court explains its reasons for ruling the evidence presented by Lee Buckner was inadmissible]

… In this case, no evidence was produced that tended to show any intent by John L. Bruckner to make the account payable upon his death to Lee J. Bruckner. Judgment affirmed.

B. ANNUITIES AND INSURANCE CONTRACTS

Reichel v. Jung

Court of Appeals of Wisconsin
237 Wis. 2d, 616 N.W.2d 118 (2000)

SNYDER, J. The children of Ronald E. Jung (Jung children) appeal from an order of the circuit court dismissing their claim seeking the proceeds of an annuity (the Annuity) owned by Ronald prior to his death. The Jung children argue that the Annuity transferred to Ronald's estate pursuant to Ronald and his wife Dianne's "Marital Property Classification Agreement." Dianne counters that the terms of the Annuity should dispose of the policy because it expressly directed ownership to pass to her as "co-annuitant."

We agree with Dianne that the terms of the Annuity control this dispute. In reaching this conclusion, we follow Wisconsin law concerning nonprobate transfers at death and joint accounts with the right of survivorship. Under Wis. Stat. § 705.20 (1995-96), the Annuity passed to Dianne as a nonprobate transfer of property, thereby defeating the marital agreement's classification of the Annuity as individual property and the will's bequest of individual property to the Jung children. In addition, under Wis. Stat. § 705.04, the Annuity constituted a joint account which transferred to Dianne as Ronald's survivor. We therefore conclude that the trial court's decision should be affirmed.

BACKGROUND

The pertinent facts have been stipulated. On April 14, 1997, Ronald and Dianne entered into a marital agreement for purposes of identifying and classifying the couple's individual and marital property. The agreement provided:

> 1. Purposes. The purposes of this Agreement are to classify and reclassify all properties, both real and personal, (including joint tenancy properties and properties held as tenants-in-common) now owned and/or hereafter acquired by either or both parties, as INDIVIDUAL PROPERTY or MARITAL PROPERTIES, as the case may be, pursuant to Sections 766.31(10) and 766.58 of the Wisconsin Statutes in order to avoid any confusion and uncertainty as to each party's ownership interests. This Agreement shall be construed in accordance with Chapter 766 of the Wisconsin Statutes.
>
> ....
>
> 3. Property Classified as Dianne's Individual Property. Both parties agree that the property described on Exhibit A attached hereto and incorporated herein by reference as though set forth in its entirety, together with all income and appreciation attributable to that property, shall be classified and reclassified as Dianne's INDIVIDUAL PROPERTY. In addition, all property acquired in exchange for any such INDIVIDUAL PROPERTY and/or acquired from the proceeds of the sale of such INDIVIDUAL PROPERTY, shall also be classified and reclassified as Dianne's INDIVIDUAL PROPERTY.
>
> 4. Property Classified as Ron's Individual Property. Both parties agree that the property described on Exhibit B attached hereto and incorporated herein by reference as though set forth in its entirety, together with all income and appreciation attributable to that property, shall be classified and reclassified as Ron's INDIVIDUAL PROPERTY. In addition, all property acquired in exchange for any such INDIVIDUAL PROPERTY and/or acquired from the proceeds of the sale of such INDIVIDUAL PROPERTY, shall also be classified and reclassified as Ron's INDIVIDUAL PROPERTY.
>
> 5. Classification of All Other Property. The parties herewith classify and reclassify all other properties of the parties, together with all income and appreciation, with the exception of those properties

> classified as the INDIVIDUAL PROPERTY of a party in accordance with the above paragraphs 3 and 4, as MARITAL PROPERTIES of the parties.

Ronald and Dianne also agreed to waive any claim they may have to the other's individual property:

> 6. Property Rights of the Survivor. Each of the parties hereby waives, bars and absolutely relinquishes any and all rights which he or she may have under the law (regardless of the jurisdiction) with respect to the INDIVIDUAL PROPERTY of the other party upon the death of the other party. Without limiting the generality of the foregoing, this waiver shall include any and all elective rights under Chapter 861 of the Wisconsin Statutes or any other similar statute in any other jurisdiction where the parties may reside, it being the intention of the parties to absolutely bar any right of either party in the INDIVIDUAL PROPERTY of the other party. This paragraph is intended to apply to all rights and property interests acquired as a result of the parties' marriage, including but not limited to rights of intestate succession, dower and curtesy, rights to elect against the will, election of deferred marital property, election of augmented marital property estate treatment, and election against the augmented estate; provided, however, that this paragraph shall not divest the surviving party of his or her one-half (1/2) interest in all MARITAL PROPERTY, acquired in accordance with paragraph 5 of this Agreement.
>
> Each party shall join in the execution and filing of any instrument or conveyance and take any other action necessary to relinquish or otherwise avoid the effects of the laws of any jurisdiction conferring any right or interest relinquished above, if the other party's legal representative or successor in interest so requests.
>
> However, nothing in this Agreement shall restrict the right of either party to voluntarily provide for the other party in accordance with his or her overall estate plan.

The agreement further allowed for transfer of record title upon request consistent with Ronald and Dianne's property classification:

> 7. Change of Record Title. In the event record title to property classified as a party's INDIVIDUAL PROPERTY is titled in the name of the other party or in both parties' names, each party agrees upon request to transfer record title to the party in whose name the asset has been classified as his or her INDIVIDUAL PROPERTY.

Exhibit B of the marital agreement enumerates items of property identified as Ronald's individual property. Included among these items is Prudential Annuity No. 98-623-456 (the Annuity) with an estimated fair market value of $ 182,813.

The Annuity lists Ronald as the first annuitant, Dianne as co-annuitant and the Jung children as primary beneficiaries. Under a provision entitled "Ownership and Control," the Annuity reads:

> Unless we endorse this contract to say otherwise: (1) the owner of the contract is the Annuitant (the First Annuitant, if two are named); (2) while any annuitant is living the owner alone is entitled to (a) any contract benefit and value, and (b) the exercise of any right and privilege granted by the contract or by [Prudential]; and (3) if two annuitants are named and the First Annuitant dies while the Co-Annuitant is living, the Co-Annuitant will become the Owner. (Emphasis added.)

On the same date of the marital agreement's execution, Ronald executed his will. The will provides in relevant part:

> SECOND. I give, devise and bequeath all my household furniture and furnishings, jewelry, wearing apparel, automobiles and all other articles of household or personal use or ornament of which I may die possessed, to my wife, Dianne M. Jung, if living, or if she shall not be living, then equally to my children then-living in such properties as my personal representative in my personal representative's sole discretion shall determine.
>
> THIRD. I hereby ratify and confirm that my wife, Dianne M. Jung, owns all of the individual property classified by us pursuant to a Marital Property Classification Agreement, bearing even date.... To the extent at the time of my death we own any marital property, I hereby declare that my wife, Dianne M. Jung, owns a one-half (1/2) interest in all marital property and I intend that this Will dispose only of my interest in such marital property.

> FOURTH. I give, devise and bequeath the entire rest, residue and remainder of my estate equally to my children and to the then-living descendants, by right of representation, of any deceased child of mine. At the present time I have five (5) children whose names are as follows: Timothy A. Jung, Teresa J. Reichel, Thomas L. Jung, Tamara A. Hall and Todd M. Jung.

Thus, the will conveyed Ronald's interest in his personal effects to Dianne and bequeathed all other property, including his individual property, to the Jung children.

On April 29, 1997, Ronald died. He was survived by Dianne and the Jung children. Following his death, the representative of Ronald's estate, Teresa Reichel, demanded that Dianne relinquish her ownership interest held in the Annuity.

On August 14, 1998, the Jung children brought this action against Dianne, requesting the court to transfer her interest in the Annuity to Ronald's estate. The Jung children then sought a motion for summary judgment seeking the proceeds of the Annuity. After the parties submitted briefs supporting their respective positions, the circuit court ruled in Dianne's favor. The court was persuaded by language contained in the Annuity indicating that if the first annuitant died, the co-annuitant would become owner. The Jung children appeal.

DISCUSSION

Motions for summary judgment are reviewed using the same methodology used by the trial court. See M & I First Nat'l Bank v. Episcopal Homes Management, Inc., 195 Wis. 2d 485, 496, 536 N.W.2d 175 (Ct. App. 1995). We will not repeat this well-known methodology here except to observe that summary judgment is appropriate when there is no genuine issue of material fact and the moving party is entitled to judgment as a matter of law. See M & I, 195 Wis. 2d at 496-97.

The issue in this case is what document controls the disposition of the Annuity-the Annuity itself or Ronald and Dianne's marital agreement. The Jung children argue that the marital agreement is dispositive based on the breadth of its terms. They contend that by retaining ownership of the Annuity, Dianne has violated paragraphs six and seven of the agreement because: (1) she has failed to relinquish her rights in Ronald's individual property; (2) she never executed an instrument or conveyance with respect to Ronald's individual property; (3) she did not take any action to avoid the effects of relinquishing her right to Ronald's property; and (4) she did not transfer record title of

Ronald's individual property to his estate. Because the Annuity is listed under Exhibit B of the marital agreement as Ronald's individual property, the Jung children maintain that Dianne's claim of ownership is defeated.

Dianne counters that the terms of the Annuity govern because they provide that upon the first annuitant's death, "the Co-Annuitant will become owner." Therefore, once Ronald died, Dianne became the owner. Dianne also points out that the marital agreement permits her retention of the Annuity because it states that "nothing in this Agreement shall restrict the right of either party to voluntarily provide for the other party in accordance with his or her overall estate plan."

Standing alone, the Annuity no doubt prescribes transfer of ownership to Dianne as the co-annuitant upon the death of Ronald, the annuitant. The Annuity's language is clear in this regard and the Jung children do not dispute its terms nor do they seek reformation of the contract.

On the other hand, the marital agreement affirmatively sets forth that Ronald's and Dianne's individual property shall belong to each of them separately and that each "absolutely relinquishes any and all rights which he or she may have under the law … with respect to the INDIVIDUAL PROPERTY of the other party upon the death of the other party." Included among Ronald's individual property is the Annuity. The marital agreement's language, however, is tempered by a further provision stating that the marital agreement shall not restrict either party from "voluntarily providing for the other party in accordance with his or her overall estate plan." The agreement does not further explain what an "overall estate plan" entails.

The parties would have us determine which document controls by looking solely at the terms of each. Such an exercise, however, reveals conflicting directions from each document. To resolve this conflict, we consider two Wisconsin Statutes which address the transfer of property upon the property owner's death.

The first statute is Wis. Stat. § 705.20, entitled "Nonprobate transfers on death." The statute reads:

> (1) A provision for a nonprobate transfer on death in an insurance policy, contract of employment, bond, mortgage, promissory note, certificated or uncertificated security, account agreement, custodial agreement, deposit agreement, compensation plan, pension plan, individual retirement plan, employee benefit plan, trust, conveyance, deed of gift, marital property agreement, or other written instrument of

> a similar nature is nontestamentary. This subsection governs a written provision that:
>
> ....
>
> (c) Any property controlled by or owned by the decedent before death which is the subject of the instrument passes to a person whom the decedent designates either in the instrument or in a separate writing, including a will executed either before or at the same time as the instrument, or later.

Id. (emphasis added).

Although an annuity is not enumerated within Wis. Stat. § 705.20(1), we nonetheless believe it falls under the language "other written instrument of a similar nature" because it has similar characteristics to the other items listed. While often issued by insurance companies, an annuity is more accurately classified as an investment, not an insurance policy. See Prudential Ins. Co. v. Howell, 29 N.J. 116, 148 A.2d 145, 148 (N.J. 1959). Like a pension plan, an annuity confers a right to receive payments over a period of time. See Grochowski v. Larson, 196 Wis. 2d 231, 235, 538 N.W.2d 802 (Ct. App. 1995). Like many securities, an annuity contract is conceived by submitting an application and a single payment of the policy's principal. See 19 George J. Couch, Cyclopedia of Insurance Law § 81:2 (2d rev. ed. 1983). As is true with many investment tools, co-owners (or co-annuitants) and beneficiaries may be established. We conclude that an annuity qualifies as a "written instrument of a similar nature."

Under Wis. Stat. § 705.20(1)(c), a nonprobate transfer applies to any property owned by the decedent prior to death which is "the subject of the instrument" and which "passes to a person whom the decedent designates ... in the instrument." The instrument here, the Annuity, contains such a provision. It states that "if two annuitants are named and the First Annuitant dies while the Co-Annuitant is living, the Co-Annuitant will become the Owner." Ronald designated Dianne as a co-annuitant with a right to ownership upon his death. Consistent with § 705.20(1)(c), the Annuity's language calls for transfer of ownership upon Ronald's death to Dianne and therefore avoids any contrary testamentary designation.

We pause to observe that Wis. Stat. § 705.20(1) does specifically mention a "marital property agreement" and would apparently lend support to the Jung children's claim. In Ronald and Dianne's case, however, their marital agreement does not purport to transfer property upon the death of the other. Rather, the agreement seeks to classify their property and, in Ronald's case, works in conjunction with his will which he executed on the same day as the agreement. Ronald's will is what calls for the conveyance of his individual property to the Jung children as beneficiaries of the remainder of his estate. The will therefore provides the means by which the Jung children seek the proceeds of the Annuity. However, conveyance of the Annuity through Ronald's will is precisely what a § 705.20(1) nonprobate transfer seeks to avoid. Section 705.20(1) precludes the transfer of property according to a testamentary arrangement where a contractual agreement provides otherwise.

Wisconsin Stat. § 705.20(1) is identical to the language presented by § 101 of the Uniform Nonprobate Transfers on Death Act of the Uniform Laws Annotated (U.L.A.). The U.L.A. comments following § 101 describe the purpose and scope of the above provision:

> This section is a revised version of former Section 6-201 of the original Uniform Probate Code, which authorized a variety of contractual arrangements that had sometimes been treated as testamentary in prior law. For example, most courts treated as testamentary a provision in a promissory note that if the payee died before making payment, the note should be paid to another named person; or a provision in a land contract that if the seller died before completing payment, the balance should be canceled and the property should belong to the vendee. These provisions often occurred in family arrangements. The result of holding such provisions testamentary was usually to invalidate them because not executed in accordance with the statute of wills. On the other hand, the same courts for years upheld beneficiary designations in life insurance contracts. The drafters of the original Uniform Probate Code declared in the Comment that they were unable to identify policy reasons for continuing to treat these varied arrangements as testamentary. The drafters said that the benign experience with such familiar will substitutes as the revocable inter vivos trust, the multiple-party bank account, and United States government bonds payable on death to named beneficiaries all demonstrated that the evils envisioned if the statute of wills were not rigidly enforced simply do not materialize. The Comment also observed that because these provisions often are part of a business transaction and are evidenced by a writing, the danger of fraud is largely eliminated.

> Because the modes of transfer authorized by an instrument under this section are declared to be nontestamentary, the instrument does not have to be executed in compliance with the formalities for wills; nor does the instrument have to be probated, nor does the personal representative have any power or duty with respect to the assets.
>
> The sole purpose of this section is to prevent the transfers authorized here from being treated as testamentary.

Unif. Nonprobate Transfers on Death Act § 101 cmt., 8B U.L.A. 200 (1993).

In short, these comments explain how certain contractual arrangements have been treated as testamentary regardless of contractual language addressing the transfer of rights and ownership upon the death of the contract creditor. The purpose of Unif. Nonprobate Transfers on Death Act § 101 is to take such contractual arrangements out of the realm of probate and to permit the terms of the contract to be upheld. We believe the same holds true in this case.

Although disputes between annuity contracts and marital property agreements are uncommon, our reliance on the language in Wis. Stat. § 705.20 is not unprecedented. In Orr v. Petersen, 28 Cal. App. 4th 1742, 34 Cal. Rptr. 2d 449, 457 (Cal. Ct. App. 1994), the California court of appeals addressed a similar dispute arising from the death of an annuity holder. In that case, the decedent was survived by his wife Loretta and by a child from a previous marriage. The decedent's will made no bequest to Loretta and instead bequeathed all of his property (his personal effects and the "residue" of his estate) to his child and her family. See Orr, 34 Cal. Rptr. 2d at 452. The will did not mention two annuity contracts which the decedent and Loretta had purchased. The contracts themselves identified the decedent as "annuitant" and "owner" and Loretta as "joint owner." The contracts also stated, "If there is more than one owner, at the death of the first owner payment will be made to the surviving owner. If the deceased owner's spouse is the surviving owner, then the surviving spouse will become the owner." Orr, 34 Cal. Rptr. 2d at 454. The court concluded that this language was sufficient to establish a nonprobate transfer of funds to the decedent's spouse.

In reaching its conclusion, the Orr court relied upon a statute identical to Wis. Stat. § 705.20 and to Unif. Nonprobate Transfers on Death Act § 101. California Prob. Code § 5000(a) (West 2000) recognizes the validity of nonprobate transfers upon death provided "in an insurance policy, contract of employment, bond, mortgage … or other written instrument of a similar nature." The court found this section applicable to "written provisions" that direct that "money or other benefits due to, controlled by, or owned by a decedent before death shall be paid after the decedent's death to a person whom the decedent designates" in the written instrument. Cal. Prob. Code § 5000(b)(1); cf. § 705.20(1)(a). The court concluded that the annuity contracts at issue "fit the broad description" of § 5000 and that the written instructions for payment to the surviving owner upon the death of the other owner or spouse should be given effect. See Orr, 34 Cal. Rptr. 2d at 457. This holding is consistent with our decision.

In addition to its reliance on the nonprobate transfer statute, the Orr court reviewed a statute pertaining to joint accounts with the right of survivorship. The statute, Cal. Prob. Code § 5302(a) (West 2000), provides that "sums remaining on deposit at the death of a party to a joint account belong to the surviving party or parties as against the estate of the decedent unless there is clear and convincing evidence of a different intent." The court found that an annuity fit the definition of a joint account under Cal. Prob. Code § 5122(a) (West 2000) because an annuity, like an account, involves a "deposit of funds between a depositor and a financial institution." Id. The court also found the issuer of the annuity, Metropolitan Life Insurance Co., to be a "financial institution" because, while not a "bank, savings and loan or credit union," it was a "like organization" since it held the deposit in substantially the same manner and for the same purpose as funds deposited in traditional banking institutions. See Cal. Prob. Code § 40 (West 2000); Orr, 34 Cal. Rptr. 2d at 456. Thus, pursuant to § 5302(a), the annuities in Orr belonged to the surviving account holder upon the annuitant's death, and not to the annuitant's estate.

California's law on joint accounts has a parallel in Wisconsin. Wisconsin Stat. § 705.04(1) provides that joint account funds belong to the surviving party unless there is clear and convincing evidence of a different intention "at the time the account is created." Wisconsin Stat. § 705.01(1) also similarly defines "account" and "financial institution" as California has. In addition, Wisconsin and California law shadows the U.L.A.'s language on the rights of survivors under joint accounts. See Unif. Multiple-Person Accounts Act §§ 12, 1, 8B U.L.A. 178, 169-70 (1993).

In this case, while the Annuity is not referred to as an account within the terms of the contract, we nonetheless find compelling the analysis proffered in Orr. An annuity, like a traditional bank account, is opened by depositing funds into a financial organization. Like a savings bank account and a certificate of deposit, an annuity can earn interest which is payable to the owner. A savings account or certificate of deposit is an investment tool analogous to an annuity. Here, although the issuer of the Annuity, Prudential Insurance Co., may not be a traditional bank or savings institution, it provides a similar function. Additionally, like a joint bank account, the Annuity contains a clause giving the co-annuitant the right of survivorship upon the annuitant's death.

Wisconsin Stat. § 705.04(1) is applicable here. The Annuity constitutes a "joint account" because the sums of money in the Annuity transferred ownership to Dianne upon Ronald's death. It is clear that no other intention was evidenced at the time the Annuity was created. See id. While the Jung children would argue that the marital agreement and will express a different intent, as a joint account such later intentions do not enter the equation. See id. Therefore, we conclude that as a joint account, the Annuity circumvents the conflicting language presented by the marital agreement and the will.

Aside from the terms of the marital agreement, the Jung children seek refuge in the policy argument that the "efficiency" of marital property agreements is threatened if they are not strictly followed. They contend that if the trial court's decision stands, a marital agreement that classifies property as one spouse's individual property and requires the other spouse to relinquish that property would have virtually no effect.

We agree that in some cases a marital agreement must yield to the terms of a previously agreed-upon contractual arrangement. As we have determined, under Wis. Stat. § 705.20, a contractual arrangement that creates a nonprobate transfer of property will defeat a marital agreement that does not make such a transfer. Under Wis. Stat. § 705.04(1), a joint account with the right of survivorship will defeat a marital agreement that seeks to transfer funds otherwise.

We acknowledge that this result places the onus on married couples to be knowledgeable of the terms of contractual arrangements which are included within their marital agreements. This result, however, does not strike us as particularly troubling because it will encourage married couples to become more aware of the terms of their prior contractual arrangements and to express more clearly their intentions in planning their estate.

In this case, if Ronald had desired ownership of the Annuity to pass to his children and not to Dianne, he could have authorized such a change by removing Dianne as a co-annuitant. As the Annuity provides, "If a First Annuitant and a Co-Annuitant are named, we will remove one from the contract upon: (1) receipt of your written request to remove that annuitant ...." We are not convinced that the purposes of the marital property agreement are subverted by upholding the terms of the Annuity. Order affirmed.

IV. REVOCABLE TRUSTS

A. THE TRUST CONCEPT

The trust is a remarkable Anglo-American legal mechanism that allows the owner of property to transfer the responsibility for managing property to one party and the right to enjoy the property to another according to rules devised by the original owner. The basic premise of the trust is that ownership can be divided into *legal* and *equitable* title. The creator of the trust (called the *settlor*, or, sometimes, the *trustor*) transfers property (called the *trust res*) to the *trustee* who acquires *legal title.* The trustee then holds the property for the benefit of the *beneficiary* (or *beneficiaries)* who possess equitable title which gives them the right to enjoy the benefits of the property but not to control it.

A trust can be created during the life of the settlor (called an *inter vivos* trust) or it can be created by will (in which case it is called a *testamentary* trust). There can be a single beneficiary, or there can be multiple beneficiaries. Moreover, the interests of the beneficiaries can be divided between present and future interests. If S places $500,000 in trust with the stipulation that the trustee pay A the income for the remainder of her life, and then following her death, to pay the income to B for the rest of her life, and after her death, to transfer the remainder of the trust res to C free of the trust, A is the present beneficiary and B and C are future beneficiaries. If the trust comes to an end without disposing of all of the property, then the trust res reverts back to the settlor or his successor.

There is no limitation to the number of roles that one individual or one entity can play in a given trust, except that no one can hold both the entire legal interest and the entire equitable interest. If S transferred the trust res and legal title to A to act as trustee of a trust created for the sole benefit of A, no trust would come into existence. There is also no requirement that the trust be created by a writing (unless the trust res includes real property, in which case the Statute of Frauds requires one), and there is no absolute requirement that the settlor use the term “trust” in setting up the arrangement.

Trusts never fail for want of a trustee. If the settlor fails to name a trustee (as in the case of a testamentary trust), one will simply be appointed. If a trustee dies or resigns or simply refuses the position, a court with jurisdiction over the trust res can always name a replacement trustee. When the trust res is transferred from the settlor to the trustee by means of a writing, the writing is called the *trust instrument* and that document normally sets out the rules by which the trust will be operated by the trustee. The trustee owes a fiduciary duty to all of the beneficiaries, including a duty to account for the activities of the trust. If the trustee fails to satisfy his commitments, the beneficiaries, and not the settlor, have the power to enforce the trust.

Trusts can also be revocable by the settlor (or someone else) or irrevocable. Revocable trusts give the settlor an opportunity to reconsider his or her decision, but irrevocable trusts have distinct tax advantages and creditor protection features not available when the trust is irrevocable. In a *living trust*, discussed below, the settlor of a trust can name himself or herself as both trustee and present beneficiary, so long as a different future beneficiary is named. (The living trust is now the most common form of will substitute.) When this happens, the document (or oral statement) creating the trust is called a *declaration of trust.* Many of the details of trusts law are discussed in the next chapter.

Wis. Stat. 701.01. [Trusts] Definitions.

As used in this chapter, unless the context indicates otherwise:

(1) BENEFICIARY.

"Beneficiary" means a person who has a beneficial interest in a trust.

(2) CHARITABLE AND PRIVATE TRUST.

To the extent that trust income or principal presently or in the future must be used by the trustee exclusively for a charitable purpose as defined in s. 701.10 (1), the trust is a "charitable trust"; any other trust is a "private trust", provided it is for the benefit of a person sufficiently identifiable to enforce the trust.

(3) COURT.

"Court" means the court having jurisdiction.

(4) PROPERTY.

"Property" means an interest in real or personal property.

(5) SETTLOR.

"Settlor" means a person who directly or indirectly creates a living or testamentary trust or adds property to an existing trust.

(6) TESTAMENTARY AND LIVING TRUST.

"Testamentary trust" means a trust subject to the continuing jurisdiction of the court assigned to exercise probate jurisdiction; "living trust" means any other trust, including a testamentary trust removed to this state from another state.

(7) TRUST.

"Trust" means an express living or testamentary, private or charitable trust in property which arises as a result of a manifestation of intention to create it.

(8) TRUSTEE.

"Trustee" means a person holding in trust title to or holding in trust a power over property. "Trustee" includes an original, added or successor trustee.

Wis. Stat. 701.02. Purposes for which trusts may be created.

A trust may be created for any lawful purpose.

Wis. Stat. 701.03. Passive trusts abolished.

Except as provided in s. 706.08 (4), every trust, to the extent it is private and passive, vests no title or power in the trustee, but the beneficiary takes a title corresponding in extent to the beneficial interest given the beneficiary. A trust is passive if the title or power given the trustee is merely nominal and the creating instrument neither expressly nor by implication from its terms imposes active management duties on the trustee.

Wis. Stat. 701.05. Title of trustee; interest of beneficiaries.

(1) Unless the creating instrument expressly limits the trustee to a lesser title or to a power, the trustee takes all title of the settlor or other transferor and holds such title subject to the trustee's fiduciary duties as trustee.

(2) If a trustee of a private trust has title to the trust property, a beneficiary has both a right to have the trustee perform the trustee's fiduciary duties and an equitable interest, present or future, in the trust property. If a trustee of a private trust holds only a power over property, a beneficiary has a right to have such trustee perform the trustee's fiduciary duties.

(3) In a private or charitable trust where the trustee takes all title of the settlor or other transferor and holds such title subject to the trustees fiduciary duties as trustee, any interest expressly retained by the settlor or not effectively disposed of to others remains in the settlor, or the settlors successors in interest, as an equitable reversionary interest and to this extent the settlor, or the settlors successors, are beneficiaries of the trust. In a private trust where the trustee takes all title of the settlor or other transferor and holds such title subject to the trustees fiduciary duties as trustee, any interest, present or future, created by the settlor in any other person is an equitable interest and such person is a beneficiary of the trust.

McMahon v. Standard Bank and Trust Co.

Court of Appeals of Wisconsin
550 N.W.2d 727 (1996)

BROWN, J. In this case we address complex questions involving passive trusts, living trusts and attempted testamentary dispositions. James J. McMahon alleges that his wife set up an invalid trust four years before her death. He argues that Phyllis's trust should be characterized as an invalid testamentary attempt because she retained complete control over the trust property even though she transferred title to the trustee. He asserts that the proper remedy is to return the title to her estate, completely vesting the trust property with her estate. Alternatively, he contends that the trust was passive because, by keeping control over the property, Phyllis did not grant any real authority to the trustee. He asserts that the remedy for this passive trust is to likewise deliver all of the trust assets to Phyllis's estate. The trust's beneficiaries, Judy Joy Almquist and George Edward Vick, who are Phyllis's children from an earlier marriage, not only contest these arguments on the merits, but have also cross-appealed primarily contending that the trust was a valid living trust.

While we affirm the circuit court's ultimate decision that the children are entitled to the trust property as the trust directs, we reach that conclusion on different grounds. Contrary to the circuit court's legal conclusion that this trust was a passive trust and that the law operated to vest the assets with the children, we hold that the trustee's duty to deliver the trust property to the children when Phyllis died made it a living trust and that this valid trust operates to deliver title to the children. Under the living trust statute, §701.07, STATS., James's arguments about the validity of the trust must be rejected because a valid living trust cannot be declared an attempted testamentary disposition or a passive trust as a matter of law.

We have gathered the facts from the uncontested parts of the record and the stipulation that the parties filed with the circuit court. Phyllis and James married in 1956. In 1969, the couple purchased a cottage at Alta Vista Estates in Lake Geneva. Although they titled the property in Phyllis's name alone, James contends that he contributed to the down payment and upkeep, mortgage and taxes through the years.

In 1990, Phyllis transferred the property, via a quit-claim deed, to the trust which is the subject of this case. The Standard Bank and Trust Company of Hickory Hills, Illinois, helped her form the documents and served as trustee. Under the trust agreement, Phyllis retained substantial control over the property even though she gave title to the trustee. She retained a "100% beneficial interest" and "full right of assignment." Moreover, the standard form language of the trust agreement explained that Phyllis "shall have the management of said property." At her death, however, the agreement directed that the property should pass in equal shares to her children, George and Judy.

Phyllis originally signed the trust documents on January 25, 1990. But two weeks later, Standard Bank informed her that to make the trust valid under Wisconsin law, the trustee must retain some control over the corpus. Accordingly, on February 7, 1990, Phyllis amended the trust agreement to require Standard Bank, as trustee, to supervise the payment of property taxes. Nonetheless, Phyllis was required to remit the tax bills and payments to Standard Bank and agreed to indemnify the trust company for any losses resulting from any dereliction of these duties.

In March 1993, Phyllis died intestate. Under Illinois law, James would normally be entitled to one-half interest in the Alta Vista property; the other half would be shared by George and Judy. See ILL. ANN. STAT. ch. 755, para. 5/2-1(a) (Smith-Hurd 1992). The distribution of this portion of her estate, however, was frustrated by the trust which directed that all of the Lake Geneva property be transferred to her children. Thus, in September 1993, James filed suit against Standard Bank and the children seeking to have the trust quashed.

Before we turn to the circuit court's findings, we review some of the basic principles of trust law arising in this case. A trust is a fiduciary relationship involving property. As a result of a trust, the person who holds title to the property, the trustee, has to perform duties on behalf of the beneficiaries. See Northwestern Nat'l Ins. v. Midland Nat'l Bank, 96 Wis. 2d 155, 172, 292 N.W.2d 591, 600 (1980) (quoting RESTATEMENT (SECOND) OF TRUSTS §2 (1959)).

A trust has three elements: a trustee, a beneficiary and trust property. Sutherland v. Pierner, 249 Wis. 462, 467, 24 N.W.2d 883, 886 (1946). The person who establishes the trust is commonly referred to as the settlor. RESTATEMENT (SECOND) OF TRUSTS §3(1) (1959).

A settlor can create a trust in two ways. First, she or he can designate in a will that the estate, or a portion of it, be placed into a trust as part of the probate process. Such trusts are known as testamentary trusts. Alternatively, a settlor can place property in a trust during her or his lifetime and possibly designate that the trust property be given to the beneficiaries at death. This arrangement is known as an inter vivos, or living, trust. See generally GEORGE G. BOGERT & GEORGE T. BOGERT, THE LAW OF TRUSTS & TRUSTEES §1, at 12 (2d ed. rev. 1984). In many jurisdictions, moreover, the settlor of a living trust may make the trust revocable. Thus, a living trust can serve as a useful means of passing property to heirs without a will or probate. The settlor can effectively retain control of the trust property while alive and then have the trustee deliver the property to the intended heirs at death. See id. §1061, at 219.

Although living trusts and wills are separate and distinct legal forms, they share many characteristics because they both serve to pass property to heirs. Under both arrangements, the settlor (testator) will retain substantial power over the estate property during life and the ultimate transfer to the beneficiaries (heirs) will only occur at death. See IA AUSTIN W. SCOTT & WILLIAM F. FRATCHER, THE LAW OF TRUSTS §57-57.1 (4th ed. 1987). Indeed, one can understand why Justice Holmes once described how living trusts may "certainly have a very testamentary look" in the much quoted case of Bromley v. Mitchell, 155 Mass. 509, 30 N.E. 83, 84 (Mass. 1892).

Nonetheless, whether living or testamentary, revocable or irrevocable, all trusts are generally subject to certain common law or statutory rules of construction. One rule which plays a role in this case is that the settlor must give the trustee a certain degree of power over the trust property. When the settlor fails to do this and leaves the trustee with no power over the property, the trust is described as passive. Most jurisdictions, including Wisconsin, have abolished passive trusts. See IA SCOTT & FRATCHER, supra §67; see also §701.03, STATS.

The flaw in a passive trust is that legal title to the trust property is controlled by a trustee who is otherwise unable to do anything with the property. When a trust is formed, the legal and equitable interests are separated: the legal title goes to the trustee and the equitable interest goes to the beneficiaries. But if the trustee is not given any duties along with the title, the beneficiaries may be harmed because the trustee has no authority to act in their best interest. See BOGERT & BOGERT, supra §206, at 27.

We believe there are several rationales that support abolishing passive trusts. First, this awkward separation of legal and equitable interests may create practical difficulties for the beneficiaries who, for example, may want to make changes to the trust property but cannot because the title lies with the trustee. See id. Second, as the children explained at oral argument, passive trusts may be used to disguise the actual ownership of property. Thus, the children theorize that abolishing such trusts helps avoid potentially fraudulent or illegal activity.

The jurisdictions that abolish passive trusts also establish a remedy. These statutes are often referred to as "statutes of uses." They operate to take legal title from the passive trustee and deliver it to the beneficiaries. See BOGERT & BOGERT, supra §206, at nn.5 & 10 (collecting authority including §701.03, STATS.); cf. §701.13(3), STATS., (permitting judicial dissolution of trusts when administration and continuation become impractical).

With these principles in hand, we will now detail the arguments brought before the circuit court. James pursued two theories. Noting that Phyllis had retained full control over the trust property, he raised the argument that this trust was an invalid testamentary attempt. He further explained that the trust agreement could not be constructively read as a valid will because it did not meet all legal requirements. For example, it was not signed before two witnesses. See ILL. ANN. STAT. ch. 755, para. 5/4-3(a) (Smith-Hurd 1992). Accordingly, he claimed that the trust agreement had no legal significance and title to the property should be returned to Phyllis's estate. Alternatively, he argued that the trust was an invalid passive trust under §701.03, STATS. Since Phyllis's trustee had no real management duties over the trust property, James claimed that the trust should be executed to vest title with the person who did have control and was the designated primary beneficiary, namely, Phyllis.

The children responded with three theories. First, under Patton v. Patrick, 123 Wis. 218, 101 N.W. 408 (1904), they argued that Standard Bank's property tax responsibilities were enough to make the trust "active" and not subject to the rule against passive trusts. They also counterclaimed, arguing that the trust was a valid living trust under §701.07, STATS. Third, regardless of the definition of the trust, they claimed that the proper remedy in this case was to simply vest title with the surviving beneficiaries, namely, Judy and George.

The circuit court agreed with James's argument that the trust was passive. It rejected the children's claim that the trustee's duty to pay property taxes was enough to render the trust active. The circuit court distinguished Patton, which stated that giving the trustee the single duty of paying property taxes was enough to make a trust active. See

Patton, 123 Wis. at 222, 101 N.W. at 409. The circuit court found that Phyllis's trustee had no real responsibility for paying property taxes; at most, it was just putting checks into an envelope and sending them to the county. To the contrary, the circuit court believed that the trustee in Patton was also required to collect payment from the leaseholders of the trust property and then use these funds to pay the property taxes. See id. The court reasoned that the extra duty of tracking down payment from third parties required of the Patton trustee presented a different situation from the subject trust because Phyllis's trustee simply had to ask her for the needed funds.

The circuit court then went forward and determined the effect of its finding. It examined the cases applying Wisconsin's passive trust statute and concluded that they established a rule that all passive trusts are abolished and the legal title goes to the beneficiary. See Janura v. Fencl, 261 Wis. 179, 185, 52 N.W.2d 144, 147 (1952). Because Phyllis died, the circuit court found that the remaining beneficiaries were the children. It directed that they be given title to the trust property.

James now renews the claims he made before the circuit court. He again argues that the trust was an invalid testamentary attempt, an issue which the court never reached. And while he agrees with the circuit court's conclusion that the trust was passive, he claims that it erred when it found that the remedy was to place the trust assets with the children. He argues that the proper remedy was to vest it with Phyllis because she remained the actual owner of the property at the time the invalid trust was formed. On the other side, the children attack the circuit court's legal conclusion that this trust was passive. Moreover, regardless of whether the trust was active or passive, the children contend in their cross-appeal that the trust was a valid living trust.

The issues the parties raise require us to apply the trust agreement to the statutes governing trusts and testamentary dispositions. The interpretation of a statute is a question of law and we owe no deference to the circuit court's conclusions. See Paul M.J. v. Dorene A.G., 181 Wis. 2d 304, 310, 510 N.W.2d 775, 777 (Ct. App. 1993). Moreover, while Phyllis entered into this trust with an Illinois company, the location of the trust property determines the applicable law governing the trust and we will apply Wisconsin law. See Boyle v. Kempkin, 243 Wis. 86, 90, 9 N.W.2d 589, 591 (1943).

We begin with the children's main argument. They contend that §701.07, STATS., the living trust statute, dictates the outcome of this case. They argue that the plain language requires that we dismiss both of James's challenges. The statute provides in relevant part:

Living trusts. (1) VALIDITY. A living trust, otherwise valid, shall not be held invalid as an attempted testamentary disposition, a passive trust under s. 701.03, or a trust lacking a sufficient principal because:

(a) It contains any or all of the following powers, whether exercisable by the settlor, another person or both:

....

4. To control the administration of the trust in whole or in part;

Section 701.07 (children's emphasis). Under their theory, Phyllis's trust is a valid living trust because she gave the trustee the responsibility of transferring the trust property to her beneficiaries when she died. The language they cite above explains that Phyllis's decision to retain substantial power of "administration" over the trust property until her death cannot be grounds for declaring the trust an attempted testamentary disposition or, similarly, a passive trust. See §701.07(1)(a)4.

James first responds to the children's theory that the living trust statute answers whether Phyllis's trust was an invalid testamentary attempt. Although he does not dispute that the plain language of the statute could be read to dismiss his claim, he contends that case law prevents us from reaching such a result. He argues that these cases hold that a trust may indeed be deemed void as an attempted testamentary disposition if the settlor retains too much management control. We thus turn to the case law and legislative history to see what they say, and to see if they can be harmonized with the plain language of the living trust statute.

The story begins over sixty years ago with the supreme court's decision in Warsco v. Oshkosh Sav. & Trust Co., 183 Wis. 156, 196 N.W. 829 (1924). There, the settlor placed a certificate of deposit in a living trust. Through the trust documents, he reserved the power to withdraw income from the account and to change trustees. At death, he directed that the balance be paid to the beneficiary, his wife. When the settlor died, the trustee paid the balance to the beneficiary according to the terms of the trust. See id. at 158-59, 196 N.W. at 829-30.

The settlor's estate, however, claimed that the trust was invalid. The supreme court agreed. But instead of specifically articulating whether this trust was passive or was an attempted testamentary disposition, the court looked to basic trust principles to deem the trust invalid. It focused on how the settlor had reserved "complete control of the trust property." Id. at 161-62, 196 N.W. at 831. In the case of a bank deposit, the court explained that this settlor's power to demand "every cent" from his deposit equated to having complete control. See id. at 160, 196 N.W. at 830. The court further reasoned that a trust requires trust property. Hence, even though this settlor delivered title to the trustee, because he failed to relinquish actual control over the property, no trust property was present and the trust failed. See id. at 162, 196 N.W. at 831.

If Warsco were the law today, James would win. If the settlor's failure to relinquish control over the trust property is the true sign of validity, then we would hold Phyllis's trust invalid because she reserved essentially all administrative power over the trust property.

However, in 1931, the legislature enacted §231.205, STATS., a predecessor to the current living trust statute. See Laws of 1931, ch. 216, §1. While we have reproduced the entire statute at the margin, the key language allowed the settlor to reserve the "right to revoke, amend, alter or modify the trust" and also withdraw sums from the trust property without risk that the trust would be declared void as an "invalid trust" or an "attempted testamentary disposition." Section 231.205, STATS., 1933. The legislature's apparent response to the Warsco case seems therefore to extinguish James's claim that the plain language of the living trust statute does not apply to Phyllis's trust.

Still, supreme court cases subsequent to the first living trust statute cast some doubt over its scope. For example, in Koppelkam v. First Wis. Trust Co., 240 Wis. 254, 256, 3 N.W.2d 350, 351 (1942), the estate administrator claimed that under Warsco, the decedent had made an invalid testamentary disposition of property because he had made his living trust revocable. The supreme court rejected this argument and held that Warsco did not establish "revocability" as the test for whether a living trust was valid. See Koppelkam, 240 Wis. at 258-59, 3 N.W.2d at 352. The court confirmed that Warsco instead turned on the degree of control that the settlor retained over the trust property. See Koppelkam, 240 Wis. at 259, 3 N.W.2d at 352.

But that estate administrator's claim that Warsco was about revocability exemplified the confusion that Warsco and the legislature's living trust statute created among the bar up through the 1940s. There was dispute over what Warsco stood for and, more importantly, what the legislature intended to do when it enacted the living trust statute in 1931. Was the first living trust statute designed only to allow a settlor to make the trust revocable, or was it also directed at the issue James raises about the settlor's attempt to retain power over the trust property? For example, in Tucker v. Simrow, 248 Wis. 143, 21 N.W.2d 252 (1946), the court seemed to further suggest that the living trust statute addressed only revocability because there it wrote that Warsco held that a settlor who retained "substantially entire control of the property" has attempted to make a testamentary disposition, not a living trust. See id. at 145, 21 N.W.2d at 252; see also Kathryn H. Baldwin, Comment, Trusts--Direction and Control Permissible--Statutory Construction, 1943 WIS. L. REV. 127, 130-31 (arguing that Koppelkam revealed that Warsco was still good law).

Fourteen years later, in Otterson v. Fraser (Estate of Steck), 275 Wis. 290, 81 N.W.2d 729 (1957), the supreme court finally had the opportunity to directly address the relationship between Warsco and §231.205, STATS., 1933, and settle the controversy about what the living trust statute did. Here, the court ruled that the statute changed the rule of Warsco regarding when a living trust would be deemed a testamentary disposition. See Otterson, 275 Wis. at 295-96, 81 N.W.2d at 732. The statute expanded the rights of the settlor to not only reserve the power to revoke the living trust in whole or part, but it also permitted the settlor to retain veto power over the trustee's decision-making. See id. at 296-97, 81 N.W.2d at 732-33.

But the supreme court's conclusion that §231.205, STATS., 1933 , allocated veto power to the settlor of a living trust does not exactly answer James's claim. Phyllis retained much more than veto power over the trustee; she reserved for herself direct management control over the trust property. The discussion in Otterson about how the living trust statute allows a settlor to retain power over "approval or disapproval of the trustee's recommendations" is thus only marginally relevant to the controversy over Phyllis's trust. See Otterson, 275 Wis. at 297, 81 N.W.2d at 733.

The legislature has, however, made two sets of comprehensive amendments to the living trust statute since the Otterson decision. While this case presents the first opportunity to gauge the effect of these amendments, which were enacted in 1955 and 1969, we are confident that the newer statutory language authorizes a settlor to retain much more than veto authority without risk that the trust will be deemed void as an attempted testamentary disposition.

The written history of the 1955 amendments described the concerns of the legal community over the direction of the supreme court decisions. The bar believed that a policy which strictly construed living trusts to determine if they were testamentary attempts would discourage the use of these "flexible estate planning tools." See Memorandum from T.L. Tolan, Jr. (of the drafting committee) to Senator Harry F. Franke, Jr., 5-6 (Sept. 15, 1954). The drafters thus designed the 1955 living trust statute to have "less strict requirements than some of the cases have demanded so far as living trusts are concerned," but to still avoid the risk of "chicanery." See id. at 5.

Moreover, in 1969, the legislature again restructured and renumbered the living trust statute. Laws of 1969, ch. 283, §17 (creating §701.07, STATS.). Most important to the issue of testamentary dispositions, the legislature added language authorizing settlors of living trusts to retain the power "to control the administration of the trust in whole or in part." See id. (§701.07(1)(d)). Given the case law and legislative history leading to these amendments, we believe that the legislature intended the 1969 changes to further embellish the settlor's power over the property placed in a living trust.

With the new changes, not only could settlors retain veto power as the earlier statutes permitted, but they could also retain full management control over the property if they desired. We reach this conclusion by placing great emphasis on the legislature's choice of the word "administration" in what became §701.07(1)(a)4, STATS., 1971, to describe the powers that could be retained by the settlor of a living trust. As Webster's dictionary explains, "administration" means:

2 b: performance of executive duties: MANAGEMENT, DIRECTION, SUPERINTENDENCE
... 3 a: the management and disposal under legal authority of the estate of an intestate or of a testator having no competent executor b: the management of an estate of a deceased person by an executor c: the management of an estate (as of an infant) by a trustee or guardian legally appointed to take charge of it

WEBSTER'S THIRD NEW INTERNATIONAL DICTIONARY 28 (1976). We believe that by using the word "administration," the legislature intended to authorize a settlor of a living trust to maintain power over the trust property equal to that normally associated with a trustee.

Accordingly, since the few amendments since 1969 have not affected this subsection of §701.07, STATS., we conclude that James's argument about the testamentary character of Phyllis's trust fails. Even though Phyllis retained more than substantial control over the trust property, her trust remains valid. The living trust statute expressly permits a settlor to retain administrative control over the trust property and not risk having the trust declared void as an attempted testamentary disposition. See §701.07(1)(a)4.

Having disposed of James's argument that the trust was an invalid testamentary attempt, we still face his alternative argument that our above conclusion about the management power granted to settlors through §701.07, STATS., has no role in the analysis of whether Phyllis's trust was a passive trust. James contends that we cannot read the living trust statute in isolation. Although James does not argue that §701.07 is ambiguous, he does assert that we may not construe the statute in a way which conflicts with the passive trust statute, specifically the following language:

Passive trusts abolished. ...Every trust, to the extent it is private and passive, vests no title or power in the trustee, but the beneficiary takes a title corresponding in extent to the beneficial interest given the beneficiary. A trust is passive if the title or power given the trustee is merely nominal and the creating instrument neither expressly nor by implication from its terms imposes active management duties on the trustee.

Section 701.03, STATS. (emphasis added). James contends that we cannot read the living trust statute to allow a settlor of a living trust to retain nearly full direction and control over the trust property, thereby not giving any power to the trustee. In his view, this reading would render the passive trust statute meaningless. James argues that the "every trust" language within §701.03 applies to every trust, including living trusts. "Had the legislature intended to nullify §701.03," James complains, "it would have been done by revocation, not by the creation of a contrary provision."

So while we face no claim that §701.07, STATS., in and of itself is ambiguous, its interrelation with §701.03, STATS., results in disagreement about the proper interpretation of the living trust statute. See Hurst v. State, 72 Wis. 2d 188, 195, 240 N.W.2d 392, 397 (1976). We will therefore turn back to the history of the living trust statute. This time we will strive to harmonize it with the statutory prohibition against passive trusts. See generally id. at 196, 240 N.W.2d at 397.

At the outset, we observe that James's argument would have much more weight if the earlier versions of the living trust statute were still in effect. Consider how a student commentator assessed the 1955 amendments:

In amending subsection (1) of 231.205, the legislature made the reserved powers "exercisable by the settlor or another or both." The plain meaning of this language seems to be that the powers may be reserved to the settlor, to the trustee, to the beneficiary, or to any other person. It seems clear that the problem to which the statute is addressed is the Statute of Wills, not problems of merger or passive trusts.

David S. Ruder, Comment, The Testamentary Nature of Revocable Inter Vivos and Life Insurance Trusts--Liberalizing Legislation in Wisconsin, 1956 WIS. L. REV. 313, 316 (emphasis added; author's emphasis removed; footnote omitted).

However, the amendments since 1955 have subsequently addressed the passive trust issue that the above commentator spotted and James now raises. After the 1955 amendments, the living trust statute that the commentator discussed began as follows:

Life use by settlor of trusts; eligibility for bequests and devises; powers. (1) Any instrument declaring or creating a trust, when otherwise valid, shall not be held an invalid trust, or an attempted testamentary disposition, because it contains any of the following powers, whether exercisable by the settlor or another or both:

Section 231.205, STATS., 1957. But in the 1969 amendments, the legislature reshaped the introductory section, adding specific language addressing passive trusts, when it created what is currently §701.07, STATS.:

LIVING TRUSTS. (1) VALIDITY. An instrument creating a living trust shall not be held invalid as an attempted testamentary disposition or a passive trust because it contains any or all of the following powers, whether exercisable by the settlor, another person or both ....

Laws of 1969, ch. 283, §17 (emphasis added). While one might expect the legislature to redefine the passive trust statute if it wanted to create an exception for living trusts, as James argues it would, the legislature seems to have taken the alternative route. It concluded that the best way to protect people forming living trusts from challenges that they had written a passive trust was to write and place an exception into the living trust statute.

Unfortunately, we were unable to locate much commentary describing why the legislature expanded the living trust statute to protect these trusts against claims that they were passive. The only explanation that the Legislative Reference Bureau "analysis" of 1969 Assembly Bill 653 provides is that the amendments were "a recodification of the law on trusts."

One would surmise, therefore, that we could identify a Wisconsin case prior to 1969 which states the rule that these amendments were designed to codify. But we have not found that case.

We have located one treatise, however, which provides some guidance. It describes how some jurisdictions have held that a trustee's duty to transfer title of the trust property to the beneficiaries at the death of the settlor is sufficient to make the trust into an active trust, not subject to the prohibition against passive trusts. Most importantly, the authors place Wisconsin in that class. SCOTT & FRATCHER, supra

§69.1, at n.4. These authors specifically contend that Boyle v. Kempkin, 243 Wis. 86, 9 N.W.2d 589 (1943), provides such a result. We agree with their analysis and hold that Boyle, at least on its facts, stands for the proposition that a trustee's duty to deliver title to the beneficiaries of a trust at the death of the settlor is a sufficient duty to mark the trust as an active trust.

The settlor in Boyle owned real estate in Racine county. Similar to what Phyllis did, he transferred title of the property to a trust and instructed the trustee to hold the property for his benefit and then to divide the property among his beneficiaries when he died. After the settlor died, the trust beneficiaries sued the settlor's estate seeking enforcement of the trust. See id. at 88-89, 9 N.W.2d at 591.

While the supreme court acknowledged that "no active duties were given to the trustee to perform," it held that the passive trust statute only operated to execute the use for the period of the settlor's life. See id. at 90, 9 N.W.2d at 591. It further explained that title was left with the trustee to the extent necessary to enable him to perform its specified duties. Thus, the court determined that the trustee in Boyle retained enough title to enable it to transfer whatever remained of the trust property when the settlor died. See id. at 90-91, 9 N.W.2d at 591-92.

In the same section of this treatise, the authors cite a case from the South Carolina Court of Appeals which provides a more thorough explanation of the relationship between the passive trust rules and living trusts. See SCOTT & FRATCHER, supra §69.1, at n.4. While that case was decided after the 1969 amendments, we find the South Carolina court's reasoning equally descriptive and persuasive.

In Ramage v. Ramage, 283 S.C. 239, 322 S.E.2d 22 (S.C. Ct. App. 1984), the settlor deeded her property to two of her nephews in trust. Their only duty was to transfer the property back to her estate once she died. The purpose of this arrangement was to protect the settlor from the pressure of other relatives asking her to sell them land. Id. at 24-25.

After the settlor died, the nephews refused to carry out their duties as trustees. They argued that the trust was passive and invalid under South Carolina's Statute of Uses. See id. at 26 (citing S.C. CODE ANN. §21-27-20 (Law. Co-op. 1976), amended, §62-7-107 (Law. Co-op. 1987)). The court of appeals, however, concluded that the Statute of Uses did not apply because these trustees did have a duty. They were required to hold the property until the settlor died and then transfer it back to her estate. See Ramage, 322 S.E.2d at 26.

The Wisconsin Supreme Court's analysis in Boyle together with the South Carolina Court of Appeals' analysis in Ramage suggest that a statute abolishing passive trusts cannot completely abolish a living trust even when the settlor grants no duty to the trustee that would be performed during his or her lifetime. This was the rule that the living trust statute seemingly codified. Where §701.07, STATS., states that a living trust cannot be deemed a passive trust because the settlor has retained (and thus not granted to the trustee) administrative control over the trust property, it is expressing the conclusion reached by the Boyle and Ramage courts.

Our conclusion that the passive trust statute does not apply to living trusts nonetheless leaves us with James's concern that such an interpretation effectively guts the passive trust statute. In fact, we still have not addressed the circuit court's conclusion that Phyllis's trust was a passive trust under Patton, 123 Wis. at 222, 101 N.W. at 409, because Phyllis did not give the trustee any real authority over the property.

We are confident, however, that our analysis is soundly grounded in the legislative history and interpretive case law. The legislature apparently has concluded that the problems which the passive trust statute is targeted at, such as potential impracticality of the trust or possible fraud, are not significant concerns in the context of living trusts.

Moreover, our discussion about the living trust statute reveals that the Patton decision is not at all relevant to a determination of whether Phyllis's trust is a valid living trust. The trust in Patton was a testamentary trust. The trust was formed only after the settlor died. See id. at 219, 101 N.W. at 408. This is a key factor because whether the settlor is still alive is the hallmark of the living trust. Quite simply, when the settlor is alive, the trustee in a living trust has the duty to stand by in case the settlor dies. This duty to wait is the active duty that the Boyle and Ramage decisions focus on.

So, while our holding somewhat curtails the passive trust statute, it by no means renders this statute meaningless because it will still be a factor in determining the validity of other types of trusts.

In conclusion, the living trust statute, §701.07, STATS., controls this case. Under it, we must reject James's claims that this trust was invalid as either an attempted testamentary disposition or as a passive trust because Phyllis retained complete control over the property. In accord with the terms of the trust, Phyllis's children are entitled to the property. We therefore affirm the circuit court's ultimate determination that title be given to the children, not to Phyllis's estate.

B. LIVING TRUSTS AS WILL SUBSTITUTES

As the above case indicates, the use of a revocable trust created during the settlor's lifetime has become a widely used will substitute. The following statute reflects the decision in Wisconsin and elsewhere that trusts of this nature, while highly testamentary in character, are not to be treat as testamentary documents. The case that follows illustrates the history of this development and its consequences.

Wis. Stat. 701.07. Living trusts.

(1) VALIDITY. A living trust, otherwise valid, shall not be held invalid as an attempted testamentary disposition, a passive trust under s. 701.03, or a trust lacking a sufficient principal because:

(a) It contains any or all of the following powers, whether exercisable by the settlor, another person or both:

1. To revoke, modify or terminate the trust in whole or in part;

2. To exercise a power or option over property in the trust or over interests made payable to the trust under an employee benefit plan, life insurance policy, or otherwise;

3. To direct, during the lifetime of the settlor or another, the person to whom or on whose behalf the income or principal shall be paid or applied;

4. To control the administration of the trust in whole or in part;

5. To add property or cause additional employee benefits, life insurance, or other interests to be made payable to the trust at any time.

(b) The principal consists of a designation of the trustee as a primary or direct, secondary or contingent beneficiary under a will, employee benefit plan, life insurance policy or otherwise; or(c) The principal consists of assets of nominal value.

(2) ELIGIBILITY TO RECEIVE ASSETS. A living trust shall be eligible to receive property from any source.

(3) CREDITORS' RIGHTS. If a settlor retains a power to revoke, modify or terminate which is exercisable in the settlors favor, except when such power is exercisable only in conjunction with a person having a substantial adverse interest, the trust property to the extent it is subject to such power is also subject to the claim of a creditor of the settlor. This subsection shall not apply to trust property to the extent it is exempt from claims of creditors under other statutes.

In re Estate of Steck

Supreme Court of Wisconsin

275 Wis. 290, 81 N.W.2d 729 (1957)

Martin, C. J. Vincent Steck died February 16, 1954, at the age of seventy-eight, leaving his widow as his sole survivor. On September 18, 1951, he had executed a trust agreement (predated September 17, 1951) with the Marine National Exchange Bank, transferring to said bank securities appraised at his death at $283,006.44. These assets remained in the sole possession of the trustee.

The trust agreement provided that the net income therefrom was to be distributed to the donor as long as he lived, and upon his death to the donor's wife during her lifetime, subject to his power of appointment reserved therein to be exercised by his will. It also gave the trustee the right to invade the corpus on behalf of the widow if that should be deemed necessary to provide for her reasonable care and support. Upon the widow's death the remaining trust assets were to be distributed equally to remaindermen consisting of nieces and nephews of Vincent Steck and two grandnieces of his wife.

The trustee was given broad powers of administration and investment. The donor reserved the power of revocation and modification and a measure of control over investments during his lifetime. The donor subsequently executed two amendments to the trust agreement which are not material here.

On September 18, 1951, after execution of the trust agreement, Vincent Steck executed his last will and testament in which he gave to his wife certain personal property and effects, exercised the power of appointment reserved to him under the trust agreement to the extent of giving her the sum of $15,000, and specifically declined to exercise such power with respect to the balance of the trust estate. The remainder of his estate was designated as his "residuary estate" and was devised to the Marine National Exchange Bank, as trustee of the trust referred to, to be added to and become a part of the corpus of said trust. With respect thereto it was stated in paragraph 4 of the will:

"It is not my intention that 'my residuary estate' shall be received by said Marine National Exchange Bank as a testamentary trustee or upon a testamentary trust, but the devise and bequest of 'my residuary estate' is made to the aforesaid trust of September

17, 1951, as a distinct legal entity already in existence at the time of the execution of this will."

The will was admitted to probate April 8, 1954, at which time the widow testified as to proof of heirship and H. Morley Fraser was appointed executor. On April 28, 1954, Martha Steck filed her election not to take under the will. On June 4, 1954, she filed her petition for amendment of proof of will alleging that the trust instrument was testamentary in character and should be admitted as Vincent Steck's last will and testament and that the will already admitted should stand as a codicil thereto.

Basically it is appellant's contention that the trust instrument was executed in accordance with the requirements of the statute of wills and thus is a valid testamentary disposition. The question presented is not whether the trust created by Vincent Steck may be interpreted as testamentary, but whether it can be interpreted as an inter vivos trust, which is what Vincent Steck expressly intended it to be. If his intention can be carried out we must do so.

Appellant relies upon Warsco v. Oshkosh Savings & Trust Co. (1924), 183 Wis. 156, 196 N. W. 829, where it was held that to constitute a valid trust there must be an alienation of the donor's property in such a way as to cause a benefit to accrue to a cestui que trust* unless prevented by a condition subsequent resulting from a lawful revocation of the trust. In that case the agreement was held not to constitute a valid conveyance in trust because the donor had retained full dominion over the trust res, the trustee being a mere agent to hold the property.

After the decision in that case, sec. 231.205, Stats., was enacted, which provides:

> "Any instrument declaring and creating a trust shall not, when otherwise valid, be held to be an invalid trust or an attempted testamentary disposition of property because the grantor or creator of the trust reserved to himself, to be exercised by him during his lifetime, the right to revoke, amend, alter, or modify the trust instrument in whole or in part, or to require that sums from the trust principal be paid to or used for him either at his request or in the discretion of the trustee. Nothing in this section shall be construed as altering or changing in any way the existing law or rules of law relating to the taxation of transfers of property in trust."

---

* *Cestui que trust* is a now somewhat dated term for beneficiary.

It is argued that the statute did not have the effect of changing the rule since the holding of the Warsco Case was reaffirmed in 1945 by Tucker v. Simrow, 248 Wis. 143, 145, 21 N. W. (2d) 252, and appellant quotes therefrom the following language:

"The doctrine of Koppelkam v. First Wisconsin Trust Co. 240 Wis. 254, 3 N. W. (2d) 350, and Warsco v. Oshkosh Savings & Trust Co. 183 Wis. 156, 196 N. W. 829, is to the effect that, where substantially entire control of the property disposed of is retained by the person making the deposit until his death, a testamentary disposition has been attempted and any document making such disposition must satisfy the statute governing execution of wills."

In that case Mrs. Simrow gave to her bank a paper containing instructions to pay to specified persons, in case of her death, the amounts in her savings and checking accounts. There was no contention that these instructions constituted a trust. The position of the appellant was that they constituted a valid contract between the bank and Mrs. Simrow for the benefit of third persons, in the nature of the creation of a joint account or the deposit of certificates of deposit jointly payable to the depositor and a third person. The court held that the instructions did not constitute such a contract but were attempted testamentary dispositions, ineffective because their execution did not comply with the statute of wills. We cannot interpret the language quoted above as having any effect on the rules relating to trusts, since the document in the Simrow Case was in no sense a trust instrument and sec. 231.205, Stats., was neither involved nor considered.

Appellant's argument that sec. 231.205, Stats., if held to change the rule of the Warsco Case, is unconstitutional, has no merit.

In creating the trust Vincent Steck reserved to himself during his lifetime the income therefrom and the right to revoke, amend, alter, or modify the trust instrument in whole or in part. The reservation of such powers is permitted by sec. 231.205, Stats., and the trust is not to be deemed testamentary on that ground. In addition the donor reserved the power of appointment by will and the right to subject to his approval the trustee's recommendations with respect to the retention, sale, or other disposition of the trust estate.

Appellant cites Restatement, Trusts, p. 175, sec. 57 (2), where it is stated:

"Where the settlor transfers property in trust and reserves not only a beneficial life estate and a power to revoke and modify the trust but also such power to control the trustee as to the details of the administration of the trust that the trustee is the agent of the settlor, the disposition so far as it is intended to take effect after his death is testamentary and is invalid unless the requirements of the statutes relating to the validity of wills are complied with."

At page 179 the following comment is made on subsection (2):

"The rule stated in subsection (2) is applicable, however, only where the settlor reserves such power of control that the transferee is his agent. The intended trust is not testamentary merely because the settlor reserves power to direct the trustee as to the making of investments or the exercise of other particular powers, or power to appoint a substituted trustee."

As found by the trial court, the trust agreement gave to the trustee broad and extensive administration and investment powers. Paragraph 9 thereof states that "The trustee in its administration hereunder shall have full and complete authority to do any and all things necessary for the orderly and efficient administration of the trust estate, and without limiting the generality thereof by the following enumeration, shall, to that end, be clothed with the absolute rights, powers, and discretions:" To retain indefinitely all trust assets, to invest and reinvest without restriction, to permit trust funds to remain uninvested, to carry any and all of the assets in its own name, to vote stock, to borrow money, to lease or exchange property, to pay, settle, or compromise claims against the trust estate, etc.

The donor required only that upon the trustee's periodic analyses of the assets it should communicate to him its recommendations based thereon in writing "and the donor may within thirty days thereafter by notice in writing to the trustee prescribe the investment thereof and/or instruct the trustee in respect of the retentions, sales, and dispositions if any so recommended." If the donor should fail to so prescribe or instruct the trustee, the trustee was to put its recommendations into effect.

This instrument was drawn by competent legal counsel. It would do violence to the words used therein to say that the investment control so reserved by the donor made the trustee his mere agent. The donor did not retain the power to deal with the trust as he pleased; his control over the investments was limited to approval or disapproval of the trustee's recommendations. Even where the powers conferred on the trustees by the trust instrument were to be exercised only upon written instructions of the settlor, in Stouse v. First Nat. Bank (Ky. 1951), 245 S. W. (2d) 914, 918, 32 A. L. R. (2d) 1261, 1267, the validity of the trust was upheld under the rule of the Restatement. It was there said:

Reservation by the settlor of power to approve investments likewise has been held not to impart testamentary character to a trust. [Citing cases.]

"Both Scott and Bogert recognize that the degree of reserved control is the determining factor in the question of whether an instrument creates a valid trust or only a mere agency. See Scott on Trusts, sec. 57.2; Bogert on Trusts and Trustees, secs. 103, 104.

"We are of the opinion that the power reserved by [the settlor] to control the trustees in their administration of the trust, which power could be exercised only within the limits and in accordance with the terms of the trust instrument, was not of such a degree as to reduce the trustees to the status of agents."

Nor does the reservation by the donor of the power of appointment make the trust invalid. The trustee's powers were no more affected thereby than by the donor's retention of the power to revoke.

The trust created by Vincent Steck contained all the necessary elements defined in Sutherland v. Pierner (1946), 249 Wis. 462, 467, 24 N. W. (2d) 883, as follows:

1) A trustee, who holds the trust property and is subject to equitable duties to deal with it for the benefit of another; (2) a beneficiary, to whom the trustee owes equitable duties to deal with the trust property for his benefit; (3) trust property, which is held by the trustee for the beneficiary."

Marine National Exchange Bank, an experienced corporate fiduciary, received the trust principal upon execution of the trust agreement, accepted the duties of management therein conferred, and exercised them for the benefit of the donor for approximately two and one-half years before his death. This was no mere "illusory device;" it was in every sense an active trust, taking effect and serving a proper purpose during the life of the donor. The fact that the trust instrument also contained testamentary provisions does not change its character from that of an inter vivos trust to that of a last will and testament.

The mere fact that the agreement provided for disposition of the trust property upon the settlor's death was not regarded as a circumstance of any importance in view of the creation of rights during his lifetime. See 1 Bogert, Trusts and Trustees, sec. 103; 1 Scott, Trusts, p. 338, sec. 57.1." Koppelkam v. First Wisconsin Trust Co. (1942), 240 Wis. 254, 257, 3 N. W. (2d) 350.

Appellant contends that because the will bequeaths the residue of Vincent Steck's estate to the trustee, the trust was incorporated in the will by reference. This is exactly what the testator did not do, expressly stating in his will that it was not his intention that the residue should be received by the trustee as a testamentary trustee but as the trustee of a "distinct legal entity already in existence." To apply the doctrine of incorporation by reference in this situation would be to ignore that expressed intent.

It is further contended that to hold this trust instrument a valid inter vivos trust is to open the door to fraud upon the widow. The argument has no place here. As stated by the trial court, "There has been no allegation by the petitioner that any fraud existed in the execution of the trust instrument in question and the court can find no evidence to sustain such finding had the allegation been made."

In establishing the trust Vincent Steck provided that his widow should receive the entire income from its assets, almost $12,000 yearly, and the right to invade the corpus should her needs require it. This hardly evinces an intention to deprive his wife of her just share in his estate, even though, as the trial court commented, "he may have had some apprehension and concern as to the manner in which she was to receive the same."

The fact that the widow received less at his death under the trust than she would have if he had disposed of all his personal property by will is not in itself indicative of fraud on her.

. . . the amount of proof necessary to stamp such a transfer as fraudulent depends in every instance upon the particular facts existing in each case." Sederlund v. Sederlund (1922), 176 Wis. 627, 634, 187 N. W. 750.

There is neither allegation nor proof of fraud and the trust being otherwise valid, the determination of the trial court must stand. Order affirmed.

C. POUR OVER WILLS

Individuals frequently combine the use of wills and trusts through the device of the pour over will. Typically, this is done by creating and funding an inter vivos trust and then by executing a will to that devises the residue of the settlor's estate to the trustee of the trust to be held under the terms of the original trust. For example, in the case of *In re Estate of Williams,* 221 Wis. 2nd 597, 586 N.W.2d 699 (Wis. App. 1997), the testator created a trust for the benefit of a number of "art-oriented and religious organizations" and then executed a will devising most of her substantial estate to the trust. Pour over wills are often used in conjunction with living trusts so that the will can transfer all non-trust assets into the trust following the settlor's death. The following statutes govern such transfers in Wisconsin.

Wis. Stat. 701.08. Transfers to living trusts.

(1) VALIDITY AND EFFECT. The order of execution of a living trust instrument and a will or other instrument purporting to transfer or appoint property to the trust evidenced by the trust instrument shall be disregarded in determining the validity of the transfer or appointment. No reference in any will to a living trust shall cause assets in such trust to be included in property administered as part of the testator's estate; nor shall it cause the trust or any portion thereof to be treated as a testamentary trust.

(2) GOVERNING TERMS. Property transferred or appointed by a will or by a beneficiary designation under an employee benefit plan, life insurance policy or other instrument permitting designation of a beneficiary to a living trust, the terms of which the testator or designator was the sole holder of a power to modify, shall be administered in accordance with the terms of the trust as they may have been modified prior to the testator's or designator's death, even though the will or beneficiary designation was not reexecuted or republished after exercise of the power to modify, unless the will or beneficiary designation expressly provides otherwise. Such property transferred or appointed to a living trust, which is subject to a power of modification requiring action or consent of a person other than the testator or designator, shall be administered in accordance with the terms of the trust instrument as they exist at the execution of the will or beneficiary designation, unless expressly otherwise provided. If the will or beneficiary designation expressly provides that the property shall be administered in accordance with the terms of the trust instrument as they may be modified thereafter, the will or beneficiary designation need not be reexecuted or republished after exercise of the power to modify.

(3) DISPOSITION WHEN NO EXISTING LIVING TRUST. If at the death of a testator a living trust has been completely revoked, or otherwise terminated, a provision in the testator's will purporting to transfer or appoint property to such trust shall have the following effect, unless the will provides otherwise:

(a) If the testator was a necessary party to the revocation or other termination of such trust, the provision in the testator's will shall be invalid;

(b) If the testator was not a necessary party to the revocation or other termination of such trust, the provision in the testator's will shall be deemed to create a testamentary trust upon the terms of the living trust instrument at the time the will was executed or as otherwise provided where sub. (2) is applicable.

Wis. Stat. 701.09. Transfers to testamentary trusts.

(1) TESTAMENTARY TRANSFER TO TRUST OF ANOTHER. A transfer or appointment by will shall not be held invalid because it is made to a trust created, or to be created, under the will of another person if the will of such other person was executed, or was last modified with respect to the terms of such trust, prior to the death of the person making the transfer or appointment and such other persons will is admitted to probate prior to, or within 2 years after, the death of the person making the transfer or appointment. Property included in such a transfer or appointment shall not be considered property subject to administration as part of the other person's estate but shall pass directly to that other persons testamentary trustee, be added to the designated trust and administered as a part thereof.

(2) INVALID TESTAMENTARY TRANSFER. If such a transfer or appointment by will is not accepted by the testamentary trustee of such other person or if no will of such other person which meets the conditions specified in sub. (1) is admitted to probate within the period therein limited, and if the will containing such transfer or appointment by will makes no alternative disposition of the assets, the will shall be construed as creating a trust upon the terms contained in the documents constituting the will of such other person as of the date of death of the person making the transfer or appointment by will.

(3) LIFE INSURANCE PROCEEDS TRANSFERRED TO TRUST OF INSURED. A trustee named or to be named in the will of an insured person may be designated beneficiary of an insurance policy on the life of the insured if the designation is made in accordance with the terms of the policy. After admission of the insured's will to probate and issuance of letters to such trustee, the insurance proceeds shall be paid to the trustee to be administered in accordance with the terms of the trust as they exist at the death of the insured, and the proceeds may be commingled with other assets passing to the trust. Insurance proceeds paid to a testamentary trustee because of his or her designation as life insurance beneficiary shall not be subject to death tax to any greater extent than if the proceeds were payable to a beneficiary other than the insured's estate. The proceeds shall be inventoried for tax purposes only and shall not be subject to taxes, debts or charges enforceable against the estate or otherwise considered assets of the insured's estate to any greater extent than if the proceeds were payable to a beneficiary other than the insured's estate.

(4) EMPLOYEE BENEFITS TRANSFERRED TO TRUST OF EMPLOYEE. A trustee named or to be named in the will of an employee covered by any employee benefit plan or contract described in s. 815.18 (3) (j) or any annuity or insurance contract purchased by an employer that is a religious, scientific, educational, benevolent or other corporation or association not organized or conducted for pecuniary profit may be designated payee of any benefits payable after the death of the employee if the designation is made in accordance with the terms of the plan or contract. After admission of the employees will to probate and issuance of letters to the trustee, the death benefits shall be paid to the trustee to be administered in accordance with the terms of the trust as they exist at the death of the employee, and the benefits may be commingled with other assets passing to the trust. Death

benefits paid to a testamentary trustee because of his or her designation as payee are not subject to the death tax to any greater extent than if the benefits were payable to a beneficiary other than the employees estate. The benefits shall be inventoried for tax purposes only and are not subject to taxes, debts or charges enforceable against the estate or otherwise considered assets of the employees estate to any greater extent than if the benefits were payable to a beneficiary other than the employees estate.

(5) TRANSFER OF OTHER PROPERTY. Property other than that described in subs. (3) and (4) may be made payable to or transferred to a trustee named or to be named in the will of the transferor.

Wis. Stat. 701.115. Future interests in revocable trusts.

(1)

(a) In par. (b), "revocable trust" means a trust that the grantor, at the time of death, was alone empowered to change or revoke, by law or under the instrument creating the trust, regardless of whether the grantor then had the capacity to exercise the power.

(b) Unless a contrary intention is found, if a person has a future interest in property under a revocable trust and, under the terms of the trust, the person has the right to possession and enjoyment of the property at the grantors death, the right to possession and enjoyment is contingent on the persons surviving the grantor. Extrinsic evidence may be used to show contrary intent.

(2) Survivorship under sub. (1) (b) is governed by s. 854.03

(3) The rights of the issue of a predeceasing beneficiary under sub. (1) (b) are governed by s. 854.06

VI. THE INTERPLAY BETWEEN WILLS AND WILL SUBSTITUTES

Although trusts and other legal forms may function as will substitutes, statutes regulating wills do not necessarily apply to the documents that substitute for them. For example, do statutes that automatically revoke devises to a former spouse following a divorce have a similar impact on beneficially interests in a trust or a beneficiary designation in a life insurance policy? Does the slayer rule apply when a future beneficiary of a trust kills the present beneficiary? Such issues are explored in this section.

A. LIVING TRUSTS AND THE LAW OF WILLS

Wis. Stat. 701.25. Applicability of general transfers at death provisions.

Chapter 854 **[Transfers at Death--General Rules]** applies to transfers at death under trust instruments.

Wis. Stat. 701.26. Disclaimers of nonprobate transfers.

(1) A recipient may disclaim, under s. 854.13, any of the following:

(a) All or part of an interest in a joint tenancy, upon the death of another joint tenant.

(b) All or part of an interest in survivorship marital property, upon the death of the other spouse.

(c) All or part of an interest that is created by a nontestamentary instrument and transferred at death, upon the death that causes the transfer.

(d) All or part of any other interest transferred under a governing instrument, as defined in s. 854.01 (2)

(2) A recipient may disclaim, under s. 700.27, all or part of any interest transferred under an inter vivos governing instrument, as defined in s. 700.27 (1) (c)

In re Estate of Cayo

Court of Appeals of Wisconsin
117 Wis. 2d 154, 342 N.W.2d 785 (1983)

Opinion by Hansen. This is an appeal from a judgment dismissing a petition for construction of a will and living trust brought by Meghan M. Cayo's guardian ad litem. The main issue before us is whether sec. 853.25(1), Stats., applies to a parent's failure to provide for a child in a living trust drafted prior to the child's birth. Because sec.

853.25(1) pertains only to the omission of children born or adopted after the making of a will, not of a trust, we affirm the probate court's dismissal.

On September 6, 1977, Linda Rudy Cayo executed a will and revocable living trust naming her son, James R. Cayo, as sole beneficiary. On June 25, 1978, Linda's daughter, Meghan M. Cayo, was born. On August 18, 1981, Linda died without changing any provisions of her will or trust.

Meghan's guardian ad litem petitioned the probate court for construction of the will and living trust. In the petition, the court was urged to find that Meghan was entitled to one-half of Linda's estate, both under the will and the trust, pursuant to sec. 853.25(1), Stats. In addition, the court was asked to find the living trust as testamentary in nature, placing it within the language of the statute. In the alternative, the court was requested to impose a constructive trust* for Meghan because Linda had mistakenly failed to include Meghan in her estate.

Pursuant to sec. 853.25(1), Stats., the probate court included Meghan as a beneficiary of the will. However, because the probate court concluded sec. 853.25 was expressly limited to wills, it declined to include Meghan in the trust. The court also declined to impose a constructive trust.

The trial court concluded the statute was limited to wills. Because statutory construction involves a question of law, this court owes no deference to the trial court's conclusion. Engineers & Scientists of Milwaukee, Inc. v. City of Milwaukee, 38 Wis. 2d 550, 554, 157 N.W.2d 572, 574 (1968). In this case, we agree with the probate court's interpretation of the statute. Section 853.25(1), Stats., reads.:

CHILDREN BORN OR ADOPTED AFTER MAKING OF THE WILL. If a testator fails to provide in his will for any child born or adopted after the making of the will, that child is entitled to receive a share in the estate of the testator equal in value to the share which the child would have received if the testator had died intestate, unless: (a) the testator left all or substantially all of his estate to the mother of the child, or (b) the testator eliminated all of his children known to him to be living at the time of execution of the will from any share under the will, or (c) the testator provided for the subsequently born or adopted child by transfers outside the will and the intent that the transfers be in lieu of a testamentary gift is either shown by statements of the testator

* A constructive trust is an equitable remedy that can be imposed to prevent unjust enrichment or an unjust result. While it shares certain characteristics with an ordinary trust, a constructive trust is technically not a trust.

or inferred from the amount of the transfers and other circumstances, or (d) in any other case it appears from the will or evidence outside the will that the omission was intentional. If a child entitled to a share under this section dies before the testator, and the child leaves issue who survive the testator, the issue who represent the child are entitled to his share.

Meghan's guardian ad litem contends that since there is no evidence that her mother intentionally excluded her from the trust provision, she should be included by virtue of this statute. We disagree.

When a statute is not ambiguous, the words of the statute must be given their obvious and ordinary meaning. Hucko v. Jos. Schlitz Brewing Co., 100 Wis. 2d 372, 376, 302 N.W.2d 68, 71 (Ct. App. 1981). The statute specifically states "[i]f a testator fails to provide in his will for any child born or adopted after the making of the will . . . ." Sec. 853.25(1), Stats. (Emphasis added.) This statute does not contemplate a settlor's failure to provide for his or her unborn children in a trust. The statutory language pertains only to wills. Therefore, we hold the statute does not contemplate the omission of children born or adopted after a trust is executed.

Meghan's guardian ad litem next argues the trust should be viewed as a testamentary disposition allowing the court to construe the trust as a will and placing the trust within the provisions of sec. 853.25(1), Stats. However, the guardian ad litem defeats his own argument by citing Estate of Steck, 275 Wis. 290, 81 N.W.2d 729 (1957). The court in Steck affirmed the trial court's determination that a valid inter vivos trust was not a testamentary disposition. The guardian ad litem drives the final nail into this argument when he cites sec. 701.07(1), Stats., which sets forth factors that will not make a living trust a testamentary disposition. Although the trust in issue has several of the factors set out in sec. 701.07 (1), it remains a valid living trust. It is unambiguous in that its sole beneficiary is James. No other beneficiary is mentioned. The trust cannot be viewed as an attempted testamentary disposition and will not be modified to include Meghan as a beneficiary. To do so would violate the intention of the settlor.

Finally, Meghan's guardian ad litem urges this court to impose a constructive trust on the estate for her benefit. The supreme court has recently set forth the limited circumstances in which a constructive trust may be imposed. The legal title must be held by someone who in equity and good conscience should not be entitled to beneficial enjoyment. Title must also have been obtained by means of actual or constructive fraud, duress, abuse of a confidential relationship, mistake, commission of a wrong, or by any form of unconscionable conduct. Wilharms v. Wilharms, 93

Wis. 2d 671, 679, 287 N.W.2d 779, 783 (1980). The only factor which could be applicable to this case is mistake. Such a mistake would refer to a mistake of fact made at the time the trust was executed and not a subsequent change of circumstances. See 89 C.J.S. Trusts, §74 (1955). However, the evidence in the record indicates that prior to her death, Linda was warned by her attorney to make changes in both her will and trust. Yet, she failed to do so. Linda's failure to include Meghan in the trust was a mistake of judgment on her part, not a mistake of fact. Since there is no evidence in the record that Linda mistakenly omitted Meghan at the time the trust was drafted, we affirm the trial court's decision not to impose a constructive trust.

Taylor v. Marshall & Isley Trust Co.

Court of Appeals of Wisconsin
256 Wis. 2d 695, 647 N.W.2d 468 (2002)

PER CURIAM. Dolores A. Pokrzywinski's godchildren appeal from the trial court's granting of summary judgment in favor of Marshall & Ilsley Trust Company and Thomas N. Tuttle, Jr. The trial court concluded that Marshall & Ilsley and Tuttle were not negligent in the establishment or administration of Pokrzywinski's trust. The godchildren claim that Marshall & Ilsley and Tuttle were negligent because they breached their duties to: (1) fund Pokrzywinski's trust with all of her assets; and (2) inform Pokrzywinski that her marriage would invalidate her estate plan. We affirm.

I. Background

Dolores A. Pokrzywinski contacted Marshall & Ilsley Trust Company in April or May of 1998 to establish a trust. Jennifer Torti, a certified public accountant for Marshall & Ilsley, met with Pokrzywinski on May 11, 1998. Pokrzywinski told Torti that she wanted to establish a trust because she could no longer manage her finances. Torti explained how a revocable trust worked, the services Marshall & Ilsley would provide, and the fees for the services. Torti also suggested that Pokrzywinski consult an attorney to set up a pour-over will and recommended Attorney J. Patrick Ronan.

Torti and Thomas N. Tuttle, Jr., a trust administrator, met with Pokrzywinski on May 14, 1998, to establish the trust. Pokrzywinski told Torti and Tuttle that she wanted to place her Smith Barney brokerage account and her Marshall & Ilsley bank accounts into a trust so that Marshall & Ilsley could pay her bills and manage her investments.

Pokrzywinski signed the trust documents and the Dolores A. Pokrzywinski Revocable Trust was established.

Article I of the trust provided:

> The Grantor transfers to the Trustee the assets described in Schedule A attached, receipt of which is acknowledged by the Trustee, together with any additional assets which may be deposited by the Grantor or any other person, in trust, for the purposes and upon the terms set forth below.

There was no Schedule A; however, according to Pokrzywinski's instructions, Marshall & Ilsley transferred the Smith Barney brokerage account and Pokrzywinski's Marshall & Ilsley bank accounts into the trust.

Article IV of the trust imposed further duties upon the trustee, Marshall & Ilsley:

> The Trustee shall keep all assets safely; collect income and the proceeds of sales, maturities and redemptions; distribute net income and principal as directed by the Grantor. Grantor's instructions, whether in verbal, written or electronic form, to the Trustee, if believed to be genuine, shall be binding. The Trustee shall provide the Grantor with periodic accounting statements and a summary of Trust income for tax purposes.

Finally, Article VII of the trust indicated that the remaining assets would be distributed to Pokrzywinski's estate upon her death.

J. Patrick Ronan met with Pokrzywinski on May 19, 1998, to discuss estate planning. Pokrzywinski told Ronan that she wanted some of her property to pass to specific charities and the remainder of her property to pass to her godchildren. Ronan told Pokrzywinski that a pour-over will, in conjunction with the trust, would allow Pokrzywinski to realize her plan and that "regardless of her situation[,] including whether she married or not married, [the] Trust would distribute [her assets] to those heirs as she so desired."

Accordingly, Ronan executed an amendment to Article VII of Pokrzywinski's trust that left the residue of the trust to four of Pokrzywinski's godchildren. Ronan also executed a pour-over will that would transfer Pokrzywinski's non-trust assets into the trust upon Pokrzywinski's death: "I give the residue of my estate to the Trustees of the DOLORES A. POKRZYWINSKI REVOCABLE TRUST."

Pokrzywinski married Leonard Rush, Sr., on September 5, 1998. By operation of law, Pokrzywinski's marriage impliedly revoked her will. See Wis. Stat. §853.11(2).* Tuttle was aware that Pokrzywinski and Rush were going to be married and was informed of the marriage after it took place. Rush also informed Ronan that he and Pokrzywinski had married. Pokrzywinski died on October 1, 1998.

At the time of Pokrzywinski's death, approximately forty percent of her assets, or $416,205, had been transferred to the revocable trust. Because Pokrzywinski's marriage impliedly revoked her will, she died intestate. Pokrzywinski had no children; thus, the remaining assets, or about sixty percent of her estate, passed to her husband, Rush.

Pokrzywinski's godchildren filed a suit against Marshall & Ilsley and Tuttle. They claimed that Marshall & Ilsley was negligent because it breached a duty to transfer all of Pokrzywinski's assets into the trust. They also claimed that Marshall & Ilsley was negligent because it breached a duty to warn Pokrzywinski that her marriage to Rush would impliedly revoke her will and invalidate her estate plan.

Marshall & Ilsley and Tuttle moved for summary judgment. The trial court granted the motion. It determined that Marshall & Ilsley's and Tuttle's duties as trustees were limited to the scope of the powers given to them by the trust. Thus, the court concluded that Marshall & Ilsley and Tuttle did not have a duty to fund the trust with all of Pokrzywinski's assets because the only duty created by the trust was a duty to distribute the assets upon Pokrzywinski's death. The court also determined that the godchildren's failure-to-warn claim was unsuccessful. It concluded that the godchildren could not prove the elements of causation or damages because they could not show that Pokrzywinski's "intent after marriage was the same as when she drafted the pour-over will."

II. Analysis

Our review of the trial court's grant of summary judgment is de novo, and we apply the same standards as did the trial court. Green Spring Farms v. Kersten, 136 Wis. 2d 304, 315-317, 401 N.W.2d 816, 820-821 (1987). First, we examine the pleadings to determine whether a proper claim for relief has been stated. Id., 136 Wis. 2d at 315, 401 N.W.2d at 820. If the complaint states a claim and the answer joins the issue, our inquiry then turns to whether any genuine issues of material fact exist. Id. Wisconsin

* This provision has been repealed since the date of this decision, and a post-execution marriage no longer has the effect of revoking a valid pre-marital will. Ed.

Stat. §802.08(2) (1999-2000) sets forth the standard by which summary judgment motions are to be judged:

> The judgment sought shall be rendered if the pleadings, depositions, answers to interrogatories, and admissions on file, together with the affidavits, if any, show that there is no genuine issue as to any material fact and that the moving party is entitled to a judgment as a matter of law.

First, the godchildren claim that Marshall & Ilsley was negligent because it breached a duty to identify and transfer all of Pokrzywinski's assets into the trust. We disagree.

The existence and the scope of a legal duty are questions of law that we review without deference to the trial court. Kramschuster v. Shawn E., 211 Wis. 2d 699, 703, 565 N.W.2d 581, 583 (Ct. App. 1997). Generally, the nature and the extent of the duties of the trustee are determined by the terms of the trust. See Saros v. Carlson, 244 Wis. 84, 88, 11 N.W.2d 676, 679 (1943) ("It is a trustee's paramount duty to … comply with the terms of the trust."); Restatement (Second) of Trusts §164 (1959) ("The nature and extent of the duties and powers of the trustee are determined by … the terms of the trust."). In this case, Marshall & Ilsley's duty to collect Pokrzywinski's assets was clearly spelled out in Article I of the trust:

> The Grantor transfers to the Trustee the assets described in Schedule A attached, receipt of which is acknowledged by the Trustee, together with any additional assets which may be deposited by the Grantor or any other person, in trust, for the purposes and upon the terms set forth below.

Marshall and Ilsley's duties were further spelled out in Article IV of the trust:

> The Trustee shall keep all assets safely; collect income and the proceeds of sales, maturities and redemptions; distribute net income and principal as directed by the Grantor…. The Trustee shall provide the Grantor with periodic accounting statements and a summary of Trust income for tax purposes.

Nowhere does it say that Marshall & Ilsley was required to collect all of Pokrzywinski's assets and deposit them into the trust. Rather, under the terms of the trust, the assets were to be deposited at the direction of the Grantor, Pokrzywinski.

Here, Pokrzywinski directed Marshall & Ilsley to deposit her Smith Barney brokerage account and her Marshall & Ilsley bank accounts into the trust. That it did. There is no evidence that Pokrzywinski directed Marshall & Ilsley to place any other assets into the trust. Accordingly, Marshall & Ilsley acted in accordance with the terms of the trust and we see no duty to transfer all of Pokrzywinski's assets into the trust.

The godchildren, however, rely upon Estate of Erlien v. Erlien, 190 Wis. 2d 401, 527 N.W.2d 389 (Ct. App. 1994), to argue that Marshall & Ilsley was required to collect all of Pokrzywinski's assets because, under Wisconsin law, a trustee is required to undertake duties that are not specifically included in the trust document. Thus, they argue the duty to gather assets and transfer them to a trust is so basic that it does not need to be "spelled out" in the trust document. We disagree. While the godchildren are correct in stating that a trustee has duties not included in the trust document, the rule does not apply here, where the trustee's duties are specifically included in the trust document, for the reasons set forth below.

In Erlien, we concluded that the trustee of a testamentary trust has a duty to ensure that the personal representative of an estate transfers all property to the trust to which the beneficiaries are entitled. Erlien, 190 Wis. 2d at 417-419, 527 N.W.2d at 394-395. We recognized this duty based upon statutory provisions governing testamentary trusts: Wis. Stat. §701.16(1) and Wis. Stat. §856.29. Id.

In contrast, Pokrzywinski established an inter vivos revocable trust. As noted above, Marshall & Ilsley's duty to fund Pokrzywinski's trust was defined by the terms of the trust. Thus, we need not resort to statutory or other extrinsic authority. See Restatement (Second) of Trusts §164 (1959) (the nature and extent of a trustee's duties are determined by the nature of the trust relationship "in the absence of any provision in the terms of the trust") (emphasis added). Accordingly, Erlien is distinguishable and we decline to impose a duty upon Marshall & Ilsley to collect all of Pokrzywinski's assets absent such a provision in the trust. See Scott v. Quarles, 197 Wis. 327, 330, 222 N.W. 235, 237 (1928) ("Courts in the exercise of equity powers may not enlarge, modify, or defeat the terms of the trust, saving and excepting only in cases where it shall appear that it is necessary to preserve the corpus of the trust.").

Second, the godchildren rely upon McCoy v. First Wisconsin National Bank, 142 Wis. 2d 750, 419 N.W.2d 301 (Ct. App. 1987), to argue that a trustee has a duty to warn a grantor of "easily identifiable impediments or pitfalls." See id., 142 Wis. 2d at 757, 419 N.W.2d at 305. Thus, the godchildren argue that Marshall & Ilsley had a duty to warn Pokrzywinski that her marriage to Rush impliedly revoked her will and invalidated her estate plan. Again, we disagree.

In McCoy, Elizabeth McCoy established an inter vivos trust with the First Wisconsin National Bank. Id., 142 Wis. 2d at 751, 419 N.W.2d at 303. The trust provided that when McCoy died, the corpus of the trust would transfer to the executor of McCoy's will or the administrator of McCoy's estate. Id., 142 Wis. 2d at 751-752, 419 N.W.2d at 303. At a meeting with the Bank and the Wisconsin Academy of Sciences, Arts, and Letters, McCoy told the Bank's trust officers that she wanted the corpus of her trust to go to the Academy. Id., 142 Wis. 2d at 752, 419 N.W.2d at 303. After the meeting, McCoy wrote a letter to the Academy's president confirming that the corpus of her trust was to pass to the Academy. Id. McCoy then sent a copy of the letter to the Bank. Id. The Bank put the letter in McCoy's file, but did not contact McCoy or take any action to amend the trust. Id.

McCoy died intestate and her estate claimed the corpus of the trust under the terms of the trust agreement. Id., 142 Wis. 2d at 753, 419 N.W.2d at 303. The trial court held that the trust had not been effectively amended; thus, the corpus of the trust could not pass to the Academy. Id.. We concluded that the Bank breached its duty of vigilance when it failed to advise or warn McCoy that the letter was insufficient to amend the trust. Id., 142 Wis. 2d at 757, 419 N.W.2d at 305. We made this determination based upon: (1) the Bank's knowledge of McCoy's intent to make the Academy the trust beneficiary, which was clearly revealed at a meeting and in a letter; (2) the language of the trust agreement, which required "an 'instrument in writing delivered to the Trustee'" to amend the trust; and (3) the Bank's expertise in trust matters. Id. Thus, we concluded that: "the Bank had a duty to at least warn McCoy regarding easily identifiable impediments or pitfalls if her intent was to make the Academy the beneficiary of her trust upon her death, an intent not found in the trust document." Id.

This case, however, is distinguishable from McCoy. First, in McCoy, we determined that the Bank had a duty to warn of easily identifiable impediments or pitfalls because the grantor made her intent to amend the trust agreement clear-she clearly made her wishes known to the Bank at a meeting and subsequently submitted a letter to the bank confirming her desire to amend the trust. In contrast, Marshall & Ilsley had no notice, written or otherwise, that Pokrzywinski wished to amend any part of her trust or estate plan. Here, the only knowledge that Marshall & Ilsley had was the minimal knowledge that Pokrzywinski had married. This simply does not rise to the level of knowledge that the Bank had in McCoy. Accordingly, it does not follow that Pokrzywinski's marriage created an easily identifiable impediment or pitfall of which Marshall & Ilsley had a duty to warn.

Moreover, there was no language in Pokrzywinski's trust that required Marshall & Ilsley to inform Pokrzywinski of possible problems with her estate plan. Indeed, such language would require Marshall & Ilsley to dispense legal advice and engage in the unauthorized practice of law. See Doe v. Condon, 341 S.C. 22, 532 S.E.2d 879, 882 (S.C. 2000) "Whether a will or trust is appropriate in any given situation is a function of legal judgment."); Green v. Huntington Nat'l Bank, 4 Ohio St. 2d 78, 33 Ohio Op.

2d 442, 212 N.E.2d 585, 587-588 (Ohio 1965) (bank that provided legal advice on estate planning engaged in the unauthorized practice of law). Pokrzywinski's attorney, Ronan, drafted Pokrzywinski's will and told Pokrzywinski that "regardless of her situation[,] including whether she married or not married, [the] trust would distribute [her assets] to those heirs as she so desired."

Marshall & Ilsley had no duty to warn Pokrzywinski that her marriage would invalidate her estate plan and the trial court properly granted Marshall & Ilsley's and Tuttle's motion for summary judgment.

B. WILL SUBSTITUTES AND TAXES

Estate of Sheppard v. Schleis

Supreme Court of Wisconsin
324 Wis. 2d 41, 782 N.W.2d 85 (2010)

Abrahamson, C.J. This is an appeal of an order and judgment from the Circuit Court of Washington County, Patrick J. Faragher, Judge. This court granted the Estate's petition to bypass the court of appeals pursuant to Wis. Stat. §§808.05 and 809.60 (2007-08).

Jessica Schleis was named as the recipient of two accounts, one a "Payable on Death" (P.O.D.) account, the other a "Transfer on Death" (T.O.D.) account, totaling over $3 million in the name of James F. Sheppard, the decedent.[1] For ease of discussion, we will refer to both accounts as P.O.D. accounts.

This action was brought by the Estate of James F. Sheppard, deceased, against the defendants, Jessica Schleis (the named recipient of the two accounts); her parents, James Schleis and Mary Jo Schleis (who signed an agreement with the Estate stating that "required estate taxes" would be paid out of the accounts); and XYZ Financial Institutions (named under Wisconsin's Fictitious Name Statute, Wis. Stat. §807.12, as

[1] [Ed. note: James F. Sheppard was the founder of the Milwaukee-based sandwich store chain, Cousins Subs, which he started with his cousin, William Specht.]

the institutions that currently have on deposit the funds from the two P.O.D. accounts). The Estate seeks reimbursement from these defendants of the federal and state estate taxes generated by the P.O.D. accounts.

The circuit court granted summary judgment to the defendants, holding that "the obligation to pay estate and inheritance taxes rests on the estate and the personal representative, not the defendants." As to the Wisconsin estate tax, the circuit court concluded that Firstar Trust Company v. First National Bank of Kenosha, 197 Wis. 2d 484, 541 N.W.2d 467 (1995), "deals with the issue completely" and that the Estate's claim that the defendants were obligated to pay a portion of the Wisconsin estate tax generated by the P.O.D. accounts is not maintainable under state law.

The circuit court also rejected the Estate's claim for apportionment of estate taxes because no Wisconsin apportionment statute exists and the court declined to create a common-law equitable apportionment rule. As to the Estate Tax Withholding Agreement signed by Mary Jo Schleis and James Schleis and the Estate for the "required estate taxes" to be paid from the P.O.D. accounts, the circuit court concluded that "the so called agreement does not provide a cognizable remedy," because "there is no federal or state withholding procedure" for P.O.D. accounts.

On appeal from the judgment and order of the circuit court, this court must address four issues: (1) When a decedent dies leaving no will, must a recipient of a P.O.D. account reimburse the Estate for a portion of the federal estate taxes attributable to a P.O.D. account? (2) When a decedent dies leaving no will, must a recipient of a P.O.D. account reimburse the Estate for a portion of the Wisconsin estate taxes attributable to a P.O.D. account? (3) When a decedent dies leaving no will and no Wisconsin statute directs apportionment of estate taxes, does the court apply a common-law limited equitable apportionment rule requiring a recipient of a P.O.D. account to reimburse the Estate for a portion of the federal and state estate taxes attributable to a P.O.D. account? (4) Does an agreement signed by parents of a minor recipient of a P.O.D. account impose liability on the parents or the minor to reimburse the Estate for a portion of the federal and state estate taxes attributable to a P.O.D. account?

We conclude that payment of the federal estate tax is to be made by the Estate under 26 U.S.C. §2002 (2006), which provides that an estate pays the estate tax on non-probate property. The P.O.D. accounts at issue do not fall within 26 U.S.C. §§2207B and 2036 or any other exception to the general rule that an estate pays the federal estate tax generated by non-probate assets. We further conclude that the Estate must pay the Wisconsin estate taxes generated by the P.O.D. accounts.

In Wisconsin the court has applied the burden-on-the-residue rule for state estate taxes unless the testator directs otherwise. The court declines to establish a common-law equitable apportionment rule. Furthermore, the agreement signed by Mary Jo and James Schleis, parents of Jessica Schleis, to retain 50% of all sums payable on the P.O.D. accounts "for the purpose of paying required estate taxes" is not enforceable against the Schleises. Accordingly, we affirm the order and judgment in favor of the defendants.

I

For the purposes of this appeal, the facts are not in dispute. James F. Sheppard, the decedent, established two payable on death (P.O.D.) accounts prior to his death. Sheppard designated his goddaughter, Jessica Schleis, as the recipient of these two P.O.D. accounts on his death. James Sheppard died without a will on July 2, 2007, with a total estate valued at approximately $12 million. The P.O.D. accounts designating Jessica Schleis as the recipient were worth approximately $3.8 million at the time of Sheppard's death.

Jessica Schleis was a minor, 17 years old, when James Sheppard died. Jessica's mother, Mary Jo Schleis, communicated with the attorney for the Estate on July 19, 2007. The Estate's attorney, who also represents the Estate before this court, advised Mary Jo Schleis that federal and Wisconsin estate tax obligations would attach to the recipient of the P.O.D. accounts.

At the suggestion of the Estate's attorney and with the advice of their own attorney, Jessica's parents signed, with Jessica's knowledge, an "Estate Tax Withholding Agreement," dated September 3, 2007. The agreement provided that 50% of all sums would remain on deposit in the accounts for the purpose of paying "required estate taxes." The Estate then supplied the Schleis family with information the Estate had regarding the P.O.D. accounts and with two death certificates, and refrained from taking any action to impede Jessica Schleis's ability to withdraw from the accounts. Because Jessica Schleis was a minor, her parents petitioned the circuit court on September 13, 2007, to be appointed her guardians.

As part of the guardianship proceeding, the circuit court appointed a guardian ad litem for Jessica Schleis. The guardian ad litem advised the Estate's attorney that she had advised the Schleis family that Jessica Schleis was not responsible for payment of federal or state estate taxes because the P.O.D. accounts were not part of the residuum of the probate estate and that as guardians of Jessica's estate the Schleises could remove all funds from the P.O.D. accounts.

On October 30, 2007, Mary Jo Schleis and James Schleis were appointed guardians for Jessica. The Schleises withdrew the entire balance from the P.O.D. accounts on November 12, 2007. While guardianship proceedings were ongoing, the Schleises retained a second attorney who on November 26, 2007, advised the Estate's attorney that she believed the Estate Tax Withholding Agreement was not binding on her clients, Mary Jo and James Schleis.

On January 17, 2008, the Estate's counsel advised counsel for the Schleises that the Estate maintained the position that Mary Jo Schleis, James Schleis, and Jessica Schleis were responsible to pay their share of all federal and Wisconsin estate taxes and that their obligation was joint and several. The Estate brought this suit seeking reimbursement of estate taxes from Mary Jo Schleis, James Schleis, and Jessica Schleis. Jessica Schleis reached the age of majority on February 18, 2008.

II

In reviewing a circuit court's decision granting summary judgment, this court applies the same methodology as the circuit court. Under Wis. Stat. §802.08(2), summary judgment must be entered "if the pleadings, depositions, answers to interrogatories, and admissions on file, together with the affidavits, if any, show that there is no genuine issue as to any material fact and that the moving party is entitled to a judgment as a matter of law."

III

The first issue is whether the Internal Revenue Code provides the Estate a right to recover a portion of federal estate taxes from the recipient of a P.O.D. account. We begin with a brief review of the applicable Internal Revenue Code provisions.

First, 26 U.S.C. §2002 states that the executor of a decedent's estate shall pay federal estate taxes imposed by 26 U.S.C. §§2001 et seq., whether the taxes are attributable to probate or non-probate property. Section 2002 simply states, "The tax imposed by this chapter shall be paid by the executor." Section 20.2002-1 of the Regulations elaborates to explain that an executor's or administrator's duty to pay federal estate tax applies to the "entire tax, regardless of the fact that the gross estate consists in part of property which does not come within possession of the executor or administrator. . . . " 26 C.F.R. §20.2002-1 (2009).

Thus the probate estate (the portion of the estate within the executor's possession) pays all of the federal estate taxes even if a portion of the total tax is generated by property that has passed to a recipient through a non-probate transfer (such as a P.O.D. account) and did not come under the executor's control or possession.

Four federal statutory provisions, 26 U.S.C. §§2206-2207B, set forth exceptions to the general rule of 26 U.S.C. §2002 that the probate estate pays the federal estate tax. These four exceptions permit the estate to seek reimbursement for a portion of the federal estate taxes paid from a recipient of a non-probate asset. The four exceptions are as follows:

Section 2206: Life Insurance Beneficiaries
Section 2207: Liability of recipient of property over which decedent had power of appointment.
Section 2207A: Right of recovery in the case of certain marital deduction property.
Section 2207B: Right of recovery where decedent retained interest.

The Estate argues that the last exception, 26 U.S.C. §2207B, applies in the present case. Section 2207B states that if the value of property is included in the gross estate on which estate tax has been paid, by reason of 26 U.S.C §2036, then the decedent's estate has a right of recovery from the person receiving the property equal to the same ratio that the value of the property bears to the taxable estate. Section 2207B(a) provides as follows:

Right of recovery where decedent retained interest.

(a) Estate tax.

(1) In general. If any part of the gross estate on which tax has been paid consists of the value of property included in the gross estate by reason of [26 U.S.C. §2036] (relating to transfers with retained life estate), the decedent's estate shall be entitled to recover from the person receiving the property the amount which bears the same ratio to the total tax under this chapter [26 U.S.C. §§2001 et seq.] which has been paid as--

(A) the value of such property, bears to

(B) the taxable estate.

(2) Decedent may otherwise direct. Paragraph (1) shall not apply with respect to any property to the extent that the decedent in his will (or a revocable trust) specifically

indicates an intent to waive any right of recovery under this subchapter with respect to such property.

To determine whether the Estate has a right of recovery under §2207B, we must therefore examine whether the value of the P.O.D. accounts at issue was included in James Sheppard's gross estate pursuant to 26 U.S.C. §2036. Only if the P.O.D. accounts were included in the gross estate pursuant to §2036 does §2207B apply, giving the Estate a right to seek reimbursement from Jessica Schleis for a portion of the estate taxes.

Section 2036 governs transfers made during a decedent's lifetime in which a decedent retained the right to income from the property or the right to determine who shall receive the property or income from the property. Section 2036(a) provides as follows:

Transfers with retained life estate

(a) General Rule. The value of the gross estate shall include the value of all property to the extent of any interest therein of which the decedent has at any time made a transfer (except in the case of a bona fide sale for an adequate and full consideration in money or money's worth), by trust or otherwise, under which he has retained for his life or for any period not ascertainable without reference to his death or for any period which does not in fact end before his death--

(1) the possession or enjoyment of, or the right to the income from, the property, or

(2) the right, either alone or in conjunction with any person, to designate the persons who shall possess or enjoy the property or the income therefrom.

Section 2036 applies where a decedent makes "a transfer" by trust or otherwise during his life retaining for his life, or any period not ascertainable without reference to his death, the income or the right to designate the persons who shall possess or enjoy the property or the income. Section 2036 operates to impose a portion of the federal estate tax on property that a decedent transferred during his or her life but in which the decedent retained an economic benefit until his death. See Helvering v. Bullard, 303 U.S. 297, 300, 58 S. Ct. 565, 82 L. Ed. 852 (1938); Hassett v. Welch, 303 U.S. 303, 310-12, 58 S. Ct. 559, 82 L. Ed. 858, 1938-1 C.B. 490 (1938).

To determine whether the P.O.D. accounts at issue are included in the gross estate under 26 U.S.C. §2036, we must determine whether the decedent made "a transfer" during his life by creating the P.O.D. accounts.

Under Wisconsin law governing P.O.D. accounts, the creation of a P.O.D. account does not amount to a transfer of property by the decedent to the recipient during the decedent's life. When a depositor opens a P.O.D. account, he or she names a recipient who is to receive the property in the account at the time of the depositor's death. The depositor is not required to notify the recipient when the account is opened or when the recipient is named. Wis. Stat. §705.26. Prior to the depositor's death, the depositor maintains control over the principal and income of the accounts and can change the P.O.D. recipient at any time. The depositor can remove all the assets from a P.O.D. account and close the account at any time before his or her death, without notifying the P.O.D. recipient. The recipient has a right to the account only if the account exists at the death of the depositor and the recipient survives the depositor.

Section 2036 applies to a transfer with a retained life estate. A property interest must be transferred during the owner's lifetime in order for a life estate to be retained. The P.O.D. account does not constitute such a transfer. During his or her lifetime the depositor is the owner of the P.O.D. account and controls the income, the principal, and the right to decide who gets the property at the depositor's death. With a P.O.D. account the depositor remains the owner during his or her life, transfers nothing during his or her life, and retains total interest in the property during his or her life. The depositor continues to control the principal and the income and could close the account or change the recipient at any time without even notifying the recipient of a change or the existence of the account. The depositor did not transfer any ownership rights or any rights to income during his life.

The recipient of a P.O.D. account does not possess a remainder interest. The recipient has only the potential expectancy of receiving the proceeds if the depositor makes no change in the nature of the account or in naming the recipient of the account and the named recipient survives the depositor. There is no transfer to the recipient involved in the creation of a P.O.D. account during the decedent's lifetime as required by 26 U.S.C §2036.

The Estate argues for a broad definition of "a transfer" under 26 U.S.C. §2036 to include the creation of a P.O.D. account. The Estate argues that the ownership right the decedent relinquished was the right to include the P.O.D. accounts in his probate estate. This argument would create an overly broad definition of a transfer. The Estate's definition would appear to require that virtually all nonprobate assets be included under 26 U.S.C. §2036.

Arguing that such a transfer does take place, the Estate relies on an Indiana court of appeals case, Burke v. Cleland, 702 N.E.2d 1078 (Ind. Ct. App. 1998). The Cleland case is not helpful to our analysis. Cleland turns on the language of the instruments used by a testator to transfer property to beneficiaries. The Indiana court did not analyze 26 U.S.C. §2036. It simply stated that an inter vivos trust was included in the gross estate under §2036.

In Cleland, the testator's will and an inter vivos trust each contained a clause directing the payment of federal estate taxes, and the two clauses were conflicting. The beneficiaries under the inter vivos trust (executed after the will) and the will were different. Conflict arose about who should pay the federal estate taxes generated by the property in the inter vivos trust.

The Indiana court of appeals held that the last instrument in time, the inter vivos trust, would control when there was an unambiguous tax provision in both a will and an inter vivos trust. The inter vivos trust instrument provided that upon request of the testator's personal representative, the trustee would pay all federal and state death taxes. The Indiana court held that this pay-all-taxes clause rebutted Indiana's presumption of apportionment. Accordingly, the inter vivos trust was responsible for the federal estate tax.

The analysis in Cleland, where a specific provision by the testator provided for payment of taxes by the trust, does not apply to the present intestate case. The general rule that the residual estate pays the estate tax is not displaced by any instructions of the decedent.

The Estate relies on other cases holding that the decedent had made a transfer for purposes of 26 U.S.C. §2036. For example, the Estate refers to Estate of Morton v. Commissioner of Internal Revenue, 12 TC 380 (1949), in which the election of a settlement option by a surviving spouse under the terms of a life insurance contract was determined to be a transfer during her lifetime that brought the proceeds within her gross estate at the time of her death. The spouse was entitled to the proceeds of the policy but elected to leave the proceeds with the insurer, receiving income with a right to invade the remainder, and naming a recipient who would receive the money on her death. The issue was whether the proceeds were included in the gross estate of the spouse even though she had not elected to receive the lump sum during her lifetime. The court considered that the spouse had made a transfer of the assets.

Another example provided by the Estate is when a decedent set up a bank account in his name as a trustee for specified recipients, sometimes called a savings account trust (or "Totten Trust"). Estate of Sulovich v. Comm'r of Internal Revenue, 587 F.2d 845

(6th Cir. 1978). The decedent gave the passbook to the parent of the recipients and authorized the withdrawal of funds. Under banking rules, the decedent retained full income and remainder rights to the account. The issue was whether the funds should be included in the decedent's gross estate, not the applicability of §2207B for apportionment of estate taxes. The court held that the decedent had not completed a gift of the assets, but that the decedent had made a transfer of the assets under either 26 U.S.C. §2036 or §2038, and that the assets were therefore included in the gross estate.

These fact patterns are different from the P.O.D. accounts where the accounts remained titled in the decedent's sole and individual name. The cases relied upon by the Estate are inapposite.

We conclude that creation of the P.O.D. accounts did not fall within the meaning of a transfer under 26 U.S.C. §2036, and therefore the estate does not have a right to recover under 26 U.S.C. §2207B. Because §§2207B and 2036 do not apply, the general rule of 26 U.S.C. §2002 applies: the residual estate pays the federal estate taxes on the P.O.D. accounts. The P.O.D. accounts are therefore not required to pay any portion of the federal estate taxes.

IV

Next, we turn to whether a recipient of a P.O.D. account must reimburse an Estate for a portion of the Wisconsin estate taxes attributable to the P.O.D. account when a decedent dies with no will. The answer is No.

We agree with the circuit court that Firstar Trust Co. v. First National Bank of Kenosha, 197 Wis. 2d 484, 541 N.W.2d 467 (1995), controls. Under Firstar Trust, the residue of the estate pays the Wisconsin estate taxes attributable to non-probate property in the absence of clear directions from the testator providing otherwise. The Estate does not separately brief the issue of liability for the Wisconsin estate tax. We conclude that under Firstar Trust, the Estate's claim against the Schleises for a portion of the state estate tax cannot be maintained under Wisconsin law.

V

The third issue is whether a common-law rule of limited equitable apportionment exists, requiring a recipient of P.O.D. accounts to reimburse an estate for a portion of the federal and state estate taxes attributable to the P.O.D. accounts when a decedent dies leaving no will.

Generally, if a decedent does not specify who pays federal or state estate taxes or does not do so effectively, state law will determine how to apportion the payment of federal and state estate taxes among the various beneficiaries. Several states have enacted statutes that determine which beneficiaries will pay federal and state estate taxes. Many states' statutes require recipients of non-probate assets to pay their pro rata share of the federal and state estate taxes. State courts have also created equitable apportionment remedies that accomplish the same result as an apportionment statute.

Wisconsin does not have an apportionment statute that directs the apportionment of federal or state estate taxes among various beneficiaries when a will or trust does not provide direction. In response to the Estate's request that the circuit court adopt an apportionment rule, the circuit court declared that "[t]here is no basis either statutorily or in the case law which would give the Court the confidence to create a remedy. More importantly, that is the province of the Supreme Court, not this Circuit Court especially under these facts. The [Estate] is asking the Court to stand the system on its head. It is the probate estate that pays the estate and inheritance taxes. To suggest that this obligation should be distributed to P.O.D. and similar accounts would have a serious negative impact on the administration of probate, generally; there would be tax obligations flowing outside of the classic probate process."

We examine three Wisconsin cases that discuss an equitable apportionment rule: Will of Uihlein, 264 Wis. 362, 59 N.W.2d 641 (1953); Estate of Joas, 16 Wis. 2d 489, 114 N.W.2d 831 (1962); and Firstar Trust Co. v. First National Bank of Kenosha, 197 Wis. 2d 484, 541 N.W.2d 467 (1995). None of the cases adopts or applies an equitable apportionment of estate taxes.

In Uihlein, the widow of the decedent chose to take her statutory one-third share of the estate rather than to take her share under the will. The widow claimed her statutory one-third share was to be calculated before federal estate taxes were paid. The effect of the widow's claim was to shift the burden of the federal estate tax to the remainder of the estate, making her share of the estate larger. The Uihlein court likened the federal estate tax to debts and expenses of administration that are to be paid by the residue before calculating the widow's share. The court rejected equitable apportionment of the federal estate tax as "unwarranted judicial legislation." Uihlein, 264 Wis. at 376. The court stated that "[t]his court in Will of Kootz [228 Wis. 306, 280 N.W. 672 (1938)] rejected the theory that our court should invoke its equity powers to achieve an apportionment of federal estate taxes which would prevent inequities . . . . We deem that it would be unwarranted judicial legislation for this court to attempt to apportion the impact of the federal estate tax . . . . The legislature has the power to enact an apportionment of federal estate tax statute providing for a different method of bearing the impact of federal estate taxes if it should determine the same desirable." Uihlein, 264 Wis. at 374, 376.

In Joas, this court considered who should pay the federal estate and Wisconsin inheritance tax relating to joint property. The will declared that the estate would pay all taxes for property that passed under the will. Because the joint property was non-probate property, that is, the property did not pass to the recipients under the will, the court held that the will's provision allocating taxes did not apply to the joint property. The court applied Wisconsin law, placing the burden of paying the federal estate tax attributable to the joint property on the residuum of the probate estate. The court declined to create an equitable apportionment rule. Finally, in Firstar Trust, the court addressed the issue of whether the residue of the estate or a trust bore the burden of the portion of the Wisconsin estate tax generated by the trust property. The court held that the burden of the state estate tax was to be borne by the decedent's probate estate and that the estate was not entitled to reimbursement from the trust for Wisconsin estate taxes paid. The court reviewed and reaffirmed prior Wisconsin case law, refusing to recognize equitable apportionment of Wisconsin estate taxes, stating: "Although some states have altered the burden-on-the-residue rule by statutory or judicially-created apportionment rules, Wisconsin is among the states that have not done so." Firstar Trust, 197 Wis. 2d at 510.

As noted there, "This court has consistently rejected the notion of judicially legislated estate tax apportionment rules." Firstar Trust, 197 Wis. 2d at 509 n.15. The Estate argues that Will of Cudahy, 251 Wis. 116, 28 N.W.2d 340 (1947), controls to make apportionment of the estate tax burden applicable to nonprobate property. The Estate misinterprets Cudahy. The issue in Cudahy was the interpretation of the decedent's will and inter vivos trust. Cudahy involved property passing under an inter vivos trust, the terms of which directed the trustee to pay all taxes on the trust property. At the same time, the decedent's will directed the executors to pay "just debts, funeral expenses and all inheritance, estate and succession taxes." The question was which entity, the trust or the estate, should pay Wisconsin inheritance taxes generated by the transfer of the decedent's interest in the trust. The court concluded that the will did not manifest the decedent's intention to provide for the payment of the taxes attributable to the beneficiaries of the trust estate, nonprobate property. The court ruled that the trust should pay the inheritance taxes; the trust disposed of the property and the trust instrument made provision for payment of taxes thereon. Cudahy, 251 Wis. at 120-21.

The Cudahy court did not hold that nonprobate assets should pay a share of inheritance taxes attributable to those assets. Cudahy was an interpretation of the decedent's intentions expressed in written documents, not an adoption of Wisconsin tax apportionment law. Cudahy is not instructive for the present case.

The Estate asks this court to recognize a common-law equitable apportionment doctrine to prevent injustice to heirs of James Sheppard and to prevent Jessica Schleis from getting a windfall. The Estate views the rule of limited equitable apportionment as promoting fairness and equality. Wisconsin does not have an apportionment statute. Wisconsin case law declines to recognize an equitable apportionment rule. The precedent is clear: In the absence of a statute or a decedent's written directions, in Wisconsin the burden of the federal and state estate taxes attributable to probate and non-probate assets falls on the residue of the estate. The rationale for the "residuary rule" has generally been that the decedent intended property transferred outside probate to be free of the usual burdens imposed on the probate estate. The burden of the federal and Wisconsin estate taxes in the instant case falls on the residue of the estate where the law has placed it. If apportionment is to be the policy of the state, then the state legislature should adopt it.

VI

The final issue relates to the Estate Tax Withholding Agreement signed by Mary Jo Schleis, James Schleis, and the Estate. The Schleises agreed that 50% of the balance of the P.O.D. accounts would remain on deposit "for the purpose of paying required estate taxes" (emphasis added). The Agreement further provides that "[i]n the event excess sums have been withheld, these monies will be distributed within 30 days following the filing of estate tax returns." The Agreement does not state that Jessica Schleis is required to pay a certain amount or portion of estate taxes. The entire text of the agreement reads as follows:

The parties agree that 50% or one-half of all payable on death accounts owned by James F. Sheppard at the time of his death will remain on deposit with the bank for the purpose of paying required estate taxes. In the event excess sums have been withheld, these monies will be distributed within 30 days following the filing of estate tax returns.

The Estate asks the court to hold that this Agreement obligates Jessica Schleis and her parents to pay a portion of the estate tax, even without determining as a prerequisite that Jessica owed any estate tax. The circuit court concluded that there is no contract binding Jessica Schleis "and further the so called agreement does not provide a cognizable remedy. There is no federal or state withholding procedure for such accounts."

The Agreement refers to "required taxes." The Schleises have no "required taxes." Because the P.O.D. accounts are not required to pay any estate taxes under federal or Wisconsin estate tax law, the Agreement creates no obligation to pay required taxes. This two-sentence document cannot be interpreted to create an independent obligation on the part of the Schleises to pay a share of estate taxes that neither they nor their daughter owed.

Furthermore, Jessica did not sign the agreement and is not a party to it. The document does not suggest that Mary Jo Schleis and James Schleis are signing in any capacity other than personally for themselves. No guardian had been appointed for Jessica, who was a minor when the Agreement was signed. Jessica is not liable for the taxes, and a guardian would not be authorized to make a gift of the taxes to the Estate without express court approval. Wis. Stat. §54.20(2)(a).

The Estate argues the Agreement is binding because Jessica did not disavow it. No agreement was made on Jessica's behalf, so there was nothing for her to disavow. Furthermore, Jessica's guardian ad litem did advise the Estate of the intent to disavow any purported agreement. By letter dated October 10, 2007, Jessica's guardian ad litem advised the Estate that under Wisconsin law, "the estate taxes would be paid out of the residue of Mr. Sheppard's estate," and that "Mr. & Mrs. Schleis cannot enter a contract regarding their daughter's money." Jessica's position has been consistent: she is entitled to all the proceeds of the P.O.D. accounts and has no obligation to pay the estate taxes.

The Estate claims the result is unjust and unfair and imposes an undue burden on James Sheppard's heirs who take through the probate estate. Federal and state law have determined where the tax liabilities fall. There is no equitable basis to impose a constructive trust as a matter of law. James Sheppard could have directed a different result but he did not.

In sum, for the reasons we set forth, we conclude that payment of the federal estate tax is the burden of the Estate under 26 U.S.C. §2002, which provides that an estate pays the estate tax on nonprobate property.

The P.O.D. accounts at issue do not fall under 26 U.S.C. §§2207B and 2036 or any other exception to the general rule that an estate pays the federal estate tax generated by nonprobate assets. We further conclude that the Estate must pay the Wisconsin estate taxes generated by the P.O.D. accounts. In Wisconsin, the court has applied the burden-on-the-residue rule for state estate taxes unless a testator directs otherwise. The court declines to establish a common-law equitable apportionment rule. Furthermore, the agreement signed by Mary Jo and James Schleis, parents of Jessica Schleis, to retain 50% of all sums payable on the P.O.D. accounts "for the purpose of paying required estate taxes" is not enforceable against the Schleises.

Accordingly, we affirm the circuit court's order and judgment in favor of the defendants.

CHAPTER 7.
AN OVERVIEW OF THE LAW OF TRUSTS

A trust can be created either during the lifetime of the settlor (an inter vivos trust) or as part of the probate process (a testamentary trust). If the former, the trust is created by the delivery of a trust instrument or a declaration of trust, and, if the latter, by a will. There are only two primary differences between the two types. First, the inter vivos trust operates independently of direct judicial oversight while the testamentary trust remains under the purview of the court that approved its creation as part of the probate process. Second, the settlor of an inter vivos trust has the capacity to play a direct role in the operation of the trust, either as trustee or beneficiary or as the holder of the power to revoke. (On the other hand, there is no requirement that the settlor retain any such involvement.) By its very nature, the testamentary trust is not subject to settlor participation. The formal requirements for trusts are minimal, and while they are normally created by a writing, the Wisconsin Supreme Court noted in *Swazzee v. Lee,* 259 Wis. 136, 47 N.W.2d 733 (1951), that oral inter vivos trusts are permitted so long as they can be proved by clear and convincing evidence.

The principal sources of the law of trusts in Wisconsin are Chapter 701 of the *Wisconsin Statutes* and the case law developed by Wisconsin courts over the past 165 years. Although 25 states and the District of Columbia have adopted the Uniform Trust Code, first promulgated in 2000 by the National Conference of Commissioners on Uniform State Laws, it has not been adopted in Wisconsin, nor, for that matter, has it been adopted in New York, California, or Texas, or in the Midwestern states of Indiana, Illinois, Iowa, Minnesota, and Wisconsin. Wis. Stat. §§701.01-701.05 are reproduced in Chapter 6.

Wis Stat. 701.24. Applicability.

(1) Except as otherwise provided in sub. (3) and s. 701.19 (9) (a), ss. 701.01 to 701.19, 701.21, 701.22, and 701.23 are applicable to a trust existing on July 1, 1971, as well as a trust created after such date, and shall govern trustees acting under such trusts. If application of any provision of ss. 701.01 to 701.19, 701.21, 701.22, and 701.23 to a trust in existence on August

1, 1971, is unconstitutional, it shall not affect application of the provision to a trust created after that date.

(2) Section 701.20 applies to every trust or decedents estate existing on May 17, 2005, and to every trust or decedents estate created or coming into existence after that date, except as otherwise expressly provided in s. 701.20 or by the decedents will or the terms of the trust. With respect to a trust or decedents estate existing on May 17, 2005, s. 701.20 (5) to (30) shall apply at the beginning of the trusts or estates first accounting period, as defined in s. 701.20 (2) (a), that begins on or after May 17, 2005.

(3) Sections 701.06 (6) (b), (c), and (d) and 701.19 (10) are applicable to a trust existing on April 11, 2006, as well as a trust created after that date, and shall govern trustees acting under such trusts. If application of any provision of s. 701.06 (6) (b), (c), or (d) or 701.19 (10) to a trust in existence on April 11, 2006, is unconstitutional, it shall not affect application of the provision to a trust created after that date.

I. ELEMENTS OF TRUSTS

All trusts, whether they are inter vivos or testamentary, must be preceded by an intention of creating a trust. Other than a resulting or constructive trust (discussed at the end of this chapter), which are not true trusts, a trust is never accidentally created. In addition, for there to be a trust, there must be a distinct and clearly identifiable trust res and a clearly defined beneficiary or beneficiaries. The naming of the trustee is not as critical, and if the settlor fails to identify a trustee, one will be appointed by the court. However, with an inter vivos trust, there must also be either a declaration of trust (that names the settlor as trustee) or a delivery of the trust res to the trustee.

A. INTENTION TO CREATE A TRUST

Wyse v. Puchner

Supreme Court of Wisconsin
260 Wis. 365, 51 N.W.2d 38 (1952)

FAIRCHILD, Justice. That a trust fund in favor of the children of Elsie Wyse's husband was created is evidenced by the following declarations in her letters. In a letter which she wrote to her attorney on October 20, 1947, she said:

'I have been thinking the matter over, and have come to the conclusion that the right thing for me to do would be to set up a fund of $5,000, the income and principal to be used toward the expenses of the children's educations. I believe this amount is about half of Mr. Wyse's insurance, and I feel it should be used for this purpose, as he was very anxious that his children should receive a good education. Please handle it directly with Mrs. Wyse, and do it in the least expensive way possible.

'During 1946 and 1947, I have sent Mrs. Wyse and the children, approximately $500 each year. However, I think it will be better at this time to clean up the entire matter by putting aside a lump sum of $5,000, so Mrs. Wyse will know exactly what she has to spend towards the children's education and support. I would like this trust to become effective as of January, 1948.'

On March 17, 1948, Elsie S. Wyse wrote the petitioner the following in a letter:

'Your Air Mail letter just arrived with the wonderful news about Frank's scholarship -- I am so thrilled & happy & proud --

'It was good of you to write me so promptly & I appreciate your thoughtfulness --

'Several months ago, when you first wrote me about Frank's college education, I had an opportunity to sell Mother's cooperative apartment in New York & I took $5,000 -- of the sales price & put it to one side marked 'Trust Fund for Frank & Kindy Wyse's education & maintenance -- ' The principal & income are to be used for this purpose -- At that time I wrote my attorney in Milwaukee -- Irving A. Puchner, Bankers Bldg. -- & asked him to establish the fund at the proper time, so you would know you had this amount to depend on -- '

The father of the children and their mother were divorced in 1938. The judgment of divorce, among other things, ordered that alimony and an allowance for support of

$250 per month be paid for the support and maintenance of the divorced wife and children. Shortly after the divorce, the father, Francis O. Wyse, married Elsie S. Wyse, who possessed a substantial independent fortune. There were no children of the second marriage. It appears that prior to the granting of said divorce and many times thereafter Francis O. Wyse and his second wife, Elsie S. Wyse, promised petitioner and agreed with her that the children should receive sufficient funds for their education and maintenance. At the time of the divorce the father of the children promised his former wife that the insurance policies on his life in the principal amount of $10,000 should remain payable to petitioner for the benefit of the children; and this fact was known to Elsie Wyse, the second wife. Subsequently said policies were made payable to Elsie S. Wyse, but with the understanding that she would provide for the education and maintenance of the children. After 1943, because of the illness of Francis O. Wyse, the father, and upon request, $775 was released from the arrearages of the alimony and support allowance. Said Francis O. Wyse died in 1945, and his insurance was paid to the said Elsie S. Wyse. Elsie S. Wyse, in recognition of her obligation to the children, in October 1947, segregated and set apart the sum of $5,000 of the sales price received from the sale of an apartment building in New York, as a trust fund for the education and maintenance of the said children, the principal and income of said fund to be used for that purpose. There was advanced to the account of Frank O. Wyse from the fund thus set up $225, $75 of which was paid to one of the cestui que trustents. Elsie Wyse died September 13, 1949, leaving a will. A claim for said trust fund in the amount of $5,600 was duly filed in the estate. Upon the foregoing facts, the court determined:

'1. Elsie S. Wyse, in October 1947 created a binding and enforceable self-declared trust in and to the sum of $5,000, the principal and income of which is for the education and maintenance of Frank O. Wyse and Clarinda C. Wyse, wards of petitioner in this action.

'2. The estate of Elsie S. Wyse is liable to petitioner for withholding said fund, including both principal and income, from the wards of petitioner.

'3. Petitioner is entitled to a judgment which shall provide:

'(a) That the Marshall & Ilsley Bank, Milwaukee, Wisconsin, be and hereby is appointed Trustee of the 'Trust Fund for Frank and Kindy Wyse's Education and Maintenance', to act in that capacity, without bond, under the terms of this judgment and further orders of this court.

'(b) That Respondents, Irving A. Puchner and Marshall & Ilsley Bank, be and the same are hereby ordered and directed to pay over from the assets of the estate of Elsie S.

Wyse, the principal sum of $4925, together with income computed at the rate of 3% from October 1, 1947 being the sum of $510.04, making in all the sum of $5435.04, to the trustee appointed pursuant to paragraph 1, hereof.

'(c) Said fund shall be designated and be for the purposes set forth in Petitioner's Exhibit 1, in this action, which is:

'Trust Fund for Frank and Kindy Wyse's Education and maintenance' -- 'The principal and income are to be used for this purpose -- '

'(d) That the trustee is hereby empowered to distribute to the beneficiaries, Frank O. Wyse and Clarinda C. Wyse, or either of them, moneys from either principal or income of said fund at such times and in such amounts as the trustee in his discretion shall determine after consultation with petitioner, Clarinda C. Wyse, and the beneficiaries with reference to their education and maintenance requirements.

' (e) That the Trustee shall furnish or cause to be furnished to this court a statement of account at the close of each calendar year, showing receipts and disbursements duly authenticated.

'(f) That the Trustee shall make application to this court respecting the disposition of any funds remaining after the purposes as set forth in paragraph 3 hereof, have been fulfilled.

'(g) That petitioner recover of respondents, Irving A. Puchner and Marshall & Ilsley Bank, executors and trustees of the estate of Elsie S. Wyse, her costs in the amount of $100.00 and disbursements of this action to be taxed before the Clerk of this Court.

The evidence on which the trial court made its findings and conclusions is of acts which will admit of no other interpretation than that the settlor of the trust retained no legal rights other than the rights as trustee over the property. There was no reservation of power to revoke. While the existence of a trust need not be declared in express terms, this trust was established by proper written evidence -- letters in writing, disclosing facts which created a fiduciary relation. In re Estate of Horkan, 193 Wis. 286, 214 N.W. 438; 26 R.C.L. 1182, 1183; 65 C.J. 231, sec. 21.

In the case of In re Brown's Will, 1930, 252 N.Y. 366, 169 N.E. 612, 614, it was said: 'While a transfer of the property to a trustee for the purposes of the settlement may be the surest way to create a trust, yet the same result will be accomplished if the owner declares that he himself holds the property in trust for the person designated, and this trust may be created either in writing or, if relating to personal property, by parol. The declaration need not be made to the beneficiary, nor the writing given to him; in fact, his ignorance of the trust is immaterial. * * *' That this doctrine has generally been followed appears from the following cases and authorities: Martin v. Funk, 75 N.Y. 134, 138; Ulmer v. Fulton, 129 Ohio St. 323, 195 N.E. 557, 97 A.L.R. 1170; Faulds v. Dillon, 231 Mich. 509, 204 N.W. 733, 737; Perry on Trusts and Trustees, 7th ed. vol. 1, p. 112, sec. 96; 65 C.J. p. 278, sec. 61. 'Whether a trust has been perfectly created is largely a question of fact in each case, and the court in determining the fact will give efficacy to the situation and relation of the parties, the nature and situation of the property, and the purposes and objects which the settlor had in view.' Perry on Trusts and Trustees, 7th ed., vol. 1, p. 124.

The learned trial judge, in discussing the case, very aptly reviewed the facts in the following statement: 'The trust in question was adequately created and defined. The intention to create a trust is made clear and all the material terms and essentials thereof are stated with sufficient certainty in the letters written and signed by the settlor, Elsie S. Wyse, from October 20th. 1947 to March 17th. 1948 and as supplemented by those which followed the latter date. The motivating reasons, all conscientiously and earnestly understood and appreciated by her, for the creation of that trust, must be accorded their significant place in the problem which she sought to respect and meet as her own. Among the elements to be noted, there are the nature of, and time between, the final illnesses of Mrs. Wyse and her husband, the purposes of her testamentary trust, the similarity of their wills with respect to their directions as to the disposition of their remains, the high regard which in her correspondence was expressed by her for her husband and in line with the same, her willingness, or anxiety, to respect and carry out all his wishes and aims toward, and for the benefit of, his two children.'

There is a suggestion of the possibility of a question arising as to whether the laws of New York or the laws of Wisconsin are to control. We pass this point with this observation: That there is no difference in the principles of law which apply to facts such as exist here as between the doctrines of the two states.

There was a motion to dismiss the appeal, but inasmuch as the executors were seeking to protect the purpose of the testatrix in providing that the residue of her estate should be devoted to cancer research, the motion was denied. We agree with the trial court that all the essentials of a definite and valid trust according to the obvious purposes and intent of the settlor are here present. No express provision for its termination was required. The general scheme of the trust is made evident, and the subject of the same and the persons to be benefited are made sufficiently clear that a court of equity can judicially determine the same and superintend the execution of the trust. It is considered that a trust was created, and that the petitioner is entitled to the relief asked for.

B. THE TRUST RES (CORPUS)

Warsco v. Oshkosh Sav. & Trust Co.

Supreme Court of Wisconsin
183 Wis. 156, 196 N.W.2d (1924)

VINJE, C. J. The plaintiff does not seek to recover for the heirs the amount of $446 spent for funeral expenses, the sum of $500 paid to Lydia Hunter, nor the sum of $10 retained by the Oshkosh Savings & Trust Company for services, but only the balance paid over to Dora E. Putzke, $2,000 of which was invested in a house and lot described in the findings.

It appears from the evidence that at the time the trust agreement was executed the deceased gave in drafts $500 to each of his nine children except Lydia Hunter, leaving him the amount turned over to the trustee. He was desirous of disposing of all his property not needed for his own maintenance. The amount so needed he wanted to keep, and he also wanted to make disposition of what remained at his death. His lawyer suggested a will, but he was opposed to wills because there was so much litigation over them. So after consultation with the lawyer and the officers of the trustee the agreement set out in the statement of facts was made. The question arises, Does it create a valid trust? It is claimed on the part of the defendants that the agreement comes within the case of Pietsch v. Marshall & Ilsley Bank, 164 Wis. 360, 160 N.W. 184. The plaintiff claims the case is not in point because there the trust was not revocable, while here it is claimed it is revocable. No difficulties arise from the fact that a trust is revocable. That does not affect its validity. McEvoy v. Boston Five Cents Sav. Bank, 201 Mass. 50, 87 N.E. 465; 26 Ruling Case Law 1206. Indeed, in an early day trusts not revocable were closely scanned by the courts to see that they were voluntary and understandingly made. 26 Ruling Case Law 1209.

In the instant case the trust is not revocable at all, but its provisions are such that the settlor may, under the terms of the trust, demand every cent from the trustee, for the agreement provides that the trustee "shall at any time, on request of said Gust Warsco, turn over and pay to him any of the moneys in its hands derived from the said certificate of deposit without the consent of the said Dora E. Putzke." In demanding all the money the trust would be executed according to its terms. A revocation implies the cessation and extinguishment of the trust, and when made operates to put an end to it, not to carry out its terms.

A valid trust implies a donor, a trustee, and a cestui que trust. The donor may be the cestui que trust or at least one of the cestuis que trustent. But there must be an alienation of the donor's property constituting the trust to the trustee and under such terms that when the trust is executed a benefit accrues to a cestui que trust unless prevented by a condition subsequent resulting from a lawful revocation of the trust. If the donor has full control and dominion over the trust property, so that according to the terms of the trust he can use it as and when he pleases, the trustee becomes his mere agent to hold title to the property, invest, sell, and collect income for him and pay as he directs. The donor has parted with no dominion over his property nor any part thereof by the terms of the trust, and such an agreement is no valid trust agreement.

In the present case the only thing the donor parted with irrevocably, and that only in case of his death before the trust property was consumed, was that the remainder of the trust property should go as directed. But that was an attempted testamentary disposition of property and not made in pursuance of the statute.

The case is identical in its main facts with the case of McEvoy v. Boston Five Cents Sav. Bank, 201 Mass. 50, 87 N.E. 465. The court there said:

"The trust in this case may be considered first in reference to its effect on the property during her life, and then in reference to its effect upon what might remain after her death. The first statement of the trust by the assignor in the assignment is in these words: 'Said trustee shall pay to me such moneys as I may demand of him at any time during my life until I have used the amount conveyed to him by me by this deed.' This gave her the right to demand any part or the whole of the money at any time, for any use that she chose to make of it. It left her the sole beneficial owner of it, with an absolute power of disposition as long as she lived. As against her, therefore, the only practical effect of the instrument during her lifetime was to give the trustee a right to collect and hold the property until she should ask for it. Her rights as beneficial owner during her life were not limited in any material way. She could revoke the trust at any time, or she could demand and receive from the trustee all the money, at any time, under the trust, and then do with it what she chose. . . . The other part of the trust created by the instrument in the present case relates solely to the disposition of the property after the assignor's death. It follows that the only material effect of the instrument was testamentary, and that it cannot be given effect under our statutes, which permit a testamentary disposition of property only by a duly executed will."

The above statement is equally applicable to this case. When the distinction between the power to revoke a trust and the retention of the complete control of the trust property or its proceeds by the terms of the trust is kept in mind difficulties vanish--the one destroys the trust, the other executes it according to its terms, and the donor need part with nothing.

In Pietsch v. Marshall & Ilsley Bank, 164 Wis. 360, 160 N.W. 184, irrevocable trusts were created and the donor did not have full control and dominion over all the trust property as the donor in this case had.

The fundamental element of a trust is that the trust property, so long as the trust lasts, is irrevocably devoted to the benefit of certain specified persons called cestuis que trustent, of whom the donor may be one. 3 Bouv. Law Dict. 3328. Someone must by the execution of the trust be benefited in a manner or degree different from that which would have resulted had no trust been created. Hence an instrument whereby the donor retains or may retain the whole beneficial interest in the trust property by the execution of the instrument according to its terms constitutes no valid trust. Russell v. Webster, 213 Mass. 491, 100 N.E. 637. In such cases the so-called trustee is only the agent of the donor. And it has uniformly been held that a devise or bequest in trust which is subject to the future directions of the donor is void unless executed in conformity with the statute of wills. See note to Atwood v. Rhode Island H. T. Co. (275 F. 513) in 24 A. L. R. 177, and cases cited.

It follows from what has been said that no valid trust was created by the instrument and that the plaintiff is entitled to possess himself of the proceeds paid to the defendant Dora E. Putzke except as previously stated, for the purpose of making distribution thereof according to law. Judgment reversed, and cause remanded for further proceedings as indicated in the opinion and according to law.

C. THE BENEFICIARY

Tharp v. Seventh Day Adventist Church

Supreme Court of Wisconsin
182 Wis. 107, 195 N.W. 331 (1923)

APPEAL from a judgment of the circuit court for Sawyer County: JAMES WICKHAM, Circuit Judge. Affirmed.

Action begun in the circuit court to construe the will of Jackson Tharp, deceased, who died leaving a will containing among others the following provision:

"I give, devise, and bequeath all of my property, real, personal, or mixed, of whatever kind and wherever situated, to J. M. Smith of Shell Lake, Wisconsin, as trustee and in trust for the following express purposes, to wit: . . . All the rest, residue, and remainder of my estate of every kind and nature to be held by my said trustee for the benefit of the Seventh Day Adventist Church, to be used principally for the publication and distribution of tracts and literature teaching its doctrine. One thousand dollars to be paid to the proper trustees of the said church on the 21st day of October of each calendar year for nineteen (19) years and the balance then remaining to be paid on the 21st day of October of the twentieth year after my decease."

As facts the trial court found:

"That the Seventh Day Adventists constitute an unincorporated religious denomination whose members maintain numerous church buildings for religious worship throughout the country and in most of the other countries of the world. Said members also maintain numerous organizations, both incorporated and unincorporated, but the words 'Seventh Day Adventist Church' do not designate nor identify any special or particular corporation, society, or organization. The local church organization is unincorporated and has as its officers an elder, a deacon, a clerk, a treasurer, and a missionary secretary. There are incorporated in each state in this country one or more corporations, each called a 'Conference,' which holds the title to all Adventists Church property within certain designated territory. There are two such corporations in this state, one of which is the defendant North Wisconsin Conference Association of Seventh Day Adventists, which holds the title to forty-four church buildings located in the Northern Peninsula of Michigan and in the northern part of this state including Sawyer county, the south line of this territory being the south line of Chippewa county.

Various union conferences, each covering the territorial jurisdiction of several local conferences, are also incorporated, one of such union conferences being the 'Lake Union Conference Association of Seventh Day Adventists,' incorporated in the state of Michigan and having territorial jurisdiction covering the states of Wisconsin, Michigan, Illinois, and Indiana. One general conference, called 'General Conference of Seventh Day Adventists,' located at Washington in the District of Columbia, is also incorporated, having territorial jurisdiction throughout the world. Each of these corporations owns in its own right certain property, and each of them, as well as the local church organizations and other persons, engage in the practice of distributing tracts and literature teaching the doctrine of the Seventh Day Adventists. Most of said tracts and literature are printed by certain other corporations affiliated with the corporations above mentioned. The power and jurisdiction of the union conference over the local conference, and the power and jurisdiction of the general conference over the union conference, is of an advisory character only and is not compulsory either as to matters of discipline, local government, or religious doctrine, and therefore the practices, methods, and teachings of the various local conferences are not necessarily the same.

All of the facts found to exist by this finding have continued to exist since the time of the making of said will. That Jackson Tharp, during his lifetime, was not a member of said Seventh Day Adventists nor a member nor an attendant of any of its local churches nor of any of said corporations. That no such local church existed in the vicinity of his residence at the time of the making of his will, although some such churches existed in neighboring communities in an adjoining county."

As conclusions of law the court held that the trust in behalf of the Seventh Day Adventist Church was "invalid, void, and incapable of execution for the following reasons:

"(a) Because it is impossible to determine from the provisions of the will, in the light of surrounding circumstances, what particular corporation, person, or organization the testator intended should receive said property. (b) Because as a private trust, in addition to its failure to identify the intended beneficiary, the trust is not fully expressed nor clearly defined by the terms of the instrument creating it; and (c) Because as a charitable or public trust, in addition to the failure to identify the intended beneficiary, no method is provided by said will to ascertain or determine what part, portion, or percentage of said bequest was intended to constitute the principal portion thereof or how the balance thereof should be used or expended, and because no power to designate the particular charitable or public purpose or purposes to be promoted thereby is given by the will to said J. M. Smith, trustee, or to any other person or persons."

From a judgment entered accordingly the defendants Seventh Day Adventist Church and the North Wisconsin Conference Association of Seventh Day Adventists appealed.

VINJE, C. J. No argument is made upon the incorrectness of the findings, so they stand as verities in the case. The legal questions raised are (a) that the circuit court should not have taken jurisdiction of the case, and (b) that the circuit court erred in holding the trust to the Seventh Day Adventist Church void for uncertainty.

Counsel for appellants rely upon the rule stated in Pietraszwicz v. Pietraszwicz, 173 Wis. 523, 529, 181 N.W. 722, to the effect that, though the circuit court has concurrent jurisdiction with the county court, yet the former will refuse to assume jurisdiction unless the lack of power to grant adequate relief in the county court is clearly shown. That is undoubtedly the general rule, but an exception has always been made to cases calling for the construction of wills. Speaking of this exception the court in Burnham v. Norton, 100 Wis. 8, 12, 75 N.W. 304, says:

"Jurisdiction of such matters has been uniformly exercised by the circuit court though specially conferred on county courts by statute. So it is said that nothing short of an express statute on the subject can change the practice in that regard." Citing Catlin v. Wheeler, 49 Wis. 507, 5 N.W. 935. See, also, Giblin v. Giblin, 173 Wis. 632, 182 N.W. 357. The trial court therefore properly exercised its jurisdiction in trying the case.

Is the bequest to the Seventh Day Adventist Church void for uncertainty? It will be seen from the findings of fact that the words "Seventh Day Adventist Church" do not signify any specific incorporated or unincorporated religious body; that there was no Seventh Day Adventist Church in the locality where testator lived; that he was not a member of or an attendant on any Seventh Day Adventist Church; that the officers of local churches consisted of an elder, a deacon, a clerk, a treasurer, and a missionary secretary; that they have no trustees and are unincorporated; that the various local and general organizations are engaged in distributing tracts and literature and that their teachings are not always the same. In view of these facts and others found by the trial court we think its conclusion that the bequest was void for uncertainty was correct. No power was given to the trustee to select an organization or church. He was required to pay to the "proper trustees."

Who were the proper trustees? The local churches had no trustees, but assuming that the word "trustees" meant officers, to what officers should he pay? Had the testator been a member of or attendant upon a local church the inference might arise that he intended his own church to be the beneficiary. But he was not connected with any Seventh Day Adventist Church, local or otherwise. It therefore becomes impossible to designate with any degree of reasonable certainty what Seventh Day Adventist Church, local or general, incorporated or unincorporated, was meant. Neither the trustee nor the court, had they otherwise the power, could determine with reasonable certainty who were the "proper trustees" or the proper church organization to receive payment. In our state the doctrine of cy pres does not obtain. Heiss v. Murphey, 40 Wis. 276; Will of Fuller, 75 Wis. 431, 435, 44 N.W. 304; Harrington v. Pier, 105 Wis. 485, 82 N.W. 345. The beneficiary must be designated with reasonable certainty or the trust fails. Holmes v. Walter, 118 Wis. 409, 95 N.W. 380. Here it was not so designated and the trust must be held invalid.

We think the case comes well within the decisions of Heiss v. Murphey, supra; Will of Fuller, supra; Harrington v. Pier, supra. Judgment affirmed.

ESCHWEILER, J. (dissenting). The will, when read in connection with the testimony taken, seems to me to clearly disclose that the testator had in mind as the primary subject of his bounty the publication and circulation of the printed matter expounding the doctrine of those who class themselves and are classified as Seventh Day Adventists for the furthering of their doctrines. This, under the authorities, is clearly a charitable trust and one that should be upheld wherever possible.* He was not so much concerned with the particular name or form of organization as he was with the doctrines of the Seventh Day Adventists; it was the latter to which his bounty was extended much more than to any particular organization.

It is also quite evident that when making this will he was not informed of the names or proper designations of the persons who could best carry out his controlling purpose and he therefore declares that his trustee shall annually pay to the "proper" trustees, whomever they shall be, the designated $1,000, undoubtedly believing that such designation could, by the time the payments were to be made, be ascertained by his trustee and thereby be made certain. There were then and are now, under the testimony and findings, persons in existence who could properly, by reason of their connection with the Seventh Day Adventists, carry out the purpose which he so evidently wanted should be done.

As has been repeatedly said, from the very nature of such charitable trusts they cannot be as definite and distinct as trusts for individuals or more particular private purposes. I can see no more substantial difficulties in the carrying out of what was the evident intention of the testator in this regard in this will than as to some at least of the provisions in the trust upheld in Rust v. Evenson, 161 Wis. 627, 155 N.W. 145; or in Giblin v. Giblin, 173 Wis. 632, 182 N.W. 357; or in Hood v. Dorer, 107 Wis. 149, 153, 82 N.W. 546,--it being always the imperative duty of the court to ascertain, if

* Charitable trusts and the subsequent significance of this opinion are discussed in Chapter 9.

possible, and then give effect, if possible, to the intention of a testator. Will of Dever, 173 Wis. 208, 210, 180 N.W. 839.

It seems to me clear that the executor of this will would have little, if any, difficulty in determining that there were persons connected with either the incorporated conference located at Washington, D. C., or some of the conferences of lesser territorial jurisdiction, who could be properly trusted with the duty of carrying out the expressed wish of the testator, and that the court should have permitted or required the trustee to have done so rather than now permitting the property to go contrary to the express declaration of the testator. In the paragraph of his will just preceding the one quoted in the majority opinion, and which, though also challenged, was upheld by the court as being valid, definite, and certain, appears the following:

"For the following express purposes, to wit: to pay bills for medical attendance, nursing, hospital bills, and support of either, each or any (as many as shall come within this provision) of my sister, nephews, or nieces, should either or any of them suffer or experience any serious injury or calamity and be financially in need of assistance. It being my desire that none of my property go to any of my relatives so long as they are in health and able to make a living for themselves."

D. THE TRUSTEE

While the trustee is a critical component of the trust, the failure of the settlor to name the trustee is not fatal to the trust if it is otherwise valid. Any time that the trustee position become open, a court with jurisdiction over the trust res can appoint an original or replacement trustee. The trustee position can be filled by a single person or entity, or there can be multiple trustees. If there is more than one trustee, the trust instrument can require unanimity on the part of the trustees, or it can require only a majority vote. The following case illustrates a variety of aspects of the trustee's function. Note that with the trust at issue in *In re Sensenbrenner* (below) there are multiple trustees, and their duties and powers are not identical. The subject of trustee powers and duties is explored in detail in Chapter 8.

Wis. Stat. 701.16. Testamentary trustees.

(1) APPOINTMENT OF ORIGINAL TRUSTEE.

(a) Trustee named in will. A trustee who is named or whose appointment is provided for in a will derives the authority to carry out the trust from the will and assumes the office of trustee upon the issuance of letters of trust by the court as provided in s. 856.29 A trustee named in a will may renounce the position by an instrument filed with the court having jurisdiction to admit the will to probate.

(b) Other original trustee. If a testamentary trust is created which fails to name a trustee, or the named trustee refuses to accept the position or predeceases the settlor and no alternate trustee is named in the will nor effective provision made for appointment of an alternate trustee, the court shall appoint a suitable person as trustee. Letters of trust shall be issued to such trustee as provided in s. 856.29

(c) Special trustee. If it appears necessary, the court can appoint a special trustee until a regular trustee can be appointed. A special trustee may be appointed without notice and may be removed whenever the court so orders. Such special trustee shall give such bond as the court requires and shall have such powers as are conferred by the order of appointment and set forth in any letters of trust issued the special trustee.

(d) Foreign trustee. If a trustee is authorized to carry out a trust created by will admitted to probate outside this state, but not also admitted to probate in this state, the foreign trustee may have recorded in the office of the register of deeds of a county in which part of the subject matter of the trust is located a certified copy of the letters of trust and filed with the register of probate of the same county a statement appointing the register of probate in his or her official capacity the trustee's resident agent for service of process. Thereafter the trustee may exercise all powers and have all the rights, remedies and defenses that the trustee would have if he or she received letters of trust from a circuit court of this state. Service of process shall be complete upon delivery of duplicate copies to the register of probate, one of which copies the register of probate shall promptly forward by registered mail to the foreign trustee.

(2) BOND. Prior to the issuance of letters of trust to an original testamentary trustee under sub. (1) or to a successor or added testamentary trustee under s. 701.17 (1), the court may require such trustee to give a bond in accordance with ch. 878 and conditioned on the faithful performance of such trustees duties. If a settlor directs that a trustee serve without bond, the court shall give effect to this direction unless it determines that a bond is required by a change in the trustee's personal circumstances since the execution of the settlors will. If the court requires a bond, and the trustee named in the will fails to furnish the required bond within a reasonable period of time after receiving notice of the bond requirement, the court may remove the trustee named in the will and appoint a successor trustee under s. 701.17 No bond shall be required of a trust company bank, state bank or national banking association which is authorized to exercise trust powers and which has complied with s. 220.09 or 223.02, nor shall a bond be required of a religious, charitable or educational corporation or society.

(3) INVENTORY. A testamentary trustee shall make and file a verified inventory of all property received from the settlors personal representative or from any other source.

(4) ANNUAL ACCOUNTING.

(a) A testamentary trustee is required to make and file a verified account annually with the court, except as provided in pars. (am) and (b) If the trustee is accounting on a calendar-year basis, the court may not require the trustee to file the annual account prior to April 15. Production of securities and other assets for examination is not necessary upon the filing of an annual account unless the court determines such production is necessary to ascertain the correctness of an account filed for a particular trust. In the case of a testamentary charitable trust a copy of the annual account filed with the court shall be filed with the attorney general.

(am) The annual accounting requirements under par. (a) do not apply to corporate trustees or to corporate cotrustees if those trustees or cotrustees agree, in their initial consent to act as trustees or cotrustees or in a subsequent filing with the register in probate for the county that has jurisdiction over the trust, to provide annual accounts to all persons interested, as defined in s. 851.21, who request those accounts by writing to the trustee or cotrustee. Each request is effective until the requester withdraws it or is no longer a person interested. A corporate trustee or cotrustee may withdraw its agreement by notifying the appropriate register in probate of its intent to do so.

(b) Except in the case of a testamentary charitable trust, the court may dispense with the requirement of an annual accounting where, due to the size or nature of the trust property, the duration of the trust, the relationship of the trustee to the beneficiaries or other relevant factors, compliance with such requirement is unnecessary or unduly burdensome on the trustee. Whether or not an annual accounting is required a beneficiary may petition the court to require an accounting and the trustee may petition for approval of the trustee's accounts on a periodic basis.

(c) Notwithstanding pars. (a), (am) and (b) the court may require an accounting at any time.

(d) Notwithstanding s. 879.47, trustees and cotrustees may submit to courts accounts in the format that they normally use for accounts submitted to beneficiaries under this subsection, if all of the information required by the court is included.

(5) FINAL ACCOUNTING. A verified final account is required upon the termination of a testamentary trust. Upon the petition of a surviving or successor trustee, a beneficiary, a personal representative of a deceased trustee or on its own motion, the court may order a verified account filed upon the death, resignation or removal of a testamentary trustee. The court may require such proof of the correctness of a final account as it considers necessary.

(6) DISCHARGE. No testamentary trustee or personal representative of a deceased trustee shall be discharged from further responsibility with respect to a testamentary trust until the court is satisfied upon notice and hearing that the requirements of this section have been met and it has received satisfactory proof that the trust property has been turned over to a successor or special trustee or, where the trust is terminated, distributed to the beneficiaries entitled to such property or turned over to a special trustee for distribution.

Wis. Stat. 701.17. Successor and added trustees.

(1) APPOINTMENT OF SUCCESSOR OR ADDED TRUSTEE. If there is a vacancy in the office of trustee because of the death, resignation or removal of a trustee, the court may appoint a successor trustee unless the creating instrument names or provides an effective method for appointing a successor. Upon the death of a sole trustee, title to the trust property does not pass to the trustee's personal representative but to the successor named in or appointed pursuant to the terms of the creating instrument or, in the case of a successor or special trustee appointed by the court, as provided in sub. (5) The court may in the exercise of a sound discretion appoint an additional trustee if necessary for the better administration of the trust, unless the creating instrument expressly prohibits such addition or provides an effective method for appointing an additional trustee. Subject to s. 701.16 (2), a successor or added testamentary trustee shall be issued letters of trust, at that trustee's request.

(2) APPOINTMENT OF SPECIAL TRUSTEE. If it appears necessary, the court may appoint a special trustee until a successor trustee can be appointed or, where a trust has terminated, to distribute the assets. A special trustee may be appointed without notice and may be removed whenever the court so orders. Such special trustee shall give such bond as the court requires and shall have the powers conferred by the order of appointment and set forth in any letters of trust issued the special trustee.

(3) POWERS OF SUCCESSOR OR ADDED TRUSTEE. Unless expressly prohibited in the creating instrument, all powers conferred upon the trustee by such instrument attach to the office and are exercisable by the trustee holding the office.

(4) POWERS OF COTRUSTEES. If one of several trustees dies, resigns or is removed, the remaining trustees shall have all rights, title and powers of all the original trustees. If the creating instrument manifests an intent that a successor trustee be appointed to fill a vacancy, the remaining trustees may exercise the powers of all the original trustees until such time as a successor is appointed.

(5) VESTING OF TITLE. A special or successor trustee is vested with the title of the original trustee and an added trustee becomes a joint tenant with the existing trustee in all trust property. The court may order a trustee who resigns, is removed or is joined by an added trustee to execute such documents transferring title to trust property as may be appropriate to facilitate administration of the trust or may itself transfer title.

In re Sensenbrenner

Supreme Court of Wisconsin

76 Wis. 2d 625, 252 N.W.2d 47 (1977)

Hansen, J. Frank J. Sensenbrenner died in 1952. His last will and testament created four equal trusts for the benefit of his four children: John S. Sensenbrenner, J. Leslie Sensenbrenner, Margaret Sensenbrenner Gilbert, and Gertrude Sensenbrenner Bergstrom. The trusts created separate limited life estates for each child with the remainder interest passing to either the child's descendants or to one of the other trusts created by the will. John S. Sensenbrenner, J. Leslie Sensenbrenner and William H. Clifford were designated as the trustees of all four trusts. John S. Sensenbrenner and J. Leslie Sensenbrenner thus held the positions of both trustee and beneficiary under their respective trusts.

Gertrude Sensenbrenner Bergstrom died in 1973. Pursuant to the last will and testament of the senior Sensenbrenner, on June 25, 1973, the assets of her trust were assigned in equal shares to the trusts created for the then three surviving children of the original settlor.

John S. Sensenbrenner died October 8, 1973, and this litigation arises out of the settlement of his trust. The will of the settlor provided that the trust terminate at the death of John S. Sensenbrenner, and, insofar as this case is concerned, that the assets be distributed among his then living children in equal shares. He was survived by four children, one of whom was F. James Sensenbrenner, Sr., the appellant in this case.

On October 8, 1973, the trust fund corpus had a market value of $2,545,545.16; comprised of stocks valued at $2,072,300.88; bonds valued at $446,646.20; and $26,598.08 cash. These assets were distributed to the remaindermen in kind. The actual transfer of the common stock occurred on April 30, 1974, and of the bonds on June 14, 1974. During the time between the death of John S. Sensenbrenner on October 8, 1973, and the actual transfer of the securities to the remaindermen, the common stock declined in value by $568,035.79, and the bonds by $26,846.61. The appellant asserts that the total loss of trust assets during this period was $595,000 and that his one-quarter interest in the trust was thus diminished by $148,750.

The appellant filed an "OBJECTION TO FINAL ACCOUNT AND DISCHARGE OF TRUSTEES." Appellant alleged that the loss in value of trust assets was occasioned by ". . . reason of the failure, refusal and neglect of the Trustees of said Trust promptly to allocate, pay and distribute said trust assets to the remaindermen beneficiaries. . . ."

He also objected to the allowance of a trust termination fee and to the discharge of the trustees until such time as they ". . . repay, reimburse, satisfy and indemnify . . ." the appellant for his alleged loss.

Judgment was entered approving and allowing the account of the trustees and trustees' termination fees. This appeal follows. Three issues are presented:

1. Under the circumstances, was the time taken by the trustees to distribute the trust assets unreasonable, so as to subject the trustees to surcharge for the depreciation in value of those assets which occurred between termination of the trust and distribution?

2. Was the termination fee allowed to the trustees fair and reasonable?

3. Were any issues regarding the Gertrude Sensenbrenner Bergstrom Trust before the trial court?

REASONABLENESS OF TIME FOR DISTRIBUTION.

The initial three trustees administered the trust assets at all times until the death of John S. Sensenbrenner. Immediately upon his death attention was given to the termination of his trust. The First National Bank of Neenah (hereinafter custodian) had long been custodian of the securities and for ease of transfer the securities were registered in the name of one of its nominees. Shortly after the death of John S. Sensenbrenner, the two remaining trustees, caused to be prepared a valuation of the trust account as of the date of death and a distribution schedule making equal allocations to the four remaindermen.

The valuation process took the balance of the month of October. During the process, the trustees concluded that a possible tax throwback problem existed and they decided to secure a legal opinion from a law firm in Chicago. The opinion was requested by the custodian bank in November, 1973, and was received in April, 1974. The final accounting was completed and submitted to the trustees on a computer print-out form.

Sometime subsequent to the submission of the valuation, the trustees or the custodian bank penciled out a proposed distribution schedule. A meeting to implement or discuss the distribution was held in late November or early December, 1973. Present were: F. Joseph Sensenbrenner, then attorney for the trustees (later to become a trustee); William H. Clifford and J. Leslie Sensenbrenner, the two surviving trustees; and representatives of the custodian bank, including James H. Lewis, vice president and trust officer of the custodian bank. As a result of that meeting, the penciled-out distribution schedules were agreed to. On or after November 8, 1973, several odd-lot sales of stocks and bonds, noted in the distribution schedule, were made.

Whether the agreement constituted a directive to the custodian bank to implement the transfers of the other securities to effectuate the distribution is a subject of controversy. At the subsequent hearing in this case, J. Leslie Sensenbrenner testified that it was his understanding that the transfer and distribution of the securities were to proceed directly as a result of the meeting, with the custodian bank handling the mechanics necessary to accomplish the distribution. Lewis was of the opinion that the agreement of the beneficiaries was needed before the actual transfer took place. The specific instructions to accomplish the required transfers were not forthcoming until late February or early March, 1974. The custodian bank sent the stocks in for transfer in late February or early March, 1974. The bonds were sent in for transfer around the middle of April, 1974. The stocks were actually distributed to the remaindermen on April 30, 1974; the bonds were distributed on June 14, 1974.

The record reflects that trustee Clifford entered the hospital in mid-December, 1973, suffering from cancer. During January and February, 1974, he sought treatment for his illness in Texas and died of a heart attack on February 5, 1974. J. Leslie Sensenbrenner, the other surviving initial trustee was eighty years of age. He was present when the preliminary distribution schedule was developed in November of 1973, but apparently left shortly thereafter to spend the winter in Florida.

At the hearing on the final account, Lewis, trust officer of the custodian bank, testified that actual transfer of the securities would take six to eight weeks. Harold J. Luedeman, expert witness for the appellant, testified that the normal amount of time for such transfers was two to three weeks. Subsequent events showed that Lewis was correct. The trust consisted of 37 stock issues and 21 bond issues.

On the foregoing facts and the provisions of the will of Frank J. Sensenbrenner the trial court made its decision and entered the following conclusions of law:

"1. That the Trustees of the John S. Sensenbrenner Trust did not, after the death of life tenant, John S. Sensenbrenner, unreasonably delay the distribution of the Trust's assets to the remaindermen-beneficiaries entitled thereto;

"2. That the Trustees of the John S. Sensenbrenner Trust are not liable for any loss of the market value of said Trust's assets from the time of the death of life tenant, John S. Sensenbrenner, until the times of the distributions thereof to the remaindermen-beneficiaries;

"3. That the Trustees of the John S. Sensenbrenner Trust are entitled to a reasonable fee for their services in terminating said Trust."

Judgment was entered terminating the John S. Sensenbrenner Trust; allowing all accounts and trustees' fees in the amount of $5,795.55, which the trial court found to be fair and reasonable; and assigning assets of the trust. The trial court viewed all of the facts and circumstances and determined that the trustees did not unreasonably delay in the distribution of the trust assets to the remaindermen. that finding and the findings of fact upon which it was based, will not be disturbed on this appeal unless contrary to the great weight and clear preponderance of the evidence or unless based upon an error of law. Estate of Scheibe, 35 Wis.2d 89, 94, 150 N.W.2d 427 (1967); Will of Mueller, 28 Wis.2d 26, 40, 135 N.W.2d 854 (1965); Estate of Gehl, 5 Wis.2d 91, 96, 92 N.W.2d 372 (1958); Welch v. Welch, 235 Wis. 282, 307, 290 N.W. 758, 293 N.W. 150 (1940); Estate of Allis, 191 Wis. 23, 33, 34, 209 N.W. 945; 210 N.W. 418 (1926).

We believe the law is clear that upon the event terminating a trust, the trustees must use due care and diligence to distribute the trust assets. The distribution must be accomplished as soon as it is reasonably possible to do so. The Restatement, 2 Trusts (2d), pp. 193, 195, sec. 345, provides:

"When the time for the termination of the trust has arrived it is the duty of the trustee to proceed with expedition to wind up the trust and distribute the estate. The trustee is entitled to take such time and such steps as are reasonably necessary for the protection of the interests of the beneficiary and for the trustee's own protection.

"The trustee is not under a duty to make a distribution of the whole estate until he has had an opportunity to make an accounting and to obtain a decree of the court approving the distribution. It is the duty of the trustee, however, to make his final accounting with reasonable promptness."

See also: IV Scott on Trusts (3d ed.), p. 2741, sec. 345.1, and 10 Bogert, Trusts & Trustees (2d ed.), p. 574, sec. 1010.

The duty to proceed with expedition in winding up the affairs of the trust estate upon termination necessarily flows from the high standards of management of a trust estate to which trustees have long been held in this state. That standard was expressed in Estate of Allis, supra, 29:

". . . A trustee occupies a position of peculiar responsibility. A trustee is selected because of confidence in his diligence, prudence, and absolute fidelity, as well as in his ability to so administer the trust as to protect those who, through infancy or other cause, are not able to protect their own interests. The performance of the duties of a trustee requires the exercise of a high degree of fidelity, vigilance, and ability. . . .

"Wisconsin early adopted the rule that trustees must exercise more than ordinary diligence and vigilance in the management of a trust estate . . . Good faith alone in making an investment will not protect a trustee. . . A trustee must also exercise diligence, prudence, and absolute fidelity."

That standard has been repeatedly applied by this court, generally expressed in terms of the requirement that a trustee act as a prudent and provident person would act under the circumstances. Estate of Poulsen, 54 Wis.2d 139, 143, 194 N.W.2d 593 (1972); Estate of Scheibe, 30 Wis.2d 116, 119, 140 N.W.2d 196 (1966); Will of Mueller, supra, 36; Estate of Martin, 21 Wis.2d 334, 341, 124 N.W.2d 297 (1963); Welch v. Welch, supra, 314.

The same standards to which the trustee is held in the ongoing management of the trust estate must, therefore, apply to the distribution of the trust assets phase of the management of the trust estate. This court has recognized that the standard of due care and diligence to which a trustee is held includes the requirement that the trustee perform his designated duties within a reasonable time after they arise. Will of Mueller, supra, 39; Will of North, 235 Wis. 639, 643, 294 N.W. 15 (1940); Estate of George, 225 Wis. 251, 256, 257, 270 N.W. 538 (1937); Will of Church, 221 Wis. 472, 481, 266 N.W. 210 (1936); Estate of Dreier, 204 Wis. 221, 227, 235 N.W. 439 (1931).

The sanction for not performing the required duty within a reasonable amount of time is a surcharge for any loss thereby caused to the trust assets. The above cited cases are all illustrative. The same sanction applies to losses caused by or incurred during an unreasonable delay in distributing trust assets. In Scott on Trusts, supra, 2741, 2742, sec. 345.1, it is stated:

"Where the trustee is not guilty of undue delay in making distribution, he is not liable to a surcharge for a depreciation of the trust property not due to any fault of his. He is not liable in such a case for interest on the trust funds, except such interest as he receives or should have received. On the other hand, if the trustee unduly delays in the winding up of the trust, he is liable for a depreciation in value of the trust property. In the case of such a delay the beneficiary can also hold him liable for interest."

See also: Restatement, 2 Trusts, supra, p. 196, sec. 345, Comment f.; Bogert, Trusts & Trustees, supra, p. 580, sec. 1010.

If a trustee is to be subject to surcharge, the depreciation must have occurred after a reasonable amount of time for distribution has passed. The general rule guiding the trial court in the determination of what constitutes an unreasonable delay is set forth in Scott on Trusts, supra, p. 2741, sec. 345.1:

"§345.1 Delay in making conveyance. When the time for the termination of the trust has arrived, it is the duty of the trustee to wind up the trust and make distribution of the trust property as soon as he reasonably can do so. Whether the trustee has been guilty of an improper delay in winding up the trust depends upon all the circumstances. Where the estate is large and where property must be sold prior to disposition, particularly where the property is not readily salable, where it is difficult to ascertain the proper distributees, or where the estate is involved in litigation, the trustee can properly take more time before the trust is wound up than where the circumstances make the winding up of the trust a simple process. The trustee, before he makes the final distribution of the whole of the trust property, is entitled to have the court pass upon his accounts and make a decree of distribution for his protection."

See also: Restatement, 2 Trusts, supra, p. 195, sec. 345; Will of Mueller, supra, 39-45.

The trial court's finding that there was no unreasonable delay in the distribution of the trust assets, as reflected in its memorandum decision and judgment was based upon three areas of consideration: (1) The nature of the trust and trust estate; (2) the character and qualities of and events affecting the trustees; and (3) the legal problems encountered during termination in regard to income tax.

The trial court characterized the trust as a "'Family Affair,'" wherein the settlor chose his two sons and a business associate as trustees rather than a corporate institution specializing in trust administration. The appellant contends that all trustees, regardless of background, are required to perform the same fiduciary obligations with the same degree of fidelity and skill, whether corporate or individual. This court has in the past recognized a distinction between individual and corporate trustees in the degree of ability to be expected in the administration of a trust estate. Guardianship of Bose, 39 Wis.2d 80, 88, 158 N.W.2d 337 (1968); Estate of Scheibe, supra, 120 (1966); Estate of Allis, supra, 29. The distinction does not mean that the due care and diligence required of the individual trustee is lessened, but rather that the standards required may not be as high as those required of a corporate trustee which holds itself out as possessing a special skill in the performance of the duties of a trustee. The finding of the trial court in this regard (i.e., that the trust constituted a "'Family Affair'") is supported by the evidence of record and the consideration of the above factor was proper, although not necessarily a controlling factor in the ultimate conclusion.

The trial court found that William H. Clifford was the "'mainstay'" of the trust; that ". . . [i]t may well be that the Trustor intended and expected the heavier burden to fall upon [him]"; that Clifford was sick on October 8, 1973, and died on February 5, 1974; and that between those two dates, Clifford carried out his duties as trustee but not with the vigor and ability of a younger man in good health. The appellant disputes all of those findings of fact except the fact that Clifford died on February 5, 1974.

The record amply supports the finding that Clifford was the "'mainstay'" of the trust. The trust instrument itself granted greater powers to the non-beneficiary trustee than to the beneficiary trustees. Clifford was the only non-beneficiary trustee. In addition, the settlor provided for the replacement of Clifford in a manner different from that to be used for the replacement of other trustees. There was a clear indication that the settlor was concerned with possible conflicts of interest of the beneficiary trustees in the management of the trust assets and thus provided that a non-beneficiary trustee was to exercise more power in those instances where conflict might arise.

Furthermore, it appears from the testimony that neither of the other trustees ever received or were to receive any fees for administering the trust. Since all trustee fees were to be paid to Clifford, it is reasonable to infer that he was to perform and did perform the majority of the work involved in administering the trust. The fact that the other surviving trustee, J. Leslie Sensenbrenner, left for Florida during the termination proceedings is a further indication that Clifford was to perform the tasks incident to distribution.

As the appellant contends, there may well be joint and several responsibility among trustees for the management of a trust. See: Guardianship of Bose, supra, 87; Will of Mueller, supra, 47. However, no doctrine prohibits one trustee from performing the majority of the duties involved and shouldering the heavier burden of the trust management. Welch, supra. While the responsibility and liability for breach of the trust relationship may not be shifted between trustees (absent a controlling provision in the trust instrument) the delegation of actual duties between them is a matter of their own concern. Guardianship of Bose, supra, 87; Abrams v. United States Fidelity & Guaranty Co., 127 Wis. 579, 584, 106 N.W. 1091 (1906). The evidence fully supports the finding of fact that Clifford was the "'mainstay'" of the trust.

The trial court found that Clifford was ill on October 8, 1973, and that he performed his duties with less vigor and ability than ordinary between that date and mid-December, when he entered the hospital. While this finding may be against the great weight and clear preponderance of the evidence, it is not of such a nature as to affect the outcome of the case. We are also of the opinion that it was proper for the trial court to give consideration to the fact that trustee, J. Leslie Sensenbrenner, was eighty years of age and spending the winter in Florida.

The trial court also found that the trustees believed that it was necessary to appoint a successor trustee to replace the deceased John S. Sensenbrenner. The trial court did not hold that it was necessary to appoint a third trustee, as the appellant contends, but that the surviving trustees believed so. The testimony of J. Leslie Sensenbrenner amply supports the finding that at least one of the trustees believed so. The finding, however, appears to be in no way critical to the trial court's ultimate holding. Even if one of the surviving trustees did believe that a third trustee must be appointed prior to distributing the assets, the record is clear that the two surviving trustees proceeded expeditiously with the preliminary steps toward distribution including the odd-lot sales, and most likely would have accomplished distribution without the appointment of a third trustee, were it not for other intervening factors.

The trial court found that the trustees had encountered a tax problem for which they sought legal advice. The appellant does not dispute the fact that a tax problem did arise prior to the distribution, but does dispute any conclusion that the tax problem was a reasonable cause for delay in distribution.

Lewis testified that during the valuation process in November, 1973, a possible income tax throwback problem arose. He was directed to secure a legal opinion concerning the problem from counsel in Chicago. The opinion was requested in November, 1973, and was finally received in April, 1974, after the distribution process had actually begun. Lewis testified that the tax problem was "[q]uite similar," but ". . . not the same" as one which had arisen during the termination of the Gertrude Sensenbrenner Bergstrom Trust. A legal opinion had likewise been requested and received concerning that trust. The appellant apparently contends that no delay was justified because the trustees already had the answer to their problem at hand. The contention overlooks the fact that in tax matters, "[q]uite similar" does not mean the exact same. Two different trusts were involved with different terminating provisions and different beneficiaries. There was no evidence that the trusts were exactly alike and that tax impacts on one would be the same for the other. Tax matters are proper consideration in the distribution phase of trust termination. See: Will of Mueller, supra, 41, 42, citing In re Kellogg's Trust, 35 Misc.2d 541, 230 N.Y.S.2d 836 (1962).

The totality of several factors, as found by the trial court, and as appear in the record, amply explain and justify the delay. These included: The solicitation of legal advice concerning a legitimately perceived income tax throwback problem; the appointment of a third trustee to replace John S. Sensenbrenner; the sickness, hospitalization and death of Clifford at a critical time during the termination proceedings; the appointment of his successor trustee; the physical absence of the surviving co-trustee; the indication that the trustees desired to obtain the approval of the remaindermen before accomplishing the actual distribution; and the solicitation and receipt of the waivers and consents from the remaindermen.

While each factor standing alone might not justify the delay in the distribution, the facts indicate that there was a continuous flow of trustee activity with regard to the termination of the trust following the death of John S. Sensenbrenner. Under all the facts and circumstances, the trial court found that it was not unreasonable delay. It cannot be said as a matter of law that the delay was unreasonable, nor is the trial court's ultimate finding against the great weight and clear preponderance of the evidence. This is not a case where no reason for the delay appears on the record, as the appellant contends. The facts and circumstances both explain and justify the delay. See: Will of Blomdahl, 216 Wis. 590, 257 N.W. 152; 258 N.W. 168 (1935).

As each determination of a reasonable amount of time for distribution must stand on its own facts, the comparison of the distribution period in the Gertrude Sensenbrenner Bergstrom Trust is of no avail to the appellant. It does not appear that the termination of that trust involved the death of one of the trustees as the termination event; nor the death of the non-relative trustee during the critical period of the distribution process. Moreover, it appears that in that termination proceeding, the legal opinion involving the income tax throwback problem there involved was acquired in a shorter time.

In the case before us, the trial court filed an extensive memorandum decision. It set forth a resume of the facts and the law and concluded that an unreasonable period of time had not elapsed in making the distribution of the trust assets. As we have stated, the trial court did not err as a matter of law in arriving at this conclusion, and it is not against the great weight and clear preponderance of the evidence.

Having reached this conclusion, the trial court then directed its attention to the following legal principles: (1) The application of the "prudent man rule" insofar as investments were concerned; (2) the determination that sec. 701.22, Stats., Distributions in kind by trustees; marital bequests., was applicable; (3) the application of the general rule that trustees need not be omniscient with regard to investment decisions; and (4) the consideration of the applicability of sec. 701.16(5), Testamentary trustees; final accounting, and sec. 881.05(2), Retention of securities by trustee. The appellant contends that these four legal principles are inapplicable and that the trial court confusedly and improperly intertwined them in its determination of whether the trustees acted with due diligence and reasonable speed in distributing trust assets upon termination of the trust. We do not consider this argument because we are of the opinion that consideration of these principles by the trial court was undertaken after and was irrelevant to its determination that the trustees did not unreasonably delay the distribution of the trust assets.

TRUSTEES' FEES.

The trial court found that the sum of $5,795.55 was a fair and reasonable closing fee to be paid to the trustees on termination of the trust. The trustees originally requested a termination fee of $25,545.55, based on one percent of the fair market value of the trust assets on October 8, 1973. The only evidence concerning a termination fee was elicited from witness Lewis who testified as to what the custodian bank's own fee schedule as a corporate trustee would have been under similar circumstances. The trial court accepted and relied on that evidence in awarding the fee. The appellant contends that the trustees, because of their lack of due diligence in distributing the assets, were entitled to no fee. If the trustees had breached their fiduciary duty in distributing the assets of the trust, this court could properly deny all compensation. Estate of Deibig, 49 Wis.2d 237, 245, 181 N.W.2d 413 (1970); Estate of Martin, 39 Wis.2d 437, 444, 159 N.W.2d 660 (1968); Joerres v. Koscielniak, 13 Wis.2d 242, 248, 108 N.W.2d 569 (1961). Since the trial court found, however, that the time period taken for distribution was reasonable, and thus that the trustees had exercised due diligence, and since that finding is not contrary to the great weight and clear preponderance of the evidence, a complete denial of termination fees is not in order.

The question remains as to whether the fee awarded was reasonable? The usual criteria for determining the amount of trustees' fees was set forth by this court in Estate of Peabody, 218 Wis. 541, 260 N.W. 444 (1935). Therein this court said at pages 545 and 546:

The character and powers of a trusteeship, the relation of such position to all duties imposed and the accompanying responsibilities must be recognized as the premise from which appellants' obligations to the trust arise and upon which the right to compensation and the extent thereof must be justified. . . The trial court seems to have been controlled or strongly moved to his decision by the custom of trust companies, when acting as trustees, of charging for their services at the rate of five per cent of the income from the estate. That method or measure of arriving at a compensation is often used. The statutes in some states provide for it. But even in those states, extraordinary services performed by a trustee may warrant additional compensation. The reckoning by a percentage basis is only used for its convenience; the question is not one of percentage, but of compensation for 'responsibility incurred and labor expended.' . . ."

and further at page 549:

". . . As has been said, in approaching this question [of compensation] consideration must be given to the whole field of operation in which the trustees acted including the elements of risk assumed, responsibility, service, and time and labor actually spent in the performance of duties arising out of the acceptance of the trust. . . ."

See also: Estate of Teasdale, 261 Wis. 248, 52 N.W.2d 366 (1952). The foregoing criteria can be properly considered in arriving at a termination fee.

The appellant argues that the trustees did not themselves handle the income tax throwback question; did not prepare the valuation of the trust assets; and did not handle the sale or re-registration of securities to effect the distribution. The record reflects, however, that the trustees did prepare the tentative distribution schedule. Moreover, the trustees caused all of the above to be accomplished, assumed the responsibility for their accomplishment and the risk of liability if they were not accomplished. The trust was in fact terminated and the assets were distributed. No lack of performance on the part of the trustees in terminating the trust was established. The trustees were clearly entitled to a reasonable termination fee.

The trial court relied on the testimony of Lewis in arriving at a reasonable termination fee for the trustees. His testimony set forth the customary fee of the bank. That was the only evidence presented to the trial court. No evidence was presented by the appellant as to how much the customary corporate fee should be reduced, if at all, in the case of individual trustees, or what factors could cause a reduction. In the absence of a finding that the trustees failed to perform their fiduciary duty and in the absence of any other evidence as to reasonableness, the trial court was entitled to consider the testimony of Lewis in determining the fee.

Considering the value of the trust estate and the problems encountered in its termination, the amount allowed by the trial court to the trustees for termination fees is not unreasonable or excessive. The matter of compensation to a trustee for services lies within the sound discretion of the trial court in view of the particular facts and circumstances in each case. Estate of Martin, supra (1968), 444; Joerres, supra, 248; Estate of Teasdale, supra, 264. That discretion was not abused in this case.

GERTRUDE SENSENBRENNER BERGSTROM TRUST.

The appellant contends that the trustees should be surcharged for their consent to an unreasonable trustee termination fee in the termination of the Gertrude Sensenbrenner Bergstrom Trust. That trust was terminated on June 25, 1973, as a result of her death. The assets of her trust were distributed in equal shares to the trusts of John S. Sensenbrenner, J. Leslie Sensenbrenner and Margaret Sensenbrenner Gilbert. The trustees at the time of her death and the distribution of her trust were John S. Sensenbrenner, J. Leslie Sensenbrenner and William H. Clifford. They requested and were allowed a trust termination fee of $17,137.01, which was based upon the valuation of the trust assets. The appellant contends that the proceedings at which the $17,137.01 trust termination fee was allowed were held upon waiver of notice executed by the trustees of the Gertrude Sensenbrenner Bergstrom Trust, who, at that time, were also the trustees for the three remaining trusts. No notice of the proceedings was given, however, to the remaindermen beneficiaries of the three trusts which received distributed assets. The appellant asserts that the failure to give him notice entitles him to raise the issue of the reasonableness of the termination fee in a challenge to the final accounting in the John S. Sensenbrenner Trust. The question is not whether he was entitled to raise the issue, but whether he did raise the issue at the hearing. Our examination of the records leads us to conclude that the issue was not raised.

The trial court in its memorandum decision stated:

"All briefs filed contain 'statements of fact' not brought into evidence. Objector's brief has discourse concerning alleged improprieties in the handling of the Gertrude Sensenbrenner Trust, which matter was not before the Court."

A review of the record indicates that there was no issue relative to the Gertrude Sensenbrenner Bergstrom Trust termination fees before the trial court at the hearing on the petition for termination of the John S. Sensenbrenner Trust. The formal objection of the appellant served on the trustees and filed with the trial court stated no objection to the termination of the Gertrude Sensenbrenner Bergstrom Trust. At the commencement of the hearing counsel for the appellant specifically advised the trial court that the matters before it were the objection to the proposed termination fee in the John S. Sensenbrenner Trust and an objection ". . . with respect to the loss of market value in the seven months' delay in the distribution of the assets . . ."

During the hearing no testimony or evidence was received in reference to the termination fees allowed in the Gertrude Sensenbrenner Bergstrom Trust. The first time the issue was raised was in the appellant's brief filed with the trial court after the hearing. The trial court, in view of the facts that the issue had not been previously raised and argued, and that no evidence concerning the issue was introduced, properly declined to consider the issue. Howard v. State Farm Mut. Auto L. Ins. Co., 70 Wis.2d 985, 994, 236 N.W.2d 643 (1975); Hasley v. Black, Sivalls & Bryson, Inc., 70 Wis.2d 562, 569, 570, 235 N.W.2d 446 (1975); Pipkorn v. Brown Deer, 9 Wis.2d 571, 580, 101 N.W.2d 623 (1960).

The judgment of the trial court is affirmed.

II. LIMITATIONS ON THE BENEFICIARY'S INTEREST

Trusts frequently require trustees to distribute the income from the trust res at regular intervals to the trust's present beneficiary or beneficiaries. While the trustee may have discretion in how to invest the assets of the trust, once the income is earned, the trustee has no choice but to distribute it to the beneficiary, who is then free to use the income as he or she (or it) chooses. This also ordinarily means that the income from the trust can be attached by the beneficiary's creditors. Trusts of this nature are known as *mandatory* trusts. It is also permissible for the settlor to give the trustee discretion as to how and when to make distributions from the trust. Such trusts are known as *discretionary trusts.* At the same time, it is possible for the settlor to prohibit the beneficiary from alienating (i.e., transferring) the beneficial interest in the trust, either voluntarily or involuntarily. This prevents the beneficiary from "cashing in" his interest in exchange for a lump sum. It also makes it impossible for the beneficiary's creditors to attach the income stream out of trust. (Nothing, of course, can be done to prevent creditors from pursuing claims against the beneficiary once the distribution is made.)

A. SPENDTHRIFT TRUSTS

Spendthrift trusts are trusts, usually mandatory trusts, which contain restraints on the alienation of the beneficiary's interest. This objective is obtained by asserting a so-called *spendthrift* clause in the trust instrument. As a result, the beneficiary cannot voluntarily alienate (i.e., transfer) his interest in the trust to another party, and the creditors of the beneficiary cannot directly attach the beneficial interest. Although spendthrift trusts would appear to run contrary to the traditional hostility of American law to the imposition of restrictions on the right to alienate property, such provisions have been an important part of United States trust law since their use was sanctioned by the United States Supreme Court in the middle of the nineteenth century in the case of *Nichols v. Eaton,* 91 U.S. 716 (1875).

Note that Wis. Stat. 701.06(6), below, specifically prohibits the use of a spendthrift clause as a creditor protection device when the settlor is also the present beneficiary. (Such trusts are known as self-settled asset protection trusts). While there has been a recent movement in some states to accept such trusts (provided that they operate prospectively), they are not permitted in Wisconsin. Also, in Wisconsin, there appears to be no presumption in favor of a spendthrift trust when the trust instrument fails to contain a spendthrift clause.

Central to the concept of a spendthrift trust is the understanding that the beneficiary's right to alienate the beneficial interest, either voluntarily or involuntarily, is restricted. As a result, such trusts provide some measure of protection for the beneficiary against his or her creditors. While the legitimacy of the spendthrift trust is no longer in doubt in the United States (though they are still prohibited in many common law countries), it is also widely accepted that some types of creditors of the beneficiary should be permitted to assert claims directly against the trust, the spendthrift clause notwithstanding. Foremost among such creditors are family members—especially the spouse and minor children—which the beneficiary is presumably legally obligated to support.

Wis. Stat. 701.06. Spendthrift provisions and rights of creditors of beneficiaries.

(1) INCOME BENEFICIARIES. A settlor may expressly provide in the creating instrument that the interest in income of a beneficiary other than the settlor is not subject to voluntary or involuntary alienation. The income interest of such a beneficiary cannot be assigned and is exempt from claims against the beneficiary until paid over to the beneficiary pursuant to the terms of the trust.

(2) PRINCIPAL BENEFICIARIES. A settlor may expressly provide in the creating instrument that the interest in principal of a beneficiary other than the settlor is not subject to voluntary or involuntary alienation. The interest in principal of such a beneficiary cannot be assigned and is exempt from claims against the beneficiary, but a judgment creditor, after any payments of principal have become due or payable to the beneficiary pursuant to the terms of the trust, may apply to the court for an order directing the trustee to satisfy the judgment out of any such payments and the court in its discretion may issue an order for payment of part or all of the judgment.

(3) DISCLAIMER OR RENUNCIATION NOT AN ASSIGNMENT. A disclaimer or renunciation by a beneficiary of part or all of his or her interest under a trust shall not be considered an assignment under sub. (1) or (2)

(4) CLAIMS FOR CHILD SUPPORT. Notwithstanding any provision in the creating instrument or subs. (1) and (2), upon application of a person having a valid order directing a beneficiary to make payment for support of the beneficiary's child, the court may:

(a) If the beneficiary is entitled to receive income or principal under the trust, order the trustee to satisfy part or all of the claim out of part or all of payments of income or principal as they are due, presently or in the future;

(b) In the case of a beneficiary under a discretionary trust, order the trustee to satisfy part or all of the claim out of part or all of future payments of income or principal which are to be made pursuant to the exercise of the trustee's discretion in favor of such beneficiary.

(5) CLAIMS FOR PUBLIC SUPPORT. Notwithstanding any provision in the creating instrument or subs. (1) and (2), if the settlor is legally obligated to pay for the public support of a beneficiary under s. 46.10, 49.345, or 301.12 or the beneficiary is legally obligated to pay for the beneficiary's public support or that furnished the beneficiary's spouse or minor child under s. 46.10, 49.345, or 301.12, upon application by the appropriate state department or county official, the court may:

(a) If such beneficiary is entitled to receive income or principal under the trust, order the trustee to satisfy part or all of the liability out of part or all of payments of income or principal as they are due, presently or in the future;

(b) Except as otherwise provided in par. (c), in the case of a beneficiary under a discretionary trust, order the trustee to satisfy part or all of the liability out of part or all of future payments of income or principal which are to be made pursuant to the exercise of the trustee's discretion in favor of such beneficiary;(c) In the case of a beneficiary under a discretionary trust who is a settlor or a spouse or minor child of the settlor, order the trustee to satisfy part or all of the liability without regard to whether the trustee has then exercised or may thereafter exercise the trustee's discretion in favor of the beneficiary.

(5m) TRUST FOR DISABLED INDIVIDUAL.

Subsection (5) does not apply to any trust that is established for the benefit of an individual who has a disability which has continued or can be expected to continue indefinitely, substantially impairs the individual from adequately providing for his or her own care or custody, and constitutes a substantial handicap to the afflicted individual if the trust does not result in ineligibility for public assistance under ch. 49 A trustee of a trust which is exempt from claims for public support under this subsection shall notify the county department under s. 46.215 or 46.22 in the county where the disabled beneficiary resides of the existence of the trust.

(6) SETTLOR AS BENEFICIARY.

(a) Notwithstanding any provision in the creating instrument and in addition to the remedies available under subs. (4) and (5) where the settlor is a beneficiary, upon application of a judgment creditor of the settlor, the court may, if the terms of the instrument require or authorize the trustee to make payments of income or principal to or for the benefit of the settlor, order the trustee to satisfy part or all of the judgment out of part or all of the payments of income or principal as they are due, presently or in the future, or which are payable in the trustee's discretion, to the extent in either case of the settlors proportionate contribution to the trust.

(b) A beneficiary of a trust may not be considered a settlor solely because of a lapse, waiver, or release of any of the following:

1. A power described under par. (c)

2. The beneficiary's right to withdraw part of the trust property, to the extent that the value of the property affected by the lapse, waiver, or release in any year does not exceed the greater of the amount in:

a. Section 2041 (b) (2) or 2514 (e), Internal Revenue Code of 1986.

b. Section 2503 (b), Internal Revenue Code of 1986.

(c) A beneficiary of a trust is not a settlor, has not made a voluntary or involuntary transfer of the beneficiary's interest in the trust, or does not have the power to make a voluntary or involuntary transfer of the beneficiary's interest in the trust solely because the beneficiary holds or exercises, in any capacity, any of the following:

A presently exercisable power to consume, invade, appropriate, or distribute property to or for the benefit of the beneficiary if the power is any of the following:

a. Exercisable only on consent of another person holding an interest adverse to the beneficiary's interest.

b. Limited by an ascertainable standard, such as health, education, support, or maintenance of the beneficiary.

2. A presently exercisable power to appoint any property of the trust to or for the benefit of a person other than the beneficiary, a creditor of the beneficiary, the beneficiary's estate, or a creditor of the beneficiary's estate.

3. A testamentary power of appointment.

4. A presently exercisable right described in par. (b) 2.

(d) A beneficiary of a trust is not a settlor solely because the beneficiary is entitled to nondiscretionary distributions from the trust.

(7) SUBSEQUENT MODIFICATION OF COURT'S ORDER. Any order entered by a court under sub. (4), (5) or (6) (a) is subject to modification upon application of an interested person.

(8) EXEMPT ASSETS. Assets of a trust, to the extent they are exempt from claims of creditors under other statutes, shall not be subject to sub. (4), (5), or (6) (a)

Resop v. McCoy (In re McCoy)

Bankr., W. D. Wis.
464 B.R. 832 (2011)

Opinion by Robert D. Martin. MEMORANDUM DECISION

The plaintiff trustee seeks turnover of the interest in a trust. The defendant debtor contends that the trust is a "spendthrift trust" and that her interest in it is not part of her bankruptcy estate. A hearing on cross motions for summary judgment was held September 13, 2011. The parties have agreed to the following facts:

On April 6, 2000, Shirley McCoy, the debtor's mother, executed the McCoy Living Trust ("McCoy Trust" or "Trust.") The debtor is a beneficiary of this Trust, and Kevin McCoy, one of the debtor's sons, is the sole trustee of this Trust. The relevant language of the Trust is:

Article 13, Section 2. Beneficiary's Right to Direct Retention of Distributions in Trust

> *Whenever a distribution is authorized or required to be made by a provision of this Article to a beneficiary, then the beneficiary may direct the Trustee in writing to retain such distribution in trust as follows:*
>
> *a. The Beneficiary's Right to Income*
>
> *The Trustee, during the life time of the beneficiary, shall pay to or apply for the benefit of the beneficiary from time to time and at the beneficiary's written direction all of the net income from this trust.*
>
> *b. The Beneficiary's Right to Withdraw Principal*

The Trustee shall pay to or apply for the benefit of the beneficiary such amounts from the principal as the beneficiary may at any time request in writing. No limitation shall be placed on the beneficiary as to either the amount of or reason for such invasion of principal.

. . .

Article 13, Section 3. Disposition of Trust Property

All trust property not previously distributed under the terms of this trust shall be maintained in trust for a period not to exceed twenty years after the date of my death and distributed only according to the directions found in this section.

a. Division Into Separate Trusts

The Trustee shall divide the balance of trust property into equal trusts, with one separate trust for each of my children named in this Article.

. . .

g. Administration of the Trust share for Julie McCoy

1. Annual Pecuniary Distribution Free of Trust

Beginning the First January 1st after the date of my death, the Trustee shall distribute $20,000.00 to my daughter, Julie McCoy annually free of trust.

Shirley McCoy amended the trust on September 6, 2002, as follows:

SECOND AMENDMENT TO THE SHIRLEY J McCOY LIVING TRUST DATED APRIL 6, 2000 This amendment dated September 6, 2002

. . .

According to the terms of my living trust dated April 6, 2000, I amend the Agreement as follows: . . .

C. Creditor Protection. I amend Article 13, to include a new Section 4, which shall read:

Section 4. Creditor Protection.

All payments of income and principal, including withdrawal rights, shall be privileged and may be exercised only by the Trustee at its sole discretion. Distributions under this Article shall not be subject to the

> *claims of any creditor or to legal process and may not be voluntarily or involuntary alienated or encumbered, except by specific Order by a Court of competent jurisdiction for reasons allowed by law. Any such Order shall cite this Section and the law specifically or the Trustee shall deny such forced distribution.*

On November 10, 2009, Shirley McCoy died. Pursuant to the terms of the Trust, on January 1, 2010, the debtor received a distribution in the amount of $20,000.00 "free of trust." Later that year, on October 27, 2010, she filed a voluntary petition under chapter 7. The debtor disclosed her interest in the trust on the bankruptcy schedules as a contingent interest valued at $0. On December 21, 2010, the bankruptcy trustee demanded that the debtor turn over the trust distribution that was available to her as of January 1, 2011. The debtor informed the bankruptcy trustee that she would not be turning over any trust distributions because Kevin McCoy would be exercising his discretion as trustee to withhold trust distributions from her.

The bankruptcy trustee commenced this adversary proceeding on March 3, 2011. In her Motion for Summary Judgment, she argues that she is entitled to an order directing the turnover of the debtor's share of the trust "as trust payments have become due and payable to the debtor pursuant to the terms of the trust." The McCoy Trust has a net worth of $1,669,712.00.

Summary judgment is appropriate "if the pleadings, the discovery and disclosure materials on file, and any affidavits show that there is no genuine issue as to any material fact and that the movant is entitled to judgment as a matter of law." See Celotex Corp. v. Catrett, 477 U.S. 317, 322, 106 S. Ct. 2548, 91 L. Ed. 2d 265 (1986). The primary purpose of summary judgment is to avoid trial where there is no genuine issue of material fact in dispute. See Trautvetter v. Quick, 916 F.2d 1140, 1147 (7th Cir. 1990). A bankruptcy trustee has the burden in turnover proceedings to prove by a preponderance of the evidence that the property sought is in fact property of the bankruptcy estate and that the debtor has possession of it. In re Smith, 2011 Bankr. LEXIS 390, 2011 WL 345865, *1 (Bankr. S.D. Ind. Feb. 2, 2011).

11 U.S.C. §541 provides that the estate is comprised of "all legal or equitable interests of the debtor in property as of the commencement of the case." 11 U.S.C. §541(a)(1). However, the Code excludes certain interests. 11 U.S.C. §541(c)(2) provides that "a restriction in the transfer of a beneficial interest of the debtor in a trust that is enforceable under applicable nonbankruptcy law is enforceable in a case under this

title." This means that "spendthrift trusts" and similar interests are excluded from the bankruptcy estate. In re Kedrowski, 284 B.R. 439, 449 (Bankr. W.D. Wis. 2002).

The Seventh Circuit Court of Appeals interpreted §541(c), when applicable, to "take the corpus of each spendthrift trust out of the definition of 'property of the estate' of the debtor." Magill v. Newman, 903 F.2d 1150, 1152 (7th Cir. 1990). The court reasoned that a contrary decision would drain the spendthrift trusts of any meaning and ignore the Bankruptcy Code provision. Id. The spendthrift trust in Newman provided discretionary distributions of net income or portions of the corpus to Newman until he reached age 50, when the trust would terminate and the trustee would distribute to Newman the assets of the trust estate "absolutely and free from trust." Id. at 1151. A spendthrift clause prevented Newman from alienating his interest or anticipating his interest in the income or corpus of any trust estate. Id. Newman filed for bankruptcy at age 45. Id. The Court of Appeals concluded that §541(c)(2) was applicable and Newman's interest in the trust was not part of his bankruptcy estate. The trust "clearly and effectively directed that the corpus not become a part of the debtor's estate until he reached age 50 and that the debtor and his creditors be prevented from anticipating the debtor's interest in the corpus until that time." Id. at 1152. The court acknowledged that the outcome might be different had the debtor already reached the age of 50. Id. at 1153.

The McCoy Trust provides that upon the settlor's death, all trust property not previously distributed is to be divided into separate trusts for each of the settlor's children. Article 13, Section 3(a). The trustee is to distribute $20,000 to each child "annually free of trust" beginning the first January 1st after the settlor's death. Article 13, Section 3(c) - (g). Each of these separate trusts will terminate 20 years after the settlor's date of death. See Id. By the Seventh Circuit Court of Appeal's reasoning in Newman, as long as the spendthrift clause is valid and enforceable under applicable nonbankruptcy law, the debtor's interest in the corpus does not constitute property of the bankruptcy estate. The annual payments of $20,000.00 are not as straightforward.

What constitutes "property of the estate" is decided by federal law; but the extent of the debtor's legal or equitable interests in property as of the commencement of the case is determined by state law. In re Mitchell, 423 B.R. 758, 763 (Bankr. E.D. Wis. 2009) (quoting Matter of Yonikus, 996 F.2d 866, 869 (7th. Cir. 1993)). The subject Trust was created in Wisconsin, the debtor resides in Wisconsin, and the parties do not dispute that Wisconsin law applies. Wisconsin law affirms spendthrift protection for beneficiaries. Wisconsin statute §701.06(2) provides that "[t]he interest in principal of a beneficiary other than the settlor is not subject to voluntary or involuntary alienation. The interest in principal of such beneficiary cannot be assigned..." The Creditor Protection Provision under Amended Article 13 seems to conform to this statute.

The spendthrift provision must be "enforceable under applicable nonbankruptcy law," including in this case, Wis. Stat. §701.06(2). But, otherwise enforceable limitations on transfer of trust funds do not prevent a creditor from gaining a court's order to turn over trust property that is "due or payable" to a non-settlor beneficiary: "... a judgment creditor, after any payments of principal have become due or payable to the beneficiary pursuant to the terms of the trust, may apply to the court for an order directing the trustee to satisfy the judgment out of any such payments ..." Wis. Stat. §701.06(2).

The bankruptcy trustee reads "due or payable" to encompass every instance in which the trustee is to make a scheduled payment to the beneficiary. She submits that the Creditor Protection Provision in Amended Article 13, Section 4, does not override the provisions for annual $20,000.00 payments or payments directed by the beneficiary, nor does it override the language of Wis. Stat. §701.06(2). The bankruptcy trustee relies on In re Thomas M. Calaway, Jr., 2000 WL 33950024, (Bankr. W.D. Wis. June 30, 2000), an unpublished decision from this district issued by Judge Utschig.

The debtor interprets "due or payable" to mean that a creditor can seize payments only when they are actually distributed to the beneficiary or when the trustee has no discretion to withhold them. She submits that unlike Calaway, the Trust provisions do not conflict with the statute. No payments are currently "due or payable" because under the Creditor Protection Provision, the trustee has the "sole discretion" to make payments and has chosen to withhold them from the debtor. Our case is distinguishable from Calaway. In Calaway, the bankruptcy trustee sought the ultimate distribution of the trust res "at the time a distribution is actually made." Id. at *1. In this case, the bankruptcy trustee requests the turnover of the debtor's annual distribution. Judge Utschig concluded that Wis. Stat. §701.06(2) did not preclude turnover once the debtor was eligible for the ultimate distribution of the trust res. Id. at *3. His conclusion is consistent with Newman and other interpretations of §541(c)(2), because a spendthrift clause is no longer effective once a trust terminates. In Calaway, the court did not order turnover of discretionary income distributions to the beneficiaries. Here, the plaintiff seeks discretionary distributions of the debtor's share of the trust res. Calaway does not compel a conclusion that the bankruptcy trustee is entitled to any annual distribution.

The debtor is correct that the Creditor Protection Provision gives the trustee discretion to make payments under the trust. The language of the amendment states that "[a]ll payments of income and principal, including withdrawal rights, shall be privileged and may be exercised only by the Trustee at its sole discretion." Amended Article 13, Section 4. This amendment supersedes the mandatory payment provisions in Article 13. The Wisconsin Supreme Court has held that in construing a trust, as with a will, the language should be construed to give effect to the intention of the settlor. Dei v. Dei (In re Dei Revocable Living Trust), 2004 WI App. 21, *P6, 269 Wis. 2d 543, 674 N.W.2d 681 (citing Welch v. Welch, 235 Wis. 282, 306-07, 290 N.W. 758 (Wis. 1940)). That intention may be ascertained from the language of the instrument, considered in the light of the surrounding circumstances. Id. That rule is elementary in the construction of trusts not created by will. Welch, 235 Wis. at 307. The late Ms. McCoy intended the Creditor Protection Provision to give Kevin, as trustee, discretion over "all payments" in the trust, including otherwise mandatory payment provisions and withdrawal rights of the debtor.

If the trustee has the sole discretion to withhold payments of principal to beneficiaries under the Trust, when are they "due or payable" under §701.06(2)? Is "due or payable" merely a common legal phrase that was adopted in the statute without much consideration? Section 701.06(2) was written in the disjunctive, which seems to suggest either requisite is sufficient. "Due" would seem to require an obligation to pay presently. But if "payable" means that the ability to have it paid exists, potential discretionary distributions, even if undeclared, would suffice. But this would lead to a limitless ability of creditors to pursue discretionary payments of the trust res. That is contrary to the statute's manifest intent. Without any instructive court interpretation of "due or payable" and without a clear meaning to seize upon, bankruptcy courts have looked for the intent of the drafters. For example, in In re Fraley, the court construed "due or payable" to include a lump sum already paid to a debtor in settlement of a worker's compensation claim, because construing the exemption statute more narrowly would contradict the statute's intent to protect beneficiaries. In re Fraley, 148 B.R. 635, 637 (Bankr. M.D. Fla. 1992).

Because there is no helpful legislative history of Wis. Stat. §701.06, the statute can only be construed in light of the its apparent purpose. That purpose seems to include different treatments for interest payments, distribution of principal, and protection of self-settled trusts.

The Wisconsin Legislature desired to protect income distributions subject to anti-alienation clauses. Wis. Stat. §701.06(1) provides as follows:

> Spendthrift provisions and rights of creditors or beneficiaries.
>
> (1) A settlor may expressly provide in the creating instrument that the interest in income of a beneficiary other than the settlor is not subject to voluntary or involuntary alienation. The income interest of such beneficiary cannot be assigned and is exempt from claims against the beneficiary until paid over to the beneficiary pursuant to the terms of the trust.

But, the Legislature chose to place substantial limitations on anti-alienation clauses contained in self-settled trusts. Wisconsin Statute §701.06(6) provides:

> (6) Settlor as beneficiary, (a) Notwithstanding any provision in the creating instrument and in addition to the remedies available under subs. (4) and (5) where the settlor is a beneficiary, upon application of a judgment creditor of the settlor, the court may, if the terms of the instrument require or authorize the trustee to make payments of income or principal to or for the benefit of the settlor, order the trustee to satisfy part or all of the judgment out of part or all of the payments of income or principal as they are due, presently or in the future, or which are payable in the trustee's discretion, to the extent in either case of the settlor's proportionate contribution to the trust. Wis. Stat. §701.06(6) (emphasis added).

This provision is intended essentially to prohibit self-settled spendthrift trusts. See In re Bogue, 240 B.R. 742, 750 (Bankr. E.D. Wis. 1999).

The contrast between the language in these two provisions and that of §701.06(2):

> A settlor may expressly provide in the creating instrument that the interest in principal of a beneficiary other than the settlor is not subject to voluntary or involuntary alienation. The interest in principal of such a beneficiary cannot be assigned and is exempt from claims against the beneficiary, but a judgment creditor, after any payments of principal have become due or payable to the beneficiary pursuant to the terms of the trust, may apply to the court for an order directing the trustee to satisfy the judgment out of any such payments and the court in its discretion may issue an order for payment of part or all of the judgment. Wis. Stat. §701.06(2) (emphasis added).

suggests that the legislature intended relatively more spendthrift protection for principal distributions. Judgment creditors may apply for an order to satisfy judgment out of any "payments of principal" that have become "due or payable." Courts are given flexibility to grant or deny such applications, acknowledging perhaps that certain situations would call for satisfaction of judgment while others would not.

Construing this subsection in light of the whole, the phrase "due or payable" was intended to mean mandatory payments under the terms of the trust - those that a beneficiary is entitled to receive, or payments that have been declared by a trustee with discretion to do so.

The subsection is silent as to whether, after an initial principal payment is made to the beneficiary debtor, the protection is lost as to a creditor seeking the court's aid. However, a Restatement of Trusts asserts that "after income or principal from a spendthrift trust has actually been distributed to a beneficiary, it becomes subject to creditors' claims." Restatement, Third, of Trusts §58 cmt. d (2003). This indicates that generally only payments that have been distributed become subject to the claims of creditors, rather than all subsequent payments of principal that may be distributed. Therefore, even if the debtor received one principal payment, as long as any subsequent payment she is entitled to receive remains in trust, it is still protected. Only payments that the trustee declares he will make or that the debtor actually receives will lose the spendthrift protection. There is no reason to believe that the Wisconsin Legislature sought to depart from this general rule.

In this case, the debtor's interest in the trust principal is excluded from the bankruptcy estate because the spendthrift clause is "enforceable under applicable nonbankruptcy law." While Wisconsin law allows judgment creditors to apply for payments of principal notwithstanding a spendthrift clause, no such payments are "due or payable" here. The bankruptcy trustee is not entitled to a turnover of the payments that the trustee has chosen to withhold from the debtor. For these reasons, the bankruptcy trustcc's motion for summary judgment is DENIED, and the debtor's motion for summary judgment is GRANTED.

In re Trust of Talmage

Court of Appeals of Wisconsin

223 Wis. 2d 266, 588 N.W.2d 927 (1998)

VERGERONT, J. Harrold McComas and Wayne Lueders, co-trustees of the W. David Tallmadge Trust, appeal the trial court's construction of the Last Will and Testament and Codicil of Marion Tallmadge, which created the trust. The disputed provision concerns the trustees' obligations with respect to Loren Tallmadge, the minor daughter of David Tallmadge. Loren cross-appeals, contending that the trial court erroneously determined the trustees had fulfilled their duties to her under the trust as construed by the trial court and also contending that the court erred in denying her relief under §701.06(4), Stats., which governs claims for the support of children of trust beneficiaries. We conclude that the trial court erroneously construed the will to include David's dependents as primary beneficiaries, and that Loren, like David's other issue, belongs instead to the secondary class of beneficiaries. With the trustees' obligations thus construed, Loren does not present an argument that they have not fulfilled their duties to her. We also conclude that the trial court did not erroneously deny Loren relief under §701.06(4). We therefore affirm the trial court's order dismissing her petition, although we reach a different conclusion on the correct construction of the will and codicil than did the trial court.

BACKGROUND

Marion Tallmadge's Last Will and Testament and Codicil (collectively, the will) created a trust out of the residue of her estate, designated as the W. David Tallmadge Trust. David was Marion's only surviving child. Paragraph A of the fifth article of the codicil is the subject of this appeal. It provides:

> (A) So long as my son shall live, the trustees shall pay to or apply for the benefit of my son such part of the annual net income from his trust fund as the disinterested and non-subordinate trustee or trustees shall, after a thorough consideration of the expenditures made by him within the current year for his support, maintenance and other necessities and the support, maintenance, education, travel and other necessities of those dependent on him for support, deem wise and expedient and in his best interests. Any part or all of the balance of the annual net income of the trust fund may, in the discretion of the disinterested and non-subordinate trustee or trustees, be paid over and distributed to or applied for the benefit of the issue of my son, or one or more of them, each for his undivided account, in such proportions as the disinterested and non-subordinate trustee or trustees may deem advisable. The balance of the net income of the trust fund not so paid over to or applied for the benefit of the issue of my son, as aforesaid, may be added to any subsequent income payments from such fund and, until so distributed, may be regarded for all purposes as part of the principal of such fund, subject, in the discretion of the disinterested and non-subordinate trustee or trustees, to again being regarded as income and being distributed at any later date to any person or persons to whom current income of the trust fund may be distributed.

Paragraph B of this article permits the trustees to distribute payments from the principal of the trust to David during his lifetime, and is not at issue.

The will was probated in Waukesha County and has been administered by the probate division of the circuit court of that county. Loren is the minor daughter of David and

Laura Tallmadge, David's estranged third wife. Loren lives with her mother in California. At the times relevant to this dispute, David has been incarcerated in California. Laura initiated a petition for construction of the trust and to compel support in the circuit court of Waukesha County on her own behalf and in her capacity as legal guardian for Loren. The petition asked for a finding that the trustees were obligated under the terms of the trust to pay for the benefit of Laura and Loren amounts that the California courts had ordered as child and spousal support; that the trustees were obligated by §701.06(4)(a), Stats., to pay the child support payments for Loren's benefit; and that the will entitled not only David, but also Laura and Loren, as persons dependent upon David for support, to priority over that of David's adult children.

After a trial to the court, the court entered written findings of fact and conclusions of law, and an order denying the petition. The court construed Paragraph A to create two categories of income beneficiaries, the first consisting of David and those dependent upon him for support and the second consisting of the issue of David. The court found that Loren was a dependent of David, and Laura was a dependent to the extent that there is a California court order for her spousal maintenance. The court also found that the trust was discretionary and the trustees had declined to make child or spousal payments for appropriate reasons, those being: the Charles E. Albright Trust was a non-discretionary trust available for those purposes; Loren had received some distributions from the Tallmadge Trust; there was a dispute between Laura and David; and Laura was not protected by §701.06(4), Stats. The court noted that, although it was dismissing the petition, it would consider Loren's renewed request for child support payments from the Tallmadge Trust, if those sums were not available from the Albright Trust or another source.

The trustees appealed the trial court's construction of the will, and Loren cross-appealed the court's decision that the trustees acted appropriately in refusing to make the child support payments and in its decision to dismiss the petition without ordering the trustees to make the child support payments under §701.06(4), Stats. Laura has been voluntarily dismissed as a party to the appeal and cross-appeal.

DISCUSSION

We first consider the trustees' contention that the trial court erroneously construed Paragraph A because the first category of beneficiaries under that paragraph consists only of David, not his dependents, and Loren is included only in the second class of beneficiaries along with his other issue. The construction of a testamentary document presents a question of law, which we review de novo. Furmanski v. Furmanski, 196

Wis. 2d 210, 214, 538 N.W.2d 566, 567 (Ct. App. 1995). The object of will or trust construction is to determine the intent of the testator or settlor. Id. at 215, 538 N.W.2d at 568. We determine the intent from the language of the document itself, considered in light of the circumstances surrounding the testator or settlor at the time the document was executed. Id. The language of the document is the best evidence of the testator's or settlor's intent, and we therefore look first to the language of the document. Id. If there is no ambiguity in the language of the document, there is no need to look further to determine the testator's or settlor's actual intent. Id.

We conclude that the language in the first sentence of Paragraph A unambiguously provides that the trustees have an obligation, as they "deem wise and expedient and in his best interests" to pay net trust income only to David or apply it for only his benefit. It is true that in deciding what is "wise and expedient and in his best interests," the trustees have an obligation to consider the "expenditures made by him within the current year for his support, maintenance and other necessities and the support, maintenance, education, travel and other necessities of those dependent upon him for support." However, that does not impose on the trustees a duty to treat David's dependents the same as David: it does not make his dependents primary beneficiaries, as David is. Loren is included under the second sentence of Paragraph A, under which the trustees have the discretion to make distributions from the balance of the net trust income to, or for the benefit of, David's issue.

In its comments from the bench, the trial court focused on the language that provides for "applying for David's benefit" the net trust income, and the language that the trustees must consider his expenses for the current year, for not only his support, but also for the "support, maintenance, education, travel and other necessities of those dependent on him for support." It is this language that, in the trial court's view, obligates the trustees to treat David's dependents as primary beneficiaries, giving them a priority over his other issue. Loren emphasizes this argument on appeal.

However, we cannot agree with this construction. The payment to David or application of funds for his benefit is to be made after a "thorough consideration of the expenditures made by him within the current year for his support … and the support … of those dependent on him for support." The explicit condition is that David is expending for his dependents, and the trustees take those expenditures into account in deciding how much to pay to David or apply to his benefit. While the trustees may make payments on David's behalf rather than paying him directly, that authority is also tied to a consideration of David's expenditures for his support and for his dependents' support within the current year.

The trial court's comments also indicate it perceived good reasons for treating David's minor, dependent child differently from his adult children, and Loren repeats this point on appeal. But our task is to construe the language of the will. That language does treat David's dependent issue differently than it treats his non-dependent issue to the extent that David's expenditures for his dependent issue's support are to be considered by the trustees in carrying out their duties to David under the first sentence of Paragraph A. However, all David's issue are treated the same by the plain terms of the will in that the trustees have the discretion to make distributions to them from the balance of the annual net income, after fulfilling their duty to David. Of course, the fact that an issue is a minor and is not being supported by David may properly enter into the trustees exercise of their discretion under the second sentence of Paragraph A. But we cannot conclude that the will imposes on the trustees a duty to give priority to David's dependent issue over his non-dependent issue.

On her cross-appeal, Loren argues that the trial court erred in ruling that the trustees had fulfilled their duty to make distributions to Loren. As we understand this argument, it is premised on the trial court's ruling that Loren, as a dependent, was a primary beneficiary along with David under the first sentence of Paragraph A. Loren does not argue that the trustees have not fulfilled their duty if Loren is not a primary beneficiary. Since we have concluded that she is not, we do not consider this argument further. Loren's second argument on cross-appeal is that the trial court erroneously denied her claim for relief under §701.06(4), Stats.

In its oral decision, the trial court reasoned that the statute authorizes it to order the relief Loren seeks but does not require it to do so. The court stated that it was reluctant to invade this trust if there were other funds available for child support, but it was fully prepared to do so if there were not. The court was aware that there were efforts to obtain payments for the court-ordered child support from the Albright Trust and was of the view "that would come through." However, in the event it did not, the court made it clear that it would consider a reapplication of Loren's request under §701.06(4) for an order for payment from the Tallmadge Trust. Loren contends that §701.06(4) does not permit a court to require that a claimant exhaust other means of satisfying the child support order before granting relief.

Before the appellate briefing was completed, the trustees filed a motion to dismiss Loren's cross-appeal on the ground that the statutory issue was moot because the Milwaukee County Circuit Court entered an order on September 3, 1997, providing that the Albright Trust shall pay child support arrears, as well as David's court-ordered monthly child support commencing August 1997, if not paid by him voluntarily or recovered from other sources. In an order dated April 22, 1998, we declined to dismiss the cross-appeal, and instructed the parties to address the mootness issue in their briefs.

The trustees assert in their responsive brief on the cross-appeal that they understand that as a result of the order entered by the Milwaukee County Circuit Court all past due child support owed to Loren has been paid, her monthly court-ordered support continues to be paid, and neither the Albright trustees nor David is seeking to overturn that order. Loren has argued, however, that there is no guarantee that these payments will continue, and if we do not decide the correctness of the trial court's application of §701.06(4),Stats., she may be precluded from making this same argument should she need to apply to the court for payment from the Tallmadge Trust under §701.06(4) at some future time. Because it appears that there has been and continues to be litigation concerning David's child support obligations and whether he is meeting them, and because we cannot conclude on this record that the payments from the Albright Trust will continue until Loren is no longer a minor, we address the §701.06(4) issue.

The proper construction of a statute is a question of law, which we review de novo. See Lincoln Sav. Bank, S.A. v. DOR, 215 Wis. 2d 430, 441, 573 N.W.2d 522, 526 (1998).The aim of all statutory construction is to discern the intent of the legislature. Id.

We begin with a reading of the language of the statute, and if that is not ambiguous, our task is to apply that language to the task at hand. Id. We agree with the trial court that §701.06(4)(b), Stats., does not require a court to order trustees to satisfy a child support order, but rather provides that the court "may" so order under the conditions established in the statute. Section 701.06(4). The ordinary meaning of "may" is permissive. See City of Wauwatosa v. County of Milwaukee, 22 Wis. 2d 184, 191, 125 N.W.2d 386, 389 (1963). See also Grohmann v. Grohmann, 180 Wis. 2d 690, 695, 511 N.W.2d 312, 314 (Ct. App. 1993), aff'd on other grounds, 189 Wis. 2d 532, 525 N.W.2d 261 (1995) (§701.06(4)(b) "grants courts the authority to order trustees to satisfy a child support obligation directly from discretionary payments that the trustees have decided to authorize").

Therefore, the question before us is whether the trial court properly exercised the discretion granted it by the statute. We affirm discretionary decisions if the trial court considered the relevant facts, applied the correct law, and used a rational process to reach a reasonable result. See State v. Gudenschwager, 191 Wis. 2d 431, 440, 529 N.W.2d 225, 229 (1995). We conclude that the trial court properly exercised its discretion in requiring Loren to first request satisfaction of the child support order from the Albright Trust. The court correctly recognized that the trustees of the Tallmadge Trust had discretion concerning distributions to Loren. Based on the evidence presented, the court considered it likely that the Albright Trust would make the court-ordered payments, and there was in fact a court order issued to that effect within three months of entry of this trial court's decision. It is reasonable for a court ruling on an application under §701.06(4), Stats., to consider whether there are other sources to satisfy the court-ordered child support obligation.

We reject Loren's argument that the court's decision is inconsistent with the purpose of the statute. The purpose of the statute, evident from its plain language, is to provide a means of satisfying court-ordered child support obligations that does not depend on direct payment by the parent, when the parent is the beneficiary of a trust. The trial court's decision is consistent with this purpose because it permits Loren to reapply if the Albright Trust does not satisfy her claim. Section 701.06(4), Stats., does not require that courts order trustees to satisfy claims regardless of other means available, and we may not read such a requirement into the statute. Loren describes the effect of the trial court's decision as "placing an unreasonable legal and financial burden on the child," and permitting the "deadbeat parent" to "win a war of attrition." It may be that in some circumstances, a court's decision that a claimant under §701.06(4), Stats., must first seek other resources for satisfaction of a child support order would be unreasonable, but that is not the case here.

In summary, we agree with the trustees that the trial court erroneously construed the first sentence of Paragraph A to include David's dependents as primary beneficiaries of the trust, along with David. It is the second sentence of Paragraph A, not the first, which governs the trustees' duties with respect to Loren and to David's other issue. Loren does not advance an argument that the trustees have not fulfilled their duty to her under the instrument as we have construed it. We also conclude that the trial court properly interpreted §701.06(4), Stats., and properly exercised its discretion in denying Loren's statutory claim but permitting her to reapply. We therefore modify the trial court's decision concerning the construction of Paragraph A, and, as modified, affirm the order dismissing Loren's petition.

B. DISCRETIONARY AND SUPPORT TRUSTS

In a purely discretionary trust, the trustee is permitted to use his or her own judgment, subject to a general reasonableness requirement, to determine how much of the trust res, whether from income or principle to distribute. Normally, neither the beneficiary nor a creditor can force a trustee to make a distribution, if the trustee concludes that no distribution is necessary. The support trust is a type of discretionary trust, except that the trustee or trustees of a support trust are required to provide the beneficiary with such distributions as are necessary for the individual's support in the style to which he or she has been accustomed. In the case of a support trust, creditors who provided the beneficiary with services essential to his or her support, like food or medical services, were also traditionally viewed as having the ability to penetrate the shield provided by the spendthrift clause. However, as the following case, which involves a support trust, suggests, a court is not necessarily obligated to order payment to such creditors out of the corpus of the trust.

In re Walker's Will

Supreme Court of Wisconsin
266 Wis. 134, 63 N.W.2d 78 (1954)

Claim against the trustee of a spendthrift trust to recover compensation for services rendered to the spendthrift as a practical nurse.

W. W. Walker and Annette Walker, his wife (hereinafter referred to as "Mrs. Walker"), executed a joint will. W. W. Walker died December 1, 1947, a resident of the city of Wausau, and under such joint will, which was then admitted to probate, Mrs. Walker received the entire estate. Mrs. Walker died at the age of eighty-three on January 20, 1949, survived by her daughter, Isabell Downey, and her son, James Gordon Walker (hereinafter referred to as "Gordon"). The joint will provided that upon Mrs. Walker's death one half of her estate was to go outright to the daughter, Isabell Downey; and the other half was placed in a spendthrift trust to be administered for the benefit of the son, Gordon. The original inventory value of the assets of this spendthrift trust was $50,011.60. The Wisconsin Valley Trust Company, of Wausau, which was the executor under the joint will, was named as trustee of the trust. The trust empowered and directed the trustee:

"To use the net income therefrom, and so much of the principal as may be reasonably necessary, for the support and maintenance of our son, James Gordon Walker, so long as he lives."

Gordon's son, Gordon Walker, Jr., was named as remainderman to take any balance that might be left after the death of Gordon. At the time of his mother's death on January 20, 1949, Gordon was approximately fifty-four years of age. He had been a stonecutter by occupation and had contracted silicosis, and in addition to the silicosis he was afflicted with ailments of the heart and liver and had been in bad health for several years. Gordon's wife had separated from him in 1945 or 1946. He was always in difficult financial circumstances and in debt. As one witness described him, Gordon "was an all-around good fellow and quite a drinker."

The claimant, Anna B. Lyons, is a married woman who, at the time of the trial, in 1953, was forty-eight years of age, and the mother of five grown children. From 1932 to 1947, Mrs. Lyons and her husband operated a tavern near Stevens Point, and Gordon met her there in 1937 for the first time. Gordon was a friend of Mr. Lyons and they hunted, fished, and drank together. Sometime thereafter Mrs. Walker also made the acquaintance of Mrs. Lyons, and at the time of the death of Gordon's father Mrs. Lyons did some work for Mrs. Walker in connection with the funeral. After the Lyons' tavern was disposed of in 1947, Gordon boarded in the Lyons' home in Amherst, Wisconsin, for some time. In April, 1948, Mrs. Walker deeded to Mrs. Lyons, subject to a life estate in favor of Gordon, a 160-acre farm near Amherst, which Mrs. Walker had purchased with her own funds (not those of the trust). Mrs. Walker was then of advanced age and in declining health. Mrs. Lyons testified that the consideration for the conveyance to her of the deed for the farm was "money I [Mrs. Lyons] spent at the home, in rendering my services to her up until the time of her death, and taking care of her up until the time of her death." It does not appear what money was spent by Mrs. Lyons in behalf of Mrs. Walker. If any money had been so spent by her, it is doubtful if it would have been anything but a trifling sum.

Mrs. Walker's home was in Wausau, and sometime after the conveyance of the farm to Mrs. Lyons, Mrs. Walker was confined by illness at a Wausau hospital, and then was taken by ambulance to her home. Mrs. Lyons came up from Amherst and rendered service in caring for her, the period of which does not appear in the record. Then, in October, 1948, Mrs. Walker was taken to the farm home in Amherst, and Mrs. Lyons, Mrs. Walker, and Gordon resided in such home until Mrs. Walker's death three months later.

Gordon and Mrs. Lyons continued to reside in the farm home from the date of Mrs. Walker's death on January 20, 1949, until Gordon's death on August 22, 1952. Gordon's health continued to decline during such period, and by 1950 his illness was such as to confine him to bed a large part of the time, although he was up and around on occasion. During 1951, he was confined to bed practically all of that year, although in that year he did make one trip by automobile to Wausau to see the trustee. During the approximate eight months he lived in 1952 he was continuously bedridden. Mrs. Lyons supplied practical-nursing services to him during all of his long illness. She was a large woman weighing during the time 194 to 213 pounds and was able to lift him in and out of bed in caring for him. There is no question but that she did take good care of Gordon and that the nursing services rendered by her were burdensome and disagreeable.

The farmhouse on the 160-acre farm was of brick construction but needed extensive repairs, improvements, and remodeling, and the funds for so doing were supplied by the trustee out of the trust estate, although Gordon had but a life estate in the premises, title being vested in Mrs. Lyons subject to such life estate. Such improvements increased the value of the premises by $2,000. Mrs. Lyons and Gordon sold off 150 acres of the farm for $3,500, retaining the 10 acres on which were located the house and other farm buildings. Gordon sold off a big barn and the lumber from some other farm buildings which were torn down, but the record is silent as to what became of the money received therefor as well as the $3,500 from the sale of the 150 acres.

Gordon received from his mother's estate some of the household furniture in the Wausau home which was brought down to the farm home at Amherst, and on March 10, 1949, he executed a bill of sale for such furniture, together with silverware, fishing tackle, jewelry, and linens to Mrs. Lyons, which bill of sale recited a consideration of $200, which sum Mrs. Lyons testified she paid to Gordon in cash.

The trustee advanced $1,400 to Gordon in order to enable him to purchase a half interest in a cottage located on Lake Emily about one mile from the farm, the other half of the cottage being owned by Mrs. Lyons. In addition, some of the lumber from the granary and woodshed on the farm which were torn down went into the building of the cottage. On May 11, 1950, Gordon, by bill of sale, assigned his one-half interest in the cottage to Mrs. Lyons. Mrs. Lyons testified that she paid Gordon $1,400 for such half interest in the cottage, but no proof to substantiate such statement was offered in evidence.

In April or May, 1951, the trustee purchased a new Pontiac automobile for Gordon, paying $2,804.45 for it. Mrs. Lyons testified that about one year before Gordon died, which would be only some three or four months after the car had been purchased, she bought it from Gordon, but again there is no proof in the record substantiating her claim that she paid Gordon for such car other than her own testimony.

Throughout the duration of the trust, prior to Gordon's death, the trustee advanced $250 per month to Gordon. In addition to that, the trustee paid the taxes on the farm real estate, the fuel bills, extensive drug and doctor bills, and other bills. In spite of such payments of $250 per month, Gordon was continually bringing pressure upon the trustee for further advances. Mrs. Lyons often accompanied Gordon on these trips to Wausau to bring pressure on the trustee to extract money from the trust. One such successful extraction was the obtaining of money to pay for the expenses of a proposed trip to the Black Hills in South Dakota, which trip was never taken, nor intended to be taken. Mrs. Lyons testified that she knew that Gordon was not intending to take the trip when he requested the money for it, but that she did not disclose this to the trustee because of a threat that Gordon had made to her.

During the period from Mrs. Walker's death on January 20, 1949, to Gordon's death on August 22, 1952, the trustee advanced in cash payments directly to Gordon $17,475.50, and paid bills incurred by him in the sum of $13,231.89, so that the total disbursements amounted to $30,707.39.

Mrs. Lyons referred to the house on the farm as her home and stated that her husband and daughter also resided there with her as well as Gordon, but not all of the time. After the tavern had been sold in 1947, the occupation of Mr. Lyons was that of an itinerant painter but the record does not disclose how much of the time he was at home on the farm or the length of his absences away.

Mrs. Lyons was familiar with the fact that any bill Gordon approved was promptly paid by the trustee. Nevertheless, she never at any time submitted any bill for personal services for herself to the trustee or made any demand for payment for services, unless the conversation which took place between her and H. G. Beck, vice-president of the Wisconsin Valley Trust Company (the trustee), in either August or September, 1950, can be considered such a demand.

In August or September, 1950, Mr. Beck made a trip down from Wausau to the farm to see Gordon in order to find out how he was getting along. Such trip was made entirely at Mr. Beck's own volition without any request from Gordon or Mrs. Lyons that he come. Gordon was in bed when Mr. Beck arrived, but was able to sit up on the bed with his feet on the floor when talking to Mr. Beck. The testimony of Mrs. Lyons and Beck differ as to the exact conversation which then took place, but, in view of the findings and judgment of the trial court, the version of Beck must be accepted on this appeal. Beck's testimony as to such conversation is as follows:

"While we were sitting there, Gordon said, 'I wish Ann [Mrs. Lyons] could get something out of this trust;' and, Ann spoke up and she said, 'Yes, who is going to pay me for my services?' And, I said, 'I don't know. I think you need a lawyer.' And then I said, 'Whatever you do, be sure you put it in writing, because we just had a case where a claim for $4,800 was filed against the estate of a decedent, and it was overruled by the court, because there was nothing in writing.'"

Sometime after such conversation Mrs. Lyons employed Attorney Herman J. Glinski of Stevens Point, who drafted an agreement, dated November 9, 1950, between Gordon and Mrs. Lyons, which agreement recited that since January 19, 1949, Mrs. Lyons had been providing "attention, care, and nursing" to Gordon and "has not been adequately compensated." The agreement then provided that Gordon agreed to pay Mrs. Lyons for her services at the rate of $50 per week from January 19, 1949, until such services should be terminated by a ten-day written notice served upon her, and stated that no part of said sum had been paid. The agreement did not specify when the $50 per week was to be payable. This instrument was signed by both Gordon and Mrs. Lyons but was not brought to the attention of the trustee until after Gordon's death, and the trustee knew nothing about the employment of Attorney Glinski and the execution of such agreement until after such death.

On May 22, 1952, Gordon employed Attorney Clifford W. Peickert of Stevens Point, who drafted a will for Gordon by which he bequeathed his entire estate to Mrs. Lyons and named her executrix without bond. (Gordon then had no property because by that time Mrs. Lyons already had obtained title to his household furniture and miscellaneous personal effects, the half interest in the cottage, and the Pontiac automobile.) At the same time Gordon also executed a promissory note to Mrs. Lyons, payable on demand, in the sum of $8,500, but Mrs. Lyons testified that she knew nothing of the existence of such note until after Gordon's death, Attorney Peickert having possession of the same in the meantime.

After Gordon's death, Mrs. Lyons filed her claim in writing against the trust, dated October 21, 1952, in the sum of $9,300, being for nursing services, care, and attention rendered to Gordon during the period from January 19, 1949, through August 22, 1952, at $50 per week. The trustee refused to pay such claim and a hearing was held thereon. Thereafter, the trial court rendered a memorandum opinion under date of May 16, 1953, in which the evidence was reviewed at length, and the conclusion stated that the claim should be denied. Formal findings of fact and conclusions of law were thereafter entered, two of which conclusions of law being as follows:

"There never was any contract, express or implied, by the Wisconsin Valley Trust Company as trustee to pay for Ann's services rendered to Gordon.

"There never was a breach of trust by the trustee in carrying out the provisions and terms of the trust established under the will of Annette Walker, deceased."

Pursuant to such findings of fact and conclusions of law, judgment was entered on June 5, 1953, denying the claim. From such judgment Mrs. Lyons has appealed.

Currie, J. The written agreement entered into between the claimant, Mrs. Lyons, and Gordon, the life beneficiary of the spendthrift trust, dated November 9, 1950, wherein Gordon agreed to pay claimant $50 per week for her services, is of no legal significance under the decision of this court in Will of Razall (1943), 243 Wis. 152, 9 N. W. (2d) 639.

Claimant in the Razall Case sought to recover from the trustee of a spendthrift trust for necessary legal services supplied to the life beneficiary and this court in its opinion stated (p. 154):

It is also clear, however, that the beneficiary cannot go out and hire his own attorney with no notice to the trustee and thus impose the obligation to pay on the trustee. He must first request help from the trustee. Until he does, there is no basis for a claim against the trust estate and neither is there any basis for interference by the court. Sec. 187, Restatement, 1 Trusts, provides:

"'Where discretion is conferred upon the trustee with respect to the exercise of a power, its exercise is not subject to control by the court, except to prevent an abuse by the trustee of his discretion.'

"Until the trustee has refused assistance to the beneficiary there can be no question of an abuse of discretion. The record is not clear as to whether a demand was made on the trustee, and if so, when it was made. The case must therefore be remanded to the county court for further proceedings." (Emphasis supplied.)

In the instant case Gordon's written agreement to pay Mrs. Lyons $50 per week was not binding upon the trustee. Counsel for claimant apparently concede this as they base their case largely on the following statement appearing in Restatement, 1 Trusts, p. 389, sec. 157:

"Although a trust is a spendthrift trust or a trust for support, the interest of the beneficiary can be reached in satisfaction of an enforceable claim against the beneficiary,

"(a) . . .

"(b) for necessary services rendered to the beneficiary or necessary supplies furnished to him;"

It is urged in behalf of claimant that the nursing services supplied by Mrs. Lyons to Gordon were "necessary services," and, as no evidence was offered in behalf of the trustee to rebut the testimony adduced in behalf of claimant that such services were reasonably worth $50 per week, the claim of Mrs. Lyons must be allowed as a matter of law. However, we do not deem the case to be as simple as that in view of this court's decision in Estate of Ray (1936), 221 Wis. 18, 265 N. W. 89, rehearing denied, 221 Wis. 22, 266 N. W. 239.

In Estate of Ray, supra (p. 19), one Charles Ray, by his will, bequeathed $100,000 in trust to a trustee "to apply the income thereof, as may be necessary in its opinion, for the support, and maintenance as well as comfort of my said sister and to apply any part of the principal for her comfort if that seem necessary in the opinion of said trustee." Miss Ray, the sister, was totally blind and resided and was cared for at the sanatorium and clinic of claimant Waukesha Spa, Inc. Charles Ray had died in 1926, and the Spa each week rendered bills to the trustee for the board, room, and incidental expenses of Miss Ray and her attendant until Miss Ray died on August 21, 1934. After her death, the Spa filed a claim against the trust in the sum of $2,500 for services of the medical staff of the Spa rendered to Miss Ray during the period from May 21, 1927, to her death. This was the first information that the trustee had that there was any claim for services rendered to Miss Ray which was not included in the weekly statements previously submitted. The trial court disallowed the claim, and, on the appeal, this court affirmed. In the opinion upon the motion for rehearing this court quoted the extract from Restatement, 1 Trusts, p. 389, sec. 157, hereinbefore set forth, and the further quotation from Restatement, 1 Trusts, sec. 187, appearing in the extract from the opinion in the Razall Case hereinbefore set forth, and other authorities, and then went on to say (p. 26):

"There was no attempt made in this case to show that the trustee had in any manner or to any extent failed or neglected to perform its full duty and to carry out the provisions of the will under which it acted. It cannot be held under the facts of this case that there was any abuse of the discretion vested in the trustee. That the interest of a beneficiary in a trust fund or the income therefrom may be reached in a certain limited class of cases seems to be well established, but the facts of this case do not bring it within the purview of that rule of law. Here the claimant was rendering weekly bills; it never advised the trustee that it was rendering any other service than that charged for in the bills which upon their face seemed to include everything necessary for the comfort and maintenance of the beneficiary. If the claimant had furnished medical service, and at the end of the week or when the next bill was rendered, had included and charged therefor and the trustee had refused to pay a reasonable bill, an entirely different situation would have been presented. Here the claimant withheld from the trustee for seven years any knowledge or information that it was furnishing anything for the maintenance and comfort of the beneficiary other than what was specified in its weekly statements. Any opportunity for the trustee to investigate or to exercise its discretion, which it was required to do in the interests of the parties entitled to the remainder of the income, was destroyed.

"It may be argued that the trustee should exercise a reasonable discretion with respect to the bill covering a period of seven years as well as one covering a period of seven days. While this argument sounds plausible, it overlooks the fact that the trustee must be given reasonable opportunity for the exercise of the power conferred upon it. Under the facts in this case it had no such opportunity. There was no liability in a suit at law, and under the circumstances of this case a court of equity will not enforce payment out of income in the hands of the trustee." (Emphasis supplied.)

As we analyze the decision in Estate of Ray, it is evident that the claim for medical services was not disallowed on the ground that they were not necessary services to the beneficiary of the trust, but rather that the claimant was by its own conduct precluded from claiming compensation therefor. Such conduct consisted of the fact that for over seven years claimant rendered weekly bills to the trustee for the board, room, and incidental expenses of the beneficiary and her attendant without ever once during the beneficiary's lifetime making any claim for the medical services being rendered. By such conduct of withholding any information from the trustee that medical services were being rendered, the trustee, as pointed out in the decision, was prejudiced because it was prevented thereby from making any investigation during the lifetime of the beneficiary to ascertain the true facts, and from exercising any discretion with respect to its duty to supply medical services to the beneficiary. While this court in its opinion in that case does not use the term "estoppel," nevertheless, that seems to be the basis upon which the claimant's claim was denied. We believe that this same principle is applicable to the fact situation in the instant case.

Counsel for Mrs. Lyons seek to distinguish the case of Estate of Ray, supra, from the one at bar on the ground that in the former case the trustee had no knowledge that the medical staff of the Spa was rendering medical services to Miss Ray, while in the instant case the trustee did know that Mrs. Lyons was rendering services to Gordon. However, while Mrs. Lyons did not conceal the fact that she was rendering services to

Gordon, and the trustee had full knowledge of such fact, her conduct was such as to induce the trustee to believe that she had been and was being compensated for such services apart from direct payments from the trust to her, and that she was not expecting to be compensated further by the trust. By such conduct, the trustee here, as in the Ray case, was precluded until after the death of the life beneficiary from making any investigation during the life of the beneficiary. The trustee was fully justified by reason of the peculiar fact situation which existed in entertaining the belief it had throughout the time the services were being rendered by Mrs. Lyons that no claim was to be made therefor by her against the trust. In the first place there are the facts which strongly indicated to the trustee that she had been, and was being, otherwise fully compensated for her services. Not only did such facts induce such belief on the part of the trustee, but they have impressed the trial court and this court in the same manner. We summarize such facts as follows:

(1) When Mrs. Walker conveyed the farm to Mrs. Lyons in the spring of 1948, Mrs. Walker was eighty-two years old and in ill-health so that it was unlikely that she would survive but a few months, and the value of the interest in the farm conveyed to Mrs. Lyons was greatly in excess of any services Mrs. Lyons was likely to render to Mrs. Walker during the few remaining months of her life. From this the trustee could readily conclude that part of the consideration for the deed of the farm was care to be rendered to Gordon whose health was also such that he could not be expected to live very long.

(2) The trustee made extensive improvements to the residence on the farm which increased its value by approximately $2,000 most of the benefit of which went to Mrs. Lyons rather than Gordon.

(3) The belief of the trustee that Mrs. Lyons had received Gordon's share of the sale of the 150 acres of the farm, and of the buildings and lumber therefrom which had been sold off from the remaining 10 acres.

(4) The transfer to her of the household furniture, the half interest in the cottage for which the trustee had expended $1,400, and the turning over of the brand new Pontiac car for which the trust had paid $2,804.45.

(5) Gordon was being paid $250 per month cash during all the period for which Mrs. Lyons claimed services, and in addition received extra cash payments. Practically all of Gordon's expenses, except food, were being paid for by the trust. Besides, Mrs. Lyons, and part of the time her husband and daughter, were benefiting from payments of bills for fuel, etc., and from whatever Gordon spent out of the $250 per month for food. The $250 per month should have been adequate to pay for all food consumed in

the household and leave a balance which Gordon could have paid to Mrs. Lyons if he chose to do so. (Mrs. Lyons' explanation of what Gordon did with his monthly allowance was that it all went for food and liquor bills.)

(6) Gordon's life estate in the farm gave him the right to exclusive possession during his lifetime. However, Mrs. Lyons, and part of the time her husband and daughter, occupied it as their own home. (Counsel for claimant state that it is customary when hiring a practical nurse to supply her with board and lodging, but that which Mrs. Lyons and her family were receiving went far beyond this.)

In the light of this summarized factual background, the failure of Mrs. Lyons during the lifetime of Gordon to make any demand upon the trustee for payment is particularly significant. She knew that it was the practice of the trustee to promptly pay any bills submitted for goods or services furnished to Gordon, if approved by the latter. Such conduct on her part not only misled the trustee into believing that she did not intend to demand compensation from the trustee, but prevented the trustee from making any timely investigation into many of the foregoing enumerated facts. By waiting until after Gordon's death to present her claim, Mrs. Lyons effectively prevented the trustee from questioning Gordon as to such matters as the disposition of the proceeds of the 150 acres of farmland and the farm buildings which were sold in which he had a life estate; as to whether Mrs. Lyons had actually paid him for the transfer of title to the half interest in the cottage, the furniture, and other items of personal property, and the new Pontiac car; and as to the extent to which Mrs. Lyons and members of her family benefited from the $250 per month cash payments to Gordon and the other expenditures the trustee made for maintaining the household. Such conduct on the part of Mrs. Lyons in making no claim until after Gordon's death was also prejudicial to the trustee in another way. If the trustee had known from the start that she was expecting compensation, it might well have decided that instead of making the extensive improvements to the farm home and paying the other comparatively large payments for maintaining Gordon in such home including the $250 per month cash payments, and in addition thereto paying Mrs. Lyons at the rate of $50 per week, Gordon's maintenance and care could better be supplied in some other manner. The silence of Mrs. Lyons deprived the trustee of exercising its discretion in this respect.

Much stress is placed by counsel for Mrs. Lyons on the conversation which took place between Beck, the officer of the trust company, and Mrs. Lyons in August or September, 1950, at the farm home, but we deem the trial court rightly minimized the legal significance of such incident. It is true that Mrs. Lyons on that occasion did say something about unpaid wages. Beck, being undoubtedly startled by such remark, told her that she had better consult a lawyer. This incident happened approximately two years before Gordon's death, and yet Mrs. Lyons concedes that she never again mentioned the subject to the trustee.

When a lawyer was consulted, he drafted an agreement between Gordon and Mrs. Lyons, not between the trustee and Mrs. Lyons, and the existence of such agreement was never made known to the trustee until after Gordon's death. This is strong evidence that Mrs. Lyons was looking exclusively to Gordon and not to the trustee for compensation.

The learned trial court relied upon such evidence in determining as a fact, in his memorandum opinion, that there was no expectation by Mrs. Lyons, when she rendered the services to Gordon, of being paid therefor from the trust by the trustee. While there may be cases, in which one who supplies a necessary service to a beneficiary of a spendthrift trust might be entitled to recover against the trustee of such trust without having had the specific expectation of being paid by the trust at the time such services were rendered, we deem the lack of such expectation is fatal to claimant's claim in the instant case. This is because she had knowledge of the existence of the trust at the time she rendered the services and nevertheless, according to the determination of the trial court, elected to look exclusively to Gordon for payment.

Furthermore, under the rule of our decision in Estate of Ray, supra, claimant's conduct was such as might well be held to estop her as a matter of law from asserting her claim against the trust after the death of the spendthrift beneficiary, because the trustee would have been misled thereby to its prejudice in the manner hereinbefore pointed out if the claim were now to be allowed.

C. THE ENFORCEMENT OF TRUSTS

Wis. Stat. 701.14. Circuit court procedure in trust proceedings.

(1) GENERALLY. A proceeding in the circuit court involving a living or testamentary trust may be commenced by a trustee or other person interested in the trust and, except as otherwise provided in this chapter, all probate procedure governing circuit courts, so far as it may be applicable, shall apply to such proceeding.

(2) NOTICE. If notice of a trust proceeding to a person interested in the trust, to the person's representative or guardian ad litem as provided in s. 701.15 or to other persons, is required by law or deemed necessary by the court, the court shall order such notice to be given as prescribed in s. 879.05 except that service by publication shall not be required unless ordered by the court. The court may order both personal service and service by publication on designated persons. Proof of service shall be made as provided in s. 879.07 Persons interested in the trust, on behalf of themselves, or their representatives or guardians ad litem as provided in s. 701.15, on behalf of themselves and those whom they represent, may in writing waive service of notice and consent to the hearing of any matter without notice. Waiver of notice or an appearance by any person interested in the trust or the persons representative or guardian ad litem as provided in s. 701.15 is equivalent to timely service of notice.

(3) ATTORNEY FOR PERSON IN MILITARY SERVICE. At the time of filing a petition for a trust proceeding, an affidavit shall be filed setting forth the name of any person interested in the proceeding who is actively engaged in the military service of the United States. Whenever it appears by the affidavit or otherwise that any person in the active military service of the United States is interested in any trust proceeding and is not represented by an attorney, or by an attorney-in-fact who is duly authorized to act on the persons behalf in the matter, the court shall appoint an attorney to represent the person and protect the persons interest.

(4) VENUE. A proceeding involving a living trust shall be governed by ss. 801.50 to 801.62 so far as applicable and shall be regarded as a civil action for that purpose.

Wis. Stat. 701.15. Representation of others.

Except as otherwise provided in ss. 701.12 and 701.13 (1), in a trust proceeding in the circuit court:

(1) POWER TO CREATE OR EXTINGUISH. The sole holder or all co-holders of a power of revocation or a general power of appointment as defined in s. 702.01 (3) may represent any or all persons whose interests are subject to such power.

(2) GUARDIAN AD LITEM; VIRTUAL REPRESENTATION.

Subject to sub. (1), the court may appoint a guardian ad litem for any person interested who is legally incapacitated, unascertained or unborn if such person is not already represented by a fiduciary having no adverse interest in the proceeding. A guardian ad litem may represent 2 or more such persons where they have a substantially identical interest in the proceeding. The court may dispense with or terminate the appointment of a guardian ad litem for such person if there is a legally competent person who is a party to the proceeding and has a substantially identical interest in it.

Wis. Stat. 701.23. Removal of trusts.

(1) REMOVAL TO FOREIGN JURISDICTION. Unless the creating instrument contains an express prohibition or provides a method of removal, a circuit court having jurisdiction of a trust created by a will admitted to probate in such court may, upon petition of a trustee or a beneficiary with the consent of the trustee and after a hearing as to which notice has been given to the trustee and other interested persons, order removal of such trust to another state where the court finds that such removal is in accord with the express or implied intention of the settlor, would aid the efficient administration of the trust or is otherwise in the best interests of the beneficiaries. Such order may be conditioned on the appointment of a trustee in the state to which the trust is to be removed and shall be subject to such other terms and conditions as the court deems appropriate for protection of the trust property and the interests of the beneficiaries. Upon receipt of satisfactory proof of compliance with all terms and conditions of the order, the court may discharge the local trustee from further responsibility in the administration of the trust.

(2) REMOVAL TO THIS STATE. Unless the creating instrument contains an express prohibition against removal or provides a method for removal, a court may, upon the petition of a foreign trustee or beneficiary with the consent of the trustee, appoint a local trustee to receive and administer trust property presently being administered in another state. The local trustee may be required to give bond conditioned on the faithful performance of his or her duties or to meet any other conditions required by a court in the other state before permitting removal of the trust to this state.

In re Estate of Becker

Supreme Court of Wisconsin

56 Wis. 2d 356, 202 N.W.2d 681 (1972)

Beilfuss, J. The contentions of the appellants-trustees raise the following issues:

1. Does the county court have subject matter jurisdiction of this proceeding?

2. Did the trial court properly deny the trustees' motion for summary judgment, motion to quash, and the plea in bar?

The facts as they appear in the pleadings, affidavits and documents in support and in opposition to the motions are as follows:

J. H. Becker & Sons, Inc., is a corporation which owns and operates a funeral home in Milwaukee, Wisconsin. The founder, J. H. Becker, Sr., died in 1949. After his death all of the corporate stock (250 shares) was owned and held in equal proportions by his five children, Roy J. Becker, Joseph A. Becker, Carl R. Becker, Mary Helen Peters and Louis A. Becker. These children were not only the sole stockholders but each one was a director and officer of the corporation.

Roy J. Becker, the president of the corporation, died on July 21, 1965. He had never married and left a will which, after providing for a few relatively minor bequests, created a testamentary trust with two major objectives. He was "anxious to have one of . . . [his] nephews engage in . . . [his] profession to wit: that of mortician." One of his nephews, Charles J. Peters, III, had completed his education and training as a mortician and was employed by the corporation as a mortician at the time of the testator's death. The county court held that Charles J. Peters, III, qualified under the terms of the will and that upon the termination of the trust he was to receive all of the stock of the testator in the corporation. The will further provided that income of the trust (if not needed for the education of the nephew who qualified as a mortician) was to be divided annually and equally among his remaining twelve nieces and nephews. The trust is to terminate in 1975 and the corpus is likewise to be distributed to the remaining nieces and nephews. The appellants, Carl R. Becker, an attorney and a stockholder, and Mary Helen Peters, a stockholder, were named executors and trustees.

The net estate after the payment of the specific legacies, debts, inheritance tax and costs of administration was approximately $250,000. The stock in the Becker corporation was appraised at $50,000. On November 10, 1965, the four remaining directors of the corporation executed new employment contracts for themselves. Carl R. Becker and Mary Helen Peters voted as executors of the Roy A. Becker estate as well as in their individual capacity. It is also claimed that Carl R. Becker usurped the functions of president of the corporation by designating himself chairman of the board, a nonexistent position. These contracts called for a yearly salary of $30,000 to be paid to Louis A. Becker, Joseph A. Becker and appellant Carl R. Becker, and a yearly salary of $10,000 to be paid to appellant Mary Helen Peters, all commencing on January 1, 1966. The contracts also provided for an annual bonus of five percent of the gross sales of the corporation to be paid to Louis A. and Joseph A. Becker; plus the contracts required the corporation to pay health and life insurance premiums for the four directors-officers.

For comparison purposes, the records of the corporation on file herein reveal the following compensations paid by the corporation in the years 1964, 1965 and 1966:

	Salary	Bonus	Dividend
Roy J. Becker			
In 1964	$30,000	5% gross profits	$4,000
In 1965			
In 1966	Deceased		
Louis A. Becker			
In 1964	$30,000	5% gross profits	$4,000
In 1965	Same	Same	
In 1966	Same	Same	
Joseph A. Becker			
In 1964	$30,000	5% gross profits	$4,000
In 1965	Same	Same	
In 1966	Same	Same	
Carl R. Becker (Appellant)			
In 1964	$3,300	$2,000	$4,000
In 1965 at least	3,300		
In 1966	30,000		
Mary Helen Peters (Appellant)			
In 1964	$2,520	$2,000	$4,000
In 1965	2,520		
In 1966	10,000		

In 1964 and 1965, salaries, bonuses and dividends were declared by corporate resolution. Only the 1966 salary was entered into by contract on November 10, 1965.

Thereafter the corporation sustained a severe operating loss and this included a substantial loss of income to the Roy J. Becker trust. In March of 1970, all of the salaries were renegotiated after a lawsuit was instituted by the corporation against all of its directors and officers. Carl R. Becker took a reduced salary

of $22,500 per year, effective date July 1, 1969. Louis' and Joseph's salaries were increased to $36,500 and their bonuses were changed from five percent of the gross profit to 10 percent of the net profit. Generous retirement benefits were also provided. The record indicates no change in Mary Helen Peters' $10,000 salary.

The petition filed by the respondents as beneficiaries of the trust alleged, among other things, that the trustees hold legal title to 50 shares of stock of the corporation, and individually they each own 50 shares, so that together they have voting control of 150 shares of stock. Further, that the trustee, Carl R. Becker, controls the voting of his co-trustee, Mary Helen Peters, so that in fact he controls all 150 shares; and that they have both used their power and control for their own benefit and to the detriment of the trust. The petition also alleges that the salary, bonus, and health and life insurance contracts are detrimental to the trust and beneficial to the trustees individually. The amended petition sets forth that appellants are not only trustees but also stockholders, officers and directors of the corporation. Their actions in respect to these positions caused a conflict of interest since their acts were inconsistent with their respective duties; and their actions as trustees were done in bad faith, were willful and intentional -- all being to the detriment of the trust.

The appellants' first contention is that the county court does not have subject matter jurisdiction over the claims against them as trustees. Sec. 253.10, Stats., gives the probate division of the county court subject matter jurisdiction to hear the instant case. Sec. 253.10 (1) and (2) (a), provides in part:

"Probate jurisdiction. (1) The jurisdiction of the county court shall extend to the probate of wills . . . and of administration on the estates . . . and to any other cases authorized by law; . . . to all cases of constructions of wills admitted to probate in such court; and to all cases of trusts and trust powers created by will admitted to probate in such court, including administration under ch. 323 of trusts created in accordance with s. 231.49 (1); . . .

"(2) (a) The county court shall have concurrent jurisdiction to hear, try and determine all matters and controversies which may arise between any . . . trustee appointed by such court and any other person relating to title to or interest in real and personal property so far as such matter or controversy is incidental to and necessary for the complete administration of the estate, . . . or trust, and regardless of who has possession of the property or in whose name it may be, to the same extent and with like effect as such matters and controversies may be heard, tried and determined in courts of general jurisdiction."

The action here is against the trustees of the Roy J. Becker Trust. It is not a stockholders' derivative suit, nor an action against the corporation nor against its directors or officers. The action seeks only the trustees' removal and an accounting therein for their bad faith acts in respect to administering the trust. The trust in question was created by Becker's will and admitted for probate in the county court in 1965. We believe the appellants have misconstrued the action and the nature of relief sought. The fact that the trustees also acted in other capacities and participated in the management of the corporation does not cause the respondents' action to fail nor taint the probate court's jurisdiction. In such management the appellants are still trustees and accountable as such. Estate of Teasdale (1952), 261 Wis. 248, 52 N. W. 2d 366. A trustee in operating a business is still also acting as a trustee. Estate of Teasdale, supra, at page 263, citing Estate of Peabody (1935), 218 Wis. 541, 546, 260 N. W. 444.

Sec. 253.10, Stats., gives the county court jurisdiction to hear, try and determine this controversy. The appellants have moved to quash the petition upon the grounds the facts stated are insufficient to constitute a cause of action and a defect of parties in that the corporation was not named. The appellants' motion to quash is equivalent to a demurrer. Estate of McKillip (1971), 53 Wis. 2d 202, 191 N. W. 2d 856, citing In re Estate of Holden (1875), 37 Wis. 98. When a motion to quash a petition has been made, as here, the petition and documents attached thereto must state facts sufficient enough to entitle the petitioner to the relief sought. And, as a corollary rule, the facts stated in the petition are assumed to be true and are entitled to a liberal construction. Estate of McKillip, supra. Here the petition seeks their removal and an accounting because of their bad faith actions in their simultaneous positions and duties as trustees, shareholders, directors and officers of the corporation. If these and other allegations contained in the petition can be proven, respondents will be entitled to have the appellants removed and to account therein. Estate of Martin (1968), 39 Wis. 2d 437, 159 N. W. 2d 660, and (1963), 21 Wis. 2d 334, 124 N. W. 2d 297. As Scott in his treatise on Trusts (3d ed.), p. 1592, sec. 193, states:

". . . Where shares of stock are held in trust, the trustee having legal title to the shares can exercise the powers of a shareholder. He is under a duty to the beneficiaries, however, to exercise these powers for the benefit of the trust. . . ."

And Scott further states in sec. 193.2 at page 1601:

"The trustee will be held accountable by the court if in the exercise of his power of control over the corporation he acts for his own interest rather than for the interest of the beneficiaries. Thus he will be held accountable where he abuses his power of control by procuring his election as an officer of the corporation and the payment to him of a salary or other compensation . . ., a trustee who holds shares of stock in trust and holds other shares individually may be guilty of a breach of trust in forwarding his own interest rather than those of the beneficiaries. . . ."

Based on the record in the instant case, and assuming the facts alleged are true, and giving it a liberal construction, the petition does state facts sufficient enough to entitle the petitioners to the relief sought. Appellants also complain in their motion to quash that the corporation is a necessary party to this action. The corporation is not a necessary party nor a real party in interest. The action is brought by the beneficiaries of the trust estate against the appellants only as trustees for breach of their fiduciary duties. The trustees by their own choosing accepted directorships and official positions in the corporation. If these positions caused conflicting fiduciary duties of loyalty they were of appellants' own making. The fact that their actions caused these duties to overlap, intermix and solidify does not change the present cause of action nor require the corporation to be joined. The action is still against the trustees of the testamentary trust for removal and accounting to the trust because of their actions as trustees and not as corporate director or officers.

The appellants also appeal from that portion of the order denying their plea in bar to the amended petition. They argue that since they were also executors of the Becker estate, and since they filed an accounting of that estate which was duly allowed and approved by the county court, and because they were then discharged as executors -- the doctrine of res judicata bars the petitioners' right to maintain these proceedings for removal and an accounting. Again, respondents are not seeking the appellants' removal and an accounting therein as executors, but rather as trustees of the trust. A trustee's status and position is completely different from that of an executor under the eyes of the law. The petition here seeks relief against the trustees and not the executors nor the corporation. The law is clear that a trustee is required to account for his doings as a trustee of the trust. Will of Gabel (1954), 267 Wis. 208, 64 N. W. 2d 853. The status and duties of an executor vis-a-vis a trustee are totally distinct and different from each other. The plea in bar was properly overruled. The major issue is whether the trial court erred in denying appellants' motion for summary judgment.

Sec. 270.635, Stats., providing for summary judgment, does not confer a right to summary judgment but rather confers on the trial court a discretionary power to grant it or deny it. Zimmer v. Daun (1968), 40 Wis. 2d 627, 162 N. W. 2d 626. Since it is within the court's discretion, an order denying the motion will not be reversed until it appears that the trial court abused its legal discretion or has not exercised it. Hardscrabble Ski Area v. First Nat. Bank (1969), 42 Wis. 2d 334, 166 N. W. 2d 191. A motion for summary judgment should be denied when either a substantial issue of fact to be tried exists, or if the inferences to be drawn from the credible evidence are doubtful and uncertain, and ". . . Likewise, when there is credible evidence which under any reasonable view will either support or admit of an inference in support or in denial of a claim of either party, it is for the jury to draw the proper inference and not for the court to determine which of two or more permissible inferences should prevail. . . ." Voysey v. Labisky (1960), 10 Wis. 2d 274, 277, 278, 103 N. W. 2d 9, and Elder v. Sage (1950), 257 Wis. 214, 42 N. W. 2d 919. If the trial court had a doubt as to whether all of the material facts are presented or some are in dispute, or believes different reasonable inferences may be drawn, or that the affidavits are not sufficient, either quantitatively or qualitatively, to raise a legal question -- then the trial court should not consider the legal question. Murphy v. Miller Brewing Co. (1971), 50 Wis. 2d 323, 184 N. W. 2d 141.

In this case the respondents seek the appellants' removal as trustees and an accounting therein for damages sustained to the trust because of appellants' said actions. The basis of this action rests on the rule that a trustee still has a strict duty of loyalty to the trust even though the will or trust instrument gives the trustee broad powers of discretion. These powers must still be exercised according to the law and consistent with the duties and obligations as a trustee of the trust. Estate of Gehl (1958), 5 Wis. 2d 91, 92 N. W. 2d 372, and Will of Gabel, supra. In Dick & Reuteman Co. v. Doherty Realty Co. (1962), 16 Wis. 2d 342, 349, 114 N. W. 2d 475, this court has quoted Magruder v. Drury as follows:

"'It is a well-settled rule that a trustee can make no profit out of his trust. The rule in such cases springs from his duty to protect the interests of the estate, and not to permit his personal interest to in anywise conflict with his duty in that respect. The intention is to provide against any possible selfish interest exercising an influence which can interfere with the faithful discharge of the duty which is owing in a fiduciary capacity.'"

In the instant case the trial court stated:

". . . The court in ruling insofar as summary judgment is concerned, on the basis of Cadden v. Milwaukee County (1969), 44 Wis. 2d 341, . . . To this court the basic and sole issue that is going to determine everything is the question of fact going to the law which imposes an absolute loyalty upon the trustee or any fiduciary to his trust . . . most of the arguments today are going to the question of the interval, good or bad, of the corporation, and that is secondary and can be used only in evidence of the status and attitude of the trustees . . . With the amended answer before the court, admitted as if it were a demurrer, there is something to adjudicate before this court and truly a serious issue. We are at a point where we haven't real facts decided by cross-examination. . . ."

It is evident that the trial court, in exercising its discretion, was of the opinion there were factual disputes to be resolved concerning the trustees' loyalty. Such disputed facts do exist. The appellants' affidavit states that the allegation of their control over the actions of the stockholders and directors is untrue, but the record shows that Carl R. Becker (trustee-appellant) sent a letter to Attorney Knoeller on October 22, 1965, in which he made an admission as to his control over the actions of the stockholders and directors, and his desire to advance his own personal interests. The letter states in part:

"Dear Mr. Knoeller:

". . . Because this meeting was so called, I decided for the protection of my interests to 'call' both stockholders and directors meeting for the pre-arranged date. . . .

"The agreement to employ me as general manager runs to the end of 1971 or a period of five years with compensation at the basic salary of $30,000.00 payable weekly. It contains no provision for bonus on sales. After 1971 it provides employment on consultative basis for five years at $10,000.00 per year payable weekly.

"I told Louis and Joe at the meeting, and I repeat here, that I will not back down on my insistence upon this contract for my employment.

"In the past the decisions of Louis and Joe with Roy on all phases of the business, notably their salaries and bonuses, was in their joint control and Mary Helen and I had no alternative but to yield thereto; and we did so. Louis and Joe may not concur in the wisdom or necessity of the company employing me, but the majority now in control believe it to be not only desirable but necessary. Louis and Joe must yield to this decision just as Mary Helen and I did to theirs in the past."

Then on May 28, 1969, Carl R. Becker sent a letter to Joseph A. Becker stating that from 1965 through 1968 an audit of the funeral home's records show that there has been a very substantial loss of income to the Roy J. Becker Trust.

From the affidavits and pleadings in support of and in opposition to the motion, it appears that there are substantial issues of fact to be tried. There are questions as to whether an actual conflict of interest existed, that is, the trustees' personal interests vis-a-vis the trust's interests; and whether they acted in bad faith, plus whether they breached their fiduciary duty of loyalty. We do not believe the trial court abused its discretion in denying the motion. It cannot be said under the facts of this case that only a question of law exists or that as a matter of right summary judgment should have been granted to the appellants.

III. REVOCATION AND MODIFICATION OF TRUSTS

A. THE CLAFLIN DOCTRINE

If a trust is created as a revocable trust, terminating or modifying the trust is a relatively simple matter, since the individual with the power of revocation simply has to exercise that power. The power to modify may have been reserved as well, or else the trust can be revoked and then re-created with modifications. However, the modification of an irrevocable trust is a more complicated matter, but under certain circumstances irrevocable trusts can be modified or even prematurely terminated. If the settlor is still alive and all of the beneficiaries agree, the parties can collectively agree to terminate or modify the trust. In that situation, the trustee has no grounds to object to the termination of the relationship.

On the other hand, if the settlor is no longer present, then the situation becomes more complicated. Even if the trust is irrevocable, it may be terminated without settlor consent if the trust has proven to be unproductive (in the sense of yielding too little income to achieve its purpose). Furthermore, even if the trust is productive, if termination of the trust would not be contrary to a *material purpose* of the trust as established by the testator, then the beneficiaries alone can decide to terminate the trust, if their agreement is unanimous. This latter principle is usually known as the *Claflin doctrine,* after the Massachusetts case of *Claflin v. Claflin,* 149 Mass. 19, 20 N.E. 545 (1889).

In that case, the plaintiff was the beneficiary of a testamentary trust which had been created by his late father and which was designed to pay him the interest until he reached age 30, at which point he was to receive the principal free of trust. Upon reaching age 21, the beneficiary sued to terminate the trust on the grounds that he was the sole beneficiary and that he preferred to receive the principal now rather than later. The court refused to grant the request for termination on the grounds that ensuring the beneficiary a continuous source of income was a material purpose of the trust and that this could not be assured if the trust were dissolved prior to his reaching that age. As a general rule, spendthrift provisions were traditionally viewed as *material purposes,* and thus spendthrift trusts were never candidates for early termination. If, however, no *material purpose* remained, the trust was properly terminated even over the objections of the trustee.

Wis. Stat. 701.12. Revocation, modification and termination of trusts with consent of settlor.

(1) By written consent of the settlor and all beneficiaries of a trust or any part thereof, such trust or part thereof may be revoked, modified or terminated, except as provided under s. 445.125 (1) (a) 2. To 4.

(2) For purposes of this section such consent may be given on behalf of a legally incapacitated, unascertained or unborn beneficiary by the court after a hearing in which the interests of such beneficiary are represented by a guardian ad litem. A guardian ad litem for such beneficiary may rely on general family benefit accruing to living members of the beneficiary's family as a basis for approving a revocation, modification or termination of a trust or any part thereof.

(3) Nothing in this section shall prevent revocation, modification, or termination of a trust pursuant to its terms or otherwise in accordance with law or prevent conversion of a trust to a unitrust under s. 701.20 (4g).

Wis. Stat. 701.13. Modification and termination of trusts by court action.

(1) ANTICIPATION OF DIRECTED ACCUMULATION OF INCOME. When an accumulation of income is directed for the benefit of a beneficiary without other sufficient means to support or educate himself or herself, the court on the application of the beneficiary

or the beneficiary's guardian may direct that a suitable sum from the income accumulated or to be accumulated be applied for the support or education of such person.

(2) APPLICATION OF PRINCIPAL TO INCOME BENEFICIARY. Unless the creating instrument provides to the contrary, if a beneficiary is entitled to income or to have it applied for the beneficiary's benefit, the court may make an allowance from principal to or for the benefit of such beneficiary if the beneficiary's support or education is not sufficiently provided for, taking into account all other resources available to the beneficiary.

(3) TERMINATION. In the case of a living trust whose settlor is deceased and in the case of any testamentary trust, regardless in either case of spendthrift or similar protective provisions, a court with the consent of the trustee may order termination of the trust, in whole or in part, and the distribution of the assets that it considers appropriate if the court is satisfied that because of any substantial reason existing at the inception of a testamentary trust or, in the case of any trust, arising from a subsequent change in circumstances, including but not limited to the amount of principal in the trust, income produced by the trust and the cost of administering the trust, continuation of the trust, in whole or in part, is impractical. In any event, if the trust property is valued at less than 50,000, the court may order termination of the trust and the distribution of the assets that it considers appropriate.

(4) MARITAL DEDUCTION TRUSTS. In a trust where the income beneficiary also has a general power of appointment as defined in s. 702.01 (3) or where all accumulated income and principal are payable to such beneficiary's estate, any termination, in whole or in part, of the trust under sub. (3) can only be ordered in favor of such beneficiary.

(5) CHARITABLE TRUSTS.

(a) In this subsection, "participate or intervene in any political campaign" includes the publishing or distributing of statements.

(b) Subsections (2) and (3) do not apply to a trust under which a future interest is indefeasibly vested in any of the following:

1. The United States or a political subdivision for exclusively public purposes.

2. A corporation that is organized exclusively for religious, charitable, scientific, literary or educational purposes, including the encouragement of art and the prevention of cruelty to children or animals, no part of the net earnings of which inures to the benefit of any private shareholder or individual and no substantial part of the activities of which is carrying on propaganda or otherwise attempting to influence legislation, and that does not participate or intervene in any political campaign on behalf of any candidate for public office.

3. A trustee or a fraternal society, order or association operating under the lodge system, provided the principal or income of such trust is to be used by such trustee or by such fraternal society, order or association exclusively for religious, charitable, scientific, literary or educational purposes or for the prevention of cruelty to children and animals, and no substantial part of the activities of such trustee or of such fraternal society, order or association is carrying on propaganda or otherwise attempting to influence legislation, and such trustee or

such fraternal society, order, or association does not participate or intervene in any political campaign on behalf of any candidate for public office.

4. Any veterans organization incorporated by act of congress, or of its departments or local chapters or posts, no part of the net earnings of which inures to the benefit of any private shareholder or individual.

(6) OTHER APPLICABLE LAW. Nothing in this section shall prohibit modification or termination of any trust pursuant to its terms or limit the general equitable power of a court to modify or terminate a trust in whole or in part.

In re Hamburger's Will

Supreme Court of Wisconsin
185 Wis. 270, 201 N.W. 267 (1924)

This is an action involving the construction of a will. The county court of Milwaukee County made an order by which the trustees under the will of Nathan Hamburger, Sr., were directed to transfer to the petitioner, Nathan Hamburger, Jr., 1,000 shares of the common stock of Gimbel Bros., Inc., out of about 23,000 shares held by them as such trustees, and to pay to Nathan, Jr., the dividends, if any, from the 1,000 shares, since they had notice of an assignment of those shares to the petitioner by his mother, Bertha Hamburger Behal, formerly Bertha Hamburger. This order was made in a proceeding by Nathan seeking a construction of the will and a judgment directing the trustees to deliver to him the shares of stock which had been assigned to him by his mother. Two of the trustees approved the gift, but the appellant declined on the ground of lack of authority.

The testator, when a lad of thirteen, entered the employ of Adam Gimbel, who was the founder of the business which has for so many years borne the name of Gimbel Brothers. In 1883 he was admitted as a partner, and at the time of his death in 1910 was a vice-president and was in charge of the Milwaukee store. Five of the seven sons of Adam Gimbel are living and connected with the business, as are also nine of his grandsons. The grandsons are all vice-presidents and stockholders of the corporation. Nathan, Jr., is the only son of the testator. He entered the employ of Gimbel Brothers, Inc., in January, 1923, and became twenty-one years of age in May of that year; holds an executive position in the Philadelphia store, and desires to have a substantial interest in the business. The corporation of Gimbel Brothers, Inc., took over the business originally conducted by the firm of Gimbel Brothers. The partnership agreement provided that the sons of the partners might be taken into the business when twenty-three years of age, if of good character and sound business ability, after serving five years of apprenticeship, or, if they had a college degree, three years of apprenticeship. Nathan did not have a college degree.

The will is a lengthy document consisting of nineteen articles. It was dated March 30, 1908, and there is also a codicil dated June 28, 1910, revoking two former codicils. The most important article, here involved, is number XVI, which is as follows:

"All the rest, residue, and remainder of my property and estate of whatever kind and nature and wherever situated, real, personal, and mixed, which I may own at the time of my death, I give, devise, and bequeath to my said executors, in trust, upon the trust that they hold and invest the same and pay the net income thereof to my beloved wife, Bertha Hamburger, for her own sole use and benefit so long as she may live, and subject only to this bequest in trust for and during the life of my said wife, the principal of this bequest is given, devised, and bequeathed to my wife to become her sole and separate estate, to be disposed of by her, by will or otherwise; and if she do not so dispose of it, to become upon her death part of her intestate estate; and the gift, devise, and bequest made to my said wife in this will are in lieu of dower and other claim against my estate which my wife might have in the absence of this will; and I will and direct that the gift, devise, and bequest made in this article of my will shall in any event include and carry no less than two thirds of the appraised value of my estate, and that the other gifts and bequests in this will made shall, if necessary, be proportionately reduced in order to make the amount given by this article of my will at least such two-thirds portion of my estate."

In the other paragraphs of the will there are numerous bequests providing for relations and charities, and there is careful provision for the appointment of executors and their successors in case of resignation or death. Other facts will be stated in the opinion.

JONES, J. It is first contended by the plaintiff's counsel that by the terms of the will the life interest and the remainder are merged in the widow; that the language of the will clearly evidences a gift of the principal directly to her without the intervention of trustees; that she was given the title and all the rights incident to the title, including the right of disposition by will or in any other way she might choose. Reliance is also placed on the clause, "and if she do not so dispose of it, to become upon her death part of her intestate estate." It is further argued that, since the life estate and the remainder merged in the widow, the trust is terminable by her.

The Wisconsin case principally relied on for this claim is Holmes v. Walter, 118 Wis. 409, 95 N.W. 380. There the language of the will was: "After the payment of my just debts and funeral expenses, I give, devise, and bequeath to my beloved wife Mary, in trust for herself and my children, all of my estates, both real and personal, with full power to continue my business if for the best interest of my estate." All of the children were minors, with the exception of one, when the suit was brought. It will be observed that, as compared with the will now before us, the language relied on to create the trust was rather vague and uncertain. In the lower court it was held that the will created a mere passive or dry trust and that it must be considered as if there were no trust at all and that the property was given direct to the beneficiaries. On appeal, in an opinion by Mr. Justice MARSHALL, it was held that the devise and bequest were not made absolutely to the trustee, the widow, but for herself and her children, and that all were to share equally in the benefits of the trust; that it was evident that the trust concerned more than the mere title and that the immediate use and possession were not intended to go to the beneficiaries. It was held that the trust was not void as indefinite or uncertain; that it was not a dry or passive trust. The judgment of the lower court was reversed, and the trust was not terminated. In discussing the question whether the trust was void for uncertainty because no time was stated for its termination, it was said:

"Again, since the will contains no prohibition, express or implied, against terminating the trust, and all parties that can be interested are in esse, when all are sui juris they can by uniting cause its termination, subject to the restraints contained in secs. 2089 and 2091, Stats. 1898 (citing cases). The mere fact that the trust is in terms perpetual does not affect it. That feature is not objectionable so long as it does not offend against the prohibition against suspending the absolute power of alienation. 1 Perry, Trusts, §23."

This language is much relied on by counsel for the respondents. It will be observed that this quotation has the qualification "since the will contains no prohibition, express or implied, against terminating the trust." This is a condition often referred to in cases cited by the respondents, and attention is called to it in a later opinion by Mr. Justice MARSHALL. Will of Rice, 150 Wis. 401, 453, 136 N.W. 956, 137 N.W. 778. Counsel also rely on authorities from other jurisdictions and especially on decisions of the supreme judicial court of Massachusetts, and the following cases are cited: Bowditch v. Andrew, 8 Allen (Mass.) 339; Inches v. Hill, 106 Mass. 575; Whall v. Converse, 146 Mass. 345, 15 N.E. 660; Sears v. Choate, 146 Mass. 395, 15 N.E. 786; Langley v. Conlan, 212 Mass. 135, 98 N.E. 1064; Eakle v. Ingram, 142 Cal. 15, 75 P. 566; Tilton v. Davidson, 98 Me. 55, 56 A. 215; Armistead's Ex'rs v. Hartt, 97 Va. 316, 33 S.E. 616. In these cases, for various reasons the courts held that the trusts might be terminated, and in Sears v. Choate, supra, a case often cited, the rule in Massachusetts was thus stated:

"There is no doubt of the power and duty of the court to decree the termination of a trust, where all its objects and purposes have been accomplished, where the interests under it have all vested, and where all parties beneficially interested desire its termination. Where property is given to certain persons for their benefit, and in such a manner that no other person has or can have any interest in it, they are in effect the absolute owners of it, and it is reasonable and just that they should have the control and disposal of it unless some good cause appears to the contrary."

It seems hardly necessary to review in detail the cases. An examination of them will show that one or more of the following considerations led the court to terminate the trust: All the interests had become vested in the beneficiary or beneficiaries, and no third person could be interested; or all the purposes of the trust had been accomplished; or there was no express or implied prohibition of the termination; or it was a mere dry trust and all the beneficiaries desired its termination; or such events had transpired after the execution of the will as had not been and could not have been anticipated by the testator, which rendered the continuance of the trust unnecessary.

In Claflin v. Claflin, 149 Mass. 19, 20 N.E. 454, a testator by his will, after liberal provisions for a son, gave one third of the residue of his personal estate to trustees in trust "to sell and dispose of the same and to pay the proceeds thereof to my son in the manner following, viz.: $10,000 when he is of the age of twenty-one years, $10,000 when he is of the age of twenty-five years, and the balance when he is of the age of thirty years." The trustees paid over $10,000 to the son when he became twenty-one years of age, and thereupon he filed a bill in equity to obtain the rest of the fund. In the opinion the court reviewed the case of Sears v. Choate, supra, and other cases, and in the opinion it was said:

"We have found no expression of any opinion in our Reports that provisions requiring a trustee to hold and manage the trust property until the beneficiary reached an age beyond that of twenty-one years are necessarily void if the interest of the beneficiary is vested and absolute (citing cases). This is not a dry trust, and the purposes of the trust have not been accomplished if the intention of the testator is to be carried out. . . . In the case at bar nothing has happened which the testator did not anticipate, and for which he has not made provision. It is plainly his will that neither the income nor any part of the principal should now be paid to the plaintiff. . . . The existing situation is one which the testator manifestly had in mind and made provision for; the strict execution of the trust has not become impossible; the restriction upon the plaintiff's possession and control is, we think, one that the testator had a right to make; other provisions for the plaintiff are contained in the will, apparently sufficient for his support, and we see no good reason why the intention of the testator should not be carried out."

The decision in this case was followed in Young v. Snow, 167 Mass. 287, 45 N.E. 686, where under the will the trust fund was to remain in the hands of trustees for twenty years from the testator's death and provision was made for the use of the income during that period. The court said:

"None of these provisions are repugnant to law or contrary to public policy. The testator, therefore, had the right to make the disposition of his property which he did make, and it is the duty of the court, so far as it has jurisdiction, to carry out the trust. Although the interests created under the trust have all vested, and all the parties interested request that the trust be terminated and the trustee consents, the objects and purposes of the trust have not been accomplished, nor has their accomplishment been made impossible. . . . While the will vests the fund in the testator's four children, it does not give them an absolute estate, and then impose restrictions and conditions repugnant to the estate, but gives an ownership qualified by the directions that the property is to remain for a time in the hands and control of the executors as trustees. Whether the testator made these provisions for one purpose or another is immaterial, since he had the right to order as he did. Under our decisions, such provisions are not void, and are to be carried out."

In Hoffman v. New England T. Co. 187 Mass. 205, 72 N.E. 952, the court said:

"But there are other grounds for refusing the petition. Plainly the testator intended that the trust should continue until the death of both of his nieces Mary and Laura. And whatever may be the law elsewhere, that provision in this commonwealth is legal. Claflin v. Claflin, 149 Mass. 19, 20 N.E. 454. It is also plain that nothing has happened which the testator did not anticipate, and for which he has not made provision. The language used by FIELD, J., in the case above cited is applicable here: 'It cannot be said that these restrictions upon the plaintiff's possession and control of the property are altogether useless, for there is not the same danger that he will spend the property while it is in the hands of the trustees as there would be if it were in his own.'" See, also, McCoy v. Natick, 237 Mass. 99, 129 N.E. 381; Forbes v. Snow, 245 Mass. 85, 140 N.E. 418.

In former decisions of this court it has been uniformly held that it is the duty of the courts in cases of this kind to uphold the intentions of the testator despite the wishes of the beneficiaries. In Bussell v. Wright, 133 Wis. 445, 113 N.W. 644, the court said, though the beneficiaries were willing to terminate the trust:

"The paramount question is, What was the intention of the testator respecting the execution of the trust as gathered from an inspection of the will? If it appears from the will that the intention of the testator was that the trustee should execute the trust founded, courts have no power to frustrate that intention and devise a different method of execution. This would be to substitute the judgment of the court for the judgment of the testator in the distribution of his bounty. The rule that the intention of the testator must govern has been often laid down by this court and other courts, and further discussion of it would seem unnecessary."

In closing the opinion the court said:

"To order a termination of the trust in the case before us, or make other provisions for the execution of it than those clearly defined on the face of the instrument creating the trust, would be a clear disregard of the intention of the testator."

We might quote, if it were necessary, at great length from the opinion in the well-known case of Will of Rice, 150 Wis. 401, 136 N.W. 956, 137 N.W. 778, where the beneficiaries asked the court to approve an agreement between them by which a trust was to be terminated and other disposition of the property of the testator, than that designated in the will, provided for. It was held that the court was powerless to carry out a plan devised by beneficiaries under the will by which their scheme could be substituted for that of the testator. In this opinion there is an elaborate discussion of the inviolability of the testamentary trust, the sacredness of the right to make a will, and the duty of the courts to uphold that right. Will of Dardis, 135 Wis. 457, 115 N.W. 332, is another case in which this court rejected a stipulation by the beneficiaries by which a distribution of the estate different from that prescribed in the will was proposed, and it was said the testator's "right is recognized to direct at least the method of management and disposal of his property after his decease, which courts cannot be compelled to disregard to accommodate the wishes of some or even all parties having pecuniary interest in the property." See, also, Guardianship of Reeve, 176 Wis. 579, 186 N.W. 736; Estate of Staab, 166 Wis. 587, 166 N.W. 326.

We cannot agree with counsel for the plaintiff that the equitable and legal estates created by the will merged in the widow and that she became the absolute owner. It was the manifest intention of the testator to create a trust, giving the control and management of the residue to trustees during the life of the widow. Although she was given a legal estate in the remainder, by the plain language of the will, that estate was subject to the trust. The will was evidently drawn by able counsel, and, since the bequest of the principal was made subject to the trust, those words cannot be read out of the will. In determining whether the absolute estate passed to the widow we cannot disregard the intent of the testator. He had accumulated by his personal effort a very considerable fortune. It seems clear to us that in disposing of it by will his paramount object was to make certain that during her life his widow should have every comfort suitable to her, rank in life.

Next to this purpose was the desire to make suitable provision for his only son, Nathan, then a small boy. He had doubtless observed enough of the vicissitudes of life to realize that it often happens that fortunes accumulated by the industry and economy of a lifetime may be lost, in the hands of persons inexperienced in business affairs, in a twelvemonth. He therefore made very careful and elaborate provision for such care and preservation of his estate during the life of his widow as to guard against such possibilities. The widow was not appointed to act as trustee alone, but two other trustees in whom he had confidence were named. It is a matter of common knowledge, as the testator doubtless appreciated, that the possession of large wealth when a boy reaches his majority is sometimes a misfortune rather than a blessing. Realizing this, in article VII of the will he bequeathed to his trustees, in trust, stock of the par value of \$75,000, afterwards by codicil made \$100,000, for the benefit of Nathan, but provided that the net income thereof should be paid to the widow to be used for his care and support until he was twenty-four years of age. In this article it was further provided that one third of the principal might be paid over to the son at that time if he desired to go into business, but this was left wholly in the discretion of two or all of the trustees to determine whether it would be safe to do so, and this discretion as to the final payment was to continue until he was thirty-five years of age. This article VII, containing very careful provisions for the benefit of Nathan, covers nearly three pages of the printed case, and includes the following clause:

"And I purposely make no further provision for my son during the life of my wife until my son reaches the age of twenty-four years, knowing that my wife, so long as she lives, will, out of provision made for her in this will, provide for my son should anything be required in addition to the income in this article provided."

It is argued by counsel for the respondents that this paragraph shows an intention that the widow should not be precluded from aiding her son by the use of some of the large capital in the residue of the estate. But article VII was in the nature of a provision, made by the testator himself, for Nathan's going into business at the age of twenty-four, subject to the very careful restrictions imposed. The widow had $100,000, received from life insurance, and the very liberal income from the trust fund. If any inference is to be drawn from article VII it would seem to us rather unfavorable than favorable to the theory that the widow had any right under the will to assign to Nathan the stock in question. As bearing on the intent of the testator, it is of some significance that in the codicil it is provided that if any deficiency arose in the income for paying certain annuities specified in the will for his mother and brother, the deficiency should be made good out of the residue of the estate, by the trustees. The testator meant not only that the trustees should discharge their duties toward the widow and Nathan, but that they must continue in the management of the estate and hold the residue in order that they might meet possible obligations to others.

In article XVIII it was directed that none of the stock be sold before 1910, and that if afterwards any was sold the first opportunity to buy be given to those who had composed the firm of Gimbel Brothers prior to the formation of the corporation, and that after 1910 the trustees were directed, in their judgment, to hold or sell the stock. Here was another indication of the intention that the trust should not be terminated at the will of the beneficiaries. On the contrary, that it should continue until the objects of the will should be accomplished, and among the objects in his mind there seemed to be the discharge of a moral duty he owed to his former partners.

Great stress is placed by the respondents' counsel on the following clause in article XVI:

"The principal of this bequest is given, devised, and bequeathed to my wife to become her sole and separate estate to be disposed of by her, by will or otherwise; and if she do not so dispose of it, to become upon her death part of her intestate estate."

It is claimed that this gave to the widow the absolute power of disposal of both income and remainder at any time by will or otherwise. This language must be construed in connection with what precedes it, in which the residue is given to trustees upon the trust that they hold and invest the same and pay the net income to the widow so long as she may live, and the clause quoted above is expressly made subject to this trust.

The language relied on was broad enough to permit the disposal of the remainder by will or assignment or otherwise to take effect on her death. It is argued by the appellant's counsel, with some reason, that the words "by will or otherwise" related to the form of the disposal; that these words do not describe the thing which may be conveyed but the manner of conveyance; that the thing to be conveyed was the remainder, but subject to the trust.

Counsel for the respondents follow their theory to its logical conclusion and argue that the widow could at any time after her husband's death have disposed of the entire residue of the estate. This means that she could have turned it over to her son or to a second husband; that in order to obtain an expected higher income she could have invested it in speculative stocks or securities and thus frustrated the plan cherished by her husband for her security. We cannot agree that the will admits of any such construction. It is true that effect should be given to every word and clause, if possible, so long as they are not inconsistent with the general intent of the will as a whole. The cardinal rule is to find out the intention of the testator and give it effect, and to this rule all others are subordinate. To ascertain the intention expressed in the will the whole document must be construed together. Our view as to the intention of the testator, in this case, has been already sufficiently stated.

We hold that the legal and equitable estates have not merged; that it was the testator's intention, as expressed in the will, to create a trust to continue during the life of his widow, whether the beneficiaries desired such continuance or not; and that such intention controls. It follows that the will does not authorize the termination of the trust at this time, since the plan and the purpose contemplated by it have not been fulfilled or completed; and that, construing the will as a whole, it contains an implied prohibition against the termination of the trust until such objects are accomplished.

Order reversed. The cause is remanded to the county court for further proceedings in accordance with this opinion.

B. INSUFFICIENT TRUST RES

If a trust produces so little income that it provides no particular benefit, the trust can be terminated and distributed directly to the beneficiaries. This principle recognizes that an inadequately funded trust cannot be accomplishing a material purpose of the settlor and thus his or her consent is not needed to terminate the trust. However, issues sometimes arise in regard to what constitutes an equitable division of the trust assets among the beneficiaries, as the following case illustrates.

Schmidt v. Higgins

Court of Appeals of Wisconsin
171 Wis.2d 771, 495 N.W.2d 103 (1992)

PER CURIAM. Margaret Schmidt appeals from a judgment equally distributing trust assets between herself, as the settlor's surviving spouse, and the settlor's children. The issue is whether the circuit court is compelled to apply an actuarial table to compute Margaret's distributable share. Because we conclude that the circuit court exercised its discretion in distributing the trust assets under sec. 701.13(3), Stats., we affirm.

The decedent, Arnold W. Schmidt, created a revocable inter vivos trust to be funded by the assets in his estate. Upon Schmidt's death, the trust was divided into three equal shares. One third was distributed to Margaret. The next third was distributed among his children from a prior marriage. The remaining third, which is the disputed share, remained in trust, with Margaret having a life estate in the income with a limited power to invade the principal, and the children as remaindermen. The parties agreed that the trust was inadequately funded and thus, could not fulfill the settlor's intent. Therefore, the circuit court dissolved the trust and the personal representative requested the court to distribute the remaining third under sec. 701.13(3), Stats. The circuit court divided the remaining share equally between Margaret and the children. Margaret appeals.

Section 701.13(3), Stats., provides that the circuit court shall distribute the "[trust] assets as it considers appropriate...." We conclude that sec. 701.13(3) empowers the circuit court to exercise its discretion in distributing the assets.

> [A] discretionary determination must be the product of a rational mental process by which the facts of record and law relied upon are stated and are considered together for the purpose of achieving a reasoned and reasonable determination. It is recognized that a trial court in an exercise of its discretion may reasonably reach a conclusion which another judge or another court may not reach, but it must be a decision which a reasonable judge or court could arrive at by the consideration of the relevant law, the facts, and a process of logical reasoning.

Hartung v. Hartung, 102 Wis.2d 58, 66, 306 N.W.2d 16, 20-21 (1981).

Margaret contends that the circuit court abused its discretion by arbitrarily dividing the remaining share equally, rather than following the settlor's intent by valuing her life estate and her power to invade. She requested the circuit court to apply the actuarial table to value her interest which would have resulted in a distribution of at least seventy-eight percent of the remaining share to her and twenty-two percent for the settlor's children. The respondents objected to the admissibility of the actuarial table, claiming it is unsubstantiated and not subject to cross-examination. They also claim that a present value calculation from the table lacks foundation absent expert testimony.

Margaret contends the circuit court abused its discretion because by dividing the remaining share equally, it achieved the same result as if the decedent died intestate. See sec. 852.01(1)(a)2., Stats. Margaret acknowledges that the circuit court was not required to apply the actuarial table to value her share. The circuit court acknowledged that it considered the actuarial table. Because we conclude that sec. 701.13(3), Stats., requires only that the circuit court exercise its discretion, we examine the record to determine whether it did so.

The circuit court reasoned that the $80,000 in the remaining share was insufficient to accomplish the settlor's dual objectives of supporting Margaret during her lifetime, and upon her death, dividing the remaining principal among the children. However, it sought to distribute the remaining share according to the settlor's intent. Because the settlor divided two-thirds of the estate equally between Margaret and the children by distributing half to each, the circuit court reasoned that it also should divide the remaining one-third equally.

While the circuit court's distribution could have been different, we are to look for reasons to sustain a circuit court's exercise of discretion. See Brandt v. Witzling, 98 Wis.2d 613, 619, 297 N.W.2d 833, 836 (1980). The circuit court considered the facts of record, the statutory authority for its decision, and the possibility of using the actuarial table. The result reached - an equal division because that was the settlor's general intent - is logical and reasonable. Under Hartung, that is all that is required. Whether another court or this court might have decided differently is irrelevant. Judgment affirmed.

C. THE WISCONSIN RULE AGAINST PERPETUITIES

Third party interests in land (like contingent remainders and what are called executory interests outside of Wisconsin) and contingent beneficiary interests in trusts (discussed below) were traditionally affected by the common law Rule against Perpetuities. The rule, as it finally developed, stated that to be valid an interest must vest or fail within a life in being plus twenty-one years following the time of its creation. If there was even a possibility that it might not vest (or fail), the interest was void at the time of its creation, and what happened subsequently was completely irrelevant to its fate.

The harshness of the rule and the remorseless way in which it was enforced (at least in lore) ultimately led to its reformulation, first by a series of interpretive canons that made it less likely that interests would be viewed as unvested, then by adopting a wait and see approach that voided only those interests that actually vested outside of the perpetuities period, then by substituting a fixed period of years for the common law's "life in being plus 21 years," and finally to the abolition of the rule altogether in many jurisdictions. Today, only Alabama still follows the common law rule in all situations.

From the beginning, Wisconsin was an outlier in regard to the Rule against Perpetuities. In the 19th century, the state's Supreme Court ruled that the Rule applied only to interests in real property and not personalty, thus making Wisconsin a jurisdiction in which it was theoretically possible to create a perpetual trust composed of personal property. Although the Wisconsin legislature brought personal property back under the rule in the 1920's, it also adopted its own unique version of the rule. The new Wisconsin rule, still in effect, extended the perpetuities period to a life in being plus thirty years, and also crafted an exception for remote interests that did not affect the alienation of property. So, as long as someone could acquire the complete interest in land subject to future interest or to property is a trust res, it was irrelevant when the attached contingent interest might vest. While it is not technically true, as sometimes claimed, that the Rule against Perpetuities has been abolished in Wisconsin, the state's early decision to focus on the alienability of property rather than the problem of remote vesting, made the Rule less of a bugaboo in Wisconsin than it was in other jurisdictions.

Wis. Stat. 700.16. Perpetuities and suspension of power of alienation.

(1)

(a) A future interest or trust is void if it suspends the power of alienation for longer than the permissible period. The permissible period is a life or lives in being plus a period of 30 years.

(b) If the settlor of a living trust has an unlimited power to revoke, the permissible period is computed from termination of such power.

(c) If a future interest or trust is created by exercise of a power of appointment, the permissible period is computed from the time the power is exercised if the power is a general power as defined in s. 702.01(3) even if the power is exercisable only by will; in the case of other powers the permissible period is computed from the time the power is created but facts at the time the power is exercised are considered in determining whether the power of alienation is suspended beyond a life or lives in being at the time of creation of the power plus 30 years.

(2) The power of alienation is suspended when there are no persons in being who, alone or in combination with others, can convey an absolute fee in possession of land, or full ownership of personalty.

(3) There is no suspension of the power of alienation by a trust or by equitable interests under a trust if the trustee has power to sell, either expressed or implied, or if there is an unlimited power to terminate in one or more persons in being.

(4) This section does not apply to limit any of the following:

(a) Transfers, outright or in trust, for charitable purposes;

(b) Transfers to literary or charitable corporations;

(bm) Transfers to a veterans memorial organization under s. 84.09 (5r);

(c) Transfers to any cemetery corporation, society or association;

(d) Transfers, outright or in trust, to the state society of physicians and surgeons incorporated under the law of this state, when the transfer is for the advancement of medical science;

(e) Transfers to any person pursuant to ch. 703; or

(f) Employees trusts created as part of a plan or contract as described in s. 815.18 (3) (j)

In re Will of Walker

Supreme Court of Wisconsin
258 Wis. 65; 45 N.W.2d 94 (1950)

Opinion by Brown. Appeal from a judgment of the County Court of Milwaukee County: M. S. Sheridan, Judge. Judgment affirmed as it affects personalty and reversed as it affects realty and cause remanded for further necessary proceedings consistent with the opinion. Costs for printing respondent's entire brief allowed

The direction to divide the interest from the trust estate among the great nephews and great nieces annually shows the testatrix's intent that the estate should be kept productive of income. This necessarily requires investment of cash assets and management of all investments. Over so long a trust period as that specified by the testatrix she must have anticipated that changes affecting the productivity of original investments would occur. Without some expression of hers to the contrary it cannot be supposed that she meant her trustee to be powerless to alter or adjust the corpus of the trust estate to retain its productivity. If she meant him to make and to manage investments, as obviously she did, she must, when she has not expressed herself otherwise, be deemed to have given him the ordinary powers of management. Of these one of the most common and necessary is the discretion to shift investments by purchase and sale as the conditions affecting them make advisable.

Upon such reasoning, in which we concur, the learned county court found that it was "the intent of the testatrix, the creator of said trust, that such power exist in the trustee of said trust, though not expressly granted by the language of her will," in so far as the securities and other personal property are concerned. The court, however, declined to apply the reasoning to the real estate saying, in a written opinion,

". . . the weight of authority seems to be that trustees have no power to sell land for the purpose of reinvesting the proceeds unless that power is expressly granted by the will. This limitation is no doubt a vestige of feudal conception of landholding which did not consider land a commodity of barter and sale as it is in modern society. The court will follow the weight of authority and hold that no power of sale, either express or implied, is contained in this will authorizing the trustee to sell the real estate contained in said trust."

Thereupon the court made findings that a grant of power to sell the real estate could not be implied from the language of the will. In this finding which, of course, is actually a conclusion of law we consider that the court was in error. It is self-evident that the testatrix herself did not distinguish between personalty and realty in her creation of the trust or her instructions to the trustee. As far as the language of her will is concerned the estate is a unit, however composed, and whatever she said applied alike to both classes of property. We do not think any distinction can properly be drawn because she used the word "interest," which technically would apply only to the income from personalty, not realty, but which (still technically) would include only the return on the bonds and debentures in her estate and would leave out the dividends from her shares of corporate stock (appraised at $18,646.07, -- not a negligible amount), as well as the farm rents. In this instance her term "interest" must be taken as the equivalent of "income."

Testatrix's language, then, being equally applicable to her personal and her real property, and making no distinction between them, cannot produce opposite results unless there is some significant difference in the character of her real-estate holdings to warrant the belief that she meant them to be differently treated, or some rule of law prevents implying a power to sell realty. The trial court relied on such a supposed rule of law.

The farm in question had not been occupied by the testatrix or any member of her family for about twenty-five years. The number of beneficiaries both at the time she executed her will and when she died, to say nothing of the possibility of after-born children, precludes the supposition that she wanted the farm preserved as a home for them. There is no indication that it had any sentimental value to her. She had formerly contracted to sell it and was now leasing it to tenants. There was no reference to it in the will. All the circumstances lead to the conclusion that she viewed it as an asset of no different standing than her cash, stocks, and bonds.

Conceding that English cases and the earlier American cases which follow them support the court's conclusion, we note that their doctrine arose in, and was appropriate to, a rigid society where family lands were preserved intact to be handed down to the eldest son; but the reason for treating that which is a mere investment in land differently from one in securities or other form of personalty disappears in our very flexible society where land is an article of commerce and the rule of primogeniture has never been recognized. Under the circumstances of this will and of the estate with which it deals we find no reason to say that the testatrix withheld from her trustee powers in respect to one sort of property which she had granted, by implication, in the other.

Respondent has cited the following passage from Prof. Scott's work on trusts, which we consider expresses the modern and the better American law:

"The courts today are more ready to find that a power of sale is conferred upon the trustee than were the courts in England at common law. In the case of land, at least, the English courts were reluctant to infer an intention to give trustees a power of sale, since land was not ordinarily dealt with as a subject of commerce, passing freely from hand to hand, but was rather handed down in the family from generation to generation whenever possible.

In England at common law the inference was that the trustee had no power to sell land unless it could be affirmatively determined from the language of the trust instrument as interpreted in the light of all the circumstances that the settlor intended to confer such a power. It is fair to say that in the United States today the inference is that the trustee has a power to sell land unless it appears from the language of the trust instrument as interpreted in the light of all the circumstances that the settlor intended that the land should be retained in the trust." 2 Scott, Trusts, p. 1022, sec. 190. We hold, therefore, that the will contains an implied discretionary power in the trustee to sell the realty, as well as the personalty, of the trust estate.

Though the land or the personal property may thus be alienated by the trustee, of course the proceeds of the sale are subject to the trust and appellant argues that the residuary clause of the will is void because the trust, itself, runs beyond the permitted period. New York, for instance, has a statute, 40 McKinney's Consol. Laws of New York, Personal Property Law, art. 2, sec. 11, forbidding suspension of the absolute ownership of personal property for more than a designated period, and it may be assumed that the present trust would offend such a statute. Wisconsin, however, has no comparable legislation. Only secs. 230.14 and 230.15, Stats., exist, and they have often been construed to the effect that they prohibit only the suspension of power to alienate, not the suspension of absolute ownership. If the trustee has power to sell, which he may exercise within the time specified by the statute, the trust is not void under our statutes even though the trust in the converted fund is perpetual. *Holmes v. Walter* (1903), 118 Wis. 409, 421, 95 N. W. 380; *Becker v. Chester* (1902), 115 Wis. 90, 115, 91 N. W. 87, mot. denied, 115 Wis. 147, 91 N.W. 650; *Will of Butter* (1941), 239 Wis. 249, 255, 1 N. W. (2d) 87.

Appellant submits that it is undesirable for trusts to endure for longer periods than that set by the statute on alienation and that when, in 1925, Wisconsin took from the above New York statute the words "Limitations of future or contingent interests in personal property are subject to the rules prescribed in relation to future estates in real property" and inserted them in sec. 230.14, we imported the New York law, of which they formed a part, forbidding restraint on the absolute ownership of property. Concerning the desirability of prolonged trusts we express no opinion. That is a matter for the legislature. Concerning the alleged importation into Wisconsin law of the omitted portion of the New York statute we are very sure that the legislature did no such thing. With the whole New York statute before it, the fact that the Wisconsin legislature left out the part concerning suspension of ownership argues strongly that our legislature did not want it and, by taking only the sentence quoted, directed Wisconsin courts to apply to future or contingent interests in personal property the prevailing *Wisconsin* rules applicable to such estates in real property. Such rules, as the Wisconsin cases already cited show, do not confine the duration of trusts to any prescribed period.

We conclude then, that a discretionary power of sale is given to the trustee by implication arising from the language of the will and from the circumstances of the case; that the power pertains to the sale of both real and personal property in the trust estate; that because of such power of sale the absolute power of alienation has not been suspended by the provision identified *"Third (4)"* of the will; and that such section is a valid testamentary disposition of both the real and the personal property. The judgment of the learned county court is therefore affirmed in so far as it dealt with personalty and reversed in so far as it dealt with realty.

Other issues of law are treated in the briefs but the decision sustaining *Third (4)* makes it unnecessary to discuss them The briefs of both parties exceeded fifty pages and each has applied according to rule and to sec. 251.264, Stats., for the allowance of costs of printing his entire brief. The questions involved have been difficult and the briefs on each side have been unusually helpful and are no longer than required for the careful analysis of which we have had the benefit. We allow respondent the costs applied for and regret that it is not possible to recognize appellant's assistance to us in like manner. Judgment affirmed as it affects personalty and reversed as it affects realty and cause remanded for further necessary proceedings consistent with the opinion.

IV. RESULTING AND CONSTRUCTIVE TRUSTS

Resulting trusts and constructive trusts are not true trusts, but are equitable and legal remedies invoked by courts to prevent injustice or to provide a justification for directing the transfer of property to the rightful owner or possessor. A resulting trust is essentially a reversionary interest that comes into existence when a regular trust fails or makes an incomplete disposition of the trust property. For example, when a previously operational trust fails for the sudden absence of a qualifying beneficiary (as when the last qualifying beneficiary dies but the trust instrument contains no provision for the termination of the trust), a new *resulting trust* arises automatically. Under the resulting trust, the trustee is required to return the remainder of the trust res to the settlor or to whomever holds the settlor's reversionary interest.

Historically, a special sort of *resulting trust* came into existence when an individual purchased land on behalf of another in his or her own name. (This was usually done to conceal the identity of the true purchaser from the seller.) Since the property was usually titled in the name of the agent-purchaser, the so-called *purchase money resulting trust* prevented the agent from simply keeping the property. When the agent was the spouse or child of the party paying the purchase price (or some other "natural object of the purchaser's bounty), no trust arose. However, this type of resulting trust no longer exists in Wisconsin. (See Wis. Stat. §701.04, below).

A *constructive trust* is a more general equitable remedy that involves the fiction of a court-imposed trust over property that has been obtained through fraud or some other unlawful means (including intentionally killing an ancestor or a devisee.) Under the "terms" of the constructive trust, the holder of the ill-gotten gain is required to return or convey the property immediately to the lawful or more deserving owner. Whether or not to impose a constructive trust is normally a matter left to the court's discretion.

A. PURCHASE MONEY RESULTING TRUSTS

Wis. Stat. 701.04. Purchase money resulting trusts abolished.

(1) If title to property is transferred to one person and all or part of the purchase price is furnished by another, the latter may not enforce a purchase money resulting trust.

(2) Creditors of the person furnishing all or part of the purchase price may enforce a resulting trust, in proportion to the amount of purchase price furnished, to the extent necessary to satisfy their demands, unless an intent to defraud creditors is disproved.

(3) Nothing in this section shall affect the right to enforce a valid express trust or to establish a constructive trust based on fraud, undue influence, breach of confidential relationship or other appropriate grounds.

Masino v. Sechrest

Supreme Court of Wisconsin
268 Wis. 101, 66 N.W.2d (1954)

Fairchild, C. J. The questions to be determined on this appeal relate to the sufficiency of the complaint and the admissibility of evidence. Does the complaint state a cause of action, and did the circuit court commit error in sustaining the respondents' demurrer to the offer of evidence by appellants and in granting the respondents' motion to dismiss the complaint?

Appellants assert the existence of a "constructive trust" favorable to them, arising out of the circumstances under which respondents acquired and now hold the legal title to the real estate involved; and contend that such a trust is raised in equity in respect of property which has been acquired originally without fraud and where it is against equity that it should be retained by the persons holding it. The respondents stand on the proposition that where one purchases and pays for land and places the legal title in the name of another by having the seller convey to such other, the title to the land vests in the grantee free from any trust, although he took with the understanding that he was to convey to the purchaser's children.

The trial court bases its decision on sec. 231.07, Stats., which provides that:

"When a grant for a valuable consideration shall be made to one person and the consideration therefor shall be paid by another, no use or trust shall result in favor of the person by whom such payment is made; but the title shall vest in the person named as the alienee in such conveyance, . . ."

The trial court, in its decision, finds in effect that because it is alleged in the complaint that the mother, Rose Masino, paid the purchase price, and that at her direction the deed was put in the name of the eldest daughter and her husband without consideration, a resulting trust is pleaded; and that since resulting trusts are abolished by sec. 231.07, Stats., plaintiffs have no cause of action. It is true that a purchase-money resulting trust arises at common law where one person pays the purchase price for land but has it deeded to another who gives him no consideration. Such a resulting trust arises in favor of the payor merely because he has paid the purchase price. An inference is made by law from the character of the transaction that the payor did not intend that the grantee should have the beneficial interest in the land. The result is that the beneficial interest springs back to the purchaser of the land. If the grantee refuses to reconvey, the purchaser may plead a resulting trust, in which case he has to show merely that he made the payment, in order to benefit from the inference implied by law; and it is for the grantee to prove that there was a gift meant if he wishes to rebut the presumption of law. Purchase-money resulting trusts were first abolished in this country by statute in the state of New York; and subsequently some other states have enacted similar statutes derived from the New York statute.

In a New York case, Foreman v. Foreman, 251 N.Y. 237, 241, 167 N. E. 428, Judge Cardozo said: "The statute has put an end to the rule at common law that where a grant is made to one for a consideration paid by another a trust results inevitably and always, by force merely of the payment, irrespective of intention (Garfield v. Hatmaker, 15 N. Y. 475, 477; Scott, Resulting Trusts in Purchase of Land, 40 Harv. L. Rev. 675). The conveyance is operative according to its terms if nothing else is proved. The statute has no effect, however, on trusts constructively imposed as a consequence not of payment alone, but of payment in combination with other or extrinsic equities. As to this, the decisions are uniform and ample. 'It is only the common-law trust for the benefit of an individual from whom the consideration for a grant issues, and resulting from the fact of payment of the consideration, and having no other foundation, that the statute abolishes' (Carr v. Carr, 52 N. Y. 251, 260; Gage v. Gage, 83 Hun, 362; Jeremiah v. Pitcher, supra [26 App. Div. 402; affd., 163 N. Y. 574]; Leary v. Corvin, supra [181 N. Y. 222, 229]; Wood v. Rabe, supra [96 N. Y. 414]; Scott, Conveyances upon Trusts not Properly Declared, 37 Harv. L. Rev. 653, 661, 669; Costigan, The Classification of Trusts, 27 Harv. L. Rev. 437; cf. as to resulting trusts, Perry on Trusts, sec. 124, and as to constructive trusts, the same author, sec. 166). "Enough and ample there is here to put the case for the plaintiff in the field uncovered by the statute. His equity does not grow out of payment and nothing more. It is reinforced by words of promise, by the relation of man and wife, and by unequivocal acts of confirmation and performance. In such circumstances, the plastic remedies of the chancery are moulded to the needs of justice."

However, a resulting trust can arise only in favor of the payor by reason of his payment; it cannot arise in favor of a third-party beneficiary. And appellants here do not contend that a trust results in favor of Rose Masino (or her heirs), the person who allegedly paid the purchase price. Appellants make the following allegations (in part):

". . . following her [the mother's] death the said defendants in violation of the trust and confidence placed in them and with intent of unjustly enriching themselves, fraudulently claimed the property herein described to be their own to the prejudice of the plaintiffs herein and contrary to the oral trust imposed by the said Rose Masino prior to her death. "That said actions of the said defendants in claiming title to said properties are contrary to the intentions of the deceased and the understanding of said defendants and is such an abuse of the confidence reposed in them by the deceased as to constitute unconscionable conduct which in equity and good conscience said defendants should not be permitted or allowed to enjoy; that said defendants should not be permitted to claim the purchase of such lands to their unjust enrichment where another has paid valuable consideration therefor and where said defendants have violated the confidence and duty to perform the trust reposed in them by the said deceased; that such conduct is inconsistent with the character of a purchaser."

It is clear that what is being pleaded here is a constructive trust based on unjust enrichment. In the instant case, the statute of frauds prevents the enforcing of an express trust showing the affirmative intent of the parties because there was no written manifestation of the alleged agreement. From its origin one of the most important uses of the trust has been for the purpose of settling family affairs. Such agreements were often in parol, and where an unenforceable agreement in parol is attended by certain special circumstances, equity resorts to the remedial device of a constructive trust to accomplish justice. The underlying principle of a constructive trust is the equitable prevention of unjust enrichment which arises from fraud or the abuse of a confidential relationship. ". . . a constructive trust arises if, but only if, it is shown that the transferee was guilty of fraud or the abuse of a confidential relationship, or if the transfer was made in contemplation of death, or is in the nature of a mortgage." 3 Scott, Trusts, p. 2358, sec. 481.3. See Krzysko v. Gaudynski, 207 Wis. 608, 242 N. W. 186; Schofield v. Rideout, 233 Wis. 550, 290 N. W. 155. In Popp v. Froelich, 223 Wis. 168, 172, 270 N. W. 38, Mr. Justice Nelson, in discussing a transfer of absolute title to land, said: "If Ernest Froelich claimed absolute title to the lands, equity no doubt would decree a trust." Among other references, he quoted from Restatement, 1 Trusts, p. 140, sec. 45:

"(1) Where the owner of an interest in land transfers it inter vivos to another in trust for a third person, but no memorandum properly evidencing the intention to create a trust is signed, and the transferee refuses to perform the trust, the transferee holds the interest upon a constructive trust for the third person, if, but only if,

"(a) the transferee by fraud, duress, or undue influence prevented the transferor from creating an enforceable interest in the third person, or

"(b) the transferee at the time of the transfer was in a confidential relation to the transferor, or

"(c) the transfer was made by the transferor in contemplation of death."

The statutes applicable to the instant case are sec. 240.06 and sec. 240.07 of the Wisconsin statutes. Sec. 240.06 provides:

"No estate or interest in lands, other than leases for a term not exceeding one year, nor any trust or power over or concerning lands or in any manner relating thereto shall be created, granted, assigned, surrendered, or declared unless by act or operation of law or by deed or conveyance in writing, subscribed by the party creating, granting, assigning, surrendering, or declaring the same or by his lawful agent thereunto authorized by writing."

Sec. 240.07, Stats., states the exceptions to that ruling:

"Section 240.06 shall not be construed to affect in any manner the power of a testator in the disposition of his real estate by a last will and testament nor to prevent any trust from arising or being extinguished by implication or operation of law."

Under the allegations, the daughter, Mary Masino Sechrest, and her husband knew of the mother's wishes and accepted the deed with the understanding that the mother desired to "maintain her property for the benefit of her children." When the mother placed the deed in her eldest daughter's name and that of her husband, she was relying upon more than a bare parol promise made by a grantee to a grantor. The confidence which the mother reposed in her eldest daughter had its origin in their relationship, and that relation was a moving cause in influencing the mother to place the deed in the names of the eldest daughter and her husband for the benefit of all of her children.

It is alleged that the daughter admitted that the property herein referred to was the property of the deceased, Rose Masino; and that there was no attempt on the part of Mary Sechrest or her husband to claim said property prior to the death of the mother. However, after her mother's death, Mary Sechrest, and her husband, repudiated the oral understanding under which they received the deed, and claimed the property as their own. Where, in a settlement of family affairs, then, the mother deeded land to her eldest daughter and her husband to be held in trust for "the benefit of her children" under an oral understanding, and where the trustees repudiate the agreement, the children, as beneficiaries, upon the mother's death, have an equitable claim on the trust res which they may realize through equity's provision for imposing a constructive trust based on unjust enrichment.

Equity regards as wrongful acts to which it attributes the same or similar effects as those which follow from actual fraud, and grants the same or similar relief as is granted in cases of real fraud. Even if Mary Sechrest and her husband did not actively procure the conveyance, under the allegations their fraud consisted in their holding the property contrary to the terms of the agreement, and they were guilty of constructive fraud upon the mother, Rose Masino, and of tort upon the other children of the family who were the intended beneficiaries. In 3 Scott, Trusts, p. 2364, sec. 486, it is said that "Where B obtained the land by a promise which he never intended to perform, it is held that he holds the land upon a constructive trust for C. The same result has been reached in many cases where B was at the time of the conveyance in . . . confidential relation to A." In the same text, vol. 1, p. 268, sec. 45.2, it is also said:

"Where A transfers land to B who orally agrees to hold it in trust for or to convey it to C, and at the time of the transfer B is in a confidential relation to A, it is held that B can be compelled to hold the land upon a constructive trust for C. . . . Where, however, B did not obtain the property by undue influence, and is guilty only of an abuse of the confidential relation in subsequently failing to perform his promise, it is more difficult to say that he thereby commits a tort to C. Undoubtedly he should not be permitted to keep the land, since he would be unjustly enriched if he were permitted to keep it; but it is arguable that he should hold it upon a constructive trust for A rather than for C. It is held, however, without much consideration for the niceties of the question involved, that C rather than A is entitled to the land." (Emphasis supplied.)

Since a constructive trust, which is based on unjust enrichment, is construed from the circumstances surrounding the transaction, independent of the intention of the parties, parol evidence of the agreement is admissible, not to enforce the agreement, but to prove that the grantee has been unjustly enriched by his repudiation of the agreement. The proving of the contract is incidental. The purpose of the parol evidence is to prove unjust enrichment, and in the instant case, the unjust enrichment is alleged to have arisen from a breach of an agreement arising out of a confidential relationship. "It is not the promise only, nor the breach only, but unjust enrichment under cover of the relation of confidence, which puts the court in motion." Sinclair v. Purdy, 235 N. Y. 245, 253, 139 N. E. 255.

The trial court recognizes the element of confidential relationship existing between Mary Masino Sechrest, the grantee, and Rose Masino, the grantor, where he says: "It [the deed] was placed in their names by the direction or request of Rose Masino, because of the trust and confidence she reposed in them." He then adds: "Such confidential . . . relationship is not essential to establish a constructive trust. The essential element is that the transfer must be induced by fraud, duress, or undue influence." But confidential relationship as an element of fraud is one of the grounds for raising a constructive trust based on unjust enrichment; and it is present in the allegations of this case.

With reference to the importance of confidential relation, and because our law has followed enactments of New York, we call attention to a ruling made by the New York court of appeals in Goldsmith v. Goldsmith, 145 N. Y. 313, 316, 39 N. E. 1067, in affirming a lower court ruling where a mother conveyed to her son her house and lot, he giving no other consideration than a verbal promise to hold the premises for the benefit of the mother and the other children and to give the latter shares therein. The court said: "It is quite evident that this was an arrangement founded upon the relation of mother and son, and brothers and sisters, involving the trust and confidence growing out of that relation, and intended as a settlement of the family affairs."

We are of the opinion that the complaint states facts sufficient to constitute a cause of action for relief in equity under a constructive trust, and that the plaintiffs are entitled to their day in court.

B. CONSTRUCTIVE TRUSTS

Hendricks v. McCormick Memorial Home

Supreme Court of Wisconsin
204 Wis. 277, 234 N.W. 886 (1931)

This action was commenced by plaintiff, Marie Hendricks, on the 29th day of May, 1929, against the defendants, for the purpose of having a resulting trust decreed in her favor in certain lands, constituting the homestead of the plaintiff, because she herself had paid the purchase money for the land, and the deed thereto had been taken in the name of her husband without her knowledge and consent; and for the further purpose of having the absolute title to said lands declared to be in the plaintiff. From a judgment dated the 1st day of March, 1930, dismissing the plaintiff's complaint on its merits, the plaintiff appealed.

The plaintiff is the widow and sole surviving heir at law of Matthew Hendricks, who died in September, 1928. The defendant McCormick Memorial Home is a Wisconsin corporation operating a home for the aged in Brown County, Wisconsin, and the defendant Joseph Van Bogart is the executor of the last will and testament of Matthew Hendricks, deceased.

The plaintiff and her deceased husband, Matthew Hendricks, intermarried in the year 1889 or early in 1890. At the time of the marriage both plaintiff and her husband were about fifty years of age. The plaintiff had certain property constituting her separate estate but her husband had no property. He had some indebtedness which the plaintiff paid. Early in 1890 opportunity was afforded to buy a certain forty-acre tract from the Brocktrup heirs, some of whom were minors. This forty was located near to the plaintiff's land. The forty was heirship property and was sold at public auction under the supervision of the county court. At the sale Matthew Hendricks was the highest bidder. The plaintiff was not present at the sale. Thereafter she met Henry Brocktrup at Chilton and paid to him the down payment on the deal amounting to something over a thousand dollars. At the time she told Mr. Brocktrup, who was attending to the sale of the forty for both the adult and minor heirs, that she wanted the deeds in her name.

Sometime thereafter the deeds were executed and delivered to Matthew Hendricks, he being named as sole grantee in the deeds. At the time the deeds were delivered the plaintiff was not present and had no knowledge that the deeds did not run to her. At the time of the delivery of the deeds to Matthew Hendricks he executed and delivered a purchase-price mortgage for $1,300 which was signed only by him. This mortgage was paid by the plaintiff during the next three or four years from her separate estate. At the time the deeds were delivered to Matthew Hendricks she did not consent to the title being taken in his name. More than two years after these deeds were delivered the plaintiff discovered that they did not run to her.

Upon discovering that the title was taken in the name of her husband she wanted the title put in her name but seems not to have been especially concerned since she fully realized that everything would be hers in case of his death because there were no children and she was his sole heir at law. Shortly after the purchase of the forty the plaintiff and her husband moved on to it and continued to occupy it as their homestead. The plaintiff did the major portion of the farm work and at all times actively managed the farm, due to the fact that her husband's health was not very good. In 1924 the plaintiff and her husband entered the defendant's home for the aged under an agreement to pay $50 per month for the board and accommodations given. Sometime thereafter the monthly rate per person was raised to $30, and the plaintiff, becoming dissatisfied, returned to her home. The husband, however, continued to stay at the Home for something over three years, when he too left the Home and returned to reside with the plaintiff.

After the plaintiff left the Home and while Matthew Hendricks was still residing there, he made a will which bequeathed all of his personal property to the plaintiff and devised his real estate to her for life and, after her death, to defendant McCormick Memorial Home. At the time the will was made Matthew Hendricks had no personal property and no real estate other than the forty acres purchased by the plaintiff. The reason for devising his property to the McCormick Memorial Home, as expressed in his will, was that he had lived at said Home for several years and had not had sufficient funds to pay the Home what was justly due it for board, lodging, care, and attention.

Sometime after making this will, as before stated, Hendricks returned to live with the plaintiff. The plaintiff had no knowledge that he had made a will and did not learn of it until after Matthew Hendricks' death. At all times after the purchase of the forty in question it was the homestead of the plaintiff and was continually occupied by her with the exception of the time when she resided at the Home. At the trial the plaintiff was not permitted to testify as to conversations with her deceased husband relating to the land in question.

The court's findings, briefly stated, are as follows: That the plaintiff was not present at the time of the auction sale of said land nor at the time and place of the execution of the deeds; that she provided the initial payment of $1,050 upon the purchase price of said land from her separate estate which she paid to Henry Brocktrup personally; that at the time of the payment she stated to Henry Brocktrup that she wanted the deed of the property to be put in her name because the land was being paid for with her money; that the balance of the purchase price covered by the mortgage was paid by the plaintiff out of the proceeds of her other land and out of her separate estate; that at the time of the delivery of the deeds the plaintiff was not present; and that Matthew Hendricks was named as grantee in the deeds without her knowledge and consent.

The court further found that more than two years after the purchase of the land the plaintiff learned that the deeds to the lands named her husband as sole grantee and that after obtaining such knowledge she took no steps to procure a transfer or conveyance of said land to herself from her husband or to have the deeds corrected; that the conduct of the plaintiff in failing to take steps to procure a transfer of the land to her constituted an acquiescence in the situation and in the state of the title in her husband, and that she was guilty of laches which barred her equitable rights. The court found as a conclusion of law "that no resulting trust exists in favor of the plaintiff to the lands described in said complaint." From a judgment in favor of the defendant the plaintiff appealed.

NELSON, J. The plaintiff contends that the facts found by the trial court lead to the inevitable conclusion that a resulting trust in favor of the plaintiff was thereby created, and that under the circumstances proven she is not precluded from asserting her rights under such trust even though many years have elapsed since said trust was created. The defendants contend that the plaintiff has, by long acquiescence and by her laches, lost the right to enforce such trust.

Upon the record and the contentions of counsel, it appears that but two questions must be determined in order to dispose of this appeal: (1) Under the circumstances found by the court and set forth in the statement of facts, was a resulting trust created in favor of the plaintiff? (2) If such a trust was created, has the plaintiff, by acquiescence or laches, lost the right to enforce such trust and to have the title to the land in question vested in her? The court found that the grant from the Brocktrup heirs was made to Matthew Hendricks; that the total consideration therefor was paid by the plaintiff; and that Matthew Hendricks took title to the land in his own name without the knowledge or consent of the plaintiff.

That a resulting trust was created seems too plain for controversy. Under our statutes and decisions there is no doubt that the facts found by the court admit of no conclusion other than that a resulting trust was created in favor of the plaintiff which she can now enforce unless she is excluded from such relief by the statute of limitations or by her laches and acquiescence. Our statutes relating to resulting trusts are secs. 231.07, 231.08, and 231.09. Sec. 231.07 provides that "when a grant for a valuable consideration shall be made to one person and the consideration therefor shall be paid by another, no use or trust shall result in favor of the person by whom such payment is made; but the title shall vest in the person named as the alienee in such conveyance," subject only to the rights of creditors as provided in sec. 231.08.

Sec. 231.09, however, provides as follows: "Section 231.07 shall not extend to cases where the alienee named in the conveyance shall have taken the same as an absolute conveyance in his own name, without the knowledge or consent of the person paying the consideration, or when such alienee, in violation of some trust, shall have purchased the land so conveyed with money belonging to another person."

It clearly appears that sec. 231.09 is applicable to this controversy. Under these statutes a resulting trust is created when (1) a grant for a valuable consideration is made to one person, (2) the consideration is paid by another, and (3) the alienee named in the conveyance has taken the same as an absolute conveyance in his own name without the knowledge or consent of the person paying the consideration. All of the facts necessary to the creation of a trust under sec. 231.09 were clearly and specifically found by the trial court. The facts as found by the court impel the conclusion that a trust resulted in favor of the plaintiff. The case of Fawcett v. Fawcett, 85 Wis. 332, 55 N.W. 405, in which Mr. Chief Justice LYON wrote the opinion, is strikingly similar to the present case. In that case it was held that a resulting trust was created and that the wife was not barred by any statute of limitations or by laches. The holding in the Fawcett Case has never been overruled and is controlling in this case. The Fawcett Case is absolute authority for the proposition that when the elements required by the Wisconsin Statutes concur, a resulting trust is created.

Cases like Skinner v. James, 69 Wis. 605, 35 N.W. 37, and Friedrich v. Huth, 155 Wis. 196, 144 N.W. 202, are clearly distinguishable. In the Skinner Case both the husband and wife were present when the deed, naming the husband as grantee, was delivered; and the wife knew that the deed was executed to her husband. It was held in that case that a resulting trust was not created under the statute because "the deed was taken in the name of the husband with the knowledge and consent of the wife and in her presence." In the Friedrich Case it was held that no resulting trust was created in favor of the deceased wife because when the deed of the real estate in question was executed and delivered the deceased wife was present and knew that her husband and herself were named as grantees therein and either expressly or tacitly consented to that arrangement.

Has the plaintiff, by acquiescence or laches, lost the right to enforce the trust created?

It was held in Fawcett v. Fawcett, supra, page 337, that the statute of limitations does not run against a resulting trust until after the trust has been effectually repudiated. The law laid down in that case has not been overruled and we see no reason for overruling it at this time. The question seems to have received most careful consideration by the court and by the learned Chief Justice who wrote the opinion. We hold that, under the facts as found, no statute of limitations bars the enforcement of the plaintiff's rights.

The court below found that the plaintiff was guilty of such laches that she cannot now be heard to complain or to demand equitable relief on a claim which must be pronounced stale. In so finding and concluding we think the court erred. We are inclined to believe that the court lost sight of the controlling importance of the following undisputed circumstances: The marriage of the plaintiff to Hendricks when both were past middle life; the plaintiff owned all of the property at that time; the deceased had no separate estate; the plaintiff was the active manager of the farm and performed most of the work thereon; the deceased's health was not good; the plaintiff and her husband were rather simple folk; the plaintiff continually occupied the forty as her homestead and exercised rather controlling dominion over it; the husband never asserted any interest in or claim to the forty hostile to the plaintiff's ownership. The plaintiff was not permitted to testify to conversations with or declarations by her deceased husband relating to the property, but a number of witnesses were produced who testified to repeated declarations by the deceased to the effect that he recognized the fact that the plaintiff had worked like a slave, was entitled to everything and would get everything upon his death.

These statements and declarations made to the several witnesses were not relevant to the question whether a resulting trust was created, but this testimony, it seems to us, did have a strong bearing on the question of plaintiff's acquiescence and laches. Certainly there was little reason for the plaintiff taking steps to have the property conveyed to her. Each was the sole heir of the other. His health was such that the plaintiff had every reason to believe that she would survive him. It is quite apparent that the plaintiff had no surplus funds to waste needlessly in litigation with her husband. Although many years elapsed after plaintiff obtained knowledge that the deed was taken in her husband's name, we do not think, under the circumstances of this case, that laches should be imputed to the plaintiff to defeat her rights under this trust.

Under the doctrine of the Fawcett Case, which seems to be quite in accord with the general rule, laches may be found or imputed much more easily in transactions between persons who are not husband and wife. Courts go a long way in refusing to find laches on the part of the wife in matters involving her husband, to the end that the peace and comfort of the family may not be endangered. As was said in the Fawcett Case, page 336, "under these circumstances it should not be held that she ought to have endangered the peace and comfort of the family--perhaps the very existence of their home--by engaging in a lawsuit with her husband over the title to the land in question, and that her right thereto is defeated because she did not do so. Courts of equity do not impute laches by any iron rule, but allow circumstances to govern their decision in every case."

We have given careful consideration to the findings of the court as to acquiescence and laches with the result that we are of the opinion that the court erred, under the circumstances of this case, in finding that the plaintiff acquiesced in the state of the title in her husband and lost the right to enforce the resulting trust by her delay and laches. The defendant McCormick Memorial Home has no rights or equities as beneficiary that are greater than were those of Matthew Hendricks at the time of his death. For the reasons stated the judgment of the circuit court for Calumet county must be reversed, with directions to enter judgment in favor of the plaintiff decreeing (1) the existence of said resulting trust, (2) the absolute title to the premises in question in the plaintiff Marie Hendricks, and (3) the removal of any cloud upon her title which may exist by virtue of the admission to probate of the last will and testament of Matthew

Hendricks, deceased. Judgment reversed, with directions for judgment as stated in the opinion.

C. ORAL TRUSTS AND OTHER SECRET TRUSTS

In re Estate of Liginger

Supreme Court of Wisconsin
14 Wis. 2d 577, 111 N.W. 2d 407 (1961)

Eleanor Liginger, the testatrix, executed her will June 18, 1956. She died on February 20, 1957, at the age of fifty-eight years. Edna Baker, sister of the deceased, petitioned for construction of the residuary clause of the testatrix's last will and testament and for determination that the residuary clause of the will be declared void and for a distribution of the residue according to law based upon the fact that there is no valid disposition of the testatrix's residuary estate under the terms of the will.

The trial court in the judgment determined that the testatrix intended to, and did, devise and bequeath the residue and remainder of her estate to her executor, John C. McBride, absolutely, he having the sole discretion to pay the sums in his hands to the person or persons previously indicated to him by the testatrix. The appeal is from the order, decision, and judgment construing the residuary clause of the testatrix's will.

Dieterich, J. The sole issue is whether, under the circumstances of this case, the executor takes the residue personally or in his official capacity only.

The first 10 divisions of the will bequeathed 10 specific legacies. The Eleventh division or paragraph of the testatrix's last will and testament contains the following residuary clause:

"Eleventh: I give and bequeath to my executor and trustee hereinafter named, $250 for the purpose of securing Masses for the repose of my soul and that of my dear husband.

"After having paid the inheritance and transfer tax in connection with the above bequests I give, devise, and bequeath the rest, residue and remainder of my estate to my executor.

"My executor shall pay the sums in his hands in his sole discretion to the person or persons which I have previously indicated to him.

"I nominate and appoint as executor of this my last will and testament, John C. McBride, and I direct that no bond be required of him.

"My executor is authorized to do and perform any act deemed by him to be for the best interest of the estate without any limitation whatsoever. I give my executor and trustee the broadest powers . . ."

The executor, John C. McBride, sometimes referred to in the will as executor and trustee, is an attorney. The testimony reveals that he is the scrivener of the will, was present when it was executed, and that he had received oral instructions from the testatrix relating to disposition of the residue.

The pertinent testimony of John C. McBride relating to the residue of the estate is as follows:

"Q. In other words, is it your contention that the directions as to distribution were given to you orally? A. Of what?

"Q. Court: Other than as specifically stated in the will? . . . A. Yes.

"Q. So then the will did not put in writing every specific direction that Mrs. Liginger indicated, is that right? A. Everyone that she indicated specifically is in there.

"Q. And aside from that, you have some general directions that are not included in the will? A. Yes.

"Q. The two witnesses who signed as witnesses to the will knew nothing about those oral directions, did they? A. No, they were just witnesses to the will. . . .

"Court: Mr. McBride, have you any argument or anything to present to the court?

"Mr. McBride: I have nothing to present to the court, Your Honor, excepting that I know full well what is to be done with these funds."

The final account filed February 2, 1960, with the register of probate in Milwaukee county discloses that from the estate there was available for distribution the sum of $12,944.67. John C. McBride is listed therein as a stranger and beneficiary entitled to the amount of $9,099.67. Thus, the scrivener and executor of the will, an attorney and no relative of the deceased, is the beneficiary of approximately 70 per cent of the estate.

If all the language of paragraph Eleventh of the will, relating to the disposition of the residue, is read together, it indicates a trust; the executor to be a conduit through which the residue is to flow to the person or persons previously indicated to the executor by the testatrix. That indication, according to the testimony, was oral. Testimony to establish what that indication was cannot be admitted, since there would be little security in the right to transfer property by testamentary devise or bequest if the meaning of the will could be changed by the parol declarations of the testator to scriveners or witnesses. Estate of Pierce (1922), 177 Wis. 104, 188 N. W. 78, and Will of Tousey (1951), 260 Wis. 150, 50 N. W. (2d) 454. The trust then fails for lack of a beneficiary.

The pertinent language of the will, "I give . . . the . . . residue . . . of my estate to my executor," does not mention the executor by name, but by title. It is possible that the executor named in the will may not be the executor in the event that the provisions of sec. 310.16, Stats., 1 applied. Then a question arises as to who would receive the residue if a different executor had been appointed by the court.

The precatory words used in this will, "my executor shall pay," are directed to the executor and imperative in nature. Precatory words directed to an executor indicate a trust while the same words to a devisee do not. Newhall v. McGill (1949), 69 Ariz. 259, 212 Pac. (2d) 764. The executor under the facts in the instant case receives in his official capacity and not personally. See Anno. 104 A. L. R. 121, 126. Gross v. Moore (1893), 75 N.Y. 412, 22 N. Y. Supp. 1019 (affirmed on opinion below in 1894, 141 N.Y. 559, 36 N.E. 343); Reynolds v. Reynolds (1918), 224 N. Y. 429, 121 N. E. 61; Olliffe v. Wells (1881), 130 Mass. 221.

The law does not favor the vesting of bequests of property to the executor in his official capacity where it will result in a partial intestacy. This does not overcome the weightier reasoning that unless the will clearly expresses an intention for the bequest to vest in the executor personally such a bequest is a nullity. Anno. 104 A. L. R. 114, 118, citing Thomas v. Anderson (8th Cir. 1917), 245 Fed. 642. It therefore necessarily follows that after the distribution of the respective legacies under the provisions of the will, the residue descends intestate.

The order and judgment assigning the residue of the estate to John C. McBride is reversed, and cause remanded for further proceedings consistent with this opinion.

CHAPTER 8.
POWERS AND DUTIES OF TRUSTEES

I. POWERS OF TRUSTEES

A. TRADITIONAL POWERS

The settlor has the power to grant or withhold powers to the trustee as he or she sees fit. When the trust instrument is silent on a question of trustee power, the common law of trusts recognized that the trustee implicitly possessed the scope of authority and all powers necessary and appropriate for the carrying out of the trusts' purposes. Today, Wis. Stat. §701.19 defines the ordinary limits of trustee authority.

In re Boyle's Estate

Supreme Court of Wisconsin
232 Wis. 631, 288 N.W. 257 (1939)

Fairchild, J. The petitioner seeks to modify the provisions in a will made by the testatrix for the distribution of income from two certain testamentary trusts. He is seeking an augmentation of income so that he can pay debts owed by him to others than the estate and meet obligations, which will be possible if a variation of the terms of the trust as prayed for is made. This cannot, however, be allowed. To contravene the will as prayed for would be making a disposition of property contrary to the provisions of the instrument creating the trusts; and would amount to a gift over to him of property of others, he being so situated by the terms of the will with regard to title and succession that the property not only does not belong to him but he will never be entitled to it.

A right of the petitioner to any income from the two testamentary trusts arises as it must from the provisions of the will. For while in addition to the paragraph from the will quoted in the statement of facts there is, among others, a provision that one half of the net income remaining in the hands of the trustees is to be paid over to Francis H.

Boyle, this is subject to the clause in which the testatrix requires that the notes, if not paid before her death or during the administration of the estate while probate proceedings are pending, are to be paid within five years after the trusts are set up. The court must exercise its power to prevent enlarging or modifying the terms of the trusts and preserve the corpus of the trusts. Will of Caswell, 197 Wis. 327, 222 N.W. 235; Upham v. Plankinton, 152 Wis. 275, 140 N.W. 5; Will of Rice, 150 Wis. 401, 136 N.W. 956, 137 N.W. 778; and sec. 231.21, Stats.

Little room for doubt about the purpose and the method to be used to carry out her intention can exist in the face of the plain language of the will. At the conclusion of article fourteen of the will she says it is her intention that the money owed by Francis be paid. She provides further that when paid it is to become part of the corpus of the estate. Whatever consideration may have been in the mind of the testatrix when drawing her will and codicil, it appears that the inheritance of the grandchildren and the possible inheritance of others was associated with the bequest to Francis H. Boyle.

The conserving of the estate was made of primal importance. While the provision for a sufficient income to Francis was desired, at the same time the possibility of extravagance on the part of any member of the family endangering the strength of the fortune was given consideration and was guarded against. She created a plan under which her son was to have a suitably furnished residence, a position which would pay him $200 per month, and the benefit of an income from a trust independent of and separate from the testamentary trusts. The proportion of income from all these trusts which goes to him is only during his life. The residue, with minor exceptions, she wills and directs to be added to the corpus of her estate and this direction is mandatory. The "living trust" afforded a sufficient income as she viewed it to maintain his family. The form and manner of the creation of the restrictions and limitations point to a desire for a plan under which former extravagances could no longer be indulged, and a plan under which by installments a large indebtedness of Francis to his mother's estate would gradually be paid, thus saving the estate from loss of the principal of the loans at least. The trustees cannot lawfully accede to the demands of the petitioner. There is to be no compromise of his indebtedness, and in the will the testatrix fixes the terms of repayment and directs the trustees to withhold enough of respondent's income from the testamentary trusts to pay the notes within five years.

The finding that it was her intention to provide for this particular beneficiary overlooks the specific requirement that out of the income which may be said to be his, he is to be obligated to reimburse the estate for moneys loaned him, and that this when collected is to take its place in property which eventually goes under the will to others than himself and is against the great weight and clear preponderance of the evidence.

He has but part of the income over and above enough to discharge his obligations on the notes, and as suggested in appellant's brief, the granting of the relief prayed for by the petitioner would violate "a decidedly fundamental part of testatrix's will." It would permit him to remain indebted to the estate while paying other creditors. In the event that petitioner were to receive the payments directed by the county court and nothing be paid upon his notes, should he die before more prosperous times with the notes unpaid, the very plan of securing the payment would be destroyed.

There is no occasion here for resorting to judicial construction. The evidence indicates the occasion for the testatrix's scheme as outlined in her will and codicil. She provided that in the event her son survived her a certain course was to be followed. After the payment of certain amounts, one half of the net income was to be for the benefit of her son during his lifetime. The other one half of the net income was to be added to the corpus of the estate. After the death of the son, assuming living issue, the trusts continue for a period of twenty-one years, or so long during said period as any issue of him survives, and the trustees are to disburse the income by applying it to the maintenance, support, benefit, care, and comfort of each of his children. When the first one of such children reaches the age of twenty-five years, and so becomes entitled to an equal portion of said net income with the others, the portion thereof to which those of said children who are still under the age of twenty-five years, in excess of the annual allowance, and the educational allowance, if any, shall accumulate to the credit of such children under the age of twenty-five years, respectively, and be held by the trustees until said children, respectively, reach the age of twenty-five years; at which time such income accruals, with accumulated interest thereon, shall be turned over to each child.

The testatrix planned building up an estate which eventually will go to her son's children, and in the event of their failure to survive, to others named in the will, a sister of testatrix, her brother, and a nephew of her deceased husband or their issue free and clear of any trust and in equal shares. The facts on which the argument in favor of the order granted by the county court is made do not raise a legal basis to support the respondent's contention.

A purpose of the testatrix to exclude the petitioner's wife, so far as possible, from the enjoyment of the money may or may not have prompted the provisions which now appear to threaten the reduction of the amount available to the wife for support of the children. The testatrix provided a home in which the petitioner and his family may live free from expense so far as taxes and upkeep are concerned. This present pressure of circumstances may result in compelling members of the now scattered family to readjust their plans and live in a proximity to each other that will enable both parents to have some association with their children, and thus approach a satisfying of the testatrix's evident desire that her son have a life approaching to normal.

The petitioner asks that if the actual terms of the trusts cannot be contravened by the court, then the court provide by its judgment that the requirements of the petitioner be taken care of by extending the five-year period within which petitioner's notes are to be paid. This again would be an invasion of the rights of others. Anticipation of benefits may possibly occur under some circumstances without contravening the express provisions of the trust instrument, but this cannot be where the one seeking the advantage has no interest against which the advance can be balanced.

Sec. 231.21 (1), Stats., provides that when the trust is expressed in the instrument creating it, every act of the trustee in contravention of the trust shall be absolutely void. The testatrix might have eliminated the petitioner entirely from sharing in any way in her estate. She chose to restrict him within certain limits for reasons which seemed to her sufficient, and within those limits the trustees must deal with him. The studied purpose of building up the corpus of the estate, which under no circumstances can ever reach the petitioner, would to a considerable extent be circumvented if the trustees were permitted to forego the obligation of collecting as much as possible of the indebtedness of petitioner to his mother's estate directly assigned to corpus which eventually goes to others. The petitioner cannot possibly place himself within reach of the provisions of sec. 231.21 (2), Stats. He has no interest which can be appropriated to him, no interest which can be sold, and nothing that can be used as a security for a loan.

We do not consider a case is presented calling upon the court to decide what the effect of a statute giving the courts power to contravene the terms of a testamentary trust might be. The case is not within the statute as written, and to comply with the requirements of the judgment, property other than petitioner's must be used, and that in any event cannot be sanctioned. Estate of Adams, 216 Wis. 77, 255 N.W. 886. The finding that the testatrix did not have in mind a change in circumstances or the possibility of the falling off of income when she made her will, is not controlling even if there was evidence to support it. There is no one now who can remake the will. It appears, however, that on August 10, 1933, she re-examined her will and in her codicil solemnly declared: "I have at the time of the preparation and execution of this codicil gone over my last will and testament and I herewith express my full satisfaction of the terms and provisions thereof." She was a woman of considerable business experience, and there is some evidence that her gross income had declined somewhat, and we must assume that she was aware that about one third of her estate would be consumed in payment of inheritance and estate taxes and expenses of administration.

The scheme of the testatrix in the preparation of the will and codicil appears and it indicates that, having in mind that her son would be embarrassed financially, she proposed to prevent the depletion of her estate. She therefore excluded him from taking any part of the corpus thereof and by the terms of the trust fixed the income "not to be susceptible of assignment, anticipation, hypothecation, or seizure by legal process." Judgment reversed.

B. STATUTORY POWERS

Wis. Stat. 701.19. Powers of trustees.

(1) POWER TO SELL, MORTGAGE OR LEASE. In the absence of contrary or limiting provisions in the creating instrument, in the court order appointing a trustee or in a subsequent order, a trustee has complete power to sell, mortgage or lease trust property without notice, hearing or order. A trustee has no power to give warranties in a sale, mortgage or lease which are binding on the trustee personally. In this section "sale" includes an option or agreement to transfer for cash or on credit, exchange, partition or settlement of a title dispute; this definition is intended to broaden rather than limit the meaning of "sale". "Mortgage" means any agreement or arrangement in which trust property is used as security.

(2) COURT AUTHORIZATION OF ADMINISTRATIVE ACTION.

(a) In the absence of contrary or limiting provisions in the creating instrument, in any case where it is for the best interests of the trust, on application of the trustee or other interested person, the court may upon notice and hearing authorize or require a trustee to sell, mortgage, lease or otherwise dispose of trust property upon such terms and conditions as the court deems just and proper.

(b) Despite contrary or limiting provisions in the creating instrument, upon application of a trustee or other interested person, a court may upon notice and hearing order the retention, investment, reinvestment, sale, mortgage, lease or other disposition of trust property if the court is satisfied that the original purpose of the settlor cannot be carried out, substantially performed or practically achieved for any reason existing at the inception of the trust or arising from any subsequent change in circumstances and the retention, investment, reinvestment, sale, mortgage, lease or other disposition of the property more nearly approximates the settlors intention.

(c) Unless authorized in the creating instrument, a trustee may not be interested as a purchaser, mortgagee or lessee of trust property unless such purchase, mortgage or lease is made with the written consent of all beneficiaries or with the approval of the court upon notice and hearing.

A representative of a beneficiary, under s. 701.15, may give written consent for such beneficiary.

(d) A trustee may not sell individually owned assets to the trust unless the sale is authorized in the creating instrument, made with the written consent of all beneficiaries or made with the approval of the court upon notice and hearing.

(3) WHEN MANDATORY POWER DEEMED DISCRETIONARY. If a creating instrument expressly or by implication directs a trustee to sell trust property and such property has not been sold for a period of 25 years after the creation of the trust, such direction to the trustee shall be deemed a discretionary power of sale.

(4) CONTINUATION OF BUSINESS BY COURT ORDER.

(am) In the absence of contrary or limiting provisions in the creating instrument, the circuit court may, where it is in the best interests of the trust, order the trustee to continue any business of a deceased settlor. The order may be issued without notice and hearing, in the courts discretion and, in any case, may provide:

1. For conduct of the business solely by the trustee, jointly with one or more of the settlors surviving partners or as a corporation or limited liability company to be formed by the trustee;

2. As between the trust and the trustee, the extent of liability of the trust and the extent of the personal liability of the trustee for obligations incurred in the continuation of the business;

3. As between beneficiaries, the extent to which liabilities incurred in the continuation of the business are to be chargeable solely to a part of the trust property set aside for use in the business or to the trust as a whole; and

4. For the period of time for which the business may be conducted and any other conditions, restrictions, regulations, requirements and authorizations as the court orders.

(e) Nothing in this subsection shall be construed as requiring a trustee to liquidate a business, including a business operated as a closely held corporation, when liquidating the business is not required by the creating instrument or other applicable law.

(4m) CONTINUATION OF BUSINESS BY DIRECTION OF SETTLOR. If the settlor directs retention of a business that is among the trust's assets in the trust document or by other written means, a trustee may retain that business during the settlors lifetime without liability.

(5) FORMATION OF BUSINESS ENTITY. In the absence of contrary or limiting provisions in the creating instrument:

(a) The court may by order authorize a trustee to become a partner under ch. 178 or 179 and transfer trust property to the partnership in return for a partnership interest.

(aL) The court may by order authorize a trustee to become a member of a limited liability company under ch. 183 and transfer trust property to the limited liability company in return for an ownership interest.

(b) The court may by order authorize a trustee to organize a corporation for any purpose permitted by ch. 180, subscribe for shares of such corporation and transfer trust property to such corporation in payment for the shares subscribed.

(c) The court may by order authorize a trustee to form a corporation for any purpose permitted by ch. 181 (d) An order under this subsection may in the courts discretion be issued without notice and hearing.

(6) REGISTRATION OF SECURITIES IN NOMINEE. Unless prohibited in the creating instrument, a trustee may register securities in the name of a nominee.

(7) PROXY VOTING OF STOCK. Unless the creating instrument contains an express prohibition or specifies the manner in which the trustee is to vote stock in a corporation or certificates of beneficial interest in an investment trust, the trustee may vote such stock or certificates by general or limited proxy, with or without power of substitution.

(8) PLATTING LAND. In the absence of contrary or limiting provisions in the creating instrument, the court may by order authorize a trustee to plat land which is part of the trust, either alone or together with other owners of such real estate. In such platting the trustee must comply with the same statutes, ordinances, rules and regulations which apply to a person who is platting the persons own land. The order under this subsection may in the courts discretion be issued without notice and hearing.

(9) JOINT TRUSTEES.

(a) In the absence of contrary or limiting provisions in the creating instrument, any power vested in 3 or more trustees may be exercised by a majority. This paragraph shall not apply to living trusts created prior to July 1, 1971, or to testamentary trusts contained in wills executed or last republished prior to that date.

(b) A trustee who has not joined in exercising a power is not liablc to an affected person for the consequences of the exercise unless the trustee has failed to discharge the trustees duty to participate in the administration of the trust. A dissenting trustee is not liable for the consequences of an act in which the dissenting trustee joins at the direction of the majority of the trustees if the dissenting trustees dissent is expressed in writing to the other trustees at or before the time of the joinder.

(10) RESTRICTION ON EXERCISE OF POWERS.

(a) Except as provided in par. (c), a person may not exercise any of the following powers conferred upon him or her in his or her capacity as trustee:

1. The power to make discretionary distributions of trust principal or income if the distributions are to himself or herself or for the discharge of his or her legal obligations.

2. The power to make discretionary allocations of receipts or expenses as between principal and income if the allocations are in his or her favor.

(b) If a power under par. (a) is conferred upon more than one person as trustee, a person who is not disqualified to act under par. (a) may exercise the power for the benefit of the person who is disqualified to act, unless the creating instrument expressly provides otherwise. A special trustee appointed by a court may exercise a power under par. (a) for the benefit of the disqualified person if no other trustee is qualified to exercise the power.

(c) Paragraph (a) does not apply if any of the following applies:

1. The person is also the settlor of the trust, and the trust may be revoked or amended by the settlor.

2. The terms of the creating instrument specifically limit the scope of the power to expenditures and distributions of income or principal on the basis of an ascertainable standard relating to the persons health, maintenance, support, or education such that the person would not be subject to tax under section 2041 or 2514 of the Internal Revenue Code as a result of having or exercising the power.

3. The person is the spouse, widow, or widower of the settlor of the trust, and a marital deduction has been allowed for federal gift or estate tax purposes with respect to the trust property that is subject to the power.

4. The creating instrument negates the application of par. (a) with respect to the power or indicates that provisions that are similar to par. (a) do not apply.

(d) Section 701.24 (3) governs the applicability of this statute.

(11) PROTECTION OF 3RD PARTIES. With respect to a 3rd person dealing with a trustee or assisting a trustee in the conduct of a transaction, the existence of trust power and its proper exercise by the trustee may be assumed without inquiry. The 3rd person is not bound to inquire whether the trustee has power to act or is properly exercising the power; and a 3rd person, without actual knowledge that the trustee is exceeding the trustees powers or improperly exercising them, is fully protected in dealing with the trustee as if the trustee possessed and properly exercised the powers the trustee purports to exercise. A 3rd person is not bound to assure the proper application of trust property paid or delivered to the trustee.

II. TRUSTEE DUTIES

A. FIDUCIARY DUTIES OF TRUSTEES AND EXECUTORS

As the holders of property for the benefit of others, trustees and personal representatives in probate are treated as fiduciaries and thus owe a higher duty of care to the beneficiaries than a normal marketplace service provider. When there is a breach of fiduciary duty, fiduciaries are personally liable to compensate the trust or the estate for any losses that result. Wisconsin courts have recognized that trustee liability can be waived as a result of a voluntarily negotiated *exculpatory clause*, but such clauses are frowned upon. It is also not clear as to whether duties can be waived completely or if they can be waived by institutional trustees, like bank trust departments. See, for example, *Hammes v. First Nat Bank & Trust Co.,* 102 Wis. 2d 719, 308 N.W.2d 419 (Wis. App. 1981).

Fiduciary duties have been defined by statute by the Uniform Fiduciary Duty Act which is now Wis. Stat. §112.01 (reproduced below). Wis. Stats. §§112.02-.03; 112.07-.09; and 112.11 also deal with the boundaries of fiduciary duty. The general good faith duty owned by trustees is discussed in the case below from the era of the Great Depression.

Wis. Stat. 112.01. Uniform Fiduciaries Act

(1) DEFINITIONS. In this section unless the context or subject matter otherwise requires:

(a) "Bank" includes any person or association of persons, whether incorporated or not, carrying on the business of banking.

(b) "Fiduciary" includes a trustee under any trust, expressed, implied, resulting, or constructive, personal representative, guardian, conservator, curator, receiver, trustee in bankruptcy, assignee for the benefit of creditors, prime contractor or subcontractor who is a trustee under ch. 779, partner, agent, officer of a corporation, public or private, public officer, or any other person acting in a fiduciary capacity for any person, trust, or estate.

(c) A thing is done "in good faith" within the meaning of this section, when it is in fact done honestly, whether it be done negligently or not.

(d) "Person" includes a corporation, limited liability company, partnership, or other association or 2 or more persons having a joint or common interest.

(e) "Principal" includes any person to whom a fiduciary as such owes an obligation.

(3) APPLICATION OF PAYMENTS MADE TO FIDUCIARIES. A person who in good faith pays or transfers to a fiduciary any money or other property which the fiduciary as such is authorized to receive, is not responsible for the proper application thereof by the fiduciary; and any right or title acquired from the fiduciary in consideration of such payment or transfer is not invalid in consequence of a misapplication by the fiduciary.

(5) TRANSFER OF NEGOTIABLE INSTRUMENT BY FIDUCIARY. If any negotiable instrument payable or endorsed to a fiduciary as such is endorsed by the fiduciary, or if any negotiable instrument payable or endorsed to a fiduciary's principal is endorsed by a fiduciary empowered to endorse such instrument on behalf of his or her principal, the endorsee is not bound to inquire whether the fiduciary is committing a breach of the fiduciary's obligation as fiduciary in endorsing or delivering the instrument, and is not chargeable with notice that the fiduciary is committing a breach of the fiduciary's obligation as fiduciary, unless the endorsee takes the instrument with actual knowledge of such breach or with knowledge of such facts that the endorsee's action in taking the instrument amounts to bad faith. If, however, such instrument is transferred by the fiduciary in payment of or as security for a personal debt of the fiduciary to the actual knowledge of the creditor, or is transferred in any transaction known by the transferee to be for the personal benefit of the fiduciary, the creditor or other transferee is liable to the principal if the fiduciary in fact commits a breach of the fiduciary's obligation as fiduciary in transferring the instrument.

(6) CHECK DRAWN BY FIDUCIARY PAYABLE TO 3RD PERSON. If a check or other bill of exchange is drawn by a fiduciary as such, or in the name of a fiduciary's principal by a fiduciary empowered to draw such instrument in the name of his or her principal, the payee is not bound to inquire whether the fiduciary is committing a breach of the fiduciary's obligation as fiduciary in drawing or delivering the instrument, and is not chargeable with notice that the fiduciary is committing a breach of the fiduciary's obligation as fiduciary unless the payee takes the instrument with actual knowledge of such breach, or with knowledge of such facts that the payee's action in taking the instrument amounts to bad faith. If, however, such instrument is payable to a personal creditor of the fiduciary and delivered to the creditor in payment of or as security for a personal debt of the fiduciary to the actual knowledge of the creditor, or is drawn and delivered in any transaction known by the payee to be for the personal benefit of the fiduciary, the creditor or other payee is liable to the principal if the fiduciary in fact commits a breach of the fiduciary's obligation as fiduciary in drawing or delivering the instrument.

(7) CHECK DRAWN BY AND PAYABLE TO FIDUCIARY. If a check or other bill of exchange is drawn by a fiduciary as such, or in the name of a fiduciary's principal by a fiduciary empowered to draw such instrument in the name of his or her principal, payable to the fiduciary personally, or payable to a 3rd person, and transferred by the 3rd person to the fiduciary, and is thereafter transferred by the fiduciary, whether in payment of a personal debt of the fiduciary or otherwise, the transferee is not bound to inquire whether the fiduciary is committing a breach of the fiduciary's obligation as fiduciary in transferring the instrument, and is not chargeable with notice that the fiduciary is committing a breach of the fiduciary's obligation as fiduciary, unless the transferee takes the instrument with actual knowledge of such breach, or with knowledge of such facts that the transferee's action in taking the instrument amounts to bad faith.

(8) DEPOSIT IN NAME OF FIDUCIARY AS SUCH. If a deposit is made in a bank to the credit of a fiduciary as such, the bank is authorized to pay the amount of the deposit or any part thereof upon the check of the fiduciary, signed with the name in which such deposit is entered, without being liable to the principal, unless the bank pays the check with actual knowledge that the fiduciary is committing a breach of the fiduciary's obligation as fiduciary in drawing the check, or with knowledge of such facts that its action in paying the check amounts to bad faith. If, however, such a check is payable to the drawee bank, and is delivered to it in payment of or as security for a personal debt of the fiduciary to it, the bank is liable to the principal if the fiduciary in fact commits a breach of the fiduciary's obligation as fiduciary in drawing or delivering the check.

(9) DEPOSIT IN NAME OF PRINCIPAL. If a check is drawn upon the account of a fiduciary's principal in a bank by a fiduciary, who is empowered to draw checks upon his or her principal's account, the bank is authorized to pay such check without being liable to the principal, unless the bank pays the check with actual knowledge that the fiduciary is committing a breach of the fiduciary's obligation as fiduciary in drawing such check, or with knowledge of such facts that its action in paying the check amounts to bad faith. If, however, such a check is payable to the drawee bank and is delivered to it in payment of or as security for a personal debt of the fiduciary to it, the bank is liable to the principal if the fiduciary in fact commits a breach of the fiduciary's obligation as fiduciary in drawing or delivering the check.

(10) DEPOSIT IN FIDUCIARY'S PERSONAL ACCOUNT. If a fiduciary makes a deposit in a bank to the fiduciary's personal credit of checks drawn by the fiduciary upon an account in his or her own name as fiduciary, or of checks payable to the fiduciary as fiduciary, or of checks drawn by the fiduciary upon an account in the name of his or her principal if the fiduciary is empowered to draw checks thereon, or of checks payable to his or her principal and endorsed by the fiduciary, if the fiduciary is empowered to endorse such checks, or if the fiduciary otherwise makes a deposit of funds held by the fiduciary as fiduciary, the bank receiving such deposit is not bound to inquire whether the fiduciary is committing thereby a breach of his or her obligation as fiduciary. The bank is authorized to pay the amount of the deposit or any part thereof upon the personal check of the fiduciary, including checks payable to the bank, without being liable to the principal, unless the bank receives the deposit or pays the check with actual knowledge that the fiduciary is committing a breach of his or her obligation as fiduciary in making such deposit or in drawing such check, or with knowledge of such facts that its action in receiving the deposit or paying the check amounts to bad faith, and the bank paying the check is not bound to inquire whether the fiduciary is committing thereby a breach of his or her obligation as fiduciary.

(11) DEPOSIT OR SAFE DEPOSIT BOX RENTAL IN NAME OF ESTATE OR TWO OR MORE FIDUCIARIES. When a deposit is made in a bank account or a safe deposit box or storage space rented, in the names of 2 or more persons as trustees or personal representatives, or in the name of an estate having 2 or more personal representatives, and a check is drawn upon the account, or access to the safe deposit box or storage space is sought by any one or more of the fiduciaries authorized by the other fiduciary or fiduciaries to draw checks upon the account, or to enter the safe deposit box or storage space, neither the payee nor the other holder nor the bank is bound to inquire whether it is a breach of trust to authorize the fiduciary or fiduciaries to draw checks upon the account, or to enter the safe deposit box or storage space, and is not liable unless the circumstances are such that the action of the payee or other holder or the bank amounts to bad faith.

(12) NOT RETROACTIVE. The provisions of this section shall not apply to transactions taking place prior to June 4, 1925.

(13) CASES NOT PROVIDED FOR IN SECTION. In any case not provided for in this section the rules of law and equity, including the law merchant and those rules of law and equity relating to trusts, agency, negotiable instruments and banking, shall continue to apply.

(14) UNIFORMITY OF INTERPRETATION. This section shall be so interpreted and construed as to effectuate its general purpose to make uniform the law of those states which enact it.

(15) SHORT TITLE. This section may be cited as the "Uniform Fiduciaries Act".

(16) INCONSISTENT LAWS REPEALED. All acts or parts of acts inconsistent with this section are repealed.

United States Bank v. Sullivan

United States Circuit Court of Appeals, Seventh Circuit
69 F.2d 412 (1934)

Appeal from the District Court of United States for the Eastern District of Wisconsin; Ferdinand A. Geiger, Judge

SPARKS, Circuit Judge.

The facts as found by the court are not in dispute. On February 7, 1929, decedent Frank J. Sullivan entered into a trust agreement with the United States National Bank and Trust Company of Kenosha, hereafter referred to as the Bank, whereby it was to act as trustee of certain funds to be derived from insurance upon decedent's life, for the benefit of appellees who are his wife and children. Decedent, a resident of Wisconsin who had been a shoe merchant, died on March 9, 1930, leaving a will naming the Bank as executor of his estate, and as trustee of his testamentary trust. The Bank thereafter acted in both capacities. At the time of his death decedent owed the Bank $1,335 on an unsecured note or open account, and $20,000 upon a note secured by a mortgage upon the building owned by decedent in which he was conducting a retail shoe business at the time of his death. The Bank as trustee received on decedent's life insurance policies the following amounts:

$2,031.00	March 15, 1930
15,130.05	March 19, 1930

27,500.67 March 20, 1930

5,140.33 April 1, 1930.

On March 20, 1930, the Bank as trustee purchased from itself the mortgage note paying itself $20,000 out of the insurance trust funds, and without having a disinterested appraisement of the note or the real estate securing it. At that time the real estate was worth $19,837.18, and was subject to a street improvement lien of $4,150 with six per cent. annual interest due thereon from June 29, 1928, of which lien the Bank had knowledge.

On May 3, 1930, the Bank as executor purchased from the Continental Bank of Chicago for a consideration of $5,000, 150 shares of the Bank's capital stock of the par value of $3,000, using funds of the trust to pay for it. This in turn on the same day was delivered by the Bank as executor to itself as trustee of the insurance trust for a consideration of $6,000. Having already paid $5,000 to the Continental Bank out of the trust funds, an additional sum of $1,000 was taken from the trust funds by the Bank as trustee and credited to itself as executor, as an asset of the estate. At that time the book value of the stock, without discount for loans, notes, furniture and fixtures did not amount to $6,000.

On October 3, 1930, the Bank as trustee purchased from itself as executor, the furniture, fixtures and stock of the retail shoe business which was being conducted by decedent at the time of his death in the building covered by the mortgage which had been purchased by the Bank as trustee from itself as Creditor. The purchase price agreed upon was $12,000, but the price paid was $12,200, which amount the trustee obtained by the sale of valid mortgage notes belonging to the trust. The trustee conducted the business with a loss of $4,988, of which $2,918.14 was due to depreciation of inventory.

On November 13, 1932, the Bank suspended business and was taken over by the Comptroller of the Currency who named appellant Taylor as receiver. On January 6, 1933, the Comptroller made an assessment upon each shareholder of the Bank for 100% of the par value of his stock.

The money obtained from the sale to the trustee of the three items referred to was applied by the executor toward the payment of creditors' claims and expenses of administration, including the Bank's unsecured claim of $1,335.18, and its charge for services as executor in the sum of $943.08.

The estate of decedent was administered under the jurisdiction and authority of the Kenosha County Court whose appraisers on May 8, 1930, appraised the real estate covered by the mortgage at $24,000.

On December 31, 1932, appellant receiver filed in the Circuit Branch of the Kenosha County Court a petition for discharge of the Bank as trustee, submitting a final account of the trust for approval, and asking that a new trustee be appointed and that the Bank as trustee be released from further liability upon its compliance with whatever terms the court might decree. Among the investments shown in the report were the three items now in controversy totaling $38,200. Appellees filed objections to the allowance of those items, and brought this action for the purpose of having the trust estate reimbursed to the extent of those investments.

The District Court found and decreed that the three investments objected to were not suitable and proper investments for trust purposes under the trust, and were not made with such discretion as would tend to safeguard the preservation of the fund and the procurement of a just income therefrom, but were made in hazardous types of investments from which little could be expected in earnings, or in the safe return of the principal.

The District Court further found that by reason of the position of the Bank and its acceptance of its various positions and relationships to the trust estate, and to the cestuis que trust, and to itself as creditor, it necessarily could not exercise a wise discretion in the performance of its duties as trustee of the insurance trust, and could not and did not exercise that degree of discretion, diligence, prudence, and fidelity with respect to the controverted investments which is required of a trustee in the administration of trust estates.

The court thereupon concluded that appellees should recover the amount demanded with six per cent interest per annum from November 1, 1932, the last date of return of earnings to the trust which the court found reasonable and fair, to November 13, 1932, the date the Bank suspended business.

The conclusions of law further set forth in detail the method by which appellees' claim was to be enforced against the indemnity fund in the hands of the State Treasurer, concerning which no objections are raised here in case the claim is held to be valid.

The question presented is whether each of the items above referred to was proper trust investment under the provisions of the first paragraph of the trust agreement which reads as follows:

"Upon maturity of any and all policies held hereunder, by death of party of the first part, Trustee shall present for collection such policies, and upon receipt of the proceeds therefrom shall thereupon and thereafter invest, reinvest and keep invested the same in such investments as Trustee in its wise discretion shall deem proper, without confining Trustee to what are known as legal investments for Trustees under the laws of the state of Wisconsin, with authority in Trustee to alter, vary, change, transfer and retransfer investments and reinvestments from time to time in the absolute discretion of the Trustee, and with special authority in Trustee to purchase as investments in the trust hereby created, securities or other properties, real or personal, which may be a part of the estate of the party of the first part at the time of his death."

It is contended by appellants that the questioned investments were authorized by the trust agreement which expressly gave to the trustee absolute discretion in the selection of investments without confining him to what are known as legal investments as required by the Wisconsin statutes, and which also gave him express authority to purchase assets of decedent's estate.

The general propositions of law upon which appellants rely may be admitted, that is to say, it was the duty of the trustee to carry out the intention of the creator of the trust, and in so doing, if it conducted itself faithfully, and exercised a sound discretion, it cannot be held liable. It was not liable for a mere error of judgment in making any investment unless the error were of so gross a nature as to show bad faith or lack of sound discretion. If a trustee acts within his powers, good faith is a defense to a charge of mistaken judgment. If a trust provision gives the trustee wide powers of investment he may exercise his sound discretion within those limits, and his actions with respect thereto are not to be tested by considerations of what may be termed "hindsight" judgment.

In applying these principles to a grant of power to a trustee, such power must be construed in the light of other well established law governing the actions of trustees. Discretion to a trustee does not mean an arbitrary or unlimited or absolute discretion, but a reasonable one. He must use judgment and prudence, and if no limits are placed on his discretion, he must nevertheless invest the funds according to approved rules for trust investments. Pabst v. Goodrich, 133 Wis. 43, 113 N.W. 398, 14 Ann. Cas. 824; Estate of Allis, 191 Wis. 23, 209 N.W. 945, 210 N.W. 418.

A trustee shall not be permitted to benefit himself in dealings with the trust estate. Such transactions are not merely prima facie invalid, but negative any idea of good faith and free consent. Shaw v. Crandon State Bank, 145 Wis. 639, 129 N.W. 794; Will of Leonard, 202 Wis. 117, 230 N.W. 715, 83 A.L.R. 712; Ludington v. Patton,

111 Wis. 208, 86 N.W. 571. Good faith alone will not protect a trustee, but he must also exercise diligence, prudence, and absolute fidelity. Wisconsin has consistently adhered to the strict rule with reference to the liability of trustees as early adopted by New York, rather than the more liberal rule adopted in Massachusetts. Estate of Allis, supra.

There is no doubt that the Bank, under the will and the insurance trust agreement had a right to act in both capacities of executor and trustee, notwithstanding the fact that it was a creditor of decedent. Indeed the obvious intention of decedent was that it should so act, but nevertheless it must be considered that it was also the intention of decedent that the Bank in thus acting should comply with the well-known principles of law governing such transactions. We do not say that the law brands such transactions as void on their face, but it does scan them very closely, because of the temptations which are inherently present. We may assume without admitting that the investments are not void as to the beneficiaries merely because the trustee failed to secure the permission of the court to make them or its approval afterwards, although, as conceded by appellants, an order of the proper court expressly directing such investments would have eliminated this controversy. However, the fact that they were never ordered or approved was quite properly considered by the court, together with all the other pertinent facts in determining whether there was bad faith or a lack of sound discretion. While the law of Wisconsin governs this case, the principle of law here involved is the same in Wisconsin as it is in Massachusetts, that is to say, a trustee is liable for an error of judgment in making an investment if the error is so gross as to show that he either acted in bad faith or failed to exercise sound discretion. Taft v. Smith, 186 Mass. 31, 70 N.E. 1031, Pine v. White, 175 Mass. 585, 56 N.E. 967.

Appellants contend, however, that the District Court did not pass upon the real question presented which was whether there had been an abuse of trust powers, but that the court's findings and decree are based upon lack of power of the trustee to act without the express direction of a court, due to the various inconsistent capacities in which it was acting. We think this construction of the court's findings and conclusions is not warranted. The court not only found that under the circumstances presented it was impossible for the Bank to exercise sound discretion, or good faith, but it also found that it had not exercised that sound discretion and judgment which the law required. We think the first finding is supported in principle at least. Shaw v. Crandon State Bank, supra. It will be noted that the District Court in this case did not lay it down as a general rule that one acting in the triple capacity of trustee, executor, and creditor could in no event exercise a sound discretion, but it held that under the circumstances of this case the Bank was unable to, and did not exercise a sound discretion. Aside from its inability to do so, the Bank is liable if it failed to exercise sound discretion, and we think there is substantial evidence to support the court's decree in that respect.

Admitting that the trust agreement authorized the trustee to purchase assets of the estate, yet that authority was not mandatory, nor did it warrant the Bank in paying therefor more than they were worth, nor in conducting the trust in a manner different from that authorized by the laws of Wisconsin. While appellants in their argument admitted that they did not controvert the findings of fact, it is only fair to say that they contend that the court did not find that the store building was worth only $19,837.18, but that it merely found that witness Carlson testified to that fact. As a matter of fact, he testified that it was worth that amount free of encumbrances. We think appellants are in error in their construction of that finding, which reads, "That on the twentieth day of March, 1930, in accordance with the testimony of witness (Carlson) * * * the said property was worth $19,837.18." If that finding is prefaced with the words, "The court finds," as it should be when construing it, it is quite obvious that the court itself made the finding of value and based it on the testimony of Carlson. It is quite true that Carlson was the only witness who testified for appellees on valuation, but it is also true that he was the only disinterested witness who testified on that subject for either side. There was an appraisement of this real estate made by the Bank's discount committee at the time the mortgage was sold to the trust. This committee was made up of officers and directors of the Bank, and the amount of that appraisement is not disclosed by the record.

With respect to the sale of bank stock to the trust, the evidence shows that the Continental Illinois Bank of Chicago held it with other collateral aggregating $274,000, as security for an indebtedness of decedent to that bank of $301,000. The record discloses no appraisement. Decedent's estate was insolvent, and the Continental Bank was bound to sustain a loss, and the fact that it sold the bank stock under those circumstances to the executor for $5000 certainly constitutes quite substantial evidence that that was all it was worth. When the executor immediately turned this stock into the trust fund for $6000 and credited the assets of the estate with $1000 from which the Bank's unsecured claim and its charge for services were paid, a substantial basis was created for the court's conclusion that there was a lack of sound discretion on the part of the trustee in participating in the transaction.

The appraised value of the shoe store, if any, was not shown. The court found that the Bank as executor agreed to sell it to itself as trustee for $12,000. We assume, as no doubt the trial court did, that this was the estate's appraised value. This is in a measure confirmed by the testimony of the Bank's president who said that it was turned over to the trust for $12,200 which was approximately the appraised value. It will be borne in mind that this was practically seven months after decedent's death, and so far as the record discloses there were no other prospective purchasers. This court will take judicial knowledge, as no doubt the trial court did, that during those seven months values were declining rapidly, and commercial enterprises of all kinds were generally regarded as extremely hazardous. If all the property of the estate were appraised at the same time, it was within a short time after decedent's death, and under the circumstances enumerated we think the court was warranted in finding that there was a lack of sound discretion on the part of the trustee. Decree affirmed.

B. DUTY OF LOYALTY

Berg v. Berg

Court of Appeals of Wisconsin
163 Wis. 2d 524, 472 N.W.2d 247 (1991)

Per Curiam. Vernon R. Berg, Sr. ("Berg Sr."), appeals from an order and judgment removing him as trustee and committeeman of certain trusts and awarding Isabelle Berg her attorney's fees in petitioning for his removal. The issues are whether the trial court abused its discretion in removing Berg Sr. as trustee and committeeman and in awarding attorney's fees. We conclude it did not abuse its discretion and affirm.

Berg Sr. founded a substantial farm equipment business. In 1961, 2,497 shares of stock for Berg Industries, Inc., were transferred into a trust. Berg Sr. and the Marine National Exchange Bank of Milwaukee were named as trustees. Vernon Berg, Jr. ("Berg Jr.") was the donor and Edward and William Berg (Berg Jr.'s only children at the time) were the initial beneficiaries.

In 1983, Berg Jr. petitioned to remove Berg Sr. as trustee. The petition was granted. Berg Sr. moved to have the order vacated. Isabelle Berg, Berg Jr.'s wife and a beneficiary under the trust, petitioned to remove Berg Sr. as trustee in the event the order was vacated. The trial court granted Berg Sr.'s request to vacate the order removing him as trustee but suspended him as trustee and committeeman pending resolution of Isabelle's petition.

Following a trial, the court removed Berg Sr. as trustee and committeeman because of self-dealing to the detriment of the trust, alcohol abuse, sexual harassment and his attitude toward the trust. It awarded Isabelle attorney's fees for bringing the petition. We conclude that the trial court properly removed Berg Sr. as trustee and committeeman because of self-dealing and his announced intention to destroy the trust. We reject the other bases for removing him. The award of fees was proper.

"A trustee may be removed in accordance with the terms of the creating instrument or the court may, upon its own motion or upon a petition by a beneficiary or cotrustee, and upon notice and hearing, remove a trustee who fails to comply with the requirements of this chapter or a court order, or who is otherwise unsuitable to continue in office." Section 701.18(2), Stats. A petition to remove a trustee is addressed to the discretion of the court, and the court's action may not be reversed absent an abuse of discretion. Will of Gabel, 267 Wis. 208, 211, 64 N.W.2d 853, 855 (1954). When determining whether an abuse occurred, we do not balance the evidence as if we were a trial court. Estate of Gehl, 5 Wis.2d 91, 96, 92 N.W.2d 372, 376 (1958). We will not disturb the trial court's findings unless they are clearly erroneous. Section 805.17(2), Stats.

Berg Sr. first argues that the trial court exceeded its authority under Wisconsin law by reviewing and second-guessing his role in the business world. To the contrary, the trial court has broad authority to remove a trustee who is "unsuitable to continue in office." Section 701.18(2), Stats.

Berg Sr. also claims that "so long as he managed the business for the overall growth and prosperity of the business he was free to do what he pleased -- subject, always, to The Marine's oversight."

We disagree. A trustee has a strict duty of loyalty to the trust even though the will or trust instrument gives the trustee broad powers of discretion. These powers must be exercised according to law and consistent with the duties and obligations as trustee of the trust." Gehl at 98, 92 N.W.2d at 376. A trustee is not relieved of the result of self-serving conduct by the fact that he acted in good faith and without loss to the trust. Gabel, 267 Wis. at 211, 64 N.W.2d at 855. A trustee can make no profit out of the trust. His duty is to protect the interests of the estate and not permit his personal interest to conflict with this duty. Estate of Becker, 56 Wis.2d 356, 367, 202 N.W.2d 681, 686-87 (1972).

Berg Sr. attacks the trial court's conclusion that paying himself royalties on a patent after it expired was a ground for his removal. He contends that he had the right to make day-to-day management decisions about the companies which included whether to pay himself bonuses. We disagree. Paying oneself unauthorized royalties conflicts with a trustee's duty to protect the interests of the estate. We conclude the trial court acted within its discretion in removing Berg Sr. as trustee on the ground that he made unauthorized royalty payments to himself.

Berg Sr. also attacks the trial court's conclusion that his claims for salary and rent justify his removal as trustee. He testified that he believes he is entitled to salary of $400,000 per year from 1984 to 1988, and to rent of $21,000 yearly from December 1984.

Berg Jr. contends that it is improper and a conflict of interest for Berg Sr. to claim salary that he would have to negotiate with himself as trustee and with the directors he would elect and control. However, this conflict of interest was created by the trust document in designating Berg Sr. as trustee and in directing the trustees to take all actions necessary to employ him as chief executive officer. See Gehl, 5 Wis.2d at 97, 92 N.W.2d at 376 (conflict of interest between trustees and beneficiaries not ground for removal of trustee where testator credited conflict). The only basis for concluding that Berg Sr.'s salary and rent claims justify his removal as trustee would be if the claims were excessive. See RESTATEMENT (SECOND) OF TRUSTS see. 170 comment o (it is not necessarily improper for "trustee to receive compensation as officer of a corporation, shares of which he holds in trust, even though the shares represent a controlling interest, if he performs necessary services as such officer and receives no more than proper compensation for such services") (emphasis added). Berg Jr. points to no evidence indicating that Berg Sr.'s salary claim is improper for the services performed, or that his rent claim is excessive.

The trial court found that Berg Sr. is an alcohol abuser who, by his own admission, drinks before lunch and dinner. His wife testified that she carries out the bottles, about a half liter a day. The court found that Berg Sr.'s vindictiveness and office behavior is precipitated by alcohol abuse. RESTATEMENT (SECOND) OF TRUSTS sec. 107 comment b (1959) provides that habitual drunkenness is a ground for removal of a trustee. Berg Sr. does not dispute the finding that he abuses alcohol but rather argues that to justify his removal an additional showing must be made that his consumption of alcohol interfered with his ability to be a trustee or a competent officer or director of the company.

Numerous employees testified to the adverse effects Berg Sr.'s drinking had on the company. Barbara Becker testified that he would leave work at 11 or 11:30 a.m. and return anywhere from 1:30 to 3:00 p.m. She observed that he had been drinking, since he would slur his speech, she could smell alcohol on his breath, and he would forget what he had told her in the morning. At times he was loud or abusive. She thought that the office ran more efficiently since Berg Sr.'s removal because "we don't have all this fear over you all the time; you can relax and do your work and enjoy your work." Barbara Burr testified that it was very difficult to get any work done in the afternoon because Berg Sr. would be talking and telling jokes. She attributed his change in attitude from the morning to afternoon to his drinking. Other employees gave similar testimony.

We conclude that insufficient evidence exists that Berg Sr.'s alcohol consumption adversely affected his ability to run his company or the trust. That he abuses alcohol does not automatically mean his ability to run the company and trust is impaired. No evidence was offered that his alcohol abuse had in fact impaired decisions he made for the business or the trust.

We reach the same conclusion with respect to claims of sexual harassment. Barbara Burr, Jean Voss and Dawn Susa testified that Berg Sr. told jokes and made remarks of a sexual nature. We agree with the trial court that sexual harassment lawsuits by disgruntled and insulted women would not be in the trust's best interest, but no evidence was offered that such lawsuits have been brought or threatened.

The trial court found that Berg Sr.'s allegiance toward the trust has changed and "bitterness now motivates Senior to destroy the Trust." Berg Sr.'s wife testified that he often told her he intends to totally destroy the trust and seek revenge, and that he is spending its money, taking it out of the trust for legal fees, and he is going to do that "right down to the very last cent." Employee Ed Miller testified that Berg Sr. fired certain employees to teach Berg Jr. a lesson. Evidence supports the trial court's finding concerning Berg Sr.'s allegiance. This finding not only supports the decision to remove him as trustee but, in our view, is a compelling reason. To retain a trustee bent on destroying the trust would be intolerable.

Berg Sr. next argues that the trial court erred in removing him as committeeman. The trial court reasoned that because he was removed as trustee, he should not retain the power to influence who is retained to act as corporate trustee as he would not act in the best interests of the trust as a committeeman.

The committee is created by the trust document and the committee has authority to appoint a successor to the initial corporate trustee. The reasons for removal of Berg Sr. as committeeman listed in the trust document are death, resignation or inability to act. None of these reasons applies. However, courts of equity have exclusive jurisdiction of cases involving trusts and the conduct of those appointed to execute them. Will of Stack, 217 Wis. 94, 98, 258 N.W. 324, 325 (1935).

Courts exercising equity powers have the duty of taking such action upon their own motion as is necessary to carry out the intention of the trust's creator. Id. We conclude that the trial court acted within its authority in removing Berg Sr. as committeeman, even though it did so for reasons not specified in the trust document. Allowing Berg Sr. to remain a committeeman would have permitted him to attempt to influence the corporate trustee in a manner contrary to the best interests of the trust. Bitterness motivates him to destroy the trust. To allow Berg Sr. to use his position or the committee to destroy the trust is as intolerable as allowing him to accomplish the same destruction as a trustee.

The last issue is whether the trial court abused its discretion in ordering Berg Sr. to pay Isabelle's attorney's fees for bringing the petition for his removal. The parties agree that the issue is governed by In re Pirsch, 148 Wis.2d 425, 435 N.W.2d 317 (Ct. App. 1988). Pirsch held that before attorney's fees can be ordered paid by a trustee, there must be a finding of bad faith, fraud or deliberate dishonesty. Id. at 433, 435 N.W.2d at 321. Bad faith is a finding of fact. Id. at 434, 435 N.W.2d at 321. The trial court is in a better position than an appellate court to determine what motivated the trustee's actions. Id., 435 N.W.2d at 322.

The trial court found that Berg Sr.'s actions constituted bad faith. We must uphold that finding unless it is clearly erroneous. Section 805.17(2), Stats. None of the parties offer a definition of bad faith. In another context, the supreme court has define bad faith as "deceit, duplicity, and insincerity." Anderson v. Continental Ins. Co., 85 Wis.2d 675, 691-92, 271 N.W.2d 368, 376-77 (1978). The trial court based its bad faith finding primarily on Berg Sr.'s handling of the patent royalties. Although it found he was not trying to be "out and out dishonest with the Trust," it noted in its June 6, 1989, memorandum decision that Berg Sr. did not disclose his taking the royalty payments to the board of directors. We conclude that the finding of bad faith is supported by this evidence as well as by Berg Sr.'s stated intention to destroy the trust and to take money out of the trust for legal fees "down to the very last cent." Berg Sr.'s brief contains unusual, unduly harsh and derogatory comments about the opposing parties and the trial court. Such comments do disservice to the parties, the trial court and this court.

Judgment and order affirmed.

C. TRUST MANAGEMENT AND THE DUTY TO DIVERSIFY

Unless limited by the trust instrument, the trustee has a duty to invest the assets of the trust in a prudent manner. In the past, trustees were expected to be extremely conservative when it came to investments and were often limited to a narrow range of extremely safe (or at least what were perceived to be extremely safe) investments. Today, consistent with modern portfolio theory, trustees are expected to place a greater emphasis on the diversity of investments with a mixture of safe and moderately risky investments (with a goal of higher returns). However, even under the old "prudent man standard" trustees were expected to diversify their investments, as the following case illustrates. The modern theory of trustee investment is currently embodied in the Uniform Prudent Investor Act and the Uniform Prudent Management of Institutional Funds Act, which are codified in Wisconsin at Wis. Stat. §881.01 and §112.11, respectively.

Wis. Stat. 881.01. Uniform prudent investor act

(1) DEFINITION. In this section:

(a) "Beneficiary," with respect to a guardianship of the estate, means a ward for whom a guardian of the estate has been appointed and, with respect to a conservator, means a person for whose estate a conservator has been appointed.

(b) "Fiduciary" means a personal representative, trustee, conservator, or guardian of the estate.

(2) PRUDENT INVESTOR RULE.

(a) Except as provided in s. 112.11 and except as otherwise provided in par. (b), a fiduciary who invests and manages assets owes a duty to the beneficiaries to comply with the prudent investor rule set forth in this section.

(b) The prudent investor rule, a default rule, may be expanded, restricted, eliminated, or otherwise altered by the provisions of a will, trust, or court order. A fiduciary is not liable to a beneficiary to the extent that the fiduciary acted in reasonable reliance on the provisions of the will, trust, or court order.

(3) STANDARD OF CARE; PORTFOLIO STRATEGY; RISK AND RETURN OBJECTIVES.

(a) A fiduciary shall invest and manage assets as a prudent investor would, by considering the purposes, terms, distribution requirements, and other circumstances of the estate, trust, conservatorship, or guardianship. In satisfying this standard, the fiduciary shall exercise reasonable care, skill, and caution.

(b) A fiduciary's investment and management decisions about individual assets shall be evaluated, not in isolation but in the context of the portfolio as a whole and as a part of an overall investment strategy having risk and return objectives reasonably suited to the estate, trust, conservatorship, or guardianship.

(c) Among circumstances that a fiduciary shall consider in investing and managing assets are those of the following that are relevant to the estate, trust, conservatorship, or guardianship or its beneficiaries:

1. General economic conditions.

2. The possible effect of inflation or deflation.

3. The expected tax consequences of investment decisions or strategies.

4. The role that each investment or course of action plays within the overall portfolio, which may include financial assets, interests in closely held enterprises, tangible and intangible personal property, and real property.

5. The expected total return from income and the appreciation of capital.

6. Other resources of the beneficiaries.

7. Needs for liquidity, regularity of income, and preservation or appreciation of capital.

8. An asset's special relationship or special value to the purposes of the estate, trust, conservatorship, or guardianship or to one or more of the beneficiaries.

(d) A fiduciary shall make a reasonable effort to verify facts relevant to the investment and management of assets.

(e) A fiduciary may invest in any kind of property or type of investment consistent with the standards of this section.

(f) A fiduciary who has special skills or expertise, or who is named fiduciary in reliance upon the fiduciary's representation that the fiduciary has special skills or expertise, has a duty to use those special skills or expertise.

(4) DIVERSIFICATION. A fiduciary shall diversify investments unless the fiduciary reasonably determines that, because of special circumstances, the purposes of the estate, trust, conservatorship, or guardianship are better served without diversifying.

(5) DUTIES AT INCEPTION. Within a reasonable time after accepting a fiduciary appointment or receiving assets, a fiduciary shall review the assets and make and implement decisions concerning the retention and disposition of assets, in order to bring the portfolio into compliance with the purposes, terms, distribution requirements, and other circumstances of the estate, trust, conservatorship, or guardianship and with the requirements of this section.

(6) LOYALTY. A fiduciary shall invest and manage the assets solely in the interest of the beneficiaries.

(7) IMPARTIALITY. If an estate, trust, conservatorship, or guardianship has 2 or more beneficiaries, the fiduciary shall act impartially in investing and managing the assets, taking into account the differences between the interests of the beneficiaries.

(8) INVESTMENT COSTS. In investing and managing assets, a fiduciary may incur only costs that are appropriate and reasonable in relation to the assets, the purposes of the estate, trust, conservatorship, or guardianship, and the skills of the fiduciary.

(9) REVIEWING COMPLIANCE. Compliance with the prudent investor rule is determined in light of the facts and circumstances existing at the time of a fiduciary's decision or action and not by hindsight.

(10) DELEGATION OF INVESTMENT AND MANAGEMENT FUNCTIONS.

(a) A fiduciary may delegate investment and management functions that a prudent fiduciary of similar skills could properly delegate under the circumstances. The fiduciary shall exercise reasonable care, skill, and caution in all of the following:

1. Selecting an agent.

2. Establishing the scope and terms of the delegation, consistent with the purposes and terms of the estate, trust, conservatorship, or guardianship.

3. Periodically reviewing the agent's actions to monitor the agent's performance and compliance with the terms of the delegation.

(b) In performing a delegated function, an agent owes a duty to the estate, trust, conservatorship, or guardianship to exercise reasonable care to comply with the terms of the delegation.

(c) A fiduciary who complies with the requirements of par. (a) is not liable to the beneficiaries or to the estate, trust, conservatorship, or guardianship for the decisions or actions of the agent to whom a function was delegated.

(d) By accepting the delegation of a function from the fiduciary of an estate, trust, conservatorship, or guardianship that is subject to the law of this state, an agent submits to the jurisdiction of the courts of this state.

(11) PHRASES INVOKING STANDARD OF THIS SECTION. The following phrases or similar phrases in a will, trust, or court order, unless otherwise limited or modified, authorize any investment or strategy permitted under this section: "investments permissible by law for investment of trust funds"; "legal investments"; "authorized investments"; "using the judgment and care under the circumstances then prevailing that persons of prudence, discretion, and intelligence exercise in the management of their own affairs, not in regard to speculation but in regard to the permanent disposition of their funds, considering the probable income as well as the probable safety of their capital"; "prudent man rule"; "prudent trustee rule"; "prudent person rule"; and "prudent investor rule."

(12) APPLICATION TO EXISTING ESTATES, TRUSTS, CONSERVATORSHIPS, AND GUARDIANSHIPS. This section applies to estates, trusts, conservatorships, and guardianships of the estate existing on, or created on or after, April 30, 2004. As applied to estates, trusts, conservatorships, and guardianships of the estate existing on April 30, 2004, this section governs only decisions or actions occurring after that date.

(13) UNIFORMITY OF APPLICATION AND CONSTRUCTION. This section shall be applied and construed to effectuate its general purpose to make uniform the law with respect to the subject of this section among the states that have enacted this uniform legislation.

Wis. Stat. 881.015 Investment companies, investment trusts and collective investment vehicles.

(1) In this section:

(a) "Collective investment vehicle" means an investment vehicle authorized for the collective investment of trust funds, including vehicles under 12 CFR 9.

(b) "Investment company" means an open-end or closed-end management investment company registered under 15 USC 80a-1 to 80a-64.

(c) "Investment trust" means an investment trust registered under 15 USC 80a-1 to 80a-64.

(2) In addition to other investments authorized by law for the investment of funds held by a fiduciary, or by the instrument governing the fiduciary relationship, a bank or trust company acting as a fiduciary, agent or otherwise may, in the exercise of its investment discretion or at the direction of another person authorized to direct investment of funds held by the bank or trust company as fiduciary, invest and reinvest in the securities of, or other interests in, an investment company, investment trust or collective investment vehicle, so long as the portfolio of the investment company, investment trust or collective investment vehicle consists of investments not prohibited by the governing instrument. In the absence of an express provision to the contrary, when a governing instrument directs or requires investment in obligations of the U.S. government or an agency of the U.S. government, a bank, trust company, trust department trustee or other fiduciary may invest in these obligations either directly or in the form of securities of, or other interests in, an investment company, investment trust or collective investment vehicle, if the portfolio of the investment company, investment trust or collective investment vehicle consists of obligations of the U.S. government or an agency of the U.S. government and repurchase agreements fully collateralized by these obligations.

(3) If the requirements of this subsection are met, a bank or trust company may invest or reinvest funds under sub. (2) in the securities of, or other interests in, an investment company, investment trust or collective investment vehicle, notwithstanding the fact that the bank or trust company or an affiliate of the bank or trust company provides services to the investment company, investment trust or collective investment vehicle such as those of an investment adviser, custodian, transfer agent, broker, registrar, paying agent, sponsor, distributor, administrator, manager or otherwise and receives compensation for those services. In order to invest or reinvest funds under sub. (2) in the securities of, or other interests in, the investment company, investment trust or collective investment vehicle for which the bank, trust company or affiliate provides services, the bank, trust company or affiliate shall disclose in writing the basis upon which any compensation for such services is calculated, whether expressed as a percentage of asset value or otherwise. The disclosure shall be made by prospectus, account statement or otherwise and shall be delivered, at least annually, to all persons to whom statements of account for the invested or reinvested funds are provided.

Wis. Stat. 881.016 Employees and agents of a fiduciary.

Unless prohibited by the terms of the instrument governing a fiduciary relationship, a fiduciary may employ attorneys, accountants, investment advisers, agents or other persons, even if they are associated with the fiduciary, to advise or assist the fiduciary in the performance of the fiduciary's duties. The fiduciary may act without independent investigation upon their recommendations or, instead of acting directly, employ one or more agents to perform any act of administration, whether or not discretionary. If the terms of the governing instrument do not address the authority of the fiduciary to delegate the fiduciary's duties, all of the following apply:

(1) The fiduciary may delegate some, but not all, of the fiduciary's duties to an agent.

(2) The employment of an agent by the fiduciary does not relieve the fiduciary of liability for acts of the agent that, if done by the fiduciary, would result in the liability of the fiduciary.

(3) The employment of an agent by a fiduciary does not relieve the fiduciary of the fiduciary's duty to use reasonable care in selecting and retaining the agent.

Wis. Stat. 881.02 Construction; court orders; written instruments.

Nothing contained in this chapter shall be construed as authorizing any departure from, or variation of, the express terms or limitations set forth in any will, agreement, court order, or other instrument creating or defining the fiduciary's duties and powers.

Wis. Stat. 881.03 Jurisdiction of court.

Nothing contained in this chapter shall be construed to affect the power or jurisdiction of any court of the state of Wisconsin in respect to trusts and trustees, nor as restricting the power of a court of proper jurisdiction to permit a fiduciary to deviate from the terms of any will, agreement or other instrument relating to the acquisition, investment, reinvestment, exchange, retention, sale or management of fiduciary property.

Wis. Stat. 881.04 Investments under prior laws not affected.

Nothing contained in this chapter shall affect any investment made prior to the enactment hereof or any amendment hereof or affect any rights or interests established, accrued or created thereunder or affect any suit or action pending when this chapter or any amendment hereof becomes effective.

Wis. Stat. 881.05 Retention of securities by trustees.

(1) Unless the trust instrument or a court order specifically directs otherwise, a trustee shall not be required to dispose of any property, real or personal, or mixed, in the estate or trust, however acquired, until the trustee determines in the exercise of a sound discretion that it is advisable to dispose of the same; but nothing herein contained shall excuse the trustee from the duty to exercise discretion at reasonable intervals and to determine at such times the advisability of retaining or disposing of such property.

(2) Any heir or beneficiary shall have the right at any time to file an application with the court in which said estate or trust is being administered for the purpose of compelling the sale of such property so held, and to compel the investment of the proceeds in other investments which are in accordance with this chapter. Upon the filing of such application said court shall conduct a hearing, after giving to all persons interested in said estate or trust such notice as shall be designated by said court, and upon such hearing said court shall enter an order thereon directing the retention or sale of such property as may be for the best interests of said estate or trust.

Wis. Stat. 881.06 Law governing existing instruments.

Subject to s. 881.01 (12), this chapter shall govern fiduciaries, including personal representatives, guardians of the estate, conservators, and trustees acting under wills, agreements, court orders, and other instruments now existing or hereafter made.

In re Mueller's Trust

Supreme Court of Wisconsin
28 Wis. 2d 26, 135 N.W.2d 854 (1965)

Wilkie, J. Three major issues are presented on this appeal:

1. Did the trial court err in determining that the cotrustees had a duty to diversify the single asset of the trusts, the Worthington stock, and that this duty was breached by the failure to sell in October or November of 1961?

2. Are the beneficiaries of the trusts estopped from making any claim against appellant?

3. Is appellant entitled to indemnification or contribution from his co-trustee as to any part of the amount of his surcharge on the two testamentary trusts?

Diversification of the Trusts.

The trial court concluded first that the trustees should have diversified the investments of the three trusts within a reasonable time after October 18, 1958, when the THIRD and FOURTH article trust accounts were approved, and second, that the trustees should have disposed of 80 percent of the Worthington stock in October or November of 1961.

We first consider the trustees' duty to diversify.

A basic rule of trust administration is that a trustee should diversify investments so as to minimize the risk of loss. The Restatement, 1 Trusts (2d), p. 541, sec. 228, provides:

"Except as otherwise provided by the terms of the trust, the trustee is under a duty to the beneficiary to distribute the risk of loss by a reasonable diversification of investments, unless under the circumstances it is prudent not to do so."

Appellant first turns to the terms of the trust instruments and argues that the trustees had the power, under these instruments, to retain the Worthington common stock. However, the inter vivos trust instrument did not authorize the retention of any stock whatsoever and only Mueller common stock could have been retained under the express terms of the article THIRD and FOURTH trusts.

As to both the article THIRD and FOURTH trusts the will provided:

"[Article FIFTH] (c) Said trustees may in their discretion participate in and make any payments required by any proceedings for the reorganization, refinancing, dissolution, or other transactions, including the acquisition of stock rights when offered, and may accept substituted or distributed stocks and securities, in respect of any corporate securities subsisting in said trusts." (Emphasis added.)

Article 6 of the inter vivos trust contained an identical provision. Thus the trust instruments authorized the acceptance of substitute stock (Worthington), but contained no express authorization to retain the substituted stock.

While there is no express provision authorizing the trustees to retain the substituted stock, if the Worthington stock was substantially equivalent to Mueller, the trustees under both the article THIRD and FOURTH trusts (but in no event under the inter vivos trust) could have retained the Worthington stock once it was received in the exchange for Mueller. But as appellant himself admitted, Worthington was a considerably different corporation in terms of size, variety of products, and ownership. Accordingly, the stocks were obviously different and it cannot be seriously contended that the stocks were substantially equivalent.

As a further contention in support of his position that the express terms of the testamentary trust instrument (as distinguished from the inter vivos trust instrument) authorized the trustees to hold onto the Worthington stock, appellant cites another provision of the will, to wit article FIFTH, par. (b), which provides:

"My trustees shall have power in their discretion to take, receive, hold, administer, collect, invest, and reinvest the assets of said trust estates, with full power to bargain, sell, and convey at such prices and upon such terms as to them may seem best, or to exchange or otherwise realize upon any or all of the assets of said trust estates as and when said trustees, in their discretion, deem it advisable. . . ." (Emphasis added.)

Relying on In re Allis's Estate, Estate of Allis, and Welch v. Welch, appellant contends that this language, while not specifically sanctioning retention of the substituted stock, was broad enough to have permitted the trustees to do so without regard to any statutory limitations. In these three cases, this court held that where sweeping powers are given in regard to investing and reinvesting the trust assets, the trustees are not bound to comply with specific statutory limitations on retention of particular investments. But even with such broad powers, this court held that the trustees are still required to act as prudent and provident persons would act under similar circumstances.

In Allis the will granted the trustees:

"'. . . full power and authority in their discretion to invest, reinvest and employ said real estate and generally manage the same; to continue the same as it is invested at the time of my death -- and especially as invested in the E. P. Allis Company, or to change such investments; to receive and collect such profits and income thereof, and to dispose of the net income as follows.'"

In Welch the trust deed provided that:

"'Said trustees, their survivors and successors, shall have full power and authority to grant, bargain, sell, convey and otherwise dispose of the whole or any part of said property and to invest and reinvest the proceeds of any sales thereof, and to convert personal property into real property and real property into personal property as they may deem for the best interests of the trust estate, . . .'"

A comparison of the above-quoted provisions of the Mueller will (Article FIFTH (b)) discloses that the trustees (as to the article THIRD and FOURTH trusts) may well have been empowered to retain the Worthington stock without complying with statutory regulations in regard to the type or class of security retained. However, in the last analysis, and as the Allis and Welch cases held, regardless of the trust provisions the ultimate question as to the two testamentary trusts and the inter vivos trust is whether or not the trustees acted prudently in retaining the Worthington stock.

Therefore, we now turn from a consideration of the effect of the terms of each trust instrument to an analysis of whether the action of the trustees in not diversifying each of the three trusts was prudent. The late Andrew Carnegie once admonished: "Put all your eggs in one basket and watch the basket." This may be good advice for some investors, but it is not the prevailing rule governing the investment practices of trustees. The rule is diversification. The exception is to retain the stock.

Is there any guide in the statutes as to what is prudent? Ch. 320, the trust-fund-investment chapter, was amended on August 1, 1959, to adopt the "prudent man" investment rule. To begin with this statute provides:

"Executors, administrators, guardians and trustees may invest the funds of their trusts in accordance with the provisions pertaining to investments contained in the instrument under which they are acting, or in the absence of any such provision, then within the limits of the following standards:"

Then follow subsections (1) and (2). Sec. 320.01 (1) provides that the fiduciary shall:

". . . exercise the judgment and care under the circumstances then prevailing, which men of prudence, discretion and intelligence exercise in the management of their own affairs, not in regard to speculation but in regard to the permanent disposition of their funds, considering the probable income as well as the probable safety of their capital. . . ."

Sec. 320.01 (2) qualifies (1) by limiting (with certain qualifications not relevant here) the holdings in common stock to 50 percent of the total market value of the fund. Thus, in trusts subject to the provisions of sec. 320.01 (2), the statutes themselves forbid investment in common stock in excess of 50 percent of the fund. This is true of the inter vivos trust.

It appears that the standards set forth in sec. 320.01 (1) and (2), Stats., do not apply to the two testamentary trusts in the instant case in view of the authority vested in the trustee by the provisions above cited. On the other hand these standards do apply to the inter vivos trust where there was no similar provision in the trust instrument.

Respondents also point out that the statutes prior to August 1, 1959, limited investments in one stock to only 20 percent of the trust fund. 14 Since the trial court concluded that the Worthington stock in the trusts should have been sold in October or November, 1961, the provisions of this section were not in effect at the time and have no bearing on any legislative standard of what is prudent. This is true even though the trial court's determination that the trustees should have sold 80 percent of Worthington is apparently based, in part, on the provisions of this statute and, in part, on the fact that the objectors claim that the trustees had a duty to dispose of 80 percent of the stock.

Since the trial court concluded that the stock in all three trusts should have been diversified to the extent of 80 percent of the holdings of Worthington, the statutes, even as to the inter vivos trust, do not control what is prudent, and the determination as to whether or not the conduct of the appellant was prudent, in the last analysis, is governed as to all three trusts by the fundamental rules regarding diversification. The basic rule of diversification applies to both the making of investments and the retention of investments. In the Restatement, 1 Trusts (2d), p. 548, sec. 230, comment j, it is stated, in part:

"Diversification. Except as otherwise provided by the terms of the trust, the trustee is under a duty to the beneficiary to distribute the risk of loss by disposing of investments included in the trust at the time of its creation which, although otherwise proper investments for the trustee to retain, are improper because not properly diversified. Compare §228. Thus, if a testator bequeaths all his property in trust and more than half of his estate consists of the bonds of a particular railroad, the trustee is ordinarily under a duty to sell some of the bonds and to invest the proceeds in other securities, so that the estate will not include an undue proportion of the securities of a single corporation."

The trial court picked October 16, 1958, the date of the approval of the trustees' accounts in the article THIRD and FOURTH trusts, as the date when the trustees' duty arose to diversify by selling the Worthington stock in all three trusts. In essence, the court's conclusion is based entirely on the application of the fundamental rules requiring diversification of trust investments.

There is no point in considering whether the duty to diversify actually arose back in 1954 when the Worthington stock was first received. The objectors concede that the "Order of October 18, 1958, approving prior accounts had the effect of relieving the trustees from their prior duty to diversify." (Emphasis added.) It is the duty arising thereafter that the objectors contend for and which the trial court found. Once the duty to diversify arises the trustees should perform that duty as soon as they can reasonably do so. Fixing the exact deadline for diversification is an extremely difficult task and the general rule guiding the court in making that determination is set forth in 2 Scott, Trusts (2d ed.), p. 1548, sec. 209, where it is stated:

". . . it is ordinarily impossible to fix that moment [of the period within which he should have sold] with any exactness, at least where no time within which the trustee must sell the property is fixed in the trust instrument. Probably the only rule is that the court will use its common sense and determine what under all the circumstances it is fair to say that the trustee ought to have received if he had done his duty in selling the property within a reasonable time."

The trial court concluded that it was mandatory for the trustees to dispose of 80 percent of the stock no later than October or November of 1961. In arriving at this conclusion the trial court made certain findings of fact, which on review will be sustained unless against the great weight and clear preponderance of the evidence.

As a director of Worthington, appellant was aware of antitrust actions within the electrical industry. The status of certain treble-damage suits against Worthington was discussed at a directors' meeting on October 18, 1961. Appellant attempts to minimize this knowledge by maintaining that he did not feel that Worthington would become involved in a significant number of suits. It may well be that Worthington's ultimate involvement in the suits was negligible. But the trial court's decision (Findings No. 10 and No. 11, and Conclusion No. 2) did not rest on this alone; it was not unreasonable for the trial court to have concluded that this information had at least a small bearing on the question of whether and when it was prudent to sell Worthington.

In addition, by virtue of his corporate office, appellant was aware that Worthington was in a profit squeeze. (Findings No. 10 and No. 11, and Conclusion No. 2). The percentage of income before taxes to billings had dropped from 7.18 percent in 1960 to 4.87 percent in 1961. Earnings dropped from $4.42 in 1960 to $3.40 in 1961. Dividends were also cut and the price of Worthington stock dropped approximately 50 percent between September, 1961, and December, 1962. Appellant counters that it was not only Worthington but the whole capital-goods industry that was involved in a profit squeeze. But this analysis ignores the possibility of investing in another segment of the market. Appellant also points out that the backlog of Worthington's unfilled orders was greater in 1961 than in 1960. But this is no particular advantage if profits are down.

Commencing on October 18, 1961, the date of the Worthington board of directors' meeting, the appellant resumed the sale of his personally held Worthington stock. (He had sold 20,500 shares from 1954 through 1958 with no sales after that date until those in 1961.) All told, in the months of October and November of 1961, he sold 13,000 shares so that by the end of these sales he had disposed of 53.2 percent of his total holdings of 62,850 shares, leaving 29,380 shares. He received an average price of approximately $51 per share on these 1961 sales. No trust shares of Worthington were sold until 1963.

Appellant maintains that the corpus of the trust would have been significantly reduced by the payment of the state and federal income taxes on any sales of Worthington (in 1961 or otherwise), and that the trial court ignored these tax consequences in arriving at its twofold conclusion: The duty to diversify and the mandatory sale date of 1961. The Mueller Furnace Company stock had a tax basis of zero in the THIRD and FOURTH article trusts, and five cents a share in the inter vivos trust. The respective bases were transferred to the Worthington stock under the tax-free reorganization in 1954. Although the tax factor is one which can be properly considered in passing on the prudence of the trustee's actions, the trial court not only made no mention of it in its conclusions, findings, or decision, but expressly indicated during the trial that "the tax angle has nothing to do with the propriety of the accounts." However, the failure of the trial court to consider any income-tax ramifications is not grounds, of itself, for reversal in this case. This is because the trial court could still have properly concluded, relying on the general rule calling for diversification in connection with appellant's knowledge of Worthington's financial condition, that it was imprudent to retain the stock even if he had considered the possible tax implications. This is not to say that the tax aspect is unimportant; rather it is to say that under the circumstances any tax advantages gained by not diversifying were outweighed by the factors requiring the sale of part of the Worthington stock.

At the trial, appellant introduced many investment digests, analyses, and bulletins he had received which indicated, in somewhat glowing terms, that Worthington was a sound investment. But a trustee cannot ignore the rule requiring diversification merely because a particular stock is a prudent investment in terms of quality.

It is apparent from its decision and findings, that the trial court placed much emphasis on the fact that appellant Mueller disposed of a considerable block of his personal holdings of Worthington in the fall of 1961, while not making similar disposals of the stock in the trusts. However, although appellant did sell 13,000 shares in October and November, he retained 29,380 shares, or 46.8 percent of his original holdings in the company. No further sales were made until August of the next year. In addition, the mere fact that appellant sold some of his own Worthington stock does not mean that retaining the stock in the trusts was imprudent per se. The sale has a bearing on the present case only if the same reasons which prompted it would also dictate a diversification of the trusts. Because he was in a 90 percent tax bracket, appellant claims that he sold the Worthington stock, upon the suggestion of his financial adviser, in order to invest in municipals. Even assuming, then, that it was to his advantage to dispose of his Worthington holdings, this does not mean that it was not to the advantage of the beneficiaries to sell. Mrs. Mueller, the income beneficiary of the THIRD article and inter vivos trusts, was in the 65 percent bracket herself. Arguably, it would have been equally as sound to invest in municipals to give her a tax break also. But this is somewhat conjectural.

Appellant believes that a recent New York case, In re Kellogg's Trust, controls the present situation. In Kellogg, the trust assets consisted of most of the stock of a holding company which in turn held stock of a family corporation and title to the family estate. A new tax law subsequently necessitated the dissolving of the holding company, and the assets passed directly to the trust. The beneficiaries objected to the trustee's account, claiming that it was improper to retain the stock of the family corporation as the sole asset. After considering all the relevant facts, the court found that the trustee had acted prudently. Kellogg can be distinguished on three grounds without discussing all the unique facts in the case. First, the court concluded that the stock could be retained under the terms of the trust agreement. This was not the case here. Second, New York law does not place the emphasis on diversification that Wisconsin law does. Third, in Kellogg the trustee had confidence that the long-range prospects of the business were good, whereas here the trustee had so little confidence in Worthington that he sold a sizeable block of his own stock.

The trial court found as a matter of fact (Finding No. 13) that appellant retained the Worthington stock in the trusts primarily for voting-control purposes. But since there were over 1,600,000 shares of Worthington stock outstanding, of which only a little more than 15,000 were held by the trust, this could hardly have been a "paramount consideration." In addition, the fact that he had disposed of over half of his personal holdings is inconsistent with this purportedly avowed purpose. Furthermore, there was no evidence adduced which affirmatively demonstrated that voting control played any part in his decision. Therefore, this particular finding is against the great weight and clear preponderance of the evidence.

However, keeping in mind that diversification is the general rule, it cannot be said, in light of the information possessed by appellant concerning the financial affairs of Worthington, that the trial court erred in concluding that 80 percent of the stock should have been sold in the fall of 1961.

Estoppel.

The trial court concluded (Conclusion No. 3) that, "None of the beneficiaries of the trusts are estopped" from making a claim against appellant Mueller. Appellant attacks this as error.

As previously discussed, the beneficiaries of the two testamentary trusts concede that they are barred in these proceedings from questioning the prudence of retaining the Worthington stock as the sole asset prior to October 16, 1958, the date the accounts were approved. However, they do not concede that they are barred from questioning the prudence of retaining the stock in those two trusts after that date.

The general rule is that a beneficiary who, with knowledge of the facts, has acquiesced in the carrying of certain securities by the trustee is precluded from obtaining relief for a breach of trust for holding them. The key fact of which the beneficiary must have knowledge is that the specific asset, the retention of which he now complains was imprudent, was held by the trust.

With reference to the inter vivos trust, there is no evidence that any of the beneficiaries were aware that the Worthington stock was the sole asset in the trust. It was reasonable, therefore, for the trial court to conclude that none of the beneficiaries of that trust is estopped from objecting to the appellant's failure to diversify.

With reference to the article THIRD and FOURTH trusts, none of the beneficiaries, with the exception of Jean Mueller, knew of the status of the trust assets. Whether Jean Mueller is estopped because of her knowledge that Worthington continued as the sole asset of these trusts gained from her signing of the annual accounts, presents a moot question because in any event the other beneficiaries were not estopped from objecting to the failure to diversify these trusts.

Liability of Cotrustee.

After concluding (Conclusion No. 4) that appellant and respondent Jean Mueller were each at fault in the THIRD and FOURTH article trusts and thus equally responsible to the other beneficiaries, the trial court decided that Mrs. Mueller was entitled to indemnity from appellant for any liability on her part but that appellant had no corresponding right of indemnity against her because he was "substantially more at fault."

While she does not specifically attack the conclusion that she was at fault, respondent Jean Mueller devotes much time in her discussion of the indemnity issue to the proposition that she was in no way culpable. Since the question of indemnity does not even arise unless she actually was at fault, her argument along those lines will be treated, for the purposes of this opinion, as a challenge to the trial court's decision.

According to the Restatement, a cotrustee is liable to beneficiaries for a breach of trust committed by another cotrustee if he:

". . .

"(b) improperly delegates the administration of the trust to his co-trustee; or

". . .

"(d) by his failure to exercise reasonable care in the administration of the trust has enabled his co-trustee to commit a breach of trust; . . ."

These clauses are illustrated as follows:

"[b] A and B are co-trustees. A directs B to invest the trust funds without consulting with A. In breach of trust B invests in shares of stock. A is liable for breach of trust."

"[d] A and B are co-trustees. A improperly permits B to have the sole custody and management of the trust property and makes no inquiry as to his conduct. B is thereby enabled to sell the trust property and embezzle the proceeds. A is liable for breach of trust."

It should be noted that the breaches in the examples involved affirmative conduct on the part of one of the trustees. In the clause (b) example, one trustee actually directed the other to manage the trust, while in the clause (d) illustration the trustee was guilty of embezzlement. In the present case, there is no evidence that respondent Jean Mueller expressly authorized appellant to handle the trust affairs. It appears that any fault on the part of appellant was passive rather than active. But there is no good reason why subsection (b) should not apply when the one trustee impliedly consents to letting the other do the administering, or why (d) would not apply in a situation where the breach results from mere omission.

Professor Scott says:

"Where there are several trustees, each of them is under a duty to participate in the administration of the trust and to use reasonable care to prevent a co-trustee from committing a breach of trust. Even if one trustee does not affirmatively delegate the administration of the trust to his co-trustee, he is liable if by his failure to exercise reasonable care in supervising the conduct of his co-trustee he allows him to commit a breach of trust."

Respondent Jean Mueller was content to let appellant alone handle the trust affairs from the date of its inception. The record shows that she made no inquiries of him regarding trust affairs subsequent to the time the Worthington stock was acquired in 1954. Having assumed the position of trustee, she was bound to perform the duties required of her, and cannot escape liability merely because she relied entirely on the cotrustee to actually run the show. Any other result would drive cotrustees into the weeds for safety's sake.

Having established that respondent Jean Mueller was at fault, the question of whether appellant is entitled to indemnity or contribution from her is reached.

The general rule is that when two trustees are liable for a breach of trust, each is entitled to contribution from the other except that:

"(a) if one of them is substantially more at fault than the other, he is not entitled to contribution from the other but the other is entitled to indemnity from him; . . ."

The Restatement lists four factors to be considered in determining whether one trustee is substantially more at fault than the other:

"(1) whether he fraudulently induced the other to join in the breach of trust; (2) whether he intentionally committed a breach of trust and the other was at most guilty of negligence; (3) whether because of his greater experience he controlled the conduct of the other, as in the case where he was an attorney and the other was a person without business experience who was accustomed to rely upon his judgment; (4) whether he alone committed the breach of trust and the other is liable only because of an improper delegation, or failure to exercise reasonable care to prevent him from committing a breach of trust, or neglect to take proper steps to compel him to redress the breach of trust."

Respondent Jean Mueller considers the following example given in the Restatement to control the present case:

"A and B are trustees for C. B permits A to assume the sole management of the trust. A purchases securities which are not proper trust investments. B does not know of or consent to the purchase. The securities are sold at a loss of $1000. If A makes good the loss he is not entitled to recover anything from B. If B makes good the loss he is entitled to recover $1000 from A."

But since her consent was required before any trust assets could be sold, Jean Mueller knew that the Worthington stock was the sole asset of the trust, and knew that no sales of Worthington were being made to diversify the trust. As a trustee she was bound, as much as appellant, to diversify the trust assets unless it was imprudent to do so.

One trustee is not more at fault so as not to be entitled to contribution merely because he was more negligent or active than the other. The mere fact that the other trustee did not actively participate in the breach does not necessarily put him in the position of being substantially less at fault.

We conclude, therefore, that Harold Mueller was not "substantially more at fault" than Jean Mueller. It follows that, although each is surcharged for the entire amount of the charge as to the two testamentary trusts where they were cotrustees, if the appellant pays the entire amount he is cntitled to a contribution from Jean Mueller of half that amount. If she pays the entire amount then she is entitled to contribution from appellant of half the amount. In other words, they should share equally in these particular surcharges.

A minority of the court, including the author of this opinion, would affirm the lower court and hold that the appellant was "substantially more at fault" because of the fact that for whatever motive he sold a substantial block of his own Worthington stock in October or November of 1961 (after not making any personal sales of Worthington since 1958) without discussing with his cotrustee the fact of these sales or the advisability of selling or retaining the trust holdings in Worthington.

Judgment reversed as to that part ordering Harold P. Mueller to indemnify Jean Mueller with respect to the surcharges and interest thereon imposed under the testamentary trusts pursuant to paragraph 1 of the judgment; paragraphs 1 and 3 of the judgment affirmed; paragraph 4 vacated and cause remanded for revision thereof in a manner not inconsistent with this opinion. Costs on this appeal to be awarded to appellant as against respondent Jean Mueller and to other respondents as against appellant.

D. DUTY TO DIVIDE PRINCIPAL AND INTEREST

When there are both present and future beneficiaries, if the present beneficiary is entitled to the income of the trust, the present beneficiary will benefit most from an investment strategy that focuses upon maximizing current income. In contrast, the future beneficiary will benefit most from a strategy that increases principal rather than income. Because the trustee owes a duty to both, he and she has to balance the investments so that neither beneficiary is favored over the other (unless, of course, the trust instrument so dictates). Balancing these interests can be quite challenging and all that is required of the trustee is a good faith effort to do so.

Recently, the unitrust has emerged as a mechanism that greatly facilitates this duty. Under the unitrust, rather than receive the annual income of the trust, the present beneficiary each year receives a fixed percentage of the trust res (usually in the 2-5% range). This way, the form of the trustee's investments are immaterial to the future beneficiaries since the compensation of the present beneficiary is not dependent on a high present rate of yield. A great deal of current Wis. Stat. §701.20, which, as can be seen below, is by far the longest and most detailed portion of the Wisconsin trust statutes, is devoted to the unitrust and a procedure that can be used to convert old-style trusts to unitrusts.

Wis. Stat. 701.20. Principal and income.

(2) DEFINITIONS. In this section:

(a) "Accounting period" means a calendar year, unless a fiduciary selects another 12-month period, and includes a portion of a calendar year or other 12-month period that begins when an income interest begins or that ends when an income interest ends.

(b) "Beneficiary" means a person who has a beneficial interest in a trust or an estate and includes, in the case of a decedents estate, an heir, a legatee, and a devisee and, in the case of a trust, an income beneficiary and a remainder beneficiary.

(c) "Fiduciary" means a personal representative or a trustee and includes an executor, administrator, successor personal representative, special administrator, and a person performing substantially the same function as any of those.

(d) "Income" means money or property that a fiduciary receives as current return from a principal asset. "Income" includes a portion of receipts from a sale, exchange, or liquidation of a principal asset, to the extent provided in subs. (10) to (24) (e) "Income beneficiary" means a person to whom net income of a trust is or may be payable.

(f) "Income interest" means the right of an income beneficiary to receive all or part of net income, whether the terms of the trust require it to be distributed or authorize it to be distributed in the trustees discretion.

(g) "Mandatory income interest" means the right of an income beneficiary to receive net income that the terms of the trust require the fiduciary to distribute.

(h) "Net income" means the total receipts allocated to income during an accounting period, minus the disbursements made from income during the period, plus or minus transfers under this section to or from income during the period.

(i) "Person" means an individual; corporation; business trust; estate; trust; partnership; limited liability company; association; joint venture; government; governmental subdivision, agency, or instrumentality; public corporation; or any other legal or commercial entity.

(j) "Principal" means property held in trust for distribution to a remainder beneficiary when the trust terminates or property held in trust in perpetuity.

(k) "Remainder beneficiary" means a person entitled to receive principal when an income interest ends.(L) "Sui juris beneficiary" means a beneficiary not under a legal disability. The term includes all of the following:

1. A court-appointed guardian of a beneficiary who is adjudicated incompetent.

2. An agent for an incapacitated beneficiary.

3. A court-appointed guardian of a minor beneficiary's estate or, if there is no court-appointed guardian, the parents of the minor beneficiary.

(m) "Terms of a trust" means the manifestation of the intent of a settlor or decedent with respect to a trust, expressed in a manner that admits of its proof in a judicial proceeding, whether by written or spoken words or by conduct.

(n) "Trustee" includes an original, additional, or successor trustee, whether or not appointed or confirmed by a court.

(3) FIDUCIARY DUTIES; GENERAL PRINCIPLES.

(a) In allocating receipts and disbursements to income or principal or between income and principal, and with respect to any matter within the scope of subs. (5) to (9), a fiduciary:

1. Shall first administer a trust or estate in accordance with the terms of the trust or the will, even if there is a different provision in this section.

2. May administer a trust or estate by the exercise of a discretionary power of administration given to the fiduciary by the terms of the trust or the will, even if the exercise of the power produces a result different from a result required or permitted by this section.

3. Shall administer a trust or estate in accordance with this section if the terms of the trust or the will do not contain a different provision or do not give the fiduciary a discretionary power of administration.

4. Shall add a receipt or charge a disbursement to principal to the extent that the terms of the trust and this section do not provide a rule for allocating the receipt or disbursement to principal or income or between principal and income.

(b) In exercising the power to adjust under sub. (4) (a) or a discretionary power of administration regarding a matter within the scope of this section, whether granted by the terms of a trust, a will, or this section, a fiduciary shall administer a trust or estate impartially, based on what is fair and reasonable to all of the beneficiaries, except to the extent that the terms of the trust or the will clearly manifest an intention that the fiduciary shall or may favor one or more of the beneficiaries. A determination in accordance with this section is presumed to be fair and reasonable to all of the beneficiaries.

(4) TRUSTEE'S POWER TO ADJUST.

(a) A trustee may adjust between principal and income to the extent the trustee considers necessary if the trustee invests and manages trust assets as a prudent investor, the terms of the trust describe the amount that may or must be distributed to a beneficiary by referring to the trusts income, and the trustee determines, after applying the rules in sub. (3) (a), that the trustee is unable to comply with sub. (3) (b) (b) In deciding whether and to what extent to exercise the power conferred by par. (a), a trustee shall consider all factors relevant to the trust and its beneficiaries, including the following factors to the extent they are relevant:

1. The nature, purpose, and expected duration of the trust.

2. The intent of the settlor.

3. The identity and circumstances of the beneficiaries.

4. The needs for liquidity, regularity of income, and preservation and appreciation of capital.

5. The assets held in the trust; the extent to which they consist of financial assets, interests in closely held enterprises, tangible and intangible personal property, or real property; the extent to which an asset is used by a beneficiary; and whether an asset was purchased by the trustee or received from the settlor.

6. The net amount allocated to income under the other subsections of this section and the increase or decrease in the value of the principal assets, which the trustee may estimate in the case of assets for which market values are not readily available.

7. Whether and to what extent the terms of the trust give the trustee the power to invade principal or accumulate income or prohibit the trustee from invading principal or accumulating income, and the extent to which the trustee has exercised a power from time to time to invade principal or accumulate income.

8. The actual and anticipated effect of economic conditions on principal and income and effects of inflation and deflation.

9. The anticipated tax consequences of an adjustment.

(c) A trustee may not make an adjustment:

1. If possessing or exercising the power to make an adjustment would disqualify an estate tax or gift tax marital or charitable deduction in whole or in part.

2. That reduces the actuarial value of the income interest in a trust to which a person transfers property with the intent to qualify for a gift tax exclusion.

3. That changes the amount payable to a beneficiary as a fixed annuity or a fixed fraction of the value of the trust assets.

4. From any amount that is permanently set aside for charitable purposes under a will or the terms of a trust and for which an estate tax or gift tax charitable deduction has been taken unless both income and principal are so set aside.

5. If possessing or exercising the power to make an adjustment causes an individual to be treated as the owner of all or part of the trust for income tax purposes, and the individual would not be treated as the owner if the trustee did not possess the power to make an adjustment.

6. If possessing or exercising the power to make an adjustment causes all or part of the trust assets to be included for estate tax purposes in the estate of an individual and the assets would not be included in the estate of the individual if the trustee did not possess the power to make an adjustment.

7. If the trustee is a beneficiary of the trust.

8. If the trust has been converted under sub. (4g) to a unitrust.

9. If the trust is an express unitrust, as defined in sub. (4j) (a) (d) If par. (c) 5., 6., or 7. applies to a trustee and there is more than one trustee, a cotrustee to whom the provision does not apply may make the adjustment unless the terms of the trust do not permit the exercise of the power by that cotrustee.

(e) A trustee may release the entire power conferred by par. (a) or may release only the power to adjust from income to principal or the power to adjust from principal to income if the trustee is uncertain about whether possessing or exercising the power will cause a result described in par. (c) 1. to 6. or if the trustee determines that possessing or exercising the power will or may deprive the trust of a tax benefit or impose a tax burden not described in par. (c)

The release may be permanent or for a specified period, including a period measured by the life of an individual.

(f) Terms of a trust that limit the power of a trustee to make an adjustment between principal and income do not affect the application of this subsection unless it is clear from the terms of the trust that the terms are intended to deny the trustee the power of adjustment conferred by par. (a)

(4c) NOTICE TO BENEFICIARIES OF PROPOSED ACTION.

(b) A trustee may, but is not required to, obtain approval of a proposed action under sub. (4)(a) by providing a written notice that complies with all of the following:

1. Is given at least 30 days before the proposed effective date of the proposed action.

2. Is given in the manner provided in ch. 879, except that notice by publication is not required.

3. Is given to all sui juris beneficiaries who are any of the following:

a. Income beneficiaries currently eligible to receive income from the trust.

b. Eligible to receive, if no powers of appointment were exercised, income from the trust if the interest of all of those eligible to receive income under subd. 3. a. were to terminate immediately before the giving of notice.

c. A recipient, if no powers of appointment were exercised, of a distribution of principal if the trust were to terminate immediately before the giving of the notice.

4. States that it is given in accordance with this subsection and discloses the following information:

a. The identification of the trustee.

b. A description of the proposed action.

c. The time within which a beneficiary may object to the proposed action, which shall be at least 30 days after the giving of the notice.

d. The effective date of the proposed action if no objection is received from any beneficiary within the time specified in subd. 4. c. (c) If a trustee gives notice of a proposed action under this subsection, the trustee is not required to give notice to a sui juris beneficiary who consents to the proposed action in writing at any time before or after the proposed action is taken.

(d) A sui juris beneficiary may object to the proposed action by giving a written objection to the trustee within the time specified in the notice under par. (b) 4. c. (e) A trustee may decide not to take a proposed action after the trustee receives a written objection to the proposed action or at any other time for any other reason. In that case, the trustee shall give written notice to the sui juris beneficiaries of the decision not to take the proposed action.

(f) If a trustee receives a written objection to a proposed action within the time specified in the notice under par. (b) 4. c., either the trustee or the beneficiary making the written objection may petition the court to have the proposed action approved, modified, or prohibited. In the court proceeding, the beneficiary objecting to the proposed action has the burden of proving that the proposed action should be modified or prohibited. A beneficiary who did not make the written objection may oppose the proposed action in the court proceeding.

(g) For purposes of this subsection, a proposed action under sub. (4) includes a course of action or a decision not to take action under sub. (4)

(4g) CONVERSION TO UNITRUST.

(a) Subject to par. (d), a trust may be converted to a unitrust in any of the following ways:

1. By the trustee, at his or her own discretion or at the request of a beneficiary, if all of the following apply:

a. The trustee determines that the conversion will enable the trustee to better carry out the purposes of the trust.

b. The trustee provides notice in the same manner as provided in sub. (4c) (b) of the trustees intention to convert the trust to a unitrust, and the notice advises how the unitrust will operate, including the fixed percentage under par. (c) 1. and any other initial determinations under par. (c) 4. that the trustee intends to follow.

c. There is at least one sui juris beneficiary under sub. (4c) (b) 3. a. and at least one other sui juris beneficiary under sub. (4c) (b) 3. b. or c.

d. Every sui juris beneficiary consents to the conversion to a unitrust in a writing delivered to the trustee.

e. The terms of the trust describe the amount that may or must be distributed by referring to the trust income.

2. By a court on the petition of the trustee or a beneficiary, if all of the following apply:

a. The trustee or beneficiary has provided notice under sub. (4c) of the intention to request the court to convert the trust to a unitrust, and the notice advises how the unitrust will operate, including the fixed percentage under par. (c) 1. and any other initial determinations under par. (c) 4. that will be requested.

b. The court determines that the conversion to a unitrust will enable the trustee to better carry out the purposes of the trust.

(b) In deciding whether to convert the trust to a unitrust under par. (a) 1., the trustee shall consider all relevant factors under sub. (4) (b) 1. to 9. (c)

1. If a trust is converted to a unitrust under this subsection by the trustee or a court, notwithstanding sub. (3) (a) 1. and 4. and s. 701.21 (4) the trustee shall make distributions in accordance with the creating instrument, except that any reference in the creating instrument to "income" means a fixed percentage of the net fair market value of the unitrusts assets, whether such assets otherwise would be considered income or principal under this section, averaged over a preceding period determined by the trustee, which is at least 3 years but not more than 5 years, or the period since the original trust was created, whichever is less.

2.

a. Subject to subd. 2. b., if the trust is converted to a unitrust under par. (a) 1., the trustee shall determine the fixed percentage to be applied under subd. 1., and the notice under par. (a) 1. b. must state the fixed percentage. If the trust is converted to a unitrust under par. (a) 2., the court shall determine the fixed percentage to be applied under subd. 1.

b. Any fixed percentage under subd. 1. that is determined by a trustee may not be less than 3 percent nor more than 5 percent.

3. After a trust is converted to a unitrust, the trustee may, subject to the notice requirement under sub. (4c) and with the consent of every sui juris beneficiary, do any of the following:

a. Convert the unitrust back to the original trust under the creating instrument.

b. Change the fixed percentage under subd. 1., subject to subd. 2. b.

4. After a trust is converted to a unitrust, a trustee may determine or change any of the following:

a. The frequency of distributions during the year.

b. Standards for prorating a distribution for a short year in which a beneficiary's right to payments commences or ceases.

c. The effect on the valuation of the unitrusts assets of other payments from, or contributions to, the unitrust.

d. How, and how frequently, to value the unitrusts assets.

e. The valuation dates to use.

f. Whether to omit from the calculation of the value of the unitrusts assets unitrust property occupied by or in the possession of a beneficiary.

g. The averaging under subd. 1. to a different preceding period, which is at least 3 years but not more than 5 years.

h. Any other matters necessary for the proper functioning of the unitrust.

5. The trustee may not deduct from a unitrust distribution expenses that would be deducted from income if the trust were not a unitrust.

6. Unless otherwise provided by the creating instrument, the unitrust distribution is considered to have been paid from the following sources in the order of priority:

a. Net income, determined as if the trust were not a unitrust.

b. Ordinary income for federal income tax purposes that is not net income under subd. 6. a.

c. Net realized short-term capital gains for federal income tax purposes.

d. Net realized long-term capital gain for federal income tax purposes.

e. Principal.

7. A court may, on the petition of the trustee or a beneficiary, do any of the following:

a. Change the fixed percentage that was determined under subd. 2. by the trustee or by a prior court order.

b. If necessary to preserve a tax benefit, provide for a distribution of net income, determined as if the trust were not a unitrust, that exceeds the unitrust distribution.

c. Average the valuation of the unitrusts assets over a period other than that specified in subd. 1.

d. Require the unitrust to be converted back to the original trust under the creating instrument.

8. Conversion to a unitrust under this subsection does not affect a provision in the creating instrument that directs or authorizes the trustee to distribute principal or that authorizes a beneficiary to withdraw a portion or all of the principal.

(d)

1. A trust may not be converted under this subsection to a unitrust if any of the following applies:

a. The creating instrument specifically prohibits the conversion.

b. Payment of the unitrust distribution will change the amount payable to a beneficiary as a fixed annuity or a fixed fraction of the value of the trust assets.

c. The unitrust distribution will be made from any amount that is permanently set aside for charitable purposes under the creating instrument and for which an estate or gift tax charitable deduction has been taken, unless both income and principal are so set aside.

d. Converting to a unitrust will cause an individual to be treated as the owner of all or part of the trust for income tax purposes and the individual would not be treated as the owner if the trust were not converted.

e. Converting to a unitrust will cause all or a part of the trust assets to be subject to estate or gift tax with respect to an individual and the trust assets would not be subject to estate or gift tax with respect to the individual if the trust were not converted.

f. Converting to a unitrust will result in the disallowance of an estate or gift tax marital deduction that would be allowed if the trust were not converted.

g. A trustee is a beneficiary of the trust.

2. Notwithstanding subd. 1., if a trust may not be converted to a unitrust solely because subd. 1. g. applies to a trustee, a cotrustee, if any, to whom subd. 1. g. does not apply may convert the trust to a unitrust under par. (a) 1., unless prohibited by the creating instrument, or a court may convert the trust to a unitrust under par. (a) 2. on the petition of a trustee or beneficiary.

(e) A trustee may release the power conferred by par. (a) 1. if the trustee is uncertain about whether possessing or exercising the power will cause a result described in par. (d) 1. b. to f. or if the trustee determines that possessing or exercising the power will or may deprive the trust of a tax benefit or impose a tax burden not described in par. (d) 1. The release may be permanent or for a specified period, including a period measured by the life of an individual.

(4j) EXPRESS UNITRUSTS.

(a) In this subsection "express unitrust" means any trust that by its governing instrument requires the distribution at least annually of a unitrust amount equal to a fixed percentage of the net fair market value of the trust's assets, valued at least annually, other than a trust solely for charitable purposes or a charitable split-interest trust under section 664 (d) or 170 (f) (2) (B) of the Internal Revenue Code.

(b) The following apply to an express unitrust:

1. To the extent not otherwise provided for in the governing instrument, the unitrust amount of not less than 3 percent nor more than 5 percent may be determined by reference to the net fair market value of the trust's assets averaged over a preceding period determined by the trustee, which is at least 3 years but not more than 5 years.

2. Distribution of such a fixed percentage unitrust amount of not less than 3 percent nor more than 5 percent is a distribution of all of the income of the unitrust and is an income interest.

3. Such a distribution of a fixed percentage of not less than 3 percent nor more than 5 percent is a reasonable apportionment of the total return of the trust.

4. A trust that provides for a fixed annual percentage payout in excess of 5 percent per year of the net fair market value of the trust is considered to be a 5 percent express unitrust, paying out all of the income of the unitrust, and to have paid out principal of the trust to the extent that the fixed percentage payout exceeds 5 percent per year.

5. The governing instrument may grant discretion to the trustee to adopt a consistent practice of treating capital gains as part of the unitrust distribution, to the extent that the unitrust distribution exceeds the income determined as if the trust were not a unitrust, or it may specify the ordering of such classes of income.

6. Unless the terms of the trust specifically provide otherwise, a distribution of the unitrust amount is considered to have been made from the following sources in the following order of priority:

a. Net income determined as if the trust were not a unitrust.

b. Ordinary income for federal income tax purposes that is not net income under subd. 6. a.

c. Net realized short-term capital gains for federal income tax purposes.

d. Net realized long-term capital gains for federal income tax purposes.

e. Principal.

7. The trust document may provide that assets used by the trust beneficiary, such as a residence or tangible personal property, may be excluded from the net fair market value for

computing the unitrust amount. Such use may be considered equivalent to the income or unitrust amount.

8. In the absence of contrary provisions in the governing document of an express unitrust, the provisions of sub. (4g) (c) 1., 4., and 5. apply.

(4k) POWER TO TREAT CAPITAL GAINS AS PART OF A DISTRIBUTION. Unless prohibited by the governing instrument, a trustee may cause gains from the sale or exchange of trust assets, as determined for federal income tax purposes, to be taxed for federal income tax purposes as part of a distribution of income that has been increased by an adjustment from principal to income under sub. (4), of a unitrust distribution, of a fixed annuity distribution, or of a principal distribution to a beneficiary.

(4m) JUDICIAL REVIEW OF DISCRETIONARY POWER.

(a) Nothing in this section creates a duty to make an adjustment under sub. (4) or to convert a trust to a unitrust under sub. (4g) Unless it determines that the decision to make an adjustment or to convert to a unitrust was an abuse of the fiduciary's discretion, a court may not grant relief from any decision a fiduciary makes regarding the exercise of a discretionary power conferred by sub. (4) or (4g) (am) An action taken under sub. (4) or (4g) is not an abuse of a fiduciary's discretion if the fiduciary gave written notice of the proposed action under sub. (4c) and did not receive a timely written objection to the notice. It is not an abuse of discretion not to exercise the power to adjust under sub. (4) or to convert under sub. (4g)

(b) A fiduciary's decision is not an abuse of discretion merely because the court would have exercised the power in a different manner or would not have exercised the power.

(c) If the court determines that a fiduciary has abused the fiduciary's discretion, the remedy shall be to restore the income and remainder beneficiaries to the positions that they would have occupied had the discretion not been abused, according to the following rules:

1. To the extent that the abuse of discretion has resulted in no distribution to a beneficiary or in a distribution that is too small, the court shall order the fiduciary to distribute from the trust to the beneficiary an amount that the court determines will restore the beneficiary, in whole or in part, to the beneficiary's appropriate position.

2. To the extent that the abuse of discretion has resulted in a distribution to a beneficiary that is too large, the court shall place the beneficiaries, the trust, or both, in whole or in part, in their appropriate positions by ordering the fiduciary to withhold an amount from one or more future distributions to the beneficiary who received the distribution that was too large or by ordering that beneficiary to return some or all of the distribution to the trust.

3. To the extent that the court is unable, after applying subds. 1. and 2., to place the beneficiaries, the trust, or both in the positions that they would have occupied had the discretion not been abused, the court may order the fiduciary to pay an appropriate amount from its own funds to one or more of the beneficiaries, the trust, or both.

(d) Upon petition by the fiduciary, the court having jurisdiction over a trust shall determine whether a proposed exercise or nonexercise by the fiduciary of a discretionary power conferred under this section will result in an abuse of the fiduciary's discretion. The petition must describe the proposed exercise or nonexercise of the power and contain sufficient information to inform the beneficiaries of the reasons for the proposal, the facts upon which the fiduciary relies, and an explanation of how the income and remainder beneficiaries will be affected by the proposed exercise or nonexercise of the power. A beneficiary who challenges the proposed exercise or nonexercise of the power has the burden of establishing that it will result in an abuse of discretion.

(5) DETERMINATION AND DISTRIBUTION OF NET INCOME. In the case of an estate of a decedent or after an income interest in a trust ends, the following rules apply:

(a) A fiduciary of an estate or of a terminating income interest shall determine the amount of net income and net principal receipts received from property specifically given to a beneficiary under the rules in subs. (7) to (30) that apply to trustees and the rules in par. (e) The fiduciary shall distribute the net income and net principal receipts to the beneficiary who is to receive the specific property.

(b) A fiduciary shall determine the remaining net income of a decedent's estate or a terminating income interest under the rules in subs. (7) to (30) that apply to trustees and by:

1. Including in net income all income from property used to discharge liabilities.

2. Paying from income or principal, in the fiduciary's discretion, fees of attorneys, accountants, and fiduciaries; court costs and other expenses of administration; and interest on death taxes, but the fiduciary may pay those expenses from income of property passing to a trust for which the fiduciary claims an estate tax marital or charitable deduction only to the extent that the payment of those expenses from income will not cause the reduction or loss of the deduction.

3. Paying from principal all other disbursements made or incurred in connection with the settlement of a decedents estate or the winding up of a terminating income interest, including debts, funeral expenses, disposition of remains, family allowances, and death taxes and related penalties that are apportioned to the estate or terminating income interest by the will, the terms of the trust, or applicable law.

(c) A fiduciary shall distribute to a beneficiary, including a trustee, who receives a pecuniary amount not determined by a pecuniary formula interest at the legal rate set forth in s. 138.04 on any unpaid portion of the pecuniary amount for the period commencing one year after the decedents death or after the income interest in the trust ends. The interest under this paragraph shall be distributed from net income determined under par. (b) or from principal to the extent that net income is insufficient. For purposes of this paragraph, the deferred marital property elective share amount elected by a surviving spouse under s. 861.02 (1) is a bequest of a specific amount of money not determined by a pecuniary formula.

(d) A fiduciary shall distribute the net income remaining after distributions required by par. (c) in the manner described in sub. (6) to all other beneficiaries, including a beneficiary who receives a pecuniary amount determined by a pecuniary formula.

(e) A fiduciary may not reduce principal or income receipts from property described in par. (a) because of a payment described in sub. (25) or (26) to the extent that the will, the terms of the trust, or applicable law requires the fiduciary to make the payment from assets other than the property or to the extent that the fiduciary recovers or expects to recover the payment from a 3rd party. The net income and principal receipts from the property are determined by including all of the amounts the fiduciary receives or pays with respect to the property, whether those amounts accrued or became due before, on, or after the date of a decedents death or an income interests terminating event, and by making a reasonable provision for amounts that the fiduciary believes the estate or terminating income interest may become obligated to pay after the property is distributed.

(6) DISTRIBUTION TO RESIDUARY AND REMAINDER BENEFICIARIES.

(a) Each beneficiary described in sub. (5) (d) is entitled to receive a portion of the net income equal to the beneficiary's fractional interest in undistributed principal assets, using values as of the distribution date. If a fiduciary makes more than one distribution of assets to beneficiaries to whom this subsection applies, each beneficiary, including one who does not receive part of the distribution, is entitled, as of each distribution date, to the net income the fiduciary has received after the date of death or terminating event or earlier distribution date but has not distributed as of the current distribution date.

(b) In determining a beneficiary's share of net income, the following rules apply:

1. The beneficiary is entitled to receive a portion of the net income equal to the beneficiary's fractional interest in the undistributed principal assets immediately before the distribution date, including assets that later may be sold to meet principal obligations.

2. The beneficiary's fractional interest in the undistributed principal assets must be calculated without regard to property specifically given to a beneficiary and property required to pay pecuniary amounts not determined by a pecuniary formula.

3. The beneficiary's fractional interest in the undistributed principal assets must be calculated on the basis of the aggregate value of those assets as of the distribution date without reducing the value by any unpaid principal obligation.

4. The distribution date for purposes of this subsection may be the date as of which the fiduciary calculates the value of the assets if that date is reasonably near the date on which assets are actually distributed.

(c) If a fiduciary does not distribute all of the collected but undistributed net income to each person as of a distribution date, the fiduciary shall maintain appropriate records showing the interest of each beneficiary in that net income.

(d) A trustee may apply the rules in this subsection, to the extent that the trustee considers it appropriate, to net gain or loss realized after the date of death or terminating event or earlier distribution date from the disposition of a principal asset if this subsection applies to the income from the asset.

(7) WHEN RIGHT TO INCOME BEGINS AND ENDS.

(a) An income beneficiary is entitled to net income from the date on which the income interest begins. An income interest begins on the date specified in the terms of the trust or, if no date is specified, on the date an asset becomes subject to a trust or successive income interest.

(b) An asset becomes subject to a trust:

1. On the date it is transferred to the trust in the case of an asset that is transferred to a trust during the transferor's life.

2. On the date of a testators death in the case of an asset that becomes subject to a trust by reason of a will, even if there is an intervening period of administration of the testator's estate.

3. On the date of an individual's death in the case of an asset that a 3rd party transfers to a fiduciary because of the individuals death.

(c) An asset becomes subject to a successive income interest on the day after the preceding income interest ends, as determined under par. (d), even if there is an intervening period of administration to wind up the preceding income interest.

(d) An income interest ends on the day before an income beneficiary dies or another terminating event occurs, or on the last day of a period during which there is no beneficiary to whom a trustee may distribute income.

(8) APPORTIONMENT OF RECEIPTS AND DISBURSEMENTS WHEN DECEDENT DIES OR INCOME INTEREST BEGINS.

(a) A trustee shall allocate to principal an income receipt or disbursement other than one to which sub. (5) (a) applies if its due date occurs before a decedent dies in the case of an estate or before an income interest begins in the case of a trust or successive income interest.

(b) A trustee shall allocate to income an income receipt or disbursement if its due date occurs on or after the date on which a decedent dies or an income interest begins and it is a periodic due date. An income receipt or disbursement must be treated as accruing from day to day if its due date is not periodic or it has no due date. The portion of the receipt or disbursement accruing before the date of death or an income interest begins must be allocated to principal and the balance must be allocated to income.

(c) An item of income or an obligation is due on the date the payer is required to make a payment. If a payment date is not stated, there is no due date for the purposes of this section. Distributions to shareholders or other owners from an entity, as defined in sub. (10), are due on the date fixed by the entity for determining who is entitled to receive the distribution or, if no date is fixed, on the declaration date for the distribution. A due date is periodic for receipts or disbursements that must be paid at regular intervals under a lease or an obligation to pay interest or if an entity customarily makes distributions at regular intervals.

(9) APPORTIONMENT WHEN INCOME INTEREST ENDS.

(a) In this subsection, "undistributed income" means net income received before the date on which an income interest ends. "Undistributed income" does not include an item of income or expense that is due or accrued or net income that has been added or is required to be added to principal under the terms of the trust.

(b) When a mandatory income interest ends, the trustee shall pay to a mandatory income beneficiary who survives that date, or to the estate of a deceased mandatory income beneficiary whose death causes the interest to end, the beneficiary's share of the undistributed income that is not disposed of under the terms of the trust unless the beneficiary has an unqualified power to revoke more than 5 percent of the trust immediately before the income interest ends. In the latter case, the undistributed income from the portion of the trust that may be revoked must be added to principal.

(c) When a trustees obligation to pay a fixed annuity or a fixed fraction of the value of the trust's assets ends, the trustee shall prorate the final payment if and to the extent required by applicable law to accomplish a purpose of the trust or its settlor relating to income, gift, estate, or other tax requirements.

(10) CHARACTER OF RECEIPTS.

(a) In this subsection, "entity" means a corporation, partnership, limited liability company, regulated investment company, real estate investment trust, common trust fund, or any other organization in which a trustee has an interest other than a trust or estate to which sub. (11) applies, a business or activity to which sub. (12) applies, or an asset-backed security to which sub. (24) applies.

(b) Except as otherwise provided in this subsection, a trustee shall allocate to income money received from an entity.

(c) A trustee shall allocate the following receipts from an entity to principal:

1. Property other than money.

2. Money received in one distribution or a series of related distributions in exchange for part or all of a trusts interest in the entity.

3. Money received in total or partial liquidation of the entity.

4. Money received from an entity that is a regulated investment company or a real estate investment trust if the money distributed is a capital gain dividend for federal income tax purposes.

(d) Money is received in partial liquidation:

1. To the extent that the entity, at or near the time of a distribution, indicates that it is a distribution in partial liquidation.

2. If the total amount of money and property distributed in a distribution or series of related distributions is greater than 20 percent of the entity's gross assets, as shown by the entity's year-end financial statements immediately preceding the initial receipt.

(e) Money is not received in partial liquidation, nor may it be taken into account under par. (d) 2., to the extent that it does not exceed the amount of income tax that a trustee or beneficiary must pay on taxable income of the entity that distributes the money.

(f) A trustee may rely upon a statement made by an entity about the source or character of a distribution if the statement is made at or near the time of distribution by the entity's board of directors or other person or group of persons authorized to exercise powers to pay money or transfer property comparable to those of a corporation's board of directors.

(11) DISTRIBUTION FROM TRUST OR ESTATE. A trustee shall allocate to income an amount received as a distribution of income from a trust or an estate in which the trust has an interest other than a purchased interest, and shall allocate to principal an amount received as a distribution of principal from such a trust or estate. If a trustee purchases an interest in a trust that is an investment entity, or a decedent or donor transfers an interest in such a trust to a trustee, sub. (10) or (24) applies to a receipt from the trust.

(12) BUSINESS AND OTHER ACTIVITIES CONDUCTED BY TRUSTEE.

(a) If a trustee who conducts a business or other activity determines that it is in the best interest of all the beneficiaries to account separately for the business or activity instead of accounting for it as part of the trusts general accounting records, the trustee may maintain separate accounting records for its transactions, whether or not its assets are segregated from other trust assets.

(b) A trustee who accounts separately for a business or other activity may determine the extent to which its net cash receipts must be retained for working capital, the acquisition or replacement of fixed assets, and other reasonably foreseeable needs of the business or activity and the extent to which the remaining net cash receipts are accounted for as principal or income in the trusts general accounting records. If a trustee sells assets of the business or other activity, other than in the ordinary course of the business or activity, the trustee shall account for the net amount received as principal in the trusts general accounting records to the extent the trustee determines that the amount received is no longer required in the conduct of the business.

(c) Activities for which a trustee may maintain separate accounting records include:

1. Retail, manufacturing, service, and other traditional business activities.

2. Farming.

3. Raising and selling livestock and other animals.

4. Management of rental properties.

5. Extraction of minerals and other natural resources.

6. Timber operations.

7. Activities to which sub. (23) applies.

(13) PRINCIPAL RECEIPTS. A trustee shall allocate to principal:

(a) To the extent not allocated to income under this section, assets received from a transferor during the transferors lifetime, a decedents estate, a trust with a terminating income interest, or a payer under a contract naming the trust or its trustee as beneficiary.

(b) Money or other property received from the sale, exchange, liquidation, or change in form of a principal asset, including realized profit, subject to subs. (10) to (24)

(c) Amounts recovered from 3rd parties to reimburse the trust because of disbursements described in sub. (26) (a) 7. or for other reasons to the extent not based on the loss of income.

(d) Proceeds of property taken by eminent domain, but a separate award made for the loss of income with respect to an accounting period during which a current income beneficiary had a mandatory income interest is income.

(e) Net income received in an accounting period during which there is no beneficiary to whom a trustee may or must distribute income.

(f) Other receipts as provided in subs. (17) to (24)

(14) RENTAL PROPERTY. To the extent that a trustee accounts for receipts from rental property in accordance with this subsection, the trustee shall allocate to income an amount received as rent of real or personal property, including an amount received for cancellation or renewal of a lease. An amount received as a refundable deposit, including a security deposit or a deposit that is to be applied as rent for future periods, must be added to principal and held subject to the terms of the lease and is not available for distribution to a beneficiary until the trustees contractual obligations have been satisfied with respect to that amount.

(15) OBLIGATION TO PAY MONEY.

(a) An amount received as interest, whether determined at a fixed, variable, or floating rate, on an obligation to pay money to the trustee, including an amount received as consideration for prepaying principal, must be allocated to income without any provision for amortization of premium.

(b) A trustee shall allocate to principal an amount received from the sale, redemption, or other disposition of an obligation to pay money to the trustee more than one year after it is purchased or acquired by the trustee, including an obligation whose purchase price or value when it is acquired is less than its value at maturity. If the obligation matures within one year after the trustee purchases or acquires it, an amount received in excess of its purchase price or its value when the trust acquires it must be allocated to income.

(c) This subsection does not apply to an obligation to which sub. (18), (19), (20), (21), (23), or (24) applies.

(16) INSURANCE POLICIES AND SIMILAR CONTRACTS.

(a) Except as provided in par. (b), a trustee shall allocate to principal the proceeds of a life insurance policy or other contract in which the trust or its trustee is named as beneficiary, including a contract that insures the trust or its trustee against loss for damage to, destruction of, or loss of title to, a trust asset. The trustee shall allocate dividends on an insurance policy to income if the premiums on the policy are paid from income, and to principal if the premiums are paid from principal.

(b) A trustee shall allocate to income proceeds of a contract that insures the trustee against loss of occupancy or other use by an income beneficiary, loss of income, or, subject to sub. (12), loss of profits from a business.

(c) This subsection does not apply to a contract to which sub. (18) applies.

(17) INSUBSTANTIAL ALLOCATIONS NOT REQUIRED. If a trustee determines that an allocation between principal and income required by sub. (15) (b), (18), (19), (20), (21), or (24) is insubstantial, the trustee may allocate the entire amount to principal unless one of the circumstances described in sub. (4) (c) applies to the allocation. This power may be exercised by a cotrustee in the circumstances described in sub. (4) (d) and may be released for the reasons and in the manner described in sub. (4) (e) An allocation is presumed to be insubstantial if:

(a) The amount of the allocation would increase or decrease net income in an accounting period, as determined before the allocation, by less than 10 percent.

(b) The value of the asset producing the receipt for which the allocation would be made is less than 10 percent of the total value of the trust's assets at the beginning of the accounting period.

(18) DEFERRED COMPENSATION, ANNUITIES, AND SIMILAR PAYMENTS.

(a) In this subsection, "payment" means a payment that a trustee may receive over a fixed number of years or during the life of one or more individuals because of services rendered or property transferred to the payer in exchange for future payments. The term includes a payment made in money or property from the payers general assets or from a separate fund created by the payer, including a private or commercial annuity, an individual retirement account, and a pension, profit-sharing, stock-bonus, or stock-ownership plan.

(b) To the extent that a payment is characterized as interest or a dividend or a payment made in lieu of interest or a dividend, a trustee shall allocate it to income. The trustee shall allocate to principal the balance of the payment and any other payment received in the same accounting period that is not characterized as interest, a dividend, or an equivalent payment.

(c)

1. In this paragraph, "plan income" means any of the following:

a. With respect to payments received from a plan that maintains separate accounts or funds for its participants or account holders, such as defined contribution retirement plans, individual retirement accounts, Roth individual retirement accounts, and some types of deferred compensation plans, either the amount of the plan account or fund held for the benefit of the trust that, if the plan account or fund were a trust, would be allocated to income under pars. (b) and (d) for that accounting period, or 4 percent of the value of the plan account or fund on the first day of the accounting period. The trustee shall, in his or her discretion, choose the method of determining "plan income" under this subd. 1. a., and may change the method of determining "plan income" under this subd. 1. a. for any subsequent accounting period.

b. With respect to payments received from a plan that does not maintain separate accounts or funds for its participants or account holders, such as defined benefit retirement plans and some types of deferred compensation plans, 4 percent of the total present value of the trusts interest in the plan as of the first day of the accounting period, based on reasonable actuarial assumptions as determined by the trustee.

2. For each accounting period of a trust in which the trust receives a payment but no part of any payment is allocated to income under par. (b), the trustee shall allocate to income that portion of the aggregate value of all payments received by the trustee in that accounting period that is equal to the amount of plan income that is attributable to the trusts interest in the plan from which payment is received for that accounting period. The trustee shall allocate the balance of any payments to principal.

(d) If, to obtain an estate or gift tax marital deduction for an interest in a trust, a trustee must allocate more of a payment to income than provided for by this subsection, the trustee shall allocate to income the additional amount necessary to obtain the marital deduction.

(e) This subsection does not apply to payments to which sub. (19) applies.

(19) LIQUIDATING ASSET.

(a) In this subsection, "liquidating asset" means an asset whose value will diminish or terminate because the asset is expected to produce receipts for a period of limited duration. The term includes a leasehold, patent, copyright, royalty right, and right to receive payments during a period of more than one year under an arrangement that does not provide for the payment of interest on the unpaid balance. The term does not include a payment subject to sub. (18), resources subject to sub. (20), timber subject to sub. (21), an activity subject to sub. (23), an asset subject to sub. (24), or any asset for which the trustee establishes a reserve for depreciation under sub. (27)

(b) A trustee shall allocate to income 10 percent of the receipts from a liquidating asset and the balance to principal.

(20) MINERALS, WATER, AND OTHER NATURAL RESOURCES.

(a) To the extent that a trustee accounts for receipts from an interest in minerals or other natural resources in accordance with this subsection, the trustee shall allocate them as follows:

1. If received as nominal delay rental or nominal annual rent on a lease, a receipt must be allocated to income.

2. If received from a production payment, a receipt must be allocated to income if and to the extent that the agreement creating the production payment provides a factor for interest or its equivalent. The balance must be allocated to principal.

3. If an amount received as a royalty, shut-in-well payment, take-or-pay payment, bonus, or delay rental is more than nominal, 90 percent must be allocated to principal and the balance to income.

4. If an amount is received from a working interest or any other interest not provided for in subd. 1., 2., or 3., 90 percent of the net amount received must be allocated to principal and the balance to income.

(b) An amount received on account of an interest in water that is renewable must be allocated to income. If the water is not renewable, 90 percent of the amount must be allocated to principal and the balance to income.

(c) This subsection applies whether or not a decedent or donor was extracting minerals, water, or other natural resources before the interest became subject to the trust.

(d) If a trust owns an interest in minerals, water, or other natural resources on May 17, 2005, the trustee may allocate receipts from the interest as provided in this subsection or in the manner used by the trustee before May 17, 2005. If the trust acquires an interest in minerals, water, or other natural resources after May 17, 2005, the trustee shall allocate receipts from the interest as provided in this subsection.

(21) TIMBER.

(a) To the extent that a trustee accounts for receipts from the sale of timber and related products in accordance with this subsection, the trustee shall allocate the net receipts:

1. To income to the extent that the amount of timber removed from the land does not exceed the rate of growth of the timber during the accounting periods in which a beneficiary has a mandatory income interest.

2. To principal to the extent that the amount of timber removed from the land exceeds the rate of growth of the timber or the net receipts are from the sale of standing timber.

3. To income or principal or between income and principal if the net receipts are from the lease of timberland or from a contract to cut timber from land owned by a trust, by determining the amount of timber removed from the land under the lease or contract and applying the rules in subds. 1. and 2.

4. To principal to the extent that advance payments, bonuses, and other payments are not allocated under subd. 1., 2., or 3. (b) In determining net receipts to be allocated under par. (a), a trustee shall deduct and transfer to principal a reasonable amount for depletion.

(c) This subsection applies whether or not a decedent or transferor was harvesting timber from the property before it became subject to the trust.

(d) If a trust owns an interest in timberland on May 17, 2005, the trustee may allocate net receipts from the sale of timber and related products as provided in this subsection or in the manner used by the trustee before May 17, 2005. If the trust acquires an interest in timberland after May 17, 2005, the trustee shall allocate net receipts from the sale of timber and related products as provided in this subsection.

(22) PROPERTY NOT PRODUCTIVE OF INCOME.

(a) If a marital deduction is allowed for all or part of a trust whose assets consist substantially of property that does not provide the surviving spouse with sufficient income from or use of the trust assets, and if the amounts that the trustee transfers from principal to income under sub. (4) and distributes to the spouse from principal in accordance with the terms of the trust are insufficient to provide the spouse with the beneficial enjoyment required to obtain the marital deduction, the spouse may require the trustee to make property productive of income, convert property within a reasonable time, or exercise the power conferred by sub. (4) (a) The trustee may decide which action or combination of actions to take.

(b) In cases not governed by par. (a), proceeds from the sale or other disposition of an asset are principal without regard to the amount of income the asset produces during any accounting period.

(23) DERIVATIVES AND OPTIONS.

(a) In this subsection, "derivative" means a contract or financial instrument or a combination of contracts and financial instruments that gives a trust the right or obligation to participate in some or all changes in the price of a tangible or intangible asset or group of assets, or changes in a rate, an index of prices or rates, or another market indicator for an asset or a group of assets.

(b) To the extent that a trustee does not account under sub. (12) for transactions in derivatives, the trustee shall allocate to principal receipts from and disbursements made in connection with those transactions.

(c) If a trustee grants an option to buy property from the trust, whether or not the trust owns the property when the option is granted, grants an option that permits another person to sell property to the trust, or acquires an option to buy property for the trust or an option to sell an asset owned by the trust, and the trustee or other owner of the asset is required to deliver the asset if the option is exercised, an amount received for granting the option must be allocated to principal. An amount paid to acquire the option must be paid from principal. A gain or loss realized upon the exercise of an option, including an option granted to a settlor of the trust for services rendered, must be allocated to principal.

(24) ASSET-BACKED SECURITIES.

(a) In this subsection, "asset-backed security" means an asset whose value is based upon the right it gives the owner to receive distributions from the proceeds of financial assets that provide collateral for the security. The term includes an asset that gives the owner the right to receive from the collateral financial assets only the interest or other current return or only the proceeds other than interest or current return. The term does not include an asset to which sub. (10) or (18) applies.

(b) If a trust receives a payment from interest or other current return and from other proceeds of the collateral financial assets, the trustee shall allocate to income the portion of the payment that the payer identifies as being from interest or other current return and shall allocate the balance of the payment to principal.

(c) If a trust receives one or more payments in exchange for the trusts entire interest in an asset-backed security in one accounting period, the trustee shall allocate the payments to principal. If a payment is one of a series of payments that will result in the liquidation of the trusts interest in the security over more than one accounting period, the trustee shall allocate 10 percent of the payment to income and the balance to principal.

(25) DISBURSEMENTS FROM INCOME. A trustee shall make the following disbursements from income to the extent that they are not disbursements specified in sub. (5) (b) 2. or 3.:

(a) One-half of the regular compensation of the trustee and of any person providing investment advisory or custodial services to the trustee.

(b) One-half of all expenses for accountings, judicial proceedings, or other matters that involve both the income and remainder interests.

(c) All of the other ordinary expenses incurred in connection with the administration, management, or preservation of trust property and the distribution of income, including interest, ordinary repairs, regularly recurring taxes assessed against principal, and expenses of a proceeding or other matter that concerns primarily the income interest.

(d) Recurring premiums on insurance covering the loss of a principal asset or the loss of income from or use of the asset.

(26) DISBURSEMENTS FROM PRINCIPAL.

(a) A trustee shall make the following disbursements from principal:

1. The remaining one-half of the disbursements described in sub. (25) (a) and (b)

2. All of the trustee's compensation calculated on principal as a fee for acceptance, distribution, or termination, and disbursements made to prepare property for sale.

3. Payments on the principal of a trust debt.

4. Expenses of a proceeding that concerns primarily principal, including a proceeding to construe the trust or to protect the trust or its property.

5. Premiums paid on a policy of insurance not described in sub. (25) (d) of which the trust is the owner and beneficiary.

6. Estate, inheritance, and other transfer taxes, including penalties, apportioned to the trust.

7. Disbursements related to environmental matters, including reclamation, assessing environmental conditions, remedying and removing environmental contamination, monitoring

remedial activities and the release of substances, preventing future releases of substances, collecting amounts from persons liable or potentially liable for the costs of those activities, penalties imposed under environmental laws or regulations and other payments made to comply with those laws or regulations, statutory or common law claims by 3rd parties, and defending claims based on environmental matters.

(b) If a principal asset is encumbered with an obligation that requires income from that asset to be paid directly to the creditor, the trustee shall transfer from principal to income an amount equal to the income paid to the creditor in reduction of the principal balance of the obligation.

(27) TRANSFERS FROM INCOME TO PRINCIPAL FOR DEPRECIATION.

(a) In this subsection, "depreciation" means a reduction in value due to wear, tear, decay, corrosion, or gradual obsolescence of a fixed asset having a useful life of more than one year.

(b) A trustee may transfer to principal a reasonable amount of the net cash receipts from a principal asset that is subject to depreciation, but may not transfer any amount for depreciation:

1. Of that portion of real property used or available for use by a beneficiary as a residence or of tangible personal property held or made available for the personal use or enjoyment of a beneficiary.

2. During the administration of a decedents estate.

3. Under this subsection if the trustee is accounting under sub. (12) for the business or activity in which the asset is used.

(c) An amount transferred to principal need not be held as a separate fund.

(28) TRANSFERS FROM INCOME TO REIMBURSE PRINCIPAL.

(a) If a trustee makes or expects to make a principal disbursement described in this subsection, the trustee may transfer an appropriate amount from income to principal in one or more accounting periods to reimburse principal or to provide a reserve for future principal disbursements.

(b) Principal disbursements to which par. (a) applies include the following, but only to the extent that the trustee has not been and does not expect to be reimbursed by a 3rd party:

1. An amount chargeable to income but paid from principal because it is unusually large, including extraordinary repairs.

2. A capital improvement to a principal asset, whether in the form of changes to an existing asset or the construction of a new asset, including special assessments.

3. Disbursements made to prepare property for rental, including tenant allowances, leasehold improvements, and broker's commissions.

4. Periodic payments on an obligation secured by a principal asset to the extent that the amount transferred from income to principal for depreciation is less than the periodic payments.

5. Disbursements described in sub. (26) (a) 7. (c) If the asset whose ownership gives rise to the disbursements becomes subject to a successive income interest after an income interest ends, a trustee may continue to transfer amounts from income to principal as provided in par. (a)

(29) INCOME TAXES.

(a) A tax required to be paid by a trustee based on receipts allocated to income must be paid from income.

(b) A tax required to be paid by a trustee based on receipts allocated to principal must be paid from principal, even if the tax is called an income tax by the taxing authority.

(c) A tax required to be paid by a trustee on the trusts share of an entity's taxable income must be paid proportionately:

1. From income to the extent that receipts from the entity are allocated to income.

2. From principal to the extent that:

a. Receipts from the entity are allocated to principal.

b. The trusts share of the entity's taxable income exceeds the total receipts described in subds. 1. and 2. a.

(d) For purposes of this subsection, receipts allocated to principal or income must be reduced by the amount distributed to a beneficiary from principal or income for which the trust receives a deduction in calculating the tax.

(30) ADJUSTMENTS BETWEEN PRINCIPAL AND INCOME BECAUSE OF TAXES.

(a) A fiduciary may make adjustments between principal and income to offset the shifting of economic interests or tax benefits between income beneficiaries and remainder beneficiaries which arise from:

1. Elections and decisions, other than those described in par. (b), that the fiduciary makes from time to time regarding tax matters.

2. An income tax or any other tax that is imposed upon the fiduciary or a beneficiary as a result of a transaction involving or a distribution from the estate or trust.

3. The ownership by an estate or trust of an interest in an entity whose taxable income, whether or not distributed, is includable in the taxable income of the estate or trust or of a beneficiary.

(b) If the amount of an estate tax marital deduction or charitable contribution deduction is reduced because a fiduciary deducts an amount paid from principal for income tax purposes instead of deducting it for estate tax purposes, and as a result estate taxes paid from principal are increased and income taxes paid by an estate, trust, or beneficiary are decreased, each estate, trust, or beneficiary that benefits from the decrease in income tax shall reimburse the principal from which the increase in estate tax is paid. The total reimbursement must equal the increase in the estate tax to the extent that the principal used to pay the increase would have qualified for a marital deduction or charitable contribution deduction but for the payment. The proportionate share of the reimbursement for each estate, trust, or beneficiary whose income taxes are reduced must be the same as its proportionate share of the total decrease in income tax. An estate or trust shall reimburse principal from income.

(31) LIMITS ON LIABILITY.

(a) If a trustee sends to all beneficiaries a written communication relating to the trust, any action against the trustee that is based on the subject of the written communication shall be commenced within 2 years after the trustee sends the written communication or be barred.

(b)

1. A written communication is sent to a sui juris beneficiary on the date on which the written communication is delivered personally to the sui juris beneficiary or on the date on which the written communication is postmarked if mailed to the sui juris beneficiary at his or her last-known address.

2. A written communication is sent to a beneficiary who is not a sui juris beneficiary on the date on which the written communication is delivered personally to the beneficiary's parent or legal guardian or on the date on which the written communication is postmarked if mailed to the beneficiary's parent or legal guardian at his or her last-known address.

(c) The identity of all of the beneficiaries shall be determined on the date on which the written communication is sent.

(d) Paragraph (a) does not apply to an action based on fraud or misrepresentation with respect to the written communication.

Wis. Stat. 701.21. Income payments and accumulations.

(1) DISTRIBUTION OF INCOME. Except as otherwise determined by the trustee or a court under s. 701.20 (4g) with respect to unitrust distributions, if a beneficiary is entitled to receive income from a trust, but the creating instrument fails to specify how frequently it is to be paid, the trustee shall distribute at least annually the income to which such beneficiary is entitled.

(2) PERMITTED ACCUMULATIONS. No provision directing or authorizing accumulation of trust income shall be invalid.

(3) CHARITABLE TRUST ACCUMULATIONS. A trust containing a direction or authorization to accumulate income from property devoted to a charitable purpose shall be subject to the general equitable supervision of the court with respect to any such accumulation of income, including its reasonableness, amount and duration.

(4) DISPOSITION OF ACCUMULATED INCOME. Income not required to be distributed by the creating instrument, in the absence of a governing provision in the instrument, may in the trustees discretion be held in reserve for future distribution as income or be added to principal subject to retransfer to income of the dollar amount originally transferred to principal; but at the termination of the income interest, any undistributed income shall be distributed as principal.

Wis. Stat. 701.22. Distributions in kind by trustees; marital bequests.

In case of a division of trust assets into 2 or more trusts or shares, any distribution or allocation of assets as an equivalent of a dollar amount fixed by formula or otherwise shall be made at current fair market values unless the governing instrument expressly provided that another value may be used. If the governing instrument requires or permits a different value to be used, all assets available for distribution, including cash, shall, unless otherwise expressly provided, be so distributed that the assets, including cash, distributed as such an equivalent will be fairly representative of the net appreciation or depreciation in the value of the available property on the date or dates of distribution. A provision in the governing instrument that the trustee may fix values for purposes of distribution or allocation does not of itself constitute authorization to fix a value other than current fair market value.

In re Will of Clarenbach

Supreme Court of Wisconsin
23 Wis. 2d 71, 126 N.W.2d 614 (1964)

DIETERICH, J. The crux of the instant appeal is the interpretation to be placed upon clause 7 (G) of the trust provisions of the will, which reads:

"(G) I hereby grant to my executors the power to determine how all receipts, whether realized or accrued (inclusive of stocks, rights, securities received upon reconversion or upon reorganization, or other securities) and all disbursements, whether paid or accrued, shall be charged or apportioned as between income and principal in making current or final distributions, and the decision of the executors shall be final and not subject to question by any court or by any beneficiary hereof."

While the above-quoted clause speaks of executors and not trustees, it is conceded that the trustees succeeded to the same discretionary power conferred upon the executors.

The appellant trustees contend in effect that irrespective of whether or not they consider profits realized from the sale of trust corpus securities to be income or corpus, they have the uncontrolled discretion under this clause to distribute such part of these profits to themselves so long as they do not abuse their discretion. They point to the fact that they have not distributed all of such profits to themselves but only approximately half thereof and that this moderation on their part absolves them from any charge of abuse of discretion. The guardian ad litem, on the other hand, contends that the clause must be construed as conferring upon the trustees the discretion to determine in good faith whether any particular receipt of the trust is income or principal from an accounting standpoint; and, only after having made the decision in good faith that a particular receipt is income, may the trustees lawfully distribute the same to themselves as the life beneficiaries of the trust.

The Uniform Principal and Income Act was adopted in Wisconsin in 1957, and sec. 231.40 (3) (b) of that act provides that, "Any profit . . . resulting upon any change in form of principal shall enure . . . upon principal." The instant profits from sale of trust securities fall into that category. However, sec. 231.40 (2) authorizes the person creating a trust to vary this provision of the act by granting discretion in the trustees to apportion receipts contrary to the other provisions of the act. 1 In these two respects, the act is but a codification of the common law of this state which existed prior to its enactment.

However, in another respect the Uniform Principal and Income Act (sec. 231.40, Stats.) operated so as to materially change the common law of Wisconsin. This is the provision of sec. 231.40 (5) (a) which provides that stock dividends "shall be deemed principal." As pointed out in Will of Allis (1959), 6 Wis. (2d) 1, 94 N.W. (2d) 226, prior to enactment of the act in 1957, Wisconsin followed the Pennsylvania rule with respect to apportioning stock dividends between trust principal and income, and this often presented an acute accounting problem. The instant will was drafted prior to enactment of the act, and the fact that Wisconsin followed the Pennsylvania rule with respect to stock dividends may well have been one of the reasons which prompted testatrix to include clause 7 (G) in her will. This probability is one of the factors that motivates this court toward adopting the interpretation of that clause advanced by the guardian ad litem.

Another fact is that nowhere else in the will is there any provision which grants discretion to the trustees to invade the corpus, even to a limited extent, for the benefit of the life beneficiaries. However, the interpretation advanced by the trustees would convert clause 7 (G) into exactly that type of device. We cannot bring ourselves to the opinion that this was what the testatrix intended by that clause.

It is our considered judgment that the purpose of clause 7 (G) was to protect the trustees from any liability after they exercised their good-faith judgment that a particular receipt was to be treated as either income or principal for accounting purposes, or for the purpose of apportionment between the life beneficiaries and remaindermen. We, therefore, so construe it and reject the broader interpretation advanced by the trustees.

It might be argued that the guardian ad litem has not adduced any proof that, interpreting clause 7 (G) as we do, there has been any abuse of discretion by the trustees, viz., a failure to make a good-faith decision that $10,000 of the $19,858.63 of the profits realized from the sale of trust securities constituted trust income and not principal. We consider that the account filed by the trustees, together with their arguments on the issue of abuse of discretion advanced on this appeal, clearly establish that the trustees did not make a good-faith decision that the $10,000 of profits constituted income and not principal. In the recapitulation at the end of the account all the profits from the sale of securities are lumped together under the one item "Capital Gains -- 1962, $19,858.63," although earlier in the account there is a detailed table showing the cost, the selling price, and the profit realized on each sale of stock. The account further shows that $5,000 of these profits was disbursed to each of the two life beneficiaries on December 31, 1962, the disbursement being labeled "Cap. Gains Dist." No profit realized on the sale of these securities was in round figures, but all were amounts ending in odd cents. No attempt was made by the trustees to allocate the $10,000 to any particular stock or stocks sold. There is no logical reason why an even figure of $10,000 should have been segregated out of the $19,858.63 total profits as being income and the remaining $9,858.63 be treated as principal. The only justification advanced by the trustees for this arbitrary distribution was that they were given discretion to do this by clause 7 (G).

The trustees place great reliance upon Dumaine v. Dumaine (1938), 301 Mass. 214, 16 N.E. (2d) 625. There, a trust clause bearing some similarity to clause 7 (G) of the trust in the instant action was broadly construed as permitting a partial invasion of principal. This result was not reached by the application of any different principle of law than we have herein acknowledged. If the person creating the trust intended such broad interpretation of the particular trust clause, then there is no breach of trust in the trustees' acting pursuant to such clause so broadly interpreted.

However, there are three facts that are different in the Dumaine Case which may have influenced the Massachusetts court in interpreting the clause before it as it did. First, there was no change made in the Massachusetts law after the inception of the trust with respect to how stock dividends were to be apportioned between income and principal. At all times Massachusetts followed the simple rule that stock dividends were principal and not income. Also, profits from sale of assets composing the trust principal were to be treated as principal. Therefore, it is arguable that the trustor by the clause must have intended it as a power to invade receipts from such sources else the clause would serve no purpose. Second, the Dumaine Case clause did not have the parenthetical words "(inclusive of stocks, rights, securities received upon reconversion or upon reorganization, or other securities)" found in clause 7 (G) of the Clarenbach trust which indicates the particular type of situation the testatrix in the instant action had in mind in granting discretion to her trustees. Third, in the Dumaine trust, the trustees had discretion to pay out trust income to the life beneficiaries for their needs, or to accumulate it. The Massachusetts court in its opinion emphasized this particular wide discretion in arriving at the broad interpretation it did with respect to the clause bearing similarity to clause 7 (G) of the instant trust. This is not the situation involved in the instant appeal, and consequently the Dumaine Case is not controlling. Thus we affirm the judgment of the trial court.

GORDON, J. (dissenting). I respectfully dissent. In my opinion, clause 7 (G) of the will gave to the trustees the power to determine whether capital gains on the sale of the trust property should be attributed in whole or in part to principal or to income. This is precisely what the testatrix had in mind when she granted her trustees power to determine "how all receipts . . . shall be . . . apportioned as between income and principal." I know of no reason why this discretionary power should not be fully respected by the court. The fact that the testatrix went on to say that the decision shall not be "subject to question by any court or by any beneficiary hereof" merely serves to stress the breadth of the trustees' discretion.

The increment which results from the sale of trust securities at a price beyond their cost is not so intrinsically a part of corpus as to make the trustees' decision erroneous, at least in the absence of affirmative proof thereof. Tax authorities, accountants, and financial experts can find ample substance for debate in attempting to analyze the trust nature of profits. For example, see Hills, The Law of Accounting and Financial Statements, p. 173, sec. 5.3:

[79] "The terms 'income,' 'earnings,' 'profits' and their derivatives have not been so adequately classified or defined by the courts or the accountants that one may be distinguished from another with any certainty."

Leading legal scholars have recognized that it is within the proper sphere of a trust instrument to permit profits from the sale of trust securities to be ascribed to income. Bogert put the matter clearly when he said:

"Obviously the settlor may direct the disposition of profits, or give to his trustee power to allocate them in his discretion."

Bogert, Trusts and Trustees (2d ed.), p. 375, sec. 823. See also 3 Scott, Trusts (2d ed.), p. 1775, sec. 233.5. The aforesaid rule is entirely consistent with the Uniform Principal and Income Act as adopted in Wisconsin. Sec. 231.40 (2), Stats., expressly provides that a settlor may grant discretion to a trustee to apportion receipts and expenses and that such discretion "shall control."

In my opinion, Mrs. Clarenbach intended to give to her trustees the power to determine what was principal and what was income. While this is not an absolute discretion, there is applicable thereto what the Massachusetts court said in Dumaine v. Dumaine (1938), 301 Mass. 214, 223, 16 N.E. (2d) 625, 630:

"The discretion conferred is not an empty one. It confers an important responsibility to make a determination which, if honestly exercised, calls for no revision by the court."

There has been no showing of fraud, bad faith, or dishonest conduct on the part of the trustees, and, therefore, I believe that the exercise of the broad powers which were awarded to them by the testatrix should not be disturbed.

I am authorized to state that Mr. Justice FAIRCHILD and Mr. Justice WILKIE join in this dissent.

E. DUTY TO ACCOUNT

In re Trust Estate of Martin

Supreme Court of Wisconsin

39 Wis. 2nd 437, 159 N.W.2d 660 (1968)

The questions involved arise out of litigation in the closing of a trust. This court has had this case on a prior appeal and the background facts are reported in its opinion in Estate of Martin (1963), 21 Wis. 2d 334, 124 N. W. 2d 297. Only sufficient facts are now given to pose the new questions.

The testator Charles R. Martin died June 24, 1941, and was survived by his wife Nellie Martin and two children of their marriage; he was also survived by a child and two children of a deceased child of a previous marriage. The estate consisted of a farm and other income-producing property. The widow was appointed administratrix with the will annexed, which will bequeathed to her the use and income of the real estate and the personal property for life and gave the remainder equally to the testator's children. The will also provided for a trustee.

The widow, as administratrix, administered the estate for almost ten years and then transferred the property to herself as life tenant. During this time O. E. Richards acted as trustee, treating the property subject to the life estate and the remainder as the trust res. The character of such a trust was explained in our prior opinion. Upon the death of the widow, Mr. Richards was appointed administrator of her estate. However, shortly before the widow's death several of the remaindermen petitioned for the removal of Richards as trustee and he thereupon petitioned the court for the approval of his account covering the entire ten-year period of his trusteeship.

On the first appeal, this court reversed the approval of the account by the county court and sent the case back for further accounting. On remand, an amended account was filed and additional objections were filed. Upon hearing, the new account of the trustee was approved and allowed up to June 12, 1964. As part of the final decree the trial court also: (1) Allowed the trustee his fees in the sum of $5,560.85; (2) charged the trustee personally with his accountant's bill for services of $7,863.14; (3) charged the trustee personally with $7,515.44 for his attorney's fees (other attorney's fees of $1,989.20 were charged to the estate as a proper trustee's expense); and (4) charged the trustee personally with the remaindermen's attorney's fees of $11,819.85 and accountant's fees of $377.50.

The trustee Richards has appealed from that part of the decree which required him to pay the remaindermen's attorney's and accountant's fees. The remaindermen filed a cross appeal from that part of the decree which allowed: (1) The trustee his fees, and (2) certain items of trust disbursements amounting to $7,463.11, which had previously been disallowed for lack of proof.

Hallows, C. J.

Were the trust disbursements properly allowed?

In its decision of December, 1965, the trial court disallowed a total of $7,463.11 in disbursements from the Fincher-Martin Farm Account because of insufficient detail as to whom the payments were made and for what purpose. On January 19, 1967, these disbursements were in effect allowed on the ground of the trustee's good faith and because the farm operation showed no loss.

We think neither of these reasons is a valid basis for approving these items in the accounting. In our first opinion concerning this trust, we stated it was the duty of a trustee to keep clear, distinct and accurate records of all trust transactions and good faith in the performance of the trustee's duty was not sufficient. A trustee is not handling his own funds but funds of others and he must always be able to make a full accounting of his stewardship. When a trustee's accounts are not clear and accurate, all presumptions are against him and the obscurities and doubts are to be taken adversely against him. This rule has long been the law in Wisconsin.

See Will of Leonard (1930), 202 Wis. 117, 230 N. W. 715; and in other jurisdictions, see Jones v. Green (1936), 41 N. M. 46, 63 Pac. 2d 1042; Wootton Land & Fuel Co. v. Ownbey (8th Cir. 1920), 265 Fed. 91; Villa Site Co. v. Copeland (1920), 91 N. J. Eq. 503, 111 Atl. 39, 13 A. L. R. 356; and Purdy v. Johnson (1917), 174 Cal. 521, 163 Pac. 893.

It may be true if a loss is shown in the operation of the trust that it is easier to apply the presumption for the failure to keep accurate and complete accounts and thereby reduce or eliminate the loss; but the converse is not true that because there is no loss shown if the disputed items are allowed that therefore they should be allowed. Besides, actual loss in management or operation of a trust may have nothing or little to do with the amount of the disbursements or the inability to account. A trustee must keep complete accounts and make an accurate accounting of a successful as well as an unsuccessful trust. Here in several respects the accounts were "completely incomplete."

We do not think because the trustee by secondary evidence was able to prove other disbursements to the satisfaction of the court that, therefore, these questioned disbursements in all probability were in fact proper and should be allowed. Such reasoning is a species of the good-faith argument and is not sufficient because a trustee should always act in good faith. The trustee in this case has been given ample opportunity to prove his management of the trust. These claimed disbursements amounting to $7,463.11, being unsupported by sufficient evidence, must be disallowed in the accounting. This has the effect of surcharging the trustee since he has claimed the disbursements in his account.

It is argued that if the trustee is surcharged for these disallowed disbursements, the surcharge should be limited to three fourths of the amount of the disbursement because one remainderman with a one-fourth interest did not join in the cross appeal. We do not think this case is similar in principle to Will of Roebken (1939), 230 Wis. 215, 283 N. W. 815, relied on by the trustee. There, several heirs joined with the executor in opposing a surcharge and lost. Under those circumstances they were not entitled to the benefit upon losing their contention. In the instant case, one remainderman neither joined nor opposed the position of the trustee. We think the trustee is not entitled to partial credit on his liability because of such inaction in this accounting proceeding. The trustee's duty to account should not be bifurcated.

Trustee's Compensation.

The county court awarded the trustee compensation in the amount of $5,560.85 because he actually performed services as trustee, he was honest and acted in good faith without fraud or intention or deliberate wrong and his derelictions related to the failure to keep accounts and make an accounting. We disagree. It seems the trial court thought the trustee should receive his normal compensation for the services performed but should be charged with the remaindermen's attorney's and accountant's fees, which were caused by his dereliction. It is not an entirely unreasonable view but we think the better view is to deny compensation in cases where a trustee does not faithfully fulfill his trust. The keeping of accurate accounts is as important as care in management. The trustee was a banker and for long periods of time kept no accounts of some of the activities of the trust. He knew the importance of keeping accurate financial records of other people's money. His way of managing a trust has led to two appeals to this court over an accounting which should not have required an appeal.

It is within the power of the court to reduce or deny compensation. As Bogert states in his work Trusts & Trustees 2d, p. 404, sec. 980, "The sum is allotted for an execution of the trust with the highest degree of good faith and with ordinary skill and care. It follows that if the administration of any particular trustee falls below this level, his compensation should be reduced or even forfeited entirely." It is true in Will of Leonard, supra, the misconduct of the trustee was more aggravated than that found by the trial court in this case, but the discretion of the trial court to deny compensation for unfaithful service is not restricted to bad faith or gross and inexcusable negligence or willful dereliction of duty. On the other hand, the reduction of compensation or its denial is not a penalty for breach of trust but is based upon the failure to perform the trust with ordinary skill and care and with the highest degree of good faith. See Joerres v. Koscielniak (1961), 13 Wis. 2d 242, 108 N. W. 2d 569; also Estate of Teasdale (1952), 261 Wis. 248, 52 N. W. 2d 366. We do not think on this record the trustee is entitled to receive any compensation for his work.

The remaindermen's attorney's and accountant's fees.

The trial court in its comprehensive opinion painstakingly passed upon every objection to the items in the account. This was drudgery and time consuming but it had to be done. From these items, no appeal has been taken. The court denied the trustee his expenses for his attorney and accountant and this finding is not in issue on this appeal. However, the court surcharged the trustee with the attorney's fees and accountant's fees of the remaindermen on equitable grounds and this action is claimed to be error.

The court considered it was not taxing costs for the amount of the fees but was surcharging the trustee and based its decision on the equitable proposition that the trustee had needlessly caused the remaindermen to incur these expenses to attain a proper accounting which they had a right to have. The trustee argues the trial court had no such equitable power and that this so-called surcharge is in effect a taxing of costs not authorized by the statute and especially cannot be justified under sec. 271.14, Stats., because no mismanagement or bad faith was found. The trustee also relies on Estate of Cole (1899), 102 Wis. 1, 12, 78 N. W. 402, which contains language that counsel fees to persons who may be interested in a trust fund are not recoverable "either from the trustees personally or out of such fund."

On first impression there would seem to be merit in surcharging or making a trustee personally responsible for causing needless expenditures on the part of the remaindermen. However, where the trustee's conduct is not found to be in bad faith but only substandard performance of his duty, we think that although compensation for his work may be denied he ought not in equity be personally liable for expenses he caused the remaindermen. By analogy, sec. 271.14, Stats., would seem to be a guideline.

We think the expenses of the remaindermen for their attorney and accountant are properly paid out of this estate. We realize the trial court considered this procedure in this case would penalize to some extent the remaindermen for obtaining an accounting which they have a right to have without such expenditure of money. The trial court would have avoided this result by surcharging the trustee for these items. Thus while the trustee would not pay the remaindermen directly as costs, he would pay the estate which is then used as a conduit to pay the remaindermen.

It is true the Cole Case stated that fees of remaindermen could not be paid out of the trust fund, but that statement has become eroded during the years and such fees were allowed in Estate of Hoyt (1963), 22 Wis. 2d 209, 125 N. W. 2d 350, and in Estate of Sheldon (1946), 249 Wis. 430, 24 N. W. 2d 875, because of "equitable extraordinary circumstances." However, we do not read Estate of Hoyt as allowing attorney's fees for the remaindermen against the trustee personally. Nor do we hold that in every case such a remainderman's expenses are chargeable to the trust. There may be cases within the equitable power of the court when a trustee should be charged personally with expenses he needlessly causes through his conduct, but we need not now decide what facts will call forth such relief.

We must, therefore, reverse the final decree of the trial court with directions to disallow disbursements in the final account in the amount of $7,463.11, to disallow the trustee any compensation, and to allow the attorney's and accountant's fees of the remaindermen in the sum of $11,819.85 and $377.50 respectively from the trust estate. The final decree is reversed, and the cause remanded for further proceedings consistent with the directions in the opinion; no costs to either party.

III. REMOVAL OF TRUSTEES

Traditionally, absent a provision in the trust instrument authorizing removal, trustees could not be removed from their position except in very limited circumstances. Respect for the wishes of the settlor made courts reluctant to order the removal of a existing trustee, absent evidence of a breach of fiduciary duty or of an inability to work with other trustees in a situation where there were co-trustees. So long as the trustee performed its fiduciary duties, beneficiaries had no right to petition for the removal of a trustee simply because they preferred a proposed replacement. One of the most debated issues in the contemporary law of trusts is whether or not there should be a mechanism for removing a trustee solely because of unsatisfactory investment results. The Uniform Trust Code contains such a provision. More traditional approaches, like that of Wisconsin, do not.

Wis. Stat. 701.18. Resignation and removal of trustees.

(1) RESIGNATION. A trustee may resign in accordance with the terms of the creating instrument or petition the court to accept the trustee's resignation and the court may, upon notice and hearing, discharge the trustee from further responsibility for the trust upon such terms and conditions as are necessary to protect the rights of the beneficiaries and any cotrustee. In no event shall a testamentary trustee be discharged from further responsibility except as provided in s. 701.16 (6)

(2) REMOVAL. A trustee may be removed in accordance with the terms of the creating instrument or the court may, upon its own motion or upon a petition by a beneficiary or cotrustee, and upon notice and hearing, remove a trustee who fails to comply with the requirements of this chapter or a court order, or who is otherwise unsuitable to continue in office. In no event shall a testamentary trustee be discharged from further responsibility except as provided in s. 701.16 (6)

Wis. Stat. 701.16. Testamentary trustees.

[The full text of § 701.16 can be found in Chapter 7.]

(6) DISCHARGE. No testamentary trustee or personal representative of a deceased trustee shall be discharged from further responsibility with respect to a testamentary trust until the court is satisfied upon notice and hearing that the requirements of this section have been met and it has received satisfactory proof that the trust property has been turned over to a successor or special trustee or, where the trust is terminated, distributed to the beneficiaries entitled to such property or turned over to a special trustee for distribution.

A. REMOVAL OF TRUSTEE WITH CONSENT OF THE SETTLOR

In re Trust of Charitable v. Bowen

Court of Appeals of Wisconsin
240 Wis. 2d 55, 622 N.W.2d 471 (2000)

NETTESHEIM, J. Eric J. Weinberger appeals from a circuit court order removing him as a co-trustee of the Catherine H. Bowen Charitable Trust and appointing another in his stead. The order was premised upon Wis. Stat. §701.12(1) (1997-98), which permits revocation, modification or termination of a trust upon the written consent of the settlor and all beneficiaries.

On appeal, Weinberger argues that his removal under Wis. Stat. §701.12(1) violated an express provision in the trust agreement that barred modification of the trust. Instead, Weinberger argues that he could only be removed for cause pursuant to Wis. Stat. §701.18(2). And since the court did not conduct any factual inquiry as to cause for his removal, Weinberger asks that we reverse the order.

We agree with the circuit court that Wis. Stat. §701.12(1), not Wis. Stat. §701.18(2), applies to this case. Therefore, we affirm the order.

HISTORY

The relevant facts are brief and undisputed. We take them from the petition which initiated this action. Catherine H. Bowen established the Catherine H. Bowen Charitable Trust under a trust agreement dated September 12, 1988. Catherine named her son John F. Bowen as one co-trustee and Weinberger, who was married to her granddaughter Jennifer, as the other co-trustee. The trust included the following provision at Article III:

> Revocation or Amendment of Trust. It is the intention of the Grantor that any transfer to any Trust created under this Trust Agreement shall constitute an irrevocable gift without possibility of reverter. *This Trust is irrevocable and neither the Grantor nor any other person shall have the power to alter, amend or modify this Trust Agreement except as specifically provided in paragraph 3.8, below*. (Emphasis added.)

After the trust was created, Jennifer commenced a divorce action against Weinberger. As a result, Bowen, the co-trustee, asked Weinberger to resign as a co-trustee. Weinberger refused. Consequently, Catherine and all of the trust beneficiaries commenced the instant action by written petition asking the circuit court to substitute a new co-trustee in place of Weinberger. The petition was brought pursuant to Wis. Stat. §701.12(1), which authorizes the revocation, modification or termination of a trust upon "written consent of the settlor and all beneficiaries." In the alternative, the petition sought Weinberger's removal for cause pursuant to Wis. Stat. §701.18(2).

The parties submitted written briefs and oral arguments to the circuit court. In a bench decision, the court ruled that Wis. Stat. §701.12(1) was the controlling statute. Since Catherine and all of the beneficiaries had consented in writing to the modification of the trust as required by the statute, the court ordered Weinberger's removal as a co-trustee. Weinberger appeals.

STANDARD OF REVIEW

We first address our standard of review. The trial court record in this case consists of the written petition, the parties' written briefs and the transcript of their oral arguments. The parties did not seek, and the circuit court did not conduct, a formal trial. Thus, we have a "paper record." In such a setting, we need not give any special deference to the trial court's findings or rulings because we are in as good a position as the trial court to address the issue. See Racine Educ. Ass'n v. Racine Bd. of Educ., 145 Wis. 2d 518, 521, 427 N.W.2d 414 (Ct. App. 1988); see also State ex rel. McMillian v. Dickey, 132 Wis. 2d 266, 281 n.15, 392 N.W.2d 453 (Ct. App. 1986).

Moreover, in this case we are required to apply the statutes at issue to a particular set of facts. That exercise presents a question of law which we decide independently of, and without deference to, the trial court's ruling. See Midwest Developers v. Goma Corp., 121 Wis. 2d 632, 651, 360 N.W.2d 554 (Ct. App. 1984). Thus, our review is de novo.

Despite our de novo standard of review, we value a trial court's decision. See Scheunemann v. City of West Bend, 179 Wis. 2d 469, 475-76, 507 N.W.2d 163 (Ct. App. 1993). Here the circuit court has provided us with a well-reasoned decision that is helpful and informative on the issue.

DISCUSSION

We begin by setting out the two statutes at issue. Wisconsin Stat. §701.12(1) provides:

> By written consent of the settlor and all beneficiaries of a trust or any part thereof, such trust or part thereof may be revoked, modified or terminated, except as provided under s. 445.125 (1) (a) 2. to 4.

Wisconsin Stat. §701.18(2) provides in pertinent part:

> Removal. A trustee may be removed in accordance with the terms of the creating instrument or the court may, upon its own motion or upon a petition by a beneficiary or cotrustee, and upon notice and hearing, remove a trustee who fails to comply with the requirements of this chapter or a court order, or who is otherwise unsuitable to continue in office.

In this court, the parties renew their trial court arguments. The petitioners contend that Wis. Stat. §701.12(1) plainly and unambiguously governs the issue because Catherine and all of the trust beneficiaries have, by their written petition, consented in writing to the modification substituting another in place of Weinberger as a co-trustee. Weinberger argues that the trust provision prohibiting modification or amendment of the trust agreement precludes the application of §701.12(1). Instead, Weinberger contends that the petitioners' only recourse was to seek his removal for cause pursuant to Wis. Stat. §701.18(2), which he argues is the more specific statute under the circumstances of this case. See Gillen v. City of Neenah, 219 Wis. 2d 806, 822, 580 N.W.2d 628 (1998) ("Where general and specific statutory provisions are in conflict, the specific provisions take precedence.").

We reject Weinberger's argument. We agree with the circuit court's holding that Wis. Stat. §701.12(1) clearly and unambiguously allows for the revocation, modification or termination of a trust upon the written consent of the settlor and all the trust beneficiaries. That, of course, is precisely what occurred in this case. The circuit court also correctly observed that the statute does not limit its application to only certain situations. Rather, the court concluded that the statute applies "to any scenario ... where the trust may be silent or may be ambiguous or has an express bar against amendments."

Weinberger argues that the circuit court's ruling overrides the intent of the settlor as expressed in the trust agreement. He cites to case law which holds that a court is obligated to uphold the intent of the settlor. See Upham v. Plankinton, 152 Wis. 275, 283-84, 140 N.W. 5 (1913), and In re Charitable Trust, Oshkosh Found., 61 Wis. 2d 432, 442, 213 N.W.2d 54 (1973). We, of course, accept this fundamental principle of the law of trusts. And we further accept that, in most cases, the trust document will control on this question because the settlor is deceased. See, e.g., Upham, 152 Wis. at 277.

But here the settlor is still living and her current intent as to who should serve as a co-trustee is unequivocally expressed via her written consent to the removal of Weinberger and her desire to substitute another in his stead. We cannot discern any sound reason why the settlor and all of the beneficiaries should be precluded from modifying the terms of a trust if all are in agreement that such action is appropriate. By its enactment of Wis. Stat. §701.12(1), the legislature also apparently could discern no such reason. In short, the statute, and our application of it to this case, honors the intent of the settlor.

Weinberger further argues that Wis. Stat. §701.18(2), permitting removal of a trustee for cause, not Wis. Stat. §701.12(1), is the operative statute in this situation. We acknowledge that a plain and unambiguous statute such as §701.12(1) may be rendered ambiguous by its interaction with other statutes. See McDonough v. DWD, 227 Wis. 2d 271, 278, 595 N.W.2d 686 (1999). In that situation, we read the statutes in pari materia, attempting to give meaning to both. See McDonough, 227 Wis. 2d at

279-80. In addition, we note that a statute which is plain on its face may also be rendered ambiguous by the context in which it is sought to be applied. See Roehl v. American Family Mut. Ins. Co., 222 Wis. 2d 136, 145, 585 N.W.2d 893 (Ct. App.), review denied, 222 Wis. 2d 676, 589 N.W.2d 630 (Wis. Dec. 15, 1998) (No. 98-1207-FT).

But we agree with the circuit court that the two statutes serve different purposes. On the one hand, Wis. Stat. §701.12(1) allows a settlor and all of the trust beneficiaries to revoke, modify or terminate a trust if all are in agreement. Such a removal need not be premised on any cause. On the other hand, Wis. Stat. §701.18(2) provides a means for removing a trustee where the conditions envisioned by §701.12(1) do not exist. However, in that setting, the trustee can be removed only upon a showing of cause. Thus, §701.18(2) would apply where the settlor and all of the trust beneficiaries are not in agreement that removal is appropriate, or where the settlor is no longer living and therefore unable to provide written consent to the removal as required by §701.12(1).

In summary, Wis. Stat. §701.12(1) is not rendered ambiguous by its interaction with Wis. Stat. §701.18(2) or by its application to the facts of this case. Therefore, we reject Weinberger's argument that by allowing for his removal under §701.12(1), we are defeating the legislative purpose served by §701.18(2). We agree with the circuit court that the two statutes serve different purposes in different situations.

CONCLUSION

We uphold the circuit court's ruling that Wis. Stat. §701.12(1) was the controlling statute in this case. Therefore, we affirm the order removing Weinberger as a co-trustee and substituting another in his stead.

B. REMOVAL OF TRUSTEE WITHOUT SETTLOR CONSENT

Bramen v. Angelopulos

Court of Appeals of Wisconsin

315 Wis. 2d 768, 762 N.W.2d 863 (2008)

HIGGINBOTHAM, P.J. Richard Bramen appeals an order of the circuit court finding him unsuitable to serve as the trustee of the Estate of Bernadetha Monroe. Bramen contends that the circuit court failed to give proper consideration to Monroe's wishes in appointing a trustee; failed to follow the statutory framework of a removal proceeding, thereby denying him the opportunity to challenge the allegations against him; and failed to articulate sufficient reasons for its finding that Bramen was unsuitable. Bramen further contends that the record does not support the court's finding of unsuitability. We reject these arguments and affirm.

Background

Bernadetha Monroe executed a will in 1996. The will made specific bequests to her sister Delia Grayson, nephew Richard Bramen, niece Lavonne McKeehan and great nieces Michelle Mostert and Renee Angelopulos. The will established a trust to distribute the remainder of her estate to these same relatives over time. It named Grayson trustee of the trust. The will specified that if Grayson were to die or otherwise be unable to act as trustee, nephew Richard Bramen would become the trustee, and, subsequently, if Bramen were unable to act as trustee, her great niece Danielle Mostert would become trustee.

Monroe died on April 13, 2003. Grayson, for reasons of her own ill health, requested that Bramen be appointed co-personal representative of the Monroe Estate and co-trustee of the Monroe Trust. All of the named beneficiaries of the will signed letters consenting to the informal administration of the will and to the appointment of Bramen as co-personal representative and co-trustee. On May 6, 2003, the will was admitted into informal administration and the probate court issued letters recognizing the status of Grayson and Bramen as co-personal representatives and co-trustees.

Grayson died on July 2, 2003, leaving Bramen as the sole personal representative and trustee of the Monroe Estate. By the terms of Grayson's will, Bramen assumed the responsibilities of personal representative of Grayson's estate and trustee of a trust created by the will.

In November 2004, Monroe's great niece, Renee Angelopulos, filed a motion to remove Bramen as personal representative, alleging several grounds for removal, which are discussed later in this opinion. Angelopulos filed a demand seeking formal proceedings to address her motion. No immediate action was taken on Angelopulos's November 2004 motion for removal.

On June 9, 2006, Bramen filed a demand for formal proceedings in the Monroe Estate, which was approved by the probate court. Bramen also filed a final account of the Estate that day, and petitioned for approval of the final account, for entry of final judgment and for his appointment as trustee of the Estate. Bramen also submitted to the court a request for reimbursement of certain expenses and fees.

On June 28, 2006, Angelopulos filed a second motion to remove Bramen as personal representative, the grounds for which are discussed later in this opinion. Angelopulos also submitted a separate filing detailing her objections to Bramen's request for reimbursement of expenses and fees.

On August 2, 2006, the circuit court held a hearing to take evidence on the motion to remove Bramen as personal representative, and to review the petition for final judgment on the Estate. After hearing the evidence, the court, in a bench ruling, approved the final account with certain amendments, and found that Bramen was unsuitable to serve as trustee. The court ordered the Estate and Bramen's lawyer to find an appropriate institutional trustee to manage the trust. North Central Trust Company was later appointed as trustee.

Bramen moved for reconsideration of the court's judgment. Bramen argued that the court's findings were insufficient to support the conclusion that he was unsuitable to serve as trustee, and were contrary to the wishes of the testator. Angelopulos also filed a motion for reconsideration, asking the court to issue a written order elaborating on its finding of unsuitability. The court denied Bramen's motion and granted Angelopulos's motion, issuing a written order giving the reasons for its decision. Bramen appeals. Additional facts are provided in the discussion section.

Discussion

As a preliminary matter, the parties dispute whether the circuit court's order removed Bramen as trustee or instead declined to appoint him as trustee. Bramen argues that the circuit court's order was one of removal because the probate court had already appointed him co-trustee of the Monroe Estate in May 2003. Angelopulos and the Estate (hereinafter, "Angelopulos") argue that the order should be treated as one declining to appoint Bramen as trustee because Bramen never assumed the duties of the position. We agree with Bramen.

As noted, Bramen was appointed co-trustee in May 2003, and later became the sole trustee upon Grayson's death. Bramen's appointment as trustee was made pursuant to WIS. STAT. §§701.16(1) and 856.29 (2005-06). Together, these statutes provide for the appointment of a trustee named in a will when the estate is admitted into probate by issuance of letters of trust, before the trust takes effect. Thus, regardless of whether Bramen had ever assumed the responsibility of managing the trust, he already held the office of trustee pursuant to §§701.16(1) and 856.29, and the court's action should therefore be considered an order removing Bramen from that office. With the foregoing discussion in mind, we address briefly Bramen's argument that the circuit court's order failed to give sufficient weight to Monroe's testamentary wishes. We agree with Bramen that in Wisconsin a testator retains the right to appoint whomever he or she wishes as trustee. See Svacina v. East Wis. Tr. Co., 239 Wis. 436, 443-44, 1 N.W.2d 780 (1942). "[N]o discretion is vested in courts with respect to refusing to grant letters testamentary [appointing a trustee or personal representative] to the persons nominated in a will, unless such persons are expressly disqualified, or unless such discretion is vested by law." Id. at 446.

However, once a trustee is appointed, the trustee has certain duties to the estate and its beneficiaries and the manner by which the trustee executes those duties is subject to the supervision of the court. See WIS. STAT. §701.18(2); see also Klauser v. Schmitz, 2003 WI App 157, P7, 265 Wis. 2d 860, 667 N.W.2d 862. The testator's designated trustee may be removed only for violating the terms of the will, the provisions of Chapter 701 of the Wisconsin statutes, a court order, or for being "otherwise unsuitable to continue in office." Sec. 701.18(2). Thus, the statutory scheme evinces a strong presumption in favor of the testator's designated trustee, permitting removal of the trustee only upon proof of a ground specified under §701.18(2). The focus of our review is therefore not on whether the court granted "sufficient weight" to Monroe's wish to appoint Bramen as trustee, but on whether the court correctly determined that grounds existed for Bramen's removal. Thus, we turn our attention to the question of whether statutory grounds existed for Bramen's removal as trustee.

Standard of Review

The decision to remove a testamentary trustee is addressed to the sound discretion of the circuit court. See First Wis. Nat'l Bank of Oshkosh v. Circuit Court for Fond du Lac County, 167 Wis. 2d 196, 201, 482 N.W.2d 118 (Ct. App. 1992). We may not disturb a decision addressed to the circuit court's discretion absent an erroneous exercise of that discretion. Connor v. Connor, 2001 WI 49, P18, 243 Wis. 2d 279, 627 N.W.2d 182. A circuit court erroneously exercises its discretion "if the record indicates that the circuit court failed to exercise its discretion, if the facts of record fail to support the circuit court's decision, or if this court's review of the record indicates that the circuit court applied the wrong legal standard." Id. (citation omitted).

Removal Procedure and Opportunity to Challenge Grounds for Removal

Bramen contends that the court committed reversible error by proceeding under the incorrect removal statute and by denying him sufficient opportunity to refute the grounds for his removal. Bramen argues that the court erred in citing as authority for its action the removal of personal representative statute, WIS. STAT. §857.15, instead of the removal of trustee statute, WIS. STAT. §701.18(2). Bramen then confusingly argues that the circuit court failed to follow the procedure set forth under the removal of personal representative statute, §857.15, which requires that the court hold a hearing at which the personal representative may "show cause why the personal representative should not be removed." Finally, Bramen appears to contend that, even if the "show cause" procedure in §857.15 does not apply, the circuit court nonetheless denied him the opportunity to contest the allegations that formed the basis for his removal. We reject these arguments.

We acknowledge that the circuit court erred in citing the removal of personal representative statute, WIS. STAT. §857.15, when the order was one removing Bramen as trustee, an action authorized by WIS. STAT. §701.18(2). It is clear that the court correctly proceeded under the removal of trustee statute, demonstrated by the language of the order, which plainly states that Bramen is being removed as trustee, and by its timing, which came at the closing of the Estate when a personal representative was no longer needed and responsibility for managing the assets of the Estate was about to pass to the trustee.

In any event, we reject Bramen's argument that the court's citation to the wrong statute is reversible error because the court's analysis was consistent with the legal standard set forth in WIS. STAT. §701.18(2). Moreover, his apparent suggestion that once the court cited the wrong statute, WIS. STAT. §857.15, it was obligated to follow the "show cause" procedure set forth in this statute is also mistaken. The court's order, while incorrectly citing §857.15, was issued pursuant to the removal of trustee statute, §701.18(2), not §857.15, and thus any specific procedural requirements of §857.15 do not apply.

We also reject Bramen's argument that, even if the court was not required to follow the "show cause" procedure, he was denied a meaningful chance to challenge the allegations against him. The hearing transcript shows that Bramen was given a full opportunity to contest the alleged grounds for removal. Both Angelopulos's motions for removal and Bramen's request for appointment had put the issue of Bramen's status as trustee before the court prior to the hearing. Among the allegations made in Angelopulos's motions for removal were that Bramen had submitted excessive reimbursement requests, an issue that was explored at the hearing, as our later discussion demonstrates, and about which Bramen himself gave testimony.

Sufficiency of Grounds to Support Removal

Wisconsin courts have long adhered to the rule "'that every citizen making a will has the right to select according to his own judgment the person or persons whom he would have execute it.'" Schmitz, 2003 WI App 157, 265 Wis. 2d 860, P8, 667 N.W.2d 862 (quoting Svacina, 239 Wis. at 442). Thus, courts have "'no discretion ... with respect to refusing to grant letters testamentary to the persons nominated in a will'" as personal representative or trustee "'unless such persons are expressly disqualified, or unless such discretion is vested by law.'" Id. However, courts may remove a personal representative or a trustee for grounds provided by statute. Schmitz, 2003 WI App 157, 265 Wis. 2d 860, P7, 667 N.W.2d 862 (citing Holzhauer v. Zartner, 183 Wis. 506, 509, 198 N.W. 363 (1924)).

As noted, WIS. STAT. §701.18(2) sets forth the grounds upon which a trustee may be removed from his or her position. The statute provides that, upon the motion of a beneficiary or co-trustee, a court may remove a trustee who fails to comply with the requirements of the trust statutes or a court order, "or who is otherwise unsuitable to continue in office." Sec. 701.18(2). The ground upon which the circuit court removed Bramen was that he was "otherwise unsuitable to continue in office." The question of whether to remove a trustee is ultimately addressed to the discretion of the circuit court. See Schmitz, 2003 WI App 157, P7, 265 Wis. 2d 860, 667 N.W.2d 862. The circuit court's written order, which restated many of the court's oral findings, provided the following explanation for its conclusion that Bramen was unsuitable to serve as trustee:

> In this case by virtue of the terms of the will/trust there is a potential conflict between Mr. Bramen as potential trustee and also as the recipient of interest income from the trust. That potential conflict in and of itself does not disqualify Mr. Bramen or make him unsuitable, but it is a contentious factor in this particular estate. This potential conflict of interest was a factor in my decision finding Mr. Bramen unsuitable.
>
> While Mr. Bramen has more than the average man's expertise in investing, he has less than an expert's expertise such as a bank trust department investing in a trust which is long-term and which has to balance the need for income to some beneficiaries with increasing the assets or principal for the remaindermen. Taking into account Mr. Bramen's acts as personal representative, the Court finds that this trust could be run more efficiently and expertly with a commercial trust department from a suitable banking institution rather than Mr. Bramen personally.
>
> Mr. Bramen filed claims against the estate for reimbursement for various charges he had incurred. These included having one of his employees clean the

> Bernadetha Monroe house; another claim for reimbursement was for cell phone charges that he claimed were made in the course of his capacity as personal representative for the estate. I find those fees to be improper and based on the totality of the circumstances I find that Richard Bramen is unsuitable to serve as trustee.
>
> Therefore, the Court finds Mr. Bramen is unsuitable to serve as trustee under all of the evidence introduced at this hearing. The Court further finds that a commercial trust department would be better suited to balance the equities involved between the interest income heirs and the remaindermen who will inherit the balance of the trust once the interest income heirs are deceased.

Bramen contends that these findings are insufficient to support the circuit court's determination that he is unsuitable to serve as trustee. He further maintains that the record as a whole does not contain sufficient evidence for the court's unsuitability determination. We assume without deciding that the circuit court's explicit findings in this case do not provide a sufficient basis for a determination of unsuitability. However, this fact does not necessitate reversal. "An erroneous exercise of discretion exists if the trial court failed to exercise its discretion or if there was no reasonable basis for its decision." Rechsteiner v. Hazelden, 2008 WI 97, P28, 313 Wis. 2d 542, 753 N.W.2d 496 (citation omitted). When the court fails to provide an adequate explanation for a discretionary decision, we may nonetheless uphold the circuit court's decision if, upon examination of the record, the facts support the court's exercise of discretion. Franke v. Franke, 2004 WI 8, P55, 268 Wis. 2d 360, 674 N.W.2d 832. In reviewing the circuit court's decision to remove Bramen as trustee, we therefore examine the record as a whole in addition to the circuit court's explicit findings to determine whether the court committed reversible error.

We observe that some of the circuit court's reasons for removal stated in its written decision are not relevant to the matter of unsuitability or to any other ground for removal provided by statute. For example, the court listed as grounds for the determination a "potential conflict of interest" arising from the testator's naming of Bramen as both trustee and beneficiary of the trust. However, the supreme court in Gehl v. Hansen, 5 Wis. 2d 91, 97, 92 N.W.2d 372 (1958), rejected an argument that a conflict of interest established by the testator's choice to name a beneficiary of a trust as the trustee was grounds for unsuitability. The Gehl court reasoned that the conflict "was created by the testator," and therefore was presumed to have been within the contemplation of the testator. See id.

We also question the court's suggestion that Bramen's level of expertise in investing is legitimate grounds for its determination of unsuitability. And the fact that the commercial trust department of a bank would, in the court's view, run the trust "more efficiently and expertly" than Bramen is irrelevant to whether Bramen is unsuitable to serve as trustee. However, based on other findings the circuit court made in its written and oral rulings and on the evidence of record, we conclude that Bramen's conduct as personal representative provided sufficient grounds for the court to determine that Bramen was unsuitable to serve as trustee.

Bramen submitted a reimbursement request of $2,194.22 to the Estate for the compensation he paid his secretary, Ruby Crozier, to clean Bernadetha Monroe's house. Bramen's request claimed that Crozier worked ten to fourteen hours a day for twenty-three days cleaning the house. Bramen sought reimbursement at Crozier's weekly secretarial salary for the days Crozier spent cleaning the house. At the hearing, Bramen justified the expense, explaining that the house was in "deplorable" condition.

Bramen also submitted a reimbursement request to the Estate for charges on a cell phone purchased to conduct the business of the Monroe and Grayson Estates. Bramen bought a monthly plan for the phone that included 250 minutes of airtime for $29 per month. Additional airtime beyond the allotted 250 minutes was subject to additional charges. From April 2003 to December 2004, Bramen ran up approximately $4,745 in charges for excess minutes. Bramen testified that the excess minutes were used "talking to people about unclaimed ... property" and other matters related to the Monroe and Grayson Estates. The court in the Grayson matter awarded Bramen $1,639 toward the cell phone charges. Bramen submitted copies of his phone bills to the Monroe Estate, but did not provide an itemized report detailing all incoming and outgoing calls. Bramen testified that such a report was not available from his wireless provider.

The circuit court found that Bramen's assertion that Crozier spent twenty-three days of ten- to fourteen-hour days cleaning the house to be "incredible," and that the reimbursement request was "improper." The court noted that Monroe's house was only 1,300 square feet in area, and that Bramen's wife helped Crozier with the cleaning. The court found the amount requested to be "unreasonable and unjustified" and determined that $800 was a reasonable figure for cleaning Monroe's house. The court then subtracted $500 already paid by the Grayson Estate to clean Monroe's house, and awarded Bramen $300.

The court also questioned Bramen's claim that the business of the Estate required the amount of cell phone time used, and asked why Bramen did not change his plan to one with more minutes instead of paying thousands of dollars in overage fees. We observe that during one month, July 5, 2003, through August 4, 2003, Bramen used 3,451 extra minutes, or approximately 57 hours, of airtime over his monthly plan minutes.

Bramen does not challenge these findings, and we conclude that they support a reasonable view that Bramen was unsuitable to serve as trustee. The court's findings that Bramen made excessive reimbursement requests as personal representative support a reasonable inference that Bramen would use his position as trustee to benefit personally from the trust, and otherwise would not protect the corpus of the trust for all of its beneficiaries.

In sum, we therefore conclude that the circuit court's order was one removing Bramen as trustee, and that the circuit court afforded Bramen a sufficient opportunity to challenge the basis for the motion to remove him as trustee. We also conclude that excessive reimbursement requests submitted by Bramen to the Estate provided sufficient grounds for the circuit court to conclude within its discretion that Bramen was unsuitable to serve as trustee. We therefore affirm.

CHAPTER 9.
CHARITABLE TRUSTS

That a trust is charitable provides it with a number of benefits. Although this is less important in Wisconsin than in other states, charitable trusts were historically viewed as exempt from the Rule against Perpetuities. Moreover, charitable trusts were to a degree exempt from the specific beneficiary requirement, because they could be enforced by the state itself through the office of the state Attorney General. Finally, assets assigned to charitable trusts have traditionally been exempt from estate and state inheritance taxes. (Although the taxation of charitable trusts is not a primary focus of this section, many of the cases below are "tax" cases.)

I. CREATING CHARTIBLE TRUSTS

Not every trust that is for a benevolent or selfless purpose is a charitable trust. Traditionally, to be legally "charitable," a trust had to be created for the benefit of the public and be designed for the "relief of poverty, advancement of education, advancement of religion, promotion of health, governmental or municipal purposes or any other purpose the accomplishment of which is beneficial to the community." As can be seen below, this standard has been incorporated into the Wisconsin statute defining charitable trusts. As the following early case illustrates, Wisconsin looks to the state's English legal heritage to determine the meaning of the term *charitable*. The Statute of Elizabeth, discussed in the following case, was also known as the Charitable Uses Act. It was enacted by the English Parliament in 1601, and has provided the inspiration for most American efforts to define charitable entities.

A. WHAT MAKES A TRUST CHARITABLE?

Wis. Stat. 701.10. Charitable trusts. (defined)

(1) VALIDITY. A charitable trust may be created for any of the following charitable purposes: relief of poverty, advancement of education, advancement of religion, promotion of

health, governmental or municipal purposes or any other purpose the accomplishment of which is beneficial to the community. No gift to charity, in trust or otherwise, is invalid because of indefiniteness. If a particular charitable purpose is not indicated and the trustee is not expressly authorized by the creating instrument to select such a purpose, the trustee has an implied power to select one or more charitable purposes. If a particular charitable purpose is not indicated and no trustee is named in the creating instrument, the court may appoint a trustee with such an implied power to select or may direct that the property be transferred outright to one or more established charitable entities.

Webster v. Morris

Supreme Court of Wisconsin
66 Wis. 366, 28 N.W. 353 (1886)

[In a portion of this decision not reproduced in Chapter 5, Justice Cassoday examined the validity of a provision in the will of testator, Hiram W. Webster that appeared to be an attempt to create a charitable trust from the residue of his estate. The provision in question stated, as follows:

"Fifteenth. It is my will, and I direct, that in case my estate exceeds the legacies mentioned in this, my will, that the surplus or remainder of my estate be appropriated and used by my executors in aid or encouragement of charitable purposes; and if in their judgment there should be a sufficient amount of said surplus, I would recommend that the same be used to establish a school in Omro, or some place in Winnebago county, Wisconsin, for the education of young persons in the domestic and useful arts; but in case there is not enough of my estate to meet the above legacies, that the deficit may be borne pro rata between the legatees, except my beloved Louisa M.

The court concluded:

8. By the fifteenth paragraph of the will the testator, in effect, willed and directed that in case his estate exceeded the legacies therein mentioned, then the surplus or remainder of his estate should be appropriated and used by his executors in aid or encouragement of charitable purposes; and if, in their judgment, there should be sufficient amount of said surplus, then he recommended that the same should be used to establish a school in Omro, or some place in Winnebago county, "for the education

of young persons in the domestic and useful arts." We have already seen that a bequest for "charitable purposes," standing alone, is too vague and indefinite to be carried into execution. This, as we have noticed, is upon the theory that courts are confined to the exercise of judicial powers, and hence have no authority to devise a particular scheme or plan of charity. But here the general words are followed by others indicating a particular scheme or plan for the expenditure. What effect is that fact to have upon the validity of the bequest? In Thomson v. Shakespear, supra, **[1 De G., F. & J. 399 (1860)]** the general words which might otherwise have been construed to be charitable were restricted, by the words which preceded them, to the Shakespear premises. "It is a universal rule of construction, founded in the clearest reason," said BLACK, C. J., "that general words in any instrument or statute are strengthened by exceptions and weakened by enumeration." Sharpless v. Mayor, 21 Pa. 147. That rule has been applied by this court. Wis. Cent. R. Co. v. Taylor Co. 52 Wis. 37, 91, 8 N.W. 833. Thus, according to Lord BACON, "all words, whether they be in deeds or statutes, or otherwise, if they be general, and not express and precise, shall be restrained unto the fitness of the matter and the person." Broom's Leg. Max. 646. See, also, Thorpe v. Thorpe, 1 Ld. Raym. 235; Moore v. Magrath, 1 Cowp. 9; Roe v. Vernon, 5 East 51; Morrell v. Fisher, 4 Exch. 591; Wood v. Rowcliffe, 6 Exch. 407.

The same rule was recently applied to the description in a bill of sale in Minnesota. McAlpine v. Foley, 25 N.W. 452. "Thus the word 'benevolent,' intrinsically considered, includes more than legal charities, but its signification may be narrowed by the context" so as only to include charities. De Camp v. Dobbins, 31 N.J. Eq. 671. So, it has been held in this state that where a power of attorney is given for a particular purpose, general words therein are not to be construed at large, but merely as giving general powers for carrying into effect the special purpose for which the power was given. Rountree v. Denson, 59 Wis. 522. It is now universally admitted that in construing a will the rule is to read it in the ordinary and grammatical sense of the words employed, unless some obvious absurdity, or some repugnance or inconsistency with the declared intentions of the testator, to be extracted from the whole instrument, should follow from so reading it. "Then the sense may be modified, extended, or abridged, so as to avoid those consequences, but no further." Abbott v. Middleton, 7 H.L. Cas. 115, and cases there cited. "Quite consistently with this rule, words and limitations may be supplied or rejected, when warranted by the immediate context or the general scheme of the will, but not merely on a conjectural hypothesis of the testator's intention, however reasonable, in opposition to the plain and obvious sense of the instrument." Ibid.; Thellusson v. Rendlesham, 7 H.L. Cas. 494; In re Northern's Estate (Salt v. Pym), L. R. 28 Ch. Div. 157; Scott v. West, 63 Wis. 529, 552, 24 N.W. 161.

Applying the foregoing principles to the paragraph of the will here in question, and assuming, for the present, that the establishment of a school of the character there indicated is a charitable purpose, then, as it seems to us, we are authorized to hold that the particular charitable purpose which the testator directed his executors to use such residue of his estate in aiding and encouraging, was in the establishment of such school. After expressing his "charitable purposes" generally, he recommends a scheme for its exercise in the establishment of the school, in case the amount of such surplus is sufficient for that purpose in the judgment of his executors. No other scheme is suggested, and, as we have seen, the court is powerless to devise one. It follows that the intention of the testator, as expressed in that paragraph of the will, is to be wholly defeated, unless we construe the word "recommend" to mean something more than is ordinarily implied by it; and, in view of the context, and the authorities cited, we think we may give it the meaning of command or direction to use such surplus to establish the school in the event indicated. Knox v. Knox, 59 Wis. 172, 18 N.W. 155.

The language of the will seems to contemplate a school of the character indicated, to be incorporated. The mere fact that the corporation was not in esse on the death of the testator in no way frustrates the trust. To establish such a school is to give it a legal existence--that is to say, a corporate existence. In re Taylor Orphan Asylum, 36 Wis. 534; Dodge v. Williams, 46 Wis. 70 at 100, 50 N.W. 1103; Gould v. Taylor Orphan Asylum, 46 Wis. 106, 50 N.W. 422; Gray's Rule against Perpetuities, sec. 607, and cases there cited. It is to be established by the executors in their capacity as trustees. It could not be established by executors until there were executors, and there could be no executors until the death of the testator. They are to appropriate and use such surplus funds as may be in their hands for that purpose in the event indicated. The authorities cited fully sanction the legality of such appropriation and use of funds by trustees in the establishment of such a school. The same authorities hold that such bequest is not void for remoteness, nor against the rule of perpetuities. Santa Clara F. Academy v. Sullivan, (Ill.) 6 N.E. 183. The legal title to such surplus estate is vested in the executors. Scott v. West, 63 Wis. 529, 24 N.W. 161. It will remain in them until they establish such school--that is, give it a legal corporate existence. It will then become vested in such corporation. Being thus continually vested, the doctrine of remoteness is inapplicable, upon the principles already suggested.

9. May the establishment of such a school be properly regarded as a charitable purpose? In Kendall v. Granger, supra, it was said by Lord LANGDALE, M. R., that a charitable purpose "must be either one of those purposes denominated charitable in the statute of Elizabeth, or one of such purposes as the court construes to be charitable by analogy to those mentioned in that statute." Among the "purposes denominated charitable" in that statute were gifts for "relief of aged, impotent, and poor people;"

and for "schools of learning, free schools, . . . scholars in universities; . . . education and preferment of orphans; . . . aid and help of young tradesmen, handicraftsmen," etc. 2 Stats. at Large, 708, ch. 4. So, according to Mr. Perry, charitable trusts include all gifts in trust for educational purposes in their ever-varying diversity, as well as gifts for the relief and comfort of the poor, the sick, and the afflicted. 2 Perry on Trusts, secs. 687, 697. In Vidal v. Girard, supra, **[43 U.S. 127 (1844)]** it was held, in effect, that donations for the establishment of colleges, schools, and seminaries of learning, and especially such as were for the education of orphans and poor scholars, were charities, in the sense of the common law. Besides, it is to be a literary corporation, which, as well as charitable corporations, is excepted from the operation of the statute. Sec. 2039, R. S.; Santa Clara F. Academy v. Sullivan, supra. county, Wisconsin, for the education of young persons in the domestic and useful arts," was a charitable purpose, within the judicial sense. Treat's Appeal, supra **[30 Conn. 113];** McAllister v. McAllister's Heirs, supra **[46 Vt. 272]**; Craig v. Secrist, supra **[54 Ind. 419]**. Especially is this so, since there is no restriction or limitation as to the class of young persons to be thus educated. In other words, it is to be a public school of the character indicated.

10. The scheme for using such surplus in the establishment of such school is, upon the principles already stated, sufficiently definite and certain to be carried into execution in the event named, and must therefore be regarded as valid. If such residue should of itself be insufficient for the purpose of fully establishing such school, and such school can be established by the use of such residue and other funds contributed from other sources, under the charge and management of a proper corporation organized for the purpose, then we see no valid reason why such residue may not be so used in the establishment of such school. Of course, if such residue should, in the opinion of the executors, be insufficient of itself to establish such school, and sufficient funds from other sources are not secured, then such surplus would go to the persons entitled under the statutes.

B. CHARITABLE INTENT

As Wis. Stat. §701.10(1) indicates, Wisconsin courts are to be liberal in their willingness to recognize an intention to create a charitable trust.

In re Estate of Raulf

Supreme Court of Wisconsin
28 Wis. 2d 514, 137 N.W. 2d 416 (1965)

Conrad Raulf, a resident of Winnebago County, Wisconsin, died testate on January 9, 1959. His will, dated September 13, 1957, disposed of his estate in part by specific bequests, but the bulk of it went into a residuary testamentary trust of which First National Bank in Oshkosh is the trustee.

The will provides that the trust is to continue during the lifetime of Charles Raulf, a brother, and Lillian Raulf, wife of Charles Raulf, with all of the income therefrom to be paid to Charles Raulf during his lifetime, and upon his death 50 percent of the income to be paid to Lillian Raulf during her lifetime, with the other 50 percent to be paid to diverse beneficiaries, including "Milwaukee Lodge Benevolent and Protective Order of Elks #46 of the United States of America (to be used only for charitable purposes) Two (2%) percent thereof." The foregoing trust is to continue until the death of the last to survive of Charles and Lillian Raulf, at which time the trust is to terminate and the principal distributed to designated beneficiaries, including "the Milwaukee Lodge Benevolent and Protective Order of Elks #46 of the United States of America (to be used for charitable purposes) Ten (10%) percent thereof."

Both Charles and Lillian Raulf survived the testator. Charles Raulf died on November 18, 1964, and thus the bequest of two percent of trust income payable to the Milwaukee Lodge of Elks #46 became operative. A judgment in the Conrad Raulf estate was entered on December 27, 1961, authorizing the trustee to pay federal and state income and death taxes. The will itself expressly imposed the burden of valid state and federal death taxes upon the estate. The First National Bank in Oshkosh, as executor, paid the federal estate taxes and Wisconsin inheritance taxes on an estimated basis, treating the remainder interest in the trust estate which was granted to Milwaukee Lodge of Elks #46 as a charitable bequest for tax purposes.

The federal taxing authorities requested the executor to furnish information regarding the charter and bylaws of the Elks Lodge and also the action taken by such lodge to designate the charitable uses to be made of its portion of the trust estate. The Elks Lodge refused to furnish the executor with such information, whereupon the executor petitioned the county court of Winnebago county for an order requiring the Elks Lodge to supply the requested data and to take the appropriate action. The county court entered an order on March 22, 1962, requiring the Elks Lodge to show cause why it should not comply with the petition of the executor and trustee. The Elks Lodge filed an answer and attached thereto a copy of the constitution and statutes of the National Order of Elks, a copy of the charter, bylaws and rules of order of the Elks Lodge and alleged that it is not a condition precedent to the establishment of its rights as a legatee and beneficiary that it make a determination evincing a specific charitable use for its bequests.

On February 5, 1965, the trial court decided that the testator's intent was to create a public charitable trust. While the trial court also ruled that the Milwaukee Elks Lodge by resolution could designate a specific purpose for which its share of the proceeds was to be used, the court further concluded that the Elks Lodge did not qualify to administer the trust. The court ordered that the administration of the trust would be by trustees appointed by the court and under the supervision of the court.

Gordon, J. Each of the two bequests to the Elks Club was expressly limited by the testator as to the purpose for which it was to be used. In one instance, the will contained the words "to be used only for charitable purposes;" in the other instance, the same expression without the word "only" was employed. The trial court interpreted these gifts to be impressed with a restriction that they be used for public charitable purposes. In view of the language of the instrument, we must agree with that conclusion. Estate of Lawrence (1964), 22 Wis. (2d) 624, 126 N. W. (2d) 517; Will of Richter (1934), 215 Wis. 108, 254 N. W. 103. We interpret the words of this will to establish that the testator intended to make a charitable bequest, and under all the circumstances it must be construed to be a public charitable gift rather than a private charitable gift or a noncharitable one. Estate of Brandenburg (1961), 13 Wis. (2d) 217, 108 N. W. (2d) 374; Estate of Rowell (1946), 248 Wis. 520, 22 N. W. (2d) 604.

In Estate of Bletsch (1964), 25 Wis. (2d) 40, 130 N. W. (2d) 275, we recognized that the court will endeavor to carry out a charitable purpose which is manifested in a testament. If a private type of charity is intended by a donor, the instrument must offer reasonably clear support for such concept. This court will not presume an intention that a charitable bequest is to be available for private charitable purposes. Harrington v. Pier (1900), 105 Wis. 485, 82 N. W. 345. This is true no matter how worthy may be the institution or the private charity involved. The testator in the case at bar did not create a formal trust, but we have held that the words "in trust" are not essential in the establishment of a charitable trust. Maxcy v. Oshkosh (1910), 144 Wis. 238, 249, 128 N. W. 899, 128 N. W. 1136; Restatement, 2 Trusts (2d), p. 215, sec. 351, ch. 11. Cf. Estate of Silverthorn (1957), 274 Wis. 453, 457, 80 N. W. (2d) 430.

In Estate of Bletsch (1964), 25 Wis. (2d) 40, 47, 130 N. W. (2d) 275, we commented as follows concerning the doctrine of cy pres:

"In our opinion, it is sufficient if there is a bequest to a charity. In a sense, it can perhaps be said that a charity always receives the gift in trust for its purposes."

Sec. 231.11 (7) (d), Stats., asserts the legislative policy of our state to be as follows:

"Where the fulfillment of the special purpose expressed in a trust or other gift for charitable or public purposes is or becomes impracticable, impossible or unlawful, it shall be the duty of the courts by a liberal construction of the trust or gift to ascertain the general purpose of the donor and to carry it into effect in the nearest practicable manner to the expressed special purpose; provided, however, that the right of visitation of a living donor shall not be held to be impaired by anything contained in this subsection."

The appellant has objected to the court's appointment of trustees and has urged that trustees (if they are found to be needed) be selected from amongst the leadership of the appellant fraternal order. In the absence of a contrary intent determinable from the instrument, it is ordinarily within the province of the county court to select trustees and to fix the conditions and terms of the trust's administration. See Estate of Rowell (1946), 248 Wis. 520, 525, 526, 22 N. W. (2d) 604; Restatement, 2 Trusts (2d), pp. 286, 287, sec. 397, ch. 11. We recognize that tax considerations may have formed the impetus for this litigation. Nevertheless, the taxing agencies are not parties before this court, and we do not purport to reach any determination concerning the taxability of the interests herein. Order affirmed.

C. MIXED PURPOSE TRUSTS

A trust cannot be a charitable trust if it is for the benefit of the settlor or the settlor's family, even if the purpose of the trust met the normal criteria for "charitable." The following case addresses the question of whether or not a trust that permits otherwise eligible family members to share in its benefits can be a charitable trust.

In re Estate of Frautschy

Supreme Court of Wisconsin
84 Wis. 2d 644, 267 N.W.2d 300 (1978)

Day, J. This is an appeal from two probate court orders determining the Wisconsin inheritance taxes in the estate of Bertie M. Frautschy. The estate's personal representative since March 14, 1976 has been the respondent, First National Bank of Monroe (hereafter personal representative). The probate court determined that a bequest in the deceased's will, establishing the "John Cowles Frautschy Scholarship Fund," was exempt from taxation as a charitable trust. The appellant, Wisconsin State Department of Revenue (department) contends that the trust was not exempt.

The question is whether the bequest of funds for a scholarship trust for needy post-high school students is exempt from inheritance taxation under sec. 72.15(1), Stats. 1973, where the scholarships are available to male Protestant Monroe high school graduates and certain relatives of the deceased.

On December 7, 1974, Bertie M. Frautschy died testate, leaving a net estate of $146,465.35 before taxes. Article XII of her will provided that the residue of the estate would be held in trust for the establishment of the "John Cowles Frautschy Scholarship Fund." John Cowles Frautschy was Mrs. Frautschy's son who died at age ten. As of May 11, 1976 the income from the fund was $6,300.00 per year.

The pertinent portions of the will establishing the scholarship are as follows:

"XII. All of the rest, residue and remainder of my estate, of every kind and nature, wheresoever situated, I give, devise and bequeath to my trustee hereinafter named for the purpose hereinafter set forth:

"Said trustee shall hold, invest and administer the trust fund in accordance with the provisions of this my Last Will and Testament, and for the purpose of establishing a scholarship fund to be known as the JOHN COWLES FRAUTSCHY SCHOLARSHIP FUND.

"The income from said fund shall annually be paid to a deserving male graduate or male graduates of Monroe High School, Monroe, Wisconsin except as otherwise noted herein. . . .

"I specifically restrict the awarding of this scholarship to male Protestant graduates of Monroe High School, except as otherwise stated herein.

"In making their selection, I direct that they shall consider need as paramount and that scholastic excellence shall not necessarily be a factor. I make this provision for the reason that many times students who do not attain scholastic honors in High School are capable of doing excellent University work. . . .

"In the event the children of NATHAN FRAUTSCHY, STANLEY THOMAS and WILLIAM EPLING show interest in a college education, and if in the judgment of the committee are deserving, it is my hope that the committee will give them favorable consideration in making the award of scholarship hereunder, provided that they may do so consistent with the terms hereof. The requirement of being a graduate of Monroe High School shall not apply to such children. Except for the children of the persons named, the awards shall be confined to male graduates of Monroe High School at Monroe, Wisconsin." (Emphasis supplied.)

The people mentioned for special scholarship consideration were all related by blood or marriage to the testatrix. Nathan Frautschy was the nephew of Chester D. Frautschy, the husband of the testatrix, who predeceased her. William Epling is a grand-nephew of the testatrix. Stanley Thomas is the husband of the testatrix's great grand-niece.

On the basis of the underlined clause the department disallowed the scholarship trust as a charitable gift.

The probate court found that the language underlined above in the will that,

". . . it is my hope that the committee will give them [the relatives] favorable consideration in making the award of scholarship hereunder . . ."

was precatory and of no effect. The department agrees that this language was precatory.

On June 3, 1976 the trial court determined that the trust was charitable and ordered the department to refund $18,747.85 in inheritance taxes to the estate.

On June 7, 1976 the department moved for rehearing on the inheritance tax determination, claiming that the scholarship trust was not exempt because part of the money from the trust had been awarded to someone who was going to attend an out-of-state college. This latter argument is not raised on this appeal.

On July 13, 1976 the probate court reaffirmed its previous decision. The department appeals from the June 3, 1976 and July 13, 1976 orders.

Sec. 72.11(1) (a), Stats. 1973 provides for an inheritance tax on the transfer of property to any distributee from a person who dies while a resident of this state, unless the property is exempted by another section of the statutes. Sec. 72.15(1) (a)2, Stats. 1973 exempts transfers to ". . . voluntary associations organized . . . solely for religious, humane, charitable, scientific or educational purposes . . ."

A determination of whether the transfer to the trust is exempt hinges on statutory construction.

". . . tax exemptions . . . are matters of legislative grace; . . . taxation is the rule and exemption the exception . . ." Estate of Thomas, 1 Wis.2d 402, 405, 84 N.W.2d 68 (1957).Even where the exemption is for a charitable purpose, the clear and unambiguous language of the statute must control. The court can not resort to an implied exemption. Estate of Price, 192 Wis. 580, 584, 585, 213 N.W. 477 (1927). The courts look with favor upon charitable bequests and the statute exempting such bequests should be construed to favor exemption. Estate of Johnston, 186 Wis. 599, 601, 602, 203 N.W. 376, 377 (1925).

Both parties to this appeal rely on Will of Chafin, 210 Wis. 675, 247 N.W. 325 (1933). In that case John Chafin died testate and part of his will provided that $72,692.13 of his estate should be put in trust for the establishment of the "Chafin Farm Home." The trust provided that the farm home was to be ". . . a home for poor neglected boys in which to educate them and teach them farming and other useful . . . occupations . . ." Chafin at 210 Wis. 676.

The bequest for the establishment of the home was conditioned on the name of the farm never being changed and on the further requirement that certain named persons be allowed to reside at the home. If Chafin's nephews, nieces or sisters-in-law were in need, the trustees of the farm were to either provide for their support or put them in the farm home temporarily or permanently. Anytime Chafin's brother-in-law, David Shultis, wanted to stay at the farm home he could do so as long as he obeyed the rules of the home.

Miss May B. Senger, who was not a relative of Chafin's, could go to the home for a vacation or become a temporary or permanent resident of the farm home. Even if May Senger was not a resident of the farm home she had the right, under the will, to receive periodic payments from the farm home's endowment fund.

If any of the above conditions of the will were not complied with, the farm home trust would be void and the trust funds would revert to Chafin's heirs.

Chafin is readily distinguishable from the case at bar for at least two reasons. First, in Chafin the trustees were required to house Miss Senger and Mr. Shultis at the farm home and to make periodic payments to Miss Senger. If the trustees did not comply with these requirements, the trust became void. Second, Shultis and Senger had a right to the housing and payments regardless of need. The Chafin trust was instituted, at least partly, for private purposes. The private purposes were shown by the benefits that were required to be given to relatives and non-relatives alike, regardless of need.

In a number of federal cases relatives benefited from a will or inter vivos instrument creating a charitable, educational or religious trust. In each of these cases, the testator or settlor asked or required that relatives be considered or given a preference, but generally the trust funds were still held to be deductible. In Schoellkopf v. United States, 124 F.2d 982 (2nd Cir. 1942) the trust instrument listed one of its objects as "The care of needy men, women and children" Schoellkopf at 124 F.2d 985. The trust allowed, but did not require that worthy descendants of the settlor's father be included as beneficiaries. The trust did not even give the descendants a preference in receiving benefits. The court stated that the possible benefits to relatives did not prevent the trust from being charitable under 26 U.S.C. §23(n) (2), Revenue Act of 1928.

In Estate of Agnes C. Robinson, 1 T.C. 19 (1942), the will created a trust for the benefit of needy persons. The trustee had absolute discretion in the choice of beneficiaries, but the will expressed the wish that friends and relatives of the testatrix be given preference. In administering the trust, the trustees made payments to seven cousins of the testatrix and seven unrelated persons. The payments to relatives totaled $2,190.00 to relatives and $2,160.00 to non-relatives. The tax court held that the bequest for the trust was charitable despite the fact that relatives were beneficiaries and given a preference. In reaching this decision, the court noted that the purpose of the trust was charitable and that the relatives receiving benefits had to be in impecunious circumstances. Robinson at 1 T.C. 23, 24.

In Estate of Waller, 39 T.C. 665 (1963), the trustees were authorized, in their uncontrolled discretion, to make distributions to anyone who was in need of financial aid, or to any young person who needed financial aid to attend a school or college. The trustees were instructed to give preference to relatives, former employees and children of employees of the donors to the trust. Relying on language in the trust instrument stating its purpose, the court held that the trust was exclusively for charitable or educational purposes. Waller at 39 T.C. 673, 674. In Estate of Sells, 10 T.C. 692, 699, 701 (1948), funds for a trust created by a holographic will were held to be deductible from the gross estate because of their religious and educational purposes. The trust provided for a $200.00 annual payment to a church and for other income to be given for scholarships, with nieces and nephews of the testatrix getting preference for the scholarship funds. The trustees followed the instructions in the trust, and during the first two years of trust administration paid $2,500.00 of $2,900.00 of trust benefits to the nieces and nephews. Despite this fact, the court reasoned that the trust was to be in perpetuity and that with time an increasingly large share of the scholarship funds would go to non-relatives. The court held that under these circumstances the trust only expressed a preference for relatives and that the bequest was deductible from the gross estate. Sells at 10 T.C. 701.

In other cases charitable deductions have been denied for expenditures used to establish inter vivos trusts from which relatives could benefit. In Amy Hutchinson Crellin v. C. I. R., 46 B.T.A. 1152 (1942), a trust was set up primarily to educate relatives of the deceased. In James Sprunt Benev. Trust. v. Comm., 20 B.T.A. 19 (1930), the trust instrument recited that a primary purpose was to pay full or partial support "on liberal lines" to any direct descendant of the settlor's parents who would serve as a minister in the Southern Presbyterian Church.

We discuss these federal cases, but do not find all of them persuasive in interpreting the Wisconsin statute at issue here. We find the tax court cases persuasive only for the general proposition that a testamentary or inter vivos trust is not necessarily less charitable because relatives of the settlor may become beneficiaries of the trust. Relatives may be beneficiaries and the trust will still be charitable or educational so long as: (1) The trustees are not required to pay benefits to relatives, and; (2) The relatives may only benefit from the trust on the same basis of need as non-relatives. Schoellkopf at 124 F.2d 985.

In this case the trustees are not required to give scholarships to relatives of the testatrix. The parties agree that the language in the will concerning the relatives is only precatory. Even if relatives of the deceased are given scholarships they must meet the same need requirements as other scholarship applicants. The testamentary trust in this case opened the class of potential beneficiaries to include relatives as well as male graduates of Monroe high school, but the relatives must still meet the same need requirements to get scholarships. It was brought out at oral argument that as a practical matter there were very few relatives who were even possible beneficiaries of the trust. Nothing in the trust or the record indicates that this trust was set up for other than bona fide charitable and educational purposes. Orders affirmed.

D. DISCRIMINATORY TRUSTS

Although it does not appear to have been an issue in the above case, the beneficial interest of the *Frautschy* trust was limited by gender (male) and religion (protestant). (It was also limited to graduates of a particular high school, but that is permitted with charitable trusts.) Whether or not a charitable trust, enforceable by the state, can be subject to such restrictions has been the source of considerable debate over the past 50 years. While it is clear that an agency of the state government cannot administer a trust whose purpose would clearly be unconstitutional if embraced by the state, *Evans v. Newton,* 382 U.S. 296 (1966), it is not clear that a privately administered charitable trust that discriminates on the basis of immutable characteristics is per se invalid. *In re Estate of Wilson*, 59 N.Y.2d 461, 465 N.Y.S.2d 900, 452 N.E.2d 1228 (1983).

In the past, especially in cases involving discrimination on the basis of gender or religion, courts have been willing to use *cy pres,* not to remove the discriminatory features, but instead to remove all vestiges of state involvement. Trusts for the support of traditionally disadvantaged groups (like racial and religious minorities and women) are clearly more likely to upheld as legitimate than trusts that discriminate against such groups by specifically excluding them from benefits for which they would otherwise be eligible. There appear to be virtually no Wisconsin cases that address this issue, and most of the authority from other jurisdictions is not of recent vintage.

Of course, if the discrimination required by the trust is prohibited by applicable civil rights laws, those provisions are simply unenforceable. The above case of *Evans v. Newton* notwithstanding, the inability to enforce discriminatory restrictive provisions will not necessarily require the termination of the trust. In most situations, there is a presumption that the settlor's primary motive for the charitable trust was to create a benefit for the public and not to perpetuate forms of discrimination. In such circumstances, the charitable trust will normally survive but will be administered under less discriminatory terms. For example, a trust to provide scholarships for white males from a particular high school that is to be administered by the local school board, can be modified so that any student, regardless of race or gender, is a potential beneficiary.

II. THE MODIFICATION OF CHARITABLE TRUSTS

Wis. Stat. 701.10. Charitable trusts. (modification provisions)

(2) MODIFICATION AND TERMINATION.

(a) If a purpose of a charitable trust is or becomes impractical, unlawful or impossible, the court may order the trust continued for one or more other charitable purposes designated by the settlor or, in the absence of such designation, order the property devoted to one or more other charitable purposes either by continuing the trust or by distributing the property to one or more established charitable entities. In determining the alternative plan for disposition of the property, the court shall take into account current and future community needs in the general field of charity within which the original charitable purpose falls, other charitable interest of the settlor, the amount of principal and income available under the trust and other relevant factors. The provisions of this subsection do not apply insofar as the settlor expressly provides in the creating instrument for an alternative disposition if the original trust fails; nor do they apply to gifts by several persons to a charitable entity on a subscription basis if the court finds that the donors intended their gifts to be limited to the original purpose and such purpose fails initially.

(b) If any administrative provision of a charitable trust or part of a plan set forth by the settlor to achieve the settlors charitable purpose is or becomes impractical, unlawful, inconvenient or undesirable, and a modification of such provision or plan will enable the trustee to achieve more effectively the basic charitable purpose, the court may by appropriate order modify the provision or plan.

(c) If a charitable trust is or becomes uneconomic when principal and probable income, cost of administration and other relevant factors are considered, or in any event if the trust property is valued at less than 50,000, the court may terminate the trust and order outright distribution to an established charitable entity in the general field of charity within which the charitable purpose falls.

(d) It is the purpose of this subsection to broaden the power of the courts to make charitable gifts more effective. In any situation not expressly covered the court shall liberally apply the cy pres doctrine.

(e) The settlor if living, the trustee, the attorney general and an established charitable entity to which income or principal must be paid under the terms of the trust shall be persons interested in any proceeding under this subsection.

A. ADMINISTRATIVE DEVIATION

In some situations the problem with the continued operation of a charitable trust lies not with the trust's purpose, but with the rules by which it is administered. In these circumstances, an otherwise impractical charitable trust can be made practical by changing the terms by which it is to operate. If this situation arises, the trustee can petition the court with jurisdiction over the trust and request permission to alter the administrative rules. However, there are times when the line be administrative and substantive is difficult to determine, whether the trust is private or charitable. In *In re Pulitzer's Estate,* 249 N.Y.S. 87 (Surr. Ct. 1931). a New York court ruled that a requirement that the assets of a testamentary trust be invested in stock of the company that published the Pulitzer newspapers was an administrative requirement rather that a substantive purpose of the trust, even though the evidence suggested that continued family control of the company (through the trustees, who were the sons of Joseph Pulitzer) was one of the reasons the trust was created.

Administrative deviation is a lesser power than the power of *cy pres* (discussed below) which allows the court to change the substantive purpose of the trust if certain conditions are met.

Estate of Robinson v. Webster

Supreme Court of Wisconsin
248 Wis. 203, 21 N.W.2d 391 (1946)

Proceedings on petition of Irving P. Robinson against Jean J. Mowrey and others as trustees, for termination of a charitable trust created by the will of Florence Porter Robinson, deceased. From an interlocutory judgment terminating the trust, directing trustees to render a final account and turn the trust personal property over to the register of probate for distribution to the heirs of the testatrix, when determined by proof of heirship, the trustees appeal.

Florence Porter Robinson died July 14, 1926, leaving a will which was duly offered for probate in the county court of Milwaukee County. Objection was made to its allowance on the grounds that the testatrix was mentally incompetent, and that it was procured by exercise of undue influence by persons unknown. No evidence was offered to support the claim of undue influence. After a full hearing and explicit findings of the mental competency of the testatrix the county court on August 23, 1929, entered judgment admitting the will to probate and establishing it "as a valid will." Appeal was taken to this court and the judgment was affirmed without opinion April 1, 1930. (Will of Robinson, 201 Wis. 656, 229 N. W. 911.) A motion for rehearing was made by contestants and denied.

The will left the property of the testatrix, after a few specific bequests, in trust to persons named therein as trustees, who were duly appointed as trustees and received the property of the testatrix from the executor of the will on April 29, 1937, and they and their successors have since administered the estate in furtherance of the purposes of the trust. It is to be noted in this connection also that the final order or judgment of the county court "settling" the executor's account contained provisions distributing to the trustees the personal estate of the testatrix and assigning to them the real estate "to be held and administered" by them "in accordance with the terms and provisions" of the will, particularly referred to and incorporating the provisions by reference in the order.

The will, after the specific bequests, gave all of the property of the testatrix "and all increment thereon" in trust to three named women friends "for the establishment and founding in the University of Wisconsin of a professorship of American history" upon the condition the trustees should arrange with the Regents of the University for the founding and establishing of such professorship, to be maintained perpetually and to be held by a woman with rank and emoluments of a full professor and that she receive a salary of "not less than $ 6,000" a year. The will further provided that the succeeding trustees should always be women. It provided further that if such chair should not be arranged for with the Regents of the University of Wisconsin, the trustees endeavor to make arrangements for the founding of such professorship with the authorities of the University of Chicago; and if for any reason it should become impossible within five years to arrange with either the Regents of the University of Wisconsin or the governing authorities of the University of Chicago to found such professorship, then the property should be distributed "as provided by the statute in cases of intestacy." The will provided that the trustees should add income to corpus until the fund should produce an income of $ 6,000 a year when this income should be paid over to the Regents of the University of Wisconsin (or Chicago) "to be paid by them to the professor who shall occupy said professorship."

Following the admitting of the will to probate the Board of Regents of the University of Wisconsin on June 21, 1930, passed a resolution that it should and thereby did "accept all of the benefits arising from the trust created" in the will, and directing and empowering the president of the university and the secretary of the Board of Regents to take all steps necessary "for the establishment and maintenance of such professorship in accordance with the terms" of the will.

On March 4, 1931, the Board of Regents adopted another resolution reciting that whereas the will provided that arrangement for the said professorship in the University of Wisconsin "to be effective must be made within a period of five years from and after the death of the testatrix," the board "shall and hereby does establish and found a professorship of American history in said university to be maintained in accordance with the terms and provisions" of the will, and directing the president and secretary of the board and the president of the University of Wisconsin and their successors to take all steps necessary for such maintenance, and the resolution expressly adopted and confirmed the act of the board in passing the resolution of June 21, 1930.

Minutes of the meetings of the Board of Regents show that on June 18, 1937, a motion was passed that the board reconsider its action "accepting the bequest" and on June 19th a motion was passed that the bequest "be rejected." It should perhaps be stated that President Dykstra had requested an opinion of the attorney general whether the board could rescind its action accepting the benefits of the will and that the attorney general had given his opinion that it could not, and that the board was informed of the giving of the opinion; that it may also be noted that Governor La Follette, after the adoption of the motion for rejection, by letter requested the attorney general "to appear and represent the state in all actions or proceedings concerning the bequest to the University of Wisconsin under the will of Florence Porter Robinson, and to do all things necessary or convenient to insure the benefit of said bequest to the university" and that pursuant to this request the attorney general, with consent of the court, filed herein a brief amicus curice for consideration on the instant appeal.

On June 19, 1944, the heirs of the testatrix petitioned the court for a judgment terminating the trust created by the will on the ground that it was impossible or impracticable of execution. Hearing was had upon this petition and, so far as the record discloses, the petition was decided upon the files and records of the county court in the instant case, including several annual accounts of the trustees and the record of the acts of the Board of Regents of the University of Wisconsin in reference to the bequest for the establishment of the professorship. Acting County Judge Bucklin who heard the matter filed an opinion and made specific findings of fact by which he found that the trust property had deteriorated from about $ 50,000 originally to property of the present value of $ 25,000 to $ 30,000; that the income of the property has never equaled the expense of administration and the income is constantly diminishing; and that the resolutions of the Board of Regents rescinding their actions respecting acceptance of the trust imposed on the board by the will operated as a "lawful withdrawal" of their acceptance. The findings recite the provision of the will that "if it becomes impossible or impracticable for the trustees to arrange for the establishment or maintenance of such professorship" the trust property shall be "divided and distributed as provided by the statutes in cases of intestacy." The judgment entered determines that the trust created by the will "is now impossible or impracticable of fulfillment within the meaning of the said will;" that the trust is terminated; and that the trustees account for and deliver to the register of probate the residue of the trust property so that further proceedings may be had to the end that it may be assigned and distributed among the heirs at law of the testatrix to be determined by proof of heirship to be made.

Fowler, J. From the foregoing statement of facts it appears that the will of Florence Porter Robinson was duly admitted to probate by the county court of Milwaukee County, and the judgment so admitting it was affirmed by this court. The will created a charitable trust and the judgment before us for review terminated that trust as "impossible or impracticable of fulfillment" and adjudged that the trust property be distributed to the heirs at law of the testatrix as they shall be determined by the county court upon proofs of heirship later to be made.

The will provides for two sets of trustees, one set consisting of three women trustees whose duty it is to manage the trust property and add its income to the corpus until a sufficient corpus is accumulated to yield an income of $6,000 a year and that they then pay that income to the Regents of the University of Wisconsin, and the other set consisting of the Regents of the University of Wisconsin whose duty it is to establish and to maintain out of income received from the women trustees, a professorship to be held by a woman and pay over to the occupant of the professorship the $6,000 income when it is received by them. That two kinds of trustees may exist together is indicated in 1 Bogert, Trusts and Trustees, p. 372, sec. 122.

The judgment of the court terminating the trust is proper if a finding of fact is permissible that the trust property cannot possibly ever amount to enough by adding income to corpus to yield $6,000 annually. 4 Bogert, Trusts and Trustees, p. 2914, sec. 997, note 61; p. 2930, sec. 1002, note 32; Will of Stack, 217 Wis. 94, 100, 101, 258 N. W. 324. But from what was said and done in the Stack Will Case and in the case of Estate of Thronson, 243 Wis. 73, 75, 9 N. W. (2d) 641, when it appears that if the main purpose of a will creating a trust cannot be accomplished by continuing the management of the trust according to the direction of the will but may be accomplished by deviating the management from that specified by the will, deviation should be ordered by the court having supervision of the trust in order to effect the main purpose.

It is plain that the main purpose of the instant will was to procure the establishment of the professorship and its maintenance from the income eventually to be accumulated from the trust property. Such deviation is expressly authorized in case of charitable trusts by sec. 231.11 (7) (d), Stats. The statute reads:

"Where the fulfillment of the special purpose expressed in a trust or other gift for charitable or public purposes is or becomes impracticable, impossible or unlawful, it shall be the duty of the courts by a liberal construction of the trust or gift to ascertain the general purpose of the donor and to carry it into effect in the nearest practicable manner to the expressed special purpose. . . ."

The brief of the attorney general filed herein as amicus curiae points out that the expense of the administration of trust funds by the University of Wisconsin is .00147 of the corpus, less than $30 a year for administering $20,000. The annual account of the trustees filed in the county court shows gross income of $692.31 from the trust property in the year 1943. Offsetting this are expenditures for attorney's fees, $500, trustees' fees, $225, inheritance tax, $100, and incidental expenses $48, aggregating $923. The 1944 account shows gross income $603.87, and offsetting this are items for bond of trustees, $135, trustees' fees, $300, attorney's fees, $476, incidental expenses, $94, total $1,005. The total of attorney and trustee fees for the eight years the trustees have had charge of the trust property is $4,421.

If the property were administered for $30 a year it is obvious that sometime its accumulations would yield an income of $6,000 a year. The finding of the trial court that the trust property will never yield $6,000 a year is based on the hypothesis that the management of the trust property will be continued as specified in the will. We cannot say that this finding is not supported by the evidence. But it is obvious that if the property is taken over in trust by the Regents of the University to manage the expense of the present management above mentioned will be obviated, and as above stated the main purpose of the will will eventually be accomplished.

From the trial judge's written opinion it appears that he was of opinion that the passing of the motion of the Board of Regents rescinding their acceptance of the trust imposed on them by the will operated as a lawful withdrawal of their acceptance and left no possibility of the professorship being established and that this was a ground for termination of the trust.

The briefs of the appellants and of the attorney general contend that the Board of Regents having once accepted the trust imposed on them by the will had no power to withdraw their acceptance. The case of Maxcy v. Oshkosh, 144 Wis. 238, 128 N. W. 899, 128 N. W. 1138, supports this contention. There is no difference in principle between the case of the city of Oshkosh having no right to refuse to carry out a charitable trust that it has accepted and the Regents of the University having no such right. Drury v. Natick, 10 Allen (92 Mass.), 169; Attorney General v. Lowell, 246 Mass. 312, 141 N. E. 45; Kibbe v. Rochester (D. C.), 57 Fed. (2d) 542, support the proposition. It is to be noted that Drury v. Natick, supra, was considered in the Oshkosh Case, supra, as supporting the decision there made. The cases of Langdon v. Congregational Society of Plymouth, 12 Conn. 113, and Hansen v. Oregon Humane Society, 142 Or. 104, 18 Pac. (2d) 1036, also inferentially support the proposition that the regents had no power to rescind their resolutions of acceptance, as the defendants in these cases were corporations whose existence would continue indefinitely, and the same reason for applying the rule of those cases to them applies to a municipal corporation.

It is true that in the cases above cited the municipalities actually received the trust property, while here the regents have as yet received nothing. But the trustees have been administering the property in reliance on the acceptance of the regents, and the trust has been administered by the court relying on such acceptance. Under these circumstances the regents had no power to rescind their resolutions of acceptance. It is also to be noted that as the University of Wisconsin authorities by acceptance of the trust of establishing and maintaining a professorship as provided for by the will, and thereby preventing the managing trustees of the trust from negotiating with the authorities of the University of Chicago to establish the chair and carry out the trust, is estopped from declining the trust after the five-year period for creating the trust had expired.

However, while the Board of Regents had no power to rescind their acceptance of the trust, their acceptance of their trusteeship did not impose on them the duty of administering the trust imposed on the women trustees. Their acceptance imposed the duty of establishing and maintaining the professorship free from the burden of administering the trust property. It is in the discretion of the regents now to refuse to take on themselves that burden if they see fit to do so.

Under the circumstances we consider that the judgment of the county court should be reversed with direction to the county court to vacate the judgment under review and to tender to the Regents of the University of Wisconsin appointment as successor trustees to the women trustees with all the powers and subject to all the duties of such trustees; and with provision that if the Board of Regents accept such appointment judgment be entered dismissing the instant petition; and with provision that if the Board of Regents decline such appointment the judgment under review be reinstated.

The judgment of the county court is reversed with direction for further proceedings in accordance with the opinion. No costs will be allowed in this court except the appellants will pay the clerk's fees.

B. CY PRES

Cy pres refers to a court's inherent equitable power to revise the terms of a charitable trust when concerns of fairness and justice so dictate.

Estate of Bletsch

Supreme Court of Wisconsin
25 Wis. 2d 40, 130 N.W.2d 275 (1964)

GORDON, J. The trial court analyzed the evidence and determined that the testator's purpose was "to help crippled children through Masonic charitable organizations of the state of Illinois." The following conclusion of law was entered:

"That the only organization whose operations closely reflect the intent of the deceased is in the 'Shriners Hospital for Crippled Children' located in Chicago, Illinois."

The designated beneficiary in the instant case is non-existent; this gave rise to a latent ambiguity which made it appropriate to examine the extrinsic evidence. In Estate of Gibbs (1961), 14 Wis. (2d) 490, 496, 111 N.W. (2d) 413, this court explained that there are two classes of latent ambiguity:

"One, where there are two or more persons or things exactly measuring up to the description in the will; the other where no person or thing exactly answers the declarations and descriptions of the will, but two or more persons or things answer the description imperfectly. Extrinsic evidence must be resorted to under these circumstances to identify which of the parties, unspecified with particularity in the will, was intended by the testator."

The trial court had before it the testimony of Mr. Koerner, who described the origins of the language which was later used by the testator in his will. The extrinsic evidence also included a description of the physical disability of the testator's daughter.

The appellant urges that the instant case is controlled by Tharp v. Seventh Day Adventist Church (1923), 182 Wis. 107, 195 N.W. 331. There the gift was to the

"Seventh Day Adventist Church" for use in publishing and distributing literature of the church. Evidence was received in that case which demonstrated that the Seventh Day Adventists constituted a religious denomination with numerous "conferences." Although there were two incorporated "conferences" in Wisconsin holding title to church property, the testator was not a member of either. The court held that it was impossible to determine which group the testator had in mind, and therefore the bequest failed. Similarly, in the instant case, appellant argues that it is impossible to determine which group Jack Bletsch intended to benefit.

The findings of the trial court in the case at bar are different from those in the Tharp Case. Here the trial court found that there was a distinct charitable purpose on the part of the testator and, using the will and the extrinsic evidence adduced, it found that the Shriners' Hospital for Crippled Children was the only one which closely reflected the testator's plan. In our opinion, this finding is not against the great weight or clear preponderance of the evidence.

The trial court applied the cy pres doctrine. That doctrine, as defined in Saletri v. Clark (1961), 13 Wis. (2d) 325, 329, 108 N.W. (2d) 548, is this:

"Very briefly stated, when a charitable purpose cannot be fulfilled according to its terms, equity will attempt to do the next-best similar charitable thing. That is the cy pres doctrine."

The appellant urges that the cy pres doctrine is not applicable in Wisconsin. We recognize that this contention is supported in a number of earlier Wisconsin decisions. For example, in the Tharp Case, Mr. Chief Justice VINJE stated flatly, at page 112: "In our state the doctrine of cy pres does not obtain." One of the cases relied upon in the Tharp Case is Harrington v. Pier (1900), 105 Wis. 485, 82 N.W. 345. The Harrington Case, however, falls considerably short of sustaining the broad, sweeping statement as to cy pres contained in the Tharp Case. In the Harrington Case, the court said, at page 503:

"When it is said that the doctrine of cy pres does not prevail in this state, that does not refer to those liberal rules of judicial construction of charitable trusts, by courts of equity, which prior to the statute of Elizabeth were applied in chancery, and of which such statute is only confirmatory, but to the prerogative power exercisable where such statute prevails. Courts here, as anciently, look with favor upon all donations to charitable uses, and give effect to them where it is possible to do so consistent with rules of law, . . ."

In England, at common law, there were two doctrines of cy pres. One was judicial cy pres; the other was known as prerogative cy pres. Under the latter doctrine, the king, in the exercise of his prerogative power, could, in certain cases, ignore a testator's intention and dispose of a man's property as the king wished. There was no duty on the part of the king (other than moral) to honor the testator's wishes. It is this prerogative doctrine of cy pres which has been disavowed in the United States.

The distinction between prerogative cy pres and judicial cy pres is significant because in the former the purposes to which the king might apply the property could be diametrically contrary to the intentions of the decedent; however, in judicial cy pres the court's principal burden was to effectuate as closely as possible the testator's plan. We doubt that the courts of Wisconsin ever truly intended to disavow judicial cy pres.

That the rejection of the cy pres doctrine was limited to the prerogative type of case is demonstrated by Mr. Chief Justice ROSENBERRY'S observations in First Wisconsin Trust Co. v. Board of Trustees (1937), 225 Wis. 34, 43, 272 N.W. 464:

". . . in some of the earlier cases the cy pres doctrine was repudiated. It is quite clear that what was repudiated was the prerogative power exercised by the chancellor, not as a judge, but as a representative of the Crown."

Although it was not so denominated, judicial cy pres was, in effect, applied by the court in Estate of Briggs (1926), 189 Wis. 524, 208 N.W. 247. There, at page 534, the court wrestled with the Tharp Case and sought to distinguish it. That the cy pres concept was tacitly followed in the Briggs Case is implicit from the following portion, at page 529:

"While it may be conceded that a bequest to a particularly denominated hospital might ordinarily be deemed lapsed where such hospital is in fact non-existent (which would also be true as to a given church or school under the same circumstances), nevertheless, if from all the surrounding facts and circumstances it can reasonably be gathered that the object of the testator was centered not in the aims of one hospital or one church or one school, but upon a general scheme to promote a given cause, then such named hospital, church, or school may be deemed a mere agency for administrative purposes, and if the agency fails, a chancellor will not permit the purpose to fail, but will supply a new agency in the form of a trustee, to carry out the testator's intention."

The hesitation reflected in the Wisconsin decisions to use cy pres openly while at the same time actually applying its doctrine was commented on in a note in 1947

Wisconsin Law Review, 467. In the note, the author, Thomas G. Godfrey, observed, at page 468:

"Although the trial court went to some length in establishing definitely that this was a charitable trust, the Supreme Court focused its attention upon the interpretation of the content and purpose of the trust. In so doing the court again demonstrated that, although it will not recognize or use the cy pres doctrine as it is used by the majority of other jurisdictions in the United States, when it utilizes the doctrine of liberal construction provided by statute, it is using basically the same theory."

The doctrine of cy pres is preserved in the American Law Institute's Restatement of Trusts. Restatement, 2 Trusts, p. 1208, sec. 399. See also 5 Page, Wills (Bowe-Parker rev.), p. 239, sec. 41.33.

While most of the descriptions of cy pres confine its operation to charitable "trusts," there is no sound reason for the requirement that there be a formal trust, as such. In our opinion, it is sufficient if there is a bequest to a charity. In a sense, it can perhaps be said that a charity always receives the gift in trust for its purposes. In Estate of Briggs (1926), 189 Wis. 524, 208 N.W. 247, there was a gift to the "Young Women's Christian Association of Wisconsin." Although no express trust was created, the court treated the matter as a charitable trust. Instead of saying that gifts to charities are necessarily in trust, we deem it better to rule that the doctrine of judicial cy pres is available when there is a gift to a charity -- without requiring that there be a formal trust.

The Wisconsin legislature, in 1933, enacted sec. 231.11 (7) (d), Stats. This subsection reflects a legislative intention both to preserve the cy pres doctrine and also to apply it even though the gift to the charity is not expressly in trust. This subsection provides as follows:

"Where the fulfillment of the special purpose expressed in a trust or other gift for charitable or public purposes is or becomes impracticable, impossible or unlawful, it shall be the duty of the courts by a liberal construction of the trust or gift to ascertain the general purpose of the donor and to carry it into effect in the nearest practicable manner to the expressed special purpose; provided, however, that the right of visitation of a living donor shall not be held to be impaired by anything contained in this subsection."

We do not believe that a bequest to a charity must fail when those purposes are clearly evidenced and there is in existence an identifiable beneficiary whose charitable or public program and goals are reasonably close to those expressed by or attributable to the testator. Cy pres remains a sound and useful doctrine.

We expressly withdraw the statement quoted above from the Tharp Case; we also consider as no longer controlling those cases which reject judicial cy pres as applied to charitable bequests. Judgment affirmed.

In re Oshkosh Foundation

Supreme Court of Wisconsin
61 Wis. 2d 432, 213 N.W.2d 54 (1973)

Hansen, J. The trustee puts three arrows to its bow in seeking to enlarge the geographical limits of the trust agreement from the city limits to the school district limits. Two arrows fall short of the target, and the third cannot be fitted to this bow.

I. Cy pres doctrine.

At the hearing, the trustee contended that the cy pres doctrine warranted the amendment of the trust agreement to include inhabitants and residents of the school district living outside the city limits. The trial court agreed. Cy pres is the common-law doctrine, codified by statute in this state, that provides "'. . . when a charitable purpose cannot be fulfilled according to its terms, equity will attempt to do the next-best similar charitable thing.'" At common law and under the statute, a finding is required that complying with the trust's stated purpose has become impossible, unlawful or impracticable. No argument is here made that the purpose of the trust has become either impossible or illegal. Rather it is claimed that compliance with the trust has become "impracticable" because it has become "unfair." The italicized words are not synonyms. The trustee, in substance, claims only that the use of school district limits would be more useful and desirable than the use of city limits as prescribed in the trust. But cy pres does not warrant a court substituting a different plan for that set forth in the trust solely because trustee or court, or both, believe the substituted plan to be a better plan. Where it was neither claimed nor established that there was a lack of qualified scholarship recipients or charitable requests within the limits set by the trust, there is no basis for holding that it has become, in the words of the statute, "impracticable, impossible or unlawful" to comply with the express terms and limits of the trust.

II. Equitable approximation.

On appeal, the trustee suggests that, while the trial court used the cy pres doctrine, its permitting amendment of the trust rests rather on the applicability of the doctrine of approximation or equitable deviation. Both a new statute, and one in effect at the time of this petition, embody the common-law concept. This corollary to cy pres derives from the two-part character of a trust agreement, and refers to conflicts developing between the two, with courts, at common law or by statute in this state, to give preference to dispositive provisions over administrative directives. However, this doctrine, it follows, is used or usable only to give preference to dispositive over administrative provisions. It permits only the amending of administrative terms in a trust. In the case before us, the class of beneficiary limitation is not such an administrative provision. The provision requiring members of the foundation committee to be residents of the city of Oshkosh would be such an administrative provision. But, for equitable approximation or deviation to become applicable, some conflict between the committee residency requirement and the purposes of the trust would have to be located. We find no such conflict. No evidence was introduced that the committee would be unable to serve its purpose or fulfill its function without nonresident committee members. Equitable approximation or deviation means only that, where there is a conflict between a dispositive provision and an administrative direction, the latter is to give way. Where there is no conflict, the equitable approximation or deviation doctrine is not available to vary the details of administration which the trust prescribes.

III. Reasonable interpretation.

On appeal, during oral argument, the trustee-respondent argued that it was an entirely reasonable interpretation of the provisions of the trust for the trustee to aid charitable agencies serving both residents and inhabitants of the city of Oshkosh and persons residing outside the city limits. The reference was to acknowledged contributions from the foundation to United Fund agencies, the Winnebago County Association for Retarded Children, Big Brothers of Winnebago County and Mercy Hospital, all of which serve nonresidents as well as residents of the city of Oshkosh. Arguably, the same issue of inclusion under a reasonable interpretation of the trust provisions, left unchanged, might be raised as to nonresident students attending schools within the city. However, this is the arrow that cannot be fitted to this bow. Even if the issue of reasonable interpretation of trust provisions had been raised at the hearing, the trial court would have been required, as is this court, to hold that the interpretation of the provisions of a charitable trust is not before the court in an action to change or alter the trust. This is not a petition for construction of the terms of a trust. It is a petition to change the class of beneficiaries served by the trust and the composition of the foundation committee. While not an action to break the trust, it is an action to amend and alter the trust by enlarging its provisions. In an action for change, there is neither invitation nor reason to consider what is a reasonable interpretation of the terms of the trust, left unchanged.

As one court has put it, the clearly expressed intention of the maker of the trust ". . . should be zealously guarded by the courts, particularly when the trust instrument reveals a careful and painstaking expression of the use and purposes to which the settlor's financial accumulations shall be devoted. . . ." We hold that neither the doctrines of cy pres nor equitable approximation apply to the petition before us. As to the matter of reasonable interpretation, we hold that construction of the terms of the trust is not before us in an action for amending the trust. So holding, reversal is required, with directions to the trial court to dismiss the petition of the trustee. Order reversed, and cause remanded with directions to dismiss the petition of the trustee for the Oshkosh Foundation.

C. ENFORCEMENT OF CHARITABLE TRUSTS

Traditionally, the enforcement of charitable trusts was the exclusive province of the state attorney general, which meant that the settlor of an inter vivos charitable trust retained no authority to enforce the terms of the trust. However, under Wis. Stat. §701.10, the settlor, or a group of co-settlors, have the authority to enforce the trust, so long as they contributed 50% or more of the trust res.

Wis. Stat. 701.10. Charitable trusts. (Enforcement provisions)

(3) ENFORCEMENT; NOTICE TO ATTORNEY GENERAL.

(a) A proceeding to enforce a charitable trust may be brought by:

1. An established charitable entity named in the governing instrument to which income or principal must or may be paid under the terms of the trust;

2. The attorney general in the name of the state upon the attorney generals own information or, in the attorney generals discretion, upon complaint of any person;

3. Any settlor or group of settlors who contributed half or more of the principal; or

4. A cotrustee.

(b) In a proceeding affecting a charitable trust, notice must be given to the attorney general, but, except as provided in sub. (2), notice need not be given where the income or principal must be paid exclusively to one or more established charitable entities named in the governing instrument.

(4) ESTABLISHED CHARITABLE ENTITY. As used in this section, "established charitable entity" means a corporation, unincorporated association or trust operated exclusively for a charitable purpose defined in sub. (1)

Estate of Sharp

Supreme Court of Wisconsin

63 Wis. 2d 254, 217 N.W.2d 258, (1974)

Hanley, J. The briefs of the parties raised numerous issues on appeal. The court, however, will confine ourselves to the following which we deem controlling:

1. Whether the attorney general had the right to intervene in this estate proceeding.

2. Whether the judgment of the court vacating its orders entered on September 8, 1967, and December 28, 1967, approving the accounts of the trustees for the years ending August 31, 1964, August 31, 1965, August 31, 1966, and August 31, 1967, and removing the appellant as trustee thereof are void for want of subject matter jurisdiction.

Right of the attorney general to notice of and intervention in estate proceeding.

Wisconsin, unlike numerous states, has specifically circumscribed the powers and duties of the office of the attorney general. Art. VI, sec. 3 of the Wisconsin Constitution limits those powers and duties to those "prescribed by law." This constitutional principle has been interpreted by the courts in numerous decisions as removing from the office of the attorney general any powers and duties which were found in that office under common law. State ex rel. Beck v. Duffy (1968), 38 Wis. 2d 159, 163, 156 N. W. 2d 368; State ex rel. Jackson v. Coffey (1963), 18 Wis. 2d 529, 118 N. W. 2d 939; State v. Snyder (1920), 172 Wis. 415, 179 N. W. 579. The attorney general is devoid of the inherent power to initiate and prosecute litigation intended to protect or promote the interests of the state or its citizens and cannot act for the state as parens patriae. See generally: Christenson, The State Attorney General, 1970 Wis. L. Rev. 298. Such power must be specifically granted by the legislature. Unless the power to prosecute a specific action is granted by law, the office of the attorney general is powerless to act.

The attorney general contends that the right to notice of and intervention in estate proceedings involving a public charitable trust finds its basis in the statutes, namely secs. 231.34, 317.06 and 324.18 (1) (b), Stats. 1967. Such, however, is not the case.

Initially, the attorney general's reliance on sec. 231.34, Stats. 1967, is unavailing. Sec. 231.34, Stats. 1967, merely imbues the office of the attorney general to enforce public charitable trusts.

"231.34 Enforcement of public trust. (1) An action may be brought by the attorney-general in the name of the state, upon his own information or upon the complaint of any interested party for the enforcement of a public charitable trust.

"(2) Such action may be brought in the name of the state by any 10 or more interested parties on their own complaint, when the attorney-general refuses to act.

"(3) The term 'interested party' herein shall comprise a donor to the trust or a member or prospective member of the class for the benefit of which the trust was established."

See generally: Bogert, Trusts and Trustees (2d ed.), p. 323, sec. 411. The power to enforce a public trust is not, however, so broad as to permit the attorney general to intervene in estate proceedings. While the powers of the attorney general under sec. 231.34, Stats. 1967, are broad enough to include actions or proceedings involving the invalidation, termination, administration or enforcement of the terms of a public charitable trust after its creation, said actions or proceedings do not involve intervention in the estate proceedings of the settlor of said public charitable trust.

Similarly, sec. 317.06 (4), Stats. 1967, fails to imbue the attorney general with the power to intervene in or have notice of estate proceedings in which a public charitable trust is involved. Sec. 317.06 (1), Stats. 1967, required that every trustee of a charitable trust account yearly to the court having jurisdiction thereof. Sec. 317.06 (4), Stats. 1967, merely required that such an accounting would not be final except upon notice to the attorney general.

"(4) No action of the court upon such account shall be final except it be upon notice mailed to the attorney general and published under s. 324.20."

This subsection was created under this court's rule-making power, Supreme Court Order, 271 Wis. xi and is inapplicable to estate proceedings.

Finally, sec. 324.18 (1) (b), Stats. 1967, which provides for notice to the attorney general in all hearings or proceedings in which a public charitable trust is involved:

"(b) Notice of all hearings or proceedings where a public charitable trust is involved shall be mailed to the attorney general at least 20 days before the hearing or proceeding."

fails to create a power or duty in the office of the attorney general to intervene in or right to notice of estate proceedings in which a public charitable trust is involved. Sec. 324.18 (1) (b), Stats. 1967, was promulgated pursuant to the supreme court's rule-making power, sec. 251.18, Stats., in 1956, Supreme Court Order, 271 Wis. xi, in order to simplify the procedure and promote the speedy determination of litigation in the courts of Wisconsin. The purpose of said supreme court order was not to create a right or power in the office of the attorney general to intervene in or notice to all hearings or proceedings where a public charitable trust is involved. Such an action is without the power of the supreme court, sec. 251.18. Only the legislature may create or limit the non-constitutionally created powers and duties of the attorney general.

It is clear then that the Wisconsin legislature has not granted to the attorney general the power to intervene in estate proceedings, there being no statutory enactment to that effect. Similarly it is clear that the attorney general is not, as it contends, an interested party who, in absence of statutory notice, is not bound by the judgment of the probate court.

"The main objective of probate proceeding is the orderly distribution of the property of deceased persons. The court of the domicile of the deceased has jurisdiction over the property within its territorial jurisdiction. The jurisdiction of the court in probate is in rem. As such, the judgment binds all persons having a property interest when statutory notice requirements have been complied with." Estate of Hatzl (1964), 24 Wis. 2d 64, 67, 68, 127 N. W. 2d 782, 129 N. W. 2d 249. See also: Estate of Evans (1957), 274 Wis. 459, 471a, 80 N. W. 2d 408, 81 N. W. 2d 489.

Since the attorney general, as the representative of the state, is not party interested in the estate proceedings, then notice to him was not necessary and the proceedings are res adjudicata as to him. Estate of Hatzl, supra; Estate of Evans, supra; Estate of Steuber (1955), 270 Wis. 426, 71 N. W. 2d 272; sec. 324.18, Stats. 1967.

Since in the opinion of the court, the attorney general is not a person interested in the estate proceeding, and since there being no averments of fraud, nor a motion under sec. 269.46, Stats., by a party interested in the estate, the judgment of the court entered on February 27, 1967, approving the coexecutors' accounts, distributing the property of the estate to Robert C. Smith and Robert H. Flatley as coexecutors must be affirmed. The judgment of the trial court entered on December 11, 1970, modifying the judgment of the court entered on February 27, 1967, is void for want of jurisdiction.

Accounting.

On September 30, 1970, Judge McHenry likewise modified the orders of the court which had been entered on September 8, 1967, and December 28, 1967, approving the trustees' final accounts for the years 1964-1966 and 1967 respectively. Such action by the court was likewise in error and must be reversed.

The trustees herein complied with sec. 317.06, Stats. 1967, which required them to account to the court having jurisdiction thereof. The yearly trustees' accounts were filed with the court and, after notice to the attorney general, a hearing was held. At said hearings the trustees appeared personally and the attorney general appeared for the state. The attorney general objected to said trustees' accounts -- especially to the trustees' fees charged -- and the objections were overruled by the court. Final orders were then entered approving the trustees' accounts for the periods therein included.

After the final orders overruling their objections and approving the trustees' accounts for the years 1964-1966 and 1967 respectively, the attorney general failed to prosecute an appeal pursuant to sec. 274.09, Stats. Rather the attorney general, knowing of the imminent retirement of Judge Kehoe, did nothing until after said retirement. The attorney general then applied to the court pursuant to sec. 269.46 to be relieved of said orders previously obtained against him. Absent however from said affidavit and motion were any allegations of mistake, inadvertence, surprise or excusable neglect.

On February 21, 1968, Judge Nier ordered the cotrustees to show cause why the orders of the court entered on September 8, 1967, and December 28, 1967, should not be vacated. Judge Nier additionally ordered:

"That the final judgment and orders referred to above in numbered paragraphs 1, 2 and 3 be and hereby are vacated pending further order of this court and hearing on this order."

The trial court took no further action until September 30, 1970 -- more than thirty-four months after the original order -- when Judge McHenry modified the previous orders of that court.

Initially, it is obvious that the trial court erred in relieving the attorney general from an order in absence of an affidavit and motion alleging mistake, inadvertence, surprise or excusable neglect. The power to grant relief from such a final order more than sixty days after the end of the term of the court at which it was rendered is limited solely to cases of mistake, inadvertence, surprise or excusable neglect. Loomis v. Rice (1875), 37 Wis. 262; Estate of Callahan (1947), 251 Wis. 247, 257, 29 N. W. 2d 352; Glassner v. Medical Realty, Inc. (1964), 22 Wis. 2d 344, 351, 126 N. W. 2d 68; Tuszkiewicz v. Lepins (1968), 41 Wis. 2d 102, 105, 163 N. W. 2d 188. Since no such allegations were made, it was error to grant relief.

Similarly, any action by the trial court under sec. 269.46 (1), Stats., is limited to a period of one year after notice of the judgment or order. Tuszkiewicz v. Lepins, supra. After the passage of that period of time, the trial court is without subject matter jurisdiction to take any further action. Harris v. Golliner (1940), 235 Wis. 572, 294 N. W. 9; Vande Voort v. Stern, supra; State Central Credit Union v. Bayley, supra. Since it is conceded that the September 30, 1970, actions of the trial court were without the one year period under sec. 269.46 (1), and since there are no allegations of fraud, said actions modifying said judgment are void for want of subject matter jurisdiction.

The attorney general contends that the trial court suspended the orders of the court entered on September 8, 1967, and December 28, 1967, on February 21, 1968, and that, pursuant to sec. 269.28:

". . . the presiding judge may suspend the order, in whole or in part, during the pendency of a motion to the court to modify or vacate the order."

and thus extended that period of time in which the motion must be decided. Such contention is without merit for while the court may suspend the effect of its orders, it may not extend that period of time during which it has jurisdiction to release a party from such a final order.

This court has previously held that it is without jurisdiction to vacate a judgment or order on statutory grounds more than a year after notice of entry of judgment. Similar to sec. 270.49, Stats., the motion must be made and decided within a specific period of time (herein one year). Harris v. Golliner, supra. However unlike sec. 270.49, the court may not extend the period of time in which such action may be taken under sec. 269.46 (1). Boyle v. Larzelere (1944), 245 Wis. 152, 159, 13 N. W. 2d 528. The court's jurisdiction to so act is limited to a period of one year after notice of the judgment or order and may not be extended either by virtue of sec. 269.45 or sec. 269.28.

Thus, since the actions of the trial court on September 30, 1970, were without the jurisdiction of the court, said actions must be vacated and the case remanded with directions to reinstate the orders of the trial court entered on September 8, 1967, and December 28, 1967, approving the trustees' final accounts for the years 1964-1966 and 1967 respectively. Judgment reversed and cause remanded with directions.

D. HONORARY TRUSTS

Honorary trusts are trusts that are not charitable, but at the same time cannot be enforced as private trusts because there is no identifiable living human beneficiary. However, the trusts are considered generally beneficial, and thus are allowed to operate under certain conditions. The range of honorary trusts is quite narrow and have been traditionally limited to trusts for the maintenance of graves, trusts for sponsoring religious masses for the dead, and trusts for the care of particular animals (as opposed to trusts for the humane treatment of animals generally, which are recognized as a form of charitable trust. *Dane Cty. Humane Socy. v. Union Trust Co.*, 271 Wis. 59, 72 N.W. 2d 698 (1955)). In each of these situations, the beneficiary is not legally capable of enforcing the terms of the trust. Nevertheless, such trusts were traditionally permitted, subject to the restrictions contained in Wis. Stat. §701.11. Moreover, the Wisconsin Supreme Court has held that trusts for the saying of masses are charitable trusts if the religious services are open to the general membership of the sponsoring denomination. *Kavanaugh v. Watt*, 143 Wis. 90, 126 N.W.2d 692 (1910).

Wis. Stat. 701.11. Honorary trusts; cemetery trusts.

(1) Except under sub. (2), where the owner of property makes a testamentary transfer in trust for a specific noncharitable purpose, and there is no definite or definitely ascertainable human beneficiary designated, no enforceable trust is created; but the transferee has power to apply the property to the designated purpose, unless the purpose is capricious. If the transferee refuses or neglects to apply the property to the designated purpose within a reasonable time and the transferor has not manifested an intention to make a beneficial gift to the transferee, a resulting trust arises in favor of the transferors estate and the court is authorized to order the transferee to retransfer the property.

(2) A trust may be created for maintaining, keeping in repair and preserving any grave, tomb, monument, gravestone or any cemetery. Any cemetery company, association or corporation may receive property in trust for any of those purposes and apply the income from the trust to the purpose stated in the creating instrument.

(3)

(a) A trust described in sub. (2) is invalid to the extent it was created for a capricious purpose or the purpose becomes capricious.

(b) If the assets of any trust described in sub. (2) are valued at less than 5,000 and the court finds that the cost of operating the trust will probably defeat the intent of the settlor or if the trustee, including a cemetery company, association or corporation, named in the creating instrument is improperly described, the court may order distribution of the assets on terms which will as nearly as possible carry out the settlors intention.

Krawcyzk v. Bank of Sun Prairie

Court of Appeals of Wisconsin

161 Wis. 2d 792, 468 N.W.2d 773 (1991)

Eich, C. J. Edmund Krawcyzk, a special trustee appointed to recover funds misappropriated from a cemetery perpetual care trust fund, appeals from a summary judgment dismissing his action against the Bank of Sun Prairie, William Livingston, the bank's trust officer, and Virginia Surety Co., Livingston's insurer. For ease of exposition, we will refer to the defendants collectively as "the bank."

Krawcyzk had sued the bank, the fund's former trustee, claiming that it had improperly transferred the trust's assets to the corporate owner of the cemetery. The bank defended on grounds that it was required to pay over the funds by sec. 157.11(9)(e), Stats., which provides that anyone having control of cemetery trust funds "shall upon demand deliver [them] to the cemetery corporation," and the trial court found in the bank's favor.

The issue is whether the transferee corporation, Wanderer's Rest, Inc., is a "cemetery corporation" within the meaning of the statute. We hold that it is not and we therefore reverse the judgment and order.

The facts are not in dispute. The Milwaukee County probate court established a trust fund for the perpetual care and maintenance of Wanderer's Rest Cemetery, using a bequest of approximately $331,000 earmarked for that purpose. Several years later, the court amended the trust to provide that only Wisconsin banks would be eligible to serve as trustees of the fund. The Bank of Sun Prairie eventually succeeded to that position. Wanderer's Rest Cemetery is owned by Wanderer's Rest, Inc., a for-profit, Wisconsin business corporation organized under ch. 180, Stats. Raymond Turner is the owner and sole shareholder of the corporation. In 1986, the bank was informed by

Turner's and the corporation's attorney that it was being discharged as trustee and that the trust funds were to be transferred to Thompson & McKinnon, a New York brokerage firm. This was done, and Turner eventually dissipated the funds.

Krawcyzk was appointed special trustee to recover the misappropriated money. He sued the bank, claiming that it was negligent and breached its fiduciary duty to the trust when it transferred the funds to "unauthorized persons and entities" in violation of the probate court order that required that the trust funds be held only by "a bank or trust company having its principal place of business in Wisconsin." The bank moved for summary judgment, claiming that it was absolved from any liability because, once the demand was made, it was required by sec. 157.11(9)(e), Stats., to deliver the trust fund to Wanderer's Rest, Inc. As indicated, the motion was granted.

In summary judgment cases, we employ the same analysis as the trial court. In re Cherokee Park Plat, 113 Wis. 2d 112, 115-16, 334 N.W.2d 580, 582 (Ct. App. 1983). Where there are no issues of material fact, as is the case here, summary judgment is an appropriate means of raising and deciding the legal issues in the case. Smith v. State Farm Fire and Cas. Co, 127 Wis. 2d 298, 300, 380 N.W.2d 372, 373 (Ct. App. 1985). We decide these issues de novo. Green Spring Farms v. Kersten, 136 Wis. 2d 304, 315-17, 401 N.W.2d 816, 820-21 (1987).

Chapter 157, Stats., regulates the funding, operation, maintenance and management of cemeteries. The regulations are designed "to promote and foster perpetual care of cemetery lots and graves, by permitting cemetery associations to receive moneys in trust for that purpose, and to safeguard and protect such funds thereafter." Wauwatosa Cemetery Ass'n v. City of Wauwatosa, 224 Wis. 34, 36-37, 271 N.W. 402, 403 (1937). "Cemetery associations" are special entities created by statute to operate and manage cemeteries. See, generally, secs. 157.061-157.11.

Section 157.11(9)(e), Stats., deals with funds received by cemeteries -- by "the trustees of [cemetery] association[s]" -- for perpetual care. It provides, among other things, that anyone having custody of "any cemetery care trust fund . . . shall upon demand deliver it to the cemetery corporation to be handled as provided in this section." Sec. 157.11(9)(e). Krawcyzk argues that the bank and the trial court were wrong to rely on the statute as a defense to his action because Wanderer's Rest, Inc., is not a cemetery corporation within the meaning of its terms. We agree. The phrase "cemetery corporation" must be read in light of the remainder of the chapter. State ex rel Wis. State Journal v. Circuit Court for Dane County, 131 Wis. 2d 515, 519-20, 389 N.W.2d 73, 75 (Ct. App. 1986). While "cemetery corporation" is not defined in ch.

157, Stats., the word "corporation" is. It means "the cemetery association having charge of a cemetery." Sec. 157.061(2).

As we have noted, cemetery associations are special entities created under ch. 157, Stats., to operate and care for cemeteries, and they may exist independently of the cemetery's ownership. Wanderer's Rest, Inc., is not such an entity. It is a ch. 180, Stats., for-profit business corporation which owns the real property on which Wanderer's Rest Cemetery is located. The bank contends that by applying the statutory definition of "corporation" in sec. 157.061(2), Stats., to the two-word phrase "cemetery corporation" in sec. 157.11(9)(e), we are reading the word "cemetery" out of the latter statute. They argue that the legislature's use of the additional modifying word "cemetery" must indicate that it intended the statute to apply to "any corporate body operating a cemetery, whether organized under ch. 157 [or] 180."

Our primary objective in interpreting a statute is to achieve a reasonable construction that will effectuate the statutory purpose. Barnett v. LIRC, 131 Wis. 2d 416, 420, 388 N.W.2d 652, 654 (Ct. App. 1986). As we have noted, the purpose of the regulatory scheme embodied in ch. 157, Stats., is to ensure perpetual care of cemeteries. And the bank's interpretation -- that the legislature intended to allow any corporation, whether for-profit or not-for-profit, and whether or not it is bound by the regulations and safeguards of ch. 157, to demand and receive a payout of the perpetual care trust funds -- is contrary to that purpose.

The payment-on-demand provisions of sec. 157.11(9)(e), Stats., neither require nor authorize payment to entities other than ch. 157 cemetery associations -- bodies charged and regulated by law to operate and care for cemeteries and the funds acquired by them, in trust and otherwise, to aid in the discharge of those duties. Since Wanderer's Rest, Inc., is not such an association, it follows that Krawcyzk's action is not subject to dismissal under the statute and that summary judgment was improperly granted. Judgment and order reversed and cause remanded for further proceedings.

E. CHARITABLE FOUNDATIONS

The management of charitable trusts and similar legal entities can create special challenges for trustees. Wis. Stat. §701.105 addresses many of those issues, especially those that are tax-related.

Wis. Stat. 701.105. Private foundations.

(1)

(a) In the administration of any trust which is a private foundation, as defined in section 509 of the internal revenue code, a charitable trust, as defined in section 4947 (a) (1) of the internal revenue code, or a split-interest trust as defined in section 4947 (a) (2) of the internal revenue code, all of the following acts shall be prohibited:

1. Engaging in any act of self-dealing as defined in section 4941 (d) of the internal revenue code, which would give rise to any liability for the tax imposed by section 4941 (a) of the internal revenue code.

2. Retaining any excess business holdings as defined in section 4943 (c) of the internal revenue code, which would give rise to any liability for the tax imposed by section 4943 (a) of the internal revenue code.

3. Making any investments which would jeopardize the carrying out of any of the exempt purposes of the trust, within the meaning of section 4944 of the internal revenue code, so as to give rise to any liability for the tax imposed by section 4944 (a) of the internal revenue code.

4. Making any taxable expenditures as defined in section 4945 (d) of the internal revenue code, which would give rise to any liability for the tax imposed by section 4945 (a) of the internal revenue code.

(b) This subsection shall not apply either to those split-interest trusts or to amounts thereof which are not subject to the prohibitions applicable to private foundations by reason of the provisions of section 4947 of the internal revenue code.

(2) In the administration of any trust which is a private foundation as defined in section 509 of the internal revenue code, or which is a charitable trust as defined in section 4947 (a) (1) of the internal revenue code, there shall be distributed, for the purposes specified in the trust instrument, for each taxable year, amounts at least sufficient to avoid liability for the tax imposed by section 4942 (a) of the internal revenue code.

(3) Subsections (1) and (2) shall not apply to any trust to the extent that a court of competent jurisdiction shall determine that such application would be contrary to the terms of the instrument governing such trust and that the same may not properly be changed to conform to such subsections.

(4) Nothing in this section shall impair the rights and powers of the courts or the attorney general of this state with respect to any trust.

CHAPTER 10.
POWERS OF APPOINTMENT

A power of appointment permits the owner of property to delay or postpone the decision regarding the identity of the item's next owner. The creator of the power, the *donor*, transfers the power to the *donee* who now holds the right to pick the next owner according to criteria established by the donor at the time of the transfer. The pool of people to whom the property can be appointed is known as the *objects* of the appointment. If the donee is permitted to select himself or herself or his or her creditors, then the power is said to be *general*; if the donee is required to appoint someone else, from a pool as broad or narrow as the donor chooses, the power is *special.* (In older terminology, *special* powers were also said to be *powers in trust.)* There is also a third category of powers, known as *unclassified* powers, which includes powers that are neither *special* or *general*. Ordinarily, *unclassified powers* are powers for which the pool of *objects* is not clearly specified in the instrument creating the power.

If the donee fails to make an appointment, the property passes to the *taker in default,* if one is named in the instrument creating the power. Otherwise, in Wisconsin, the property passes in equal shares to the designated objects of the power, if they constitute a distinct class (like "children" or "nephews and nieces"). If there is no such class, the property reverts back to the donor. Futhermore, if the donor choses, the power can stipulate that the property reverts back to the donor if the donee fails to appoint a designate object.

I. OPERATION OF POWERS OF APPOINTMENT

A. DEFINITION

Wis. Stat. 702.01. Definitions.

As used in this chapter, unless the context indicates otherwise:

(1) "Creating instrument" means the will, trust agreement or other document which creates or reserves the power.

(2) "Donor" means the person who creates or reserves the power; "donee" means the person in whom the power is created or reserved; and "appointee" means the person to whom an interest is appointed.

(3) "General power" means a power exercisable in favor of the donee, the donee's estate, the donee's creditors or the creditors of the donee's estate, whether or not it is exercisable in favor of others. A power to appoint to any person or a power which is not expressly restricted as to appointees may be exercised in favor of the donee or the donees creditors if exercisable during lifetime, and in favor of the donees estate or the creditors of the donees estate if exercisable by will.

(4) "Power" means a power of appointment over legal or equitable interests in real or personal property. A power of appointment is a power created or reserved by a person having property subject to his or her disposition which enables the donee of the power to designate, within such limits as may be prescribed, the transferees of the property or the shares or the interests in which it shall be received; it does not include a power of sale, a power of attorney, a power of revocation or a power exercisable by a trustee or other fiduciary in his or her fiduciary capacity.

(5) "Special power" means a power exercisable only in favor of one or more persons not including the donee, the donees estate, the donees creditors or the creditors of the donees estate and, when exercisable in favor of a class, so limited in size by description of the class that in the event of nonexercise of the power a court can make distribution to persons within the class if the donor has failed to provide for this contingency.

(6) "Unclassified power" means a power which is neither a general power nor a special power as defined in this section.

Wis. Stat. 702.11. Irrevocability of creation, exercise and release of powers.

The creation, exercise or release of a power is irrevocable unless the power to revoke is reserved in the creation, exercise or release of the power.

Wis. Stat. 702.13. Recording instruments relating to powers.

(1) Any of the following instruments relating to powers is entitled to be recorded as a conveyance upon compliance with s. 706.05 (1):

(a) An instrument, other than a will, exercising a power;

(b) An instrument expressing consent to exercise;

(c) A disclaimer;

(d) A release.

(2) If a power is exercised by a will, a certified copy of the will and of the certificate of probate thereof may be recorded.

Wis. Stat. 702.19. Matters governed by common law.

As to all matters within the scope of those sections of ch. 232, 1963 stats., which have been repealed, and not within this chapter or any other applicable statute, the common law is to govern. This section is not intended to restrict in any manner the meaning of any provision of this chapter or any other applicable statute.

Wis. Stat. 702.21. Applicability of chapter.

The provisions of this chapter are applicable to any power existing on May 16, 1965, as well as a power created after such date.

Wis. Stat 702.22. Applicability of general transfers at death provisions.

Chapter 854 applies to transfers at death under an instrument that creates or exercises a power of appointment.

B. SPECIFIC VERSUS GENERAL POWERS OF APPOINTMENT

Note that the case below involves the Uihlein family and the use of powers of appointment. The same was true for the case of *Uihlein v. Uihlein, supra,* Chapter 5.

In re Estate of Trainer

Court of Appeals of Wisconsin

123 Wis. 2d 102, 365 N.W.2d 893 (1985)

Wedemeyer, P.J. The Wisconsin Department of Revenue (state) appeals from a judgment holding that a portion of sec. 72.01(5), Stats. (1969), was unconstitutional and that a power of appointment possessed by Mary Uihlein Trainer therefore was not includable in her taxable estate. Because the application of the statute to the facts presented would violate the estate's right to equal protection under the law, we affirm.

The facts are not in dispute. Robert A. Uihlein executed a trust agreement on December 31, 1943, wherein he granted to Trainer, his daughter, a power of appointment over certain trust assets. The provisions of the trust agreement pertinent to the resolution of this appeal read:

(b)(1) All, or any part less than all, of that portion of the trust fund contributed to the trustees by Robert A. Uihlein, donor, or allocable to contributions to the trustees by Robert A. Uihlein, donor, shall be distributed and paid to such person or persons who are included within a class which does not include any others than:

a. The spouse of Robert A. Uihlein, donor;

b. The spouse of Mary Uihlein Trainer;

c. The spouse of Robert A. Uihlein, Jr.;

d. Descendants of Mary Uihlein Trainer or her spouse;

e. The descendants (other than Mary Uihlein Trainer) or Robert A. Uihlein, donor, and the spouses of such descendants;

as Mary Uihlein Trainer shall appoint to receive the same by her last will and testament, or by an instrument in writing executed by her during her lifetime before two witnesses and acknowledged before a notary public. In exercising such power of appointment, Mary Uihlein Trainer shall specify the part of such portion of the trust fund to be distributed and paid to such person or to each of such persons. As used herein, the term "descendants" includes adopted children.

(2) Such part of the portion of the trust fund contributed to the trustees by Robert A. Uihlein, donor, or allocable to contributions to the trustees by Robert A. Uihlein, donor, which shall not be paid and distributed to any such person or persons within

such class pursuant to the exercise of the power of appointment herein granted to Mary Uihlein Trainer shall be added to and form a part of the balance of the trust fund to be divided and allocated as provided in Paragraph (c) of this Article II.

Trainer did not exercise this power of appointment either by will or by any other written instrument executed during her lifetime. Nor did she ever release or modify the power. Trainer died July 21, 1971.

The state seeks to apply sec. 72.01(5), Stats. (1969), to the power of appointment which Trainer held at the time of her death. The particular portion of the statute that is central to this appeal was added to sec. 72.01(5) by ch. 510, Laws of 1951, effective July 22, 1951. It defines the powers of appointment that will be tax exempt and specifies that if a power of appointment was created before October 21, 1942 which did not fall within the definition of the tax exempt class, the power could be tailored by modification or release to qualify as tax exempt. No provision, however, was made for modification of any powers created on or after October 21, 1942 and before July 22, 1951. The power of appointment with which we are concerned was created by Robert A. Uihlein in the December 31, 1943 trust agreement.

The trial court concluded that Trainer's power of appointment was not subject to inheritance tax for two reasons: (1) Section 72.01(5), Stats. (1969), as applied to Trainer's estate, would deny the estate equal protection of the law; and (2) at the time of her death, Trainer could not exercise the power of appointment in favor of any person outside of the exempt class defined in sec. 72.01(5). We rely on the trial court's first reason as the basis for this affirmance.

The state contends that there is no constitutional infirmity in the statutory classification created by ch. 510, Laws of 1951, i.e., the distinction drawn between powers of appointment created before and after 1942. It argues that the legislature was attempting to make Wisconsin's taxation of powers of appointment mirror the federal scheme and that the classes established have a fair and substantial relationship to the object of the legislation. The October 21, 1942 cutoff date in ch. 510 and the ability to release or modify powers of appointment, which is limited in ch. 510 to powers created before October 21, 1942, both tie in directly with the federal law. The state argues that the classifications of ch. 510 therefore are not arbitrary. We are not persuaded and conclude that the legislature's effort died aborning.

In general terms, a power of appointment is the authority to designate a beneficial interest in property. Usually, powers of appointment are considered either general or special. Under a general power, the class of permissible donees or appointees is unrestricted; under a special power, a limitation is placed on who may be the object of the appointment. The Revenue Act of 1916, which imposed the first federal estate tax, made no provision for the special treatment of property passing by a power of appointment. See Revenue Act of 1916, Pub. L. No. 271, 39 Stat. 756 (1916). The United States Supreme Court rejected an effort by the Treasury to equate a general power of appointment with a provision dealing with property held by a decedent. United States v. Field, 255 U.S. 257, 264 (1921). As a result, powers of appointment continued to pass free of estate tax under the 1916 Act.

To fill this statutory gap, Congress amended the estate tax law so that a gross estate was defined to include property passing under a general power of appointment exercised by the decedent by will. Revenue Act of 1918, Pub. L. No. 254, 40 Stat. 1057, 1097 (1919). If, however, the holder of the power could not appoint to himself or his creditors, the power was considered to be special and was exempt from estate taxation. In response to a joint congressional report which found this statute inadequate in scope and an attractive device for tax avoidance, Congress enacted sec. 403 of the Revenue Act of 1942, Pub. L. No. 753, 56 Stat. 798, 942 (1942). Under the new provision, the exemption of special powers was reduced in scope and applied only if its exercise was limited to members of a specifically described group. Section 403 of the Act provided that a special power would be tax exempt if the class of possible appointees included only "the spouse of the decedent, spouse of the creator of the power, descendants of the decedent or his spouse, descendants (other than the decedent) of the creator of the power or his spouse, spouses of such descendants" and certain charities. The 1942 amendment applied generally to estates of decedents dying after October 21, 1942, the effective date of the Act. For powers existing prior to October 21, 1942, various transitional rules were provided. For all subsequently created powers, the stricter rules became effective immediately.

No sooner had the 1942 amendment been enacted, than complaints were voiced concerning its rigidity in application and resulting impracticality. See Craven, Powers of Appointment Act of 1951, 65 Harv. L. Rev. 55, 61 (1951-52). After years of analysis and exchange of views by the various interested groups, Congress returned to its pre-1942 position by enacting the Powers of Appointment Act of 1951, Pub. L. No. 58, 65 Stats. 91, effective June 28, 1951. It liberated powers of appointment from the estate tax, except for general powers as defined by I.R.C. sec. 2041(b)(1). As a consequence, the only powers subject to tax were powers exercisable in favor of the decedent, the decedent's estate, the decedent's creditors, or creditors of the decedent's estate. 5 B. Bittker, Federal Taxation of Income, Estates and Gifts sec. 128.1, at 128-7, 128-8 (1984).

Wisconsin's inheritance tax on property subject to a power of appointment has far deeper roots. By sec. 1 (5), ch. 44, Laws of 1903, the legislature adopted verbatim sec. 220(5), ch. 284, of the Laws of New York of 1897. New York courts interpreted this provision to include both general and special powers of appointment; their interpretation was acceded to by Wisconsin courts. The provision taxed all powers of appointment and remained intact until 1951, when ch. 510, Laws of 1951, narrowed its scope of application by creating a tax exemption. See note 1, supra. The federal Revenue Act of 1942, sec. 403, effective October 21, 1942, defined a nontaxable power of appointment as "a power to appoint within a class which does not include any other than the spouse of the decedent, spouse of the creator of the power, descendants of the decedent or his spouse, descendants (other than the decedent) of the creator of the power or his spouse, spouses of descendants" and certain charities. By the Powers of Appointment Act of 1951, effective June 28, 1951, Congress supplanted an elaborately defined class of permissible appointees with a simple definition of a taxable power of appointment.

If Wisconsin, by enacting ch. 510, Laws of 1951, was attempting to federalize its taxation of powers of appointment, as argued by the state, it was chasing a mirage rather than mirroring a federal counterpart. Chapter 510 was not enacted until after Congress drastically changed the image to be copied. Additionally, the definition of a nontaxable power of appointment contained in ch. 510 is considerably narrower than that contained in the 1942 federal act. The possibility therefore remained, even after the enactment of ch. 510, that a power of appointment designed to be nontaxable under the federal law would still be taxable under Wisconsin law. It was not until 1978, when sec. 517e, ch. 418, Laws of 1977, was enacted, that Wisconsin finally adopted the federal definition of a taxable power and thereby achieved the uniformity the state claims it desired.

From an historical perspective, we find little if any basis for the state's contention that the pre-October 21, 1942 versus post-October 21, 1942 classification created by ch. 510 had a substantial relationship to the object of the legislation. It may be true, although it is not established in the record, that the legislature intended to use the effective date of sec. 403 of the Revenue Act of 1942, October 21, 1942, to effectuate a reasonable congruence between state and federal law. Nevertheless, ch. 510 was so tardily enacted and so far removed from the federal legislation in effect when it was passed that uniformity was no longer achievable. Further, while Congress left no transitional gaps ripe for constitutional challenge, the drafters of ch. 510 created a legislative vacuum for powers created between October 20, 1942 and July 22, 1951. Powers created after July 22, 1951, could, of course, be created as nontaxable by being drafted in compliance with the newly-enacted statute. Under ch. 510, powers created before October 21, 1942, that did not comply with the definition for tax exemption could be made nontaxable by being modified or limited to comply with the definition. On the other hand, powers created on or after October 21, 1942, and before July 22, 1951, were given no opportunity to be made nontaxable.

Aside from the state's abortive and belated effort to associate Wisconsin's qualification date to that of the federal act, October 21, 1942, has no relationship whatsoever to prior Wisconsin law. We perceive no reason why October 21, 1942, was picked as the date at which the opportunity to modify noncomplying powers would be cut off. Because of the statutorily-created hiatus, Trainer was not provided the same protection or opportunity possessed by donees of powers which were created before October 21, 1942. In Will of LeFeber, 223 Wis. 393, 271 N.W. 95 (1937), the supreme court declared an emergency inheritance tax law unconstitutional because certain time periods were omitted from its application. It stated: "'[C]lassification, in order to be legal, must be rational; it must be founded upon real differences of situation or condition, which bear a just and proper relation to the attempted classification, and reasonably justify a difference of rule.'" Id. at 398, 271 N.W. at 97 (quoting Black v. State, 113 Wis. 205, 221, 89 N.W. 522, 528 (1902)). The court further stated: "'[C]lassification "must be reasonable, not arbitrary, and must rest upon some ground of difference having a fair and substantial relation to the object of the legislation, so that all persons similarly circumstanced shall be treated alike."'" Id. at 399, 271 N.W. at 97 (quoting Colgate v. Harvey, 296 U.S. 404, 423 (1935)).

As applied to the inheritance tax, there may be proper classification, and the required uniformity 'means simply taxation which acts alike on all persons similarly situated.'" Estate of Heuel, 4 Wis. 2d 400, 404, 90 N.W.2d 634, 637 (1958) (citation omitted). If the classification does not rest upon a difference between the classes which bears a fair, substantial, natural, reasonable and just relation to the objective of the act, it is a violation of the guaranty set forth in the fourteenth amendment of the United States Constitution that all citizens are entitled to equal protection of the law.

The only support for the classification proposed by the state is identification with the effective date of the federal Revenue Act of 1942, which contained a different definition of tax exempt powers and which, unlike ch. 510, augmented its objective with a continuum of transitional rules. This does not, in our opinion, constitute a sufficient basis for classification. Chapter 510 did not have the same impact on all persons similarly situated and therefore violated Trainer's and her estate's right to equal protection.

The state next argues that if ch. 510 is found to be unconstitutional, the statute it amended, sec. 72.01(5), Stats. (1949), would apply to the power, and the power therefore would be taxable. The state's argument is without merit. The trial court concluded:

Chapter 510, Laws of 1951, is arbitrary and discriminatory, and therefore unconstitutional, insofar as it denied to Mary U. Trainer or her Estate the right to release or modify a power of appointment created after October 21, 1942, and before July 21, 1951, while giving to others the right to release or modify a power of appointment created before October 21, 1942, and that being unconstitutional, it cannot be applied by the Department . . . to tax such power . . . .

The record reveals no attack on the prospective creation of classes of appointees exempt from taxation. It is only the retroactive application of the statute to powers created during the hiatal period that is the point of contention. Section 990.001(11), Stats., provides in part: "If any provision of the statutes . . . is invalid, or if the application . . . to any person or circumstance is invalid, such invalidity shall not affect other provisions or applications which can be given effect without the invalid provision or application." (Emphasis added.)

In State ex rel. Briggs & Stratton Corp. v. Noll, 100 Wis. 2d 650, 659, 302 N.W.2d 487, 492 (1981) (quoting Bence v. City of Milwaukee, 84 Wis. 2d 224, 233-34, 267 N.W.2d 25, 30 (1978)), the supreme court declared:

"There is ample precedent to permit a court to sever from [a] . . . legislative enactment that portion of an act which is unconstitutional and to declare that the remaining portion is valid. . . . [T]he determination of whether an invalid portion so infects the remainder of the legislation as to require the entire law to be invalidated is a question of legislative intent. “The inquiry is whether the "elimination of a void portion leaves a complete law in some reasonable aspect capable of being carried into effect consistent with the intention of the legislature which enacted it in connection with the void part . . . ." Estate of Zeimet, 259 Wis. 619, 623-24, 49 N.W.2d 924, 928 (1951).

By ch. 510, the legislature created some tax exempt classes of appointees. The reason behind the creation of each tax exempt class is not as important as the fact that the legislature did create them. It is obvious that the legislature intended to create them. That intent would be furthered if the prospective features of the statute were left to stand alone. We perceive no good reason to use a broadax when a scalpel is more suitable. Thus we conclude that the inability to utilize the procedural exception for modification to a tax exempt class is all that is invalid. The substantive portion of ch.

510 creating the tax exempt class remains in force as a viable part of sec. 72.01(5). Judgment affirmed.

C. EXERCISING THE POWER OF APPOINTMENT

Powers are never exercised automatically, in that they require an affirmative action on the part of the donee to effect a transfer. However, unless the instrument creating the power specifies a specific way in the which the power is to be exercised, there are an almost infinite variety of ways that exercise could occur. Ultimately, what matters is that the donee had the intent to exercise the power and took some step to do so.

Wis. Stat. 702.03. Manifestation of intent to exercise powers.

(1) Unless the person who executed it had a contrary intention, if a governing instrument, as defined in s. 854.01 (2), or an inter vivos governing instrument, as defined in s. 700.27 (1) (c), creates a power of appointment that expressly requires that the power be exercised by any type of reference to the power or its source, the donors intention in requiring the reference is presumed to be to prevent an inadvertent exercise of the power. Extrinsic evidence, as defined in s. 854.01_(1), may be used to construe the intent.

(2) In the case of other powers, an instrument manifests an intent to exercise the power if the instrument purports to transfer an interest in the appointive property which the donee would have no power to transfer except by virtue of the power, even though the power is not recited or referred to in the instrument, or if the instrument either expressly or by necessary implication from its wording interpreted in light of the circumstances surrounding its drafting and execution manifests an intent to exercise the power. If there is a general power exercisable by will with no gift in default in the creating instrument, a residuary clause or other general language in the donee's will purporting to dispose of all of the donee's estate or property operates to exercise the power in favor of the donee's estate, but in all other cases such a clause or language does not in itself manifest an intent to exercise a power exercisable by will.

Wis. Stat. 702.05. Exercise of powers.

(1) CAPACITY TO EXERCISE POWER. A power can be exercised only by a person who would have the capacity to transfer the property covered by the power.

(2) KIND OF INSTRUMENT AND FORMALITIES OF EXECUTION. A donee can exercise a power only by an instrument which meets the intent of the donor as to kind of instrument and formalities of execution. If the power is exercisable by will, this means a will executed with the formalities necessary for a valid will. A written instrument signed by the donee is sufficient if the donor fails to require any additional formalities or fails to indicate a will, but if the power is to appoint interests in land, it can be exercised only by an instrument executed with sufficient formalities for that purpose.

(3) CONSENT OF 3RD PERSONS. When the consent of the donor or of any other person is required by the donor for the exercise of a power, such consent must be expressed in the instrument exercising the power or in a separate written instrument, signed in either case by the persons whose consent is required. If any person whose consent is required dies or becomes legally incapable of consenting, the power may be exercised by the donee without the consent of that person unless the donor has manifested a contrary intent in the instrument creating the power.

(4) POWER VESTED IN 2 OR MORE DONEES. Unless the donor manifests a contrary intent, when a power is vested in 2 or more persons, all must unite in its exercise, but if one or more of the donees dies, becomes incapable of exercising the power or renounces, releases or disclaims the power, the power may be exercised by the others.

Wis. Stat. 702.07. Powers to be construed as exclusive.

The donee of any power may appoint the whole or any part of the appointive assets to any one or more of the permissible appointees and exclude others, except to the extent that the donor specifies either a minimum share or amount to be appointed to each permissible appointee or to designated appointees, or a maximum share or amount appointable to any one or more appointees.

In re Estate of Shepherd v. Shepherd

Court of Appeals of Wisconsin
344 Wis. 2d 440, 823 N.W.2d 523 (2012)

NEUBAUER, P.J. Ramona Czaplewski appeals from a trial court order admitting the will of her father, Donald Shepherd, to probate. Due to an attorney drafting error, the will did not contain a specific reference to the power of appointment as required under the Marital Property Agreement (MPA) executed by Donald and his predeceased wife,

Lulu Mae Shepherd. Ramona contends that without the reference to the power of appointment, the will is nonbinding and the estate should be distributed according to the MPA. Ramona also contends that the sole witness in the case, the attorney who drafted the will and the MPA, should have been barred from testifying. We reject Ramona's challenges. We conclude that the trial court properly admitted the drafting attorney's testimony as permissible extrinsic evidence of testator intent. We further conclude that the trial court did not err in admitting Donald's 2010 will to probate. We affirm.

BACKGROUND

Overview

Donald and Lulu Mae Shepherd were married on January 7, 1947. They had three children: Daniel, Steven, and Ramona. Ramona subsequently had two daughters, Rebecca Kayser and Kelly Wuttke. In 2002, Donald and Lulu Mae entered into the MPA, one provision of which governed the disposal of their property at death—to be divided equally between their three children. The MPA permitted the revision of the property distribution, provided any subsequent instrument made specific reference to the power of appointment in the MPA.

Lulu Mae died in January 2005. In 2007, Donald properly exercised his powers under the MPA to execute a will (the 2007 Will) altering the property distribution in the MPA by dividing Ramona's one-third of the property equally between Ramona and her two daughters. In March 2010, Donald executed a codicil to the 2007 Will changing the personal representative from his son Daniel to his son Steven. Less than one month later, Donald second-guessed his change in personal representative and executed a new will (the 2010 Will), which reinstated Daniel as his personal representative and also revoked all former wills and codicils. The 2010 Will made no reference to the MPA provision governing power of appointment.

Donald passed away on June 10, 2010. Daniel applied for the informal administration of Donald's 2010 Will on August 16, 2010. Ramona filed a petition for summary confirmation of interest in property under the terms of the MPA. The trial court held an evidentiary hearing on July 22, 2011, and on September 22, 2011, issued a written order admitting Donald's 2010 Will to probate, appointing Daniel as personal representative, and dismissing Ramona's petition for summary confirmation of interest in property.

Relevant Documents and Evidence

The MPA. The 2002 MPA provided that it would be binding and "in effect until final disposition of all property subject to this Agreement upon termination of the parties' marriage by death or dissolution." Pursuant to Article XIII B., all property belonging to the first spouse to die would be distributable to the surviving spouse. As to the disposition of property upon the death of the surviving spouse, the MPA instructs at Article XIII:

> C. Upon either party's death, with the other party having predeceased, all property of the surviving party, which would be subject to probate administration in the absence of this agreement, shall be distributed to those beneficiaries, in trust or otherwise, as shall be appointed in the surviving party's Will or Revocable Trust by specific reference to this power.
>
> D. If the surviving party fails to exercise this power effectively, then all of the property of the surviving party, which would be subject to probate administration in the absence of this agreement shall be distributed without probate by nontestamentary disposition, pursuant to the provisions of [Wis. Stat. §] 766.58(3)(f), ... in equal shares to our children, STEVEN E. SHEPHERD, RAMONA L. CZAPLEWSKI and DANIEL E. SHEPHERD, or to their issue by right of representation.

Thus, the surviving spouse had a general power of appointment to distribute his or her estate as desired. However, in the event of nonexercise, the property distribution would default to Article XIII D.

The 2007 Will. After Lulu Mae's death in 2005, Donald executed a will that changed the disposition of the property. This 2007 Will expressly referenced the MPA, stating: "This instrument is drafted pursuant to the power of appointment in Article XIII, Paragraph C. of a Marital Property Agreement dated April 24, 2002." The 2007 Will gifted one-third of Donald's estate to Daniel, one-third to Steven, and the final one-third was to be divided equally between Ramona and her two daughters, Rebecca and Kelly. Thus, the 2007 Will reduced Ramona's portion of Donald's estate from one-third to one-ninth.

The 2010 Codicil. In March 2010, Donald executed a codicil changing the designated personal representative of his estate from Daniel to Steven.

The 2010 Will. In April 2010, Donald second-guessed his decision to change his designated personal representative. On April 15, Donald executed a will that reinstated Daniel as the personal representative but left the disposition of property unchanged.

The 2010 Will revoked all former wills and codicils. It made no reference to the MPA provision governing power of appointment.

The Drafting Attorney's Testimony. The 2002 MPA, the 2007 Will, the 2010 Codicil, and the 2010 Will were all drafted by Attorney Karl Dovnik, the estate planning attorney who represented Donald and Lulu Mae. Dovnik was the only witness to testify at the evidentiary hearing. When questioned by the trial court about Donald's intent, Dovnik stated that Donald "had a very close relationship with his two granddaughters," and "[Donald specifically said he did not want [Ramona to receive an entire one-third, that he felt that his granddaughters deserved something from that as well because of their relationship with him." Dovnik also testified that Donald's intent in creating the 2010 Will was "to replace Steve as the personal representative now and put Dan back in charge." According to Dovnik, Donald "made it clear that he wanted disposition to be exactly the same as on that [2007] Will ... that he still wanted to share his estate with his granddaughters."

The Trial Court's Ruling

The trial court found an ambiguity as to whether the 2010 Will was intended by Donald to exercise or amend the power of appointment provision found in the 2007 Will. Thus, the trial court considered the circumstances surrounding the execution of the 2010 Will, as well as Dovnik's testimony, the language of the MPA, the 2007 Will, and the 2010 Codicil. The trial court held that Donald intended the distribution of his estate to be governed by the residuary clause in his 2010 Will rather than the 2002 MPA. The trial court ordered that the 2010 Will be admitted to informal probate, that Daniel be appointed personal representative of Donald's estate, and that the estate be distributed as indicated in the 2010 Will, specifically: one-third of the estate to Daniel, one-third to Steven, and the final one-third be divided equally between Ramona and her daughters, Rebecca and Kelly. Ramona appeals.

DISCUSSION

Ramona raises several challenges to the trial court's order. Ramona maintains that Donald and Lulu Mae intended that the distribution of the estate would be governed by the 2002 MPA; that Donald did not intend the 2010 Will to exercise the power of appointment contained in the MPA; that the 2010 Will is unambiguous and, therefore, analysis of extrinsic evidence is improper; and that Dovnik's testimony was inadmissible hearsay and barred by Wis. Stat. § 885.16, the dead man's statute. We are not persuaded. We agree with the trial court's conclusions that the distribution of Donald's estate is governed by the 2010 Will.

I. The MPA Provides Donald with the Unilateral Right to Change the Distribution of Donald's Estate After Lulu Mae's Death.

The parties agree that the MPA enables Donald to unilaterally designate the transferees of his estate pursuant to his will; it provides him with the power of appointment. Article XIII C. of the MPA provides that "all property of the surviving party, which would be subject to probate administration in the absence of this agreement, shall be distributed to those beneficiaries, in trust or otherwise, as shall be appointed in the surviving party's Will or Revocable Trust by specific reference to this power." In the absence of an effective exercise of power of appointment, the property would be distributed in equal shares to Donald's and Lulu Mae's three children. The trial court determined, and we agree, that the language of the MPA is clear and unambiguously provides Donald with the unilateral right to change the distribution of the property after Lulu Mae's death.

II. Applying Wis. Stat. § 702.03(1), Donald's and Lulu Mae's Intent for Creating the MPA's Specific Reference Requirement Was to Prevent an Inadvertent Exercise of the Power of Appointment.

The MPA creates the specific method by which the power of appointment is to be administered. According to the MPA, "Upon either party's death, with the other party having predeceased, all property of the surviving party, which would be subject to probate administration ... shall be distributed ... as shall be appointed in the surviving party's Will or Revocable Trust by specific reference to this power." (Emphasis added.) This provision is governed by Wis. Stat. § 702.03, titled "Manifestation of intent to exercise powers," which provides:

> (1) Unless the person who executed it had a contrary intention, if a governing instrument, as defined in [Wis. Stat. §] 854.01(2), or an inter vivos governing instrument, as defined in [Wis. Stat. §] 700.27(1)(b), creates a power of appointment that expressly requires that the power be exercised by any type of reference to the power or its source, the donor's intention in requiring the reference is presumed to be to prevent an inadvertent exercise of the power. Extrinsic evidence, as defined in [§] 854.01(1), may be used to construe the intent. (Emphasis added.)

In requiring specific reference, the MPA creates a presumption that the donors intended to prevent an inadvertent exercise of the power. Ramona provides no evidence to show a contrary intent, i.e., to rebut the statutory presumption. Thus, we turn to the 2010 Will to determine whether Donald effectively exercised the power of appointment. The issue, in light of the statutory presumption, is whether Donald's disposition of his property in the 2010 Will was an inadvertent or intentional exercise of the power of appointment.

III. Donald's 2010 Will Was Intended to Exercise the Power of Appointment in the MPA.

The interpretation of a will under undisputed facts presents a legal issue that is reviewed without deference to the lower court. Caflisch v. Staum, 2000 WI App 113, ¶6, 235 Wis. 2d 210, 612 N.W.2d 385. The purpose of will construction is to ascertain the testator's intent. Lohr v. Viney, 174 Wis. 2d 468, 480, 497 N.W.2d 730 (Ct. App. 1993). Because the language of the will is the best evidence of the testator's intent, we look to it first; if there is no ambiguity or inconsistency in the will's provisions, there is no need for further inquiry into the testator's intent. Id. However, if an ambiguity or inconsistency exists in the will's language, we look to the surrounding circumstances at the time of the will's execution. Id. If an ambiguity or inconsistency still persists, we may resort to the rules of will construction and extrinsic evidence. Id. Ambiguity exists where the will's language is subject to two or more reasonable interpretations, either on its face or as applied to the extrinsic facts to which it refers. Id. at 480-81.

Ramona contends that the 2010 Will is unambiguous and, by omitting reference to the power of appointment, demonstrated Donald's intent to not dispose of his property through his will. We disagree. The 2010 Will seeks to distribute Donald's estate to identified beneficiaries in a different disposition from that set forth in the MPA, but it fails to specifically reference the power of appointment. Ramona contends that the 2010 Will must be looked at alone, and yet, her argument necessarily requires that we examine the 2010 Will in light of the presumption created by the MPA's required reference to the power. That presumption contemplates an inquiry into whether the testator intended to exercise the power—here, that inquiry is whether Donald's 2010 disposition of his estate was intentional or inadvertent. See Wis. Stat. § 702.03(1).

Here, if we were to accept Ramona's argument, the 2010 Will's distribution of the very same property to which the power of appointment relates is meaningless. If a failure to reference the power of appointment would render an instrument of execution meaningless and inoperable, it becomes reasonably plain that the testator intended the instrument to exercise the power of appointment. At the very least, it creates an ambiguity—what is the purpose of Donald's stated disposition if the 2010 Will has no effect whatsoever? Thus, the 2010 Will itself is inherently ambiguous, because it attempts to effect a distribution that, Ramona argues, is nugatory. The surrounding circumstances further confirm the ambiguity—the 2010 Will replaced the prior 2007 Will, which specifically referenced the power of appointment, stating: "This instrument is drafted pursuant to the power of appointment in Article XIII, Paragraph C. of a Marital Property Agreement dated April 24, 2002." If, after examining the surrounding circumstances at the time of a will's execution, the ambiguity or inconsistency persists, it is appropriate to resort to extrinsic evidence and the rules of will construction. See Lohr, 174 Wis. 2d at 484. In doing so, the drafting attorney's testimony concerning the statements the testator made is admissible as extrinsic evidence of the testator's intent. Id. at 485 (citing Mangel v. Strong, 51 Wis. 2d 55, 69, 186 N.W.2d 276 (1971)).

Our analysis is supported by the legislative changes to Wis. Stat. § 702.03. We note that prior to its repeal and recreation in 1998, § 702.03(1) (1995-96) stated:

> (1) If the donor has explicitly directed that no instrument shall be effective to exercise the power unless the instrument contains a reference to the specific power, in order to exercise effectively such a power the donee's instrument must contain a specific reference to the power or the creating instrument and expressly manifest an intent to exercise the power or transfer the property covered by the power.

Thus, an executing instrument was required to contain both the specific reference to the power and expressly manifest an intent to exercise the power or transfer property. See id. However, the current version of Wis. Stat. § 702.03(1), which was patterned after Uniform Probate Code §2-704 (amended 2010), simply recognizes that the specific power of appointment requirement creates a presumption that the specific reference was intended to prevent inadvertent exercise. This presumption can be overcome if it can be demonstrated that the donee had knowledge of and intended to exercise the power. See id., cmt.; see also Motes/Henes Trust v. Motes, 297 Ark. 380, 761 S.W.2d 938, 940 (Ark. 1988) (donee's intended exercise given effect despite failure to use specific reference when drafting attorney's testimony presented very strong evidence of intent).

Insofar as Ramona contends that the current statute still requires an express reference to the power of appointment, we disagree. The legislative changes to §702.03 (1995-96) reflect the increasing focus of the Wisconsin Probate Code on giving effect to the testator's intent when possible. See Howard S. Erlanger, Wisconsin's New Probate Code, Wis. Lawyer (Oct. 1998),

Here, the trial court appropriately considered the 2007 Will, the 2010 Codicil, and the drafting attorney's testimony. The 2007 Will establishes that Donald knew of and intended to exercise the power of appointment. Dovnik, the attorney who drafted all of the documents in question, testified that the failure of the 2010 Will to reference the power of appointment was due to a drafting error and not a change in Donald's intent as to the distribution of his estate. Ramona presented no evidence to refute Dovnik's testimony. Thus, the undisputed evidence establishes that Donald intended to distribute his property according to the dispositive provisions of his 2010 Will. We conclude that the evidence established Donald's intent to exercise the power of appointment provided for in the MPA through his 2010 Will.

IV. Attorney Dovnik Is Not Barred from Testifying in this Case; Wisconsin Courts Generally Allow Drafting Attorneys to Testify.

As a final matter, we reject Ramona's contention that Dovnik's testimony was inadmissible under Wis. Stat. § 885.16 and otherwise constituted inadmissible hearsay. A trial court's decision to admit or exclude evidence is a discretionary determination, and we affirm discretionary decisions if they have a reasonable basis and apply the correct law to the facts of record. Bell v. Neugart, 2002 WI App 180, ¶15, 256 Wis. 2d 969, 650 N.W.2d 52. In challenging the trial court's discretionary decision, Ramona ignores established Wisconsin law recognizing that the testimony of a drafting attorney as to the statements made to him or her by the testator is admissible on the question of intent once such extrinsic evidence becomes admissible. See Mangel, 51 Wis. 2d at 69. We nevertheless address each of Ramona's objections in turn.

Wisconsin Stat. § 885.16, the dead man's statute, provides restrictions on witness examination pertaining to transactions with deceased or insane persons. It prohibits a witness's testimony if the witness meets three conditions: (1) a specified interest contemplated by the statute, (2) the witness's testimony relates to a transaction or communication by the witness personally with a deceased individual, and (3) the opposing party derives a specified interest in the action through the deceased. Id. This court has recognized that the core meaning of § 885.16 is that it disqualifies a witness to a transaction or communication with a decedent from testifying about that transaction or communication in his or her favor, or in favor of any party to the case claiming under the witness. Bell, 256 Wis. 2d 969, ¶17.

Ramona argues that Dovnik is an interested person because how the 2010 Will is construed may cause or prevent a malpractice claim against him by beneficiaries and interested parties, specifically Kelly and Becky. However, Ramona's argument runs contrary to Wisconsin case law that a witness's interest must be "present, certain and vested, not just a remote or contingent interest" in order for Wis. Stat. § 885.16 to bar testimony. See Giese v. Reist, 91 Wis. 2d 209, 224, 281 N.W.2d 86 (1979). Because any interest in avoiding a threat of malpractice, real or imagined, would be a remote or contingent interest, the trial court properly exercised its discretion in permitting Dovnik to testify.

Ramona also argues that Dovnik's testimony was barred as inadmissible hearsay. Again, Ramona's argument fails. Wisconsin Stat. § 908.03(3) allows for an exception for evidence describing the declarant's then-existing state of mind; this exception can be used to describe declarant's intent, plan, motive, design, or mental feeling. This exception is thought of as able to "look forward in time," or, in other words, can be used to prove that the declarant later acted in conformity with a certain mental state. Jay E. Grenig & Daniel D. Blinka, Wisconsin Civil Rules Handbook § 908.03:3 (2012). The trial court did not err in permitting Dovnik to testify as to Donald's intent to dispose of his property pursuant to the disposition of his 2010 Will.

CONCLUSION

We conclude that the trial court properly ordered that Donald's 2010 Will be admitted into informal probate, that Daniel be appointed personal representative of Donald's estate, and that the estate be distributed as indicated in the 2010 Will, specifically: one-third of the estate to Daniel, one-third to Steven, and the final one-third be divided equally between Ramona and her daughters, Rebecca and Kelly. We affirm the trial court's order.

II. FAILURE TO EXERCISE A POWER

A. TAKERS IN DEFAULT

If the donee fails to exercise the power, what happens to the appointive property? The short answer is that it goes to the *taker in default*. How the taker in default is determined is, however, somewhat complicated. Under Wis. Stat. §702.15, the property goes to any individual who has received "an express gift in default" in the document that created the power. If there is no such individual named, then the property goes either to the pool of potential takers as a group, or it reverts back to the donor (or the holder of the donor's interest), depending on the intention of the donor. As a general rule, the property will revert to the donor only if the language of the instrument creating the power specifically states that the objects *only* take as a result of the exercise of the power.

Wis. Stat. 702.15. Disposition when special power is unexercised.

If the donee of a special power fails to exercise effectively the power, the interests which might have been appointed under the power pass:

(1) If the creating instrument contains an express gift in default, then in accordance with the terms of such gift;

(2) If the creating instrument contains no express gift in default and does not clearly indicate that the permissible appointees are to take only if the donee exercises the power, then to the permissible appointees equally, but if the power is to appoint among a class such as "relatives," "issue" or "heirs," then to those persons who would have taken had there been an express gift to the described class; or

(3) If the creating instrument contains no express gift in default and clearly indicates that the permissible appointees are to take only if the donee exercises the power, then by reversion to the donor or the donor's estate. But if the creating instrument expressly states that there is no reversion in the donor, then any language in the creating instrument indicating or stating that the permissible appointees are to take only if the donee exercises the power is to be disregarded and the interests shall pass in accordance with sub. (2)

Derse v. Derse

Supreme Court of Wisconsin

103 Wis. 113, 79 N.W. 44 (1899)

One Anthony Derse, on July 23, 1895, died testate, leaving real estate, consisting of 145 2/3 acres of land in Dodge county. The material part of the will is as follows: "First. After the payment of all my just debts and funeral expenses, I give, devise, and bequeath to my beloved wife, Catherine Derse, all the rest and residue and remainder of my estates, both real and personal, and to have and to hold the same for her own personal use and benefit, for and during her natural life, to all intents and purposes as if she had been the original owner. Second. I give unto my wife, Catherine Derse, the full and sole control of all my estates, both real and personal (if she should survive me), the right to devise and bequeath to the several members of my family in shares as she may see fit, at the time of making her last will and testament, to all intents and purposes as I could have done."

In the probate proceedings upon that will the county court, by order of July 21, 1896, ordered and adjudged "that all of the above-described real estate be, and the same is hereby, assigned and set over to the said Catherine Derse, widow of the said deceased, to have and to hold the same unto her, her heirs and assigns, according to the last will and testament of said deceased." The widow occupied the land up to the time of her death, on May 20, 1897, but shortly before her death made a deed of 65 2/3 acres of the said land to the defendant. She died intestate.

The children, constituting the family of the deceased Anthony and Catherine Derse, were twelve in number, eleven of whom are the plaintiffs, and the twelfth the defendant. All are of full age and sui juris. The prayer of the complaint is for construction of the will and adjudication that Catherine Derse's interest was a life estate, coupled with an imperative trust or power to dispose of the same by her will amongst the children, and, she having failed to execute such trust or power, that the court carry out the same, and adjudge said real estate to the parties to this action in equal twelfth shares.

Judgment was rendered to that effect, from which defendant appeals.

DODGE, J. That the will of Anthony Derse intended to confer a life estate upon Catherine Derse, accompanied by a power to apportion the real estate amongst the children by will, appears clear. The will was not drawn by a lawyer, and the testator was a farmer. The use of the words "for her life" are, however, very significant, whether used by a lawyer or by a layman. It may be said that almost uniformly they convey to the mind of either the idea of limitation, and we think they were so used here. The unnecessary implication of words to express rights which she would legally have without such words, by virtue of a mere life estate, is not inconsistent with the intent of such limitation, when used by such people as the draftsman and the testator in this case.

The words used do not necessarily indicate more than an intention that her control and enjoyment of the farm during her life should be uncontrolled by anyone else. They are entirely consistent with the purpose that she should enjoy the property only for her life, but during her life the children and all others should be excluded from interference therewith; and they do not suggest any thought in the testator of giving to her the additional power of disposition, during her life, which might be inconsistent with a mere life estate. The intention of the testator to confer something less than an absolute fee is further evinced by the directions given as to the disposal of the property at the death of Catherine Derse by devise and bequest.

While, of course, a direction as to whom she should devise the property might be ineffectual, if it were clear that an absolute title in fee were given to her, its presence is of much force in the construction of the preceding words, and confirms the conclusion that Anthony Derse did not intend to give the property to her absolutely, but only for her life, so that it would remain undisposed of at the time of her death. Then he was willing to leave it to her discretion how the apportionment of it should be made amongst the then-existing children, whose conditions might have substantially varied in the interval between the making of his will and the death of the life tenant. In Knox v. Knox, 59 Wis. 172, intention to limit widow's rights to her life was predicated on far less significant language.

This conclusion being reached, the duty of the court below to proceed to make the apportionment follows obviously. The second section clearly conferred upon the widow a special power in trust, as defined by sec. 2122, Stats. 1898; for under that section a "class of persons other than the grantee" was entitled to benefit from the disposition authorized by the power. Sec. 2127 provides that, "if the trustee of a power with right of selection shall die leaving the power unexecuted, its execution shall be adjudged in the circuit court for the benefit equally of all the persons designated as objects of the trust." To this effect is the judgment appealed from. Judgment affirmed.

B. DONEE RELEASE OF A POWER OF APPOINTMENT

There are some situations in which the donee of a power may choose to release the power, i.e., give up his or her right to exercise it. Sometimes this is done as a consequence of tax concerns (as when the holder of a general power exercisable only at death releases the power to avoid estate taxation), and sometimes it is done to assure that the designated taker in default will eventually own the appointive property. It is also possible for the intended donee to simply disclaim the appointment at the outset of the transaction.

Wis. Stat. 702.08. Disclaimer of powers.

The donee of any power may disclaim all or part of the power as provided under s. 700.27 or 854.13.

Wis. Stat. 702.09. Release of powers.

(1) Except as the creating instrument expressly provides that the power cannot be released or expressly restricts the time, manner or scope of release, the donee of any power may:

(a) At any time completely release the donee's power;

(b) At any time or times release the donee's power in any one or more of the following respects:

1. As to the whole or any part of the property which is subject thereto;

2. As to any one or more persons or objects, or classes of persons or objects, in whose favor such power is exercisable;

3. So as to limit in any other respect the extent to or manner in which it may be exercised.

(2) A release may be effected, either with or without consideration, by written instrument signed by the donee and delivered.

(3) Delivery of a release may be accomplished in any of the following manners, but this subsection is permissive and does not preclude a determination that a release has been delivered in some other manner:

(a) Delivery to any person specified in the creating instrument;

(b) Delivery to a trustee or to one of several trustees of the property to which the power relates, or filing with the court having jurisdiction over the trust;

(c) Delivery to any person, other than the donee, who could be adversely affected by an exercise of the power; or

(d) Recording in the office of register of deeds in the county where the property is located.

In re Cudahy's Trust

Supreme Court of Wisconsin
22 Wis. 2d 198, 125 N.W.2d 344 (1963)

Gordon, J.

"For justice, tho' she's painted blind/Is to the weaker side inclin'd." Samuel Butler, Hudibras, Part III, Canto III.

The equities of this case are strikingly in favor of Mrs. Bischoff. The latter was Mrs. Hoyt's friend, nurse, and companion for almost seven years. Mrs. Hoyt's will clearly expressed her intention to have Mrs. Bischoff enjoy the benefits which would have resulted from the testamentary exercise of her power of appointment in favor of Mrs. Bischoff. A nephew of Mrs. Hoyt, Michael J. Cudahy, vigorously supported Mrs. Bischoff's position in this court. However, regardless of the equities, if Mrs. Hoyt's partial release of her reserved testamentary power of appointment was valid when it was made in 1944 and was not revocable, it follows that her testamentary appointment of Mrs. Bischoff was invalid.

We must first resolve whether the partial release of the power of appointment was effective. The execution of the instrument by Mrs. Hoyt on February 25, 1944, was a deliberate and meaningful act. Prior to its preparation and execution, Mrs. Hoyt had the guidance of an analytical report from her lawyers; they recommended the partial release in order to diminish federal estate taxes on Mrs. Hoyt's estate. We consider that in the issue before us it is immaterial whether the tax savings which Mrs. Hoyt sought to obtain were ultimately obtained. The document had independent legal significance even though its purpose was to gain a specified tax benefit.

Mrs. Bischoff contends that Mrs. Hoyt was unable to release the reserved power of appointment because to do so would breach a contractual arrangement with her co-settlors. A trust, by its terms, may embody contractual burdens amongst those who establish the trust. However, we are unable to apply the contract theory espoused by Mrs. Bischoff to the instant trust. With reference to the shares of stock which Mrs. Hoyt transferred to the trust, she reserved the life income therefrom and also reserved the right to designate by her will who was to receive the dividends from such shares for the natural life of the appointee. Upon default in the exercise of the appointment, the trust instrument provided that the income would be enjoyed by her issue or, if none, by the surviving settlors or their issue. Mrs. Hoyt died without leaving a surviving spouse or any surviving issue.

We construe the provision for a power of appointment in the instant case to constitute a reserved property right in the settlor as distinguished from a contractual or promissory obligation with reference to the power. In our opinion, the power of appointment which Mrs. Hoyt held under the 1918 trust agreement was subject to her right to release such power in whole or in part, and this right existed pursuant to the common law. No one could claim an interest as a prospective appointee under this power of appointment. Mrs. Hoyt was free to designate any natural person or persons whom she chose to appoint, and she was not under any duty to exercise the power. This, therefore, was not a special power in trust as contemplated in sec. 232.22, Stats., and considered in Ruggles v. Tyson (1899), 104 Wis. 500, 517, 79 N. W. 766, and in Will of Uihlein (1953), 264 Wis. 362, 380, 59 N. W. (2d) 641.

Since it was not a special power in trust and since it was releasable under the common law, Mrs. Hoyt's partial release of her power was not dependent upon either the 1943 or the 1957 versions of sec. 232.495, Stats. We do not construe the 1943 statute as restricting the right of a donee of a power to release such power. The 1943 adoption of sec. 232.495 was designed to take advantage of certain federal estate-tax exemptions. See Explanation of Proposed Repeal and Re-creation of Sec. 232.495, relating to ch. 650, Laws of 1957, Wisconsin legislative reference library drafting files. This section may not be construed as abbreviating the common-law right to release powers. Under the common law, all powers were releasable except powers in trust. Simes and Smith, The Law of Future Interests (2d ed.), p. 525, sec. 1057.

Restatement, Property (1948 Supp.), p. 506, sec. 335, concludes as follows:

"All special powers of appointment can be released by the donee unless the donor in creating the power manifests an intent that it shall be non-releasable."

The authors, at page 508, report that Wisconsin statutory expressions were merely declaratory of pre-existing nonstatutory law.

Had Mrs. Hoyt been the donee of a power in trust, she could not have extinguished that power in contravention of the plan of distribution created by the donor. It is arguable that even a power in trust is releasable under the 1957 version of sec. 232.495, Stats.; however, we are not required to construe the scope of that version of the statute in the instant case. The rule which precludes the release of a power in trust does not prevent the release of a power wherein the donee is giving up something which is unqualifiedly his. In this light, Mrs. Hoyt, who was both the donor and the donee of the power, possessed the right to appoint by her will, to fail to appoint, or to extinguish her power in whole or in part.

The partial release by its own terms evidences that such action was made "irrevocably and forever." Whether Mrs. Hoyt at the time of the execution of her will was mindful of her pre-existing release, or whether she had forgotten such pre-existing document, is not of significance. Her partial release was valid when made, and she divested herself of the authority to revoke such release. The trial court correctly ruled that Mrs. Bischoff could not qualify as an appointee of the power under Mrs. Hoyt's will. Judgment affirmed.

C. RIGHTS OF CREDITORS

Because the property ownership remains with the donor of the power of appointment, the traditional rule was that the creditors of the donee had no right to reach the appointive property. However, when the power is general, rather than special, different rules apply. Case law interpreting Wis. Stat. §702.17 and its predecessors is surprisingly sparse.

Wis. Stat. 702.17. Rights of creditors of the donee.

(1) GENERAL POLICY. If the donee has either a general power or an unclassified power which is unlimited as to permissible appointees except for exclusion of the donee, the donee's estate, the donee's creditors and the creditors of the donee's estate, or a substantially similar exclusion, any interest which the donee has power to appoint or has appointed is to be treated as property of the donee for purposes of satisfying claims of the donee's creditors, as provided in this section.

(2) DURING LIFETIME OF THE DONEE. If the donee has an unexercised power of the kinds specified in sub. (1), and can presently exercise such a power, any creditor of the donee may by appropriate proceedings reach any interest which the donee could appoint, to the extent that the donee's individual assets are insufficient to satisfy the creditor's claim. Such an interest is to be treated as property of the donee within ch. 816. If the donee has exercised such a power, the creditor can reach the appointed interests to the same extent that under the law relating to fraudulent conveyances the creditor could reach property which the donee has owned and transferred.

(3) AT DEATH OF THE DONEE. If the donee has at the time of his or her death a power of the kinds specified in sub. (1), whether or not the donee exercises the power, any creditor of the donee may reach any interest which the donee could have appointed or has appointed, to the extent that the claim of the creditor has been filed and allowed in the donee's estate but not paid because the assets of the estate are insufficient.

(4) ASSIGNMENT FOR BENEFIT OF CREDITORS. Under a general assignment by the donee for the benefit of the donee's creditors, the assignee may exercise any right which a creditor of the donee would have under sub. (2).

(5) THIRD PARTIES IN GOOD FAITH PROTECTED. Any person acting without actual notice of claims of creditors under this section incurs no liability to such creditors in transferring property which is subject to a power or which has been appointed; and a purchaser without actual notice and for a valuable consideration of any interest in property, legal or equitable, takes such interest free of any rights which a creditor of the donee might have under this section.

www.ingramcontent.com/pod-product-compliance
Lightning Source LLC
LaVergne TN
LVHW062242200926
848484LV00006B/1592